The Elsewhere

The Elsewhere

On Belonging at a Near Distance:
Reading Literary Memoir from
Europe and the Levant

Adam Zachary Newton

The University of Wisconsin Press

The University of Wisconsin Press
1930 Monroe Street
Madison, Wisconsin 53711

www.wisc.edu/wisconsinpress/

3 Henrietta Street
London WC2E 8LU, England

Copyright © 2005
The Board of Regents of the University of Wisconsin System
All rights reserved

5   4   3   2   1

Printed in the United States of America

Library of Congress Cataloging-in-Publication Data
Newton, Adam Zachary.
   The elsewhere: on belonging at a near distance /
   Adam Zachary Newton.
   p.   cm.
   ISBN 0-299-20890-7 (hardcover: alk. paper)
   1. European literature—20th century—History and criticism.
2. Setting (Literature)   3. Travel in literature.   I. Title.
PN56.S48N48   2005
809´.922—dc22   2004025637

This book was published with the support of a University
Cooperative Society Subvention Grant awarded by
the University of Texas at Austin.

Mahmoud Darwish's "We Journey Towards a Home," from
Unfortunately It Was Paradise: Selected Poems, trans. Munir Akash
and Carolyn Forché (Berkeley: University of California Press, 2003)
by permission of The Regents of the University of California.

Dan Pagis's "The Art of Contraction," "Point of Departure," and
"Written in Pencil in the Sealed Railway-Car," from *The Selected
Poetry of Dan Pagis,* trans. Stephen Mitchell (Berkeley: University of
California Press, 1996) by permission of The Regents of the University
of California.

In memory of my mother
M. JOAN NEWTON
1923–2003

ר׳ טרפון והניח שתי ידיו תחת פרסותיה והיתה מהלכת עליהן עד שהגיעה למטתה.

"R. Tarfon held his hands under the soles of her feet, and she walked on his hands until she reached the couch."

Tractate Peah 1:1, 15c, Palestinian Talmud

In modern Athens, the vehicles of mass transportation are called *metaphorai*. To go to work or come home, one takes a "metaphor"—a bus or train. Stories could also take this noble name: every day, they traverse and organize places: they select and link them together; they make sentences and itineraries out of them.
    Michel de Certeau, *The Practice of Everyday Life*

To mangle a sentence into a landscape.
    Elias Canetti, *Notes from Hampstead*

If language may be regarded as an old city full of streets and squares, nooks and crannies, with some quarters dating from far back in time while others have been torn down, cleaned up and rebuilt, and with suburbs reaching further and further into the surrounding country, then I was like a man who has been abroad for a long time and cannot find his way through the urban sprawl anymore, no longer knows what a bus stop is for, or what a back yard is, or a street junction, an avenue or a bridge.
    W. G. Sebald, *Austerlitz*

Itinerary and Topography of the Book

Contents

	Preface and Acknowledgments	xi
	Introduction: Sta Viator	3
1	Place from Place, and Place from Flight: W. G. Sebald's *The Emigrants* and Aharon Appelfeld's *The Iron Tracks*	41
2	Flight from Flight, and Flight from Border: Witold Gombrowicz's *Diary* and *A Kind of Testament* and Essays and Short Fiction by Bruno Schulz	96
3	Border from Border: Elias Canetti's *The Tongue Set Free* and *The Voices of Marrakesh* and Gregor von Rezzori's *The Snows of Yesteryear*	155
4	Border from Beyond: André Aciman's *Out of Egypt* and Edward Said's *Out of Place*	207
5	Beyond from Beyond: Dan Pagis's *Abba* and Anton Shammas's *Arabesques*	240
	Notes	281
	Works Consulted	353
	Index	379

Preface and Acknowledgments

Like black borders solemnifying a letter, four events surround the writing of this book. Each, in its dislocating effect, records the inscrutable shift between here and elsewhere—between what Henry James calls the nearer distances and clearer mysteries, and their remoter, less lucid counterparts. The first is the calamity of 11 September 2001, which I witnessed at a televised distance in Austin, Texas, my home for the past decade. My true home, however, I still regard as New York City, where I grew up and which I abandoned (it felt) the year the twin towers were finished.

As had Pennsylvania Station for the generation of my grandparents newly emigrated from Eastern Europe, as had the Empire State and Chrysler Buildings for my parents, so the World Trade Center towers, their paired ascent, made that home an architectural event for me. Yet, any claim I might have made on New York as "*my* lost city" (for unlike F. Scott Fitzgerald, I was born there) was swiftly countervailed by the fact that I had not resided there for over twenty-five years. Wrenched therefore between the *nostos* of bittersweet recollection and a home no-longer-home, I journeyed to lower Manhattan a month after the attack in order to bear a different kind of witness than that of my youth. I was there, yet not there, near, but at a distance.

The second event was the untimely demise in December of the same year of the elegist W. G. Sebald, which seemed as if it were the final, black-bordered threshold in an oeuvre whose deep subject *is* threshold—the defining yet permeable verge between persons, between event and recollection, between the living and the dead, between a no-longer recoverable Europe and a Europe surviving in its stead. Suddenly, all that had felt so proximate—that forgivably proprietary fantasy we sometimes entertain that an author were writing as though just for us—felt eerily conveyed away, elevated to a firmament beyond. Ironically enough, I had planned my return to New York City in part to overlap with a public reading Sebald was to give from his soon-to-be-published novel *Austerlitz* (happily, voice and presence matched the promise of text[1]). Two months after that, on the first day of the New Year, I began a temporary stay in Paris, a city unfamiliar to me. It is also the locale where the plot of *Austerlitz* concludes, and where as a duty of homage, I felt the need to follow the traces of Sebald's perambulating narrator—at Gare d'Austerlitz, at the Bibliothèque Nationale, at the Cimetière Montparnasse. Once again, nearness and farness etched their complex, balletic figure. Sebald's books alternately license and rebuke the acts of approximation they take upon themselves (re-inscribing others' stories, retracing their footsteps), but never before had such mimesis felt so apropos.

The third event was an indirect tragedy of more intimate proportions, the sudden passing of a close friend's father. I received the news not long after my arrival in Paris, nearly coincident with the *yortsayt* of my own father, and felt obliged almost immediately to reverse my steps and return to Texas. Circling back so soon and so unexpectedly, undoing a several-thousand-mile journey by doubling it in retrograde, I thought of Sebald's narrators who sometimes lose their bearings in a kind of vertigo that graphs its own journey. Where exactly was I now, dislocated, so to say, from my newly acquired displacement? Where was home; where was elsewhere; where lay the terrain bounded by the passing of fathers, the nearness and remoteness of grief, the grip and slide of memory? How was it that *unheimlich* themes had been supervened so dramatically by unhoming events?

Re-crossing the Atlantic for the second time in little more than two weeks, newly (re)versed in the etymological kinship between "travel" and "travail," I thought I could discern a sequence in these three events; and it was this last, nearest bereavement that compelled me to consider that very possibly "home and elsewhere" stand for properties of person maybe even more than they do of place, and that those whom we approach or who recede from us define the real coordinates of belonging at either near distance or far. In the absence thus left by this third loss, the traces to be limned were not spatial but rather the very outlines of the Other. For is it not others who unseat us from what we thought was home, sending us elsewhere, and who also, we hope, redeem us from our homelessness, securing our only true and genuine place?

Preface and Acknowledgments xiii

The fourth and truly unmooring event was the death of my mother, of blessed memory, which coincided with my revisions for this book. If the word "elsewhere" is to sustain its widest possible breadth of meaning in the pages ahead, if the *longing* in "belonging" is to resonate most plangently, it is because my debt to my mother's tutelage in these regards is as incalculable as it is illimitable. She was one of the Elsewhere's most lettered citizens, and a very regent of longing. Truly, without her sensibility, and without her own idiom of inhabiting *midbar* spaces and making them speak, this book would not have come to be. It is therefore in her honor and memory—let it be for a blessing—that my vagaries of criticism locate themselves in public space, always at the nearest distance from her own example. A cemetery vigil or visit appears in each of the following six chapters; it is fitting, therefore, that the entire book stand as a kind of *matzeva* (headstone) memorializing the one who, invisibly, stands over it: "to whom he speaks, as if he still had the power to hold her"(Canetti).

Originally, I planned to conclude this book with an epilogue that would double as travelogue. I would journey to Bad Kissingen, Czernowitz, Drohobycz, Alexandria, Cairo, Ruschuk, Marraskesh, Fassuta, Jerusalem, laboring in what Simon Schama calls the archive of the feet, and give honest, foot-worn shape to *elsewhere* and *distance*. I knew full well that Sebaldian anamnesis—"it was as if I had already been this way before and memories were revealing themselves to me not by means of any mental effort but through my senses"—would remain a property of the "as if." But even so, I wanted the moral schooling of hard contact. In the end, however, it was to be a different set of cumulative journeys that would dictate my purpose, the very ones I have just described. In tribute, therefore, to those whose passing instructed me in this lesson—the perished of 11 September, the writer W. G. Sebald, a comrade's father overtaken by his fate, and most of all, my beloved mother *a"h*—I dedicate this book.

Lastly, I wish to acknowledge the claim on my sensibilities of five who have instructed me: above all, my brother Scott, who continues to teach me the elusive truth of nomadism, of "the journey of Ark" as expounded in tractate *Shabbat* 116a—"that this is not its place" means to be dislodged in both reading and religiosity, that to receive a text is to build it, and to build it is to save it from its misfortune as a book; my estimable colleagues Paul Mendes-Flohr and César Salgado, who teach me gratitude for their fidelity; my invaluable interlocutor of long standing Andrew Sekel, who teaches me *the word in speaking* over and above the spoken word; and finally, at a far distance, LCR, who taught me the elsewhere.

A portion of the second chapter has previously appeared as an essay in *Mapping the Ethical Turn: A Reader in Ethics, Culture, and Literary Theory,* ed. Todd Davis and Kevin Womack (Charlottesville: University of Virginia Press, 2001). I thank Michael Martin for assisting with the translation of Levinas's *De L'évasion;* Abraham Marcus, Harris Lenowitz, and Nissim Elbaz for their recommendations on translating Pagis's *Abba;* Susannah Heschel for her encouraging words; Erin Holman for her ample patience and keen editorial eye; and as always, for their gift of surprise, my students.

The Elsewhere

Introduction
Sta Viator

1. Midbar

Amar Rav Hisda, "Lamadnu 'makom' mi 'makom' u'makom' me'nisa' v'nisa' mi'nisa' v'nisa' mi'gevul u'gevul' mi'gevul u'gevul' mi'hutz' v'hutz' mi 'hutz'."

Rav Hisda said, "We learn 'place' from 'place', and 'place' from 'flight'; 'flight 'from 'flight', and 'flight' from 'border'; 'border' from 'border', and 'border' from 'beyond'; and 'beyond' from 'beyond'."
Tractate *Eruvin* 51a

This proposition reads like a riddle, but it is in fact an exegetical formula referring individual words in one verse to their clarifying contexts in related verses, drawn from a tractate in the Talmud that concerns boundary and movement, the nature of domain, and the mixing or pooling of areas for Sabbath observance *(eruvei tehumim)*. Through such verbal analogy, the prohibition in Exodus 16:29–30 against exceeding a certain limit while traveling on the Sabbath is elucidated with reference to two kinds of environs: places of asylum, or "cities of refuge," and places of restrictive settlement, the "cities of the Levites."[1]

Implicitly, what the formula does is to liken a demarcation within time to perimeters of space—the Sabbath as both refuge and exceptional inheritance. While its abstract topics are origin and destination, private vs. public space, travel and transport, the Talmud's overt focus here is regulatory and prescriptive. *Descriptively,* however, the mnemonic chain incises the lineaments of a story. Suppose then we were creatively to misread *place-flight-border-beyond* as a narrative kernel about dwelling and departure; as a story about the crossing of frontiers to their yonder side—perhaps to another place, or to continued flight, or perhaps to time exchanged for place; and finally, as a progression "beyond"—to an elsewhere, an otherwise-than, a place instead of place.

Flight would signify a human action, a movement in and through space. *Place, border,* and *beyond* would herald human impositions upon space that transform it into a place, a realm of memory; successively, *flight, place, border,* and *beyond* would abandon, found, and sight a given landscape.[2] Let us imagine tracking such a story—out of Talmudic bounds—within the modern, secular context of a particular kind of literary memoir. The genre would be called "*midbar,*" after the Midrash on Song of Songs 4:3 that interprets the verse "Thy speech is comely" as "Thy wilderness *(midbarekh)* / Thy utterance *(midabratekh)*," because the desert is where the divine word spoke to the multitude.[3] Homographs, "speech" and "desert" are spelled the same (MDBR) in consonantal Hebrew—as, indeed, are the words, "there" and "name," by their own shared lexeme, ShM.

"They are astray in the land; the *wilderness* has closed in on them," says Pharaoh of the Israelites in Exodus 14, which we can thus take the liberty of infusing with our own double-meaning: for the practitioners of *midbar*-writing, *speech* has closed them in, as well. As a record of a somewhere else, an estrangement at the very heart of speaking from abroad or out of bounds—elsewhere as elseword—the literature of *midbar* is be-wildered in just this double sense. Trajectories of *flight*—geographic, linguistic, biographic; the arc from *place* to *beyond* as the exodus from home to elsewhere; the syntax of route and itinerary where each slot, each "from x," represents another point of leave-taking—such tropisms could be used to describe the authorizing conditions for a set of texts that themselves may be said to have "learned place from flight, flight from border, and border from beyond."

In this respect, the texts attest to their own sojourns; they comprise the "notes" (as in the subtitle to Elias Canetti's *The Voices of Marrakesh*), composed "*after* a journey." Typically, the titles for such texts make their overriding theme unmistakable: *Lost in Translation: A Life in a New Language* (Eva Hoffmann), *Speak, Memory* (Vladimir Nabokov), *Native Realm* (Czeslaw Milosz), *The Enigma of Arrival* (V. S. Naipaul). When they do not, as in Joseph Brodsky's *Less Than One* or Norman Manea's *The Hooligan's Return* or the matter-of-fact sounding *Diary* by Witold Gombrowicz, estrangement and dislocation have likely been made to serve the uses of memoir rather than the other way around. Edmond

Jabès's *From the Desert to the Book* states the midrashic relationship here precisely: "To speak is, accordingly, to lean on a metaphor of the desert" (101).

Of course, one of the more hackneyed adages about the practices of writing and reading after modernity is that they resemble, dramatize, enact a voyage, detailing on the planes of discourse, narration, and figuration the very outward-bound experiences they project as their subject. Quest and pilgrimage tales, foundational epics, voyages, expeditions, sorties, bourgeois treks and sentimental journeys, rambles into countryside or metropole, descents into hearts of darkness: all propose a surface correlation between the topos of errancy and the machinery of textual coding. Succession in time, enchainment in space, departure, repetition, and return: all "happen" on the written page as the pen, eye, or mouth make saccadic transits from grapheme to grapheme, advancing line by line. In the reciprocal direction, "There is a rhetoric of walking," says the historian Michel de Certeau. "The art of 'turning' phrases finds an equivalent in an art of composing a path [*tourner un parcours*]" (*The Practice of Everyday Life*, 100). Text mimes travel; terrain awaits its inscription in cartography.[4]

Open a folio of the Babylonian Talmud, Vilna edition—say tractate *Eruvin* 51a, the very spot where "we learn place from place, place from fight; flight from flight, flight from border; border from border, border from beyond; and beyond from beyond"—and you will find a history of dispersal charted by the borders and margins of the printed text itself. In the center column, *mishna* and its elucidation through *gemara* composed in Eretz Yisrael and Babylon, c. 200 B.C.E. to 500 C.E.; on the right, commentary by Rabbi Shlomo ben Yitzhak (Rashi) from eleventh-century France; on the left, commentary by Tosafot composed in France and Germany, circa 1150-1300; in the left-most column, gloss and textual emendation by the Ga'on of Vilna, the Ba"H", and other scholars from Italy, Poland, and Lithuania, circa sixteenth through eighteenth centuries. Additional commentaries on a given Talmud page may also include those from eleventh century Tunisia and sixteenth century Egypt.

Open a page of a very different sort of text, say the 1934-35 essay "Discourse in the Novel" by Mikhail Bakhtin (who spent much of his life in interior exile in Kazakhstan, Savelovo, and Mordovia), and you find language described in the rhetoric of displacement as a condition of conflicting land-claims that "the speaker *populates* with his own intention," a transfer "many words stubbornly resist, others remain[ing] *alien,* sound[ing] *foreign* in the mouth of the one who appropriated them and who now speaks them." "Language," says Bakhtin, "is not a neutral medium that passes freely and easily into the private property of the speaker's intentions. Expropriating it, forcing it to submit to one's own intentions and accents, is a difficult and complicated process" (*The Dialogic Imagination,* 254). Biblically if not Talmudically speaking, Bakhtin's prosaics are the drama of Abraham, Joseph, Ruth, even Cain (called *na va'nad va'aretz,* that first vagrant and wanderer on earth), linguistically enacted. Against the backdrop of the novel, but part and parcel of *midbar* texts too, utterance in this more modern setting means relocation, settlement, exodus, distance traveled, passage from elsewhere.[5]

But then, modern readers are no less driven than the texts they read. For "readers are travelers," says de Certeau: "[T]hey move across lands belonging to someone else, like nomads poaching their way across fields they did not write, despoiling the wealth of Egypt to enjoy it themselves" (174).[6] Hitchhikers, *metaphorai* of *metaphorai,* they produce further and necessary displacements, just as the narrated adventures they traverse "do not merely constitute a 'supplement' to pedestrian enunciations and rhetorics . . . [but] in reality . . . organize walks. They make the journey, before or during the time the feet perform it" (116).[7] Reading is both anti-nostalgic—it "detach[es] texts from their lost (or accessory) origin" (169)—and willfully errant, "wander[ing] through an imposed system . . . emancipated from places" (169, 176).

After the same fashion, writing is exilic and fugitive at its very core: "born of the impossibility of one's own place, [it] articulates the constantly initial fact that the subject is never authorized by a place . . . that he is always foreign to himself" (de Certeau, *The Writing of History,* 320). For if exile promises an enabling fiction, an aesthetic gain, it does so in part because literary representation already speaks in the argot of terrain and passage. Narrative is both the mimesis of an action and its allegory, just as departure from place, reclamation of place, marking, crossing, and re-imagining of place all name features of discourse. Linguistic tropes *("tours")* enable a means of representational travel, just as expatriation, migration, diaspora, nostalgia, homecoming, traversing boundaries lend themselves to metaphor. "Writing repeats [a] lack in each of its graphs, the relics of a walk through language. It spells out an absence that is its precondition and its goal. It proceeds by successive abandonments of occupied places, and it articulates itself on an exteriority that eludes it, on its addressee come from abroad, a visitor who is expected but never heard on the scriptural paths that the travels of a desire have traced on the page" (*The Practice of Everyday Life*, 195).

Now, for a certain sort of French intellectual discourse, this penchant for reflexive interplay between vagrancy and the literary is comme il faut, or, as de Certeau might himself pun, *common-place*.[8] "Espace," "espacement," éloignement," "dehors," écart," "distance," "reserve": the vocabulary reminds us once again that the term *metaphor* itself licenses leaving one place for another. And the cultural studies theorist Homi K. Bhabha shows this predilection to be neither exclusively French nor even western European: "Metaphor, as the etymology of the word suggests, transfers the meaning of home and belonging, across the 'middle passage,' or the central European steppes, across those distances, and cultural differences, that span the imagined community of the nation-people" (*The Location of Culture*, 139).[9]

Yet, trope can be potentially reckless.[10] In *The Production of Space* Marxist philosopher Henri Lefebvre, de Certeau's and Bhabha's contemporary, sounds the cautionary note to all such practitioners of the turned phrase: "Metaphorization and metonymization [are] a 'beyond,' but a nearby one, which creates the illusion of great remoteness. Although 'figures of speech' express much, they lose and overlook, set aside and place parentheses around even more."[11] For *elsewhere*, one recalls in the Latin, corresponds to *alibi*, to pretext. Thus does one of this book's authors, André Aciman, write of his fellow *midbar*-ist, W. G. Sebald, "[he] is always elsewhere, as he is always from elsewhere. Identity is an alibi" ("Out of Novemberland"). And likewise, the literary critic Harold Bloom remarks in a related vein, "*To be different, to be elsewhere* is a superb definition of the motive for metaphor" (*Kabbalah and Criticism*, 52).[12]

Sta Viator. Pause, traveler . . . and read: "The memoirs had seemed to him like one of those evil German fairy tales in which, once you are under the spell, you have to carry on to the finish, till your heart breaks, with whatever work you have begun—in this case, the remembering, writing, and reading" (*The Emigrants*, 193).

If you poach, this passage from Sebald's memoir-novel seems to imply, you risk being caught or, at the very least, haunted. Don't the theorists tell us that while writing "plays the role of burial rite [and] constructs a *tombeau* for the dead" (de Certeau, *The Writing of History*, 100), so likewise a reader "associates texts like funerary statues that he awakens and hosts but never owns. In that way he also escapes from the law of each text in particular, and from that of the social milieu" (*The Practice of Everyday Life*, 174)?[13] But suppose instead, that by engaging such literature, trekking its itineraries of displacement, a reader hosts, and, while never owning, is still bequeathed, made legate or beholden to a calculus of literary effects determined by arrearage rather than plunder.

Call this giving shape to caesura, to the space within the pause. Instead of taking *metaphorai* to leave or return home, let us propose that *metaphorai* take us—making not only writers but also readers dispossessed in acts of imaginative possession. To adapt a formula de Certeau himself suggests for the genre of historiography, while place is dogmatic, reading—like the coming back of time—can restore or refound an ethics.[14] Is that because it breaks the spell cast by story, by writing? Or rather, because "carrying on to the finish" just means *enchantment*? And on which side of heartbreak might the ethics of reading lie—further enchantment, or sober awakening? What is the "dogma" of place, and how do readers obey or else transgress (over-go) it? What, we may ask finally, is the *practice* of reading the writing of *midbar*?

These are some of questions I wish to pose in the chapters that follow. In the spirit of de Certeau, they assert themselves "heterologically" as the rhetorical Other that forces a given discourse to think against itself (even, as in this case, against the grain of de Certeau's own), to bring to light what is in question within it. For they insinuate something slightly oblique to what is customarily called (in double genitive) "the writing of displacement"—something like Sebald's carrying on to the finish that forces enchantment to the surface. And in cutting athwart the grain, they seek their answers in a certain *practice*, specific to a certain *genre*, which seeks to restore, or at least invoke, a certain sense of *ethics*.

The remaining part of this section illustrates that practice with some additional signposts from Sebald. "Genre" and "ethics" are the subjects of the two sections that follow it. Section four explains the tropings of "elsewhere" and "belonging at a near distance." Sections five through seven are more personal in nature. And while in combination, all these stages do record a sojourn of sorts, they constitute the kind of notes that must remain on journey's hither side until it begins in earnest with chapter 1.

Of the several reviews for Sebald's *The Emigrants (Die Ausgewanderten)*, shortly after publication, excerpts from two reproduced on the book jacket of the American edition stand out in the context of the passage from it quoted above: 1) "Everything, it seems, is paid for; there is no scot-free" (Richard Eder, *Los Angeles Times*); and 2) "a deconstruction of fairy tales and a somber quarrel with Proust" (Brigitte Frase, *New York Newsday*). The first claim touches upon indebtedness. The second aligns the question of enchantment with whatever might count as a quarrel with Proust[15]—let us say, with a very modernist fascination with Time. Time is the real landfall for Proust, place merely an elsewhere—*alibi* or pre-text. For, "Proust's garden was little more than a place where he had once yearned to be elsewhere" (André Aciman, *False Papers*, 77).

From Sebald's point of view, however, "Time is an unreliable way of gauging these things; indeed it is nothing but a disquiet of the soul" (181). *The Emigrants*—four novellas of lives given over to vagrancy under the shadow of this century's two world wars—is haunted by place from first to last. Its eighty-six photographs, not least the many landscapes, but even the figures, reproductions of diaries and newspaper articles, Schulzimmerplan and Bahnhofplan, all seem to lead back to "the dogma" of place over the blandishments of time redeemed or recaptured.[16] Subsequent to its own remembering and writing, the work one takes on in reading such a book—if it is until heartbreak—must require a more vexed relationship to terrain than emancipation from places. One cannot, that is, just pass through it, or (in de Certeau's more pointed metaphor), run it the way one runs traffic lights (*The Practice of Everyday Life*, 176). The power, the pathos, the rebuke, of place is too strong. That is part of this text's sheer fatidic weight.

Let us take its opening gestures as example. What we see first is a photograph, one of many interspersed among the book's pages. It more or less approximates what we read in the first few lines of text. The place is Hingham in Norfolk County in the East of England. The church, described with reference to "its grassy graveyard, Scots pines and yews" probably denotes St. Andrews. The photograph shows what therefore appears to be a yew tree surrounded by gravestones. Yew trees tend to be long-lived, which accounts for their mythic and numinous associations in Celtic and later Christian lore.[17] Commonly found within church precincts, the Yew often predates the churches that abut it (the Fortingall Yew, for example, said to be the oldest tree in Europe, is believed to be around three thousand years old, and Fortingall itself, in Scottish Caledonia, is said by local tradition to be the birthplace of Pontius Pilate). The yew was identified with Palm Sunday in the Middle Ages, its branches used to represent palms during elaborate church services that commemorated Jesus' arrival into Jerusalem; tradition associates it with the wood of the Cross. And it figures, of course, in the meditative, elegiac poetry of place by William Wordsworth, Thomas Gray, T. S. Eliot, and Sylvia Plath.[18]

An emigrant to the English countryside and an "ornamental hermit" in his own gardens, the story's protagonist, Dr. Henry Selwyn—who has "concealed his true background for a long time" (21)—is actually Hersch Seweryn, as we discover through a self-admission that seems to hasten, if not precipitate, his suicide at episode's end. The story's initial photograph thus not only locates us in the place of emigration, the substitute for homeland; it also stands over the entire narrative as a palimpsest of buried origins, the uneasy adjacency (or overlay) of Jewish and Gentile traditions, and ever-present, inconsolable loss (the book's first word in the German edition is "Ende").[19]

When I asked where it was that he felt drawn back to, he told me that at the age of seven he had left a village near Grodno in Lithuania with his family. In the late autumn of 1899, his parents, his sisters Gita and Raja, and his uncle Shani Feldhender, had ridden to Grodno on a cart that had belonged to Aaron Wald the coachman. For years the image of that exodus had been gone from his memory, but recently he said, they had been returning once again and making their presence felt. I can still see the teacher who taught the children in *cheder*. . . . I can still see the empty rooms of our house. . . . I see myself sitting topmost on the cart, see the horses' crupper, the vast brown earth. . . . I see the telegraph wires rising and falling past the train window, the facades of the Riga houses, the ship in the docks and the dark corner on deck where we did our best to make ourselves at home in confined circumstances. The high seas, the trail of smoke, the distant greyness, the lifting and falling of the sip, the fear and hope within us, all of it (Dr. Selwyn) told me I can now live through again, as if it were only yesterday. (19)

In this premonitory and shortest of Sebald's four emigrant elegies, place is intimately connected to "the return of past selves" (17) effected in part by the narration of stories and the mimesis of photography within the narrative and prefiguring, at story's end, the work of geology and landscape themselves. "More and more, he said, he sensed that Nature was groaning and collapsing beneath the burden we placed upon it" (7). Whatever landscape means in this first requiem—haven, entombment and disinterment, margin between human and nonhuman worlds, mystery—one sojourns in it, through reading, at a cost. (Such sojourning underpins all four of Sebald's novel-memoirs,[20] a purely biographical element of the author's practiced migrancy as well as a reflection of the distinctly Romanticist legacy that informs his writing.)[21]

Yet, however complexly layered strictly within the confines of the first novella (the next chapter elaborates this intricacy of connection), this first image in Sebald's book echoes twice, quite conspicuously, in two subsequent photographs toward the end, and once again, more subtly and formalistically, in the opening photograph of the second novella. The latter is a close-up photograph, taken at ground-level, of railway lines, that launches the narrative in the text most explicitly linked to the Holocaust. It is also directly linked to the yew image—a church graveyard, and the mobile graveyard that was the *Deutsche Reichsbahn Gesellschaft*—by their being reproduced together, one above the other, on the book's front cover in the original English translation.

The other two photographs belong to the fourth and final narrative (like the account of Selwyn, an English gothic). The first is a reproduction of a landscape by Courbet, glossed with reference to the peculiar painting method of the story's protagonist, Max Ferber. The narrator has returned to Ferber's studio, the last in the text's series of such returns to former habitations, noting that "the same dull light was entering by the window, and the easel still stood in the middle of the room on the black encrusted floor, a black piece of card on it, overworked to the point of being unrecognizable. . . . [T]he model that had served Ferber for this exercise was a Courbet I had always been especially fond of, *The Oak at Vercingetorix*" (179–80). The oak in Courbet's painting reputedly indicates the place of the Celtic chieftain's last-ditch battle against Julius Caesar to keep his province free of Roman rule, thus recalling the telluric overtones in the initial photograph of the yew.

But more immediately, its mention directly precedes Ferber's unburdening of himself on the model of Henry Selwyn's: "Following this late reunion, which neither of us had expected, we talked for three whole days far into the night, and a great many more things were said than I shall be able to write down here: concerning our exile in England, the immigrant city of Manchester and its irreversible decline" (181).

Once again, the figuration of place—here absolutely uncanny since Ferber's portrait already imitates the Courbet the narrator has reproduced in the text—asks us to grapple with something other than "the relics of a walk through language." Place here—Germany, in fact—is the mark of an expulsion. It quite literally "spells out an absence." It is the abandonment by place of person, not the other way around: "To me, you see, Germany is a country frozen in the past, a curiously extraterritorial place, inhabited by people whose faces are both lovely and dreadful" (181).

The story ends with the narrator's retracing of places memorialized in the inset diary of the protagonist's mother, which tells of her childhood in Steinach and Bad Kissingen when there were once Jewish communities there. The memoirs—not a German fairy tale but rather a German-Jewish chronicle nested within the memoir of the fourth novella itself—become memento mori when their author, Luisa Lanzberg Ferber, is deported in 1941, "fate unknown" (225).[22] And thus, already subtly prepared for the resonance with the earlier photograph of a country churchyard, we come upon a dramatic two-page spread showing adjacent pictures of the Jewish cemetery in Bad Kissingen in Lower Franconia. (Known as one of the "Royal Spas of Europe," Bad Kissingen is famed for its salt springs, which were discovered in the ninth century, several hundred years after Jews first settled in Ashkenaz.)

On the left page, a gated fence with the Star of David, and an official notice reading: *"Dieser Friedhof wird dem Schutz der Allgemeinheit empfohlen. Beschädigungen Zerstörungen und jeglicher beschimpfende Unfug werden strafechtlich verfolgt"* (222). "This cemetery is recommended to the protection of the general public. Destructive damage and any insulting mischief are vigorously prosecuted." On the facing page, gravestones; the short text above, continuing on the next page, reads,

What I saw had little to do with cemeteries as one thinks of them; instead, before me lay a wilderness of graves, neglected for years, crumbling and gradually sinking into the ground amidst tall grass and wild flowers under the shade of trees, which trembled in the slight movement of the air. Here and there a stone placed on top of a grave witnessed that someone must have visited one of the dead—who could say how long ago. It was not possible to decipher all of the chiseled inscriptions, but the names I could still read—Hamburger, Kissinger, Wertheimer, Friedländer, Arnsberg, Auerbach, Grunwald, Leuthold, Seeligman, Frank, Hertz, Goldstaub, Baumblatt and Blumenthal—made me think that perhaps there was nothing the Germans begrudged the Jews so much as their beautiful names, so intimately bound up with the country they lived in and with its language. (223-24)

And with its topography, as well, its fusion of name and place: Baum, Blumen, Berg, Wald.

At this point, the narrator's own discourse picks up (almost literally) where the earlier allusion to fairy tales and heartbreak—and to remembering, writing, and reading—in the same story left off: "and I was touched, in a way I knew I could never quite fathom, by the symbol of the writer's quill on the stone of Friederike Halbleib, who departed this life on the 28th of March 1912. I imagined her pen in hand, all by herself, bent with bated breath over her work; and know, as I write these lines, it feels as if *I* had lost her, and as if *I* could not get over the loss despite the many years that have passed since her departure." (224–25). This may suggest how one may begin to understand the text's "quarrel with Proust." It is the very emplacement of *this* gravestone, the rootedness *here, in this plot*, of a whole people's presence memorialized in death, the incised glyph fusing the token for writing with the sign of an individual life once lived, that authorizes place, that insists on its "dogma."

If the narrator trespasses here through the license of transference—he has crossed boundaries (from border to beyond) that he cannot rightly arrogate for himself, the text deftly holds itself at a near and ironical distance. "*Dieser Friedhof wird dem Schutz der Allgemeinheit empfohlen. Beschädigungen Zerstörungen und jeglicher beschimpfende Unfug werden strafechtlich verfolgt,*" reads the warning, after all. Poaching is admonished.[23] Taking the license of the text's mimetic transfer, one may recall by way of contrast the famous opening scene of Dickens's *Great Expectations*—a novel, not insignificantly, with exile and outland always on its periphery—which features a cemetery, a reader, a recollected time "long before the days of photographs," a poacher, and an admonition.[24] But the figural narration in Dickens's great Bildungsroman is also perhaps party to *The Emigrants*' quarrel with novelistic discourse. An instruction in the dogma of place, Sebald's text is thus also a complex meditation on the meaning of memoir in the first person. It compels us to ask about both its uses and our duties toward it.

The question becomes, how do I *transmit* these stories and why do they exact such due from me? "Often I could not get on for hours or days at a time," writes Sebald's narrator, "and not infrequently I had unraveled what I had done.... By far the greater part had been crossed out, discarded, or obliterated by additions" (230).[25] The need to seek out *this* place, *these* burial plots in *this* cemetery, to read it, be marked by it, and then to show that mark; the obligation to leave England (the place possessed) in order to return briefly to Germany (the place abandoned), to be present in Steinach and Bad Kissingen after having read of them in a memoir; the care with which the memoirs and photographs are conveyed or transcribed;[26] and finally, the purposeful juxtaposition of those very place-names with the names of Jewish residents inscribed in stone in the cemeteries on their outskirts: this seems a very different exercise in drawing stories from graveyard letters.

The gravestones—more precisely, the photographic representations of gravestones—reprove the purely tropic operations of writing *as repeated by* reading: "relics of a walk through language and the successive abandonment of places." The reading of the memoirs *inside* the memoir would then seem to model reading as a bounden practice under the sway of place. 'I stayed in the Jewish cemetery till the afternoon, walking up and down the rows of graves, reading the names of the dead, but it was only when I was about to leave that I discovered a more recent gravestone, not far from the locked gate, on which were the names of Lily and Lazarus Lanzberg, and of Fritz and Luisa Ferber. . . . I stood before it for some time, not knowing what I should think; but before I left I placed a stone on the grave, according to custom" (225). Cemeteries, or excursions to them, figure prominently not only in *The Emigrants* (and in Sebald's writing, generally), but in André Aciman's essays and Anton Shammas's *Arabesques,* in Gregor von Rezzori's and Elias Canetti's memoirs, in the posthumously published prose fragments by Dan Pagis, in short essay-memoirs by Aharon Appelfeld as well as in *The Iron Tracks*. Bruno Schulz's last work, a set of painted murals, serves as a kind of accidental tombstone, and I suggest something similar in chapter 4 of this book in regard to Edward Said's *Out of Place*.

The genre of "memorial books" or *yizker bicher* for the ruined communities of Jewish eastern Europe represents a textual version of such vigil: placing a stone on the grave according to custom, but at a farther distance. Graveyards create a certain kind of pedestrian, who is thus restricted—according to custom—by perimeters, margins, markers, which compel him to read such places with eyes and feet, both, at a near distance. They are visitable but not habitable.[27] They mark a limit point, respectively, for place, for flight, for border, and beyond.

Returning to de Certeau's aperçu of readers despoiling the wealth of Egypt, one can suppose that he has post–Middle-Kingdom tomb-robbers in mind, but nothing gainsays inferring here as well a reference to the Children of Israel when finally given consent to leave Egypt by Pharoah: "They requested from the Egyptian silver vessels, gold vessels and garments . . . so they emptied Egypt" (Ex. 12:35). While not the outright plunder of the Shechemites recorded in Genesis 34 (which the rabbinic commentaries regard as compensation for unpaid wages), these are spoils in a fairly straightforward sense. Consider, however, the episode from the Book of Numbers in which men are sent by Moses as scouts to search the land of Canaan, which precipitates their own generation's effacement, a forty-years' wandering in the wilderness.

That decree is due to both their misprision of what they saw and their misreporting of it. In Joshua 2, which narrates a successful version of such a mission, the scouts are called *meraglim,* pedestrians, those who go by foot. In the Pentateuchal story, however, they are known as *tarim,* spies, or more simply, sightseers. "And they brought up an evil report of the land which they had searched [*taru*] unto the children of Israel, saying, the land through which we have gone to search [*latur*] is a land that devours its inhabitants" (13:31).

Their touring, a kind of poaching, projects upon the landscape their own unstable position as interpretive comers and goers. Indeed, the Talmud, in Tractate *Sotah* 34b, connects the word for "explore" in this passage, *veashperu,* with "shame," *veshapra,* or as Emmanuel Levinas annotates it from his essay "Promised Land or Permitted Land," "Those who explore the land will cover it with shame," that is, by demystifying it (*Nine Talmudic Readings,* 55). This is a more metaphorical kind of plunder, or despoliation, in de Certeau's own sense of "metaphor" as the traversal and selective organization of landscape. And as if to underscore the charged relationship between roving and reading, this particular Torah portion concludes with the commandment to wear on one's garment fringes, *tzitzit* (a word the commentaries already associate with penetrative or projective "peering" [*metzitz*], as in Song of Songs 2:9): "that you search not *(lo taturu)* after your own heart and your own eyes" (15:36). But unlike the Ark of the Covenant's holier, less prehensile mission to "seek out" *(latur)* rest for the Israelites (Num. 10:33), human hearts and eyes risk being bodily spies—they poach and roam across lands belonging to someone else.

In the episode from Numbers—"a strange tale of no return, no homecoming," notes Ilana Pardes[28]—place stands at a remove; it withholds itself, keeps its *tarim* (touristic onlookers) at bay, as it does in a much more profound sense at the conclusion of the Torah when the prophet Moses can only look but not cross over. Earlier, in Genesis 28, which treats Jacob's twenty-year personal exile, we read that taking leave of one place prompts an encounter that is really a collision: "Jacob *departed* Beer Sheva, and set out for Haran/ He *was struck by* a certain place."[29] (Called by the rabbis *kefitzat ha-derekh,* "the jumping of the road" or "the shortening of the way," Jabob's encounter *(pegiah),* is interpreted as describing a prayer experience—that Jacob traveled supernaturally fast.) Here, place leaves a remainder; it marks the person who traverses it. Rashi, the rabbinic expositor from Troyes, observes reciprocally that "the 'leaving' of a person from a place *makes an imprint"*; a void is left behind. Or as a modern commentary puts it, to collide with a place means that it has been traveling toward oneself (Avivah Zornberg, *The Beginning of Desire,* 187). In each of these examples, however, what place says is *Sta Viator.*

2. Genre

Chov zich yarn gwalgert 　in der fremd Itzt for Ich valern in der haim.	For years I wandered about 　in the world Now I'm going home 　to wander there.

　　　Itzik Manger—born 1901, Czernowitz; resided 1938–1960, Paris, London, New York; died 1969, Tel Aviv

In his classic 1966 study of American literature, *A World Elsewhere,* Richard Poirier suggested that part of writing's territorial imperative is to create environments of freedom through the power of words. Similarly named but differently conceived, *The Elsewhere* proposes instead to explore environments of desire that could at best approximate, reach only part of the way, within the often-shifting boundaries of a non-western (east, central, Balkan) Europe and a Levantine-east Mediterranean (and in one case, Maghrebi) Middle East for a group of writers often themselves on the margins of canonical discourse. This is a choice based in part upon the way each region stands "at a near distance" from a Eurocenter and thus represents a mix of periphery and crossroads, and in part upon a common store of image and theme.[30] It also reflects the interpretive demands of a particular genre, a certain kind of text, in its formal operations.

　　That genre and that text resemble the literature of travel, yet are not entirely subsumed within it. They look like prose fiction while purporting to be autobiography (memoir, by definition, is selective in both memory and focus), recalling Paul de Man's dictum that the autobiographical indicates "not a genre or a mode, but a figure of reading or of understanding" (*The Rhetoric of Romanticism,* 70). Consider the following reflections on exile by Joseph Brodsky, and Witold Gombrowicz (in acerbic reply to his fellow exile, E. M. Cioran)[31]:

Brodsky: "If one would assign the life of an exiled writer a genre, it would have to be tragicomedy.... Life in exile, abroad, in a foreign element, is essentially a premonition of your fate in book form, of being lost on the shelf among those with whom all you have in common is the first letter of your surname." (*Altogether Elsewhere,* 4, 9)

Gombrowicz: "Why has the voice of these people faded abroad? They do not roar because, first of all, they are too free.... Everything to which they were tied and everything that bound them—homeland, ideology, politics, group, program, faith, milieu—everything vanished in the whirlpool of history and only a bubble filled with nothingness remained on the surface. Those thrown out of their little world found themselves facing a world, a boundless world, and, consequently, one that was impossible to master. Only a universal culture can come to terms with the world, never parochial cultures, never those who live only on fragments of existence. Only he who knows how to reach deeper, beyond the homeland, only he for whom the homeland is but one of the revelations in an eternal and universal life, will not be incited by the loss of his homeland. (*Altogether Elsewhere*, 154–55)

The Elsewhere is thus never a blank slate, and may be as discursively unfree as the metaphysical, political, and cultural conditions it seeks to redress. It is pre-occupied: its Crusoes will always come upon the footprints of other inhabitants. This is why Bakhtin's reminders of the relentlessly territorialized realm of utterance, quoted above, are so salutary.[32] And the more pressing therefore become the claims of a distinctive modality of reading, as this section will endeavor to show in tying it to a distinctive genre—the literature of *midbar*.

De Man's essay on self-writing, "Autobiography as De-facement," begins with skepticism about any generic definition of autobiography and ends with the startling claim that the communicative values such writing seems to install or rehearse—narrative authority, a life's "truth," voice and face (metaphorically speaking)—are all formally disfigured by the very nature of the writing itself. "Language as trope," de Man insists, "is always privative."

To the extent that, in writing, we are all dependent on this language, we are ... not silent, which implies the possible manifestation of sound at our own will, but silent as a picture, that is to say eternally deprived of voice and condemned to muteness.... Death is a displaced name for a linguistic predicament, and the restoration of mortality by autobiography deprives and disfigures to the precise extent that it restores. Autobiography veils a defacement of the mind of which it is itself the cause. (*The Rhetoric of Romanticism*, 80–81)

Briefly raising historical and formal arguments (Is autobiography a specifically pre-romantic and romantic phenomenon? Can it be written in verse?), de Man argues for the symbiosis between textual form and external reference, the autobiographical project "producing" the life as much as the life can be said to determine the autobiography. Figuration is de Man's principal suspect here—the tricks of mimesis that fetter diegesis—since the question whether the referent determines the figure or the other way around is by his account strictly undecidable.

Although de Man cites Proust, the end of the mimetic tether here for my purposes might be better fastened to a writer like Joseph Conrad, famous exilic innovator of narrative form, whose autobiographic *A Personal Record* makes some telling claims in its preface that it immediately proceeds to undermine. A novelist, writes Conrad, "remains to a certain extent, a figure behind the veil; a suspected rather than seen presence—a movement and a voice behind the draperies of fiction." Conversely, in an autobiography, in an author's own "personal notes[,] there is no such veil" (12). That the trope of cloaking more or less duplicates de Man's own critical point of departure is noteworthy by itself; for no less than Conrad's storytelling, his "fiction of autobiography" (Edward Said's term) hides its narrator in the act of revealing him, as we will rediscover in chapter 4.

But the narrative machinery of Conrad's autobiography, its logic of interruption, its acts of compelled reading/writing, its twinning of novelistic and maritime apprenticeship, its dramatization of speaking author and listening reader, and, most of all, its internal pattern of repetition (family relations, dogs, allusions to other authors and their literary characters, erased and obliterated manuscripts) relentlessly anchor the experienced—the "personal"—to the figured and inscribed—the "record."

> It is sufficient for me to say (and I am saying it at length in these pages): *J'ai vécu.* I have existed, obscure among the wonders and terrors of my time, as the Abbe Sieyes, the original utterer of the quoted words, had managed to exist through the violences, the crimes, and the enthusiasms of the French Revolution. (91)

In fact, it is *never* sufficient for Conrad to say simply that he has remained alive, since the very enunciation of that existential statement is self-consciously layered through other voices (Abbe Sieyes, Jean-Jacques Rousseau, Anatole France) and the self-conscious manipulations of a fiction-writer. "I have a pretty story to tell you"; "I am afraid I interrupted you"; "Look out there!": these are some of the strategically placed interruptions by speakers inside Conrad's text that, in reflexively mimicking its own external politics of authorship and reception, impel readers to ask, with de Man, "Is the illusion of reference not a correlation of the structure of the figure, that is to say, no longer clearly and simply a referent at all but something more akin to a fiction?" (69).[33]

Another example of the instability of literary memoir might be drawn from the work of Walter Benjamin, who, like Conrad, was a fugitive, a habitué of both center and margin, and not least, an elusive memoirist. At the beginning of his "Berlin Chronicle," he admits to "how slight a role is played by people" (*Reflections*, 30) in his recollections, and in fact, they are given over almost entirely to the spirit of place so much, so that it becomes the memoir's operative trope. "The 'Berlin Chronicle' is a misnomer," comments Peter Dementz, "because it actually offers a map of coexistent apartments, meeting places, elegant salons, shabby hotels rooms, skating rinks and tennis courts; social distinctions are expressed in terms of different urban landscapes . . . and certain streets . . . are ontological thresholds" (xvii–xviii).[34]

But Benjamin's own figures speak for themselves: from "the idea of setting out the sphere of life—bios—graphically on a map" (5) to the image of a labyrinth on paper (subsequently lost) that resembles a series of family trees, as a "diagram of my life" (30).

> I am not concerned here with what is installed in the chamber at its enigmatic center, ego or fate, but all the more with the many entrances leading into the interior. These entrances I call primal acquaintances; each of them is a graphic symbol of my acquaintance with a person whom I met, not through other people, but through neighborhood, family relationships, school comradeship, mistaken identity, companionship on travels, or other such—hardly numerous situations. So many primal relationships, so many entrances to the maze. . . . This is what the sketch of my life revealed to me as it took shape before me on that Paris afternoon. Against the background of the city, the people who had surrounded me closed together to form a figure. (30)

As absolutely concrete as Benjamin's depictions are—the moldings and balustrades of the Kaiser Friedrich School, the forecourt on Tiergartenstrasse ("this Hohenzollern labyrinth"), the *Markt-Halle* whose commerce remains as obscured in memory as the sense of its name is "eroded" by being pronounced "*Mark-Talle*"—they turn the memoir itself into a labyrinth of images and "turns of phrase"—a *tourniquet,* as de Man would say, a specular "whirligig" or "revolving door" (or what Sebald, for the title of his first book, calls *Schwindel. Gefuhle*—the trick of vertigo).

The difficulties of generic definition that affect the study of autobiography repeat an inherent instability that undoes the model as soon as it is established. [The] metaphor of the revolving door helps us to understand why this is so: it aptly connotes the turning motion of tropes and confirms that the specular structure is not primarily a situation or an event that can be located in a history, but that it is the manifestation, on the level of the referent, of a linguistic structure. (70–71)

In short, even a straightforward autobiographical text cannot help but decenter and displace *precisely* those elements it takes to be most central—its own subjective authority and its readers' desire for referential stability. Now, whether one follows de Man's argument to its irrevocably melancholy conclusions or not, his attention to autobiography's discursive *tourniquet* (his own word) has the virtue of suggesting an adjoining interpretive neighborhood to de Certeau's "series of turns *(tours)* and detours that can be compared to 'turns of phrase' or 'stylistic figures'" (*The Practice of Everyday Life,* 100). That is, whether one believes with de Man that autobiography ultimately dis-figures or defaces, displaces or decenters, still the "turning motion of its tropes" is perhaps never so much its manifest theme as when those tropes express a sense of *place displaced,* the figuration of exile, expatriation, loss, and nostalgia.

In excess of its obsession with tropes, de Man's essay has the additional relevance of focusing on one trope in particular: a cemetery scene and its metonym, gravestone epitaphs. Drawn from Romanticism's great lyric autobiographer, that scene underpins William Wordsworth's *Essays upon Epitaphs,* a text, according to de Man, "that turns compulsively from an essay *upon* epitaphs to being itself an epitaph, and more specifically, the author's own monumental inscription or autobiography" (72). De Man's focus is anti-sentimental to the point of (a characteristic) grotesquerie: Wordsworth's rhetorical desire for restoration in the face of death is undone—defaced—by the properties of rhetoric, of literary language. Throwing the voice after death paradoxically mutes voice precisely when it wants voice to speak, substituting linguistic figures for things, representations "as silent as pictures." Epitaphs merely leave their readers "eternally deprived of voice and condemned to muteness" (80). Reading, in this view, is less a practice than a privation or an ordeal.

Wordsworth's own concern, however, is the *inscription* itself, not the environs, and accordingly, de Man's immediate purposes lie quite far from his and this book's as well. De Man's favored image—reading

Introduction

as some version of death—rubs shoulders with Maurice Blanchot: for instance, his metaphorization of the reader's function as a *"Lazare, veni foras,"* a summons to open the tomb of the work lodged inside the book.[35] As post-romantic mystifications that purchase their intimations of mortality too profligately, they both bow beside the kind of scene excerpted from Sebald above. For there, however self-consciously mediated—that is, placed at ever remoter distances—the allegory of reading modeled by the cemetery vigil in *The Emigrants* makes the narration of *place* the essential matter—which in this case is death enough. Memoir, therefore, not as *de-facement* but as a complex itinerary of *placement(s)*.

Gravestone inscriptions are left unrecorded by Sebald's narrator, and thus the scene waves away the reflexivity (and *vertige*) that might flag de Man's attention. It is the *staying* in the cemetery till the afternoon, the *walking up and down* the rows of graves that parallels the *reading* of the names of the dead, and, by extension, our *reading* of this memorial act. Moreover, the photographs are indeed silent, as befits the pictures they are, but by accompanying the text, they introduce us to something quite otherwise than a purely linguistic dilemma.[36] To enlist Benjamin again, from the closing paragraph of his memoir:

> The *déjà vu* effect has often been described. But I wonder whether the term is actually well chosen, and whether the metaphor appropriate to the process would not be far better taken from the realm of acoustics. One ought to speak of events that reach us like an echo awakened by a call, a sound that seems to have been heard somewhere in the darkness of past life. Accordingly, if we are not mistaken, the shock with which such moments enter consciousness as if already lived usually strikes us in the form of a sound. It is a word, tapping, or a rustling that is endowed with the magic power to transport us into the cool tomb of long ago, from the vault of which the present seems to return only as an echo. But has the counterpart of this temporal removal ever been investigated, the shock with which we come across a gesture or a word as we suddenly find in our house a forgotten glove or reticule? And just as they cause us to surmise a stranger who has been there, there are words or gestures from which we infer that invisible stranger, the future, who left them in our keeping. (*Reflections*, 59)

Of course, it is not *our* past that the memoir-literature of *midbar* confronts us with, for it is *itself* "the stranger." Benjamin's observation is self-commenting, as he illustrates in his text's closing anecdote. But it also has the knack of ringing true for the uncanniness of Conrad's memoir (in whose preface especial pressure is placed on sound and accent), or Sebald's, or Benjamin's itself, which seem at times to reach one like echoes awakened by a call.

After Benjamin, we can call the effect, *déjà entendu,* an order of shock that, while attendant upon "the turning of its tropes" we should wish along with de Man to assign as the distinguishing feature of the genre, nevertheless leaves readers at a different kind of loss than soundlessness. Notwithstanding de Man's pessimism about the generic instability of autobiography,[37] his speculations do help to clarify the connection between memoir, trope, and place, and how the dogma of place might conceivably restore an ethics. That term, used more than a few times thus far, now warrants its own clarifying location.

3. Ethics

Zora has the quality of remaining to your memory point by point, in its succession of streets, of houses along the streets, and of doors and windows in the houses, though nothing in them possesses a special beauty or raity.... This city which cannot be expunged from the mind is like an armature, a honeycomb in whose cells each of us can place the things he wants to remember. Between each idea and each point of the itinerary an affinity or contrast can be established, serving as an immediate aid to memory.
      Italo Calvino, *Invisible Cities*

Each of this book's chapters begins with an epigraph drawn from Italo Calvino's *Invisible Cities,* which anticipates a theme or detail in the analysis to follow. His book is introduced here because its framing conceit is the act of narration—more specifically, *told stories* addressed to a *soon-to-be-superseded figure* about *cities of empire*. That act, which begins in narration and ends in reading, gives shape to one dimension of what I wish to call "ethics." The narrative audience in Calvino's text is the potentate Kublai Khan, and he is, in the practical sense, Marco Polo's reader. Their intermittent colloquy circles around one of the book's recurring themes, the discourse of travel as a *vehicle* of travel, and of concentrated patterning, and imaginative repossession, and dispossession, and loss.[38]

Itself a retracing of narrative steps from texts of elsewhere like *1001 Nights* and Johnson's *Rasselas, Invisible Cities* sketches out almost on the periphery the politics of deferral, of being held at remove, that is *The Elsewhere's* true subject. After all, like Ralph Ellison's great first novel whose title assumes one readership in particular that is optically challenged (a man invisible because he can't or won't be seen), the cities are invisible only to the Great Khan, who will never see or even visit them and who must therefore defer to his informant's illocutionary authority.

And like the great Khan, readers of Calvino's book are given over to the spell (and dogma) of place, and thereby perhaps awake to possibilities of their own affectivity before it. The stories of place may bring the places nearer, but the telling ineluctably fixes their recipient at a distance. This is caused not simply by the machinery of desire, but also by the stubborn tendency for place to elude somehow easy traversals and appropriations (the sanguine truth recorded by the narrator at the end of Albert Memmi's *La Statue de Sel*, for example, for whom the famous Biblical image serves as an apt metaphor for being immobilized and stranded in the act of composition).[39] Calvino's, in short, is a book of imagined elsewheres *and* narrative perlocutionary effects. Two of its cities in particular suggest opposite poles for my own "inside narrative" of *place-flight-border-beyond:* Zaira, city of high bastions, characterized by "relationships between the measurements of its space and the events of its past" (*Invisible Cities*, 10), and Eutropia, "not one city but many, of equal size and not unlike one another, scattered over a vast, rolling plateau" (64). In the one, a mimesis of place as its own cartography,

> The city . . . does not tell its past but contains it like the lines of a hand, written in the corners of the streets, the gratings of the windows, the banisters of the steps, the antennae of the lightning rods, the poles of the flags, every segment marked in turns with scratches, indentations, scrolls. (11)

In the other, lines of escape, a fantasy of perpetual *alibi:*

> On the day when Eutropia's inhabitants feel the grip of weariness and no one can bear any longer his job, his relatives, his house and his life, debts, the people he must greet or who greet him, then the whole citizenry decides to move to the next city, which is there waiting for them, empty and good as new. . . . So their life is renewed from move to move, among cities whose exposure or delivery or streams or winds make each site somehow different from the others. (64)

Zaira: to read a place's past, which "the city soaks . . . up like a sponge and expands" (11), from its surfaces and contours; Eutopia: exile as the very meaning of desire.

Zaira, Eutropia, Diomira, Isaura, Despina, Euphemia, Zobeide, Valdrada, Baucis, Eudoxia, Clarice. Not the least of Calvino's triumphs in this book is the enchaining of instances, together with the typology that sorts and coordinates them: Cities and memory, Cities and desire, Cities and eyes, Continuous cities, Hidden cities, Thin cities. In this respect, too, *Invisible Cities* anticipates what has drawn me to particular texts of *midbar*. Wirblbahn, Prachthof, Herben, Upper Herbem, Gruendorf, Gruenfeld, Gruenwald, Rondhof, Upper Ronhof, Sternberg, Sandberg, Steinberg, Weinberg: these are the fictive towns of an indistinct, thinly realized Europe, countries left nameless, in Aaron Applefeld's *The Iron Tracks*. Hingham, Meiringen, Yverdeon, Salin-les-Bains, Gunzenhausen, Kempten, Lechbruck, Manchester, Würzberg, Steinach, Bad Kissingen: these are some of the municipalities remembered or retraced in Sebald's *The Emigrants*.

Indeed, this is why the chapter that follows couples just those two authors and just those two texts. The sheer massing of place and the way their respective narrators coordinate disparate haunts and give voice to a metaphysics of trek and abandonment, mirror—or rather introduce—this book's own method. Read together, *midbar*-memoirists and their two memoirs trace a double itinerary. This facing of texts represents another dimension of ethics, one revealed and undertaken on the plane of criticism.

It is not merely that the partners in each fabricated dialogue—Canetti and von Rezzori, or Shammas and Pagis, or Schulz and Gombrowicz, or Said and Aciman—share certain topical points of tangency with one another. It is the very antiphony of facing texts, the acoustic space of textured resonance, that gives methodological expression to "*midbar*"—the fact that such texts are never finished in themselves, always in some sense foreign to themselves, always narrating the impossibility of their own place. Ethics would therefore mean choosing a "side" of each text to face at its counterpart, implicitly calling attention to the way other possible sides conceal themselves, hide in the act of facing. Texts faced at each other always and necessarily belong at a near distance; their counterpoint is one of approach and recession (a notion treated explicitly in chapter 4).

Critically, thus, one has a performative, practical, ethical stake in the process of *metaphorein,* of being situated elsewhere, whereby both one's own relationship to text and texts' relationship to one another participate in what Roland Barthes calls "*advenience* or even *adventure*" (*Camera Lucida,* 19). It is in this regard, too, that de Certeau's formulation makes methodological sense, detaching texts from their lost or accessory origin, "combin[ing] their fragments and creat[ing] something un-known in the space organized by their capacity for allowing an indefinite plurality of meanings" (169).

And yet de Certeau's own rhetorical question gives certain pause: "Is this 'reading' activity reserved for the literary critic (always privileged in studies of reading), or can it be extended to all cultural consumers?" (169) Maybe one has to settle for being a certain kind of poacher after all, trafficking between discourses—which is finally what any responsible literary critic does when s/he compounds a simple record of a text's effects, their *advenience,* with a reading of them, one's *collision* with them. Still, what this book proposes to keep in the foreground is a certain terrain, the specification of a certain *practice* of reading as an *ethics:* how narrative literature thematizes proximity and distance as the very modes of telling and listening, the borders that enjoin effects—resistances as well as mimetic loyalties—in readers.

According to a recent essay by the critic John Guillory, reading represents an ethical practice because the pleasure it evokes was originally seen therapeutically as a "legitimate end of reading, as an end it itself" (*The Turn to Ethics,* 40). "Ethical practice" is a concept Guillory has borrowed from the work of Michel Foucault, where "ethical" names a dimension midway between the moral and the aesthetic, opening onto but keeping itself distinct from both, and "practice" denotes an agential realm more or less internally safeguarded against being usurped as an instrument of power/knowledge. But the equilibrating, autonomous function Guillory discovers in early-modern ideologies of reading ultimately gives way to a historical bifurcation between kinds of *readers*—a lay readership of self-distracted consumers on one hand, and a professional class (de Certeau would call them *clercs*) on the other, that "asceticizes" reading for the sake of political ends—its "transformative effects" on others.

And this, argues Guillory, is a cause for double lament. For in both cases, the aesthetic pleasure of the reading experience itself becomes occulted, leached of its self-improving, and therefore ethical, effect. Moreover, each version of reading fundamentally *misrecognizes* itself, lives an alienated life. In their stead and to heal the breach between them, Guillory proposes an intermediate practice based on an ethic reducible to neither the pure pleasure of consumption nor a re-moralization of reading in the service of political effects. To refine such a mode, finally, would portend reading's "self-recognition" (30).

Endorsing the link between practice and the ethical, this book views each component somewhat differently—"practice" for my purposes lying closer to de Certeau's sense than Foucault's,[40] and ethics connoting a centrifugal move outward, toward alterity rather than a centripetal motion back to self. Like Guillory, Charles Altieri outlines a version of "the ethical" that also seems to promise a most practicable theory of practice. As Guillory wants to return reading to an ethic of self-care, so Altieri takes issue with mainstream ethical criticism whose approach to literary texts (principally narrative) would turn its readers into "judicious spectators" (Martha Nussbaum's term). The effect of such criticism, Altieri writes, "is to cast literary experience as primarily a spectator sport: readers retain the distance of the easy chair even as they learn to sympathize with how agents engage their particular imagined worlds" ("Lyrical Ethics and Literary Experience").[41]

We should be concerned instead with "how and where we become situated by full participation in the energies organized by the work." "Minimally... we become attentive to the selves that are possible when we manage to deploy distinctive powers of mind and sensibility. And often the focus is much less on how we perceive or interpret the world beyond ourselves than on how we manage to achieve states of will or of satisfaction or of painful separation in relation to events and even to overall assessments about how life might be worth living" (32–33).

The gain, then, is *aesthetic* in an ethical degree, just as the foil here is an ethical criticism (Guillory's "remoralized" discourse) that risks muffling literary accents and timbres in an appeal to more or less non-textual modes of judgment. For Altieri, it is the specifically *lyrical* (rather than the narrative) that stands in the gap between cardinal values for literary experience, on the one hand, and formulations derived from ethical theory, on the other. And for Altieri, the dimension of literary experience too often scanted by ethical criticism is aesthetic transport, a *participation* in passionate states, or as he names it simply, "lyrical power." Altieri's and Guillory's notions coincide along this hinge: as agents on the move, both "passional" and "therapeutic" selves range freely through a text and, to the degree that they exercise elective mobility, become poachers and nomads by another name. But what one misses in either of these programs for reading—these practices—is a less self-invested subjectivity, in motion "toward the other" (as Levinas might say), and a sense in which a text can course ahead of or fall behind one's powers to master it, the specifically textual condition of place tied to its own displacement.

Such out-of-phase quality is what one *midbar*-writer, André Aciman, calls "palintropism." On a pilgrimage to Illiers-Combray, he explains the phenomenon in relation to Proust: "How could Marcel have ever loved such a place? Or had he never loved it? Had he loved only the act of returning to it on paper, because that was how he lived his life—first by wanting to live it, and later by remembering having wanted to, and ultimately by writing about the two? The part in between—the actual living—was what had been lost" (*False Papers*, 77).

Limited by Aciman to a property of the *apatride*'s experience, the concept of palintropism, however, seems just as efficacious for figuring and renaming an ethics and praxis of reading. For not to be at home in one's home exactly describes the dialectical relationship between kind of text and mode of reading this book names *midbar*—an ethical practice that is the calibration of distances and proximities, an always risky or adventitious treading across the terrain of textual elsewheres.[42] That term itself, however, along with "belonging" and "near distance" now requires some unpacking of its own.

4. Elsewhere

> In short, Adorno says with a grave irony, "it is part of morality not to be at home in one's home." To follow Adorno is to stand away from "home" in order to look at it with the exile's detachment. For there is considerable merit in the practice of noting the discrepancies between various concepts and ideas and what they actually produce. We take home and language for granted; they become nature, and their underlying assumptions recede into dogma and orthodoxy.
> Edward Said, "Reflections on Exile" (147)

What, then, of the dogma of place? Perhaps, if one intends to write about it, and if there is indeed to be no scot-free and place is to have its due, both "irremediably secular and unbearably historical," one should make the trip to Czernowitz oneself, in order to be disenchanted of the spell of "unreal estate" and "exilic alibi."[43] To Czernowitz, and the Bukovina of Appelfeld, von Rezzori, Dan Pagis, and Itzik Manger. To Ándre Aciman's occluded Alexandria, "The Capital of Memory." To Anton Shammas's tessellated Fassuta, "built on the ruins of the Crusader castle of Fassove, which was built on the ruins of Mifshata, the Jewish village that had been settled after the destruction of the Second Temple" (*Arabesques*, 11). To Bruno Schulz's somber Drohobycz, a place of internal exile. To Elias Canetti's Ruschuk—heteroglot and many-peopled, from whose child's vantage, "the rest of the world was known as 'Europe'," (*Memoirs*, 7); and to Marrakesh, the site of adult excursion, whose voices, half-heard and half-understood, "beyond words, deeper and more equivocal than words" (23), seem to portend the very essence of *midbar* as simultaneous speech and wilderness.

Irremediably secular and unbearably historical—that is, lined, scathed by twentieth-century nationalisms and polities—each of these locales is nevertheless both privatized and mystified in their respective memoirists' writing. The one seems actually to necessitate the other. The peculiar symbiosis between *these* texts on the one hand, and *these* places and regions on the other, suggests that what the story of *place-flight-border-beyond* betokens, finally, is an allegory of reading. A reader of this kind of elegiac writing (that, like a gravestone, marks a place and memorializes a loss) would thus always be an "addressee come from abroad" (de Certeau) or "a foreigner carrying in the crook of his arm a little book"(Edmond Jabès)—estranged, kept at bay.

The solitary reader should become, like Rousseau, a solitary walker, then, in real time and space—as in *The Emigrants,* summoned almost terrestrially to exchange the mirror for the road, to justify one kind of mimesis with another, to take up, and, not read, but walk circumspectly, at a near distance. Following Edward Said's lead above, one would thus not be taking *elsewhere* and *language* for granted either. Embodying the complementary gesture, before one effectively "stands away from" a place, one should perhaps reside there, or at least arrive at, visit, *collide* with, it.

In the present case, however, such a road remained untaken. The trip to Czernowitz was never made. But the impulse to have done so—like the biblical Jacob, to encounter, collide with a place—surfaces (im)presses as it does, because the texts themselves provoke a peculiar oscillation of desire and responsibility, the wish to luxuriate at home (textually speaking), but also to venture forth into the Real. Perhaps it is because so many of them feature a cemetery visit. Perhaps it is on account of the "stationary flight, the flight of intensity" they display—first-personal in Sebald and Appelfeld; addressive in Gombrowicz; extra-temporal and extra-territorial in Canetti and Schulz; at once mythic and ironic in Shammas and Aciman—each still *binding* one in some way to its textual calculus, so that one belongs both nearly and distantly. And it is the problematic of *belonging*—"at a near distance"—that captures not only *midbar* writers' ambivalence toward the places they have left or that have abandoned them, but the predicament of readers as well, as they take up a double position, within and outside their texts.

"Belonging" is a curious word, after all. Etymologically, it represents the intensive form of ME *"longen"* ("to go along with, accompany, appertain to") and the compound form O.E. *gelang* ("at hand or dependant on"), and thus, "To relate to, to be a dependency, adjunct, appendage, or adherent of." Yet it incorporates a morpheme whose alternate etymology (from O.E. *langian*) connotes "being or seeming long; to 'think long'," and therefore "to desire, yearn, wish earnestly." Thus in "belonging," one can hear counterpointed the senses of both *possession/relatedness* and *yearning/desire*—similar but not identical states of feeling, as Witold Gombrowicz illustrates in the following passage from his *Diary:* "not to love Poland because I was close to it, to love Argentina because I always had it a certain distance, to love it now, yes, when I was moving, tearing away . . . and in this growing distance, consumed by a furious love for what is growing more distant from me" (3:77-78). "Near distance"—a phrase rerouted from another moment in Gombrowicz's *Diary* when the author and a fellow train passenger must "rest [their] unseeing gazes on each other from a very near distance" (17)—is very nearly oxymoronic. And as such, it recapitulates the tension of near and far compacted in "be-longing."

Together, the two phrases yield a doubled, recursive effect that we might call proximity-at-a-remove on the other side of elsewhere, which captures the distinctive polarity at work in the writing of *midbar*. Not coincidentally, "belonging at a near distance" also describes the regional bivalence at play for east-central Europe and the Levant/East Mediterranean, the large-scale geographies that figure in this study over and above individual authors' allegiances. Each is a region of multiple palintropisms, and each a shadowy double of the other: Janus-faced toward "west" and "east" alike, at a near distance from "europe" and the "middle east," the one shading into a European middle east at its point of tangency, the other, into a middle-eastern Europe.[44] Historically, both have been dominated by diffuse, multi-ethnic imperial powers—Hapsburg-Austro-Hungarian and Ottoman—in whose aftermath, regional identity becomes tied as much to what is "not Europe" as to what is culturally, ethnically, linguistically autonomous, one's own.

Each region exemplifies the Bakhtinian loop between "one's own" and "half someone else's" that merges boundaries of land and language, depolarizes Occident and Orient as ratios rather than distinct cultural Imaginaries. And in the case of Shammas's Fassuta or Appelfeld's Czernowitz or Canetti's Ruschuk, the cities themselves are palimpsests, "marginocentric cities," as they have been termed (Cornis-Pope and

Neubauer, 26)—nodal points of many tongues and multiple ethnicities. Each region, whether the forward-looking "east-central Europe" or the anachronistic "Levant" asserts its right to a fictionality across or beyond more customary demarcations. The Levant and east-central Europe overwrite topographies that answer to the common-consensual yet no less constructed, entities of, say, "the Middle East" or "Mitteleuropa." In the case of a projected history of literary cultures of east-central Europe, Cornis-Pope and Nebauer, for instance, call their project a "rearticulation" of boundaries that too easily freeze, rather than free up, borders (25).

The writers of the texts that distill the cities which represent the lands that are defined by these regions—Drohobycz, Poland; Ruschuk, Bulgaria; Czernowitz, Romania-Ukraine; Alexandria, Egypt; Fassuta, Palestine-Israel; and tangentially, Marrakesh, Morocco and Buenos Aires, Argentina—are thus all alive to the prismatic light those places cast and refract: the near distances and ambiguous belonging through which homeland and diaspora become textual, narrative, and mimetic problems after they have done their work of geographical placement and displacement.

In its metonymic progression, writer-text-city-land-region also echoes the contours of place-flight-border-beyond. And the component at dead center corresponding to what remain coded allusions in the narrative kernel is, of course, *city*. Of the writers in this book, Gombrowicz writes trenchantly but also abstractly about "Poland," the nation as such; and Sebald conjures Germany as a ubiquitously spectral presence. The rest concern themselves with particular cities and towns or with Europe and the Middle East in the abstract. In my own particular case, as introduced in the next section, it is *Strzegowo,* a kind of invisible city subtracted, lifted out from the patria enclosing it, that beckons—no longer discoverable, barely a place of memory now; and thus, *only* narratable.

5. Place Name

Az man kumt iber di planken, krigt man andere gedanken.
    Yiddish saying

As this volume's author's previous book is entitled *The Fence and the Neighbor,* the saying above—which, loosely translated, means "When you climb the fence, other thoughts commence"—felt especially apropos upon realizing that in that book's ending lay the seed of the present

Introduction   31

book's beginning. Its final section, entitled "Proper Names," briefly discusses the East-European origin of the philosophers Emmanuel Levinas and Yeshayahu Leibowitz, the significance of their family-names, and the fact that Yiddish was spoken in their childhood homes. Because of the relation between family- and place-name, this section also mentions my own paternal family's original East-European name together with its history in the shtetl of Strzegowo on the Polish/German border.

The book's very last footnote cites the *Yizker buch* (the first word in Yiddish means "may he remember") published shortly after the Second World War to commemorate the town's exterminated Jewish population, which included relatives of mine. It was not until some time after climbing the fence, while browsing for online records of my grandfather's passage from eastern Europe to America that I thought to perform an internet word-search for "Strzegowo," which in turn produced the wholly unexpected discovery of an English translation of the memory book that had been published the previous year.[45]

I was familiar with the three-page account of the Novogrodsky family written by a distant cousin in the original Yiddish, but to read it anew in the language of public record was revelatory. More dramatic and heartbreaking yet were references to my family that I had overlooked in another profile, the most plangent of which is the following:

Reb Faivl Novogrodsky [my great-uncle] was one of the best types of people in Strzegowo. Perhaps it was because he was such a sick man. In the last years he was very ill and his whole life was determined by it from one attack to the next—it was mostly heart trouble. . . . Why does he remain in my memory as a sick man? Perhaps it is because of the characteristic way he spoke to me in the midst of his illness. "Reb Faivl," I used to ask him, "What is missing in your life?" And he answered, "Nothing is lacking and I have nothing." Two nights before he died I was sitting in his house. And when he came to himself after a while, he said, "What is your problem? Live, live while you are young." And a minute later: "Live, for you see what life is really about." . . . These two men, Faivl Novogrodsky and Israel Rosen are coming from the home of Yitzkhak Meir Piotrikowsky. Every evening they enjoy themselves in the office over a few lines of Gemara and a tasty glass of tea. Then they talk about many different issues, in general as well as personal ones. Reb Moyshe Shoykhet, in the sharpness of his insight calls the little table around which the three sit the "mysterious table" because they place there every secret in Strzegowo.[46]

I thought first of my late father, who had anglicized the family name, and whose last years were similarly beset by illness and heart trouble. His was an individualized though common enough story of second-generation immigrant New York—a "middle man," as Philip Roth has termed the generational standing of his own father. Of the men from the previous generation of Novogrodskys, Faivl was the sole brother of four to have lived and died in the *shtetl* itself, Henekh having left for Palestine: Itsl, my grandfather, for America: and Abba, along with his wife and son, for Warsaw on the eve of German occupation, to perish finally in Treblinka. A sadly common enough albeit individualized story of twentieth-century Jewish geography, passage, and dispossession—place, flight, border, beyond.

One felt an impossible nostalgia for environs entirely foreign, but also suddenly closer to understanding what de Certeau said about writers, transposed to the position of readers, "the constantly initial fact that the subject is never authorized by a place . . . that he is always foreign to himself." Moreover, Reb Faivl's words, though heard by me as intensely affecting, had the sound of worn cultural and literary currency. One thought of myriad elderly men gently instructing their charges, and—already in mind of literary exiles and émigrés and Jamesan cadences—of Lambert Strether's admonition to Chad Newsome in James's *The Ambassadors*—the same Strether who imposed a brake upon his own imagination when he observed, "You could deal with a man as himself—you couldn't deal with him as someone else."[47] For mimesis is a form of poaching, too.

A particular utterance recorded at that "mysterious table" in a Strzegowo that no longer exists stands out, however, on account of its mystery: "Nothing is lacking and I have nothing." An ailing and elderly Jew's echo of rabbinic wisdom, perhaps.[48] Or some more personalized equanimity. Its full meaning, finally, would have to remain one of Strzegowo's undisclosed secrets, but its distance from me—the fact that it is not and could never be in my hearing, that it was so very far from me and I from it—recalled to my mind the sigh preserved as a "sound-secret" in verses by the poet from Vilna, the "Jerusalem of Lithuania," Abraham Sutzkever.

> Zvishn klangn-soydos vas ich halt zei oych a rigl
> Soydos fun bnei- odom, shteyner, aynvoyner mit fligl,
> Oder say fun lebendike, say fun toyte blinkn—
> Mont ich mir a lebn-lang der klang un mont a tikun.
>
> [Among the sound-secrets that I keep locked up,
> Secrets of human beings, of stones, of dwellers with wings,

Introduction 33

> Whether from the glances of the living or the dead.
> The sound resounds in me all my life and demands its due.]⁴⁹

There are no more living members of my family named Novogrodsky. They are as far from me as prewar Palestine, the New York's Lower East Side on the eve of the First World War, Strzegowo and Treblinka in wartime Poland. The Strzegowo *Yizker* book recounts a story of loss made especially poignant because a whole townspeople's presence had been obliterated from the town it once claimed as home. Like the tombstones in *The Emigrants'* Steinach, only alphabetic letters remain. And like Aharon Appelfeld's own village, Zadova, near Czernowitz in the Bukovina of the former Austro-Hungarian Empire, "whose name is found only on ordnance maps" ("Buried Homeland," 48), while the town of Strzegowo perdures, the *shtetl* Strzegowo is gone forever—sunk in the past's abyss, "a darkness that gives back nothing."[50] Or if verifiable, not wistfully so—as Appelfeld and Gregor von Rezzori differentially attest in describing contemporary Czernowitz:

> I returned home with a few sentimental drawings of Czernovitz, which I had bought in a department store. They did not reflect the Czernovitz I had seen. There the potential for Jewish tourism had not been developed, as for example, it had been in Prague. In Czernowitz, the splendid temple of the city is now a place where people watch movies, gamble, and play billiards. Perhaps it's better that way—no counterfeit sentimentality. ("Buried Homeland," 56)

> You must never undertake the search for time lost in the spirit of nostalgic tourism. (von Rezzori, *The Snows of Yesteryear*, 290)

Yet not so verifiable after all. For, the same "splendid temple of the city" Appelfeld describes, von Rezzori correctly records as destroyed—("I was to learn that only the flamboyant neo-Assyrian temple of the Jews had been razed during the German occupation") (280).[51] And thus does Elsewhere license belonging at a near distance.

6. Proper Name

> The man from Asia, having settled in Africa, been driven to England, not arrived there.
>   Elias Canetti, *The Human Province*

Like most Ashkenazi families, mine can claim only a relatively short history for its surname, since it was only in the eighteenth century, under the czar, that persons formerly and traditionally identified solely by patronymic—Noson ben Meshullam, Avigdor ben Moshe haLevi, say—were required to choose a last name. This was not unlike the czarist fiat in 1896 that villages institute a market day so that thenceforward they would be known as "towns"—the destiny of Strzegowo, in fact. A minor development in Jewish history but still worth remarking, this meant that the politics of identity at the level of proper name were to be allied with that always unstable feature of Jews' quotidian experience: land. Property, in the form of place or vocation, became attached to surname (as for many of the names Sebald reads on the tombstones). And typically, as in my own family, the chosen name was a toponym. Thus, the Novogrodskys became identified by and through a place-name in Russia that translates into English as "new town."

Something to which I had never given particularly much thought: that my last name signified a place; (and was, moreover, anagramatically akin to Canetti's man from elsewhere not arrived—that is, "went on"); that it conveyed a distinction between an erstwhile habitation and one new-found; that paradoxically, its translation into English, though literal, severed an identifiable link to originally native linguistic, cultural grounds; that such a link, the name in Polish, was uncannily linked to the town Strzegowo itself (which because it had been developed so quickly was briefly given the sobriquet Novy Berlin—"New Berlin"): suddenly, all this mattered for the writing in front of me.

At the beginning of Simon Schama's *Landscape and Memory*, the author similarly initiates his history of landscape-tradition in the West personally and at ground level—"the archive of the feet" (24)—by journeying to Gilby in a forested area of northeast Poland that shares the countryside with Lithuania. It is the place where the Schama family of Jewish foresters had its roots. Yet, "Trees have roots. Jews have legs," he recalls once being admonished in his student days, as if to say, that the past has moved on; he will nevertheless make the trek, reading whatever figures and characters he can discern in the footsteps of his East-European forbears.

Schama, however, is at pains to locate his forbears as not only *from* an elsewhere but as workers *upon* it, claimants to its physicality. After a brief detour into the story of Polish poet Adam Mickiewicz—descended from Jewish converts, briefly settled before dwelling among the Polish diaspora in Paris, in Kovno, Lithuania, and whom Schama therefore claims "for a *Landsmann*" (30)—he returns to his tourist's contemplation of a bygone, Jewish-Polish-Lithuania before borders and

Baltic/Slavic divisions.⁵² "Kowno would have to remain a tantalizing distance away. But to be in my grandfather's landscape—timbered Lithuania—I did not need to cross any borders at all. When I stood on the mound at Gilby I was already there" (35).

In fact, though, he does continue the sojourn a little further on—"the detour" of the introduction's title—to a near-literal instance of what the novelist Aharon Appelfeld has called "buried homeland," a Jewish cemetery in Punsk, all but unlocatable now under the dense undergrowth that has completely covered it.

It was only by crushing the dandelions underfoot that I could feel something other soft-packed dirt. I knelt down and parted the stalks and leaves, brushed away the fuzz of their seedballs. Two inches of grizzled stone appeared, the Hebrew lettering virtually obliterated by heavy growths of tawny mustard-colored lichen. . . . I could have spent a day with a shovel and shears and exposed an entire world, the subterranean world of the Jews of Punsk. But to what end?. . . The tombs themselves were being covered, sliding gently and irrevocably into their companionable mound as verdant Lithuania rose to reclaim them. The headstones that had been lovingly cut and carved were losing any signs that human hands had wrought them. They were becoming a geological layer. I lay down and stared through the branches at the blue beyond, listened to the elms and the poplars saying an indistinct Kaddish, and thought, Well, once there was a Lithuania and no Jews and for that matter no Christians either. Then there were Jews and some of them lived about the wood and took to the rivers and the towns, and now there were no Jews and forest stands there. Perhaps Deutscher was right, I thought. Trees have roots; Jews have legs. I walked away from the mound at Punsk. (36)⁵³

One may associate Schama's apothegm with the famously diasporist George Steiner, who used it to underscore his belief in text-as-homeland rather than place; but another lesson can be drawn here, and it is both Lithuanian and Levinasian. In an essay on Judaism that alleges human freedom from "the sedentary forms of existence" whereby "other fidelities and responsibilities" are instituted through the ethical relation to similarly unbound others, Levinas (born in Kovno, emigrated to Paris) writes, "Man, after all, is not a tree, and humanity is not a forest" (*Difficult Freedom*, 23). There is place, and there is place contained within memory or by representation, and the two do not and need not necessarily coincide. Whether or not I myself would journey to East-Central Europe and the Levant (with forays to Argentina and Morocco) and study in pedestrian archives, no travel was necessary to discover this distinction between roots and legs. Language itself can walk, which is of course the double-meaning of *"midbar,"* and which my own family's surname demonstrates by having walked away from its roots, preserving their sense while effacing their reference.

On the other hand, it was not enough that the landscape itself might be heard reciting Kaddish. That was what the Strzegowo *Yizker* book was for. And that is also, albeit less mournfully but still elegiacally, how the texts of *midbar* seem to beckon, "like an echo awakened by a call, a sound that seems to have been heard somewhere in the darkness of past life," or as Benjamin similarly evokes a disturbance of the present through the past, "a rustling that is endowed with the magic power to transport us into the cool tomb of long ago, from the vault of which the present seems to return only as an echo."

7. Lightness

> One day Guido Cavalcanti left Orto San Michele and walked along the Corso degli Adimari, which was often his route, as far as San Giovanni. Great marble tombs, now in Santa Reparata, were then scattered about San Giovanni. As he was standing between the porphyry columns of the church shut fast behind him, Master Betto and his company came riding along the Piazza de Santa Reparata. Catching sight of Guido among the tombs, they said, "Let's go pick a quarrel." Guido, seeing himself surrounded by them, answered quickly: "Gentlemen, you may say anything you wish to me in your own home." Then, resting his hand on one of the great tombs and being very nimble, he leaped over it and, landing on the other side, made off and rid himself of them.
>
> Bocaccio, *Decameron* VI.9

This passage about the Florentine poet Cavalcanti is quoted by Italo Calvino as the image he wishes his readers to keep in mind for the literary attribute he will esteem as "lightness." The scene of vaulting on nimble legs over a tombstone Calvino finds emblematic of a particular literary sensibility, which for him is associated not with vagueness and the haphazard but rather precision and determination (*Six Memos for the Next Millenium*, 16). His own working method, he explains, "has more often than not involved the subtraction of weight [:]... to remove weight, sometimes from people, sometimes from heavenly bodies, sometimes from cities; above all . . . from the structures of stories and from language" (4).

It would not be misrepresenting things overmuch if I confessed to nearly the opposite tendency in my own work: to uphold (as Calvino might say) the values of pressure and weight—the weight of human encounter, the weight of interpretive obligation, the weight of words. Certainly, the image of vaulting over tombstones ill accords with the gravity underscored by emblematic scenes of cemetery visits and vigils recounted in this introduction and in later chapters. To be sure, Calvino's lightness is not Milan Kundera's (who is certainly a likelier choice as concerns the literature of *midbar*). Nor, for that matter, does it correspond to the anti-gravitational force of skepticism one finds in Joseph Brodsky or Norman Manea (whose recent contribution to the Elsewhere, a cross between Canetti and Gombrowicz, pointedly resists the unbearable heaviness of exilic identity or the idolatry of place).[54] Yet lightness in Calvino's sense represents a virtue that, if it cannot always be borne out in subject matter here, does describe the arcing effect of buttressed texts connected by airy filaments I wish to capture in this book—as Calvino says of the invisible city Ersilia, "spider-webs of intricate relationships seeking a form."

After all, nothing would be more self-canceling than to pinion the Elsewhere or ossify the supple tendons that enable "belonging at a near distance." The compassionate genius of Sebald's *The Emigrants* is its obliquity of form, its meandering method of detour. Likewise, the heart of Aciman's palintropic sensibility is its capacity to spring back. It represents for him "a sort of systematic *reversement* reminiscent of the back-sprung reflex Homeric bow, which was strung in such a way as to counter the normal curvature of the bow, reversing the curve to gain more power" (*False Papers*, 15-16). Or as Julia Kristeva remarks, the very condition of the not-at-home seems to require that one "lighten that otherness by constantly coming back to it" while also endeavoring to "merely touch it, brush by it, without giving it a permanent structure" (*Strangers to Ourselves*, 3). This is also the secret of Jacob's waking from his dream after having "collided with a certain place" in Genesis 28, as mentioned earlier. On the verse "And Jacob lifted up his legs" (29: 1), Avivah Zornberg notes, "The Targum adds an adverb, 'lightly'"; thus do "Jacob's feet, in midrashic sources, become a symbol for the conflict of lightness and gravity" (199-200). Thus also does "place" become "flight" in the positive sense of "buoyancy," and it is in the same spirit that my work proposes a commerce with the dogma of place that aims *beyond*; indeed, as the chapters progress, they trace a trajectory something like Guido's nimble vault, gravity offset by lift, a movement from weight toward lightness.

Finally, in a project like this where the rubbing between texts is as important as the interpretive friction applied to them,[55] one wants to guard against merely forced resemblance and correspondence, the kind proclaimed at its baldest by Shakespeare's Captain Fluellen: "There is a river in Macedon, and there is also a river at Monmouth . . . and there is salmons in both" (*Henry V,* iv.7). A river can indeed be found in Canetti's Ruschuk as likewise in von Rezzori's (and Appelfeld's) Czernowitz, but the two should be differentiated accordingly, whatever aquatic life they do contain.

Also, since figuration means language on the move, one does well to heed the counsel of a famously bounded American poet to be "at home in metaphor,"[56] even when the metaphors themselves bear the imprint or tattoo of the unhomed and far away. The tropings of literary memoir can be *tourniquets,* but a critical study that follows suit does so at its own risk. Ideally, if the assembled texts here have been paired aright, they discover new permutations of place, flight, border, and beyond at the margins of their encounters with one another. This, then, would be the specifically intertextual import of "belonging at a near distance" whereby one text becomes the other's elsewhere, and the resulting harmonics enhance rather than eclipse the self-subsistent melodies of each.

Sometimes, such convergences lie in wait to be heard: when, for example, Aharon Appelfeld was asked in an interview whether he knew Canetti's work, he replied, "Of course I know Canetti. He belongs to my 'family'."[57] Or when asked by André Aciman, what he thinks of "such writers as Elias Canetti and Aharon Appelfeld who, incidentally, was also born in Czernowitz," Gregor von Rezzori replies, "I admire Canetti. . . . I feel at home in his world. . . . Of Appelfeld I have read only one book and thought it brilliant." Or when von Rezzori again, in his memoir, etches an aleatory transit between central Europe and the Levant, relating that his pregnant mother spent winter months away from the Bukovina in Luxor, Egypt, and he "for a time, matured in embryonic safeness" (59); or, in the opposite direction, so to speak, when he contributes one of the blurbs in the inside cover of Aciman's *Out of Egypt.*

At bottom, though, *The Elsewhere* couples into pairs the books or writers whose attraction it wishes to register because that facing of texts accurately records their *advenience,* how they came upon (collided with) me, and, through the lens of criticism, how they come upon each other — "as if those words committed to paper had not, as it were, opened up of their own accord" (*The Emigrants,* 128). Place from Place. Flight from Flight. Border from Border. Border from Beyond.

Each of the following chapters draws a heading from that same narrative kernel, together with an epigraph from Calvino's *Invisible Cities.* In sequence, they also follow a route: from Western to eastern to central

Europe and the Balkan Peninsula (with detours to Argentina and Morocco), south to the Levant and eastern Mediterranean, circling back to the area known as the Bukovina, one of the original embarkation points. Each couples a Jewish and a non-Jewish writer (though this is more fortuitous than programmatic), and each conducts its analysis more asymmetrically than not (not every text, in other words, receives equal time). Each, finally, holds vigil at a cemetery, and asks its reader-travelers to pause before they plunder.

"Place from Place, and Place from Flight," traces two transits through an extraterritorial Europe. Though oblique to one another in several important respects, W. G. Sebald's *The Emigrants* and Aharon Appelfeld's *The Iron Tracks* are treated as parallel exercises in narrative reclamation after the calamity of dispossession. *Midbar* here is what leads up to and away from the destruction of Jewish eastern Europe, and because "elsewhere" and the meaning of "belonging" are made willfully indeterminate by these authors, a terrain, so to speak, forms around the writing of disaster.

"Flight from Flight, and Flight from Border," moves on to Poland, or rather, its metaphorical and metonymic poles, Argentina and the Galician town of Drohobycz, by looking at the writing of Polish modernists Witold Gombrowicz and Bruno Schulz, the one departing Europe on the eve of world war only to return a quarter of a century later, the other succumbing to its horrors in 1942. This longest of the book's chapters shifts between them on the pivot of two contemporaneous essays by Emmanuel Levinas, De l'évasion (1935) and "Quelques reflexions sur la philosophie de l'hitlerisme" (1934), in order to tease out the meaning of escape or exile for each writer against the background of an unstable Europe and precarious national mythos of Poland. It builds throughout upon a series of scenic tableaux drawn from Gombrowicz's Diary, Schulz's fiction, and his short essays on Joseph Piłsudski.

"Border from Border" returns to Appelfeld's native region, the Bukovina (Czernowitz), moving south to Bulgaria (Ruschuk) and Morocco (Marrakesh) via Gregor von Rezzori's *The Snows of Yesteryear* and Elias Canetti's *The Tongue Set Free* and *The Voices of Marrakesh*. Divided between liking to feel the past strange and liking to feel it familiar, both of these *dépaysées après la guerre*, central Europeans from an East that is still West and a West that looks East, take up the same Jamesian challenge to different effect: to catch the past at the right moment and at the right angle—on one side or the other of its "nearer distances and clearer mysteries."

"Border from Beyond" juxtaposes two similarly titled books by two correspondingly diasporic former-citizens of the Levant: *Out of Egypt* by André Aciman and *Out of Place* by Edward Said. The two accounts specifically designated as "memoir" by their authors, these works both banish religiosity in the name of a secularism that remains oddly hanging, incomplete. As the chapter that moves the analysis from settings in East-Central Europe, the Balkan Peninsula, and the Maghreb, to those in and around the eastern Mediterranean, this one (the shortest of the five), begins by positioning its authors relative to two expatriate Eastern Europeans and their reflections on nostalgia—Joseph Conrad, in his autobiographical travel essay, "Poland Revisited," and Svetlana Boym, in *The Future of Nostalgia*—and retrieves the notion of "counterpoint" as a critical *desideratum*.

The final chapter, "Beyond from Beyond," begins in Galilean Fassuta, migrates beyond the shores and seas of the Levant, revisits both the Bukovina before the war by way of Radautz (thirty-five miles southwest of Czernowitz), and the State of Israel afterward; receding, finally—on an interpretive horizon—*beyond*. *Arabesques* by the expatriate Israeli Arab Anton Shammas and *Abba* by the Romanian-born Israeli Dan Pagis chart the serpentine route. The questions of genre, ethics, and elsewhere are once again key for a novel (the first in Hebrew by an Arab-Israeli) that is semi-autobiographical and discreetly keeps some of its secrets, and for a series of short prose pieces I call "faces," by a poet who thus only posthumously lets himself be exiguously glimpsed.

Like the mobile sense of *midbar* itself across a range of unhomed conditions, it will be seen that "memoir" comprehends a variety of text-types in these chapters and thus tracks an odyssey of its own: from fictive autobiography to diary and essay to memoir proper to prose-poetry to autobiographical fiction.[58] One final note needs to be made on the multilingual aspect of such an itinerary: I have, except where noted, used the published translations of the many texts not written in English. Some of these are authorized by the writers themselves, as in the case of Sebald, Appelfeld, Shammas, and von Rezzori; the others, even when I deferred to them over my own translation, were checked against the originals (for example, Lillian Vallee's translation of Gombrowicz's *Diary*), in Hebrew, Yiddish, German, French, and Polish.

1

Place from Place, and Place from Flight
W. G. Sebald's *The Emigrants* and Aharon Appelfeld's *The Iron Tracks*

> In Ersilia, to establish the relationships that sustain the city's life, the inhabitants stretch strings from the corners of the houses, white or black or gray or black-and-white according to whether they mark a relationship of blood, of trade, authority, agency. When the strings become so numerous that you can no longer pass among them, the inhabitants leave: the houses are dismantled; only the strings and their supports remain. From a mountainside, camping with their household goods, Ersilia's refugees look at the labyrinth of taut strings and poles that rise in the plain. That is the city of Ersilia still, and they are nothing. They rebuild Ersilia elsewhere. They weave a similar pattern of strings which they would like to be more complex and at the same time more regular than the other. Then they abandon it and take themselves and their houses still farther away. Thus, when traveling in the territory of Ersilia, you come upon the ruins of abandoned cities, without the walls which do not last, without the bones of the dead which the wind rolls away: spiderwebs of intricate relationships seeking a form.
> Italo Calvino, *Invisible Cities*

Refugees

"That is the city of Ersilia still, and they are nothing."

So, place and the reconstructive imagination are always in some tensed relationship. Eventually, the airy inscription that makes a syntax of the spaces between structures—spiderwebs of intricate relationships—overtakes and eventually outlasts the city of Ersilia itself. Place is abandoned and rebuilt elsewhere. A writing, figured as a bare form or interstice, resides there still, after the inhabitants have moved away; its predications float free from the referents that once anchored it. The walls do not last, and the bones of the dead are dissipated by wind; only the strings and their supports remain.

That system of semaphore now defines the city space itself through the operation linguists call condensation or metaphor. The corresponding movement is centrifugal: Ersilia's emigrants relocate always "farther away"; or let us say, they displace *place from place*. And as in the Talmudic formula, *flight* measures a human action, a movement in and through space, just as *place* represents a human imposition upon it, the city named "Ersilia." Flight after flight, with every new abandonment and new founding, the urban relationships of blood, trade, authority, agency, take on more intricacy—through the network of strings that charts them and then stands in for their loss. Each successive pattern of connective filaments becomes "more complex and at the same time more regular" than its antecedents. Finally, the reweaving of connections seems goaded in part by nostalgia itself. For the migrants' periodic recognition of the city they have left behind, and from which they have dispossessed themselves, occurs in an encampment at the city's outskirts—from a near distance.

Calvino has called explicit attention to the "tension between geometric rationality and the entanglement of human lives" as the thematic principle of *Invisible Cities* as a whole,[1] something the allegory above captures precisely, and, transposed here, contrapuntally reads our first two narratives, W. G. Sebald's *The Emigrants* (*Die Ausgewanderten,* 1992) and Aharon Appelfeld's *The Iron Tracks* (*Mesilat barzel,* 1991). For, however discrepant in design and authors' biography these two texts of *midbar* may be, the webbing of "intricate relationships seeking a form" describes a formal imperative for each—the iron tracks of Appelfeld's title, the railways of a post-Shoah Europe; and the routes of *auswanderung* tracked within Sebald's four stories and by his narrator.

Properly speaking, neither is a memoir, though each purports to be so in its figural narration. While they may both thus point us back to de Man's observations about the generic instability of even straightforwardly autobiographic discourse, they can be more fairly understood not as limit-cases, but with reference to Calvino. Each rebuilds its

Ersilia elsewhere—ever, therefore, a second-order reality. Alternatively, each weaves a substitute pattern of signs. Appelfeld writes programmatically *athwart* the story of his life in order to remove it, as he says, "from the mighty grip of memory," thus to give it over "to the creative laboratory" of literary invention. "I came from a world of detailed, empirical reality, the camps and the forests. My real world was far beyond the power of imagination, and my task as an artist was not to develop my imagination but to restrain it, and even then it seemed impossible to me, because everything was so unbelievable that one seemed oneself to be fictional."[2]

The Iron Tracks is manifestly novelistic, never pretending to literary realism (the train is a repeated symbolic motif in many of his other novels). Conversely, *The Emigrants,* as its English-translation paratext phrases it, "puts the question to realism" playing between the borders of autobiography, fiction, historical chronicle, and the literature of travel. The narratives are both told in the first person. Like *The Rings of Saturn* (1995), *Vertigo* (1990), and *Austerlitz* (2001), *The Emigrants* is voiced by a fictional stand-in for the author, a German writer who has emigrated to England and who, if he does so at all, speaks about himself through an elliptical pattern of biography and figural echolocation. Indeed in its purposeful swerve toward the biographic, Sebald's method is an almost textbook example of the Baktinian precept, "I am in myself the condition of possibility for my own life, but I am not its valuable hero" (*Art and Answerability,* 106). The narrating self is an organizing presence that keeps itself in shadow, withholding itself in the very act of discovering and communicating biographic detail.

If the text's final sentence, an allusion to the mythical Parcae, beckons conspicuously beyond the quotidian—that is, in the direction of a *beyond*—its first sentence states a seemingly prosaic fact about destination—"At the end of 1970, shortly before I took up my position in Norwich, I drove out to Hingham with Clara in search of somewhere to live." Yet "Clara" soon disappears from the narrative just as "I" never assumes full clarity, and so the incipient quest-narrative clandestinely intimates a paradox. Self-exiled from Germany though I am, it will nevertheless revisit me (or I, it), through the lives of four German emigrants (exiles, refugees, expatriates), at various relational or circumstantial distances from me, whose stories come upon me (or I, them). In search of some*where*—the book's counter-Proustian agenda, let us say—I stumble into a parallelism between places and lives both of which, I discover, hold themselves at a near distance from recuperative narration.

Aharon Appelfeld betrays a comparable obliquity about himself within his fiction. He, too, withholds himself, while nevertheless evoking, as one critic puts it, "the unconscious revelation of things that come up through the reading process."³ His reticence extends to expected partisanships, as well. As has been noted often in interviews, he is an Israeli writer, a member of the *dor ha'medina* ("statehood generation," also known as *gal hadash*, "new wave") who writes an extremely spare and stylized Hebrew, which was not his first language. Yet he prefers to characterize himself as "a European, Jewish writer" in the East-Central European tradition of Kafka and Schulz and a claimant to the legacy of Proust.⁴ His closest analog in Israeli literature, according to Gila Ramras-Rauch, is probably the early modernist Uri Nissan Gnessin, who shared a similar idiom of place (in his memoir, Appelfeld names S. Yizhar, Moshe Shamir, and Haim Gouri as his "role models"). He is more popular among a readership that reads him in translation than among fellow Israelis (a novelist for professors, according to the late Yehudah Amichai, "not loved by the general populace").⁵ Despite what would seem to be a single and obsessive subject, it is indeed debatable whether his books are "about the Holocaust" in the reductive sense of such a phrase. In an interview with the author, Philip Roth deftly captured the multiple ambiguities here:

[Appelfeld's] literary subject is not the Holocaust, however, or even Jewish persecution. Nor, to my mind, is what he writes simply Jewish fiction or, for that matter, Israeli fiction. Nor, since he is a Jewish citizen of a Jewish state composed largely of immigrants, is his an exile's fiction. And, despite the European locale of many of his novels and the echoes of Kafka, these books written in the Hebrew language certainly aren't European fiction. Indeed, all that Appelfeld is not adds up to what he is, and that is a dislocated writer, a deported writer, a dispossessed and uprooted writer. Appelfeld is a displaced writer of displaced fiction, who has made of displacement and disorientation a subject uniquely his own. (*Beyond Despair*, 61)

Like Sebald, then, he is a refugee who, in looking back, sees a labyrinth of taut strings and poles that he must endlessly reweave, rising in the plain. The critic James Wood calls such echoic labor, in Sebald's case, a "concentrated patterning" of facts made fictive.⁶ And both *The Emigrants* and *The Rings of Saturn* end with evocations of weaving that in turn echo Calvino: in the one, a photograph (described, not reproduced) of three ghetto workers in Łodz sitting behind a loom, conjuring an image of the Fates; in the other, a comparison between weavers and writers, both "straining to keep their eye on the complex patterns they created . . . engrossed in their intricate designs . . . pursued into their dreams by the feeling they have gotten hold of the wrong thread" (James Wood, *The Broken Estate*, 283). In Appelfeld's novel, the strings are made of iron, whose incessant tracking (they both lead and are followed) intersects with a labyrinth of sidings and byways about which the narrator wonders at one point, "Why, then, am I going in the wrong direction?" (186).

The Iron Tracks (his thirteenth published novel) is one of Appelfeld's few longer fictions told in the first person (others are *The Age of Wonders* [*Tor Hapla'ot*, 1979] and *Katerina* [1992]).[7] Yet in the context of his work thus far, its narrator seems unsettlingly close to the author's own person in certain crucial respects, most conspicuously, choice of name: *Erwin* (Appelfeld's own) *Siegelbaum* ("Signet-tree")—like *Appelfeld* ("Roll-call-field"), a grafting of human signing practices onto nature. The narrator's voice and discourse eerily resemble the author's in the personal history "Buried Homeland," published in the *New Yorker*: "Years ago I bumped into one of them in the dark and said, in our language, 'Why do you run from me? What harm have I ever done you?' He was so startled that he went pale and said nothing" (*The Iron Tracks*, 17); "We, the survivors, smell each other out, like animals. We're drawn to one another, and at the same time, we flee from one another. My few comrades in suffering won't touch my books" ("Buried Homeland," 49).[8] Because it *is* fiction, however, and if we take Roth's point about displacement, Appelfeld's novel hails at a nearer distance the enfolded narrative impulses complexly at work in Sebald's text rather than those more visibly (albeit still elliptically) on the surface of Appelfeld's soi-disant memoir, *Story of a Life* (*Sipur hayim*, 1999).[9]

Geographically, *The Iron Tracks* marks the first of Appelfeld's fictions to *return* to postwar Europe years afterward and revisit the actual vicinity of the concentration camps. It is certainly unique in circling them by traversing the railways of Europe decades after deportation and liberation. Its compulsive centripetal curve, the protagonist's plan to find and then execute the Nazi officer who murdered his parents, keeps Europe always and necessarily at the nearest of distances. And indeed, both the incessant refiguring of an "elsewhere" together with the politics of "belonging at a near distance" might legitimately be said to comprise Appelfeld's narrative *ars poetica* in this text as well as all his others.

Within the "saga" Appelfeld says circumscribes his fiction—the "hundred years of Jewish solitude" taken on as narrative burden[10]—plots might be divided crudely into those that revolve around stasis (*Badenheim1939* [*Badenheim Ir Nofesh*], 1980; *The Retreat* [*Ha'pisgah*], 1982), and those goaded by movement (*To the Land of the Cattails* [*El Eretz Ha'gomeh*], 1986, *Layish*, 1994). Among the latter, *For Every Sin* ('*Al Kol Ha'pesha'im*, 1989), like *The Iron Tracks*, also traces its protagonist's movements in the aftermath of catastrophe; yet in its very first paragraph, it presents a character who, after being liberated, resolves to travel "back home alone, in a straight line, without twists or turns . . . never to deviate."[11] By contrast, *The Iron Tracks* proclaims a state of perpetual vagrancy at its outset: "Since the end of the war, I have been on this line, as they say: a long, twisted line stretching from Naples to the cold north, a line of locals, trams, taxis, and carriages. . . . My annual route is circular . . . a route with endless stations" (3, 11).

No doubt the politics of counterpoint between writers like Appelfeld and Sebald may warrant attention in the first place, as if it were not sufficient for textual affinities to speak first and last for themselves. That Appelfeld (b. 1932) is a Jew who barely escaped deportation to Trans-Dniestra and almost certain extermination, and Sebald (b. 1944) a non-Jewish *Bayer* one generation removed from the war, does not make a conjunction between them necessarily forced or even inapt.[12] It does make it uncommon, however. While needless to say, critical and journalistic research on both postwar German writing and (the mostly Jewishly contoured) field of Holocaust literature thrives, few comparative studies between the two domains have been ventured. The title of Ernestine Schlant's *The Language of Silence: West German Literature and the Holocaust* already signals one reason why: the relative dearth, until recently, of fiction by West Germans that treats the specifically Jewish ordeal and legacy of the Shoah mournfully or multi-dimensionally.[13]

But by no means does that fully explain the scarcity of a pairing like Appelfeld/Sebald, authors who, albeit obliquely and from disparate cultural and geographic vantages, write under the shadow of the same calamitous event. The Jewish geography of Appelfeld's fiction is determinative, whether configured dialectically and regionally, as in Sidra Ezrahi's explanatory rubric, "between Bukovina and Jerusalem," or triadically and metropolitically, as in Gila Ramras-Rauch's "Jadovo, Czernowitz, and Jerusalem." Sebald's itinerary is at once more open-ended and less axial: Lithuania, Norfolk, the South German Provinces, Switzerland, France, New York, Constantinople, Jerusalem, Munich,

Manchester. Yet both authors claim the widest expanse for literary fidelities, and thus place for each is locative but not encompassing, dogmatic (in de Certeau's sense) yet still contingent. The absolute in *The Emigrants* and *The Iron Tracks* is precisely the unplaced (and unplaceable), not the placed.

Appelfeld's awareness of Jewish assimilationism is acute. Yet he himself, the product of such background but also a well-schooled archivist of the feet, sustains a remarkable aptitude for multiple negative capabilities in the writing: formally, ideologically, mimetically. His aesthetic is a remarkable fusion of the exclusivist and the anti-parochial. Likewise, Sebald demonstrates an uncanny sympathetic imagination — with predecessor figures and countrymen like Adalbert Stifter and Walter Benjamin, but also demonstrable others from elsewhere, like Thomas Browne. Astutely, Cynthia Ozick notes what few reviews of *The Emigrants* have discerned, that Sebald, singularly among contemporary German writers, can be said to "reciprocate" the one-time, long-standing Jewish attachment to Germany and German culture. Referring to the novel's third story, which locates itself among German relations and Jewish families in New York State, she writes,

> So the immigrants, German and Jewish, mingle in America much as Germans and Jews once mingled in Germany, in lives at least superficially entwined.... The yeshiva on Amsterdam Avenue, the Solomons, Seligmanns, Wallersteins, Mrs. Litwak and the succahs on the Lower East Side: this is how Sebald chooses to shape the story of his Catholic German relations. It is as if the fervor of Uncle Adelwarth's faithful attachment to Cosmo Solomon were somehow a repudiation of Gershom Scholem's thesis of unrequited Jewish devotion [for Germany]; as if Sebald were casting a posthumous spell to undo that thesis. (37)[14]

When the narrator writes at the end of Sebald's book, "Grunwald... Goldstaub, Baumblatt and Blumenthal — perhaps there was nothing the Germans begrudged the Jews so much as their beautiful names, so intimately bound up with the country they lived in and with its language," the family name "Appelfeld" might easily insinuate itself into the roster (the unmarked graves of Appelfeld's parents have not, however, been as fortunate as the protected plots in Kissingen among which Sebald's narrator lingers[15]). It is not uncommon to hear of German/Jewish dialogues in one forum or another (not least between Germans and Israelis). In such milieus, Appelfelds and Sebalds would very likely meet at their multiple points of tangency, their overlaps, and their gaps. But needless to say, the reason they meet here in the public space of criticism has less to do with cultural or ideological politics than with the politics of literary parochialism.

No matter the symbolic capital of "German/Jewish Holocaust texts in tandem," it would not be dramatically *more* customary to come across Levantine/Central European literary pairings or Jewish-Ottoman/Gentile-Austro-Hungarian, or Israeli-Ashkenzi and Israeli-Sephardi, for that matter. Both Edward Said and André Aciman spent their childhoods in Egypt; both became émigré writers on American soil; both wrote memoirs whose titles, *Out of Place* and *Out of Egypt*, fairly cry out for affiliation (a term dear to Said's heart); and yet the claim for such dialogism will have to be staked here, in this book.

"It says something about the humanities, as institutionalized in the university," writes Bruce Robbins, "that they can both overappreciate the rootlessness of the world's Naipauls, and *for reasons that are no less institutional,* feed off . . . 'protest-authors' as well" ("Comparative Cosmopolitanisms," 250). What it says is that academic professionals routinely stage "interpretive contests" over the texts and authors that will *matter*. A cultural studies critic, Robbins is specifically concerned with the mobility of, and necessary professional self-interest in, such terms as "particular" and "universal," "situated" and "cosmopolitan." The task, he says, is to discriminate degrees; the "limits" of a term like cosmopolitanism "are among its conjunctural virtues" (260).

But it also says something about the humanities that traditions and counter-traditions alike tend toward selective paradigms even in the service of comparativism. Hence, the choices and corrective sorting for them in this book. This is precisely where a dialogical literary criticism can take its stand: to set up a gravitational field within which textual affinities *advene*—come upon each other. Here, in this "Elsewhere" designated as such, the textual pairings will thus have to make their own organic arguments for shared proximities. "As soon as we ask what it *means* to belong, or how many different ways of belonging there may be," says Robbins, we have named our problem, as interrogators of identity and the location of culture (250). This book's dialogic sights are at once more restrictive and angled on the bias. Granting, indeed identifying, the necessary particulars of *whose* homeland and *whose* diaspora—as discrepant biographic or cultural properties—we will explore how the *writings* may nevertheless belong at near distances to and from each other, prompted by critical intervention. And therefore, to resume with the first of two of them.

The Emigrants

YEW AND GLACIER, TWIG AND TEAS-MADE

"In photography," writes Roland Barthes, "the presence of the thing (at a certain past moment) is never metaphoric; and in the case of animated beings, their life as well" (*Camera Lucida*, 78). At the end of her essay about works of fiction on the Shoah that take representational liberties, Cynthia Ozick insists, "In the beginning was not the word, but the camera—and in that time, in that place, the camera did not mislead. It saw what was there to see" ("The Rights of History," 24). She is speaking of documentary photography, even or especially as recorded by Nazi cameras in the hands of Nazi technicians. Barthes evokes a metaphysic for photography, its essential melancholy or fatalism, as a record of the bygone; he attends only to Spectator and Spectrum (photograph), not Operator. "I observed that a photograph can be the object of three practices (or of three emotions, or of three intentions: to do, to undergo, to look)" (*Camera Lucida*, 19).

While James Wood (with an aside to Stendhal) ties the interpolation of photographs in *The Emigrants* to occultation, and Ozick (with an aside to Henry James) refers it to sound,[16] Sebald avers a different relation to photography when he tells an interviewer, "It was an escape route, something entirely private" (Atlas, "W. G. Sebald," 278). That is, the finding, collecting, and pondering of anonymous portraits and landscapes instigates an afterlife of the extraterritorial that brings about a second leave-taking, which becomes a kind of collision. At least that is what Sebald says about how his writing devolves from the photographs he has come across—"I think it was these photographs that eventually got the better of me" (278). In that respect, however, he plays a somewhat analogous role to Barthes's "operator"; he stands *outside* the frame of his text and its interspersed photographs.

Yet, he doesn't quite. The effect of each photo's *punctum* has already been registered before we come upon them ourselves. These are (most of them) photographs not *taken* by author or narrator but rather *encountered* by them. Certainly, a part of their function is evidentiary. They are also counter-metaphoric to the extent that they have been already placed in dialogue with figurations of text. That is, they come both before *and* after. And unlike the images in Barthes's *Camera Lucida*— almost all portraits, all authorized by artistic merit or archival status— they are embedded, situated on the plane of discourse, even if some of them admittedly are, as catalysts, *objets trouvés*.

Having initially raised some implications of its image-content in the introduction, a reckoning with Sebald's sense of *midbar* depends on the photographs themselves, or more specifically, the mediating operation between their placement in the book, on the one hand, and their effects that take place in the reading, on the other. I do not mean that the various landscapes, say, depict the far-away or the olden; that would merely entail too superficial a "use" of place. Rather, it is what Sebald and we *do* with the images that engages the dynamics of elsewhere, of belonging, and of near distance.

Perhaps one should subjectify the pronoun, however, since different readers perforce do different things with them and Sebald's (or his narrator's) own intentions for them are, because penumbral, mostly unavailable. Some examples from critical responses to *The Emigrants* may clarify, since each homes in on a particular photograph to make its general point. André Aciman, aligning himself with Sebald not only as a fellow *apatride*, as someone equally taken up by "the question of Jewish suffering," mentions two. The first is a group picture, in the third or "Ambros Adelwarth" section (p. 75 in the text), that includes the narrator's mother designated by an "x" drawn above her head, an indicator which Aciman says "tugs at the reader with the resonance of her certain death" (64). But unless he has in mind mutability generally, he has gone wide of the mark, since the narrator's mother is, we assume, Gentile. The second picture, from the same section, features roofers posing on top of the Augsburg synagogue in 1928, who have, in Aciman's words, "'Holocaust' written all over their faces." Here again, Aciman may over-reach, since one of the workmen is the narrator's uncle, Kasimir (presumably also Gentile), and nothing in the text invites us to assume that "the Jews of Augsburg who had donated the old copper roof" (*The Emigrants,* 80) are the same persons as the coppersmiths featured in the photo.

James Wood chooses, from the identical section, an indistinct picture of (or taken by) Uncle Kasimir that represents one of a handful of self-commenting images in the text, which says above it, "Then he took a camera out of his large-check jacket and took this picture, a print of which he sent me two years later, probably when he had finally shot the whole film, together with his pocket watch" (89). "The blurred photograph," comments Wood, "reminds us that we cannot read this narrator"; "[T]he tiny, pregnant detail about how it took Kasimir *two years* to shoot the rest of the film suggests a life without photographs, a life without much sense of its own visibility. And the detail of the pocket watch closes the scene like a still life, like a skull in a Renaissance painting, suggesting Time vainly controlled (by the writer who has assembled these constituents) and also lost (by these characters)" (40). The observation is acute. Yet one must also grant, unreprovingly, that it happens to coincide with Wood's interpretive agenda throughout, which is an implicit dialogue with the role of realism in contemporary fiction. In the case of Sebald, that means "the indecipherability of facts," which in turn require the most delicate of narrative procedures to recuperate them fictively.

For Cynthia Ozick, an "agenda" is just as pertinent, in a double sense. Alongside her own programmatic critical intentions, the first of two photographs she selects, once again from "Ambros Adelwarth," and also reproduced in the review, depicts a pocket diary, with the word "Agenda" engraved on it. The photograph, one of several depicting inscription of one sort or another, stands out for its Magritte-like reflexivity, but then all the more so in a critical intervention that refracts it. The second image epitomizes the most poignantly autotelic moment in the book—a projected image of the Lasithi plateau as viewed in Dr. Henry Selwyn's living-room. Selwyn recounts,

> We sat looking at this picture for a long time in silence too, so long that the glass in the slide shattered and a dark crack fissured across the screen. That view of the Lasithi plateau, held so long till it shattered, made a deep impression on me at the time, yet vanished completely. It was not until a few years afterward that it returned to me, in a London cinema, as I followed a conversation between Kaspar Hauser and his teacher, Daumer, in the kitchen garden at Daumer's home. Kaspar, to the delight of his mentor, was distinguishing for the first time between dream and reality, beginning his account with the words: I was in a dream, and in my dream I saw the Caucasus. The camera then moved from right to left, in a sweeping arc, offering a panoramic view of a plateau ringed by mountains, a plateau with a distinctly Indian look to it . . . follies, in a pulsing dazzle of light, that kept reminding me of the sails of those wind pumps of Lasithi, which in reality I have still not seen to this day. (17–18)

Mimesis, memory, repetition, stasis and movement, interior and exterior spaces, and not least a certain fatality of destiny—as in the figure of Kaspar Hauser: all these "strings," each by itself wonderfully intricate, are intertwined in this short passage, illustrating *The Emigrants*'s Ersilia-like complexity.

"Notably," Ozick writes, "this is not a landscape viewed by a fresh and naked eye. It is, in fact, a verbal rendering of an old photograph—a slide shown by a projector on a screen" (34)—not unlike a photograph of a book-within-the-book that says "Agenda" (Sebald's own, in point of fact, as he has attested in an interview). As a fiction writer who has expressed serious ambivalence about her own literary imaging of the Holocaust, Ozick voices a certain disquiet in the course of ample regard for Sebald's achievement about the propriety of lyrical (and indeed non-Jewish) elegy that wistfully conjures national catastrophe and the ghosts of its Jewish victims. In other words, she is concerned no less about the *framing* than the *haunting* of the Real. Sebald's "sublime" and "delicate" verbal renderings, a "grieving that has been made beautiful" (34), incite her caution, one also suspects, inasmuch as they are accompanied by counter-metaphors—the photographs—that nevertheless "lack the capacity to sign" (Ozick, 34).[17]

In point of fact, many of the book's photographs *do* signify, indeed they function rhetorically within it because they have a more textual (and thus isomorphic) than strictly photographic role to play as part of the narrative's semiotic machinery. Each of Sebald's readers here—Aciman, Wood, Ozick—has focalized the import of photography in *The Emigrants* in very distinctive ways, as of course they must. Indeed, what distinguishes Sebald so profoundly and aligns him so closely with Appelfeld is the ethical sophistication that *obliges* readers to refract an already prismatically constructed text.

For the photographs do participate crucially in that text's dogma—its pathos and ethos and poetics—of place. Five of the seven pictures in the first narrative, "Dr. Henry Selwyn," portray landscapes; the other two belong to prior "frames"—a photograph of lepidopterist Vladimir Nabokov clipped from a magazine, and the front page of a newspaper that the narrator comes across after Selwyn's suicide, reporting the discovery of preserved remains from the Aare glacier in the Oberland. The remains belong to Selwyn's alpine guide Johannes Naegeli missing since 1914, and recalled metadigetically by Selwyn himself in the slide-projector scene. "And so they are ever coming back to us, the dead," says the text (23) on the facing page—a refrain that haunts each of the four narratives. The newspaper by itself gestures inwardly to the text's machinery overall, since it includes printed type, hand-written notations and underlines, and its own nested photograph of a man crouching in front of the Oberaar glacier.

More easily missed, however, is the text of the newspaper article itself, in particular an adjacent story at the bottom which is too severely cropped to parse fully, but whose heading, *"L'histoire,"* and sub-heading, "*Film, légendes,*" and "*l'imagination,*" we can read, together with an incomplete line of type, "*une main tenant fermem—,*" underlined by the narrator. A photograph inside a photograph, text underneath and alongside text, this corroborative visitation from the solid world of fact is bent like refracted light, taken on a semantic detour that seems to say: we hold the past but half-firmly; it comes to us in the prehensile grasp of reportage, legend, imagination, "*l'histoire.*"[18]

We might want to read the succession of photographs in "Henry Selwyn"—one, two, three, four, five exterior settings, six, man with butterfly net, seven, man crouched in front of glacier—as telling its own story, narrating a progression from place to person to place-and-person married, then separated. But we would likely be guilty of a sedulous formalism. While a narrative logic does explain the sequence of the four narratives, the arrangement of the photographs within them, albeit careful, is not algorithmic. (And as allusions to Nabokov appear in all four stories as a unifying leitmotif for the book, one should no doubt be on guard against facile trespass of the text's mysteries.) Still, let us ponder for a little longer the photographs' participation in the "dogma of place," specifically the first snapshot, of the yew tree in the churchyard, and the last, of the Aare glacier.

What was downplayed in the brief foray into "Dr. Henry Selwyn" from my introduction is the salient detail that the yew tree picture *precedes* any discourse: it is not only the first photograph we see but the first *thing*. Absent Barthes's defensible claim again, it is extremely difficult not to see such a thing as a presence *densely* metaphoric. Death and loss, of course; elegiac and pastoral calm (an English penchant for which a non-Englishman might honor and ironize at the same time); *place* in all its stolidity and *Dasein:* these would be a few of its significations. But a scant twenty pages later, there is that majestic glacier, rising up over that man who looks almost obeisant to it, yet still cabined, cribbed, confined by text on all sides—not Sebald's, but the evidentiary prose of news report.

Directly opposite it, on the last page of the story's text, the narrator says, "At that point, as I recall, or perhaps merely imagine, the memory of Dr. Selwyn returned to me for the first time in a long while" (23). This represents the final instance in the story of a distinctive idiom that colors the narrator's discourse from the outset. "The house gave the impression" / "And I recalled the chateau . . . which made a powerful impression" / "Perhaps this impression came from the way he had of looking" / "Her facial expressions and movements gave a distraught impression" / "That view of the Lasithi plain plateau . . . made a deep impression." And also: "I recall, or perhaps merely imagine"/ "it stuck in my mind"/ "I fancied" / ·"I can still see . . . "but I may only be imagining." And, "as I recall" / "as I now realized" / "when I think back." In addition to visibility (Wood) and audibility (Ozick), *The Emigrants* has as its deep theme sensation and ideation generally—what neuroscientists call memories of memory[19]—to register rightly, recollect, and finally transmit—tell about—what stands before me. In the second novella of *The Emigrants*, "Paul Bereyter," after a series of sentences all of which begin, "I imagine him . . ." the narrator confesses, "Such endeavors to imagine his life and death did not, as I had to admit, bring me any closer to Paul, except at brief moments of the kind that seemed presumptuous to me. It is in order to avoid this sort of wrongful trespass that I have written down what I know of Paul Bereyter" (29). The question becomes, what is the difference between the first image in the story and the last, as sense-impressions similarly subject to recall and imagination?

If there is an allegorical story to be read out of this photographic frame, one suspects it is this. Nothing in the text absolutely guarantees that the yew tree pictured on the first page, if indeed it is a yew tree, is located in the St. Andrews churchyard in Hingham. The photo of the newspaper account, on the other hand, testifies exactly to what the narrator is now telling us, as he concludes the requiem for Hersch Seweryn, and corroborates what Seweryn, as Selwyn, has himself narrated a few pages prior. Which picture makes us feel more at home in the text whose first circuit *we* have just completed? Which is more proximate to us, which at a nearer distance?

One answer is that if, indeed, we *have* construed a linear, diagrammatic progression to this first story, the text must itself resume and begin again. Its pattern of strings, its intricately relational spiderweb, will seek another, more intricate form. Did we cause it to happen by reading? How could we? Selwyn can reimagine Naegeli; slides of Selwyn can remind the narrator of Nabokov as slides of Lasithi can recall the landscape in "Kaspar Hauser," which itself mimics Kasper Hauser's dream of the Caucasus; Selwyn can still see the *cheder* in Grodno, the empty rooms, the cart and horse's crupper; the narrator can recall the memory of Selwyn, and three quarters of an hour afterward comes upon a Lausanne paper that relates the release of the Bernese guide Naegeli from a seven-decades interment in the ice. But all of this happens inside a book, and we are here, apart, at a distance.

"Through the act of looking, we own these pictures, or, rather, they thrust themselves upon us," writes Luc Sante in his uncanny book *Evidence,* which among other things fabricates narratives for anonymous police photos from the turn of the last century on the verge of being discarded. "There is no place for us outside the frame . . . nowhere to stand," he says. We cannot be the viewer of such a scene. We must have forgotten: We are the subject" (99). Like Sebald, Sante has engineered this to be true by writing the book he has, directing our gaze to found photographs whose narrative gaps he fills with his own invocative prose. But Sante confines himself to the anonymous victims in police evidence photographs, and while he may seem to claim too much their like, he gestures toward the ground and contextual condition for the photos themselves: they gave witness that something had happened. The yew tree and the glacier do not—at least not in the same way. Moreover, "Trees have roots; Jews have legs," as Schama's extraterritorial-minded colleague was recollected to say. Place cannot be determinate.

One suspects Sebald's point in this first section is rather that place must leave an impression, an imprint, just as human figures leave their traces behind upon it—even if they are the frozen remains of a lone Alpine guide, "returned" to human witness. By extension—in the plain sense of a distancing—while we are not the subject of these photographs, nor are we in their room or they in ours, we are placed *by* them in some relation, an approximation as well as a remove. We are in their *aura*—an attribute that, according to Walter Benjamin's great essay on art and mechanical reproduction, "withers" in proportion to the distance between copy and original. And yet aura, as Benjamin defines it later with reference to natural objects, "is the unique phenomenon of a distance, however close it may be." "If, while resting on a summer afternoon, you follow with your eyes a mountain range on the horizon or a branch which casts its shadow over you, you experience the aura of those mountains, that branch" (*Illuminations,* 223).

In an earlier essay, "A Little History of Photography" (1931), especially pertinent to the analysis here, Benjamin says much the same thing about photographs—"What is aura actually? A strange weave of space and time: the unique appearance or semblance of distance, no matter how close the object may be"—but also, more importantly, reminds his readers of the intersubjective claims made upon them by aesthetic looking: "To perceive the aura of a phenomenon [means] to invest it with the capacity to look at us in turn."[20]

This is the burden of *The Emigrants* as well: to have us look at the yew tree and the newspaper photo, implicitly reading them as a movement and perhaps then wringing an allegorical lesson from it, while all the time they look at us in turn, having cast their aura over us. We *are* the viewers of such scenes as they reproduce. Yet *our* reckoning, our near distance from them—their impression on us—as the narrator would say, is also their subject.

Consider even the two purely indicative photographs and their accompanying text in the book's fourth section, entitled "Max Ferber." Barthes would call these photos tautological: "a pipe here is always a pipe . . . as if the Photograph always carries its referent with itself" (*Camera Lucida*, 5).

The first is of a teas-made . . . which is always a teas-made:

> When I made the tea and the steam rose from it, the shiny stainless steel contraption on its ivory-colored metal base looked like a miniature power plant, and the dial of the clock, as I soon found as dusk fell, glowed a phosphorescent lime green that I was familiar with from childhood and which I had always felt afforded me an unaccountable protection at night. That may be why it has often seemed, when I have thought back to those early days in Manchester, as if the tea maker brought to my room by Mrs. Irlam, by Gracie—you must call me Gracie, she said—as if it was that weird and serviceable gadget, with its nocturnal glow, its muted morning bubbling, and its mere presence by day, that kept me holding on to life at a time when I felt a deep sense of isolation in which I might well have become submerged. Very useful, these are, said Gracie as she showed me how to operate the teas-made that afternoon; and she was right. (154–55)

The second photo, in Kissingen, shows what appears to be a blackthorn twig operated upon by the chemical action of mineral water flowing down upon it from a salt frame. Again, the narrator draws a tight speculative circle around the object whose metaphoricity, not just reference, seems portable: "At length I sat down on a bench in one of the balcony-like landings off the gallery, and all that afternoon immersed myself in the sight and sound of that theater of water, and in ruminations about the long-term and (I believe) impenetrable process which, as the concentration of salts increases in the water, produce the strangest of petrified or crystallized forms, imitating the growth patterns of nature even as it is being dissolved" (230). Both these moments in the text (pertinently, perhaps, assigned to the text's culminating narrative) should elicit an astringency about the "privation" opened up by autobiographical discourse: "To the extent that, in writing, we are all dependent on this language, we are . . . not silent, which implies the possible manifestation of sound at our own will, but silent as a picture, that is to say eternally deprived of voice and condemned to muteness."[21] Paul de Man's choice of pronoun here assumes a continuity between writer and his Others, but in both of these passages from Sebald's text, alongside their visual aids, the intent, I believe, is to direct our gaze—as if we now have ocular proof—only to shift it elsewhere.

The twig and the teas-made remain "looking" at us. Nature and culture, water acted upon by both salts and domestic intervention, impenetrable processes that alike yield mystery together with some definable product, some *thing:* if these are twin allegories, then their function is in excess of their signifying, just like the two photographs from "Henry Selwyn." To defer to Wood's analysis, we are perhaps not meant to *read* this narrator, even at those narrative cruces where he shows us signs that we would want to work iconically but merely leave us with their lonely indexicalities[22]—as Barthes might also insist. Thus, what was termed above a densely metaphoric presence in relation to the yew tree should more properly be construed as an emptily metaphoric presence: figure as *tourniquet* or *schwindel,* a semiotic revolving door through which we keep traveling without getting anywhere.

The narrator is immersed in the sight and sound of water, seeming to share its properties. He finds genuine comfort in an artificial glow—this time beating back submersion in interior depths and mysteries. Readers, on the other hand, are purposefully kept at near distance, presuming the same principles of transference for themselves, while, if they are attentive, discovering over and over again the Law of aura that makes them Jews—if one may—not trees. Excepting these two object-images, each of *The Emigrants'* four stories contains three categories of photograph: 1) exterior scenes, 2) individual and group portraits, and 3) some sort of written text—a public notice on a cemetery gates ("Max Ferber"), a reproduction, or simulation, of diary entries ("Ambros Adelwarth"), a Schulzimmerplan and Bahnhofplan ("Paul Bereyter"), a newspaper article ("Dr. Henry Selwyn"). Yet there is no allegorical progression here. A visiting card from Ambros Adelwarth with the fateful message—"Have gone to Ithaca . . . yours ever, Ambros"—is no more iconic than the oval effigies of Luisa Lanzberg and Fritz Ferber, which are no less ordinary than the greenhouse fallen into disrepair. All equally plangent; yet, all commensurably "an echo that cannot be heard" (Ozick), though for all that, "an echo awakened by a call" (Benjamin).

The role played by photography in *The Emigrants* merits this kind of attention because it participates in the text's overall investment in aura as a necessary strangeness and distance. To be sure, additional details of its rhetoric could be scrutinized just as much—for example the off-rhyme of facing portraits, boarding-school students on the left, primary school students on the right; or the catachresis of successive snapshots of the protagonist as mobilized soldier and vacationer, bespectacled in the one, dark sunglasses in the other, heads at opposite diagonals in each; or the alliteration of five out-of-doors poses, all in "Paul Bereyter"; or the anadiplosis of architectural studies—hotel, estate, casino, pagoda, synagogue, Chrysler Building, the Old City in Jerusalem—in "Ambros Adelwarth"; or the zeugma of fire-scorched Manchester textile mills and factories and the burning of the Würzburg Residenzplatz (the latter pronounced to be a forgery, and thus a possible prompt for us to be cognizant of photography's limitations as representational "truth"). If the associative logic Sebald admits to in an interview[23] applies to the interposition of photographs too, still a case can be made for a syntax of connection, Calvino's spiderweb seeking a form.

But one does not want to be too much the Champollion here (or worse, *Middlemarch*'s Causabon), with all one's power vested in a hieroglyphic key. Ersilia's once-and-future residents, recall, "would like" for their successive approximation to be more complex and regular; but "then they abandon it and take themselves and their houses still farther away." That, too, is a lesson for formalists. Moreover, except for the brief nod to falsifiability for the Würzburg photo, the narrator never pauses to interpret the images he has chosen to enhance or "verify" his discourse.[24] The photos comment on the text more than text reads the photos. Two of the sections, "Paul Bereyter" and "Ambros Adelwarth" derive many of their photos from albums that have preceded the conversations between the narrator and his informants; that is, up until a point, documentation has already narrated these lives and so plays an analogous role to the memoirs of Luisa Lanzberg that the narrator himself interpolates. And when photography is addressed as such, it is usually symbolically, as in the following anecdote from "Max Ferber": "[I]n the 1930s there was a photographic lab assistant in Manchester whose body had absorbed so much silver in the course of a lengthy professional life that he had become a kind of photographic plate, which was apparent in the fact (as Ferber solemnly informed me) that the man's face and hands turned blue in strong light, or, as one might say, developed" (165). It is in

Sebald's prose, however, that one finds ultimate validation for the claim that place and the reconstructive imagination are always in some tensed relationship, and thus we turn to it next.

ŁODZ INTO MANCHESTER, MANCHESTER INTO JERUSALEM

First, a few coordinates for place itself. When Ambros Adelwarth says above that he has gone to Ithaca, he means the town in upstate New York, but perhaps also Cavafy's surrogate for Alexandria and literary surrogate for Odysseus's patria; more specifically, he means the sanatorium for which "Ithaca" is a metonym, and whose actual name is "Samaria" (and thus cognate with that part of the Levant Adelwarth had visited as a young man). When in the same section, as he makes his own trek to Samaria-in-Ithaca, the narrator lists the names of certain towns: Monroe, Monticello, Middletown, Wurtsboro, Wawarsing, Colchester, and Cadosia, Deposit, Delhi, Neversink and Nineveh, and shortly after, Sabattis, Gabriels, Hawkeye and Lake Tear-in-the-Clouds—"place names that have remained indelibly in my memory ever since" (107)— he sends a silent signal about the portage of place through name—New England, New Spain, New Zion, and (with must be confessed as evoking a certain personal resonance), New Town.

Toward the end of "Max Ferber," we learn that Łodz was known as the Polski Manczester; as earlier, Ferber reminiscences about Manchester when it was known as "the Industrial Jerusalem" (165). Having been sent away by his parents from certain extermination in Germany, he decides not to follow his uncle to New York but rather to begin a new life in Manchester, which "instead, reminded me of everything I was trying to forget . . . an immigrant city [whose] immigrants were chiefly Germans and Jews" (191). "[A]nd so, although I intended to move in the opposite direction, when I arrived in Manchester I had come home, in a sense, and with every year I have spent since then in this birthplace of industrialization, amidst the black facades, I have realized more clearly than ever before that I am here, as they used to say, to serve under the chimney" (192). When, in the parallel account in "Henry Selwyn," Lithuanian Jews disembark from the port they believe to be New York— "since every one of them had all booked passage to Americum, as we called it" (19)—they discover that they have in fact gone ashore in London. And in the very first pages of the book, when the narrator first glimpses Selwyn's cottage, he recalls a French château whose façade was designed by its owners to replicate that of the palace at Versailles.

When, finally, Paul Bereyter, a three-quarter Aryan, returns to Germany after a sojourn as a tutor in France, he is conscripted in the muster, stationed variously in the Greater Homeland, Poland, Belgium, France, the Balkans, Russia, and the Mediterranean; "and doubtless saw more than any heart or eye can bear" (56). After the war, he returns again to Germany, to his native town: "What moved and perhaps forced Paul to return, in 1939 and in 1945, was the fact that he was a German to the marrow, profoundly attached to his native land in the foothills of the Alps, and even to that miserable place S.[25] as well, which in fact he loathes and, deep within himself, of that I am quite sure, said Mme. Landau, would have been pleased to see destroyed and obliterated, together with the townspeople, who he found so utterly repugnant" (57).

In short, "place" is never simply itself in *The Emigrants*, but is, rather, its own emigrant (must the title confine itself to persons alone, anyway?). Place is already flight, border, and beyond, palintropically caroming off the treks made by its exiles and refugees, transposing Łodz into Manchester and Manchester into Jerusalem. Home/elsewhere, *patride/apatride*, are each other's correlatives. Thus Sebald ascribes rather to locale to begin with the state or condition of mind Aciman elaborates as the peculiar province of an exiled writer's nostalgia, which thus haunts and shadows it in an *internally* tensed relationship, place displaced from within. It is as though Ersilia, in mimicry of its inhabitants, departs from itself and rebuilds elsewhere.

And like place, so narration. Whether or not the various sequences of photographs within sections should be read as part of a concentrated patterning, the arrangement of the four stories does betoken a palpable design—from repressed Jewish origins that surreptitiously return in the shelter of a Norfolk hermitage ("Henry Selwyn"), to an internal exile and victim of Nazi Germany's racial laws and the text's second suicide ("Paul Bereyter"), to a philo-semitic emigrant in America whose life is extinguished by incapacitating sadness ("Ambros Adelwarth"), to a German-Jewish exile in England for whom Germany remains "a kind of insanity lodged in [his] head" (191). Serially, they progress from brevity to increasing length, from indirection to direction. It would seem, in other words, that the story of Dr. Henry Selwyn requires the story of Paul Bereyter, which in turn precipitates the other two, each one Janus-faced in relation to the others abutting it on either side.

But it should also be noted that the first and fourth sections narrate roughly parallel emigrant lives in England whom the text, as it were, comes upon, while the inner two concern persons more proximate to the narrator, either through propinquity (Ambros Adelwarth), or tutelage (Paul Bereyter). Great-Uncle Adelwarth, the nearest through kinship, is also the farthest away, as his story never impinges upon the narrator directly—"Not even in my thoughts did he remain present" (68)—but is rather conveyed through the reminiscences of others (Aunt Fini and Dr. Abramsky, caretaker of the sanatorium in upstate New York where Adelwarth eventually dies, and a double or reinstantiation in the text of Dr. Henry Selwyn), as Paul Bereyter's is mediated by his friend, Lucy Landau.

But Ambros Adelwarth's story is also conveyed through his own diary entries as have been incorporated by the narrator. As such, it has *its* double in the final story in the memoirs of Max Ferber's mother, Luisa—another figure circumstantially distant from the narrator yet brought intimately close through writing. "Now I am standing in the living room once again, writes Luisa." / "From there it climbs the steep Aschacher Leite, where Lazarus (Luisa writes) always got down from his calèche so the horse would not have so hard a job of it" ("Max Ferber," 194–95). "Early morning (it says), myself on deck for a long time, looking astern." / "Today (it reads two days later) a first walk through the city and into the outer districts" ("Ambros Adelwarth," 128, 137). In the nested accounts, indeed, in the spoken monologues the narrator records as well, the borders between frame narrative and the voices embedded and re-voiced within it are sedulously, but still only intermittently, demarked. Discursively, too, the book observes proprieties in distance and proximity.

Recalling de Man,[26] we remain alert to the instabilities of subjective voice in the first place (and person), the "I" forever shifting among speakers, the narrator's own timbres insinuating themselves into the accents of others. Uncle Adelwarth, for instance, writes, "For, like Death itself, the cemeteries of Constantinople are in the midst of life.... Whole districts of the city built entirely of wood.... The Jewish quarter is built the same way. Walking through it today, we turn a corner and unexpectedly have a distant view of a blue line of mountains and the snowy summit of Olympus. For one awful heartbeat I imagine myself in Switzerland or at home again" (131). Or, from the interpolated reminiscences of Max Ferber's mother: "If I think back nowadays to our childhood in Steinach (Luisa's memoirs continue at another point), it often seems as if it had been open-ended in time, in every direction—indeed as if it were still going on, right into these lines I am now writing. . . . When I think back to those days, I see shades of blue everywhere—a single empty space, stretching out into the twilight of late afternoon, crisscrossed by the tracks of ice-skaters long vanished" (207, 218). Both passages betray the narrator's hand. Much like the Residenzplatz photograph, we are invited thus to acknowledge a byplay between one's own and half someone else's—a constituent feature of records personal and public alike.

This does not, however, make *The Emigrants* Nabokovian (notwithstanding its internal allusions to butterflies or to *Speak, Memory*), or even a self-defacing autobiographical act. Sebald's point, one suspects, has less to do with the vagaries of text-and-*hors du texte* than with ratios of belonging at near distances and outlying immediacies. This text may thrust itself upon us in imitation of the effects of narrated lives upon the narrator—"The memoirs of Luisa Lanzberg have been very much on my mind since Ferber handed them over to me, so much so that . . . I felt I should make the journey to Kissingen and Steinach" (218) / "Even so, I did eventually fly to Newark on the 2nd of January 1981. This change of heart was prompted by a photograph album of my mother's which had come into my hands" (71). But we may only go so far and no farther.[27] The parentheses that briefly turn direct discourse into indirect (there are no quotation marks or *erelebte Rede*[28] in this text), the semblance of an overall serial logic, the repeated motifs of tracking: all these make us look, but, as James Wood remarks of the photo of Uncle Kasimir, then want us to turn away.

Perhaps what we are left with finally, what the text wants to teach us, are the purely interpretive junctures we establish through reading. Thus, one asks oneself how Germans and Jews are "mingled" once again in the parallel between the diaries of Luisa Lanzberg and Ambros Adelwarth, the former a delicate record of loss written on the eve of German-Jewish destruction, the latter a travelog written by the German companion of a Jewish American scion whose passing and the gradual dissolution of whose family leaves him at an encompassing loss. A similar hermeneutic may be applied to the interspersed, motivic detail of parting gestures.

"[R]ising, [Selwyn] made a gesture that was most unusual for him. He offered me his hand in farewell." (21) / "Exactly as she had described Uncle Adelwarth the day before, Aunt Fini now stood on the pavement in front of her bungalow . . . waving her handkerchief after me. As I drove off I could see her in the mirror . . . growing smaller and smaller; and, as I recall that mirror image, I find myself thinking how strange it is that no one since then

Place from Place, and Place from Flight 63

has waved a handkerchief after me in farewell." (104) / "Dr. Abramsky walked the rest of the way beside me in silence. Nor did he say a word in farewell, but described a gentle arc with the goose wing in the darkening air." (116) / "One morning when I went out to Mamaroneck, Uncle Adelwarth was gone. In the mirror of the hall stand he had stuck a visiting card with a message for me, and I have carried it with me ever since." (103) / "As I stood, irresolute in the hall, I noticed that Paul's windcheater was missing, which, as he happened to mention that morning, had been hanging there for almost forty years. I knew at that moment that Paul had gone out, wearing that jacket, and that I would never see him alive again." (61)

Or to the anamnetic substitution of place for person in similar scenes of remembered childhood, like Selwyn's reveries of Grodno or the parallel to it in "Max Ferber," when Ferber's parents drive him to the airport so that he can emigrate: "He no longer knew what the last thing his mother or father had said to him was, or he to them, or whether he and his parents had embraced or not. He could still see his parents sitting in the back of the hired car on the drive out to Oberwiesenfeld, but he could not see them at the airport itself. And yet he could picture Oberwiesenfeld down to the last detail, and all these years had been able to envisualize it with that fearful precision, time and time again" (187). Or to scenes of excursion like the passage from "Paul Bereyter," subtly back-shadowing the Bernese Oberland in "Henry Selwyn" and discreetly foreshadowing the railroad motif that stands over this entire section, in which Mme. Landau "gazed down for an eternity at Lake Geneva and the surrounding country, which looked considerably reduced in size, as if intended for a model railway" (45). This passage, in turn, can be sorted with the small fables of mimetic transfer that dot the landscape of each narrative:

The flood of memory, little of which remains with me now, began with my recalling a Friday morning some years ago when I was suddenly struck by the paroxysm of pain that a slipped disc can occasion. . . . I also remember that the crooked position I was forced to stand in reminded me, even in my pain, of a photograph my father had taken of me in the second form at school, bent over my writing. In Colmar, at any rate, said Ferber after a lengthy pause, I began to remember, and it was probably those recollections that prompted me to go to Lake Geneva after eight days, to retrace another memory that had long been buried and which I never dared disturb. (171–72)

Or, ascending one diegetic level, it can also be put it into play with the narrator's own purposeful insinuations:

When I think back to our meetings in Trafford Park, it is invariably in that unremitting light that I see Ferber, always sitting in the same place in front of a fresco painted by an unknown hand that showed a caravan moving forward from the remotest depths of the picture, across a wavy ridge of dunes, straight toward the beholder . . . so that if you half shut your eyes, the scene looked like a mirage, quivering in the heat and light. And especially on days when Ferber had been working in charcoal, and the fine powdery dust had given his skin a metallic sheen, he seemed to have just emerged from the desert scene or to belong in it. (164)

And then have it intersect with quivering allusions to other locales, other *trompe l'oeil*, half-mirage effects, in other sections of the text:

And I recalled the château in the Charente that I had once visited from Angoulême. In front of it, two crazy brothers—one a parlimentarian, the other an architect—had built a replica of the façade of the palace of Versailles, an utterly pointless counterfeit, though one which made a powerful impression from a distance. The windows of that house had been just as gleaming and blind as those of the house we now stood before. (4)

"Why, I shall never know," said Aunt Fini, "but in my mind's eye I always see Ambros crossing Lake Constance from Lindau by steamer, in the moonlight, although that can scarcely have been how it was in reality" (77). This is the same Aunt Fini who, the narrator tell us, "spoke about the past, sometimes covering the left side of her face, where she had had a bad neuralgia for weeks, with one hand" (73). Surely, Sebald wants noticed the resemblance between Aunt Fini's self-critical understanding of the reconstructive imagination and other similarly wistful utterances by Max Ferber or Henry Selwyn or Paul Bereyter. (All four protagonists as well as their intermediaries could thus also be said to participate in Sebald's dialogue with Proust.) And surely, he wants noticed the hand-to-face gesture that (either staged by the narrator or "borrowed" from another figure of melancholy like Paul Bereyter[29]) conveys a similar guardedness.

One of the text's most exquisitely embodied and delicate moments has Aunt Fini furnishing a "little history" of memory, then of narration, and then gesturally offsetting the breach she has opened up in both by turning to photographs to let them speak for themselves:

That was when Uncle Adelwarth began, now and again, to recount incidents from his past life. Even the least of his reminiscences, which he fetched up very slowly from depths that were evidently unfathomable, was of astounding precision, so that, listening to him, I gradually became convinced that Uncle Adelwarth had an infallible memory, but that, at the same time, he

Place from Place, and Place from Flight 65

scarcely allowed himself access to it. For that reason, telling stories was as much a torment to him as an attempt at self-liberation. He was at once saving himself, in some way, and mercilessly destroying himself. As if to distract me from her last words, Aunt Fini picked up one of the albums from the side table. This, she said, opening it and passing it over to me, is Uncle Adelwarth as he was then. As you can see, I am on the left with Theo, and on the right . . ." (100–101)[30]

Of course, Sebald is distracting us through the identical maneuver, for indeed we *can* see, from the photograph that meets us now on the facing page, that Fini is on the left with Theo, with Ambros sitting somberly (now we know why) in the middle. An equally subtle yet still wrenching pause is created in the Paul Bereyter section. Under a photograph of Paul vacationing from wartime muster on the Southeast European coast—whose immediately preceding text says "as Paul wrote under this photograph"—readers are presented with a minor problem of attribution: which part of the quoted discourse belongs to Paul, and which to the narrator? "[O]ne was, as the crow flies, about 2,000 km away—but from where?—and day by day, hour by hour, with every beat of the pulse, one lost more and more of one's qualities, became less comprehensible to oneself, increasingly abstract" (56). Either Paul meditatively pens all of this, or else there is a bleed between proximate yet still distinct sensibilities. Nearness and farness conduce again to strictly textual properties, and again, the discourse creates its own eddying currents, moving us ahead to the blurred photo associated with Uncle Kasimir, introduced in the text with an echo of Paul Bereyter's aside, "I often come out here, said Uncle Kasimir, it makes me feel that I am a long way away, though I never quite know from where" (89).

The introductory chapter to this book asked where such a text leaves us. Now, from inside the narrative, Paul Bereyter and Kasimir gesture off-center toward that same conjecture, pointing us also in the direction of a familiar set of terms: from where?—from place, from flight, from border, from beyond. But here, those terms spell out an allegory of reading, of positionality angled, always bent toward and away from the text's spatial coordinates, its oscillation between wedged and dislodged identity, home and elsewhere.

In the extant fragment of his lost essay on the bildungsroman, Mikhail Bakhtin focuses on Goethe's *Italienische Reise* as a narrative suspended between Romanticist and Realist optics and distinctive in its own right for a pronounced bias toward that which can be clearly *seen*. Bakhtin writes, "[T]he *word* coincided with the clearest visibility. . . . The invisible did not exist for him. But at the same time his eyes did not want to (and could not) see that which was *ready-made* and *immobile*. His eyes did not recognize simple spatial contiguities or the simple coexistence of things and phenomena" (*Speech Genres and Other Late Essays*, 28).[31] This is a viewpoint almost diametrically opposed to Sebald's, who should therefore rightly be seen in dialogue with Goethe[32] as well as Proust, that is, both retracing Goethe's steps and cutting aslant them. Sebald's perspective revises Goethe's demystifying Romantic/Realist vision and its appropriative grasp.[33] What it sees, it cannot effectively grasp. As post-Romantic memoir, *The Emigrants* recasts the merger of *Dichtung* and *Wahrheit* by making it throb with the ache of modernity.

This explains the role of recall, of impression, of imaginative "return." The invisible is all around, not least in words, and between sentences. For Goethe, the imprint of history upon landscape must be palpable; for Sebald, like transmitting a past life or a lost homeland, it fastens on to impalpabilities. The presence of photographs in the book drives that point home: this is a ghost story, and these are its specters.

And both impose hermeneutic obligations. Even when he admonishes himself to behold the foreign with "fresh, clear eyes," the one matter left unquestioned in Goethe's travel narrative is the impunity of travel itself, a proprietary standard handed over in turn to readers—under that ensign, to move across lands belonging to someone else, like nomads poaching their way across fields they did not write. No such entitlement comes with the territory in *The Emigrants*. At best, readers are allowed the way-stations of their own interpretive junctures. And even then, the text warns us away, like the cemetery sign in Kissingen, from mistaking the merely visitable for (as the jargon has it), the "deterritorializable."

Loathe to fix determinatively this or that figure in the carpet—not the more famous Jamesian conceit but rather Calvino's cryptogram for the city of Eudoxia (that also maps our final chapter), "in which you can observe the city's true form: each place in the carpet correspond[ing] to a place in the city and all the things contained in the city . . . included in the design"—one might point to two related tableaus in "Max Ferber," one naturalistic, the other symbolic, that convey this idea. Ferber, for whose painting technique Sebald borrows from the real-life English painter and expatriate German Frank Auerbach, exercises a kind of creative destruction, an art that seems at war with its own painterly possibilities (an unambiguous trope, as well, for the technology of mass slaughter)—as much *undrawing* through erasing and "excavating" with a woolen rag as compulsive *redrawing* through reapplied lines and shadings of charcoal. "He might reject as many as forty variants, or smudge them back into the paper and overdraw new attempts upon them; and if he then decided that the portrait was done, not so much because he was convinced that it was finished as through sheer exhaustion, an onlooker might feel well that it had evolved from a long lineage of grey, ancestral faces, rendered unto ash but still there, as ghostly presences, on the harried paper" (162). More than that onlooker, readers of Sebald's text may well ask themselves whether they are not also such over-drawers.

But one can object: that seems merely obvious, like the staged gesture of Aunt Fini's hand concealing half her face; or grotesque and melodramatic, like the allusions to Grünewald or the sepulchral evocations of a scarred and pitted Manchester, or the mute and uncanny cameos that appear like wraiths in gothic interiors.[34] In fact, the narrator reuses the same figure and applies it to his own over-scrupulous art of biography as though he had become Ferber twice over: "I had covered hundreds of pages with my scribble, in pencil and ballpoint. By far the greater part had been crossed out, discarded, or obliterated by additions. Even what I ultimately salvaged as a "final" version seemed to me a thing of shreds and patches, utterly botched" (231). Now the conceit seems, if anything, even more heavy-handed. Directly before it, however, is the photograph of the petrified crystallized blackthorn twig, described as the result of "the long term and (I believe) impenetrable process[,] . . . imitating the growth patterns of nature even as it is being dissolved." The photo is preceded on the overleaf by a double-page spread taking up the bulk of each page: two shots of the salt frames, whose perspectives mirror each other yet still resist unambiguous, visual parsing, as if to say "we see everything at once, and still we do not know how it is: no clear picture emerges."

The twig—meaningfully perhaps, the only unbordered photograph in the text, merely inserted into the blank space between paragraphs—is an image Sebald has used once before. In his first book, *Vertigo,* from a section on Stendhal, an itinerant Henri Beyle visits the Hallein salt mines in Salzburg and pronounces such crystallized forms to be "an allegory for the growth of love in the salt mines of the soul"—a conceit his lover, Mme. Gherardi, finds merely "pretty."[35] The maturation of the *figura* from earlier to later text is notable, since in line with Stendhal's own allegorizing, it connotes merely amorous memory's successful insulation from the actual failures of love. Remobilized in *The Emigrants,* it reads the text's own penchant for the figural, the allegorical.

Mimesis inevitably places itself at a remove, even when it does the work of re-presentation—what Emmanuel Levinas, in an early essay, formulates as letting go the prey for the shadow.[36] Sebald's idea suggests that *art* stands in allegorical relation to itself, *internally* held at bay: Ferber's redrawings from their object, Sebald's successive approximations of Ferber's life story from that life. At what necessarily further remove, then, must lie the hermeneutic gesture that also imitates even as it is being dissolved?

As before, one wants to resist playing cipher key to the text's enigma-machinery. We cannot say that we read Sebald's narrator, and while we are provided with much more information about them, we cannot say we apprehend the lives he narrates. The claim is made less in service of an inveterate, scrupled calibration for an ethics of reading than out of the posture the book seems to solicit from me. Imagining the life of Paul Bereyter, it says, risks a wrongful trespass that narrating the life story *may* put right. Narrative is thus potentially corrective, entangled though it may be with the art of losing (which is "not hard to master," in the concluding lines of Elizabeth Bishop's famous villanelle, "though it may look like (Write it!) like disaster"). Yet, in the very next section, Sebald's text tells us that the most limp memoirs can still read like *Märchen,* in which, once you are under their spell, you have to carry on to the finish with the remembering, writing, and reading.

The book mends the tears it presents but also unravels them all over again. Its Ersilia is both rebuilt and dismantled at the same time, an ambivalence left unresolved, in or outside of the fiction. The margin between imaginative reconstruction and actual person or place is of course one of several borderlines *The Emigrants* self-consciously straddles. And that border, between facts and facts made fictive, is arguably most at issue in "Paul Bereyter," the section closest in topic and vicinity to the "pulverized past of Europe,"[37] and proximate in those respects as well to Appelfeld's *The Iron Tracks*, with which it shares more than a single seam. The next two sections straddle some of them before we turn to Appelfeld's text.

TREES AND ROOTS, JEWS AND LEGS

What does representing obliquely the years 1939–1944 in Europe mean? Not to misrepresent, certainly. Nor to tell it more truthfully by telling it slant. Sebald's and Appelfeld's books, at least, make no such claim; and besides, their truth (unlike Dickinson's), denotes no "superb surprise." *The Emigrants,* as one reviewer circumspectly put it, "skirts around some great issue," which most other reviewers take to be "the Holocaust." Yet Holocaust-as-topic is ultimately imprecise where *The Emigrants* is concerned, unless it is taken as a metonym for the centripetal loss of a Europe coeval but separable from the destruction of its many murdered Jews at mid-century. Glimpses of that Europe are revealed throughout the text. The following passage from "Ambros Adelwarth," in which Dr. Abramsky reviews for the narrator the history of the Samaria Sanatorium, is representative:

> I believe it was Fahnstock's unmistakably Austrian intonation that predisposed me towards him at first. He reminded me of my father, who was from Kolomea and, like Fahnstock, came from Galicia to the west after the dissolution of the Hapsburg Empire. Fahnstock tried to re-establish himself in his home town, Linz, whilst my father tried to start up in the liquor trade in Vienna, but both fell foul of circumstances, the one in Linz, the other in Leopoldstadt. In early 1921 my father emigrated to America, and Fahnstock must have arrived in New York in the summer months, where he resumed his career in psychiatry. . . . At about the same time, my father died when a boiler exploded in a soda factory on the Lower East Side. When I was growing up in Brooklyn I missed him very much. (114)

Not the least of *The Emigrants'* threads of intricate relationships has to do with this *elsewhere* of bygone Jewish Europe: a shtetl in Grodno, the Augsburg synagogue, *Polski Manczester*. But Hersch Seweryn emigrates in England more than a decade before Hitler is elected chancellor, and Max Ferber arrives there on the eve of the war; Ambros Adelwarth belongs to an earlier generation entirely and perishes in an American sanatorium in the early 1950s. Paul Bereyter, then, alone among the text's *Ausgewanderten,* resides in that Europe in the midst of its destruction, which he witnesses directly in the motorized artillery.

So yes, in a real sense, Paul is a victim of a catastrophized Europe, called up for service by the German war machine although he is a quarter-Jew, and taking his life at his own hand forty years later by laying himself down in front of a train. Along with other Jewish families, his parents suffered the depredations of townspeople in the 1930s, long before Kristallnacht, as we eventually learn. As does Paul himself: "Paul for a long time had only a partial grasp of what had happened in S. in 1935 and 1936 and did not care to correct his patchy knowledge of the past. It was only in the last decade of his life, which he spent largely in Yverdon, that reconstructing those events became important to him, indeed vital, said Mme Landau" (54).

Yet, we come upon this information midway through the narrative, until which point only one other detail, at the narrator's imparting, suggests Paul's heritage.[38] It occurs on the section's first page, which, like the preceding narrative of "Dr. Henry Selwyn," actually commences with a photograph of what Appelfeld's novel will name "the iron tracks." We learn that Paul has either died of his own free will or else "through a self-destructive compulsion" (27) and that the motivating cause has been left out of the obituary notice. What the obituary does not omit, however, "almost by way of an aside" is that "during the Third Reich Paul Bereyter was prevented from practicing his chosen profession" (27).

"It was this curiously unconnected, inconsequential statement" (which comes to the narrator under our eyes in much the same way as does the newspaper account of Naegeli's body released from the glacier), "as much as the violent manner of his death" (27) that triggers the reconstruction we are about to read. The photograph of the tracks stands over the entire story, which, to paraphrase Ferber, thus serves under the sign of the railway. The presence of the thing, to paraphrase Barthes, is *continuously* metaphoric. Bereyter's violent death, nearly half a century after the war, unambiguously stands for that calamity and the destruction left in its wake.

Like the yew tree that reverberates in the photos of the Courbet Oak and the Kissingen graveyard from much later in the text, the railway tracks reappear in several later guises: a plan (presumably in the narrator's own hand, which he had had to copy from Paul's model on the blackboard), reproduced from his student days; a plan of the classroom in the same hand, from several pages earlier; and two photographs of automobiles, one civilian, containing Paul's family, and one military, in which Paul himself sits at the wheel. The iconicity of all these images—though they are indexically quite different—may be taken to point to a common referent: a Europe reinscribed and emplotted by the wartime imagination, the land rewritten in rectilinear by the Reich (along with its crumbled and battered aftermath, figured correspondingly by Ferber's and the narrator's compositional techniques and certain descriptions of vacated or leveled city-space).[39] Paul's fate, we could say, is bound up in its diagrams and means of transport. "[S]ystematically laid out for him in the railways" is how the text puts it and as Mme. Landau explains: "Railways had always meant a great deal to him—perhaps because he felt they were headed for death. Timetables and directories, all the logistics of railways, had at times become an obsession with him, as his flat in S. showed" (61).

The word harrows the last three pages of text like a revenant: railways, the logistics of railways, laid out for him in the railways, he would end up on the railways, *end up on the railways*. All these words are spoken by Mme. Landau, whose voice the narrator allows to end the story (another detail that distinguishes it from the other three).[40] The narrator has anticipated them, however, speaking of the Paul he knew in his youth (which would have to be several years after the war), whose speech mannerisms "gave one the feeling that it was all being powered by clockwork inside him and Paul in his entirety was a mechanical human made of tin and other metal parts, and might be put out of operation by the smallest functional hitch" (35).

It becomes clear, however, that the source of Paul's corrosive sadness is not exclusively his changed fortunes under the Nuremberg Laws or the death of his father or even his military experience. And therefore, it limits and simplifies Sebald's purposes to maintain that with Paul's suicide the Holocaust has claimed a belated victim. For no less than Henry Selwyn, Ambros Adelwarth, and Max Ferber, Paul Bereyter is "almost consumed by the loneliness within him" (44). And no less than the three parallel stories of emigrants, Paul's stages an intersection along two axes, geographic (the space of nations) and the eccentrically—that is the solitarily—human. These are lives becalmed at some *metaphysical* level, exiled because they belong, at best, apart and at a distance. But these are also Europeans whose origins and departures limn a Europe that has been irreparably disfigured by its dispossession of them—its failure to embed and emplace those who stray, drift, and wander within or away from it. A deeply submerged irony in the text, then, has Ambros Adelwarth, subsequent to all his journeys and voyages, passing away in what it is colloquially referred to as a *home*.

TEARS IN THINGS

One was, as the crow flies, about 2,000 km away—but from where?
    W. G. Sebald, *The Emigrants*

That is the city of Ersilia still, and [the refugees] are nothing.
    Italo Calvino, *Invisible Cities*

It was, I thought, particularly auspicious that the rows of houses were interrupted here and there by patches of waste land on which stood ruined buildings, for ever since I had once visited Munich I had felt nothing to be so unambiguously linked to the word *city* as the presence of heaps of rubble, fire-scorched walls, and the gaps of windows through which one could see the vacant air.
    W. G. Sebald, *The Emigrants*

> Thus, when traveling in the territory of Ersilia, you come upon the ruins of abandoned cities, without the walls which do not last, without the bones of the dead which the wind rolls away: spider-webs of intricate relationships seeking a form.
>
>   Italo Calvino, *Invisible Cities*

We are told by Mme. Landau that Paul's obsessive reading of Klaus Mann, Georg Trakl, Walter Benjamin, and other German writers who had taken their own lives convinced him that he "belonged to the exiles and not to the people of S." (59). The narrator tells us as well that when his own family moved from the village of W. to the small town of S. in 1952, it seemed liked a voyage halfway around the world; it was here, in fact, that "the patches of waste land" described above were first descried. But while self-confessedly German to the marrow (and thus inwardly compelled to return to that same town of S. after the war) Paul belongs to the exiles, not because he is a quarter-Jew and not because he was prevented from practicing his chosen profession under the Reich, but because to be from somewhere in this book is already to be an *Inswanderer,* an internal refugee.

It is worth keeping in mind that Germans who opposed National Socialism but chose silence belonged to what they called the "inner emigration" *(Daheimgebliebenen)* and that the official euphemism for mass deportations to the camps was *Abwanderung,* "exodus" or "migration." As though its seismic shifts were palpable to feet and eye, Europe bedrock has been rendered unstable under the Jewish geography that has always lain like loose topsoil upon it. "Home" sits tenuously alongside "land," fastened to impalpabilities—like the epigraphs for each section, excerpted by Sebald from sources left unannotated by him, each assigned a page of its own as if it too were homeless.[41]

This is the *aura* that hovers tremblingly above the text's surface. For both readers of this book and for the emigrants it fleetingly houses and for the Europe it conjures from abandoned cemeteries in Kissingen or the Litzmannstadt ghetto in Łodz, to "be" in that aura means the unique phenomenon of a distance, however close what we think we look at may be. And it is the ligature Sebald effects between inconsolable loss and indelibly imprinted place that invests such aura with the capacity to look at us in turn, from the remove where it resides. In the spirit of his book's envoi to Roman mythology (an allusion to the Parcae: Nona, Decuma, and Morta), this treatment of it concludes in kind. *Sunt lacrimae rerum et mentem mortalia tangunt:* "There are tears in the nature of things, and mortality touches the mind," says Aeneas as he gazes transfixed at paintings of fallen Troy *(Aeneid* 1:462). Reading *The Emigrants,* one wonders whether such tears inhere in things themselves, or, rather, derive from the *distance* in their nature that holds us at bay, even and especially in the act of our drawing nearer.

The Iron Tracks

TWENTY-TWO STATIONS, TWENTY-TWO LETTERS

"I have learned this route with my body" (3), says the narrator of Appelfeld's novel. Speculating on what that may mean exactly, we may recall the great Zionist poet of nature, Saul Tchernichovsky, who wrote,

> Man is nothing but the soil of a small country,
> nothing but the shape of his native landscape,
> nothing but what his ears recorded
> when they were new and really heard,
> what his eyes saw, before they had their fill of seeing—[42]

Appelfeld knows the poet and the poem, of course, even quoting the metaphor himself in his short memoir about returning to Czernowitz written for the *New Yorker* magazine. Erwin Siegelbaum, the fictive confessor of *The Iron Tracks,* has exchanged land for a kind of peace, we could say, in the form of interminable mobility and transport without agency. So what would be the shape of *his* native landscape?

He says that he possesses an entire continent, that he is at home in every abandoned corner, that he can claim familiarity with even places unmapped. And yet, unlike Tchernichovsky's fusion of body and terrain, he is properly an *overlander* not a footer: his body is sheathed within the "writing" that is rail transport, and if he belongs anywhere, it is to the trains that carry him over the tracks that travel under, and for, him.[43] More than their passenger, he might be said to be their *citizen,* as they in turn assume the contour of country and landscape. "A train is by nature heavy, even clumsy. But in open spaces, when it gains speed, it transforms itself, defies gravity, and soars" (5). A mobile homeland, a train is a trope extended, indeed supported by the tracks that give the book its title, for they exchange land for *routes*. This man, it appears, is nothing but *the railways*—not only the timetables, directories, logistics so important to Paul Bereyter, but the *perpetuum mobile* of conveyance forever circling and rehearsing death but still deferring it at the same time. Place from flight.

The "iron tracks" suggest an engravening upon the land, but the novel makes the repeated segmented excursion itself an explicit correlate for writing: "My annual route is circular. Actually oval. . . . It's a route with endless stations, but for me there are only twenty-two. The rest are of no consequence. I know my stations like the palm of my hand" (11). Each station, then, a letter, for the total corresponds to the number of letters in the Hebrew alphabet, each of which already doubles as a number. Like the letter "shin" concretely rendered by tefillin straps on the back of the hand, or the *hamsa*, an amulet shaped like a human palm with written characters, or the kabbalists' correspondence between letters and fingers, script and body join terrain in *The Iron Tracks* to form a palimpsest of language, selfhood, and errancy: "I live by signs, by codes whose meaning I alone know" (11)—like the mother tongue he and his "rivals" speak / "My route is fixed, more fixed every year. Imprinted on my body, it cannot be shaken" (15) /—like the iron tracks themselves. / "At the Monday fair years ago I found a ladle with the Hebrew word for milk engraved upon it. Hebrew letters in these remote places move me" (117)—like trains.

But before we proceed further, there is the small matter of the novel's title. "*Mesilat barzel*," which means path or road of iron in Hebrew,[44] should bring to mind for someone familiar with the "Judaica" (in the standard nomenclature) collected by Siegelbaum on his journeys, the title of a canonical Jewish guide to moral conduct and spiritual perfection. Composed by the eighteenth-century pietist and mystic Moshe Haim Luzzatto (also known by the acronym RaMCHaL) born Padua, 1707; died Acco in Palestine, 1747), it is entitled *Mesilat Yesharim*, "The Path of the Just" (or "straight"),[45] and lest it be heard as functioning simply as a silent echo, Appelfeld has named it in the text as such: "In the past few years, whenever I showed Stark a manuscript or an old book, he would sit and read, and in the end he would say, 'This book would have made my father very happy.' Recently it was as if the words he has used for so long had been wiped from his tongue. He now spoke in the way of his ancestors. During my last visit he reminded me of all the books I had shown him. Once I sat with him all night long, and we read *The Path of the Righteous*" (98).

Though Appelfeld's own literary idiom tends to eschew the sort of overlay *(shibbutz)* and thematic allusion to classical Jewish texts common to Israeli writers of an earlier generation and his own statehood peers,[46] the titles for some of his fictions send clear if layered signals about precursor texts: "*Annei Ha'nahar*," for instance ("the foundations of the river") sounds like *Annei Hasedeh,* "foundations of the field," a talmudic trope for telluric spirits or *genii loci; "Mikhvat Ha'or"* ("searing light") recalls the description of leprosy as a "burning by fire in the skin" in Leviticus 13. Typically, such titles bend Biblical or religious contexts to quotidian concerns, but then they cannot help but switch the polarity in the other direction as well. *Mesilat,* then—path, road—like trains or railroad ties themselves, is bordered on either side, framed by co-referents from different contexts (yet each is associable with railways), "iron" and "free from curvature."

ZALISHTSHIK AND WIRBLBAHN

But while "the path of the just" aims at transcendence, a grammar of moral ascent, "the iron tracks" is resolutely earthbound and in fact tautological. The narrative begins and ends in the town of Wirblbahn, a name that mingles the linear with the vortical. And even while the novel concludes with Siegelbaum's intent to set fire to the town, he proposes this over drinks in a dining car. The text locates him at story's end still on the iron tracks. "I had done everything out of compulsion, clumsily, and always too late" (195), reads the last sentence of the novel, almost in parody of the twinned traits of caution and enthusiasm in *Mesilat Yesharim;* and yet, one is left to wonder what he will do afterward and where he will go. Circuitous and cyclical train travel, after all, is both the form and substance of his "memoir": "It has been forty years since I first harnessed myself to those racehorses known as trains" (10) in what becomes a seemingly interminable *überflügelnd,* or outflanking. Perhaps now, therefore, he is merely one letter and one station short of twenty-two in an otherwise "endless" series.

Appelfeld's choice of title, then, overtly connects his unvarying theme about the place of Jewish tradition—how to reconcile a Jewish world before and after the Shoah—to Jewish textuality itself. Additionally, *The Iron Tracks* also marks a return to the mise en scene of Appelfeld's earliest short fiction in which errant Jews venture out of and back into forests ("Cold Spring"), monasteries ("The Last Refuge"), and hamlets ("The Station") of a postwar former Hapsburg territory whose ground has shifted utterly.[47] Like train stations in succession, like points of origin and return, or most of all like a switch-point at crossing rail lines, the novel routes *Mesilat barzel* so that it follows, meets, or otherwise intersects *Mesilat Yesharim.* As we discover in following Siegelbaum's detours and temporary stays along the "long, twisted line" (3), this is a text littered with instance after instance of what S. Y. Agnon, a precursor on the intersecting tracks of Jewish tradition and modernity, named "a book that was lost."

And like Appelfeld's text (which most certainly alludes to it), Agnon's story by that name joins text to pre-text, mirroring legatees of tradition and their testators.[48] But whereas in Agnon, books enclose each other in *shalshelet ha'kabbalah*, a "chain of tradition" that winds its way through diaspora eventually to find its terminus and haven in Jerusalem, *The Iron Tracks* lights haphazardly upon books, mezuzahs, and kiddush cups like so many fragments awaiting redemption.[49] When Siegelbaum admits compulsiveness and belatedness, even though his mission to execute his parents' murderer has proved ultimately successful,[50] we are not so sure that the parallel, albeit emancipatory mission to collect and preserve stray texts and antiquities (Siegelbaum calls them "antiques") is liable to the same charge. Agnon's is a Jewish Europe stranded between tradition and modernity, a metaphorical "Wirblbahn," so to speak. In the world of *The Iron Tracks*, conversely, it is the *objects* that have become stranded[51] because that Jewish Europe has been eradicated. It has become the Wirblbahn imagined at novel's end and announced at the beginning:

> I have sought to change the starting point of my journey. Until now I've been unable to do so. I will explain: in flat Wirblbahn, which is nothing more than a row of warehouses, a few watchmen's huts, and a wretched inn, in this accursed place, my life ended and I was reborn. The Germans brought our train to this remote station and left us here. For three days we had been bolted inside. On the third day, the train stopped moving. The wings of death had departed, but we didn't know it. The next morning someone released the bolt, and a stream of light washed over us. That was our return to life. (12)

Neighboring to the abstract and spare landscapes of Kafka—a European *Amerika?*—this continent holds itself in suspense, as though it had stopped breathing momentarily but is in no danger of expiring. "Thus it is every year. And in this repetition lies a strange hopefulness. As if our end were not extinction but a sort of constant renewal" (5). Without pressing the analogy too far, the iron tracks inscribe a Europe that perhaps most resembles Sebald's evil fairy tales in which everything—person, object, habitation—subsists under a spell. Place has been, so to speak, withdrawn from time; or reciprocally, an uncanny atemporality has been transmuted into place.[52] "The train passes through rural stations without stopping. Thank God nothing ties me to them" (23). These trains are not carriers of death, but rather a hybrid of hotel and concentration-cell in motion. They not only defy gravity and attachment, they convert the experience of time into the railway-time of arrivals and departures.

This is of course the norm for train travel, as sometime-fellow passenger Michel de Certeau notes: "The more you see, the less you hold—a dispossession of the land in favor of a greater trajectory of the eye" (*The Practice of Everyday Life*, 112).[53] But in Appelfeld, the train is a compulsive trope: "Is there an Appelfeld novel without a train?" asks one critic (Brown and Zhorowitz, *Encounter with Aharon Appelfeld*, 74). Like the motif of cigarette-smoking in "Smoke," a story from 1962, it recapitulates the industrial technology of Jewish death but sublimates it: "What would I do without that somnolent rhythm?" (30). "The trains make me free" (19). *Eisenbahn macht frei*.

People live here in this Europe, Siegelbaum visits them, but the towns and countryside through which the text meanders and realizes thinly are also not ultimately *habitable* places, but places to visit, pass through, return from. Life is strangely half-made up, unreal,[54] like the description of *eretz sham* ("Over There") conjured by Appelfeld's younger contemporary David Grossman in his 1989 novel *See Under: Love*: "The only trouble is, there's a curse on Over There. . . . There's this spell that was put on all the children and grownups and animals, and it made them freeze. The Nazi Beast did it. It roamed the country, freezing everything with its icy breath " (50). Stranded people—some of them Jews, half-Jews, quarter-Jews, some of them Jew-haters—man hotels and stations. Vagrant, usable women enter the foreground briefly and recede. Siegelbaum crosses paths with his "competitors" now and again, "six or seven in all [who] apparently follow the same circular route"; like him, "they are experienced creatures of the tracks." "For my part," he confides in us, "I am prepared for any compromise, for any division of territory" (7).

And we speculate, as before: what is that territory exactly? In what way would it be divided? Does it denote restrictively land, terrain, boundaries of towns, the borders of present and former nations? Or might it refer to the "Jewish antiquities, manuscripts, and books" that Siegelbaum and his rivals ferret out of hiding, which have survived the murdered Jews to whom they once belonged? Itinerary of an expedition: Wirblbahn, point of departure, cycles *(wirbl)* around its rails *(bahn)*, as we know. Proceeding northward to Herben and beyond it to Upper Herben, and thence, to Prachthof. From that point, Hofbaden, Saltzstein, and in quick succession, Gruenfeld, Gruenwald, and Pracht (foreshortening "Prachthof"), where Siegelbaum picks up the trail of the murderer Nachtigel ("nightingale" crossed with "to pass the night"). Express, next, to Sternberg, in which a reminiscence about a past love and fellow traveler ("she was one of ours") discloses one of only two non-Austrian place names in the text, her hometown "Zalishtshik"; the other, "Strozhnitz," follows hard upon it in a similar encounter in the subsequent chapter on the way north from Sternberg.

Then, to Gruendorf, where we learn of Rabbi Zimmel, acquaintance of Gershom Scholem to whom he will send the books, menorahs, candlesticks, and other remnants that Siegelbaum begins to collect there. Further north to the Graten mountains, where according to R. Zimmel "as far as I know, Jews never lived" (89), thence to Rondhof and Upper Rondhof on a barren, remote plateau. One hundred and twenty kilometers further on, Weinberg, where Nachtigel has retired, but Siegelbaum feels impelled to get off at Zwiren instead, when the train makes a stop there. From Zwiren to Upper Zwiren on an even more elevated and exposed plateau. Again, rather than press on straight to Weinberg, a detour to Sandberg, home of Rabbi Zimmel, and thence to Steinberg, forty kilometers from Nachtigel's home, although Siegelbaum breaks off from the iron tracks and heads south to Little Steinberg. Boarding the train again to Upper Steinberg, and finally, off the iron tracks again, a two and a half kilometer walk to Weinberg, where he shoots Nachtigel. Mission accomplished, through the forest shortcut between Steinberg and Weinberg (that "I know well," 179), to the station and the express train to distant Saltzstein. Once arrived, back to Wirblbahn, point of return and of planned conflagration.

Like the thinly sketched, flattened characters in the novel, the route is stark, transparently schematic. Every Appelfeld fiction is plainly allegorical, but the place names in this one seem especially so, being so manifestly prosaic. "Yard," "village," "bath," "circle," "salt," "stone," "mountain," "forest," "field," "star," "green," "upper," "little": all nominal components of real places, to be sure, but in serial form, suggesting a cutout Austro-Hungarian empire stripped bare to its terrestrial skeleton, as though the land, too, were constructed of (iron) tracks. Mode of transport and itinerary of places seem to share each other's properties, fugitive places[55] alike, though one moves while the other remains static . . . or seems to. From one vantage, the text outlines one all-encompassing "Wirblbahn," and Wirblbahn, as Siegelbaum reminds us, is "flat Wirblbahn." Siegelbaum, moreover, not only shares the components of his name with those of towns and villages, but is himself the same paradox of forward motion within circularity that the name of the town articulates.

Not surprisingly, then, Appelfeld's novel betrays an almost modular design. Land, person, object, and language share metaphorical equivalency. As in the case of Sebald's title, nothing obliges us to take "iron tracks" as exclusively the semiotic province of trains and rails, since it also portends variously a landscape, a personality, a cultural tradition, and its language(s), a world after catastrophe, the mechanics of transmission. Similarly, the two ongoing actions in the story, riding the trains and purchasing ceremonial artifacts and books, mutually reinforce each other in a literal economic circuit since finances earned from one enable continual pursuit of the other; each, moreover, parodically reflects more authentic expressions of community in the one, and religious practice in the other. (Sitting in a train station after he has killed Colonel Nachtigel, Siegelbaum meets a stranger who "in our language" tells him, "You can be proud of what you have done. Not everyone manages to do what you have done" [183], which, while it concerns Siegelbaum's legacy of gathered holy texts and icons, surprises even him, who expects a direct reference to the execution he has just performed.)[56]

The critic David Suchoff correctly reads the one name standing prominently apart from all the others, "Zalishtshik," as a post-Shoah rewriting of the biblical "shibboleth" where language means both cultural difference and survival, figured by a literal crossing-over. The famous incident in the Book of Judges Suchoff has in mind transpires as follows: "And the Gileadites held the fords of the Jordan against the Ephraimites: and when any fugitives from Ephraim said, 'Let me go over, the men of Gilead said unto him, are you an Ephraimite?' If he said, 'No,' they said to him, 'Say now *Sh*ibboleth": and he said "*S*ibboleth': for he could not frame to pronounce it right. Thereupon they seized him, and slew him by the fords of the Jordan: and there fell at that time of the Ephraimites forty and two thousand" (Judges 12:5–6).[57] In Zalishtshik now, Siegelbaum's former lover tells him, "There are no Jews, only Ukrainians and Poles" (71), which for Siegelbaum presents the clearest evidence that she should not go back, that no place for her remains. Yet, persuaded rather by the pull of "longings and obligations," she does return and, like a stranded Ephraimite, spends her days "on a riverbank" (72). Later in the novel, Siegelbaum recalls another of their conversations: "It seemed that she was putting herself into a kind of self-enchantment, blinding herself with illusions. I chided her: 'We don't need a house of our own, a river of our own. We must live without illusions and within ourselves.' She listened to me and fell silent. That evening her eyes were swollen, and she didn't mention Zalishtshik anymore" (146). Bertha concedes: "One mustn't yearn for a city that murdered its sons and daughters.[58] I have to wrench such yearnings from my heart and accept that I no longer have a permanent place in the world" (146). Yet, she does return, nevertheless.

Suchoff argues that such homelessness, understood linguistically, is not a privation but rather an inevitable consequence of crossing and sharing borders between one's own culture and someone else's. Endogamous local tradition, he writes, "travels the rails, crosses the river, marries others." And to be sure, that tension lies at the heart of Appelfeld's entire literary project: the "saga" of Jewish tradition that remains permeable, at its very great risk, to other voices that by the very same token allow it the obligatory encounter with otherness. Yet in the text, returning himself to the identical spot where he and Bertha argued about Zalishtshik, Siegelbaum confesses after reminiscing, "Now Sternberg is no longer Sternberg for me, just a burning space where one must not linger" (72). It seems that the very bringing back to mind of "Zalishtshik" deforms both the place and the name that bespeak the other tongue: Sternberg is no longer "Sternberg" for me.

"In political terms," adds Suchoff in a necessary qualification, "'our' river was controlled by non-Jewish nation-states in the European diaspora. The illusion of Jewish linguistic and political autonomy in Europe, magically controlled and delimited by the password of our language, was, of course, a shibboleth in the end." Of course, what constitutes 'our' language has not been simplified as a problematic by Appelfeld in his fiction, despite his having found a home not only in the State of Israel but in Hebrew. It is, as he acknowledges in interviews, an ongoing matter of personal identity as well. "German was my mother language . . . but after what happened I was always ambivalent about it. After I came to Israel, Hebrew became my mother tongue, and I studied Yiddish to avoid German. I know it now, but I am still ambivalent" (*Voices of Israel*, 132).[59] Unlike his contemporary, the German-Jewish emigrant to Palestine Yehudah Amichai (1922–2003, born Ludwig Pfeuffer), who Hebraicized both fore- and surname (the latter means "my people"),[60] "Aharon Appelfeld" registers that very ambivalence, a name half Hebrew, half German.

Immediately after the recounted episode with Bertha, Siegelbaum recalls another time a year later "on this very line" when he meets a woman who could have been her double. He tells her she looks "very similar to my friend Bertha, who has just returned to her native city of Zalishtshik," and she responds, "my mother was born in Zalishtshik" (75)—for Siegelbaum, like the force of the earlier confirmation of a no-longer-Jewish Zalishtshik, unmistakable evidence that they are "bound to each other, and not by chance" (75). It is an uncanny tableau, in no small part because all the communication takes place in writing: the woman is deaf. Siegelbaum writes down for her in his "mother tongue" his name and the name of his hometown, which we speculate to be an echo of Appelfeld's own Czernowitz. He and the woman are neighbors, she tells him; she comes from Strozhnitz (whose Jewish population along with that of its neighboring city was decimated, then ghettoized, and finally deported).[61]

Now, it is true that the text implies Sternberg has lost its luster for Siegelbaum due to romantic disappointment: "Since she left me, my hold on the world has become weaker" (72). Earlier, he has confessed the opposite tug: "If I have a grasp of anything on this earth, it is of my lost hometown. . . . Sometimes it seems that all my travels are to that place" (48). Moreover, such names and places as Zalishtshik and Strozhnitz are exclusively associated with women and with the mother tongue. "Mother tongue" represents something of an oxymoron, since Siegelbaum tells us that in his early youth his mother fell mysteriously silent. As a consequence, he is placed in the custody of his father, who distances him from his mother and maternal grandfather in order to "learn the ways of the Ruthenians." "At the age of six I spoke Ruthenian[62] like a native. My father was proud of that. The language of the Jews repelled him" (50). "I spent most of the months with my father on trains, in third class, of course, with all the wretched and oppressed, crossing through villages, rivers, and forests. He loved the Ruthenian way of life from the depths of his soul, and he would pronounce every word in their language as if her were savoring a piece of honey cake. The Ruthenians were impressed by his accent, but they guessed, of course, that he wasn't one of their own" (57). Even his father, anchored on the near side of the Jordan, can't quite escape this shibboleth.

The text's algebra becomes clearer. At the risk of schematizing it too coarsely, one can say simply that trains, wandering, and the other's language are the stuff of patrimony.[63] Conversely, the land, along with native accents, and not least, the legacy of Jewish tradition—an older and subsuming inheritance—exercise their pull through the mother. Appelfeld deftly coordinates all three through an analepsis where Siegelbaum, in his mother's care, spends a summer in her father's village.

It was a small village surrounded by tall trees, and from a distance. Grandfather's low house resembled an abandoned kennel in the heart of the forest.... [A]ttached to the house was a shed where Grandfather would sit most of the day with his books.... [T]oward evening many people would gather at his doorstep. They were tall, bearded Jews. The smell of horses wafted from their long garments, and whips never left their hands.... During those long bright summers, I learned the morning, afternoon, and evening prayers. Grandmother would sit and practice with me. She knew the prayers by heart. (54–56)

Two unobtrusive details quietly drive the distinction between mother and father, native and alien, home. Having become accustomed to living in "tunnels, caves, abandoned houses and barns on the outskirts of villages" (57) while traveling underground with father, a Communist organizer, Siegelbaum returns again to his mother's house, where his life "was confined to sitting in the yard or next to the window" (59). By contrast, it is the doorway of the house that the text associates with the opposing legacy: "Near the door [the people] paused awkwardly. Grandmother would come out and speak to them softly . . ." / "At night in the courtyard they would ring their hands and implore. Grandfather would stand in the doorway, mute as stone" (56–58).

Maternal grandfather, a rabbi, and Siegelbaum's father, fellow traveler, are in the end not wholly dissimilar, as they both preach social justice for the oppressed. But it is those liminal ports between home and elsewhere, window and doorway, that bespeak the difference in valence worth noting here, something clarified in the following chapter. Marking the first instance of the transmission of Jewish "treasures" in the narrative, an innkeeper in Pracht (one of several clandestine Jews or part-Jews in the text) asks Siegelbaum to preserve something very dear to her, "a thin mezuza, decorated with Hebrew letters" (64). "How can I keep this?" replies Siegelbaum. "I have no house, and I wander from place to place" (65). But he does keep it, the ritual marker, placed on the doorpost, that Jews reside here under the inscribed sign of the Law.[64] Suchoff records the tensions staged in this figura:

How can he continue the tradition, Erwin wonders, without marking its linguistic home, demarcating what belongs within and without? Radical nostalgia in Appelfeld's spare Hebrew prose longs for a language that will recall Judaism's pre-Holocaust diaspora origins, but comes to a contrary conclusion on the way: that the memory grounding our tradition is fleeting, broken, and never ending. . . . The most monumental, self-identical tradition, Erwin knows, is always the hidden portal to difference, no matter how nostalgically we wish to return home. . . . It is thus no accident that Erwin sleeps most soundly here, where the need to mark the threshold of the Jewish home is accepted—he takes the *mezuza* in safe keeping from Mrs. Groton—but the boundary between "our" home and that of "others" remains unfixed.

Yet while it is true these environs have typically had a narcotic effect upon him—"Only in Pracht does my body cease its gallop. . . . Were it not for the fears that drive me from place to place, I would remain here. . . . In Pracht the dreams peel away from me, like a scab from a healed wound" (61)—after receiving the "amulet," Siegelbaum bolts: "I had planned to stay at her inn another day, but my emotions prevented me . . . my throat closed, and I fled as if for my life" (65). Worse (since this episode, like many of the others, is a reminiscence narrated in the present), the place now feels robbed of its soporific benison: "I stand, but my leg won't support me. . . . I sit in the neglected station swallowing drink after drink, waiting for the next train" (65).

Actually, it is by or near the doorpost *in his childhood* that Siegelbaum admits to being overcome by sleep: "Sometimes we practiced [prayers] so long that I would fall asleep on the porch." And though strictly speaking not under the tranquillizing protection of a mezuzah, the portal between house and nature affords a similar sleep-inducing aura: "Life in stables, near the animals, was for me a lasting magic . . . as soon as the pungent odors struck my nostrils, I would collapse into sleep" (57). Further, sleep is often figured by the text as narcotic, and a means of avoidance: "Since then my days have glided over the rails with a kind of haste, as if they weren't days, but the gathering darkness of twilight. It was a profound sleep, sometimes disturbed by the pounding of hammers" (31). Thus what appears like sound sleep induced by caesura or threshold in one place becomes sedative sleep in the midst of relentless flight in another. (Nostalgic reminiscence usually prompted by stasis is almost always followed in the discourse by the act of re-boarding the train: "For hours memory flooded into my head, as if seeking to drown me. My distant childhood, lost sights, appeared before me like a melting sea of ice. Since then I no longer overstay" [36].[63])

To gather up these details now and suggest what is at play: the analysis so far has highlighted the novel's modular form in light of which the transferential link between the psychology of Siegelbaum's childhood attachments and his adult compulsion to repeat becomes a given—not because of a superficial Freudianism, necessarily, but rather from a certain schematic logic of congruence. Which parent, which language, which spatial architectonic, which competing pull, we wonder, is privileged? Which leverages greater power: particularizing tradition on one side, or a modernity hostile to cultural difference on the other? The novel over-parses. Yet clearly, even while Appelfeld has confined himself to a small set of connecting threads, Ersilia-like again, they reveal themselves to be not as diagrammatically rigid as one might suspect. They too can take the form of tangled ravelings rather than stiff and iron-tracked rectilinearity.

Siegelbaum's own route leads him into detours, we recall, and the implacability of iron tracks as a grid upon the land is offset by the feathering effect lent by the accidental gathering up of stray objects (as well as by Siegelbaum's own straying, by roads and paths, from the railway). So there is crossover, even among the text's various binary poles (mother/father; *shtetl*/third-class trains; Ruthenian/mother tongue; religious/secular; Zalishtshik/Sternberg).[66] Bertha must return to Zalishtshik to honor her "obligations" (71); in reply to the question, "Where are you going?" Siegelbaum tells Comrade Stark, "I have obligations" (43). And it is with Stark, the Communist secretary, that Siegelbaum sits all night reading *Mesilat Barzel,* "The Path of the Righteous," who also once tells him "Your work is holy. You mustn't leave these precious objects in the hands of strangers. Marvelous memories are stored up in them" (81).

The mother tongue is not alone in sharing properties with place: "Again I was with my father, dragged from hut to hut, completely submerged in the Ruthenian language" (156). Nor does the inn at Pracht have a monopoly on sleep: the inn at Gruenfeld "has the power to put my nightmares to rest" (47). "A glass of cognac separates me from my memory for a while" (9). "True, a drink and a few cigarettes can banish fear from my heart for a while, but only the train, it alone, can tranquilize me completely" (31). "Today one woman, even one who is not demanding, is enough for me, plunging me into a very deep sleep" (101). Melancholy, too, can overpower him, and when gripped by it in his sleep, he "lose[s] the power to move even a single meter" (43). To take a final example by now familiar to us, the name of the town Wirblbahn effectively means long-twisted; the railway line, as we also know, Siegelbaum describes as "long, twisted."

Jan Gross has said of the standard historiographic approach to the years 1939–1945 that it "posits that there are two separate wartime histories—one pertaining to the Jews and the other to all the other citizens of a given European country subjected to Nazi rule" (*Neighbors,* 8).

If *The Iron Tracks* superficially suggests such schematic partition, it nevertheless subjects it to internal critique. This is the novel's version of Calvino's filigree: crossover, switchback, tracks that become a helix, tradition that becomes a twisted chain, sameness that "travels the rails, crosses the river, marries others."

TRAINS INSTEAD OF LEGS

One more difficult implication of the novel's title, therefore, means that ceaseless rail travel has inadvertently *dulled* a set of overriding differences rather than sharpened them. "When I'm fortunate I meet one of my rivals on this line. For a while he tries to lose me, but I won't give in. In the end I trap him in a dark corner. It turns out that I'm mistaken. He's not a rival of mine. On the contrary, like me, he's also been tracking Nachtigel. He's been after him for years" (67). After Stark tells him that his work is holy, Siegelbaum admits that his "attraction to these godforsaken places has grown stronger. Sometimes my heart chides me for that devotion because it can distract me from my main goal: the murderer" (81). In good Conradian fashion, where center sometimes becomes periphery and periphery center,[67] the two tracks on which the story's plot positions itself—the hunt for Nachtigel and the pursuit of stranded objects—cross chiasmatically, threatening confusion.

The train, we are told at first, makes Siegelbaum free, but "in the end [they] are just a jangle of nerves" (78), which follows one of the more surprising revelations in the discourse: "Whenever anyone mentions Israel, I am filled with gloom. I would very much like to go there, to gather strength. I would return here fortified. A month in Israel would make me a brave man. It would teach me to get away from the trains and live in the forest. There I would learn to concentrate, to stay on the track, and not to despair" (78). By this point, we have become increasingly dubious of such expostulations, not least because Siegelbaum braces himself through all kinds of aids: sleep, alcohol, shaving, and especially encounter. "Two days in Stark's company restore a whole world to me" (41) / "This Italian in exile, in whose company I dwell for two or three hours, grants me, without knowing it, the feeling of home. It was as if I returned to my native city" (33) / "Strangely, a couple of hours in [Gizi's] company restores my will to live" (39). "If nightmares interrupt my sleep, I stop off for a day or two in Gruenfeld; [the inn] has the power to put my nightmares to rest" (46). "Max lets me sleep as my soul desires. Sleep in his fortress is a quiet sleep, without threats, and I lose myself in it.... A week with Max restores me to some of the hidden realms of my life" (109, 112). More important, the diction in the passage about Israel is strangely self-canceling: to get off the trains in order to stay on the track. "Track" may be meant in figuratively, but the Hebrew still says *"mesilat."*

Israel functions not as destination or terminus but stopover; "return" means not Jewish homecoming but a circling back to Europe. "'Return' in an Appelfeld story is a gesture not so much of 'going back' as of 'repeating'" says Sidra Ezrahi (181), for whom the chronotope of the road in such fiction leads only to endings deferred by a series of detours.[68] Sure enough, Israel as forest rather than sea or desert in the passage above recalls nothing so much as the familiar landscape of the Bukovina (whose forests, Appelfeld remarks in *Beyond Despair,* were "a kind of childhood where reality and legend were mingled" 12).[69] So Israel is no more an object of desire for Siegelbaum than the women he meets on his train rides, of whom he says tellingly, "Thus I repeat to myself: love for two stations and no more" (9).

His desires, like his experiences, are serial and imitative; they merely recapitulate. And thus the similar sounding projection of enchanted tranquility at Mrs. Groton's—"Sometimes I imagine I'll spend my last days here, among the tall trees that cast their long shadows on the earth. Here I will join all those beloved by me" (64)—that Suchoff reads as a figure for discovering belated shelter under tradition's canopy, still smacks of self-serving fantasy, albeit understandably so. And fantasy, Siegelbaum is told later in the story in tones that seem to echo *Mesilat Yesharim,* "is more dangerous than cognac. A person must do the right thing, without submitting a bill or expecting a reward" (75).

Appelfeld's novel is rife with such crosshatchings. The episode involving the mezuzah, for instance, that seemed so full of portent and conclusive meaning is restaged more or less unchanged several chapters later when another quasi-or clandestine Jew gives Siegelbaum an object—this time a kiddush cup engraved with the words "Holy Sabbath"—for safekeeping. "I wrapped it in its velvet cloth again. I wanted to say, I don't have a house of my own, where shall I put it? . . . The train came early, and I left him hastily, as if the earth were burning under my feet" (119). Yet again, the crosshatching here coordinates threads of resemblance and contiguity alike. "From Zwiren to Uppper Zwiren is only a half hour by train. But the atmosphere is entirely different" (120) begins the next chapter. And indeed, a scant three pages after removing the wrapping to reveal a kiddush cup, reminding himself of his purpose in traveling to this vicinity, he says: "I drew the pistol from my valise and unwrapped it. The solid piece of metal always pleases me. In the end, I sell the treasures and manuscripts, but it remains faithful to me" (122).[70]

Kiddush cup and pistol are unveiled alike through the text's own self-evident parallelism, but what elicits particular attention is the common prompt of a "quarter-Jew," who proffers the cup and thoughts of whom trigger recollection of the alternate mission to murder Nachtigel. And it is here, in these instances of lineal, albeit mixed, descent, through the mingled, blurred legacies of Jewish and non-Jewish traditions, that the novel's preoccupation with differences becomes most intriguing. And here, too, the trope of the tracks, the iron cleavage between parallel lines that somehow still manage to meet and cross, once again gets pressed into service. Early on, Siegelbaum tells us, "I confess, I have no faith in anyone outside the train. They repel me. Over the years, I've found a few friends who remain faithful and wait for me, a few women" (31).

The former do not always or even necessarily denote full, intact coreligionists, however. What appears to be the lone Jew in the Graten mountains (where R. Zimmel says "Jews never lived"), tells him that "the period of isolation was ending and the time had come to rejoin the Jewish people. The words were familiar and I understood their meaning. Despite that a barrier had descended, divided us in silence" (93).[71] While he admits to a close friendship with Rabbi Zimmel or Max Rauch from Sadgora, a Jewish haberdasher and fellow collector living in Upper Rondhof, he also speculates that he feels safe and calm in the latter's company perhaps due to "the large, well-protected room on the ground floor. The room has two exits, one of them secret" (109). Besides, Max is married to a Gentile "whose hatred for the Jews knows no bounds" (116). Siegelbaum's other "few friends" typically consist of fellow exiles like the Italian Marcello, or Jews *in some part* like August the quarter-Jew.

First, Gizi, a convert, with whom Siegelbaum has "an unspoken secret that binds us" (38). Then a Paul Bereyter–like figure "who proudly told me that his paternal grandmother had been Jewish," a "strain [that] had prevented him from being accepted in the military academy. During the war he had been sent to the Eastern Front" (47). Both these figures are interposed between recollections of Siegelbaum's parents. Then, Mrs. Groton the donor of the mezuzah, who tells him something she's never revealed to anyone: "My maternal grandmother was Jewish, and she converted" (64). Further reminiscences about his father's fellow communists and about Bertha from Zalishtshik and her "double" from Strozhnitz, and then we are introduced to Mrs. Braun, who "although half Jewish, feels completely Jewish" (78).

In chapter fifteen, we meet Mrs. Hahn, "a convert to Christianity" who understands Jews—"Jews are never pleased with themselves, and others aren't pleased with them either"—only because she admits "Because I'm one of them" (104). And in chapter seventeen, Siegelbaum briefly dilates on August the quarter-Jew, whose personal history, again, recalls Paul Bereyter: "Because of that quarter he has suffered all his life.... During the war they had sent his aged mother, a half-Jew, to a camp in Germany to improve her character. She returned from there thin and withdrawn, and she didn't speak again till the end of her life" (117–18).

The dramatis personae of the novel, predictably, divide into distinct modules: the Communist compatriots of Siegelbaum's father, Stark, Kron, and Rollman, and thus behind them, Siegelbaum's father himself; Bertha, Bella, and other women who briefly reincarnate his mother;[72] Rabbi Zimmel and Max, associated with the preservation of *shalshelet ha'kabbalah,* and thus aligned with Siegelbaum's maternal grandparents;[73] his opposite, Colonel Nachtigel, along with minor cameos of Nazi "enemies"; and finally, the set of partial or veiled Jews. All the groupings subtend each other and intermingle, Stark now being doubled with Rabbi Zimmel, now with Siegelbaum's father, for instance. But the father manifests crossover itself—as intermarriage, the merger of bloodlines. Yet at the same time, the various half, quarter, or converted Jews are all depicted as *essentially* Jewish in some way, each thus giving voice to what the historian Yosef Hayim Yerushalmi calls Jewish Lamarckism,[74] "the feeling, harbored or expressed by committed and alienated modern Jews alike, of the enormous weight, the gravitational pull, of the Jewish past, whether it be felt as an anchor or a burden" (31).

JEWS TERMINABLE AND INTERMINABLE

Yerushalmi develops the conceit in a monograph about Sigmund Freud's personal tensions around that twinned anchor/burden, *Freud's Moses: Judaism Terminable and Interminable,* the subtitle of which could easily be appended to *The Iron Tracks* as its own. Yerushalmi maintains that the true axis of Freud's *Moses and Monotheism* is not the farfetched narrative (in a letter to Stefan Zweig, Freud himself refers to the work as a "historical novel"), but rather the problem and dynamics of *tradition,* which for classical Judaism means the chain of tradition communicated orally and textually, but for Freud the fate of being repressed and therefore a compulsive return and reassertion. "Deconstructed into Jewish terms, what is Lamarckism if not the powerful feeling that, for better or worse, one cannot really cease being Jewish. . . . [This] Lamarckian assumption lies at the heart of Freud's history of the Jews" (31). For did not Freud himself, fore-echoing the fictive Erwin Siegelbaum, write in a letter to Sabina Spielrein, "We are and remain Jews. The others will only exploit us and will never understand and appreciate us?"[75]

The third part of *Moses and Monotheism* makes an argument that lies parallel to the iron tracks of Rabbi Zimmel's injunction to Siegelbaum to keep ferreting out the holy remnants that have endured holocaust, for "the day would come when people speak of my discoveries the way they speak of the Cairo Geniza" (86). Writes Freud, "The political misfortune of the nation taught them to appreciate the only possession they had retained, their literature, at its true value. Immediately after the destruction of the Temple in Jerusalem by Titus, Rabbi Yochanan ben Zakkai asked for permission to open at Yabneh the first school for the study of the Torah. From now on it was the Holy Book and the intellectual effort applied to it that kept the people together" (147). Even more pertinently—as the very exercise of transmitted patrimony— Yerushalmi cites Jakob Freud's inscription, written in *melitsah* (the tessellation of idioms from classical Jewish sources), in the Bible studied by Sigmund in his youth and now given back to him rebound in leather: "Behold, it is the Book of Books, from which sages have excavated and lawmakers learned knowledge and judgment. . . . Since then the book has been stored like the fragments of the tablets in an ark with me. For the day on which your years were filled to five and thirty I have put upon it a cover of new skin and have called it: 'Spring up, O well, sing ye unto it!'" (6 May 1891).[76]

"The book . . . was stored with me": as Yerushalmi notes, an allusion to Deut. 32:34, *ha-lo hu kamus 'imadi*, "is it not laid up in store with me, sealed in my treasuries?" The relevant point of *Freud's Moses* for a reading of *The Iron Tracks* is simply this: tradition gets transmitted through a recuperation that is the mark of incurred damage and loss. Or rather, transmission marks the double-sign of salvage and ruin. Whatever the wrong turns and dead ends of Freud's dubious theory of Judaism's historical origins, the core notion—on the eve of European Jewry's destruction—that a "national character" can be transmitted "independently of direct communication" (Freud's words) means that "'Jewishness can be transmitted independently of 'Judaism,' that the former is interminable even if the latter is terminated" (*Freud's Moses*, 90).

If the construct "Judaism Terminable and Interminable" might thus also suit the exigencies of Appelfeld's novel, clarifying a textual design that, like a train upon iron tracks, trundles over an intricately webbed, overconnected landscape, it may be helpful to return to the novel's own title. *Mesilat barzel* exactly means *Mesliat Yesharim*. Jewish exegetical tradition moves on, is therefore defined by, a set of iron tracks. "Moses received Torah from Sinai and delivered it to Joshua, and Joshua to the Elders, and the Elders to the Prophets, and the Prophets delivered it to the Men of the Great Synagogue" (Tractate *Pirke Avot* 1:1). The iron tracks deliver and they receive.

Even when circumstances mitigate this tradition's direct influence or a direct engagement with it, it will nevertheless be "stored" (as Freud's father says), either whole or in fragments. The very cadence of Jewish tradition oscillates therefore between remembering, forgetting, and remembering again (this is also the import of Grossman's *See Under: Love*). "In ancient times when the Torah was forgotten in Israel, Ezra came from Babylon and established it; again partly forgotten, and Hillel the Babylonian came again and established it; yet again partly forgotten, and R. Hiyya and his sons came up and established it" (*Tractate Sukkah 20a*, quoted in *Freud's Moses*, 88). Likewise ritual—candlesticks, mezuzah, kiddush cup—functions like the Tabernacle in the Wilderness, a portable framework to be used, stored away, used again. Indeed, the textual, ceremonial chain of tradition in *The Iron Tracks* is overtly counterpoised to the plagues of individual memory, which Siegelbaum describes as "a powerful machine that stores and constantly discharges lost years and faces" (9).

And thus the parallel between the execution of duty and the "duty" of execution. Appelfeld's novel says that in the Elsewhere of Jewish Europe after the Shoah, strange objects like pistols can lie in Jewish hands just like Jewish objects—the *haggadah* purchased from a peasant at the Rondhof fair—can lie in stranger's hands. As if implicating the link, Siegelbaum admits, "This is my strange way of making a living" (80). Sacred books and journals in Yiddish, like those in Stark's library that Siegelbaum believes to have been immolated by nuns in a post-Holocaust holocaust after his death, will in fact be preserved by them. "And what will become of the books?" asks Siegelbaum, upon entering Stark's cabin. "They are here," answers the nun. "Whoever wants to consult them can do so" (189).

Similarly, the synagogue in Sandberg that Rabbi Zimmel expects to find a ruin has all the time been watched over by a Gentile cleaning woman. "Several times vandals had been about to set the place on fire, but the woman had threatened them with divine retribution, and they were deterred. She died a few days before his arrival" (127). Not every religious Christian, the novel seems to say, will subject European Jewry to a second dispossession—on the order of, say, the cloister and its towering crucifix adjacent to Auschwitz-Birkenau erected by Carmelite nuns in 1984.[77] Bowing his head "as if my shame were revealed," Siegelbaum departs the scene of Stark's cabin, recalling the former ritual when comrades would circle it singing, "*Am Yisrael Chai*," "the Jewish people live."

"Iron tracks" thus also means the bar between Jew and Other, or between Czernowitzer and Austrian, or mother and father, or childhood and adulthood, or locale and travel, or secular and religious—a division between parallel lines, which, albeit geometrically interdicted, converge unexpectedly but perhaps also necessarily. It is Suchoff's insight to construe such intersection chiefly in terms of language, Yiddish, German, Ruthenian, the first of which, "absolutely forbidden" in Appelfeld's own household, the second, "considered not only a language but also a culture," the third, the lingua franca for most of the Bukovina's inhabitants who "were Ruthenians, and so they all spoke Ruthenian" (*Beyond Despair*, 71, 77).

Suchoff points to the moment in the text—immediately before the allusion to *The Path of the Righteous*, which thus confirms it—when Stark is revisited by the *heymish* linguistic past: "Recently it was as if the words he had used for so long had been wiped from his tongue. He now spoke in the way of his ancestors" (98), which is, confirmed by Kron, who tells Stark that he "was speaking in the way people once spoke in Jewish homes." This return, says Suchoff, is "brought back by the power of a suppressed language, subject in the end to the power of an idiom he thought had been left behind" (4). That power of tradition he calls *bilingual*, tradition having become stronger "by incorporating the force of its 'adversary' languages." His own convincingly strong (and Bakhtinian) reading of the text discloses one of its starkest antisentimental lessons: *that we don't own our most intimate treasures.*

Yet, even around this node, in the form of quotidian utterance, the text can structure a certain ambivalence. The chapter that details Siegelbaum's murder of Nachtigel features a banal colloquy between them, and the latter dies in the evident assumption that his speech partner is a fellow Austrian. Immediately following, the text stages the encounter with one of Siegelbaum's *unheimlich* doubles ("I saw with displeasure that he was one of my rivals. . . . But at that moment, he was, for some reason, like a brother to me," 183) who exhorts him to take pride in his accomplishment. "Your discoveries are all safe with Max, and when the time comes, they'll be gathered into the treasury of the Jewish people. The Jewish people aren't dust. They're the people of the book who fight for their values." But Siegelbaum merely turns away: "I wanted to shout, Be quiet. Stop making so much noise. Your words sicken me. You're an empty vessel, not a human being" (184). A distinctively Jewish accent may have resurged in Stark's party rhetoric-tinged voice, but Siegelbaum in German with Nachtigel, and Siegelbaum in Yiddish with his rival, do not sound appreciably different.

As ventured above, however, "intersection" also marks the confluence of blood. In a particularly uncanny moment, Siegelbaum fires two rounds of the pistol in an empty spot where he had earlier escorted Bertha, "to show her the landscape and the pistol" (123)—accessory linked to terrain as if it were a kiddush cup, mezuzah, or other territorially circumscribed found objects. "Strange," he says, "after every target practice, here I see many faces. All the stations bunch together and acquaintances who live many kilometers apart, Jews, half-Jews, and enemies, mingle with each other like relatives" (124). He quickly adds restrictively that such a vision "belongs to that place alone," but one can, without taking too much liberty, read it as the novel's ambivalent pronouncement on iron tracks that have either softened or warped toward each other.

"Iron tracks" lead to and from memory, and they trace a similar circuit with death at both termini. In each case, construing them spatially now, we descry spiderweblike lengths of rail as cicatrices of writing on, belonging to, the European continent—a trope of scarred physiognomy. In a no less overdetermined yet still more aggrieved fashion than Sebald's "emigrants," they thus feature the problem of *belonging*—to countries, to landscapes, to compatriots, to languages—after a lived tie to all those things has been systematically severed. The Jews of Czernowitz, Appelfeld tells us in his autobiographical pieces, wanted very much to be like the Viennese—the milieu, we don't need to be reminded, of Jakob and Sigmund Freud, the death of the latter in September 1939 coinciding with Germany's invasion of Poland. Assimilation, Appelfeld writes, "had become a way of life . . . had become our heritage" (*Beyond Despair*, 7-8). Yet in his interview with Philip Roth, he sounds the more complicated note: "I have always loved assimilated Jews, because that was where the Jewish character, and also, perhaps, Jewish fate, was concentrated with greatest force" (71).

In the "monologue with Freud" that concludes his book, Yerushalmi writes disconsolately, "You left us, Professor Freud, at the outbreak of a war whose full horror and whose devastation of a third of the Jewish people you could not have anticipated" (98). He may as well be describing the Bukovinan Jews of Appelfeld's fiction who, in contrast to Freud, however, reap the whirlwind. Or, to use Appelfeld's metaphor that chimes with his novel, in company with fellow Jews from the East and Jews from the West, found themselves standing "under an iron sky" (*Beyond Despair*, 8). In this respect, the fiction runs parallel to the unwittingly tragic dialectic of terminable and interminable Judaisms Yerushalmi finds at the core of *Moses and Monotheism*. Writes Appelfeld, "In the midst of one's march toward the enchanted realms of self-rejection, the satanic hand came and brought one back to the foundations of tribal existence and commanded one to see it through, not as an individual, and not because of one's opinions, but because one was a member of the Jewish people" (*Beyond Despair*, 10).

After the dark night of the catastrophe, the several quarter-, half-, converted, and self-rejecting Jews of *The Iron Tracks* discover an interminable Jewishness from within the midst of a terminated Jewry. Siegelbaum keeps bumping into it himself, on trains, in the courtyards of Inns, in stranded objects, in the Graten mountains where "as far as I know, Jews have never lived," on the iron tracks in its multiple guises. One gloss on it left unspecified until now, but which has surely been implicit all along, is better voiced by Yerushalmi, since it once again sets Freud and Siegelbaum in parallel. "In your psychoanalysis of history you have presented us with a haunting vision of Eternal Return more seductive, because so much more subtle, than that of Friedrich Nietzsche. Beneath the dizzying multiplicity of events and phenomena that history throws up to the surface you have discerned a pulsating repetition: patricide, repression, return of the repressed, followed by reenactment of the entire cycle, though disguised under different forms, in a seemingly endless spiral" (95). The iron tracks of recurrence interminable: Appelfeld has his own much simpler, one-word formula for it—Wirblbahn.

The last person with whom Siegelbaum speaks in the novel, with whom he discusses his plan to raze Wirblbahn to the ground, is an elderly Nazi—who gestures "in a way that reminded me, sharply, of the gesture Nachtigel made before I killed him" (193). Eerily, he approves of Siegelbaum's plan, for he reveals that he had been mustered there because of a physical disability and as a result was compelled to guard the warehouses instead of serving at the front—the same warehouses that Siegelbaum tells us in the second chapter were waiting for him and the others like him to be trundled out of the railroad cars: "Here, it turned out, stood the warehouses where we were going to work" (13). The final, bitter crosshatching of the text: "For me," says Sigelbaum at the beginning, "Wirblbahn is a mute chapter." "It was all because of a limp," says his interlocutor at the end: "After the war the soldiers returned from the front and told of signs and wonders, and you were the fool of the family. You sat in the corner, mute as a stone" (192).

The old soldier consoles himself with the illusion that had he been sent to the front, he "would have been a different man. . . . There would have been light in my life" (193). Siegelbaum nurtures no such self-deception: "If I had a different life, it wouldn't be happy. As in all my clear and drawn-out nightmares, I saw the sea of darkness, and I knew that my deeds had neither dedication nor beauty" (194). It is a subtle counterpoise. The identical place is accursed and wretched to a German soldier who misses his chance at glory by having to guard doomed Jews and to a Jew who in being left there by the Germans as they decamp escapes his doom. Siegelbaum concludes his tale by reproving the compulsion and belatedness in all he has done. The soldier feels permanently disgraced, blackened, and disfigured. "In the end he had to make a living from what his ancestors had bequeathed him, a wretched living" (193).

A stunning *tourniquet, Schwindel.* A rhetorical *Wirblbahn.* Literally fellow travelers, Siegelbaum and the soldier, German and Czernowitzer, if only for a moment, reflect each other as in a mirror. So even interminability ceases to be wholly Jewish property. After Freud's predicament filtered through Yerushalmi (the author, it should be noted, of *Zakhor: Jewish History and Jewish Memory*), this is Jews' most intimate treasure, one that they alone own.[78] Yet, once again and for the final time in the novel, the iron tracks bend, converge, and coalesce. The nuns have not set fire to Stark's cabin (of whom Siegelbaum recalls his own comment to a friend after Stark's demise, "He's returned to his ancestors" [191], preparing us for the parallel with the elderly German to come). Siegelbaum exits the text this way: "Yellow flames writhed before my eyes, mingling with black flames" (195). But why *mingled* with *black* flames? Perhaps because Wirblbahn had "blackened and disfigured" the old soldier's life. Tradition, Suchoff says, "like our common pasts, is lived through 'other' voices that lie outside its domain." Or as Elias Canetti will be quoted again in chapter 3, "All the places that words have been to! In what mouths! On what tongues! Who can, who may know them, after all these wanderings" (*The Human Province*, 97).

STRANDED OBJECT

There is, however, a remainder, something left over like a terminal stranded object in the text. At the end of his monologue with Freud, in a "provisional postscript," Yerushalmi quotes a letter from Freud's daughter to Ernest Jones in which she calls the flight of psychoanalysts from Germany in the early 1930s "a new form of diaspora." "You surely know what this word means," she continues, "the dispersion of the Jews throughout the world after the destruction of Jerusalem" (99). That does seem to be the novel's one unassailable version of Jewish interminability or interminable Jewishness. But reading it not as compulsive wandering and errancy, we can see it as the *Mesilat Yesharim* laid over the *mesilat barzel*. After centuries of their lying uneasily on the land and between borders of countries to which they did not belong, despite their near-obliteration, the dispersion of Jews is also inscribed upon the land, and the land—even the Graten mountains "where Jews never lived, even Zalistshik where "there are no Jews, only Ukrainians and Poles," even "flat Wirblbahn"—makes for more humane reading, an obligatory exegesis, because of it.

2

Flight from Flight, and Flight from Border
Witold Gombrowicz's *Diary* and *A Kind of Testament* and Essays and Short Fiction by Bruno Schulz

> When you have forded the river, when you have crossed the mountain pass, you suddenly find before you the city of Moriana, its alabaster gates transparent in the sunlight, its coral columns supporting pediments encrusted with serpentine, its villas all of glass like aquariums where the shadows of dancing girls with silvery scales swim beneath the medusa-shaped chandeliers. If this is not your first journey, you already know that cities like this have an obverse: you have only to walk a semicircle and you will come into view of Moriana's hidden face, an expanse of rusting sheet metal, sackcloths, planks bristling with spikes, pipes black with soot, piles of tins, blind walls with fading signs, frames of staved-in straw chairs, ropes good only for hanging oneself from a rotten beam. From one part to the other, the city seems to continue, in perspective, multiplying its repertory of images: but instead it has no thickness, it consists only of a face and an obverse, like a sheet of paper, with a figure on either side, which can neither be separated nor look at each other.
>
> Italo Calvino, *Invisible Cities*

Lost but European

Face and obverse, like a sheet of paper, with a figure on either side: let us imagine human countenance as itself such a page, its recto and verso two figures of authorial myth. On either side of that page, let the visages be those of Witold Gombrowicz (1904-1969) and Bruno Schulz (1892-1942), two colossi of minor modernism who turned the page of the face over and over again in their writing. Schulz, in a recently discovered letter, even went so far as to make visage seem like the wellspring of fiction. "To translate a countenance into words," he wrote, "to express it entirely, to exhaust the world that it contains—this is what attracts me: a human face as the starting point of a novel!"[1] Schulz and Gombrowicz share something else in common with the Calvino epigraph above—a fascination with *face-off*. Duels between high and low: front parlor and kitchen: a lavish, exterior façade of alabaster, serpentine, coral, and a hidden armature of rusting metal, rotten beams, soot, sackcloth beneath: both authors found such polarity endlessly apropos.

When Calvino's Moriana says "face," it specifies not a person but a place. What can be neither separated nor made to look at each other are the twin visages of the city beyond the mountain pass, Janus faces of the same *urbs*. The city as human countenance happens to be a conceit Schulz anticipated by half a century, in an essay written to commemorate the death of Jozef Piłsudski, Marshal of Poland during the interwar republic. "In the act of dying," Schulz wrote, "merging with eternity, that face flickers with memories, roams through a series of faces, ever paler, more condensed, until out of the heaping of those faces there settles on it at last, and hardens into its final mask, the countenance of Poland—forever" (*Letters and Drawings*, 62). Even more than metropolis, nation is the massing or outcrop of physiognomy.

Calvino's simple point is a lesson in perspective. Walk semicircularly, and Moriana will appear altogether different, self-opposite. But if we tilt it in the direction of Polish literary modernism and Poland under the shadow of German occupation, let us imagine both Schulz and Gombrowicz taking such a walk around their common homeland. Each, after his own fashion, belongs to Poland at a near distance. Gombrowicz founds his belonging from the vantage of a different hemisphere, securing his *point d'appui* through a lucky escape that becomes a twenty-three year exile in Argentina, where he remains "lost but European" (*A Kind of Testament*, 84). Fatefully circumscribed by the southeastern provincial town off the north slope of the Carpathians in which he was born and spent nearly the whole of his fifty years, Schultz founds belonging by imaginatively redrawing the national map as a "republic of dreams." The one, in permanent existential flight from flight; the other, in tenaciously mythopoeic flight from border.

Moving eastward and south from Sebald's and Appelfeld's western Europe to these Polish provinces of literary modernism, this chapter will configure its titular elements as the province of national Form. When the postcolonialist critic Timothy Brennan defines "the national longing for form," he has in mind the machinery of desire associated with the modern nation-state. But, as he says, the phrase also conjures "something more nebulous," an open series of predicates culminating in the "condition of belonging."[2] His exploration of nationalism moves swiftly from European hegemon to its subaltern former outposts in the Third World as the site of both a new phase of the nation and new forms, new literatures, that have recast it. Contemporary fiction in neocolonial contexts, says Brennan, is uniquely situated to mediate the give and take between premodern traditional cultures and postmodern and global networks of information and communication.

A missing context, however, in Brennan's discussion is Europe's east and central Other once called the Second World, which in this chapter we will propose as a "third possibility" between western empire and eastern colony, keeping in mind the clarion call of the great novelist of the Austro-Hungarian empire, Robert Musil, from his play, *The Enthusiasts*, "But life always makes you choose between two possibilities, and you always feel: one is missing! Always one—the uninvented third possibility." "What is Poland?" Witold Gombrowicz asks, as if in reply, and promptly answers, "It is a country between the East and the West, where Europe starts to draw to an end, a border country where West and East soften into each other. A country of weakened forms" (*A Kind of Testament*, 53). "So, in that Proustian epoch at the beginning of the century, we were a displaced family whose social status was far from clear, living between Lithuania and the former Congress Kingdom of Poland, between land and industry, between what is known as 'good society' and another, more middle-class society. These were the first 'betweens', which subsequently multiplied until they constituted my country of residence, my true home" (28).

What Poland teaches, what all "secondary cultures" teach, in Gombrowicz's view, is both a condition and its cure. The condition, one of uncritical "belonging," let us call *mimesis bound*, repetition as held hostage to the power of Form on the grandest of scales. The cure, such as it is—to be, at all costs, *unbound*—stipulates an unswerving, savagely consistent commitment to remaining always and everywhere *in between* and to refashion oneself *as* (and not just at) the border.[3]

If the major nations of France and England have "provided their natives with certain advantages" (57), Poland enables Gombrowicz to seize on the very lack of such advantages as conceivably the best kind of (bad) luck: "for men situated in minor, weaker countries . . . and bound to them sentimentally, subjugated by them, formed by them, it [becomes] a matter of life and death to break away, to keep one's distance" (57). And Argentina, Poland's figural reduplication in Gombrowicz's personal sojourn, raises the stakes of estrangement twofold: "One feels the presence of Europe there, far more forcefully than in Europe itself, yet at the same time, one is outside Europe" (84). Poland and later the Argentine become salutary *obstacle* rather than uncritical birthright. That is their simple advantage, acquiring for Gombrowicz a face he proceeded to turn into a mask or a grimace, a face at which he proceeded to make faces in return, answering Form with more form, figure with counter-gesture. In this chapter, the face that takes the place of national form will also serve as an emblem for literary form, as well as the seam between these two writers and us, their readers.

And so it is only right that in this chapter, the trope of human countenance—selfsame but also multiplied through a repertory of images—will play more than a cameo role as the writings of Gombrowicz and Schulz come into view. Facilitating and deepening that scrutiny will be two early essays by Emmanuel Levinas, *De l'évasion* (1935) and "Quelques reflexions sur la philosophie de l'hitlerisme" (1934), contemporaneous with Schulz's and Gombrowicz's own inaugural moment in literary space, and composed before Levinas began to develop his own favored trope of *le visage*. The primary focus, however, is once again versions of literary memoir: Gombrowicz's *Diary*, volumes 1–3, and *A Kind of Testament*, and Schulz's short essays on Marshal Piłsudski with reference to his fiction. Throughout, pressure will be placed on a *formal* opposition between only two possibilities, Europe and an other-than-Europe. In between that dichotomy, we find, thus marooned and elided, two Polish modernists who speak from the confines of a Europe already "othered" from within and who stand on the farther threshold of what Levinas names Europe's "bad conscience."[4] I also wish to open up a space for a particular genre or literary form—subform, really—that the alignment between nation and (novelistic) narration manages to bypass.

Citing Mikhail Bakhtin and Georgy Lukács, Brennan says that the national longing for form picks up where the specifically literary conditions of desire licensed by the novel leave off. The novel "mimicked the nation's composite structure through stratification and diversification of languages and styles, bringing together the 'high' and the 'low' within a national framework—not fortuitously, but for specific national reasons" (49-52). Even Walter Benjamin (like Bakhtin after him, a "failed questioner," according to this view), fails to appreciate the counter-European gesture and the counter-European moment, when Third World fiction binds "information to epic (or folkloric) 'experience'" (55) and "projects itself into a European setting" (56). In the last century, however, well before such renegotiated postmodern cosmopolitanism, modernist voices from Drohobycz and a Polish-accented Buenos Aries had mounted a similar projection of their own into that very same space.[5]

Another theorist of the nation and its interstices, Homi K. Bhabha also invokes Bakhtin to a certain negative effect, illustrative of the way Europe has traditionally held synoptic sway over its Others. In the oft-cited essay, "DissemiNation: Time, Narrative, and the Margins of the Modern Nation," Bhabha suggests that Bakhtin's reading of Goethe's *Italienische Reise* (1786-88) merely picks up where Goethe's totalizing view of nationhood leaves off, with both German Romantic culture-hero and Soviet critic alike endorsing "landscape as the inscape of national identity," which is thus given over to "the power of the eye to naturalize the rhetoric of *national affiliation* and its forms of collective expression" (*The Location of Culture*, 143). Bhabha, like Brennan, seeks to expose temporal gaps and discursive rifts that lie hidden in plain sight under the aspect of "fullness of narrative time and visual synchrony" (144).[6] But whether one concedes the point or not, as with Brennan's critique, such gaps and rifts get introduced with reference to a pre-given collusion between the national Imaginary and the European Novel.[7]

Gombrowicz's memoiristic writing in his *Diary* comes at the problem of mutually entangled form, literary and national, from an angle at once more oblique and less tendentious than that of these two counter-hegemonists. First published in the literary magazine *Kultura*,[8] the *Diary* is the culmination of a literary journey begun twenty years earlier in Poland. "How can one escape from what one is, where is the leverage to come from?" asks the narrator of the 1937 novel *Ferdydurke*. "Our shape penetrates and confines us, as much as from within as from without" (Mosbacher translation, 1961, 49). Slanting this metaphysic in the direction of the "national longing for form" and having replaced (but also recapitulated) Poland with Argentina, Gombrowicz calls

Trans-Atlantyk, a work published in 1953 that bridges his early fiction and his later *Diary,* a "novel directed towards Poland from the Argentine" (*A Kind of Testament,* 102).[9]

Gombrowicz declares that the subject of that novel is not actually Poland but, "as always," himself.[10] By extension, one might characterize the *Diary* itself as doubly directed from the constantly reasserted vantage point or border of selfhood: at 1) national form (Poland in its subordinate, mediate capacity); and 2) literary form (the novel as supergenre, literature's version of a "global power"). "A Pole, when confronting the East, is a Pole delineated and known in advance. A Pole with his face turned toward the West has a turbid visage, full of unclean angers, disbeliefs and secret sore spots" (*Diary* 1:14). Undistorted by the mask of fiction (or as much as autobiography can hold its internal properties of defacement at bay), and as vigorous challenge to Form, the *Diary* lends that turbid visage to a willful autobiographical act. From the other direction, it molds that act into a visage.

"Happy Frenchmen who write their diaries with tact, except that I don't believe in the value of their tact, I know that theirs is only a tactful circumvention of the problem, which is by its very nature unsociable" (*Diary* 1:34). In *A Kind of Testament* (published as conversations with Dominique de Roux in 1968), Gombrowicz says that his fiction almost writes itself. "I must admit that the forms of the novel do not interest me particularly" (72), he says. On the other hand, 'Thanks be to you, too, Almighty, for the *Diary.* . . . [I]t was only when I really started to write in the *Diary* that I felt I was wielding my pen. . . . It was as if I were accompanying my art all the way to the point where it was dropped into another person's existence and became hostile to me" (*Diary* 2:181).

Gombrowicz's memoirs possess a curious meld of public and private, elevating and substantifying the self—"I want to be a balloon, but one with ballast; an antenna, but one that is grounded" (34) in common view, "right in the newspaper in front of people" (34)—but also degrading, dissecting, abjecting it. The paradoxical goal is to free the writer from Form (or face) by directing, even grafting it upon the reader. Face, in this sense, is a constant irritant or wound. It is also one of the "secret sore spots" where Gombrowicz and Schulz keep company. Thus, Gombrowicz:

> I am completely alone in a desert. I have never seen people nor do I imagine that another man is even possible. At that very moment an analogous creature appears in my field of vision, which, while not being me, is nevertheless the same principle in an alien body. Someone identical but alien

nevertheless. And suddenly I experience, at precisely the same moment, a wondrous fulfillment and painful division. Yet one revelation stands out above the rest: I have become boundless, unpredictable to myself, multiple in possibilities through this alien, fresh but identical power, which approaches me as if I were approaching myself from the outside. (*Diary* 1:20)

And Schulz:

When I approach a new person, all of my former experiences, expectations, carefully planned tactics, prove useless. Between me and every individual I meet, the world begins anew, as if nothing had been agreed and decided upon yet. How naïve and obtuse is the scholastic, academic science of physiognomy that perceives a residue in a facial expression, a layering of multiple grimaces—mere muscle cramps. As if one had to mold expressions on faces, as if they were something else, just the grimace itself, a look, a penetrating talk, a passionate wink towards our perspicacity. ("Letter to Maria Kasprowiczowa," in *New Documents and Interpretations*, 22)

Before actually turning to Gombrowicz's and Schulz's writings in earnest, however, my treatment secures its own beachhead by returning to wartime Poland three years after Gombrowicz set sail for Argentina and pushing off an incident that begins and ends in 1942, only to recommence unexpectedly in the summer of 2001. It is a story of place, of face, and of evil German fairy tales (recalling Sebald), under whose spell one is asked to carry on to the improbable, attenuated, and disputable finish.

In November of 1942, the Jewish ghetto of Drohobycz was liquidated.[11] Bruno Schultz met his end on the nineteenth of that month on Shevchenko Street (now Czacki and Mickiewicz streets), shot in the head by SS officer Karl Günter in a revenge killing for the murder of Günter's Jewish protegé. That killing was committed by Schulz's protector, Gestapo chief Felix Landau,[12] who oversaw the murder or deportation of Drohobycz's 15,000 Jews (his random assassinations of Jewish slave laborers may have served as the model for one of the more horrific scenes in the film *Schindler's List*). But Landau's name is also remembered because he had conscripted Schulz to paint murals of scenes from Grimms' fairy tales to adorn the walls of his five-year-old son's bedroom. Schulz's last creative works, these flights of fancy materialized at the very moment that the town's Jews were being consigned to their death outside the Villa Landau, either massacred in the nearby forest of Bronice or rounded up for transport to Belzec in Drohobycz's *Umschlagplatz*.[13]

Nearly sixty years afterward, in February of 2001, the murals were discovered in a pantry of the converted Villa Landau by a filmmaker from Hamburg and a former pupil of Schulz's. In May, Israeli representatives from Yad Vashem, the museum and memorial to the Shoah in Jerusalem, arrived, either with or without permission of the authorities, removed fragments of them (according to a Ukrainian-Polish commission, roughly 70 percent), and transported them to Israel. An anguished debate among Polish, Ukrainian, and Israeli authorities and partisans ensued, which reached even the editorial page of the *New York Times* and became the subject of numerous articles in other journals.[14] The rescued/smuggled mural portions depict a princess, dwarves, a clown, a jester, and a coach driver whose triangular face is clearly that of Schulz himself. As partially recovered, the murals now lie at a permanent distance—or as Gombrowicz might put it, *amputated*—from themselves. Fragments will be displayed in a new Holocaust museum in Israel, and the rest will remain in Drohobycz, where plans have ostensibly been in the offing to turn the hundred-year-old villa into a museum in Schulz's memory.

In one of his most unembarrassed, importuning letters from 1934, Bruno Schulz writes of his need for friendship—the redemptive consummation that turns idiosyncratic whim into "reality when reflected in two pairs of eyes."[15] In the light of his final pictures' fate, he might just as well have been speaking of the redemptive revelation now forever to elude them, partially defaced in the act of recovery: "What was once a closed tight place with no further prospects now begins to ripen into colors in the distance, burst open, reveal its depths. The painted scenery takes on perspective and slides into real vistas; the wall admits us to dimensions formerly denied us; the frescoes painted on the vault of heaven come to life as in a pantomime" (*Letters and Drawings*, 54). And in his last surviving letter, to friends who were leaving their house in Drohobycz to uncertain fate in Warsaw (they never arrived), Schulz composed another uncanny fore-echo, with his characteristic self-projection: "How sad to think that at 30 Mazeppa Street, where I spent so many lovely hours, no one will be left, all of it will become mere legend. I don't know why I feel guilty toward myself, as if I had lost something and it was my own fault" (213).

Where does this art belong and to whom: in the space where it was affixed, once Poland, now Ukraine, to the municipality and the state? Spokespersons for the small remnant of Jewish Drohobycz answered emphatically in the affirmative, for they were as outraged at Yad

Vashem's rescue as the Ukrainian official who was quoted as saying, "Imagine that I would come to Jerusalem and cut off a piece of the Wailing Wall." Less invidiously, those Drohobycz-born Jews see themselves as a voice for a Jewish cultural legacy in eastern Europe that survived Nazi slaughter, and yet lives on. Not unlike the battered Drohobycz synagogue, faded, rusted, staved in, awaiting reclamation, they seek to leave intact and *in its place* the evidence of Jewish life even if it is fatally twinned with Jewish destruction. The murals, thus, serve belatedly as a kind of gravestone.

Or do the polychromes—damaged by salvage—belong rather in the place where survivors of the Shoah themselves sought refuge, and thus to the transnational inheritors of the Jewish state? For the record, a press release from Yad Vashem stated, "Most of the Holocaust survivors live in Israel, but the scattered remnants of the vibrant Jewish life, and of the suffering of the victims are scattered throughout Europe. Therefore, we have the moral right to those remnants" (Bohlen," Artwork," A1).[16] Inasmuch as the generation of human remnants ("pieces" in Nazi jargon, "displaced persons" in a more benign but still disindividuating nomenclature) were themselves subject to a profound societal ambivalence that regarded them as the most lamentable evidence of diaspora-Jewry's dead end, the motives behind such righteous intervention are neither plain nor simple. But in one sense, one could plausibly argue that behind their being whisked away to new life in Israel lies the unexpressed feeling that, left in Drohobycz, Schulz's frescoes would still bear the taint of the weak, soft, marginalized Jewish experience that gave life to them (as indeed Schulz's own meek, subservient persona emblematizes so well).[17] Only in Israel, on the model of the survivors themselves, could their remnants be rehabilitated and reinvigorated—gravestones still, but elevated, transported elsewhere.

Perhaps the most trenchant remark in this whole affair comes from the director of research at the Holocaust Documentation Committee of the Polish American Congress, who was quoted as saying, "For me, the fact that Schulz chose to use the Polish language, not German or Hebrew, is dispositive. Israel's Yad Vashem evaded that debate by its poaching" (Chotkowski, "The Battle," A26). This is poaching in its actionable, not de Certeauan, sense. The full dimensions of the murals controversy coincide with the latest stage in a public confrontation with the Shoah and its aftermath, which goes by the official name "Holocaust reparations."[18] As the generation of survivors and surviving perpetrators dies off, absconded family legacies and plundered cultural inheritance become perhaps the final crime in Europe's abandonment of its Jews yet to be adequately reckoned with—the vastest of grand larcenies, the most scandalous of dispossessions. While such debate obviously exceeds the scope of the present work, its relevance in the case of Schulz's murals does take a curious form. I would call it the forced migration of place itself—not unlike the magical teleportations of a Grimm's fairytale—whereby some portion of the walls of a Drohobycz pantry finds itself relocated to a somber mount in Jerusalem.[19]

Of course, the affair can be perceived differently. Consider for a moment a short story by Gombrowicz's, Schulz's, and Levinas's immediate contemporary, S. Y. Agnon, which we have encountered in the previous chapter in relation to Appelfeld's *The Iron Tracks*. The plot of "A Book That Was Lost" turns on a text of rabbinic commentary that is handed down or conveyed hand to hand and eventually returned from exile in eastern Europe to its new institutional home, the National Library for the Jewish people in Jerusalem. In the very midst of this anticipated homecoming, however, Agnon's story registers unmistakable ambivalence about the movement from diaspora to reclaimed center. For the land of restitution and redemption will paradoxically inscribe an absence, as the cherished book, transmitted across the generations in eastern Galicia (the same region in the former Austro-Hungarian province that encompasses Drohobycz), goes missing on its way to Jerusalem. It is, we could say, lost but European. The story of that loss coincides with another, as, in company with the book's non-arrival, the protagonist himself arrives on Jerusalem soil on the ninth of Av, the religious day of mourning in the Hebrew calendar that commemorates historical and national calamity much older than the Shoah.[20]

The questions raised by Schulz's unhoused murals go to the heart of the meaning of eastern Europe as either Jewish home or *midbar*, both before and especially after the war where its lost but European survivors pried themselves loose from a half-embedded European life. Is Bruno Schulz a Polish Jew or a Jewish Pole?[21] Are his fiction, letters, essays consequently Polish or Jewish? And how would we class his graphic work, those paintings and drawings unparticularized by alphabet, dialect, or phoneme—especially, those final, oxymoronic "commissions," princess and carriage driver to lull the son of a Gestapo chief who orders mass executions just outside? Which place, which country, which land has territorial rights to them? Which national boundaries properly encompass them?[22] Should they be resituated behind sunlit gates high atop the Hill of Remembrance on Mount Herzl, exhibited with a new face; or be left in a former pantry from within Drohobycz's hidden obverse, instead—the face of rusting sheet metal, planks bristling with spikes, pipes black with soot, behind walls with fading signs?

In paraphrase of Chotkowski's remark above, the terms *evaded* and *poaching* are, if not "dispositive," then at least impossible to ignore in the context of the present book's concerns—the latter because it recalls de Certeau, and "evaded," because it corresponds with Levinas's concept for the condition of selfhood before the upsurge of the Other's face. Recent French commentaries on Levinas's 1935 essay *On Escape* have noted the convergence of politics and ontological argument, as well as the shared semantic territory of *évasion* (escape, evasion) and *exode* (exodus) that insinuates both a foreboding of war and a personal narrative of capture and release.[23] In different though related ways, Schulz and Gombrowicz mounted a complex evasion of the constrictions of national and social identity through what Schulz called "the migration of [literary] forms."[24] To be sure, Chotkowski's use of the word veers in an altogether different direction. And yet it does suggest a family resemblance when collocated with "poaching."

On one level, at least—where the production of space meets the accident of emplacement—a diary entry by Gombrowicz transects the whole affair, while acquiring a meaning it did not originally intend:

> Paintings are not meant to be hung next to one another on a bare wall, a painting is meant to adorn an interior and be the joy of those who live with it. . . . There exists an unbearable, degrading contrast between the *intention* of each of these works of art, which wants to be the only and exclusive one, and hanging the paintings all together in this room. Yet art, not just painting, is full of such marginal clashes, absurdities, uglinesses, and stupidities which we cast outside the mainstream of our feelings. An old tenor in the role of Siegfried does not jar us, nor do frescoes we can't see, a Venus with a broken nose, or an old lady declaiming young poems. (*Diary* 1:23)

Gombrowicz's manifest concerns are the institutionalization of art, not its disfigurement as the result of competing proprietary claims. And yet, as the passage is all about the clash between intention and disposition, so it can serve effectively as a kind of commentary. For Gombrowicz's satire does capture what the mural controversy adventitiously exposed, indeed what the murals embodied in the first place as fairytale images painted by a doomed Jew to "adorn an [Nazi] interior": the "degrading contrast between the *intention* of these works of art" on the one hand, and their fate as objects within a cultural landscape on the other. For Schulz, that landscape had always been Drohobycz in Galicia, the Polish East. But now, under the auspices of irony or resurgent national destiny, it becomes a symbolic memorial to the Shoah in Jerusalem, instead. The destiny of Schulz's art does not rectify the clashing absurdity of Gombrowicz's museum scene, but rather or at most, re-situates it. Tombstones each, they differentially mark a grave that lies elsewhere.

Assuredly, the inevitable consequence of the murals' removal is that it *effaces* and partially disfigures the literal fusion between Schulz's art and the concrete presence of Drohobycz, the constant locus of his fictional world. Whether he would have been amused (to paraphrase one of the *New York Times* letters to the editor), one is best not hazarding an opinion. But it is safe to say that Gombrowicz would have been.[25] When Erwin Siegelbaum in *The Iron Tracks* says that he would like to journey to the forests in Israel in order to fortify himself, we hear it as so much self-delusion. It is a wish that Schulz neither expressed nor recorded at any time.

If he fantasized relocating to an elsewhere, it would have been to Paris,[26] not Tel Aviv. Besides occasional forays to Warsaw, Schulz did leave Drohobycz in 1917–18 to study in Vienna and again in 1936 for a three-day excursion to Stockholm and was able finally to take a three-week sojourn in France in August 1938, which, however, was largely disappointing.[27] When he periodically requests national school authorities to provide him with an extended leave of absence "to realize my literary goals" (*New Documents and Interpretations,* 14) in letters, or when he proposes that he be transferred to Lwów or Warsaw, closer to "the intellectual movements of the day [and] the stimuli and artistic aids available in the capital" (17–18), he seeks to close the gap between provincial near distance and *Polish* metropolitan proximity.

At bottom, one wonders whether Schulz would have felt at home anywhere in the world, even in Drohobycz.[28] When his countryman Gombrowicz writes, "parody allowed me to liberate Form, to tear it from weightlessness and launch it into pure space, where it became light, bold, and revealing" (*A Kind of Testament,* 42), he might be underlining the permanent advantage he had over his sometime friend. While less a parodist than a fabulist, and while he may have imagined his home-town in similar terms, in stark contrast to Gombrowicz's flight from flight, Schulz's Jewishness hemmed him in within geographical and social borders from which the only flight possible was *imaginative*. A Paris reprieve—or an even more counterfactual dream-sojourn in

Vienna, Berlin, or Prague—would have been welcome for Schulz, and he would not have had to entertain Gombrowicz's fear that "in the long run, Paris would have turned me into a Parisian, [a]nd I owed it to myself to be anti-Parisian" (84). Schulz was at once too Jewish, too provincial, too embedded by dint of character as well as fate. Moreover, being classed as un-European in his case was warrant for extermination, not liberating possibility. Repeatedly, Grombrowicz quotes from one of his novels in *A Kind of Testament*, "Day by day, my position on the European continent became increasingly precarious and equivocal." How much more so for Bruno Schulz.

Yet even if transitivity had been afforded him, Schultz would no doubt still have comported himself "in pursuit of Europe," paying little heed to Gombrowicz's warning to Polish literati that they will "never catch up with her" (*Diary* 1:26). Schulz's mission was not to "strike at European art," and he never shared the ruthless self-surgery of Gombrowicz's *cri de guerre*, "I attack Polish form because it is my form" (16).

> Thus my desire to "overcome Poland" was synonymous with the desire to strengthen our individual Polishness. I simply wanted the Pole to stop being the product "of" an exclusively collective life and "for" a collective life. I wanted to complete him. To legitimize his other pole [alas, a pun not in the original]—the pole of individual life—and stretch him between the two. I wanted to have him between Poland and his own existence—in a perspective more diacritical and full of antinomies, conscious of his internal contradictions and capable of exploiting them for his own development. (*Diary* 2:15)

Schulz was neither programmatically focused on a Polish here-and-now nor particularly burdened by the Polish past and the weight of its literary tradition. His literary heroes were contemporary, to be found across Poland's western border: "I am looking for a new author who would dazzle and enrapture me. For quite some time, I haven't found anything except Rilke, Kafka, and Mann" ("Letter to Rudolf Ottenbreit," in *New Documents and Interpretations*, 26).

But to pull back from an always tempting interface between these two preternaturally proximate writers (they are always too close for comfort), we shall return to the fantasy of literary sojourn in Paris that places them on a different footing in order to account provisionally for the foreign in both their writings. In her meditation on the "non-naturalized" citizen, *Strangers to Ourselves*, Julia Kristeva remarks,

"Nowhere is one more a foreigner than in France" (38). In that centralized, autonomous patrie, the universal is France, the normative is the French, the quintessence of European is la langue Française, and the non-standard is everything else, all that is nonlocal, nonnative, extraterritorial. By the same token, however, because ostracism confers distinction, "one is nowhere *better* a foreigner than in France" (39). Visible, exceptional, singularized, "You are a problem, a desire—positive or negative, never neutral" (39).

No matter how strange each writer may have felt temperamentally both to himself and under the national sign of Polishness (whether inside its territorial borders or without), Kristeva's book, and specifically its introduction, "Toccata and Fugue for the Foreigner," only loosely addresses the circumstantial plights of Schulz and Gombrowicz (her focus is at once more historically distant—Suppliants and Metics in ancient Greece, Ruth the Moabite—and abstractly contemporaneous guest-workers, *SOS-Racisme*). Yet, in a quasi-Levinasian move that will help us focus on a shared image of both writers, as well as prepare the ground for a discussion of Levinas, Kristeva instances the foreign face as the template for strangeness, the otherness that has already breached the barricades of the self and resides within it:

> At first, one is struck by his peculiarity—those eyes, those lips, those cheek bones, that skin unlike others, all that distinguishes him and reminds one that there is *someone* there. The difference in that face reveals in paroxystic fashion what any face should reveal to a careful glance: the nonexistence of banality in human beings. Nevertheless it is precisely the commonplace that constitutes a commonality for our daily habits. But this grasping the foreigner's features, one that captivates us, beckons and rejects at the same time. (3)[29]

While the psychological features running parallel beneath it—aloofness, scorched happiness, melancholia, irony and belief, ebullience and mask—have all been owned by that more verbal subset of outsiders, exiled or émigré artists; this is still an anonymous and marginal face, however, a face in the crowd. The foreigner, Kristeva says emphatically, is the *worker* (18).

Let us consider, by contrast, the faces and the foreignness on display in a tableau from Gombrowicz's *Diary*, volume 3, set in an Argentine train compartment—the first of seven "scenes" of facing drawn from Gombrowicz and Schulz and mediated by Levinas to be staged in this chapter.

110   *Flight from Flight, and Flight from Border*

SCENE 1: SOCIETY; OR, A RAILWAY IN ARGENTINA

That mug ten centimeters away. The teary, reddish pupils? Little hairs on this ear? I don't want this! Away! I will not go on about his chapped skin! By what right did this find itself so close that I practically have to breathe him in, yet at the same time feel his hot trickles on my ear and neck? We rest our unseeing gazes on each other from a very near distance . . . each person is curling up, rolling up, shutting, shrinking, limiting to a minimum his eyes, ears, lips, trying to be as little as possible. Their revolting, fat, veiny, droop, or dry properties fling me straight into the air, I feel as if I were leaping straight into the sky—I don't want this! This is an insult! I am insulted! The train is racing forward and suburban houses flicker by. Station. They push, they push their way in. The rain moves. Too Much. (17)

The mug may be the facial property of a *czango*. Perhaps it belongs to a Negro, Asian, Malay, Arab, Turk, Chinese. Or maybe an intellectual ("slowly the discussion is settling over us, the same one as always, the one they have learned by heart: imperialism, Cuba . . ."). The point is not so much a matter of class distinction or even ethnicity but physiognomy that is simply too close for comfort. And though the entry later on expands its *ressentiment* to the sheer *numbers* of people compressed into the same car as Gombrowicz himself, "that mug ten centimeters away" does not exactly fade from readers' sight. It stays vivid (Gombrowicz has ensured as much) partly because of the uncanny little scene that embeds it.

Against the background of the author's abiding concern with the space *between* two persons, the gauntlet-slap delivered to Gombrowicz's face is the basic fact that another faces him.[30] The slap that answers it is his counter-face grimacing in return. *Przyprawienie gęby* ("fitting someone with a mug") describes the norm of human interaction, a relentless duel of face-making, face-wearing, face-imposing. One face creates the other; a grimace responds. Both faces remain in dependent relation, face and grimace, mug and countenance, tracing a double helix of unrelenting mutual deformation. Scenes like it appear over and over in the *Diary*. Gombrowicz selects some Other out of the crowd to shadow and eventually face-off. Or else he is the object of the same ritualized phenomenon. Maybe the most risible of these is recorded in an entry for the year 1958 in volume 2:

I was walking along a eucalyptus-lined avenue when a cow sauntered out from behind a tree. I stopped and we looked each other in the eye. Her

Flight from Flight, and Flight from Border 111

cowness shocked my humanness to such a degree—the moment our eyes met was so tense—I stopped dead in my tracks and lost my bearings *as a man,* that is, as a member of the human species. The strange feeling that I was apparently discovering for the first time was the shame of a man come face-to-face with an animal. I allowed her to look and see me—this made us equal—and resulted in my also becoming an animal—but a strange even forbidden one, I would say. I continued my walk, but I felt uncomfortable . . . in nature, surrounding me on all sides, as if it were . . . watching me. (24)³¹

"Nothing but the mug," cries a character in *Ferdydurke* who is looking for authentic countenance. "Oh, give me one uncontorted face next to which to I can feel the contortion of my own face, but instead—all around me were faces that were twisted, mangled and turned inside out, faces that reflected my own like a distorting mirror . . ." (Borchardt translation, 2000, 47). Synecdochic shorthand for the heteronomy of persons, one's own face is a scandal inasmuch as it gets forced into self-consciousness and counter-move by the face of another. In the introduction to his 1962 novel *Pornografia,* Gombrowicz writes, "Man, tortured by his mask, fabricates secretly . . . a secondary domain of compensation" (8). The sufficiency of my own private physiognomy is always being interrupted or compromised by the intervening faces of others. Even if I seem finished to myself, a facing other will make me seem unfinished, de-shaped. The face is a double agent: the seat and sign of personal identity but also just another composite body part. In short, we *wear* or *share* a face; we don't own it.

Art also has a face, and it stares straight back—as demonstrated by this second anecdotal scene, set against the backdrop of Argentina's *Museo Nacional de Bellas Artes.*

SCENE 2: ART; OR, INSIDE A MUSEUM

There were ten other people besides ourselves who walked up, looked, then walked away. The mechanical quality of their movements, their muteness, gave them the appearance of marionettes and their faces were nonexistent compared to the faces that peered out of the canvas. This is not the first time that the face of art has irritated me by extinguishing the faces of the living . . . Here in the museum, the paintings are crowded, the amount crowds the quality, masterpieces counted in the dozens stop being masterpieces. Who can look closely at a Murillo when the Tiepolo next to it demands attention and thirty other paintings shout: look at us! (*Diary* 1:23)

Later in the *Diary,* Gombrowicz will call this duel of paintings, onlookers, and the space encompassing both, "Da Vinci punching Titian in the

Louvre" (90). Call this the pugilistic counterpart to Benjamin's notion of artistic aura as a "returned look"—the fact that "objects retain something of the gaze that has rested upon them" (*Illuminations*, 188, 198). Or the comic analogue to Levinas's complaint about the plastic arts that they merely reify the "caricature" reality already bears on its own face (*Collected Philosophical Papers*, 8). For Levinas, anticipating Schulz as well as Gombrowicz, painted faces (say, Klee's *Angelus Novus* as famously evoked by Benjamin) can only stare back unceasingly—visages become figures, and thus so many petrified masks. Gombrowicz, too, testifies to art's eerie alienation effect, a special case of a more general provocation: the scandal of human countenance that makes one a stranger to oneself.

As portrait or person, as cultural heritage or national form, the stranger is neither an immigrant worker nor a fellow exile, émigré, refugee. The stranger is a visage; more aptly, a face and an obverse, like two sides of a sheet of paper with a figure on either side. On one are drawn the features of the Other facing opposite; on the other, to quote Gombrowicz's very first entry for the *Diary*, are inscribed, "Monday: Me, Tuesday: Me, Wednesday: Me, Thursday: Me." When scenes like the two above are sketched in literary space, it is fair to speculate that they allegorize to one degree or another the author's keen awareness of writing in the presence of reading others. On one side of the divide, the façade of the writing Self; on the other, the aggregate mugs, reddish pupils, and tiny hairs of readerly nearness. Thus, unlike the more "tactful" French diaries to which he alludes above, Gombrowicz will treat his diary, so to speak, *proxemically*, "as an instrument of my becoming before you" (*Diary* 1:35).

In *Nations without Nationalisms*, the successor volume to *Strangers to Ourselves*, Kristeva mimics the self-assertion of citizens who define themselves with recourse to the *natio*, the fusion of origins and bloodlines: "I don't know who I am or even if I am, but I belong with my national and religious roots, therefore I follow them" [or "I am them," since the French reads "*donc je les suis*"] (2). Here, contrariwise, is Gombrowicz: "Who am I really and to what extent *am* I? I have found only one answer: I don't know who I am, but I suffer when I am deformed. So at least I know what I am not. My self is nothing but my will to be myself" (77). A coda follows: "A measly palliative! Another formula!"

Is it possible to be a Self without recourse to Form or formula? Almost as if in anticipation of Kristeva, Gombrowicz responds,"What a powerful and unfathomable dynamism! Man submitted to the interhuman is like a twig on a rough sea: he bobs up and down, plunges into the raging waters, slides gently along the surface of the luminous waves, he is engulfed by rhymes and vertiginous rhythms, and loses himself in unforeseen perspectives. Through form, penetrated to the marrow by other men, he emerges more powerful than himself, a stranger to himself" (75). He is, in a word, defaced. Penetrated to the marrow by other men, this same Man emerges estranged at the level of visage, *plus puissant que soi* (Gombrowicz) yet strangely *dévisagé*, "discountenanced" (Emmanuel Levinas).[32]

INTERLUDE 1—GOMBROWICZ AND LEVINAS

Amidst the recent cascade of writing on the Lithuanian-born French philosopher Emmanuel Levinas (1906-1996) in conjunction with other thinkers (Levinas/Buber, Levinas/Lacan, Levinas/Barth, Levinas/Bataille), one wonders why Gombrowicz has not yet been enlisted into the foremost ranks. Aside from an accomplished and demonstrated familiarity with Continental philosophy after Hegel, and even absenting for a moment the obsession with face as a recurrent figure, Gombrowicz's analysis of subjectivity and the interhuman alone should qualify for an extended *rapprochement* with Levinas. The two east-central Europeans are in an obvious sense counter-figures: on the model of the famous digressive duel in *Ferdydurke,* a Filidor/anti-Filidor outside the text. Yet just that very difference draws them close to one another as *semblables,* makes them, as Levinas would say, non-indifferent. They share a *lien* ("bond") across an *écart* ("interval, gap"),[33] proximate while at a near distance.

"Scene 3" in this chapter will feature a direct face-off between Gombrowicz and Schulz. Before that can be staged, however, the foregoing observations about Gombrowicz and Schulz in either flight or internal *midbar* will be juxtaposed with Levinas's early and tantalizingly brief philosophical accounts of "evasion" as both property of existence and historically localized effect. Levinas will thus be made to play the role of third party—in Levinasian argot, *le tiers*—subtending the two who face each other against a common horizon. He joins them there additionally as a kind of estranged countryman. For, just as Lithuania, joined to Poland in a commonwealth since the sixteenth century, subject to successive appropriations by the Third Partition of 1795 and the German and Soviet occupations of World Wars I and II, remains Poland's contiguous neighbor to the north and east, so Levinas borders Gombrowicz and Schulz, although in ways neither writer could foresee.

Ten years before he fleshed out the concepts of the ethical relation, Levinas engaged Heidegger's phenomenological ontology by proposing an alternative notion of attachment-to-being at the core of selfhood, and the individual person's consequent need for escape or *"ex-cendence"* from it. Subjective being is felt as a weight or drag, an "irremissable" fixity that, consequently, generates the desire for *flight*.[34] In 1934, one year before the essay *De l'évasion* appeared, Levinas penned a short article for a progressive Catholic journal that contemplated the clouds of Hitlerism massing over the horizon of Europe. Provocatively, and anticipating more recent critiques of Heidegger, such as those by Philippe Lacoue-Labarthe, Victor Farias, and Rüdiger Safranski,[35] Levinas analyzed the phenomenon as a crisis whose origins lay within transcendental idealism and liberal philosophy itself—inscribed (as he puts it in his 1990 preface), "within an ontology of being concerned with being ... being as gathering together and as dominating" (63).[36] In other words, both the subjective self and its projection as national and cultural body politic are seen by Levinas in parallel: self-irritated, unhappy from within, caught in a paradox of needful but impossible escape.

After briefly listing worldviews committed to ideals of freedom (Judaism, Christianity, Enlightenment liberalism, Marxism), Levinas argues that, "Man's essence no longer lies in freedom but in a kind of bondage [enchainment]" (69). "To be truly oneself does not mean taking flight once more above contingent events that always remain foreign to the Self's freedom; on the contrary, it means becoming aware of the ineluctable original chain that is unique to our bodies, and above all accepting this chaining." The humanly physical, in its own terms, can reveal an absolute position, "an adherence that *one does not* escape" (68). Extrapolating from a phenomenology of embodied identity to the conditions of state culture based on race and blood, Levinas sees in National Socialism an ideology that stands in defiance of the transcendence discovered by the subjective self in its responsibility for the other man. "Chained to his body, man sees himself refusing the power to escape from himself" (70), that is, the power to be free and alone in the face of the world. Hitlerism signifies "an awakening of elemental feelings," a social order that in turn harbors a philosophy.

The racism expressed in expansionist forms of war and conquest that also sees persons as chained to their bodies has as its source this same personally felt sense of embodiment as bondage.[37] Liberal idealism—"steeped in reason and subject to reason" (66)—always runs the risk of evading the claims of embodied existence, and thus in liberalism's own claims to totality and universality, according to Levinas, are sown the seeds of an effacement of difference that takes its most inhuman form in Hitlerism. Since Levinas wants in fact to affirm an embodied subjectivity by beginning with the "human" moored to "being," he does so by laying claim to "the value of European civilization [, which] incontestably resides in the aspirations of idealism if not its history" (*De l'évasion*, 97).[38]

"What matters is departing from being by a new path even at the risk of overturning certain notions that seem most evident to common sense and to the wisdom of nations" (97): this is the note on which that longer essay ends. In the course of outlining the direction such path will take (and perhaps fulfilling the original promise of Idealism), *De l'évasion* mounts a less overtly politicized account of the human condition than we find in the article on Hitlerism. Levinas begins from a similar vantage—the human in excess of (or lagging behind) being in its modern, universalized, anti-marginal form, the social totality. Once again, modernity is seen as "tormented with problems that suggest, perhaps for the first time, that this concern for transcendence has been abandoned" (69)—not because self and civilization are believed to be finally sufficient unto themselves (the Hitlerian mythos), but rather because a "deeper blemish," a "strange restlessness" at the root of being has made itself felt. Discerning it most emergently in the work of modernist writers, Levinas therefore borrows his operative term—*évasion*—from what he calls "the critical language of contemporary literature," where it appears, he believes, not accidentally as figure for and a symptom of "the disease of the century" (70). He does not have Gombrowicz in mind, but he may as well have.

The term also implicitly summons the figure of Heidegger, just as the entire essay, in the words of editor Jacques Rolland, "could be understood as an essay on the 'hermeneutics of agency' that lingers at the level of 'thrownness' and separates itself from the path taken by Heideggerian thought" (104). (In his preface, Rolland renders Heidegger's expression, "*es ist einem unheimlich*" as "*on est de-paysé*," that is, one is *un*-homed—the sticking point, as we shall see, for Levinas and Gombrowicz alike.) Fleeing in the face of Being itself from an existence, the thrown subject in Heidegger's thought must reckon with the authenticity of *Dasein*'s Being-toward-death. Levinas disagrees, preferring to see escape from being as "the search for an exit, but not a nostalgia for death, since death is no more a means of egress than it is solution" (73). The same analysis applies to the creative impulse, to "becoming," because it is still attached to Being even while it may aspire toward transcendence.

Whether we seek to turn away like the poet, from "vulgar realities"; or like the Romantic, from falsifying social conventions; or like the Heideggerian, from the self to its projection "ahead of itself"—in all these ways, we are still, in Levinas's view *en route*. "We are going towards the unknown, but we are still going somewhere, while in evasion we aspire to evade, to depart from the path.... Evasion is ... the need to depart from one's self, which is as much as saying the need to break the most radical and unpardonable confinement, the fact that the self is itself" (73). As in his essay on National Socialism, Levinas takes pains to italicize an *original* condition of enchainment—not escape per se (as in the conventional sense conveyed, for example, in the title of Alexandre Dumas's popular romance, *L'évasion du duc de Beaufort*). But here, that condition exceeds the identity of self and body, for it is bound up with a *surplus* of selfness. Escape first expresses itself as the resistance to sheer sensate self-presence. Selfhood is not at war with exterior or brute being, as it would be typically conceived in existentialist philosophies. Rather, the friction derives internally, at the place marked by the hyphen sign between "human" and "being." It is this "irremissable attachment" of the self to itself rather than any intrinsic lack in it that makes it *need* release from self-sameness, turns it outside and elsewhere, toward departure, liberation, *ex-cendence*.

Marshaling succinct phenomenological analyses of need, sickness, pleasure, shame, and finally nausea, Levinas comes at the problem of enchainment to one's own being as sensible, affective, embodied—that very material plane which idealism distrusts. If consciousness "chaperones our being" (79), then evasion signals our innate truancy and recalcitrance. As the weight of being is felt, as it presses on one from within, so malaise and pleasure represent distinctly physical states that dramatize the *essential* nature of escape. Both pleasure and shame evince a kind of incomplete derivative of evasion, just as malaise and nausea reveal the power of its need. Shame is not moral but rather existential: "That which becomes manifest in shame is therefore precisely the fact of being riveted to oneself, the radical impossibility of fleeing oneself in order to hide oneself from oneself" (87).

Likewise, the extremity of nausea is not measured by social embarrassment but by the fact of being excessively self-present, of being submerged beneath one's existence. It constitutes a mini-drama of ontology, "*the very experience of pure being*" (91). Feeling a concomitant impotence to depart from that presence, "the nauseous subject doesn't even *know* that vomiting is going to deliver it, since it cannot imagine a way out" (Rolland's introduction to *De l'évasion*, 41). We seem to be a long way from Gombrowicz, even from the qualmishness he vents in the *Diary*. And yet, to paraphrase Levinas's own commentator Rolland, one wishes to proceed here as a determined exteriorist, who, while he always carries within him the threat of violence, is therefore also able to bring to light what is in question in a text—especially by situating it in close proximity to a textual neighbor.

After the train pulls into Morón and having disengaged himself from "that mug" with its reddish pupils, ear-hairs, and chapped skin, Gombrowicz finds himself in line at the bus station, and suffers a paroxysm at the mass of people who surround him: "Yet they keep passing and passing, constantly coming from around a corner and passing and coming around from the corner and crossing and coming around from the corner and passing and coming around from a corner and passing and coming from around a corner until I threw up. I threw up and the guy in front of me looked and didn't say much of anything because what the heck! A crowd. I threw up again and—I am not sure that I am exaggerating—I threw up again" (*Diary* 3:19). Nausea in Gombrowicz appears to be simple loathing in the presence of others.[39] If Gombrowicz wants to evade anything, it is the tyranny of the mass, density, and numbers of people who crowd around him. "Form," he will write, "has gone mad, roused by Numbers" (*Diary* 3:39). But this is Gombrowicz at his calculatedly most narcissistic and grotesque, a mask or grimace for his readers. Perhaps one must look elsewhere for a closer correspondence between philosopher and anti-philosopher, perhaps in the common nodal point of "shame," the self's existential and unhidden nudity.

Returning, then, to Levinas's essay: as he often does in the midst of dense philosophical seriousness, Levinas adverts to a brief textual example, in this case, the famous scene in Chaplin's *City Lights* where the Little Tramp swallows a whistle. Inducing hiccups rather than nausea, being impossible to conceal, sounding an alarm with every intake and exhalation, Chaplin's whistle "makes striking the scandal of the brutal presence of his being" (87). Had Levinas been aware of it, however, he could have had equal recourse to Gombrowicz's roughly contemporaneous *Ferdydurke*, whose protagonist becomes ruthlessly subjugated to the mere fact of his body, the self-adhesion from which there is no evasion.

What Levinas will call "everything recalcitrant in the state of being" (95) becomes in *Ferdydurke* the desire for self-sufficiency that is ridiculed by the unruliness of the face to begin with, by its enslavement to one's own torso. Standing up to the top of my height, I am still mocked by the very backside that joins trunk to head. The very fact of a posterior calls consciousness down from its lofty perch. Digits and toes conduct their own duel of grimaces in repeating each other, hand to foot. There, the face is made scandalous not only by its caricature, the grimace or mug *(gęba),* but by the "calf" or "backside" *(pupa).* An otherness infiltrates the root of a person's metaphysical integrity quite independently of any human Other, for any self-project is *already* undermined by the innate surrealism of the body. "I even imagined that my body was not entirely homogeneous . . . that my head was laughing at my leg, that my leg was laughing at my head, that my finger was poking fun at my heart, my heart at my brain, that my nose was thumbing itself at my eye, my eye chuckling and bellowing at my nose—and all my parts raping each other in a an all-encompassing and piercing state of pan-mockery" (*Ferdydurke*, 2003, 3).

Subjectivity—what one cannot *not* observe, as Levinas puts it—is not so very differently embodied in Gombrowicz; indeed it is eerily akin. "I don't know who I am, but I suffer when I am deformed," he pleads. That deformation assails us from within and without: *"Ferdydurke* is existence in a vacuum, that is, nothing but existence. That is why, in this book, all the basic themes of existentialism play fortissimo" (*Diary* 1:181). To be sure, as he quickly adds, his novel "is a circus and not a philosophy." In a circus, the face is a made-up mask, animals seem human, evasion is merely simulated, shame is entirely comic, being is performance. And yet, for all that, it often reads like Levinas carnivalized, one long satire on the category of departure. (It is worth noting that the plot of *Ferdydurke* turns directly on a sequence of fugues, confinements, and abscondences—the very working-out of Form's ceaseless transitivity.) And while the rallying cry we have already heard uttered by one of its characters, "Nothing but face!" does immediately segue into the cri de coeur, "To hell with philosophy!" (Mosbacher translation, 1961, 199), Gombrowicz's novel, not least in its physiognomic aspect, still strikingly anticipates the early contours of Levinas's thought.[40]

By the time Levinas writes his philosophical essays of the 1950s and his first magnum opus, *Totality and Infinity,* in 1961, "the face" has become the favored trope and sensible image for the otherness of "the other man." The face in Levinas is a kind of sensible absolute, a "signifyingness" that testifies, very simply, to its own upsurge, the non-indicative sign (or better, site) of the infinte alterity of the facing other. That signifyingness is its very content, the "message" it sends, the trace of being exterior and "other." In Alain Finkielkraut's apt elucidation, "The face or the narrow escape. Its determining characteristic is resistance to definition, the way it never allows itself to be cornered by my most pointed questions or even by my most penetrating gaze. The Other always is more than what I know of him, always escapes my grasp. This surplus, this constant excess of the being that takes aim at the intention that would fix him, goes by the name *face*. 'To encounter a man is to be kept on alert by an enigma'" (*The Wisdom of Love*, 13). It is, without attenuating matters too much, the non-dialectical solution Levinas develops two decades later to the experimental problematic of *le besoin d'évasion*, "the need for escape." What is initially figured in the 1935 essay as the centrifugal but impossible pull of *self-ex-cendence* is reconfigured at mid-career "as a question to the Other and about the other," ethical *transcendence* (crossing over but also ascending, going beyond) as thus the very meaning for Levinas of the human.[41] "But let us say right away that it is not towards eternity that escape directs itself" (95). It will direct itself rather, in his developing thought, *toward the Other*.[42]

This is at once very near to and very far from Witold Gombrowicz. For, while both thinkers begin from the identical vantage of embodied subjectivity, Levinas's and Gombrowicz's shared terrain of visage and alterity opens onto finally incompatible vistas, the face as *"lieu original de la Révélation"* ("Quelques reflexions," 62), and the face as mimetic goad; the Other as neighbor, and the Other as *semblable*, a grimacing *hypocrite lecteur*; the *droiture* and *temimut* (rectitude) of the face-to-face, and the slant and leverage of the face-off. And of course it cannot be forgotten for a moment that Gombrowicz is a writer of fictions, a surrealist, a ringmaster, and Levinas is an academic philosopher (though in no facile way, contra academic philosophy); ethics, chastens Levinas in *Totality and Infinity*, "freezes all laughter" (200), just as aesthetic consciousness "paralyzed in its freedom, *plays*, totally absorbed in the playing" ("Reality and its Shadow," 7). Lithuanian and Pole are at right angles to each other, tangent but oblique, sober ethical metaphysician to irreverent "rhetorical" phenomenalist.

As the self-amputating "writer whose subject is Form" (*A Kind of Testament*, 154), Gombrowicz's obsession with the face-attached-to-trunk means that subjectivity for him is absolutely bound to the direct effect of signifying forms, inescapably material. Levinas, while intensely drawn to language and the aesthetic (his allusiveness, frequent lyricism, and gift for metaphor are certainly some of his signal traits), wants sensible subjective and intersubjective experience to *break through* all the social and featured forms mediating it in order to lay bare ethical presence and immediacy and event. The Levinasian face speaks datively, vocatively, imperatively, but also enigmatically—otherwise than or beyond the economy of being: it is both a visitation and a transcendence, "the site of revelation." The Gombrowiczian face lies, by contrast, ever on the knife's edge between self-identity and the "mug"—rhetorical, dogmatic, petrified[43] (and thus closer to Levinas's account of the aesthetic and rhetorical), the sign of a membranous creature that has secreted, or retreated into, a facial shell. Divesting itself of its form, the face in Levinas proclaims, "You shall not do murder." Subject to deformation from within and without, the face in Gombrowicz grimaces and gets slapped.

But distances notwithstanding, we could also point to certain meaningful proximities that follow directly from Levinas's and Gombrowicz's personal histories. Each is a displaced east-central European more or less precariously on the ground in western Europe or South America: Gombrowicz, a Pole exiled in Argentina on the eve of war, and Levinas, Lithuanian by birth, taken prisoner as a French POW in 1940 and liberated at war's end. Both are unhomed by totalitarian conquest (is it irony or mimetic rough justice that Gombrowicz escapes European fascism only to witness the rise of Peronism in Argentina—favored sanctuary, into the bargain, for former Nazi officers?). They could even be said to inhabit complementary or overlapping Europes—the secondary, weakened Europe of *A Kind of Testament* ("impaired, sickly," allowing Argentina to become a country of "early and easy form" in its stead); the "worn-out" Europe of Levinas's late essay, "Peace and Proximity." Europe was "old Europe" for both thinkers long before that phrase became a twenty-first-century American faux pas, and before Poland became an official member of the EU.[44]

This is a Europe that Levinas's two essays of the 1930s presciently interrogate, along with the weakened (if not worn-out) idealism that reflects it. Just as Hitlerism arises against a crisis in liberalism that accepts degenerate forms of the ideal and magnified versions of embodied identity, so the *besoin d'évasion* brings the self's desire for *ex-cendence* in colloquy with the material being it vainly hopes to surmount, thus recalling idealism's "first inspiration" to exceed being. In the *Diary*, Gombrowicz writes the following address to the second-person, with his mug an uncomfortable ten centimeters away from ours:

> by suggesting, somewhat in the way of a proposition, certain problems, more or less linked to me, I pull myself into them and they lead me into other secrets still unknown to me. To travel as far as possible into the virgin territory of culture, into its still half-wild, and so, indecent, places, while exciting you to extremes, to excite even myself. . . . I want to meet you in that jungle, bind myself to you in a way that is most difficult and uncomfortable, for you and for me. Don't I have to distinguish myself from current European thought? Aren't my enemies the currents and doctrines to which I am similar? I have to attack them in order to force a contradistinction and I have to force you to confirm it. I want to uncover my present moment and tie myself to you in our todayness. (*Diary* 1:35)

Gombrowicz could almost be describing Levinas's own maverick relation to Heideggerian and Husserlian phenomenology, to existentialism, to materialist philosophies, to the currents and doctrines to which he was similar but also from which he was at a distinct remove.[45] Long stretches of the *Diary* are taken up by fascinating and compelling arguments with Sartre and Lévi-Strauss among others, or with Marxism and structuralism. Here is perhaps the most exemplary passage, an almost perfect heterology to Levinasian evasion:

> Today, in today's raw times, there is no thought or art which does not shout to you in a loud voice: don't escape, don't play, don't poke fun at yourself, don't run away! Fine. I, too, in spite of everything, would also prefer not to lie to my own being. I, therefore, tried this authentic life, full of loyalty to existence in myself. But, what do you want? It can't be done. It can't be done because that authenticity turned out to be falser than all my previous deceptions, games, and leaps taken together [in near synchronicity with the Levinasian critique of Heidegger]. I, with my artistic temperament, don't understand much theory, but I do have a nose when it comes to style. . . . It seems impossible to meet the demands of *Dasein* and have coffee and croissants for an evening snack. To fear nothingness, but to fear the dentist more. To be consciousness, which walks around in pants and talks on the telephone. To bear the weight of significant being, to instill the world with meaning and then return the change from ten pesos. What do you want? I know how these contrasts come together in their theories. Slowly, gradually, from Descartes through German Idealism, I grew accustomed to their structure, but laughter and shame toss me about at the sight of it with equal strength, as in the first days, when I was still completely naïve. And even if you were to "convince" me a thousand times over, there would still always be some elementary, unbearable ridiculousness in this! (*Diary* 1:183–84)

A blend of Democritus and Diogenes, laughing philosopher and (for a time, impoverished) cynic, Gombrowicz would at first sight seem to construe evasion according to the very categories Levinas uses merely as foils: creative becoming, *epater la bourgeoisie,* the free, sovereign, and solitary self of "artistic temperament." How smoothly, really, does Levinas's sense of flight from brute attachment to being comport with a de-Polanded Pole's own self-amputation through protracted exile in Argentina, where he can be or become Polish at a safe distance from Poland; with his willed fugitiveness on the margin and hinterland; with the jarring fusion of literary stylization and homelessness?[46] Like the *Chobry* on its return to Poland he apostrophizes in the opening pages of the burlesque novel *Trans-Atlantyk,* Gombrowicz drifts and sails on super-structurally, seeming to float above any attachment to any base of belonging.

But this overlooks Gombrowicz's unique purchase on Form (not to mention his distinctive nose for style), which solders the self to itself and other selves, an enchainment that can, it seems, only be "evaded" through illusory departures that necessarily result in new bondages (chapter titles in *Ferdydurke* are: "Abduction," "Imprisonment and Further Belittlement," "Legs on the Loose and New Entrapment," ". . . Captive Again," "Mug on the Loose and New Entrapment"). Indeed, the Levinas of the two early 1930s essays is nearer to Gombrowicz than at any other stage of his philosophical development. In them, he merely glimpses the Other in passing as a possible direction that his "new path" will later take (not fully worked out until *Otherwise Than Being; Or, Beyond Essence* (1974), where the self marks the place of a primal expulsion, the Other-*in*-the self).[47] Concomitantly, Gombrowicz across the entire curve of his artistic life seems stranded—as he allowed himself to be for so long in Argentina—at the very ontological juncture Levinas captures in the analysis of "irremissable attachment." That is to say, the neighbor is never discovered by Gombrowicz as the occasion for an authentic and successful departure from the encasement of selfhood. The neighbor is simply Form made manifest in another body . . . or face.[48] If Gombrowicz wears an amulet to insulate the self (like Pascal's famous *"Mémorial"* sewn into the lining of his coat), on the inside it reads: "to break away, to keep one's distance" (*A Kind of Testament,* 57).

And if the Other can only act as exterior lure or threat, the self is left not so much bobbing on the sea of humanity as adrift within its own amnion, umbilically self-tied. For Gombrowicz, the first-person plural—the "foggy, abstract, and arbitrary 'we,'"—rather than the third—the Heideggerian "they"—poses merely a more insidious version of the first-person singular.[49] Even within that membrane or carapace, the "I" is "assailed by the limitless anarchy of Form, of human form. . . . So it was always within me . . . and I was within it (*A Kind of Testament*, 47). When Gombrowicz cries, "Give me a knife, then! I must perform a more radical operation! I must amputate myself from myself!" (*A Kind of Testament*, 58), is he not exposing something like the very marrow of Levinas's subjectivist *besoin* and *nausée*?[50] "In the identity of the self, the identity of being reveals its confining nature because it appears under the form of suffering and invites evasion. Escape is also the need to depart from one's self, which is as much as saying the need to break the most radical and unpardonable confinement, the fact that the self is the self" (*De l'évasion*, 73).

Of course, what becomes the alembic for craved-albeit-impossible evasive distillation is Gombrowicz's art, his writing and his style. As he says of parody, it should allow him "to liberate Form, to tear it from weightiness and launch it into pure space, where it [becomes] light, bold, and revealing" (*A Kind of Testament*, 42). Yet, as he tells us himself, he will still suffer when he is (de)formed, the only escape from Form being another way-station of Form. The formal transitivity of Gombrowicz's art, writes the critic Tomasilaw Longinović, permits "an endless chain of identities which are continually assumed and rejected" ("I, Witold Gombrowicz," 49), serial attachments to and detachments from national collectivities and erotic objects, temporary allegiances to countries, genres, genders.[51] Fiction, drama, diary: those are some of the various blades in the self-vivisecting Swiss Army knife Gombrowicz calls out for.

And yet, the stubborn persistence of the word "chain" in the quoted sentence above cues us yet again to the specter of Levinas. "The flight [that motivations for escape] dictate is a search for haven. It does not only involve leaving, but going somewhere. The need for escape, on the contrary, finds itself absolutely identical at all the stopping points where its adventure may take it, as if the path traveled alleviates none of its dissatisfaction" (*De l'évasion*, 71–72). Creative enunciation, however vital its impulse, however elevated its launch into pure space may be and however artful its de-tetherings, never escapes bondage-to-being; indeed, says Levinas, it aims smack at it. One hears its unmistakable throb in the following recitative from the *Diary*:

As for me: No, never, never, never. I *am*. . . . The word "I" is so basic and inborn, so full of the most palpable and thereby the most honest reality, as infallible as a guide and severe as a touchstone, that instead of sneering at it, it would be better to fall to your knees before it. I think rather that I am not yet fanatical enough in my concern with myself and that I did not know how, out of fear of other people, to surrender myself to this vocation with enough of a categorical ruthlessness to push the matter far enough. I am the most important and probably the only problem I have: the only one of all my protagonists to whom I attach real importance. (*Diary* 1:113)

The entry ends with Gombrowicz speculating that he should make a character out of himself on the order of Hamlet or Don Quixote—except that he would seem to have accomplished something like that already, since as memoirist he sounds like a modernist version of Goethe, Rousseau, or Carlyle. Or again: "And haven't I already written in this diary that this 'I want to be me' is the whole secret of personality, this will, this desire, defines our attitude toward deformation and results in the fact that deformation begins to hurt. And if external forces crush me like a wax figurine, I will remain myself as long as I agonize, protest against it. Our authentic form is contained in the protest against deformation" (*Diary* 1:225).

Perhaps the most moving riposte to this protest belongs to Bruno Schulz, more adjacent to Gombrowicz's fictional temperament than Levinas. It appears in *Cinnamon Shops (Street of Crocodiles)*, which was first published in the same year as Levinas's "Quelques reflexions," and anticipates some of Levinas's remarks on art in an essay written ten years later:

Figures in a waxwork museum, even fairground parodies of dummies must not be treated lightly. . . . Can you imagine the pain, the dull imprisoned suffering, hewn into the matter of that dummy which does not know why it must be what it is, why it must remain in that forcibly imposed form . . . ? Do you understand the power of form, of expression, of pretence, the arbitrary tyranny imposed on a helpless block, and ruling like its own tyrannical, despotic soul? You give a head of canvas and oakum an expression of anger and leave it with it, with the convulsion, the tension enclosed once and for all, with a blind fury for which there is no outlet. The crowd laughs at the parody. Weep, ladies, over your own fate, when you see the misery of imprisoned matter, of tortured matter which does not know what it is and why it is, nor where the gesture may lead that has been imposed on it forever. (*Collected Fiction*, 35)

"The characters of a novel are beings that are shut up, prisoners.... A novel shuts beings up in a fate despite their freedom" asserts Levinas in his 1948 essay, "Reality and Its Shadow"; "For here materiality is thickness, coarseness, massivity, wretchedness ... is absurd, is a brute but impassive presence; it is also what is humble, bare, and ugly" (57), he says in *Existence and Existents*, from 1947. But those essays' critique of art's illusionistic commerce with anarchy and "evasion" are a world away from both Schulz's devotion to the transmigration of forms, to figure and figuration for their own sake, and Gombrowicz's commitment to liberating form, to tearing it from weightiness.[52] More pertinently, though, as we have seen, the burden of Levinas's argument a decade earlier is the burden of self-presence—immediate, ponderous, the "weight of being crushed beneath himself" (*De l'évasion*, 94). While the human being can change expression, anger ceding perhaps to elation or languor or shame, *internal* forces (contra Gombrowicz) work upon it not unlike the fury for which there is no outlet in Schulz's wax figure. Even fairground *spectators*, in other words, experience the tension of being as enclosed within a subjectivity that cannot help but wish to "excend" itself. The self, so to speak, becomes its own tar-baby. With Gombrowicz's relentless self-exile, and perhaps *especially* within the lineaments of his creative expression, one senses that while he may desperately have desired to be ever en route—the flight that is "a search for haven"—a different category of departure—the flight *from* flight—leaves its imprint. It marks the trace of the aspiration to be elsewhere.

So rather than construe the Gombrowiczian "I" in terms of his art's free-floating quality and its endless chain of identities, it makes sense to see instead the persistent shadow of a self enchained to itself at the level of the body, an anchorage the artist both celebrates and sublimates as a perpetual departure that never gets anywhere. Remember that immediately upon the triumphalism of "My 'self' is nothing but my will to be myself," Gombrowicz adds, as if applying a more ruthless act of self-surgery, "A measly palliative! Another formula!" Tellingly in this connection, Levinas regards the self-pinioned self as gaining a "dramatic form" while losing the character of a logical or tautological one, because it suffers from its confining nature.

At the base level of Gombrowicz's successive abandonment of identities, the plane of exigent, nauseated, ongoing bondage to the isolated self, that drama may be discerned in something like Levinas's sense.

There is, of course, no "other man" for Gombrowicz, no exterior brake—which is the only *successful* escape—on self-sameness. (In the train-compartment scene, we get a fantasy of *ejection*—"their properties fling me straight into the air, I feel as if I were leaping straight into the sky"—rather than *excendence*.) Alterity is merely one more form to hold at bay. Exteriority—as Levinas will say, "outside the subject"—possesses no specifically ethical valence. Yet one can, I think, still speculate on the kind of unease, be it *malaise* or *impuissance* or *nausée* that lies at the fount of Gombrowicz's permutations of Form, however he may energetically compensate for it.[53] But how to get back to that point of origin? How to recover its parthenogenesis, so as to capture Gombrowiczian evasiveness *in its nakedness*, in its "Levinasian" guise?

In fact, it is neither possible nor necessary. Even if the dialectical impossibility of conceiving the beginning of being could somehow be made mooted, a paradox would still remain[54]: for as Levinas insists, one feels the weight of being before it is accepted.[55] It is the *contradictio in adjectio* of attempting to "seize the moment when it took on weight, and of nevertheless being cornered by the problem of its origin" (94). Be that as it may, it is the problem of origin in Gombrowicz's case that has been posed, and to the degree that we can be escorted there through his memoirs, beginnings, origin, point of departure, at some level all indicate *a place:* Poland.

At the very end of *A Kind of Testament*, Gombrowicz muses, "To return to the time before the beginning, to seek refuge in my initial immaturity . . ." He adds the confessional parenthesis, "This Immaturity is still more important to me than Form, but I haven't said much about it in this book because it isn't easy to discuss it and I would rather people looked for it in the live matter of my artistic work." And then he concludes: "But to rebel? How? Me? A servant?" (155). I have always been struck by this passage, both for its unembarrassed nostalgia (which feels so out of place amidst Gombrowicz's resolute anti-sentimentalism) and its suspicion of mastery (to which Gombrowicz was nevertheless inclined by temperament and class).[56]

Immaturity in Gombrowicz's thought typically connotes a pre-form (Schulz calls it "an embryology of form"), a formlessness, or even a respite from Form altogether. For in youth, the self and its fit in the world are as yet green and unfinished. In such a state of developmental suspension, the body feels perhaps more light than weighty.[57] Subjectivity enjoys the illusion of something other than bondage, like the deceptive evasion Levinas ascribes to pleasure. "Communion" in the interhuman church remains some distance off yet, and can be held tentatively at bay. In *A Kind of Testament* Gombrowicz ironically, but still believably, refers to his youth as "that Proustian epoch" and "those Proustian days" (28–29).[58]

He plays ceaseless variations on this theme throughout his work. *Ferdydurke,* for instance, begins with a parody of Dante, "I was halfway down the path of life when I found myself in a dark forest. But this forest, worse luck, was green" (Borchardt translation, 2000, 2). And the preface to the Filidor chapter concludes, "Let the cry be backwards!" (Mosbacher translation, 1961, 86). The late novel *Pornographia* entirely exploits the theme. In the *Diary,* he claims that "in his work, a man ascending, that is, a young man, must become an idol" (3:167). In *A Kind of Testament,* he says, "You know from my diary how difficult it was for me to break with youth. This break came very late. I continued to look and feel young until I was forty. I belong to that race of people who have never known middle age. I tasted age the moment I said farewell to youth." (122). The attraction of Argentina lies in its youthfulness and "earliness" (soon, of course, to be contorted by those magicians of national form, Eva Duarte and Juan Domingo Peron). But perhaps the most illuminating portrait of Gombrowiczian immaturity belongs to Bruno Schulz, from his review of *Ferdydurke:*

> As reality we live permanently below this plateau in a completely honorless and inglorious domain that is so flimsy we also hesitate to grant it even the semblance of existence. . . . Our immaturity (and at heart perhaps our life force), tied with a thousand knots, with a thousand atavisms, with these secondary forms, with second-class culture, resides squarely in it by virtue of obsolete bonds and alliances. . . . [Gombrowicz] thus calls us back to the lower forms, orders us once more to reshape, refight, and remodel our entire cultural childhood: to become a child, not to find salvation in these ideologies that are ever baser, ever more primitive, ever trashier, but because in developing out of the phase of his primitive naiveté, the same man has wasted, squandered, and lost the treasure of his living concreteness. All these forms, gestures, and masks have been fleshed out with what is human and contains the rudiments of the wretched but concrete and sole human condition—and Gombrowicz revindicates them, recovers them, calls them back from their long exile. (*Letters and Drawings,* 159, 162)

Immoderate, lower, degraded, rudimentary, trashy, raw: these are attendant qualities of "a time of immaturity" (and which indeed Gombrowicz himself took pleasure in recounting in his several allusions to Schulz's review in his reminiscences).[59] "Abnormal, twisted, degenerate, abominable, and solitary" is the chain of adjectives he deploys in the second chapter of *A Kind of Testament,* reminding us once again of Levinas: "Where could I find this secret blemish, which separated me from the human herd? In physical illness? But, except for some minor lung infections, quite common among boys of my age, I was in reasonably good health. . . . So what could be the cause of this inner disorder . . . ?" (*A Kind of Testament*, 37).

Sexuality may be the culprit here,[60] but in looking "for something very elementary, something low and therefore very authentic" only to return "from these wild excursions to my respectable existence," he himself points to a curious splitting at work: "How could I devote myself to these two forms of excursion? How were these things reconciled within me? The answer is that they were not. Neither of these two realities was more real than the other. I was fully immersed in both of them and I was neither one nor the other. I was "between." And I was an actor" (38). This inbetweenness, which is Gombrowicz's special form of evasion and the very motor in his "time of immaturity," is key.

Thus, it is Schulz's prescient dialectic of "obsolete bonds and alliances" and "recovering from long exile forms, gestures, and masks fleshed out with what is human" that catches our ears. For though neither Schulz nor Gombrowicz at the time could have known what the year 1939 had in store for either of them, Schulz's intimation of *belonging* hits very close to the connection between one's immaturity as a bygone phase, on the one hand, and *place as such,* on the other. Or let us say rather, the time of Gombrowicz's immaturity *is a kind of movable locale*—a state, a republic, a place that moves from flight over border to beyond. True, Gombrowicz will say "that a man annihilated by history may, in time, become a creator . . . of his own history" and that "loyalty toward oneself appears to be the last law we can still obey" (*Diary* 3:49–50). But the complex palintropism in the *Diary* between Europe and America, Poland and Argentina, discloses the unease that gives baseline *évasion* a specifically exilic and bifurcated twist.

Especially in the third volume, which covers the years between Gombrowicz's departure from Argentina ("beyond Poland, adrift")[61] and his return to Europe (but not to Poland), we encounter a series of entries that stage for us a splitting not so very far removed from the torn polarity of the Schulz murals, part residing in Drohobycz, part in the Judean hills. In death, of course, Schulz will become dismembered on the ground, wrenched between topographies, as he never was in life. Gombrowicz, on the other hand, even if only through happenstance, became permanently amputated from *natio,* the country of his belonging, and therefore evasive in whatever place he found himself. March 19, 1963, recapitulates August 22, 1939, irrespective of the twenty-four year interval, as Gombrowicz boards a ship sailing to Berlin, with a grant from the Ford Foundation in hand, the end of his South American sojourn now at hand: "Pushed by the knife of this revelation, I died immediately—yes, all my blood ran out of me in a minute. Already absent. Finished. Ready to go. That mysterious something between me and my place had been severed" (*Diary* 3:69).

So we are witness to another kind of surgery. Nations assume the guise of forms, for which their possessed and dispossessed citizens *long,* and to which they *be-long* discrepantly at near or far distances.

Argentina! Sleep, squinting, weary, again I am searching for it in myself—with all my might—Argentina! I wonder, why in Argentina I never came upon this passion for Argentina in myself. Why is it attacking me now, as I leave it? My God, I who did not love Poland for a second. . . . And now I am standing on my head to love Argentina! It is curious, too, that the word love was forbidden you until now. And now, here, you experience shameless attacks of love. Oh, oh, oh (this is difficult for me to write, difficult to edit—as always, when I increase the candor in myself, the risk of being excessive, pretentious, grows, and then stylization is unavoidable). . . . And sure—I thought—surely this is nothing more than growing farther apart: not to love Poland because I was too close to it, to love Argentina because I always had it a certain distance, to love it now, yes, when I was moving, tearing away . . . and surely because in old age one can demand love more boldly, bah, beauty too . . . because they already appear at a distance, allowing for greater freedom . . . and they are more concrete, perhaps, at a distance. Yes, and one can love one's past from a distance, as I am removed not just in time but in space . . . carried away, subject to the uninterrupted process of growing more distant, of tearing away, and, in this growing distance, consumed by a furious love for what is growing more distant from me. Argentina—the past or a country? (*Diary* 3:77–78)[62]

This is an absolutely arresting moment in the *Diary,* which despite the post-hoc analytical maneuvering appears genuinely disconcerting to its author.[63] The text in all three volumes oscillates between narrative invention and discursive polemic, all of it dramaturgical, but this is certainly the *Diary*'s most important event, not least because it repeats (and perhaps cancels) the act 1 exodus amputating him from Europe and grafting him onto the South American continent.

Several pages later, a self-described "river of events in the present," he makes landfall: "Today, the twenty-second, I touched European soil" (83). He recalls that he landed on Argentine soil on the twenty-second as well. "Twos are my number. Hail magic!"—an infrequently pronounced but still significant word in the author's lexicon, as we know from the incipit of *A Kind of Testament*, which offers "Darkness and magic" as the "big" and "powerful" words that will commingle with the smaller ones in the "drama and non-drama" of Gombrowicz's life. Leaving ship for land, "I walked to the square where there is a statue of Columbus and I glanced at the city in which, perhaps, I will settle permanently after Berlin (every word of this sentence horrifies me: 'I walked' and 'to' and 'square,' et cetera)" (*Diary* 3:83).

The darkness and magic, the waning and waxing eros, the need to "tear away" and the need to adhere haunt not only Gombrowicz's nostalgia for times past but also his habitual experience of places to which he will always belong contradictorily, estranged but somehow also bound. They shadow his art as well. "But as the years passed, my words, these written words, seem to have less and less to do with me, they are already so far away, in foreign tongues, in various editions I have rarely seen with my own eyes, in the hands of commentators about whom I know nothing. . . . I no longer have any control over this. What then is happening to me, in what language, in what country?" (*Diary* 3:194).

Indeed. To have expended so much energy in his memoirs distancing himself from Sartre only to be squeezed into a train compartment with Levinas! If "control" is at bottom Gombrowicz's *idée fixe*, he knows well enough that writing always conduces to a process or event of creative dispossession. That it is to say, with every *Diary* entry he pens, the *Chobry* sets sail again, just as the fugitive plot of *Ferdydurke* stems from the decision to compose, a scene of writing that *produces* a departure.

Certainly, the nostalgic element in Gombrowicz's writing rarely if ever escapes an ironic overlay, but it feels nonetheless palpable and authentically felt. Not the dreamy nostalgia that engenders self-deceptive disdain—the sort memorably captured by the aging denizen of a moribund Atlantic City played by Burt Lancaster in the 1981 Louis Malle movie of the same name, who in the course of reciting a litany of the city's bygone thrills, looks out toward the ocean and says, "The Atlantic Ocean was something, then; you should have seen the Atlantic Ocean in those days." Gombrowicz has seen this same ocean, too, has even sailed it twice through departure and near-return. Given his penchant for in-between states, or the space between States, perhaps the ocean is his natural element after all, not the "rough sea" of the interhuman, not even the "troubled waters of the past," but the pooling ever west of east-central as the ideal expanse on which "to keep one's distance."

Immaturity would then be the temporal analogue to that expanse, the maritime nowhere and everywhere of adolescent in-between: "I was fully immersed . . . and I was neither one nor the other. I was 'between'." Gombrowicz's nostalgia does really aim homeward, a homesickness for original dislocation. For has he not already admitted to us that his was a "displaced family," living in a series of "'betweens,' which subsequently multiplied until they constituted my country of residence, my true home" (*A Kind of Testament*, 28)? "Near distance" is the alternate and oxymoronic name for this mobile homeland of sensibility, which also functions "vertically" when we factor in the role that writing plays, especially in the *Diary:* "I want to be a balloon, but one with ballast; an antenna, but one that is grounded." This is a tethering that seems more like repose than flight from flight, or existential unrest.

It would be too facile to naturalize Gombrowicz as a literary citizen, as immigrant in the "true home" of text, and leave it at that. Psychologically and maybe even metaphysically, he cannot so conveniently be sent on leave from the inveterate "category" of departure. Geographic dispossession, as suggested above, may reorient *évasion*, but it doesn't appear to rectify it. Quite the contrary: it externalizes it into land mass, cartography, and other forms. Still, Gombrowicz's *Diary* creates its own intermediate space, which, whether it reconstitutes his "country of residence," places him in vexatious proximity to a sensed, albeit impalpable, alterity—that of his readers. When Gombrowicz contrasts his intentions for such a text with more conventional instances of it, he actually speculates on being "enabled" by those he addresses: "Let this diary be more modern and more conscious and let it be permeated by the idea that my talent can only arise in connection with you, that is, that only you can excite me to talent or, what's more, that only you can create it in me" (*Diary* 1:35).

Though sneeringly and with a grimace, perhaps it is on the plane of the *Diary* that Gombrowicz improbably enacts a scene out of Bruno Schulz's fiction to which we will come momentarily, where homelessness makes friction with another being. One may even wish to propose that the *Diary* offers Gombrowicz a Levinasian solution to his dilemma of riveted self-presence, one Levinas himself was still on the way to formulating when he wrote *De l'évasion*. Is this the ocean of the interhuman in which Gombrowicz finally subjects himself to the Other? Let us leave the question open and turn, if not for definitive answers, then to a set of scenes that move us in back in the direction of a common homeland, and in this case, internal diaspora, thus modulating from an evasive inbetweenness to the enisled fate of Bruno Schulz.

SCENE 3: LITERARY SPACE; OR, A DUEL OF
POLISH FACE SLAPPING

Before me I have Bruno Schulz in the French translation, heralded a few weeks ago by Suzanne Arlet (the poet). It is a volume of stories entitled *Traite des mannequins* (chiefly stories from *Cinnamon Shops*) published by Julliard. . . .
    Bruno.
    I have long known about this edition prepared with such painstaking effort, yet when I finally saw the book I winced. . . . He first showed up on Służewska, after the publication of *Cinnamon Shops*. He was small, strange, chimerical, focused, intense, almost feverish—and this is how our conversations got started, usually on walks. That we needed one another is indisputable. We found ourselves in a vacuum, our literary admirers were spectral. . . . After reading my first book, Bruno discovered a companion in me, for which to furnish him with the Outside without which an inner life is condemned to a monologue—and he wanted me to use him in the same way. . . . And here is where the "miss" or "dislocation," to use the language of our works, came in; for his extended hand did not meet my own. I did not return his regard, I gave him abysmally little, almost nothing of myself, our relationship was a fiasco; but perhaps this secretly worked to our advantage? Perhaps he and I needed fiasco rather than happy symbiosis. To day I can speak of this openly because he has died. (*Diary* 3:3)

The rest of this extended reflection is equally forthright, unsparing, and often brutal, as though Schulz's mug were ten centimeters away from Gombrowicz's own. Differently put, it reads almost as though the unextended hand has to summon a countenance it must deflect apotropaically, not merely by turning away Bruno's regard, but by fitting him with a "grimacing mask grown onto his face."[64] To that end, it re-enacts Gombrowicz's keen awareness of writing in the presence of reading others. Finally, it exemplifies what we have heard Schulz himself say: "As if one had to mold expressions on faces, as if they were something else, just the grimace itself, a look, a penetrating talk, a passionate wink towards our perspicacity" (*New Documents and Interpretations*, 22).

In one of his last stories, Schulz supplies a different-seeming confirmation: "You rub against somebody, attach your homelessness and nothingness to someone alive and warm. The other person walks away and does not feel your burden, does not notice that he is carrying you on his shoulders, that like a parasite you cling momentarily to his life" (*The Complete Fiction*, 298).[65] Gombrowicz mounts a sustained prophylaxis against such incubated proxy-life, the alternative to which—"fiasco"—etches into that much sharper relief the rubbing, clinging, carrying, burdening whose parasitism is also allergy. We have glimpsed Gombrowicz's grimacing in the (literal) face of exteriority before. But there, in the train compartment, it was a matter of too much body too close for comfort. Here, however—though the body is not a superfluous element, ethnically or "racially"—the gauntlet flung, the face against which it slaps, belong to the compartment of authorial adjacency, the public nearness of two writers.

We could certainly retrieve the face motif as a hieroglyphic key here. Inasmuch as the self is warped and blemished from the outside, it wears a face. Inasmuch as it can lay claim to a latency for estrangement and maculation, it wears a face. And inasmuch as subjectivity is flaunted and defended on the page, in the space of reading, the wearing and imposing of faces is something authors and readers can be said to exercise and undergo.[66] The *Diary* routinely enacts that final-most duel of grimaces. The figuration may be less distinct than magnified pupils, hairs, skin—Schulz's visage has to be conjured in the act of reading—but the self-riveted authorial subject seems to put on even more weight as it contemplates itself under the scrutiny of rival Others and an untold number of reading eyes.

But we also could have recourse to Levinas's drama of *évasion*. Only Gombrowicz perhaps could afford to speak so unguardedly, so "openly" about Schulz, who, as we have seen, still remains vulnerable to dis-integrating forces so many years after his death. Yet, once again, let us pick up on telling ornaments in Schulz's diction, specifically the arabesque of attaching one's homelessness to another. And let us also note that Gombrowicz's grimace at the Bruno Schulz before him is provoked most immediately by the text I cited in the previous section—the "Treatise on Tailor's Dummies," which asks whether we "understand the power of form, of expression, of pretence, the arbitrary tyranny imposed and ruling like its own despotic soul."

In the *Diary*'s description, Schulz comes off as nothing less than a neurasthenic, defective version of Levinas's irremissable subject.

> A tiny gnome with an enormous head, appearing too scared to exist, he was ejected from life and crouched among its peripheries. Bruno did not

acknowledge his right to exist, he sought his own annihilation—not that he wanted to commit suicide; he merely "strove" for nonbeing with all his might (and this is precisely what made him, Heidegger-style, so sensitive to being). In my opinion there was so sense of guilt à la Kafka in this striving, it was more like the instinct that moves a sick animal to separate, remove itself. He was superfluous. He was extraneous. (*Diary* 3:6)

Not that Gombrowicz isn't aware of his own part in the recapitulation of this fiasco: "I am looking at the pages I wrote about Schulz. Was he really like that? Was I really like that? O real truth, who will sprinkle salt on your tail!" (7).[67] But Schulz's own correspondence and literary output, while confirming at least a part of Gombrowicz's judgment, reminds us that he too, like his compatriot, is capable of measuring the shape of personality against the landscape of national-geographic belonging.

In fact, he does so programmatically with the figure of Marshal Piłsudski in the essay entitled "Tragic Freedom" when he writes, "The hero melts pantheistically into the historical landscape [and] forms into the face of an individual, into the spirit of Poland's history" (*New Documents and Interpretations*, 47). While he hardly has himself in mind, may we not, if only to make the point, redress Gombrowicz's earlier critique by applying the following to Schulz himself: "an individual grew a head higher than the century, a genius of love and care devoured by smallness" (46)? Of course, Schulz's trope signifies Piłsudski and, by extension, Poland. But let it, if only for a moment, raise the specter of the now justly elevated croucher among life's peripheries, the tiny gnome with an enormous head. "Bruno."

Schulz was probably as uncomfortable within his Polishness and Drohobyczness as within his Schulzness. But it is *his* unease, not Gombrowicz's. The two modernists may assume the burden of suprapersonal identity with mutual discomfiture, but they bear up differently. And thus, the gesture imposed upon Schulz forever in the *Diary* does not necessarily leave him palsied. "The accomplishment of a destiny is the stigmata of being," says Levinas (72), which also captures the fate, the consequence maybe, of literary reminiscence. Yet lived lives will always outpace their thematicization—this being one of the clarion calls of Levinas's "essay on exteriority," *Totality and Infinity*, and an incessant chime in Schulz and Gombrowicz as well.

The latter distinguishes himself according to certain specific criteria—"Bruno was a man denying himself. I was seeking myself. He wanted annihilation. I wanted realization. He was born to be a slave. I was born to be a master. He was of the Jewish race. I was from a family of Polish gentry" (3:6). As to the last—since it will define him biologically under the Reich, ultimately sanctioning his murder—Schulz makes few overt references to being a Jew in his extant correspondence; his fiction similarly mystifies or sublimates that identity. But his intellectual circle in Poland consisted largely of Jews like himself, and it was a circle the Gentile aristocrat Gombrowicz enjoyed and admired as well. And one can speculate that Schulz's professional fortunes were in some measure tied to that identity, for better after his death, possibly for worse, beforehand.

It is undeniable, however, that the murals that were to become his last graphic expression, his manuscript *The Messiah* that along with other texts and letters went missing, and the life that was violently taken from him, are all attached exclusively to the fact that he was a Jew. For all his universalist mythologic (Jerzy Ficowski's term), his literary cosmopolitanism, this "blemish" of particularity rooted him to the spot. "This is a landscape," Schulz writes in "Tragic Freedom," "permeated through and through with history, windblown by history, heavy with the past—the embodied essence of Polishness" (*New Documents and Interpretations,* 49). It is a landscape that, because of that history in its modern moment, simultaneously held him fast and deracinated, disgorged him. Had he been made of stronger stuff, one could perhaps concoct for him a retroactive counter-fable of flight—like the fictional transubstantiation he accomplishes as a character in the Israel novelist David Grossman's *See: Under Love,* or the real-life narratives of successful escape and rescue told by the Polish pianist Wadyslaw Szpilman and the Yiddish poet Avrom Sutzkever.[68] But, he was a lifelong inhabitant of a provincial Polish town. And in the final decade of his short life, the tenuousness that always underscored Jewish life in east-central Europe both imprisoned him within and amputated him from the Polish body politic—homeland insecurity, so to speak.

INTERLUDE 2—LEVINAS AND SCHULZ

In the edition of Levinas's *De l'évasion* published in 1982, Jacques Rolland appends a lengthy and truly revelatory footnote, which reads in part as follows:

This dimension of existence glimpsed in the sense of being riveted, in the sense of its character as unpardonable or as irrevocable, was attributed in the introduction to its likely philosophical origin: the Heideggerian notion of *Geworfenheit*. We wonder, nonetheless, if it does not possess an entirely different origin: "Jewishness," in the sense that Nazi anti-Semitism has recently and brutally disclosed it, possesses precisely this unpardonable character. We are thinking of an article [by Levinas] published in 1935 in the eighth number of the review of the Alliance Israelité Universelle, *Peace and Justice*, entitled "The Religious Inspiration of the Alliance" (p. 4). We recall from it these few phrases: "Hitlerism is the greatest of tests—the supreme test—that Judaism must traverse.... The *pathétique* fortune of being Jewish becomes fatality. One can no longer flee from it. The Jew is ineluctably riveted to his Judaism." A generation of young people "definitively attached to the sufferings and the joys of their respective nations ... before the reality of Hitlerism are discovering all the gravity of the fact of being Jewish"; "in the barbaric and primitive symbol of race ... Hitler has reminded us that one does not desert Judaism." The similarity of these phrases to those "On Evasion" uses to convey the way the existent is bound to its existence cannot fail to hit home. Coming from a man who will later draw attention to pre-philosophical experiences which are the sap upon which philosophical reflection nourishes, this articulation of the fundamental underpinning of "pre-philosophical experience"—viz., the trauma provoked by the first manifestations of absolute antisemitism—cannot fail to capture our attention. (*De l'évasion*, 104)[69]

Nor can it fail to capture precisely the fate of the chimerical and feverish writer, ineluctably riveted to his Jewishness (whether he understood himself to be as such from within his own embodied subjectivity or not). The irony is that of all twentieth-century Jewish writers in the diaspora, Schulz represents a kind of apogee or aphelion of, let us call it, pagan sensibility—the fiction-writer as unexampled demiurge and idolator of form. Myth in Schulz cannot really be called Judaic (or kabbalistic) in the way it can more easily for Kafka; while biblical or midrashic themes and motifs undeniably dot his fiction, they seem more Seleucid or Hellenic in their unembarrassed syncretism.[70]

How eerily poignant for Schulz's case, then, becomes a claim by Levinas in another short piece entitled "The Actuality of Maimonides," from the fourth number of the contemporaneous 1935 *Peace and Justice*: "*Paganism is a radical impotence to depart from the world*. It does not consist in denying spirits and gods, but of situating them in the world....The pagan is imprisoned in this world which suffices for itself, is closed upon itself" (quoted in Rolland's footnotes to *De l'évasion*, 119). To be sure, the express incommensurability between Judaism and paganism here must exclude Schulz, since it opposes moralities and worldviews, not rival aesthetics. Yet let us say that in the midst of the gap Levinas has sketched for us an inadvertent bond, since Schulz's work so notably bestrides the cleavage of antithetical worlds, synthesizing and harmonizing them. On the one hand, the pagan finds the world that imprisons him "solid and firm" under his feet, and that cannot describe Schulz (rather, it sounds like Kristeva or Heidegger). And yet, on the other, Schulz is himself mysteriously attached and rooted to his ambient world by both circumstance and temperament (at least in default of freedom of movement and innate *puissance*). Or more precisely, it is the *imaginative* world—"The Formation of Legends," "The Republic of Dreams," "The Annexation of the Subconscious," "The Mythologizing of Reality" (all Schulzian titles)—that holds him fast. Therein, he finds his "Tragic Freedom," (the title of a volume by the poet Kazimierz Wierzyński, which he reviews in the essay of the same name).

On the other hand, Schulz absolutely embodies Levinas's evocation of "the Jew in the world": "In the middle of the most complete confidence attributed to things, he is devoured by an undeclared uneasiness. However unshakable the world may appear to those whom one calls 'normal soul' [*esprits sains*], it contains for the Jew a trace of the provisional and of the created. This is the madness or the faith of Israel" (119). There is no "*contradictio in adjectio*" here. The full tragedy of Schulz's fate immures it, in his own words, within the "threatening and unfathomable face of history" (*New Documents and Interpretations,* 52). It is likewise linked to the fate of myriad other European Jews cleft down the middle of their beings between competing claims of belonging—to Europe and to Judaism—that could no longer be permitted to cohabit in the same body. That is, Schulz was *made* or *certified* "mad" by Hitlerism as an adherent of Israel, however gingerly he may have carried his faith. Yet, at the same time, his very last artwork attests to the fairy-tale world (evil or not, evil *and* not) in which he sought a paradoxical sanity and firm foundation, as its recent fragmentation introduces a final ironic element of detachable homelessness into his story.

The syncretism we see in Schulz's art is neither unknown to Levinas nor disallowed. For Schulz can hardly be called "pagan" in Levinas's sense, someone identified by a "fundamental incapacity to transgress the limits of the world," who "accepts" existence without "justifying" it. But he is very obviously sentenced by history to a duality or splitting around a paradox of belonging that ultimately costs him his life. And it is here that we might most effectively discern the contrasting profiles of Gombrowicz's mobile, transportable inbetweenness and Schulz's dichotomous and immutable fixity. Here, therefore, Gombrowicz's distinction between himself as Gentile and Schulz as Jew reads definitively.

But we should stop short of collapsing Schulz's dilemma into the fact of his Jewish identity, since that would hold him hostage to totality only slightly less than the political and cultural constraints that kept him riveted to Jewishness and marooned in Drohobycz. And while we would also chafe at subscribing entirely to the alternative—that his mythologized reality constituted some kind of oneiric homeland, redressing a mis-fit on the ground—we should still wish to keep it at something like a near distance. No, Galicia was neither determinist nor entirely distillate geography, neither unbearably heavy nor unbearably light.[71] Positioned somewhere in the middle of these poles (in a double sense), what it signified for Schulz was an aperture through which the longings for national form and mythmaking structures of the imagination coalesced. A Pole, a Jew, a provincial, a celebrated artist and writer, a prisoner of occupation and wartime conquest, he was not suited or destined for escape. *Because* he came from a Jewish mercantile family, *because* he was never able to escape the shallows of middle-class drudgery, and *because* his febrile literary sensibility was driven by "transmigration" in all possible forms, he was more ImagiNative than émigré or expellee.

SCENE 4: HOMELAND; OR, SCHULZIAN UTOPIA

After a great many of fate's capricious ups and downs, which I have no intention of going into here, I found myself abroad at last, in that realm of my youthful dreams I once ardently yearned for. . . . I made my return not as a conqueror but as one of life's derelicts. The intended domain of my triumphs was not the scene of wretched, inglorious, petty defeats in which I lost, one after the next, my proud and lofty aspirations. By now, I was fighting for mere survival; battered, trying as best I could to save my flimsy shell from shipwreck, blown here and there by the winds of fate. I finally came upon that middle-sized provincial town where, in the dreams of my youth . . . (*Letters and Drawings*, 228)

This is the beginning of Schulz's fragment "Fatherland," published in the December 1939 issue of the literary magazine *Sygnały*, a month after Kristallnacht. It reads like a Bildungsroman, a Polish *Ulysses*, a fantasy of prolonged departure and humbled return.[72] Only the humbled return, however, has basis in the reality of Schulz's life: brief trips to Warsaw, Vienna, Paris, but otherwise an absolutely umbilical tie to his native city, "the hard partner in Schulz's mysticism" (Adam Zagajewski, in *Letters and Drawings*, 17). We never see the speaker reenter the precincts of town, however, since, as he tells us, he is luckily diverted at the last moment by a "favoring current," which carries him ... elsewhere, another instance of "the deft interaction of circumstances, the dexterous meshing of the gears of destiny" (*Letters and Drawings*, 228) in his life. Horizontals of the outward-bound journey and back quickly fade and are overtaken by the verticalities of class mobility, which elevate him from yeoman's work to bourgeois respectability (café fiddler to concertmaster); at this point the author's own machinery of wish-fulfillment may reasonably be inferred. Then, y and x axes perfectly intersect: "My whole past of homeless wandering, the submerged misery of my former existence, separated itself from me and floated back like a stretch of country positioned crosswise against the rays of the setting sun, rising one more time over distant horizons, while the train that bore me away rounded the last curve and headed straight into the night, full-breasted with the future that thrust against its face, a swelling, intoxicating, future seasoned with smoke" (229).

Fatherland, in this fantasy, signifies the place I stumble upon in my wanderings and that adopts me and makes me its own, where I become an adult, happily married, socially aligned, professionally rewarded: "A long succession of years heavy with happiness and fulfillment lies ahead, an unending mathematical progression of joyful good times" (232). The fantasy retrospect to this prospect is mapped for us in the contemporaneous essay "The Republic of Dreams," where, standing "here on the Warsaw pavement in these days of tumult ... I retreat in my mind to the remote city of my dreams" (*Letters and Drawings*, 217). As if Schulz, and not Calvino, were composing *Invisible Cities,* the essay keeps projecting and proliferating its central conceit, a country that licenses a continual escapist reinvention. At first, the remembered realm of youth is evoked as a place paradoxically more real than other sites: "Where other towns developed into economies, evolved into statistics, quantified themselves—ours regressed into essence.... Here events are not ephemeral surface phantoms: they have roots sunk into the deep of things and penetrate the essence. Here decisions take place every moment, laying down precedents once and for all. Everything that happens here happens only once and is irrevocable. That is why such weightiness, such heavy emphasis, such sadness inheres in what takes place" (*Letters and Drawings*, 217).Town and countryside take on shape, fully open to nature's fertility and vitality, the sign not only of "the Weed," but also, unsurprisingly, of the mother, for this essay poses the maternal dream-past to Fatherland's Symbolic form-giving and adult propriety.[73] Then, impelled by the spirit of flight, in order to escape from this sleepy luxuriance and "the incubus lying heavy on the chest in a torrid noontime nightmare," the narrator, along with his gang of boys, "hit on the outlandish and impossible notion of straying farther . . . of patrolling borders both neutral and disputed . . . where we meant to dig in, raise ramparts around us . . . proclaim the Republic of the Young" (219–20).

In this stronghold, "part fortress, part theater, part laboratory of visions," Schulz spins *his* version of canonical literary antecedence grafted onto the self: "As in Shakespeare, this unleashed theater spilled over into nature, expanding into reality. . . . Like Don Quixote, we wanted to divert the channel of all those histories and romances into our own lives" (220). Finally, at the end of the essay, the bygone but still pulsing dreamscape of youth recrudesces through the auspices of a later visitor, a "director of cosmic landscapes and sceneries" who "perceived the ready contours of myth suspended over the sight" and thereupon, himself "established the exclusive domain of the fictive." "The grand theater of uncircumscribed airspace is inexhaustible in its ideas, its projects, its aerial preliminaries: it hallucinates an architecture of grandiose inspiration, an ethereal, transcendental brand of urbanistics" (222). And unlike the narrator in what Gombrowicz would call his greenness, this ingenuous dreamer makes the Republic cosmopolitan, denationalizing it, and "invites everyone to keep on working, fabricating, jointly creating: We are all of us dreamers by nature, after all, brothers under the sign of the trowel, destined to be master-builders." (223).

Fatherland and the Republic of Dreams are Drohobycz perfected and spiritualized. As the prospective realm of material reward, it grants Schulz the living and renown, the domestic rescue, he could only yearn for. As the utopian province of nostalgia and redemptive anamnesis, it marks the place, in Zagajewski's words, "where civilization, diluted in the peripheries, takes up a dialogue with the cosmos, with nature" (*Letters and Drawings*, 17).[74] The split between just these two aspects, cultural patrimony or paradise regained on the one hand, and home transubstantiated or paradise lost on the other, benignly figures the literal rent or tear in murals that now live a double/fragmented life in the unnaturally twinned cities of Drohobycz and Jerusalem. In the latter, not his home, Schulz discovers belated refuge and reclamation; in the former, the only home he ever knew, some of what he painted remains still proximate to him (he is buried anonymously in the Jewish cemetery)— his only tombstone.

SCENE 5: PHYSIOGNOMY; OR, THE FACE IN SCHULZ

It was the face of a tramp or a drunkard. A tuft of filthy hair bristled over his broad forehead rounded like a stone washed by a stream. That forehead was now creased into deep furrows. I did not know whether it was the pain. The burning heat of the sun, or that superhuman effort that had eaten into his face and stretched those features near to cracking. His dark eyes bored into me with a fixedness of supreme despair or suffering. He both looked at me and did not, he saw me and did not see. His eyes were like bursting shells, strained in a transport of pain or the wild delights of inspiration. (*The Complete Fiction*, 47)

What, finally, of the face in Schulz? Above, in scene 3, as almost in imitation of Gombrowicz himself, we made way for it, only to turn away. It appeared briefly in the earliest moments of this chapter as the possible starting point of a novel and as the countenance of Poland. Let us now follow up on these hints, and draw links among physiognomy, literary sensibility, and national belonging. With his relative obscurity, his frustration with a provincial fate, the ambient pathos of his personality, his precarious Jewishness in German-occupied Poland, if anything, Schulz was possibly even more conscious of the spell cast by the face as the emblem of vulnerable humanity and his own need to conjure and ward it off than was Gombrowicz. The surviving correspondence we possess certainly shows a writer in overdetermined relationship to readers, those whose faces he knew.[75] The fiction, from time to time, directly *aims at the face* or tentatively hovers above and before it.

It is a minor element within a minor modernism, to be sure. Unlike its counterpart in Gombrowicz, the Schulzian visage throws down no gauntlet. It does not believe in dueling. Nor does it proliferate, finding refuge in metonymy, safety in numbers. Instead, faces seem to live a wholly metaphorical life, subject to the same forces that preside over everything else in Schulz's mythified fictional world: a fundamental principle of transmigrated form, objects turned into signs, persons collapsed into allegories of themselves, private space and time contracted into further depths of privacy or else dispersed into otherness. The face appears, only to recede again—in much the same way as Gombrowicz depicts Schulz himself in *Diary*, "extraneous," "superfluous." But perhaps there lies its significance, a minor element in a minor modernism that nonetheless reads the larger-in-scale.

To that degree, it might be seen as sharing an affinity with the aspect of the foreigner that Julia Kristeva conjures in *Strangers to Ourselves*: "From heart pangs to first jabs, the foreigner's face forces us to display the secret manner in which we face the world, stare into all our faces, even in the most familial, the most tightly knit communities. . . . Between the fugue and the origin: a fragile limit, a temporary homeostasis" (3–4). The limit and homeostasis, a boundary and a steady state—these are what faces in Schulz's work epitomize. Some examples: the very first story of *Cinnamon Shops*, "August," describes the half-wit Touya, whose face "works like the bellows of an accordion. Every now and then a sorrowful grimace folds it into a thousand vertical pleats, but astonishment soon straightens it out again" (*The Complete Fiction*, 6). The simile that conveys this figure (or her face) promises a kind of plenitude, the opposite pole to which—hollowed out or contracted space—is assigned to Touya's mother, "white as a wafer and motionless like a glove from which a hand had been withdrawn" (7).

The pulse of Schulz's fiction oscillates between such fading or shrinkage and corresponding pullulations of "immoderate fertility," as in the face of the tramp or drunkard from the story "Pan."[76] The face in Schulz folds in on its own metaphoricity, producing exquisite similes that evince "both the prose's strenuous artifice and its harrowing effect."[77] The faces *are* their metaphors, wholly figural productions of language. As there must be in Gombrowicz, there are thus neither counterfaces nor mugs in Schulz's fiction. "It is part of my existence," says a character in *Sanatorium under the Sign of the Hourglass*, "to be the parasite of metaphors, so easily am I carried away by the first simile that comes along" (309),[78] a fate shared by the face as well. Human countenance is both homeless and migratory, but in each case, it presents itself vulnerably, the very sign, as in Levinas, of woundable alterity.

The counterpart to Gombrowicz's train compartment scene might therefore be something like this: "For a time I had the company of a man in a ragged railwayman's uniform—silent, engrossed in his thoughts. He pressed a handkerchief to his swollen, aching face. Later even he disappeared, having slipped out unobserved at some stop. He left behind him the mark of his body in the straw that lay on the floor, and a shabby black suitcase he had forgotten" (*The Complete Fiction*, 242). Faces continually exceed, and recede from grasp. Sometimes, they are telluric, atavistic and, typically, female: "the dark half-naked idiot girl rises slowly to her feet and stands like a pagan idol, on short, childish legs; her neck swells with anger, and from her face, red with fury, on which the arabesques of bulging veins stand out as in a primitive painting, comes forth a hoarse animal-scream, originating deep in the lungs hidden in that half-animal, half-divine breast" (*The Complete Fiction*, 7). Sometimes, they are etiolated, wan, and typically male: "Uncle Mark, small and hunched, with a face fallow of sex, sat in his grey bankruptcy, reconciled to his fate, in the shadow of a limitless contempt in which he seemed only to relax. His grey eyes reflected the distant glow of the garden, spreading in the window" (*The Complete Fiction,* 9). Human countenance can license a riotous overgrowth across its features. And it can also secure a no-man's land, a recess in the general tumult, like Dodo's face from *Sanatorium under the Sign of the Hourglass:* "His face matured early, and strange to say while experience and the trials of living spared the empty inviolability, the strange marginality of his life, his features reflected experiences that had passed him by, elements in a biography never to be fulfilled; these experiences, although completely illusory, molded and sculpted his face into the mask of a great tragedian, which expressed the wisdom and sadness of his existence" (*The Complete Fiction,* 275). Visages are "engrossed," "perspiring," "fermented," "saturated," more body than face. But they are also "submerged," "immured," so much "imprisoned matter" (recalling the fate of persons undone by figuration through art, in Levinas's critique). On the Street of Crocodiles, "pseudo-American" district of utilitarian commerce, where "reality is as thin as paper and betrays with all its cracks its imitative character" (67), half-baked and undecided, mien is mere consumerist outline, "a row of pale cut-out paper figures, fixed in an expression of anxious peering" (69). Prolonged affectivity of another sort transforms Father's face into "a petrified, tragic mask, in which the pupils, hidden behind the lower lids, lay in wait, tense as bows, in a frenzy of permanent suspicion" (75), miming that of a correlative object, a stuffed condor frozen "in the pose of a Buddhist sage, its bitter dried-up ascetic face petrified in an expression of extreme indifference and abnegation" (73).

In the last set of examples, and most extravagantly in the story "Tailor's Dummies," Schulz perhaps approximates the Gombrowiczian notion of face as something imposed rather than simply possessed, faces or expressions that "imprison" or coerce the simulacra that wear them. But then, the seeming cruelty here merely instances a special case of the general principle Schulz lays out in his published description of *Cinnamon Shops:* "a certain monism of the life substance" for which "specific objects are nothing more than mask. The life of the substance consists in the assuming and consuming of numberless masks. The migration of forms is the essence of life" (*Letters and Drawings*, 113). The human face is thus not really different in either kind or degree from the moon, which Schulz calls "that most inventive transmogrifier" (96) in the final story from *Cinnamon Shops*, "The Comet."

The visage in Schulz takes on the effects of chiaroscuro, as in the painting of Botticelli, a play of light and dark, or sfumato, as in drawings by Leonardo, a gradual shading from the substantial into the ineffable. It could thus be said to spatialize a similar notion from *Sanatorium under the Sign of the Hourglass* about time: "What it is to be done with events that have no place of their own in time; events that have occurred too late, after the whole of time has been distributed, divided, and allotted; events that have been left in the cold, unregistered, hanging in the air; homeless, and errant? Could it be that time is too narrow for all events? Could it be that all the seats within time might have been sold?" (*The Complete Fiction*, 131). In fact, answers Schulz, an axis of substitution shunts branch lines of time or supernumerary faces into a zone of irrecoverability, where they are nevertheless preserved metaphorically.[79]

Perhaps this exorbitance of metaphor, the transporting of contraband that cannot otherwise be registered (as Schulz puts it in *Sanatorium*), is what Gombrowicz meant when he charged Schulz with approaching art "as if it were a lake he intended to drown in" (*Diary*, 3:6). Without endorsing Gombrowicz's Manichean distinctions between himself and Schulz as laid out in his *Diary*, one sees that the Schulzian face does what the Gombrowiczian face cannot. It doesn't flinch or recompose itself. Passively staring back or focused on an elsewhere—not grimacing or wincing or mugging—is how it stares back. And how perhaps it stares at Poland and makes Poland seem to stare back at it, as we shall see momentarily.

How Schulz might have extended or complicated such mythopoesis is a question that remains fixed in the death mask imposed upon his own face by a Gestapo officer's bullet in 1942. Schulz's demise, as Gombrowicz coldly notes in the *Diary*, licenses a different kind of facing—something Gombrowicz had already prefigured during Schulz's lifetime, when he drew him out in an exchange of open letters, exposing his face in public.[80] But Schulz exposed himself too, it is reasonable to argue, most deliberately and masochistically in his graphic work, where preternaturally large heads (like Schulz's own) evince a studied physiognomy that also often clearly corresponds to that of the artist himself. His face, for instance, presides on the frontispiece for a collection of his draftsmanship circa 1920–21, *The Book of Idolatry*. He painted numerous self-portraits that centered upon his distinctive triangular, heavy-browed, and sidelong glancing face. Depicted so, it appears to be holding itself from itself and its viewers at (ironic?) (forlorn?) (defensive?) remove, self-belonging at a near distance.

Gombrowicz required foils and counter-faces to articulate the features of his own. To this degree, his criticism and his demeanor as public intellectual were of a piece with his art. Intersubjective space becomes an infinite regress of metonymy, the face that begets other faces as well as the face of human encounter that transposes into the face of reading. Schulz also sustains a consistency between life and art, but it corresponds to the more vulnerable, because fixable, consistency of metaphor. Faces wander extraterritorially in Gombrowicz; in Schulz, they always appear on the verge of leaving or returning home. Moreover, there is no face-*to*-face. The face is an object, *un visage trouvé*, a kind of pure passivity, held out by the fiction to be stared at, just as reading Schulz's fiction, analogously, typically feels like postcoital languor and torpid assent.[81]

Even away from his fiction, when Schulz wrote correspondence to others or answered Gombrowicz's open letter with one of his own or produced critical essays on the subconscious or the mythologizing of reality, the face—as we have seen in the letter that proposes it as a foundation for fiction—is asked to do a different kind of work than in Gombrowicz's art. And just as Jean-Paul Sartre plays an intermittent, allusive role in the *Diary* as a counter-figure for Gombrowicz's arguments with both Western Europe and western philosophy, so he now makes a cameo appearance here in the context of Schulz. "A consecration by the ceremony of the spectacle" is Sartre's description of the ethics of reading, and it accurately conveys the *ceremonial* quality of Schulz's prose, its air of *nunc stans* that put Gombrowicz so ill at ease.[82] "Kant believes that the work of art first exists as fact and that it is then seen," Sartre continues. "Whereas it exists only if one *looks* at it and if it is first appeal, pure exigence to exist.... The work of art is a value because it is an appeal" (*What Is Literature?* 57). The final scenes in this chapter are meant to propose the Schulzian bridge—face and obverse—between the pure (and passive) exigence to exist on the one hand and the might of mythic history on the other, between forms of literature and the longing for national form.

SCENE 6 AND POSTLUDE WITH LEVINAS: MYTH AND HISTORY; OR, THE FACE OF POLAND

During his lifetime [Piłsudski's] face may have been the face of an individual. Certainly, those near him knew that smile, that clouding brow, the flashes the moment lit up on his face. To us, from a distance, individual traits increasingly dim and blur, they seem to give out a radiance from within, as of larger, more massive features carrying in themselves hundreds of lost and irrecoverable faces. In the act of dying, merging with eternity, that face flickers with memories, roams through a series of faces, ever paler, more condensed, until out of the heaping of those faces there settles on it at last, and hardens into its final mask, the countenance of Poland—forever. (*Letters and Drawings*, 62)

Quoted earlier, the essay "The Formation of Legends," written on the occasion of Piłsudski's death, treats greatness in an abstract sense, but also as a counterexample to the lasting effect—personified by Napoleon—Western Europe has had over its central and eastern European other. The receding of individual features that permits a heightening of more massive ones, the merging, condensation, and heaping of Faces into Mask, the expanse of Others that silhouettes a Self: the scandal of (unifying) countenance here we recognize as the scandal of metaphor generally in Schulz. But in this essay and the other two published a year later, "At Belvedere" and "Tragic Freedom," Schulz explores a relationship superfluous to the fiction, between the machinery of mythologization and the formation of a genuine historical, and national, legend in the present moment.

Czesław Z. Prokopczyk, the editor of *Bruno Schulz: New Documents and Interpretations* (in which these essays appear for the first time), cautions against folding Schulz's essayistic discourse into the "migrational" realm of his fictional discourse, in parallel with Schulz's own fairly clear distinction between history in its presentist effect and the workings of myth. In the fiction, the seemingly distant and hieratic realm of myth interpenetrates the quotidian, "worn and tattered" world of the everyday. The very thrust of his literary imagination purposefully *mediates* the two. In the essays on Piłsudski, says Prokopczyk, no bond bridges the gap separating historical greatness (in the figure of the interwar Marshal of Poland) at its lofty height on "an acropolis of the nation" (*Letters and Drawings*, 60) from the ordinary (*New Documents and Interpretations*, 40–42).

In "The Formation of Legends," Schulz defines greatness as legend—"this entity broader and deeper than the nation, at the same time comprising the nation within itself" (*Letters and Drawings*, 60) against the "unending, zealous, subterranean work of smallness" (59) that conspires to reduce and pulverize it. "The human mass resists those who lead it to greatness, especially if that greatness spurns the wiles of seduction, does not wheedle, adulate, or promise. One must surrender one's heart to such greatness if one is to bear it. But who can make up his mind to espouse this sacrificial, unrequited, burning, sublime love? Who can take up its crushing weight for the rest of time?" (60). This essay, written shortly after Piłsudski's death on May 12, 1935, is but a year past Levinas's essay on Hitlerism and two years after Hitler's appointment as *Reichskanzler* of Germany; it is the year the Nuremberg Laws were passed. Yet, "The Formation of Legends" commemorates the lonely, Olympic heroism of Piłsudski, a "towering and inscrutable" figure who "stood beyond" his acts, by contrasting him with the distant figure of Napoleon, "a force of nature in the midst of other forces" and thus a legendary Form who "merged completely with his acts" (61). The one, left unconsumed in death by his deeds and effects, a legend whose "role in history is only beginning"; the other, "all presence and moment, like a splendid set of fireworks with a single mission: to burn itself out utterly."

The tragic irony of Piłsudski's "tragic freedom"—the discrepancy between heroic greatness in history and the national mass it transcends, spiritualizes, and indemnifies—is that after the war, in the socialist interval of the People's Republic of Poland, he was eclipsed entirely, epitomizing *perfectly* Schulz's lament that "there is some elemental pettiness in us that nibbles, gnaws, roots away at the cliff of greatness until finally its is chewed up, ground to bits, dissipated" (59). In "The Formation of Legends," Piłsudski's legacy was to be "sheer continuity," drawing "the past behind him like a vast mantle for all of Poland" (62). In actual fact, from 1944–1989, his name could be uttered publicly, if at all, only in derision.

But only slightly less ironic must be Schulz's choice of Napoleon rather than Adolf Hitler as foil for genuine greatness. Hitler is never mentioned by name in the essay, but then neither is Piłsudski. Levinas's essay attests to the mythic status that had already accreted around the new *Reichsführer*. Schulz's poses a set of antinomies that indirectly cuts to its heart: "Will to power, overweening ambition, usurpation—or ascetic humility, renunciation, total sacrifice of self? Pride in, and contempt for, human beings—or the tenderest love and worship? Self-sufficient aloofness, wrapped up in its own greatness, or the loftiest solidarity with the community? Coarseness or sublimity?" (60). Is the figure of Napoleon in that essay, then, merely a cipher for another (to use the same word Schulz employs for Piłsudski), who was also "all presence and moment," indeed with a decade more of the same in front of him? One can only conjecture.

What can be reasonably ventured, however, does not reflect well on Schulz's philosophy of history, especially in the context of the later essays "Tragic Freedom" and "At Belvedere." (These, possibly because they are reviews of fellow Poles' writings about Piłsudski, concentrate only on the formation of his legend against the backdrop of history without reference to contrastive examples, depicting the Marshal as "ready even during his life . . . a potential myth with elemental promise, unformed dynamics itself moving towards a great legend" [*New Documents and Interpretations*, 44]). Many of Schulz's observations about the history of collective myth in concert with the "great fatality of Polish history, the typical and tragic situation of her history" bear an uncomfortable, eerie resemblance to Levinas's analysis of the rise of National Socialist mythos in Germany in "Reflections on Hitlerism."

"What is History?" asks Schulz (*New Documents and Interpretations*, 43). Levinas answers: "the most profound limitation, the fundamental limitation" (65). Man, "speaking absolutely, has no history" (64). Freedom, "true freedom, the true beginning would require a true present, which always at the peak of a destiny, forever recommences that destiny" (64-65). Schulz answers his own question otherwise. For Schulz, man and history secretly conspire, like clandestine lovers: "The title of a person sometimes is a signboard, under which great and nameless forces of history arrange for themselves a 'rendezvous' leading to epoch making enterprises" (*New Documents and Interpretations*, 52).

Levinas, however, sees a new conception of man on the horizon, in which bodily identity dictates social formation and historical destiny alike, and bondage has replaced freedom.

A society based on consanguinity immediately ensues from this concretization of the spirit. And then, if race does not exist, one has to invent it. . . . It is to such a society that the Germanic ideal of man seems to promise sincerity and authenticity. . . . How is universality compatible with racism? The answer—to be found in the logic of what first inspires racism—involves a basic modification of the very idea of universality. *Universality must give way*

> *to the idea of expansion,* for the expansion of a force presents a structure that is completely different from the propagation of an idea. (69–70)

Ideas work anonymously, equalizing all who propagate and participate in them. Force works in reverse, consolidating unity through a massifying of individual and collective wills. It remains "attached to the personality or society exerting it, enlarging that person or society while subordinating the rest" (70). The universality of an order does not derive from the universality of truth, a process Levinas calls "ideological expansion;" rather, ideological expansion constitutes "the unity of a world of masters and slaves" (71).

Here, on the other hand, is Schulz on the collusion between history and mythic heroism:

> Great causes in history and epoch making operations revolve within a preverbal, extraverbal silence of history. The great moment of action, the thunderclap of strength and will that pierced the flesh of the nation—all that which we attribute today to the name of Piłsudski, was during its course, in its unarticulated actuality stripped of words, totally immersed in biology, in the elements and in vegetative restlessness. . . . In this fact, a deep irony of history expressed itself. The great moment of history, which had been anticipated by an entire century of poetry, fervent contemplations, and daydreams, . . . revealed itself as if beyond this great ideology, as an unfathomable force of nature, offering nothing in rationalizing, comprehending or predicting the great individual. As if life wanted to prove its eternal otherness, and its method of historical realizations both dissimilar from and hostile towards all possible ideology. (*New Documents and Interpretations,* 52)

History and Nature do the propagating or gestating here, providing the seedbed for the legendary individual *avant la lettre*.[83] *Apres l'histoire,* on the other hand, the task falls to the poet and prose writer, to "legalize the irrational," in Schulz's phrase, "to conjure up a compromise with the eternally unutterable" (52). As one such artisan, Schulz can hardly be assailed for his own lyrical attempt, in the Piłsudski essays, to memorialize a figure who personified Poland's brief respite from secondariness, from subordination, from "weakened form." But he may as well be describing himself, not the writer Kazimierz Wierzyński, when he rhapsodizes the poet's bending of historical realities to his rhetorical will: "With the uncanny alchemy of the word, he created a poetical dimension, a mythical reality, in which an outside chronicle of history passes through unseen into its deeper sense, in which a historical fact is lambently permeated by the philosophy of history, outside events by their own lyrical, inner cantilena" (47). This sentence is exquisitely turned, like so many of Schulz's signature stylizations. But it speaks as much to his own extravagance in distending political leadership into the grandiosity—and one must also say, recklessness—of myth, cleaving between it and everyday, ordinary reality according to principles—and a selectivity of historical judgment—that his fiction far more wisely eschews.

Under what Jacques Derrida calls *l'autre cap*,[84]—the "other heading" that is Form—both the diminutions and grandiosities of Polish history and national identity, Poland's mimeticism, its soft and secondary, weakened and derivative quality, can all be made to answer to the saving powers of myth and the artist's lyric intensity. But the shadow of Kristallnacht, of *Konzentration-lager*, of Nazi Germany's impending and inexorable conquest of central and eastern Europe, falls obliquely over these essays in a way that Schulz either did not concern himself with or else purposefully avoided. In "At Belvedere," he speaks of how, "as in a magic portrait," history "incarnates itself, enters the blood and bones of a person . . . [a]nd in a moment individual features are dispersed and dissolved in this portrait and from the abyss surfaces a threatening and unfathomable face of history" (*New Documents and Interpretations*, 52). Just as the body can be not only a happy or unhappy accident, in Levinas's words, so this merger of history and mythic person, of person and body politic, can be genuinely heroic, as in the case of Piłsudski, but also genuinely monstrous.

In his fiction, literary transcendence seems possible for Schulz, if not through the writer's attempt to escape the economy of Forms, then, as we have seen, through shapes that briefly assume a coherent physiognomy and solicit mere acknowledgment, the pathos of patch and fragment—an aching, swollen face. It would be a mistake, I think, to read the essays on Piłsudski from the same vantage. Piłsudski, the face of Poland, may leave in his place a greatness that bears the stamp of his features forever, drawing the past behind him like a vast mantle carrying Poland in its train as well, which itself assumes a countenance, a mask mantling the land. But Piłsudski is not a fictive character, the latter-day counterpart (as many Polish Jews regarded him) to the Emperor Franz Joseph, within whose Austro-Hungarian empire Poland's national identity may have remained occluded but at least untrammeled.

Similarly, while Piłsudski may not himself have been anti-Semitic, and while historically, Polish Jewry enjoyed an intermittently favorable cultural and political climate compared to the rest of Jewish eastern Europe, many political parties in the interwar Republic advocated the forced emigration of Polish Jews and aggressively pursued anti-Jewish measures "designed to eliminate them from Poland's social and economic life."[85] The massacre of Jewish Poles by their fellow Poles in Jedwabne as documented in Jan Gross's *Neighbors*, one year before Schulz's own murder, was only the most gruesome expression of such native-bred eliminationism.[86]

The merged face of Poland's hero and its own hardened mask cannot therefore innocently signal an occasion for transcendence; it does not license a liberating diasporism within the Country of Forms. (One thinks of Levinas's remarks in the essay "Persons or Figures" on Paul Claudel's "freezing" of the Pentateuch's "holy history": "A man as a person, as an agent of history seems to him less real than a figure-man, a statue-man. This freedom proper to conscious man is enveloped in a kind of sublime and sacramental fate in which instead of *being*, man *figures*" [*Difficult Freedom*, 122]; or of the transit from image to caricature to tragedy he analyzes in "Reality and Its Shadow": "In the instant of a statue, in its eternally suspended future, the tragic, simultaneity of necessity and liberty, can come to pass: the power of freedom congeals into impotence" [12].) Indeed, nothing passes more summary judgment on Schulz's rhapsodic, and escapist, fusion of myth and history than the fate of Piłsudski's legend after the war—a deformation to match its formation—and, in Schulz's lifetime and death, the coalescence of Hitler's *figura* with a truly threatening and unfathomable face of history. We need only recall the figure of Dodo from *Sanatorium under the Sign of the Hourglass* "whose mind did not register anything but the present" and whose features were "sculpted into the mask of a great tragedian." For it is also the case that "his face, under its mask of seriousness and sadness broke into frivolous smiles that fought against its usually tragic expression" (*The Complete Fiction*, 276). And yet, for all that, it is a countenance properly left to the fecund escapism of Schulz's fiction or to the spiritualized utopia of a Republic of Dreams. Poland's, between the wars and afterward, is not a face that has looked benignly on Jews like Schulz.

On Gombrowicz it has looked wryly, answering his own grimace with one superimposed upon it by him. For as mimetic farce, history always repeats itself, and since it does so through a ceaseless massing of faces, history wears not the mask of a great tragedian, but rather of Momus, God of parody and mockery. Ultimately more fortunate than

Schulz but so much more an exilic figure, Gombrowicz restlessly exposes the "debilitating mimeticism" (Dorota Głowtska, *Gombrowicz's Grimaces*) he sees at the core of Poland's history. "Having become a tyrannical and grotesque agent of history," writes Głowtska in an essay on Gombrowicz and Schulz, "the Polish tradition can only narcissistically exercise its own empty gestures, in a monstrous spectacle of self-parody" (72). Against such a trend, Gombrowicz "pitches a vision of history as a succession of forms which constantly mock each other and, in a pandemonium of universal mimicry, mutually expose their own artificiality." Anything but mythic, therefore (unless myth is relegated to the jocose) the face of Poland for Gombrowicz would be something rather on the order of the singular "portraits" by the Baroque artist Guiseppe Archimboldo, who constructed human faces out of fruits, vegetables, and fish.

In Gombrowicz's writing, the master-face of Nation or History is itself merely another duel of grimaces, whereas for Schulz, the face can sometimes offer a respite, perhaps even a lucky refuge, from the "other capital" of Form and its tyrannies—but only when it is a common, lowercase, human face, not the hypertrophic visage of Myth or Polish history. With perhaps his own nod to an ante-Napoleon French monarch dubbed "Le Grand," Gombrowicz succinctly puts his authorial and textual *puissance* this way: "*I* am a separate state." Riveted to his Jewishness on the other hand, and married forever to a town, Bruno Schulz intermittently (or continually) escaped it and Poland by sovereignly reimagining them as forms to be unmade and made up all over again. In a last, gruesome twist of fate, Schulz was permitted to dwell in fairyland within the domestic confines of the Nazi Destroyer. In Jaroslaw Anders's fitting words,

> One of the last images of Schulz recorded by Ficowski shows him lying on his back, like Michelangelo in the Sistine Chapel, painting the ceiling in the Gestapo offices in Drohobycz. What was he thinking about? Was the chrysalis finally broken? Was this the helpless insect naked in the storm that was about to crush him and his world? Or was he thinking only about the empty wall to be covered with faces, shapes, the "exuberant mildew" that seemed to hold the promise of "limitless possibilities of being?" We shall never know, and it is hard to tell which of the alternatives is more terrible to contemplate. (41)

Witold Gombrowicz was born on an estate at Maloszyce in southeast Poland, of noble lineage yet surrounded by rustics; lived in Warsaw as a teenager, a country-youth relocated among urban school-fellows; was marginalized yet again by his reluctance to be mobilized during the Polish-Soviet war of 1920; became stranded in Argentina on the eve of World War II, and remained there twenty-four years, establishing substitute but still distant ties; returned to Europe in 1963, four years before his death, an internationally recognized writer. Bruno Schulz lived, wrote, and died in the same small Galician town. Gombrowicz exchanged a European nation he regarded as minor, green, and subordinate, for a Latin American nation in which he found only its *doppelganger*. Schulz remained stuck and cramped in Jewish Southeastern Poland in the 30s and 40s—the wrong place at the wrong time. As the great elegist of Austro-Hungary Joseph Roth pronounced in his evocative little book from between the wars, *The Wandering Jews*, "as long as Jews continue to live in the countries of others, they are required to live and, unfortunately, also to die for these countries."[87] Even in life, Witold and Bruno seem to personify different rhetorical figures, metonymic homelessness on the one hand and metaphoric transmogrification of home, on the other—a distinction that can also, however, be inverted from the vantage of the place rather than the person. For Argentina functioned as Poland's substitution in Gombrowicz's cosmopolitics, just as Drohobycz assumed the metonymic mantle of distilled Polishness for Schulz.

And yet, as Dorota Głowtska observes, each writer insists on the absolute condition of his *midbar:* "Gombrowicz, *persona non grata* among his compatriots in Argentina; and Schulz, self-exiled to the republic of dreams, a wanderer in foreign lands which open up in the heart of his hometown" (*GG*, 84). Between them is suspended the countenance of Poland in the middle decades of the twentieth century, itself Janus-faced and self-estranged, haunted by the death's head of National Socialism at one end and the grimace of Communism at the Other.[88] And for these two dis/mis-located writers from within Poland and from without, metaphor and metonymy, face and grimace, serve, literally at least, as complementary ways to map its features. Europe at mid-century, nationalism as an always unstable fixture of identity, Otherness and 'the minor' as vicissitudes and exigencies within Europe (or between Europes): Gombrowicz makes us see these features as a kind of rictus; Schulz (in his fiction, at least), as a frivolous smile that fights against their usually tragic expression.

And even though Schulz's essays on Piłsudski argue for a hardening of mask onto land as the combined effect of Myth and History, we know he also said, "How naïve and obtuse is the scholastic, academic science of physiognomy that perceives a residue in a facial expression, a layering of multiple grimaces—mere muscle cramps. As if one had to mold expressions on faces, as if they were something else, just the grimace itself." Schulz understood that, akin to the land-mass and boundaries of human countenance, continents are mutable at surface level too, quietly but inexorably shifting tectonically beneath the faces imposed by them by Nation and History, home to "the agitation and turbulence *immanent* to any construction of identity, the *Unheimlichkeit* or uncanniness internal to any and every space we call home" (Santner, 5).

SCENE 7: VISAGE AS ELSEWHERE

His pale flabby face seemed from day to day to lose its outline, to become a white blank with a pale network of veins, like lines on an old map. His face seemed like the breath of a face—a smudge which an unknown passerby had left in the air. From the mist of his face, the protruding white of a pale eye emerged with difficulty, enticing me with a wink. I felt an irresistible sympathy for Emil. . . . But meanwhile, the ghost of a smile which had appeared under Emil's soft and beautiful mustache, the seed of desire which had shown in a pulsating vein in his temple, the tenseness which for a moment had kept his face concentrated, all but fell away again and his face receded into indifference and became absent and finally faded away altogether. (*The Complete Fiction*, 10)

In the writings of these two precariously situated Poles, when the Other Europe, the Minor Europe, the Unbound Europe seeks its face in the mirror, it discovers not a convincing self-portrait but rather sometimes, everything it is not: a here on its way to becoming an elsewhere, a belonging that has already slipped; a face—resembling the lineaments of an old map whose features become increasingly more difficult to read; a country of weakened forms where the East and West soften into each other—resembling a face, with a pale network of veins—like a breath of a face—like a smudge—like a wink from within a mist.

3

Border from Border
Elias Canetti's *The Tongue Set Free* and *The Voices of Marrakesh* and Gregor von Rezzori's *The Snows of Yesteryear*

Despina can be reached in two ways: by ship or by camel. The city displays one face to the traveler arriving overland and a different one to him who arrives by sea. When the camel driver sees, at the horizon of the tableland, the pinnacles of the skyscrapers come into view, the radar antennae, the white and red windsocks flapping, the chimneys belching smoke, he thinks of a ship; he knows it is a city, but he thinks of its as a vessel that will take him away from the desert, a windjammer about to cast off, with the breeze already swelling the sails, not yet unfurled, or a steamboat with its boiler vibrating in the iron keel; and he thinks of all the ports, the foreign merchandise the cranes unload on the docks, the taverns where crews of different flags break bottles over one another's head, the lighted, ground-floor windows, each with a woman combing her hair. In the coastline's haze, the sailor discerns the form of a camel's withers, an embroidered saddle with glittering fringe between two spotted humps, advancing and swaying; he knows it is a city, but he thinks of it as a camel from whose pack hang wineskins and bags of candied fruit, date wine, tobacco leaves, and already he sees himself at the head of a long caravan taking him away from the desert of the sea, toward oases of fresh water in the palm trees' jagged shade, toward palaces of thick, whitewashed walls, tiled courts where girls are dancing bare foot, moving their arms, half-hidden by their veils, and half-revealed. Each city receives its form from the desert it opposes; and so the camel driver and the sailor see Despina, a border city between two deserts.
    Italo Calvino, *Invisible Cities*

Nostography

Another ideogram with two faces, this time a border city between two deserts. But Despina's two countenances are really two vantage points, maritime and terrestrial, envisaged from complementary and reversing distances. Seafarers make out a cityscape as if they had approached by land; overland travelers descry a vista that calls up a vision of the sea. Each type of sojourner prefers an invisible city to the visible one he actually beholds. Each locates a fixed point, a tenor, using coordinates borrowed from the vehicle of the other. Each imagines a mobile oasis to offset the elemental surround of desert. And unknowingly, each—as navigator rather than tourist—performs a synthesis for the discerning third party. Sailor and camel driver bring each other close in the very act of venturing away from their customary selves. Together, they form a caduceus of near and far, native entwined with the alien.

Calvino predicates the city of Despina expressly in terms of *desire*. *Longing* at a near distance, his travelers are awash (or aground) with nostalgia for a home not naturally their own. But as with Moriana and Ersilia previously, we can divert Despina's border qualities to other environs and once again justify the promise made in the introduction to engage in a commerce with the dogma of place that aims beyond. So let Despina's allegory of here-as-elsewhere also tell a story about the machinery of memoir. Let it be about the *memoirist's* desire, about the pull of recall spurred by separation, transposed by writing, in selective dialogue with the annealed or malleable past that is recollection's "cruel partner." Let it be about a different set of discontinuities than land imagined from sea and sea from land. In an essay about memory, place, and return, the author/neurologist Oliver Sacks writes,

> It is thus, discontinuities, the great discontinuities in life that we seek to bridge, reconcile, or integrate, by recollection and, beyond this, by myth and art. Discontinuity and nostalgia are the most profound if, in growing up, we leave or lose the place where we were born or spent our childhood, if we become expatriates or exiles, if the place or the life we were brought up in is changed beyond recognition or destroyed. All of us, finally, are exiles from the past. But this is especially true for [the one] who feels himself the sole survivor and rememberer of a world forever past. ("The Landscape of His Dreams" 169)[1]

Finally, let Calvino's travelers be imagined as not two individuals but one single person at different junctures in a life. Despina would be that life, and the contrasting vantages from which it is viewed would be positioned in time, not space. A border city between two deserts in time, Despina would thus signify half a life, depending on when apprehended—in the present, or many years afterward through imaginative repossession. Sailor and camel driver become complementary halves, a narrating and narrated self, each diacritically completed by the other while still by himself necessarily partial, drawn across the border to his neighbor to borrow image and form.

The East-Central European writers Elias Canetti (1905–1994) and Gregor von Rezzori (1914–1998) take up uncomplicated residence in Calvino's mise-en-scene: two desirers, two hinged and complementary faces, twin "cities" looking upon opposing "deserts." But each is better perceived as looking at his own Despina. Each looks evocatively back upon a yesteryear that is also an elsewhere, a *temps perdu* that doubles for *espace perdue,* the one no less sought after than the other. And as the allusion to Proust intimates, each makes his own bid for redefining or refining a certain literary genre. If the chapter "Place from Place" dwelt upon a Europe extraterritorialized in something like death and haunted afterlife, obsessively circled and trod; and if "Flight from Flight" refracted inner and outer margins of the same Europe through the notion of "evasion," this time not a ceaseless circuit by rail, a *tourniquet,* but a *sens unique,* a one-way street; then "Border from Border" will concentrate on the boundaries of memoir itself.

Both Canetti's and von Rezzori's memoirs depend upon a peculiarly *exterior* sort of narrative (Canetti's resists psychological analysis in the extreme) in which the autobiographer's light is purposefully bent through the prism of formative or subordinate others. Von Rezzori regards his various works of fiction as so many "hypothetical autobiographies" that toy with alternate or "tentative" selves. In turn, he composes his nonfictional personal record in the form of five "portraits for an autobiography" each of which impinges but never comes to center directly upon him. He is not the hero of his own life (after Bakhtin), but rather its narrator, "assimilated, as it were, to its heroes" ("Author and Hero in Aesthetic Activity," 106, 112); or as von Rezzori himself puts it: "I have to mention myself, but I emerge tangentially, by the biographies of others."[2]

Canetti emerges similarly crosshatched between the weft of narrating self and the warp of mentors, progenitors, foils. Goethe may be the explicit model for the memoirs,[3] but Canetti's play of *Dichtung* and

Wahrheit, truth and poetry, owes as much to the modern novel, to Kafka, Karl Krauss, and Isaac Babel, as to Romantic autobiography.[4] One critic has suggested that his prose should be imaged as a kind of physiognomy, with writing thus brokered into an indirect commerce with the face.[5] "That is the *meaning* of the word 'human'," writes Canetti: "each person a midpoint next to countless others, who are midpoints as much as he" (*The Conscience of Words,* 43). On one hand, as "keeper of metamorphoses" (161), dedicated to "keeping people alive by means of words" (*The Human Province,* 70), Canetti develops a repertoire of what he calls "acoustic masks" assembled from the discourse of others (*Memoirs Vol.2: The Torch in My Ear,* 465). On the other hand, with an author's sovereign self-regard he can often reduce others to *just* a voice or a face, some tic or abstraction that serves the needs of self-allegory.[6]

The passage from *The Human Province* just quoted reads in its entirety: "Keeping people alive by means of words—isn't that almost the same as creating them with words?" The difference between sustaining and fabulating is critical, in fact—especially when Canetti blurs it in a work of non-fiction like *Die Stimmen von Marrakesh.* Another of his aphorisms could well serve as prospective indemnification, a pledge to be fulfilled for both that work and his three volumes of memoirs: "True writers encounter their characters only *after* they've created them" (*The Human Province,* 75). This is especially the case for *The Voices of Marrakesh,* a quasi-travel narrative almost wholly figural in its effects. (Because that text merits an extended analysis in its own right, disproportionate attention is given to Canetti over von Rezzori in this chapter.)

Like von Rezzori, Canetti evidently needed the space of literature to meet humanity half way. Or like Gombrowicz, let us say, he used it to bring humanity closer by holding it at a distance. Both memoirists are fascinated by *aura,* the quality that Walter Benjamin connects specifically to distance and gap; they also share a fascination with the principle Canetti termed *Verwandlung,* or metamorphosis. "The chaos of voices and faces in which I used to be at home has become hateful to me," he writes. "I like to experience people individually. When there are several of them, I want to have them sitting next to one another, in an order, as in a train, and I wish to decide what I look at first. Chaos has lost its attraction. I want to order and form and not lose myself in anything anymore"(57–58). Call this the Canettian version of the train-compartment in Argentina. Canetti's memoirs, especially together with *The Voices of Marrakesh* (written a decade earlier), seem designed to perform just this function: to police the borders of self and other.[7]

But this chapter does not coordinate Canetti and von Rezzori solely on their twinned merits as autobiographers. It is, rather, as *nostographers,* recollectors of bygone homelands, fellow travelers to Despina, that they most intriguingly converge.[8] As displaced central and southeastern European *dépaysées après la guerre,* each attempts to retrieve a bygone Europe on the margins and its attenuated conditions of belonging. Theirs will be not just "remembrance of a European childhood" (the subtitle for the first volume of Canetti's memoirs) but also a return to a childhood Europe, "a bygone world, golden and miraculous," (*The Snows of Yesteryear,* 16) in relation to which "The East was threateningly close" (17) and which oversaw the last stirrings of an already outmoded romanticism.

The memoirs, all 832 pages of them covering Canetti's first thirty years, conclude as Canetti leaves Austria on the eve of the *Anschluss.* The first volume, *Die gerettete Zunge: Geschichte einer Jugend* (English title, The tongue set free: history of a childhood), begins with an abandonment and ends with an expulsion; each crisis carries the curse of a parent. *The Voices of Marrakesh,* while not a search for lost time, might well be read as an outline for the void that is Canetti's sense of homeland, as the chapter later suggests. Von Rezzori preserves his native soil in fiction where he tills and tends it more carefully than he can in fact or even in memory. His *Blumen in Schnee,* "Flowers in the Snow" (inaptly replaced by its title in English, The snows of yesteryear, from the famous Francois Villon poem, "Les neiges d'antan") re-narrates successive exiles in all five of its "portraits," culminating in a revisit, sixty year later, to the "Carpathian land that remains my true home" (12)—the same terrain revisited in very different circumstances by Aharon Appelfeld in "Buried Homeland."

That home—Czernowitz in southwest Ukraine (formerly the Kingdom of Romania after the Treaty of Trianon in 1919, formerly part of the Dual Monarchy), on the river Prut at the foot of the Tatra Mountains—is to Canetti's Ruschuk—(Ruse or Roustchouk) in northeast Bulgaria (formerly part of the Turkish Empire), on the Danube bordering Romania—as windjammer is to caravan: land face is to sea face of the same kind of border city, polyglot and provincial outposts in the shadow of waning or moribund Empires. By the time each memoirist looks back at them on paper, their countenances may have still resembled their former selves, but the cities, after successive reterritorializations, have irrevocably changed.

Perhaps not surprisingly, Canetti and von Rezzori were border intellectuals at home in the world, yet seemingly unmoored in everything they wrote. "To get to know countries as if no others existed; but to get to know many" / "The towns one has lived in become neighborhoods in the towns one dies in," wrote Canetti in *The Human Province* (102, 191). Yet for all that, they remain singular cases, "minor" and still somewhat obscure internationalists, writing in the same major language, laying claim to Austrian allegiances, while still somehow remaining at an oblique angle to the established boundaries of a national literature.

Vienna and later London/Zürich became the twin poles for Canetti's artistic and cultural majority, just as German became the adopted tongue that freed his own while England became his adopted home for half a century. Yet, his Ruschuk origins with their Sephardic Ladino and Bulgarian accents signal that the minor in his case also raises the specter of ethnic and religious difference, however muted Jewish identity was to remain in his mature work.[9] For von Rezzori, the minor possesses a double valance, too. Born in that world-changing year of 1914, he, too, resided in Vienna and later West Germany in his maturity, yet he consistently indulged something like Gombrowicz's exilic sensibility of being one's own separate state, belonging, if anywhere, to what he called "the former aristocracy." "You see," he writes, "everybody who reads my books will understand that it is extremely menacing for someone to be born in a place and then to be suddenly taken from it. . . . I am genuinely the most displaced person I know" ("Conversations," 13).[10]

But like Gombrowicz, von Rezzori's upbringing was by accident of heritage and later by national conflict, consigned to a region of weakened form, as the latter puts it, "a colony deserted by its colonial masters" (*The Snows of Yesteryear*, 65). Czernowitz in the Bukovina, as we already know from the example of Aharon Appelfeld, is one of east-central Europe's marginocentric cities, the effect of continually redrawn territorial borders and shifts of national sovereignty, with a "multifarious population of not one but half a dozen nationalities, with not one but half a dozen religions, and with not one but half a dozen tongues" (36).[11] Von Rezzori's family was twice consigned to internal exile: "declared [(and déclassé)] former Austrians" within a "Balkanic backwater" after the collapse of the Hapsburg Monarchy in 1918; and the same again, upon the yoking of the Austrian rump state to Nazi Germany, twenty years afterward.

"We lived in the Bukovina—more radically than would have been the case elsewhere—as the flotsam of the European class struggle, which is what the two great wars really were" (200). Though the graft of "von" and "Rezzori" may conjure up an Austrianized lineage of Sicilian nobility—von Rezzori calls his father "a representative of the Baroque who had landed in the wrong century" (*The Snows of Yesteryear*, 157)—by the time of Gregor's birth such privilege has shrunken to the much smaller dimensions of cultivated anachronism and pseudo-feudalism in the Ruthenian hinterland. Likewise, through marital *mésalliance*, his mother forfeits her haute-bourgeois pedigree relished in a youth spent in Occidental spa culture for a peripheral and periodically refugee lifestyle in relocation camps and "other people's houses" amidst "the dubious shakiness of one of those successor states described, rather derogatorily, as the Balkans" (28).

At their closest, even if that closeness still tastes tartly of differences, Canetti and von Rezzori keep pace with each other as fellow nostographers of their own past. They knowingly reconstruct their early lives in text as a border city between two deserts, the *midbar* of birthplace and background and the *midbar* of exile and denationalization. The terminal counter-Proustian sentences of both their memoirs can thus be heard as very nearly hailing each other, ghost ship to phantom caravansary. Von Rezzori: "You must never undertake the search for time lost in the spirit of nostalgic tourism" (*The Snows of Yesteryear*, 290). Canetti: "It is true that I, like the earliest man, came into being only by the expulsion from Paradise"(*The Tongue Set Free*, 268). They mean those admonitions as chastisements for their readers as well. Peremptorily, Rezzori says, "It is also my task as a twentieth century writer to disabuse and disillusion nineteenth century readers" ("Conversations," 23). Likewise, writes Canetti, "In a diary, one talks to oneself. The man who cannot do this, who sees an audience before him, even a later one, even after his death, is a forger. Such forged diaries are not the issue here. They too can have their value. Some of them are incredibly fascinating; their interest lies in the extent of the forgery: their attraction depends on the forger's talent" ("Dialogue with the Cruel Partner," *The Conscience of Words*, 44).

Consequently, the heading for this fourth chapter of *The Elsewhere*, "Border from Border," does triple duty. It signifies the writing of nostalgia as "nostography," the return to a lost world, its components "charged like a Leyden flask with the very essence of an era" (*The

Snows of Yesteryear, 207). It insinuates either the lay and the shift of land regularly unbound or re-constellated—like the "no-man's land between the cultures of West and East" of von Rezzori's Czernowitz, with its "leadenly nostalgic character, heavy with empty longings" (*The Snows of Yesteryear*, 121), or simply civilization at a limit point—like Canetti's Ruschuk, which "began where the Turkish Empire had once ended," and from whose margins "the rest of the world was known as 'Europe'" (*The Tongue Set Free*, 5). And lastly, it refers to the autobiographical pact itself cleaved by literary memoir, a dialogue with a sometime cruel partner.[12] It therefore most especially recalls Paul de Man's troubled condition of autobiography as "not a genre or a mode, but a figure of reading or of understanding."

It must be acknowledged that readers of Canetti and von Rezzori may lay claim to a troubled condition of their own. One perhaps does not expect two such practiced cultivators of the concrete to be from time to time such zealous, even tyrannical "slaves of the abstract" (von Rezzori's phrase). The Canetti of the memoirs comes across as unnervingly self-important. His narrative stance in *The Voices of Marrakesh*, though more opaque, is no less studied. In life he was reputed to be sometimes harsh and autocratic, a trader in charisma as well as its keen analyst.[13] Once set free, he had a tongue that "reaches to hell" (*The Human Province*, 273). And while praised by many critics for his attention to particulars, his character portraits often run the risk of becoming so many metaphors of self.

With his chill powers of observation, Von Rezzori can appear similarly calculating and aloof. He describes himself in the text as prone to "a fatal indifference, an innate indolence of soul" (*The Snows of Yesteryear*, 248). Each "autobiographical portrait"—of mother, father, sister, nursemaid, and governess, exactly *because* of the studied decentering (a kind of *trompe "l'oreille"*) that frames it—bows finally before the *Diktat* of vaunted self-ambiguity, kept alive with words but also made more vulnerable that way:

> I had before me an 1873 issue of *Over Land and Sea*. From its yellowed pages rose a subtly musty whiff. A foxed steel engraving of a three-master with reefed sails in a small palm-fanned harbor in front of a background of steep volcanic cones—this lured my imagination into the airy remoteness of spiced shores. But there remained a floating core of consciousness filled with nothing but a transparent void—I would have called it my "I," had I been asked—that was neither here nor there but, instead, in an anguished and tormenting nowhere. (*The Snows of Yesteryear*, 108)[14]

One may think, perhaps contrastingly, of Nabokov's *Speak Memory*, a benchmark for nostalgic though clear-sighted reverie in which mastery of the concrete prevails over subjugation to the abstract. Or because Nabokov plays a recurrent and allusive role in *The Emigrants*, W. G. Sebald may come to mind, a kindlier, gentler purveyor of the posthumous sublime.[15]

Yet, no doubt, prose like von Rezzori's above supplies its own bona fides. And as to any ambivalence each author may generate, readers must content themselves in this chapter with the unexpected horizons, as if one were approaching Despina, discovered in the wake of critical intervention. One such landscape is a poetics of language pressed into a very special kind of service, made *representative* in the dual sense of standing for and in lieu of home and polity. That it happens to be the same language for both Canetti and von Rezzori is certainly no accident as regards their pairing here. Von Rezzori hoarded the German tongue as a linguistic inheritance that, after small exiles and repatriations whereby his family was successively redefined as distantly Romanian, then former Imperial Austrian but now Occidental, and then Eastern all over again, comes to seem the only nonspurious birthright for "a dying and largely superannuated caste" (*The Snows of Yesteryear*, 240). The contrast with Aharon Appelfeld, a fellow Czernowitzer, could not be starker.

When von Rezzori speaks of being in a state of "cultural pupation" in his youth, "from which we freed ourselves only gradually, through increasing our knowledge and deepening our insights" (239), linguistic mastery represents not the least of these instruments of liberation.[16] Canetti made himself an author in a German he had to *acquire;* many years afterward, in an address at the Bavarian Academy of the Fine Arts, he still refers to himself as "only a guest in the German language" (*The Conscience of Words*, 140).[17] Taught him by his mother, German defines his bond both to her and to those other figures of power who assume her place later in his life.

Canetti makes language an overt topic in *The Tongue Set Free,* several essays, many of his notations, and throughout *The Voices of Marrakesh*. In *The Human Province*, for example, it seems to means at least three things: 1) heterogeneity (or in Canetti's jargon, "plurinationalism") (*The Human Province*, 57); 2) penumbra—the shadow of silence lapping at the borders of language from its other side; and 3) that which substitutes for physical place when it has been subtracted or abandoned. Here are three aphoristic examples:

—The various languages you ought to have: one for your mother, which you subsequently never speak again; one which you only read but never dare to write; one in which you pray but without understanding a single word; one in which you do arithmetic and to which all money matters belong; one in which you write (but no letters); one in which you travel, and in this one you can also write letters. (*The Human Province*, 7)

—With every thought, the important thing is what it leaves unsaid, how much it loves the unsaid, and how close it comes to it without touching it. (*The Human Province*, 29)

—The language of my intellect will always remain German—because I am Jewish. Whatever remains of the land which had been laid waste in every way—I wish to preserve it in me as a Jew. *Their* destiny too is mine; but I bring along a universal human legacy. I want to give back to their language what I owe it. I want to contribute to their having something that others can be grateful for. (*The Human Province*, 53)

But perhaps a narrative example is more apropos. In *The Tongue Set Free*, Canetti portrays his elderly Bulgarian grandfather on a visit to Vienna and coordinates speaking across borders, on the one hand, with actually traversing them, on the other. As such, it offers a small parable of free and unfree modes of utterance, of "the indefatigable man" from a superseded generation who feels at home in the world, and the parent who restricts that same world to less linguistically heterogeneous, more manageably domestic confines.

One of Grandfather's most conspicuous traits was his indefatigability; he, who otherwise seemed so Oriental, was always on the move. No sooner did we think he was in Bulgaria than he popped up again in Vienna, soon taking off for Nurenberg (which he pronounced *Nürimberg* instead of *Nürnberg*). But he also traveled to many other cities, which I can't recall, because he never mispronounced their names badly enough for me to notice. How often did I run into him on *Praterstrasse* or some other street in Leopoldstadt: he was always hurrying.... He tried to speak to all people in *their* language, and since he had learned only these languages on the side, while traveling, his knowledge of them, except of the Balkan languages (which included his Ladino), was highly defective. He liked counting his languages off on his fingers, and the droll self-assurance in toting them up—God knows how, sometimes seventeen, sometimes nineteen languages—was irresistible to most people despite his comical accent. I was ashamed of these scenes when they took place in front of me, for the speech was so bristling with mistakes that he would have been flunked by Herr Tegel in my elementary school, not to mention our home, where Mother corrected our least errors with ruthless derision. On the other hand, we restricted ourselves to four languages in our home, and when I asked Mother if it was possible to speak seventeen languages, she said, without mentioning Grandfather: "No, for then you know none at all!" (*The Tongue Set Free*, 87)[18]

To speak in Canetti's world means fundamentally (as Bakhtin might put it), to *choose* a language. And choosing a language means choosing also the place to speak it, a neighborhood, a city, a nation, a land, or in Canetti's case, an entire continent. After his parents move to England in 1911, Canetti relates the following anecdote:

George, the youngest brother, was a very lovely child, with dark eyes and pitch-black hair. Father taught him his first words. Every morning, when he came into the nursery, the same dialogue always went on between them, and I listened in suspense: "Georgie?" said Father in an urgent and quizzical tone of voice, to which George replied: "Canetti"; "Two?" said my father, "Three," said the child; "Four?" said my father, "Burton, " the child, "Road," said my father. Originally, that was all there was. But gradually, our address was completed, it came, with allotted voices: "West," "Didsbury," "Manchester," "England." The last word was mine, I wouldn't give it up, I added "Europe."

Cultural affiliations and cosmopolitan fidelities ensure that, indeed, he never will give it up, a totemic kind of last word (however he may have stood European culture on its head).[19]

Von Rezzori, too, connects language with the formative figures of his early life. The most emblematic of these is certainly his wet-nurse Cassandra, an almost mythically telluric and precultural figure, fully at home in the Carpathians, possessed of a disorderly farrago of dialects, "the mediator of the reality all around" (12)—but also "the distorted funhouse-image of each of us" (13). Her physical presence is arresting—almost Schulzian in its grotesqueness—but it is her peculiar relationship to language that gives her naturalistic powers their real edge. There is orality that seems to know no borders: "Our mother neither spoke nor understood any of the local languages. Although German had been the official idiom in the Bukovina during the Austrian era, that language became increasingly mangled and incomprehensible, both to us and to the variegated nationals, the deeper one penetrated into the Bukovina. Cassandra, on the other hand, who spoke no language correctly, expressed herself in snatches of Romanian, Ruthenian, Polish, and Hungarian, as well as Turkish and Yiddish, assisted by a grotesque, grimacing mimicry and a primitive, graphic body language" (8). And there is a concomitant repudiation of written language and reading as *all* bourne and border, the undiscovered country from which no traveler returns intact:

> That certain things had been recorded between the covers of these books which could be grasped mentally and transformed into speech and knowledge by initiates in the shamanic craft of coding and decoding these runic symbols—this could only understood as a supernatural phenomenon. . . . She realized that for those who acquired it, the ability to read conferred power over those to whom the written or printed word remained a sealed mystery. But she also knew that this was a power pertaining to black-magic—that it turns against its own practitioners and transforms them into slaves of the abstract. She saw in it a truly devilish power, since its manipulators, who also were its most immediate victims, were not even aware of its nefarious effects. (33)

Cassandra's uncivilized plenitude makes her a living metaphor for physical place, embodiment, and Babel, and von Rezzori makes his compound identification with her absolute: [20]

> I cannot disassociate the memory of Cassandra from that of the landscape that nurtured her, the land whence she had come to us. . . . Cassandra could not turn away from that perspective without a deep sorrowful sigh, as if she saw herself as a wanderer on the wide dusty road between the poplars, forever drawn by her own inescapable destiny. And each time she would clasp me in her long simian arms only to thrust me away abruptly, as if pushing me out of her life. . . . And because I sensed this in my innermost self, I also took up life as if it were but a succession of leave-takings in the course of a long journey. (43)

> Even though it may be questioned whether I was actually fed at Cassandra's breast, there can be no doubt that linguistically I was nourished by her speech. (44)

> Through her speech patterns, and prodded and guided by my father, we developed a rare awareness of language, an almost maliciously acute way to listen to the spoken word and an interpretive feeling for written expression, to a degree that otherwise I have encountered only in students of Karl Krauss, whose linguistic education certainly was less fun than ours, even though it stemmed mainly from the satirical pointing up of the ridiculous and the corrupted. (45)[21]

(Coincidentally enough, Canetti was one such student.[22])

For really, what *The Tongue Set Free* and *The Snows of Yesteryear* rehearse for us is a myth of language and its mastery. It is to be sure a staple of romantic autobiography—the genesis of a writer as he gains a foothold in the terrain of expression—but it also represents a particular subgenre we might call "language-memoir."[23] As opposed to, say, Bruno Schulz, for whom imagination requires the "migration of forms" but who himself almost never left his hometown, what catalyzes Canetti's and von Rezzori's acts of autobiography is migration *in fact*—the dissolution of real borders, expatriation, exodus, an aesthetic of alienation. And while each writer superimposes upon the lived past an ordering design, enabling the autobiographic project, as de Man would say, to "produce" the life, each still makes a firm pact with realism. By circumstance, neither writer is able to stay put.

Moreover, neither writer appears isolated for very long. And so, in addition to the shared story of the tongue set free through authorship, their memoirs narrate the common thread of becoming a stranger to oneself while surrounded, overwritten (if it may be put this way) by the company of others. In his address "The Writer's Profession," Canetti says, "This I think would be the true task of the *Dichter*. That gift, once universal, but now doomed to atrophy, has to be preserved by any means possible; and the *Dichter,* thanks to that gift, ought to keep the accesses *between* people open. He should be able to become *anybody and everybody,* even the smallest, the most naïve, the most powerless person" (*The Conscience of Words,* 242).

This is the Canettian principle of metamorphosis, the topical province of literary artists like Ovid, like Kafka, but also the measure of what authors *do* when they identify with others, interrelating them, making them coalesce and exceed their borders. In place of hermetic-demiurgic freedom, we get the dual transformative power of cultural myth, which the *Dichter* appropriates "through the inspirations of his readings," on the one hand, and his own personal history, on the other, whose dramatic potential "he appropriates through his openness to people around him now." Family others, ethnic others, the otherness of language or land: each of these is another "border" to be crossed and renegotiated.

This chapter's foray into the writing of *midbar,* then, will revisit the semantic borderline that splices the word "midbar" itself, which we can think of as one more Despina with two faces, into its neighboring connotations in Hebrew, "wilderness" and "speech." But first it must pass the checkpoint separating flexible past from hard present, and so we turn there next, focusing on Canetti's *The Tongue Set Free* and notations, and von Rezzori's *The Snows of Yesteryear.* The chapter concludes with a separate discussion of Canetti's *The Voices of Marrakesh.* For of all the cities found and lost in this chapter, Marrakesh, through Canetti's strange appropriation of it, is the one that most closely resembles Despina, that city of desire.

Visitable Pasts

"I delight in a palpable imaginable *visitable* past," writes Henry James in the preface to *The Aspern Papers,* one of his most celebrated elsewhere-texts:

> —in the nearer distances and the clearer mysteries, the marks and signs of a world we may reach over to as by making a long arm we grasp an object at the other end of our own table. The table is the one, the common expanse, and where we lean, so stretching, we find it firm and continuous. That, to my imagination, is the past fragrant of all, or of almost all, the poetry of the thing outlived and lost and gone, and yet in which the precious element of closeness, telling so of connexions but tasting so of differences, remains appreciable. With more moves back the element of the appreciable shrinks— just as the charm of looking over a garden-wall into another garden breaks down when successions of walls appear. The other gardens, those still beyond, may be there, but even by use of our longest ladder we are baffled and bewildered—the view is mainly a view of barriers. The one partition makes the place we have wondered about *other,* both richly and recognizably so; but who shall pretend to impute an effect of composition to the twenty? We are divided of course between liking to feel the past strange and liking to feel it familiar; the difficulty is, for intensity, to catch it at the right moment when the scales of the balance hang with the right evenness. (*The Art of the Novel,* 164)

In James's preface, as in his novella, landscape is foreshortened to the nearer distance of street and alley—desert expanse, not a homeland lost but rather manageable interior space, and even more intimately, a table on which perhaps to eat or write. Beyond, at most, are other gardens, in adjoining or nearby villas, in the same district of the same city. A Venetian closeness defines the limits of the strange as well as the familiar. The occasional expatriate is met with, but for all its exotic and liminal promise of farther distances and obscurer mysteries (after all, Calvino's Marco Polo is Venice's native son), this border city domesticates gradations of space and time alike; it brings them inside. Venice is Despina faced in on itself, self-nostalgic, impatient with deserts of any kind.

Neither Canetti nor von Rezzori revisits his past in this manner. (But then, neither author tales his cue from Anglo-American modernism but, rather, from German novels by the likes of Mann, Musil, Joseph

Roth, and Karl Krauss.) The yesteryear-elsewheres of Czernowitz and Ruschuk elicit recollection from a vanishing point, not a nearer and clearer distance. Indeed, the regions themselves, and the personal pasts and superseded Europes they represent, seem to wander off in the very attempt made to recover them nostalgically. For example, "The core of my being had been left behind in a lost, homefelt at-homeness in Bukovina, remembrance of which I could no longer summon up; even less could I have demonstrated that it more than a phantom, an illusion, a myth of myself. I was in the Bukovina in as abstract a way as I was in that far-off exotic harbor [pictured in the old magazine] or with boys playing games... whom I fancied roaming the exotic streets of that exotic harbor town" (*The Snows of Yesteryear*, 111). It is this quality of abstraction (as von Rezzori calls it) in the midst of concrete reminiscence that bestows a kind of twilight patina on a more or less sunlit diurnal narrative.

What, then, should we make of Elias Canetti's stark claim at the beginning of *The Tongue Set Free:* "Anything I had subsequently experienced had already happened in Ruschuk" (4)?[24] No less dramatic are Canetti's vaunted powers of recall: "The events of those years are present to my mind in all their strength and freshness (I've fed on them for over sixty years), but the vast majority are tied to words that I did not know at the time."[25] We might feel warranted in seizing on such an announcement as a perfect instance of blindness masked as insight, autobiography's double-bind.[26] But Canetti simply affirms, "It seems natural to me to write them down now; I don't have the feeling that I am changing or warping anything" (10). The caravans of youth, it seems, remain palpable even when one has long since booked passage on windjammer, as do the sailing ships when one has long since crossed overland by camel.

If we are not in a position to gainsay Canetti's claim, still the entire first section of the memoirs, "Ruschuk," does support it inasmuch as the quick succession of character sketches establishes the compositional strategy for the rest of the text. In short order we meet his parents; the indigent store employee Chelebon, treated like a servant by the grandfather but actually his brother; the Armenian servant who fled to Bulgaria after witnessing his family's murder in Istanbul; *Kako la Gallinica*, the village idiot transformed into a chicken by the jeers of children; Bulgarian girls who tell fairy tales about wolves and vampires, another model for metamorphosis; Gypsies and Turks; "two grandfathers"; two younger brothers; and cousin Laurica, whom Canetti threatens to kill with the Armenian's ax, because she taunts him with writing held just out of reach.

The last of these vignettes, "The Murder Attempt," ends on a mysterious note. "No one recognized the connection between my murderous goal and the fate of the Armenian. I loved him, his sad songs and words. I loved the ax with which he chopped wood" (30). Should *we* have recognized the connection? *Would* we, had Canetti not interposed to tell us that there is one? And precisely, which connection? The "sad Armenian . . . the first refugee in my life" (12), is a semaphore thrown up by the text for just two paragraphs before he disappears entirely from it. He sings sad songs for his murdered sister as he chops wood, he turns to five-year old Canetti and smiles as he lifts his ax, he "exchange[s] a few words, but very few, and I don't know what the language was" (12).

We wonder where to establish the link. Perhaps it is the common element of violence and murder, anecdotally reported in the one case, threatened or pantomimed in the other (later in *The Tongue Set Free,* in a section entitled " Getting Ready for Prohibitions," Canetti says that the lasting effect of this event was "the actual, the primal prohibition in my life: the prohibition to kill" [27]). It may be a matter of gesture—the fact that Laurica lifts her school primers ("'Let me see the writing,' I begged the instant she appeared," [29]) far over her own head, in echo of the Armenian's movement as he lifts his ax to chop wood. It may signify language in a plainer sense, in obscure alliance with homicide and desire. Or it can simply denote garden-variety transference, and thus unnecessary to explicate in the narration.

Equilibrating the two, Canetti says plainly, "my murderous goal and the fate of the Armenian." The *goal* is voiced repeatedly and even italicized: "'*Agor vo matar a Laurica! Agor vo matar a Laurica!*'—'Now I'm going to kill Laurica! Now I'm going to kill Laurica!'" (29), an objective foiled by the intervention of Canetti's grandfather. The *fate* might mean a number of things: exile, melancholy, subservience, foreignness. Maybe the connection, finally, is just the object itself, the ax that condenses significations—a symbol of dimly understood violence, an activity accompanied by song, an instrument of rage against powerlessness, also linked with human expression, a prefiguring of the future author's pen. Alternatively, "the goal" could simply be the wish to master the power of "magic language" (22)—what von Rezzori called a "shamanic craft," a "supernatural phenomenon"—and "the fate" would portend humanity reduced through privation and extremity to pure sound.

We remain unsure of the precise connection.²⁸ But more intriguing is Canetti's emphasis that there is one, insinuating there is more to his memoirs than mere story, and demonstrating it through his own agency as *revisitor*. In "The Writer's Profession," he speaks of "the force of the characters that have come to tenant him, who do not abandon the space they now occupy in him. They react out of him, as though he consisted of them. They are his majority, articulated and conscious, they are—since they *live* in him—his resistance to death (244). So the Armenian recalled is a small battle waged against oblivion, with Canetti wielding both hatchet and jointure, the woodcraft of authorship.

Ruschuk also signifies a linguistic divide that Canetti will successfully traverse and to which his writing at this very moment in the memoirs, seven decades after leaving his birthplace, explicitly attests. He will spend only the first six years of his life in Bulgaria (as von Rezzori will spend only his first ten in Czernowitz). His departure coincides with the equally important rubicon of choosing German as retroactive mother tongue.²⁹

> I heard [fairy tales] in Bulgarian, but I know them in German; this mysterious translation is perhaps the oddest thing I have to tell about my youth, and since the language history of most children runs differently, perhaps I ought to say more about it. . . . All events of those first few years were in Ladino or Bulgarian. It wasn't until much later that most of them were rendered into German within me. Only especially dramatic events, murder and manslaughter so to speak, and the worst terrors have been retained by me in their Ladino wording, and very precisely and indestructibly at that. Everything else, that is, most things, and especially anything Bulgarian, like the fairy tales, I carry around in German. (10)

It is a strange sentence, really: "especially anything Bulgarian, . . . I carry around in German." Words carry with them the places they have been—as though they were their own saddlebags, or caravanserai, or steamboats.³⁰ But Canetti seems to be saying that carrying Bulgarian quiddity around in German vocabulary is more akin to embalming it with preservative or sheathing it with polyurethane. *"Agor vo matar a Laurica! Agor vo matar a Laurica!"* or *"Kako la Gallinica!"* the Ladino exclamations of his youth that wounded like weapons, remain with Canetti as first heard or spoken. The other events, most things, have been made to speak in a foreign tongue instead: "The vast majority tied to words I did not know at the time."

Canetti himself calls this revoicing of the past notably odd, and it certainly is when we consider that visiting the past means subjecting it to translation. It suggests something like the linguistic analog to the small lesson in perspective that commences Benjamin's *A Berlin Chronicle*. His child's eyes staring at the statuary fronting the approach to the Tiergarten, Benjamin finds not the towering figures of Frederick William III or Queen Louise but rather the *plinths* on which they stand, "since the events taking place on them, if less clear in their ramifications, were closer in space" (*Selected Writings*, 595). Exchanging, so to speak, Bulgarian figure for German plinth, Canetti likewise substitutes the nearer for the farther, without, it appears, incurring any loss in clarity.[31] As James would say, he finds delight in the nearer distances, which are also the clearer mysteries.

When von Rezzori visits his past, it is speech—in the form of Cassandra's patched and polychromic linguistic garb—that establishes its coordinates, and sound that records it nostographically. In the chapter on his governess Bunchy who becomes the counterpart to Cassandra in his adolescence, he explains why "the evocation of Bunchy's dark-colored voice and her guttural good humored laugh brings her back to me with all the fullness of her wise presence" and how it is "that she remains more vivid in my aural memory than my visual one": "—this in accordance with the former's multidimensional impact in depth, which invests the sudden sounding of a long-forgotten musical motif with the power to bring forth the very essence of an entire period, and in a richer, emotionally more lasting way than any visually remembered object" (246). A long list follows, a rendition of the varied "acoustic banalities" that counterpoint von Rezzori's "sentimental biography"—the crack of gunshots, the rhythmic creaking of saddles. Affection for his governess prompts him to reconnect with his childhood induction into the wilderness of language when Bunchy asks him to "translate for her the German-Romanian-Ukranian-Yiddish linguistic salad I had inherited from Cassandra" (247), though such translation signals that (as von Rezzori remarks in another context) this linguistic inheritance had entered the flow of time, had become history and was no longer myth. "We spoke of myths and I found myself thinking how you had opened my eyes about Cassandra's fairy tales. Up to then, everybody merely doubled over when I retold these in her own linguistic mishmash. That they contained something very beautiful, that their distortion through Cassandra's impish spirit held great fascination—only you saw this. . . . If you ask me now what I believe in, I'm tempted to say the magic of words" (255).

Beyond the magic of words, however, or rather, in a domain that has no need of sound to trigger and recapture it, lies the ramified past improbably preserved, "charged like a Leyden flask with the very essence of an era." Von Rezzori's literal re-visitation of it crowns his autobiography. He introduces it by rehearsing the history of Czernowitz, quickly noting that everything in his summary "is designated as 'former,' that is to say, not in the present, not truly existing" (276). This mythic, irreal quality, together with a hiatus of more than fifty years since he last set foot there, prompts him to muse, "It began to sound as if I had invented Czernowitz—and with it, myself" (277).

As he goes on to say, he did indeed invent such a place in the form of the fictive Czernopol that forms the background to three of his novels, the literary transposition of his hometown "as a scaffolding on which to model a mythic site in which mythical events take place" (277). But reality would have its due, and so von Rezzori, after a half a century, makes the return journey home. "Naturally, I had to assume that the Ukrainian Chernovtsy of 1989, cleansed of its hodgepodge of Swabian Germans, Romanians, Poles, Jews, Prussians, Slovaks, and Armenians, could no longer be the Czernowitz or Cernauti that I had last visited in 1936 (278). The assumption proves mistaken. Cleansed the former provincial capital had been, of both its former multiethnic population and the expected accretion of dirt and grime. Freshly painted and well-manicured it had been rendered. But it was nevertheless recognizably the hometown of von Rezzori's childhood and his memory, "tangibly real and concrete." (Sound, however, is one of the notable elements missing for him.[32])

No longer the mythic capital of memory but rather "the quintessence of a provincially solid, bright, and well-kept township," it strikes von Rezzori as nothing so much as a forgery, a conquering of the nostalgic imagination by unwittingly fictionalizing fact: "Not that it had been arrested in its evolution, but rather that it had been backdated, as it were, beyond it. The present-day Czernovtsy was a repudiation both of the interwar Cernauti and of the imperial Austrian Czernowitz. In its unaltered surface permanence it had reverted to an abstract, powerfully idyllic Belle Époque, a founders'-era dream of itself, but without spirit and life" (281). What von Rezzori beholds is a Despina despoiled of its denizens, "the stage-setting of a play that had never been produced, a cleaned-up spit-and-polish, lacquered and antiseptic city." Indeed, it was very simply a Czernowitz without Czernowitzers. Homogeneity had replaced the "furiously fermenting," multiethnic human counterpart to Cassandra's linguistic salad. The Jews that had made the city a byword for an unmistakable type of individual were conspicuous only by their absence. Stale nationalism had taken the place of a homegrown skepticism that set Czernowitz's former inhabitants apart: "Any true Czernowitzer watched an exhibition of overflowing nationalistic sentiment with no greater personal involvement than that which he reserved for the Purim masquerade put on by street urchins" (282).

Von Rezzori writes, "I was there and yet I was not" (286)—a demi-dreamscape finally undone by the rude awakening that "of all the houses in Czernowitz, of which not a stone seemed out of place, my house was the only one missing" (286). But instead of being distressed, von Rezzori finds himself oddly comforted by the notion that his childhood home had thereby turned into irreality and pure myth. "So be it!" he concludes. "It was indeed in the realm of the unbelievable and fabulous that my own Czernopol, the imagined counterpart of the factual Czernowitz, was located" (290).

What he glimpses through this wholly unexpected reencounter with a nearly exact duplicate of the past is the fundamental ir-re-place-ability of human others, their endowing of place with substance and meaning. The search for lost time, motivated perhaps by "the spirit of nostalgic tourism" (290), fails if it finds only an allegorical landscape, as if it were one of Calvino's invisible cities. The view, to adapt Henry James's images, becomes a view of barriers, the garden wall opening onto only a succession of further walls. For James, of course, it is the single partition that successfully "makes the place we have wondered about *other*" (*The Art of the Novel*, 164). This is "the precious element of closeness" vouchsafed us if we take no more than one move back.

What made Czernowitz Czernowitz, and thus *other* and proximate was its human partition, its mottled scrim of Swabian Germans, Romanians, Poles, Jews (especially Jews), Prussians, Slovaks, and Armenians—a roster to which one must also add Ruthenians (Appelfeld's quintessential Other), a former minority "in a place where there was no majority" that in von Rezzori's revisit accounts for all of Chernovtsy's present inhabitants. Cassandra is the epitome of that no longer proximate, *unvisitable* past, and her fate, we learn, was of a piece with that of the Bukovina's Jews: "for the ethnic mishmash of her component parts was as variegated as her language; it allowed neither racial classification, nor, as its consequence, relocation" (132). "Proximity" thus acquires its relational significance—both spatial and ethical—only as a category of the interhuman, or, taking a page from de Certeau, we should construe the "space" that substantifies and actuates a "place" as the sum of its demographic parts.[33]

A tableau in *The Snows of Yesteryear* sheds particularly illuminating light on this crucial element. Following his parents' divorce, resituated along with his mother and sister in the very heart of Czernowitz where they are effectively surrounded by Jewish houses and places of worship, von Rezzori recounts a brief episode very nearly Gombrowiczian in its mock-combat and spirit of face-off. Climbing up to the stable roof, and from there to the roofs of neighboring buildings, von Rezzori espies a boy a few years older "with a highly sensitive pale face under smooth black hair" who "would sit immobile and read, turning pages with a sparse motion of his thin hand" (124).

Feeling spited by having his presence go unacknowledged, von Rezzori takes up what he supposes to be a challenge: "I brought my own books to the tin roof, sat down facing him and read in imitation of him.... I read against the young Jewish scholar, so to say, in mute competition; a duel in which, however, he refused to participate." A single verbal exchange concludes the episode, "eerily, on the very day I dared to get a volume of Dostoevsky from my mother's books," after which his roof expeditions are placed under interdiction. "'What's he reading?' he asked without so much as looking at me. 'Dostoevsky,' I relied casually. 'A step forward, I'd say,' he commented with cutting irony. That was all. Nothing more; no word, no further sign of noticing me.... I never again saw my reading companion, but our encounter prompted me to read all of Dostoevsky" (124).

If we venture to see this anecdote as a kind of bridge between the language acquisition nourished by Cassandra and its more sophisticated distillation under the tutelage of Bunchy, the very outlines of Czernowitz become filled in, "spatialized"(in de Certeau's sense), by a symbolic scene of reading that doubles as a scene of encounter. That the episode is prompted by von Rezzori's chafing at being confined to his house's garden makes the comparison with James's preface that much more happily apropos. For here, indeed, "the one partition makes the place we have wondered about *other*, both richly and recognizably so." The pivot between liking to feel the past strange and liking to feel it familiar in such a moment in von Rezzori's text is engineered, through recollection, by means of the (human) figure that differentiates a (merely topographic) ground.

Canetti also returned home, to Bulgaria, in 1924, where he planned a voyage down the Danube and to stay with family in Sofia; Ruschuk, he tells us, was not to be part of the itinerary. Not surprisingly, then, the relevant chapters from *The Torch in My Ear*, "The Final Danube Voyage; The Message" and "The Orator" say almost nothing about Bulgaria the place. Characteristically, the focal point in the first chapter is an advocate/adversary, the Ruschuk physician who brought Canetti into the world and whom he unexpectedly encounters on board ship. The discourse covers territory already narrated in *The Tongue Set Free:* Canetti's scalding, when his father saved his life by returning from England; his father's sudden death, not long after being cursed by Canetti's grandfather for deciding to emigrate from Bulgaria; the burden of patrimony.

"The Orator" refers to Bernhard Arditti, one of several impassioned Zionists who zealously attempt to convince their compatriots to emigrate to Palestine. We hear of the complacent and exclusivist Sephardic community won over by Arditti's sheer fieriness and of Canetti's discovery that Ladino was not simply a "stunted language for children and the kitchen," but an instrument through which "it was possible to speak about universal matters, to fill people with such passion that they earnestly considered dropping everything, leaving a country in which they had been settled for generations, a country which took them seriously and respected them, in which they were certainly well-off—in order to move to an unknown land that had been promised them thousands of years ago, but didn't even belong to them at this point" *(The Torch in My Ear*, 362).

The chapter, however, soon becomes a vehicle for a disquisition on crowds, and ends with Canetti's reencounter with Laurica, the childhood friend whom he had tried to murder with the ax, who unaccountably attempts to disabuse him of the formative facts of his six years in Ruschuk, the very ones rehearsed by Dr. Menacemoff on the Danube steamer: that he was scalded, that his father journeyed from Manchester to rescue him, that his grandfather cursed his father. The portrait Canetti gives of Laurica is derisory and satiric (smaller than remembered, coquettish, she has even forgotten how to read) but one wonders whether Canetti's Bulgarian origins have not also been belittled in the bargain—although we have already been oddly warned: "I didn't plan to visit Ruschuk, where I had spent my earliest childhood" (*The Torch in My Ear*, 355).

It is a strange scrap of nostography, to say the least. Framed by talk of emigration on both sides. A routine sequence of counter-figures. An opportunity to refract some crucial Canettian themes. But Bulgaria itself forms the merest backdrop, and Ruschuk itself might as well have disappeared from the map. If we are to take Canetti at his word, that anything he subsequently experienced had already happened in Ruschuk, then perhaps, any sort of homecoming would be superfluous. Nostalgia, at least for those early years in Bulgaria, has no place in these memoirs. Nor, must one admit, does place itself.[34] A later chapter in the memoirs, one of its high points, may hold a clue as to why. In "Samson's Blinding" from *The Torch in My Ear*, Canetti speaks eloquently about the function of painting. "Pictures are nets," he writes.

> What appears in them is the holdable catch. Some things slip through the meshes and some go rotten. But you keep on trying, you carry the nets around with you, cast them out, and they grow smaller from their catches. However, it's important that these pictures exist *outside* a person, too; inside a human being, even they are subject to change. There has to be a place where he can find them intact, not he alone, a place where everyone who feels uncertain can find them. Whenever a man feels the precariousness of his experience, he turns to a picture. Here, experience holds still, he can look into its face. (380)

Certainly this applies to Canetti himself, who provides astonishingly powerful readings of paintings by Brueghel, Grünewald, and Rembrandt. Concluding the chapter with a description of Rembrandt's *The Blinding of Samson* as his education in the meaning of hatred, Canetti is drawn back to his childhood, and to Laurica. "I had felt hatred when very young, much too young, at five, when I tried to kill Laurica with an ax. But you don't know what you have felt: you have to see it in front of you, in others, in order to recognize and to know it. Something you recognize and know becomes real only if you have experienced it previously. It lies dormant in you, and you can't name it; then, all at once, it is there, as a painting; and something happening to others creates itself in you as a memory; now, it is real" (383). A similar principle, as we have seen, operates for Canetti's "transporting" in German of anything Bulgarian: lying dormant and undiminished, the earlier experience is somehow awakened by the later-acquired means of representation. Evidently, "anything I subsequently experienced already happened in Ruschuk" means not that the landscape of the lower Danube, with its polyglot culture, will serve as the memoirs' "rosebud" (from the film *Citizen Kane*), their trigger for memory, but rather that everything Canetti subsequently experienced requires full narration in order to carry Ruschuk forward into the rest of his life. As he says of pictures that need the viewer's experience, "That is why pictures slumber for generations: no one can see them with the experience that awakes them."

In other words, Canetti will never "go back." Unlike von Rezzori, he does not "write in order to return." "Memory," he writes in *The Human Province,* "wants to come undisturbed and in its own time, and nobody who was present *back then* should interfere with it" (26)—this includes, presumably, the rememberer himself. And thus a homecoming could never be Odyssean, let alone uncanny (like von Rezzori's or Tonio Kröger's in the short story by Thomas Mann). Canetti can only continually catapult the past into present, through a temporal Doppler shift— which is why the first volume of the memoirs concludes as it does: "It is true that I, like the earliest man, came into being only by an expulsion from Paradise."

"Paradise," in this case, also connotes group affiliation, compatriotism, determinative ties to others based on bloodline and origin, the very sort of crowd identity from which Canetti scrupulously keeps his distance. If these speculations are valid, then we must look elsewhere (indeed) for a poetics of place, having witnessed place displaced, as it were, by attention to language and reconciled memory. We must look to a more evocative and plangent Despina than Ruschuk: Marrakesh.

Notes after a Journey

The section heading is identical with the subtitle for *The Voices of Marrakesh,* and I am not the first to observe that text's eerie split between experience and recollection, and the double mediation performed by writing and the passage of time.[35] Canetti's journey to Morocco was undertaken in 1954; the book was published in 1967. If, however, one expects a memoir in the mold of his autobiographical writing, s/he will be caught by surprise. Even on a cursory reading, it is hard not to miss the book's hermeticism and abstraction, a certain fugal quality, all the more curious in light of the dramatic political upheaval in Morocco at the time (something only once and indirectly evident in Canetti's commentary). The *Aufzeignungen* are interspersed with lengthy reflections on contemporary history and politics as well as self-critical judgments about other cultures, but *The Voices of Marrakesh* reads as though it had been composed in a vacuum by a writer who belongs equally to nowhere and everywhere. After all, this is the same writer, who, when recalling how he hears about Odessa as a child, imaginatively reterritorializes vast spaces at ease:

I laid claim to the Black Sea, even though I had known it for only a few short weeks in Varna . . . Without realizing it, I had found the natural capital for that smaller town on the lower Danube; and I would have found it suitable if this Odessa had developed at the mouth of the Danube. Then, the famous voyage that had determined the dreams of my childhood, up the Danube and down again, would have stretched from Vienna to Odessa and from Odessa back to Vienna. And Ruschuk, which lay very far downstream, would have had a proper place on this route. (*The Torch in My Ear,* 516-17)

But however idiosyncratically rendered, the voyage to Morocco years later is certainly a different affair than, say, R. B. Cunninghame Graham's 1898 *Mogreb el Acksa,* a British Arabist's tour through Southern Morocco by turns romantic and bigoted, which Conrad admired and whose unembarrassed Orientalism we decry a century later.[36] Precisely what kind of text is Canetti's, then, we may ask—touristic, aesthetic, anthropologic, self-allegoric? Perhaps it is generic (say, in the tradition of Goethe's *Italian Journey* or Hebel or even Karl May), and thus, despite Canetti's own origins in the European east, given to Orientalist misprision. Or, conversely, maybe it is anti-generic, a knowing subversion that deliberately feigns blinkered sight in order to implicate readers in their own presuppositions about the familiar and the foreign. The text's title, at least, offers something of an answer to these questions inasmuch as Canetti seems explicitly concerned with voice not vision. Yet, we may very well fail to gain any surer purchase if we thus acknowledge its frank aural curiosity in the face of language it does not pretend to understand.

Compact, symbolic, narrated sometimes philosophically, sometimes prosaically, the book forms an episodic sequence of thinly interlocked stories, which may or may not yield a plot. As one critic has contrasted the organization of the notations with that of the memoirs, *The Voices of Marrakesh* is decidedly more metonymic than metaphoric.[37] Canetti's own narratorial position appears consciously blurred . . . or muffled. He is traveling with an English camera crew, identifies himself as English for simplicity's sake, converses with the Moroccans he meets only in French, treats Marrakesh Jewry almost as though he himself were not Jewish, let alone "Oriental." As a specimen of cultural discourse about alterity, the text has been pronounced both naive and self-aware. It is patently about distance on a number of planes simultaneously, cultural, spatial, personal, interpretive.

One critic, Cecile Zorach, captures a reader's dilemma very simply when she asserts that Canetti's "acceptance of distance results in a travel book that tells the reader relatively little about Marrakesh and very much about how Canetti sees man's position in the world at large"; the place it describes may remain opaque, but the act of inscription itself renders a visible "ordered whole."[38] "The visible" should probably be immediately qualified by *"the audible."* This is a point, again, so manifestly central to the text that we might rename it by conflating the second and third titles of Canetti's memoirs: *Öhrenspiel,* or "play of the ears."

Not that the desire to see does not also play a conspicuous role (after all, Canetti is accompanying a group of filmmakers). In fact, being equally present, the thematic of vision—of what Canetti can and cannot see, depicts and effaces (offers the provocation to which the intransitivity of voice) its sound over sense—supplies the rejoinder or corrective. Moreover, "man's position in the world at large" may well claim too much, since it overlooks (or underhears) the tension between *Stimmen* ("voices") and *Aufzeichnungen* ("notes"), speech and writing, that is basic to the text's architectonics throughout.

In his essay about diaries, "Dialogue with the Cruel Partner," Canetti speaks at length about travel narratives, including his own. He admits that given his own susceptibility to the chaos of communication when one does not speak the native tongue, he has never had the composure to keep a diary while traveling. "Language, otherwise an instrument that one thought one could manipulate, suddenly becomes wild and dangerous. . . . A written word about these things will rest on the paper like its own corpse" (*The Conscience of Words,* 49). (Canetti never seems to miss an opportunity to relate a given topic to mortality or to one of its correlatives, murder.[39]) He then dwells upon his own experience as a reader of travel diaries he has admired, specifically citing texts by non-Europeans: Huan Tsang, Ibn Battuta, Sei Shonagon, and Lady Murasaki.

He speaks also of "intimate encounter" but seems to have in mind the interpenetration of readers' and authors' consciousnesses rather than the anything like the small dramas of interchange that comprise the fourteen chapters of *The Voices of Marrakesh.* Yet he does say of the "spectacle" of such encounter that its two minds "touch at certain points; at others, empty spaces form between them not to be filled in any way. The similar and the dissimilar are so close together as to force one to think; nothing is more fruitful than such diaries from nearby, as one might call them" (51). Certainly, one can say that Canetti's stake in exteriority and the interhuman—"That is the *meaning* of the word 'human': each person a midpoint next to countless others, who are midpoints as much as he"—is operative for the reading posture he outlines in this essay. (One wonders, though, what he would have thought of a diary as frontal and penetrative as Witold Gombrowicz's, which bestows a very different meaning on the concept of "the cruel partner.") *The Voices of Marrakesh* is not by any reckoning a diary from nearby, let alone at a near distance. Indeed, given Canetti's Balkan origins, it might be better described instead in terms of *far closeness*.

Zorach likewise cites this same passage from the essay, but in returning to it myself I notice what immediately precedes it: a short treatise on confidentiality in which Canetti says, "There cannot be enough ruses and cautionary measures for keeping a genuine diary secret" (*The Conscience of Words*, 48). Now, any attempt to link essay to travelogue has to remain speculative.[40] For one thing, if we take Canetti's taxonomy seriously, *The Voices of Marrakesh* would correspond more closely to "Notes" than to "Diaries." And so let us resist the temptation to use the one as cipher for the other, not least because Canetti has explicitly alerted us to the virtue of encoding any self-writing and thus preserving its inviolability.

It is reasonable to suppose that a version of such concern also provides a structuring principle for the travel narrative, since one of its most unmistakable features is the leitmotiv of hiddenness and inscrutability. Secrecy, both the wish to preserve it and the desire to penetrate its confines, characterizes what the text's author hears or wishes to see—in the souk, the square, the Mellah, the Jewish cemetery—and also the mystified quality of his own discourse. At one of the narrative's important transitions, for instance, Canetti says: "In order to feel at home in a strange city you need to have a secluded room to which you have a certain title and in which you can be alone when the tumult of new and incomprehensible voices becomes too great. The room should be quiet; no one should see you make your escape there, no one should see you leave. The best thing is when you can slip into a cul-de-sac, stop at the door to which you have the key in your pocket, and unlock it without a soul hearing" (31). At such a moment, the work's fascination with bounded spaces and inner chambers becomes reflexive. Canetti's own writing will assume the dimensions of such a room, and, though we may perhaps see him make his escape there, the key stays in his pocket. Late in the text, in the chapter "Storytellers and Scribes," Canetti actually (or seemingly) indicts himself for having "dedicated himself to paper": "I live now behind the protection of desk and door, a craven dreamer.... Having seldom felt at ease among the people of our zones whose life is literature—despising them because I despise something about myself, and I think that something is paper—I suddenly found myself here among authors [storytellers of the souk] I could look up to since there was not one line of theirs to be read" (79). If we do not trust him, it is because we have taken care to remember where the key is kept.

Thus, addressing the trenchant question Zorach poses toward the end of her essay about Canetti's purposefully equivocal identity—"who is this Elias Canetti anyway? Is it the 49-year-old sojourner in Morocco? Is it the 62-year-old writer in London?"[41]—we can at least deepen it by adding, with hindsight, "Is it not also the memoirist writing a decade later?" For the Canetti who resists returning to Ruschuk is more or less continuous with the European traveler in Marrakesh who so evidently wishes to appear unanchored and so ambivalently identifies with those who are themselves a blend of root and rootless. (The figures upon whom he focuses are all either societally marginal—beggars, women—or culturally mongrel—Chinese-French, English-Italian, Moroccan-Jewish.) That is to say, the journey to the Maghreb could be slotted into the place that a hypothetical return to Ruschuk *might* have occupied: impersonal, merely or wholly semiotic.

In Claudio Magris's words, "Canetti remains the great poet of metamorphosis in his autobiography too, which conceals him even as it appears to reveal him. He visits his past, but we will never learn what happened on this journey, whether or where he rediscovered his identity" (*Essays,* 283). Or as Canetti frames a similar idea in *The Human Province:* "A man who can only stray his way home. Each time, he has to find a *different* route" (140). And "To find the path through the labyrinth of one's own time, without giving in to one's own time, and without jumping out" (265).

Besides the acoustic element, the notable feature of Canetti's title is its place-name, for this will be a record of a visit to the city of Marrakesh, not to Morocco in general. Similarly, Cunninghame Graham's *Mogreb el Acksa* never records a visit to Fez, Marrakesh, or Casablanca. The Canettian counterpart to Czernowitz is only nominally or strictly speaking Ruschuk. More loosely but also more substantially, it has to be the "invisible city" of Marrakesh, instead. And as with James's Venice, the precious element of closeness, telling so of connexions but tasting so of differences, remains appreciable.

Reenlisting what James says and reaffirming a parallelism with von Rezzori positions us in the similarly fabled Rose City, Pearl of the South. "With more moves back the element of the appreciable shrinks—just as the charm of looking over a garden-wall into another garden breaks down when successions of walls appear. The other gardens, those still beyond, may be there, but even by use of our longest ladder we are baffled and bewildered—the view is mainly a view of barriers." And so do we find Canetti's Marrakesh—an intaglio of perimeters, walls, and bounded areas that either lead to or encompass further confines.

Town squares begin and end Canetti's text in the center of which—in the secret heart of its clock (to paraphrase the title of another of Canetti's books[42])—lie the Jewish quarter, the Jewish cemetery, and the house of the Dahan family whose spokesman, Élie, possesses the same name as Canetti himself. Gerhard Melzer refers to the crucial sentence in the chapter "A Visit to the Mellah"—"I *was* the square as I stood in it. I believe I am it always" (51)—and observes,

> The "square" spoken of here is now only tangentially connected to the actual square that the traveler happens upon. *Together* with the other "squares" that play a role in *The Voices of Marrakesh,* it forms a hierarchical *complex of signs* that admits a correspondingly complex meaning. . . . The sign "square" is only *one* of numerous building blocks that together constitute the symbolic order of the text. Alleys, courtyards, houses, and apartments also mutate into carriers of hidden meaning, and even doors and furniture no longer allow themselves to be taken for granted as props. (198)

Like James's table inside the house and the garden wall without, such deceptively prosaic design serves as the tangible marker of near and far, exposed and closed, obstructed and penetrated. Unlike James, however, Canetti provides no accommodating preface or meta-commentary. The view in *The Voices of Marrakesh* may likely be mainly of barriers, and its author-narrator and we may indeed be baffled and bewildered, but barriers, bafflement, and bewilderment do not ultimately decode the text, which, as Melzer emphasizes, guards its own internal precincts as jealously as does the city it interrogates.

To adapt a conceptual axis proposed by the historian Pierre Nora, Marrakesh exists as a *milieu* for its inhabitants—a setting that is a part of everyday experience—that Canetti conveys as a *lieu*—a residual public site that presents itself symbolically, totemically.[43] Or, in de Certeau's terms, that place resolutely resists being transformed (at least by outsiders) into a space. Marrakesh does not lend itself to being easily encroached, let alone poached upon.

How fortuitous, then, that Canetti's text should begin with this sentence: "I came into contact with camels on three occasions, and each occasion ended tragically" (9). In this first chapter of the book, Canetti and a friend are in an automobile as they enter the large open square by the city wall on its far side relative to their starting point. The visit is already in medias res. They arrive late; the square is mostly empty; only a small group of people and their donkeys remains, screening, as Canetti discovers, a rabid camel tethered by three legs that is shrieking and bouncing violently. "We had gone to the market expecting to see hundreds of these gentle, curvaceous beasts. But in the huge square, we had found only one, on three legs, captive, living its last hour, and as it fought for life we had driven away" (11).

On the second occasion, Canetti does see a large caravan of camels, situated again close to a city wall, and what strikes him particularly is that "they had faces," an impression that becomes more poignant when he is told, first by a drover who has meager command of French, that the camels had journeyed for almost a month from a desert in the south, and then by a man of Marrakesh, whose "voice had a jagged quality, like the edge of a blunted knife" (12), that they were all being sold for slaughter. If this first chapter of Canetti's text maps a progression, then this second of three encounters with camels places Canetti more specifically but no less distantly: from an automobile passenger he becomes, "for the sake of simplicity," *from London*.

The final encounter returns Canetti to the El-Khemis Gate on the following Thursday, when the camel market is held. Once again, a captive creature is singled out, beaten and mutilated by its handlers, flinching and shrieking this time because it smells the butcher who has come to slaughter it. For a third time, Canetti is engaged in conversation with a local who deciphers the scene for him (and for us). In fact, the speaker reveals himself to be the same one who, the week before and in broken French, explained that the first camel was suffering from rabies. His discourse is rambling and disjointed, threading folklore about camels (their meat is tasty; they will suffocate humans in their sleep; they prefer to travel accompanied by another camel) with his own war experiences (he was wounded; his wound still hurts). The chapter ends as Canetti moves to "the other side of the square, back among the donkeys" (17), where he rejoins his cohort.

Symbolic patterning (Melzer's "cross-referencing," Zorach's "ordered whole") determines the shape of the narrative. Wounding, tethering, violence to man and beast, shrieking and jagged voices, here and elsewhere, fragmented communication, being alone or in groups, walls: these make up the signifieds for the chapter's "hierarchical complex of signs." But do they mean more than they seem to, when distilled into such terms? We could group the episode, as a concentrated prefiguring, with the three chapters that conclude the text that likewise feature images of suffering and confinement, "The donkey's concupiscence," "Sheherazade," and "The unseen." Alternatively, we can pair it directly with the final chapter in which the counterpart to the shrieking camel becomes an armless beggar in a shapeless garment, barely discernibly human, "a small, brown bundle on the ground consisting not even of a voice but of a single sound" (100). The two chapters make a neat frame of two squares, the conjoint themes of power and powerlessness, life and death, and Canetti's empathy for the voices of Marrakesh.

However we map the work, the work has already remapped more densely configured coordinates into figure and ground: camel in relation to square, square in relation to the rest of Marrakesh and southern Morocco beyond, Morocco in relation to the European and American West. Setting, thick with lived experience, has metamorphosed into dimly understood realm, an abstractable fixed point for the various pivot views an outsider brings to bear. In this first chapter and antechamber for the rest of the book, then, Marrakesh the place gets decomposed into wall and square, its voices devolve into camel-shrieks, and human language itself becomes a partial barrier. Motivated at first by a desire to see camels, Canetti and his companion, by mutual agreement, avoid speaking of them thereafter: "During the rest of our stay in the 'red city,' we did not mention camels again" (17). The episode's central figure and vanishing point is itself finally deleted from notation, despite its ostensibly "tragisch" and "unheimlich" and "verzweifelt" (despondent) thrust.[44] Many of the text's individual units follow the model, a series of cameos conjured then dismissed.

After this morbid, enigmatic introduction, the second chapter, "The Souks," offers a salubrious contrast. Its theme is display, openness, the intimacy of commerce, the comfort of material things. The narration is entirely descriptive, ethnographic, in a much more anodyne register than before. Stylistically, it speaks a kind of prose chatter that can cut either way: either as trite as it sounds—"how to bargain at an Oriental bazaar"—or a deadpan parody, its double-voiced-ness being difficult to pinpoint precisely, however. Whereas we are apprised of eloquence, argument, the ritual of negotiation, no speech is actually recorded. The gist seems to be the buyer's eventual surrender or seduction through sale. If Canetti is slyly replicating such commerce through a textual transaction, the answer remains equivocal.

Equivocality itself—of incident, image, sound, "beyond words"—becomes the declared theme of the third chapter, "The Cries of the Blind," which returns us to the unsettling pathos of "Encounters with Camels." This time, however, the seemingly straightforward narration that has escorted us through Marrakesh thus far cedes to self-critique and interrogation. Canetti pauses to reflect: "Here I am, trying to give an account of something, and as soon as I pause I realize that I have not said anything at all. A marvelously luminous, viscid substance is left behind me, defying words. Is it the language I did not understand there, and that must now gradually find its translation in me? . . . What is there in language? What does it conceal? What does it rob one of?" (23). Canetti admits that he made no effort to "learn" these human beings (as he might say) beforehand, neither their languages nor customs. "The little that one picks up in the course of one's life about every country and every people fell away in the first few hours" (23).

Perhaps Morocco represents a pre-prelapsarian realm for Canetti, before expulsion but also antedating the giving of names—a world, as it were, before language, before Bulgarian and Ladino, before Ruschuk (and thus *after* Manchester, Vienna, Zurich, after German and English). Accordingly, he has come here to fulfill the fantasy he proposes on the first page of this chapter: "A dream: a man who unlearns the world's languages until nowhere on earth does he understand what people are saying" (23). He tells us that above all he wants *sounds* to affect him. So Marrakesh must be bleached of language, the milieu of speech decomposed into a lieu of pure sound—a realm seemingly attained at the end of the book, when the single sound its "small, brown bundle" emits, as transcribed by Canetti, is "a deep, long-drawn-out, buzzing 'e-e-e-e-e-e-e'" (100).

Canetti suspects that "the creature—as it must have been . . . had no tongue with which to form the 'l' of 'Allah' and to it the name of God was abbreviated to 'e-e-e-e-e-e-e'" (101, 103). In fact, "Allah" is the single word that Canetti admits he cannot get around in "The Cries of the Blind." It constitutes the very *cry* of the blind. Echoing the scene of the caravan of camels, here there are "hundreds of them, more than one could count. . . . All the blind offer one the name of God, and by giving alms one can acquire a claim on him" (24), thus transacting another sort of trade. "They begin with God, they end with God, they repeat God's name ten thousand times a day. All their cries contain a declension of his name, but the call they have once settled on always remains the same. . . . There is a terrible defiance in this: God seemed to me like a wall they were always storming in the same place" (24). "Cries" is actually a little misleading, since only one invariable cry gets repeated endlessly by a crowd of undifferentiated mouths.

Canetti terms them "acoustical arabesques," which cleverly captures the theme-and-variations character of the cry and the human who utters it. "You commit him to memory, you know him, from now on he is there; and he is there in a sharply defined capacity; he shields himself, his cry being his border" (25). It is Canetti's perspective, however, that defines the crying blind so restrictively as "the saints of repetition" (26). And now we understand the bait-and-switch of the previous chapter's ethnography of the souk. It was to prepare us for a much less savory kind of reiteration in which Canetti also discovers an instrument of "seduction." "How much or little variety was there in the activities of the craftsmen I had watched at work in their booths? In the haggling of the merchant? In the steps of the dancer? In the countless cups of peppermint tea that all visitors here take? How much variety is there in money? How much in hunger?" (26). Even the givers are transformed through the transaction into emblems of sameness, which is how they appear or feel to those who entreat them with the identical and unwavering expression of thanks, "Allah."

We return to the beginning of the chapter. "Allah," of course, represents the single word that adulterates Canetti's dream of speechless sound. Language represents an instrument of both stealth (what does it conceal?) and thievery (of what does it rob one?). The logic of the chapter's flow seems to be:

an equivocality and depth beyond (or under) words
the fantasy of "wordlessness"
the word "Allah"
the ubiquity of the begging blind
the uniformity of the begging blind and their cries
the uniformity of every kind of commerce

If we have understood Canetti correctly here, having imagined he could cleanse himself linguistically by journeying to Morocco, he bumps up against the word "Allah," just as its utterers hurl themselves at the wall that it names, and finds himself compelled to participate in, or at least witness, another species of trade that offers a concentrated spectacle of repetition. Perhaps the dream of the man who unlearns the world's languages is the wish to use each word only once and thus hoard its purity, unspent and unadulterated through circulation (although that fantasy is implicitly critiqued by a notation written a few years later: "Can one resent a language? Perhaps, but only in that language itself. Any resentment of a language expressed in another language is suspicious" [257]).[45]

The theme, however, extends to the next chapter, "The marabout's saliva," in which we are introduced to a very different sort of *luminous, viscid substance*. Here, the respective tourist's and self-questioners' voices we have heard thus far alternate with each other, though in its anecdotal flavor, this fourth chapter chimes with the second, just as the bleakness of the third recalls the first. The marabout, a blind holy man, contentedly (at least in Canetti's estimation) chews and goes on chewing, and what he chews is currency. What could be filthier? Canetti asks himself. Was it just *my* coin that he chewed? No, it appears that the marabout conducts the ritual with *all* his almsgivers.

Reflecting on the enigma to the point of being himself stared at by others—"The astonishing creature was myself, who stood so long uncomprehending" (29)—he decides that in bringing givers' coins into contact with his saliva, the marabout "confers a special blessing on them and thus enhances the merit they have acquired in heaven through their almsgiving" (29). Later on, a passerby offers a different explanation: "'He puts the coin in his mouth to see how much you've given him'" (30). Canetti calls it nonsense, and persists in his belief. The marabout blesses him after spitting out the coin Canetti has bestowed. "The friendliness and warmth that passed across to me as he spoke were such as I had never had a person bestow on me before" (31). The chapter ends.

Now it appears that Canetti is again gladdened by the seduction of exchange. Here, also, he chooses to disregard the explanation proffered by an insider in favor of his own hypothesis, which seems self-serving on its face. This chapter and the one preceding it therefore form a contrasting pair, as do chapters 1 and 2. And so already we have become party to a fairly dense network of carryover and interconnectivity, four chapters into the text. But if our tracking of the sequence of themes and images has paid a dividend, it is fair to say at this point that the work remains calculatedly ambiguous despite, or in the midst of, its symbolic coherence.

As in the memoirs, individuals possess value for their own sake or otherwise serve as a field for Canetti's projection. Language appears similarly split between its shadows and substance. And as to the differential possibilities of proximity, Canetti seems especially careful, if still subtle, about maintaining a dialectical tension between the nearer distances and clearer mysteries, and their farther and more opaque complements. Each, however, exerts a pull on him, and it is well to remember how he defines dialectics in *The Human Province:* "a kind of false teeth" (256). And yet, he also writes there, "To write without teeth. Just try" (242).

One additional feature connects chapters 3 and 4. In "The Marabout," Canetti confesses that watching the holy man's exhaustive chewing prompts him to respond briefly in kind, such that "I felt my own mouth begin to move slightly although it contained nothing that it could have chewed" (27). In "The Cries of the Blind," Canetti records a more thoroughgoing mimicry, one of the most arresting moments in the entire text, postdating in fact the journey narrated in it:

> Back from Morocco, I once sat down with eyes closed and legs crossed in a corner of my room and tried to say "Alláh! Alláh! Alláh!" over and over again for half and hour at the right speed and volume. I tried to imagine myself going on saying it for a whole day and a large part of the night; taking a short sleep and then beginning again; doing the same thing for days and weeks, months and years; growing old and older and living like that, and clinging tenaciously to that life; flying into a fury if something disturbed me in that life; wanting nothing else, sticking to it utterly. (25)[46]

The Canettian principle illustrated here, of course, is *Verwandlung:* the poet's ability "to become *anybody and everybody,* even the smallest, the most naïve, the most powerless person." Yet, it is fitting to speculate what it means in these "foreign" circumstances to mirror such powerless people as these, whether it is nearness (empathy) or distance (power) that licenses the transformation. The irony of cultural mediation (the self turned into just another self in the presence of others); or the irony of estrangement (the self privileged in its cultivated ambiguity).

An agitated tension between the two seems to determine the whole flow of the work. Chapters 5 and 6 comprise another pair and chart newer territory by introducing into the narrative women to whom Canetti is insistently drawn thereafter. Not surprisingly, the question of whether Canetti scrutinizes or is himself the object of scrutiny becomes a dominant leitmotiv as well. "The silent house and the empty rooftops" begins with the passage quoted earlier about retreating into a secluded room, locking the door, and pocketing the key.

Canetti's musing is turned on its end by the end of the chapter. He is warned by his friend (who we surmise now to be an Englishman or American who resides in Marrakesh) not to ascend to the rooftops and casually peer into courtyards where women might be seen. Why? Not only because it is considered indelicate but also because "we may have been seen," too. "But then one's less free on the roof than on streets" (33), Canetti protests. The whole pretext for this chapter's seclusion from and above the squares, their bustle, and their blind men was to allow Canetti the luxury of silence and elevation.

> [Within:] The cat embodies the noiselessness you have been longing for. You are grateful to it for being alive: a quite life is possible, then. It is fed without crying "Allah" a thousand times a day....
>
> [Above:] You feel you could walk all over the city up there. The narrow streets present no obstacle, you cannot see them, you forget that there are streets.... The space above the rooftops is peoples with swallows. It is like a second city, except that here things happen as fast as they happen slowly in the human streets below. They never rest, these swallows.... They snatch their prey in flight; maybe the roofs in their emptiness look like a conquered land to them. (32)

What may have seemed a casually inserted detail, the swallows as a comforting substitute for swarming humans perhaps, performs an alternate, slyer function. It discloses Canetti's ulterior motive for seeking refuge on the empty rooftops: "You see, you do not show yourself on the roof. Up there, I had thought, I shall feast my eyes on the women of fable: from there I shall overlook the neighbors' courtyards and overhear their goings on" (32).

Invisible citizens, we might say. But we could more forthrightly register Canetti as *voyeur,* as *peeping tom.* And it is at this juncture that Canetti records his friend's rebuke. "The cries of the blind" begins with a freestanding excursus on language and ends with Canetti in vexed commercial and mimetic engagement with generalized humanity—his hands dirtied, so to speak. (One is reminded of the beginning of the idiosyncratic *Crowds and Power,* "The Fear of Being Touched," in which Canetti writes, "As soon as a man has surrendered himself to the crowd, he ceases to fear its touch."[47]) Just so, in this chapter, an initial speculation on privacy that seemed motivated by the increasing "crowdedness" of the narrative thus far transforms into a somewhat darker purpose as Canetti implicates himself in a different sort of desire.

And again we wonder: what are his *textual* motives? How does he wish us to regard such disclosures—as his blindness and our insight, or the other way around? The chapter ends literarily. "I watched the swallows and envied the way they went swooping at their ease over three, five, ten roofs at a time" (33). We are still not sure. The next chapter, "The Woman at the Grille" leaves us little more enlightened though far more privy to the erotic undercurrents coursing through the book. It is here that Canetti launches what will become a recurrent pattern for many incidents to follow. He tells us that "he senses" a certain meaning in the actions of the Moroccans he encounters, a meaning directed somehow at him. He personalizes and often transparently sexualizes others' doings that may in fact have little or nothing to do with him.

The unveiled "woman at the grille," whose "soft, tender, caressing voice" Canetti *senses* as speaking to him, and whose "gentle stream of phrases" Canetti *senses* as "endearments" and later as a "vague pleading . . . as if she had been saying: don't go away," is by the end of the chapter revealed to be mad. The chapter fairly overflows with lubricious references. It begins as Canetti passes a "small fountain where a youth was drinking" (32). Soon the woman's voice sounds, "as if her words issued from a fountain," a voice Canetti fears his movements might frighten away "like a bird"; later, compressing the two figures into one, he says, "those words flowed on like a little river of bird sound" (36). Toward the end of the chapter, Canetti describes several schoolboys, one of whom he uncannily links to the woman at the grille (it is he who informs Canetti, "Elle est malade dans sa tête"), another as being "exceptionally beautiful: he had a long, pale face with large, dark, very sad eyes" (39).

In between, he witnesses a ritual in which a woman presses her child's mouth against an object Canetti cannot initially see but discovers to be the shreds of a saint's robe wound around a ring, looking "as dirty as if the alley had been wiped with them" (38). Not only is the ceremony witnessed by a group of schoolchildren but so is, once again, Canetti's conspicuous scrutiny of it, which is thereupon mocked by them as they all run up to the rags and kiss them, "and their kisses were like a series of loud smacks" (37). The chapter enfolds a series of nested gestures: Canetti keeps looking indiscreetly at the woman behind the grille; veiled women look at him; the schoolchildren look at his looking and mimic what he watches; and finally and most improbably, Canetti asks one of them whether he can read French and hands him a book on the religious customs of Morocco, opened to a passage that dealt with veneration of the saints: "You can call it an accident, but he now read out to me what he and his friends had just demonstrated to me. Not that he gave any indication of being aware of this: perhaps in the excitement of reading he did not take in the meaning of the words. I praised him, and he accepted my tribute with the dignity of an adult. I liked him so much that I involuntarily associated with the woman at the grille" (38).

Whether we are dealing with an actual occurrence or not, we are assuredly being drawn into its figural transposition. At one point, Canetti pauses to wonder, "How can I describe the effect that an unveiled female face, looking down from the height of a window, has on one in this city, in these narrow streets?" (35). But unless we take him merely for a tour guide, the more germane question is: what compels you to do so in the first place? He tells us that because the women are more or less "shapeless sacks walking down the streets . . . you grow weary of trying to arrive at a firm idea of them" (35). (Whether or not they exist tenuously in themselves, the "firm idea" is a function of *Canetti's* want.) And therefore,

You dispense with women. But you do so reluctantly, and a woman who then appears at a window and even speaks to you and inclines her head slightly and does not go away, as if she had always been there waiting for you, and who then goes on speaking to you when you turn your back on her and steal away, who would so speak whether you were there or not, and always to you, always to everyone—such a woman is a prodigy, a vision, and you are inclined to regard her as more important than anything else that this city might have to offer. (35–36)

Rank exoticism, yes (all the more curious, given the book's dedication to Canetti's wife, Veza, who passed away in 1963).[48] The drift of thought recalls the marabout who goes on chewing and would so chew, as it were, whether Canetti were there or not, always to him, always to everyone. But the more general implications of it as a token of Canetti's turning encounter into aesthetic event should also be clarified with reference to a portrait of another beggar in the text, who because he radiates contentment after obtaining a doughnut, "seemed to be extremely important for the life and well-being of the square—its eating monument" (45).

Of course, it is *Canetti* who monumentalizes him—in line with the way he rarifies the marabout, totalizes the blind, eroticizes the veiled women, and personalizes all of them. He collapses the distance between them and himself at the same time as he keeps them at bay, screened behind the "wall" of his aesthetic seeing. *Macht,* to be sure (after Canetti's most famous work)—the supremacy of a detached observer; but less *Masse* than marabout-as-monument; and less person (to recall a Levinasian distinction from the previous chapter), than figure. The erotic element in particular, following the innermost pair of chapters about the Jewish quarter that compose the narrative's heart, dominates the text thereafter, except for the final, most figurally exorbitant chapter, "The Unseen."

Chapters 9 through 14 disclose a discrete narrative logic just underneath the surface, a crescendo of salacious affect and imagery (the latter, once noticed, embarrassing in its blatancy). In "Choosing a Loaf," a vignette about buying bread, the line between financial and sexual commerce blurs suspiciously:[49]

They were mature women for the most, in shape not unlike the loaves. The smell of the loaves was in my nostrils, and simultaneously I caught the look of their dark eyes. . . . From time to time, each would pick up a loaf of bread in her right hand, toss it a little way into the air, catch it again, tilt it to and fro a few times as if weighing it, give it a couple of audible pats, and then, these caresses completed, put it back on top of the other loaves. In this way, the loaf itself, its freshness and weight and smell, as it were, offered itself for sale. . . . There were men going past with bold looks in their eyes, and when one saw something that caught his fancy he stopped and accepted a loaf in his right hand. He tossed it a little way into the air, caught it again, tilted it to and fro as if his hand had been a pair of scales, gave the loaf a couple of audible pats. And then, if he found it too light or misliked it for some other reason, put it back on to of the others. But sometimes he kept it, and you sensed the loaf's pride and the way it gave off a special smell. Slipping his left hand inside his robe, the man pulled out a tiny coin, barely visible beside the great shape of the loaf of bread, and tossed it to the woman. The loaf then disappeared under his robe—it was impossible to tell where it was anymore—and the man went away. (81–82)

"The calumny" of the following chapter's title—conveniently placed in the mouth of a disreputable French colonial—alludes to the prostitution of very young girls, prompted by Canetti's attentions to beggar children who crowd around the Kutubiya cafe, one of whom "the prettiest of them all, had long been aware that I had a soft spot for her" (84). Chapter 12, "The Donkey's Concupiscence," at first seems merely to rehearse a familiar pathos about mistreated animals, until it divulges that the donkey in question possesses an enormous erection in the midst of its abjection. That he "still had so much lust in him," Canetti writes, "absolved me of the impression caused by his misery. I often think of him" (90).

Finally, in the aptly named "Sheherazade," a young married

woman is furtively pimped to Canetti by the half-French, half-Chinese proprietress of a café (who keeps a rubber truncheon behind the counter that she takes delight in exhibiting). Canetti pretends, of all things, to be a psychiatrist in order to gain her confidence.[50] Both the young woman and her husband are said by her to be kept amorously by others. The chapter ends with the truncheon displayed in front of Canetti, which he reports without commentary. "She took it out from behind the counter and swung it to and fro a couple of times. 'I keep it for Americans. It's often come in handy, believe me!" (100).

What Gerhard Melzer calls Canetti's characteristic disdain of all things corporeal, his scorn of eroticism and sexuality,[51] is either supported by this aspect of the text (if we credit Canetti with insight) or disconfirmed, rather (if we believe we catch him in a blind spot instead). Clearly, the book's psychological unconscious is possessed of its own network of alleyways and chambers.[52] As rich as the erotic ones may be for pondering Canetti's ambiguous motives, however, within the book's inner sanctum, the Jewish quarter, resides the most complex evidence of its intriguing ambiguity and its idiosyncratic calibration of the interpersonally near and far.

Mellah

"A Visit to the Mellah" (the word means "salt" in Arabic as well as Hebrew[53]) and "The Dahan Family" form a distinct pair, the fourth such in the book's succession of chapters.[54] If we wanted to make an imaginative and literary but still close-grained visit to the cultural and sociological milieu of North African Jewry just before its migration to France and Israel in the Maghreb's pre-postcolonialist moment, other books besides *The Voices of Marrakesh* offer more reliable ports of entry. The Tunisian Albert Memmi's *The Pillar of Salt*, say, or *'Akud* (Bound), by the Casablanca-born Albert Suissa, both autobiographical memoirs, offer insiders' perspectives and recollections—much like von Rezzori's reminiscence of Czernowitz or Canetti's sparse account of Ruschuk. *The Voices of Marrakesh*, within the Mellah, remains resolutely on the outside: mystified, symbolic, *deraciné*.

At more or less dead-center in his narrative, Canetti is asked, "Êtes vous Israélite?" He replies "enthusiastically in the affirmative" (58), not, as we might suppose, to declare solidarity with coreligionists, but because "It was such a relief to be able to say 'yes' to something at last, and besides I was curious as to what effect this admission would have"

(58). Presumably, the many "No's he has felt compelled otherwise to give have been responses to those who have importuned him for one thing or another—in the context of these two chapters, either Jewish beggars or their more bourgeois counterpart, Élie Dahan—young, unemployed, hoping that Canetti will facilitate his hiring fortunes, and possessed of a variant of the same name as the author himself.

Had Canetti not responded thus and were one not familiar with the details of his biography, it would require some ingenuity to gain a secure foothold on his own identity. The chapter ends, in fact, after Canetti is introduced to Élie Dahan's father, with an invitation to the festivities of Purim, which Canetti declines out of embarrassment with his "ignorance of the old customs" (76). His story of his visit to the Mellah records a similarly estranged and discomfited posture. It begins (and one should probably note that it is the only chapter whose title echoes the book's own—*Reise*), with the sheerest sort of travelogue boilerplate, not so far removed, actually, from Henry James's condescending observations about Jewish life on New York's Lower East Side in *The American Scene* (which contrast instructively with his views of Venice):

> Their heterogeneity was astonishing. There were faces that in other clothing I would have taken for Arab. There were luminous old Rembrandt Jews. There were Catholic priests of wily quietness and humility. There were wandering Jews whose restlessness was written in every lineament. There were Frenchmen. There were Spaniards. There were ruddy-complexioned Russians. There was one you felt like hailing as the patriarch, Abraham: he was haughtily addressing Napoleon, and a hot-tempered know-all who looked like Goebbels was trying to butt in. I thought of the transmigration of souls. Perhaps, I wondered, every human has to be a Jew once, and here they all are: none remembers what he was before, and even when this is so clearly revealed in his feature that I, a foreigner, can recognize it, every one of these people still firmly believes he can stand in direct line of descent from the people of the Bible. (40)

Even without the odd (tasteless?) reference to Hitler's minister of propaganda, one has to wonder what Canetti is up to here. Is this the same author who wrote, "Their [Jewish] destiny is mine too. . . . I want to give back to their language what I owe it. I want to contribute to their having something that others can be grateful for"? It *is* the author who wrote the following several years later, upon returning from Marrakesh: "It is very unpleasant for me to talk about 'Jews' because they were so strange there" (*The Human Province*, 149).[55]

Does these Jews' Jewishness transcend their ethnic heterogeneity, uniting them, along with Canetti, in something common to them all? No, in fact, it is their "way of swiftly glancing up and forming an opinion of the person going past" (40).[56] What distinguishes the Jewish residents of the Mellah is their (circum)spection: they are forever *looking*, searching out with their eyes. Even the one-eyed vendor thus catches Canetti's attention: "The eye he could not see with was atrociously swollen; it was like a threat" (43).

It is in this context that Canetti mentions the sole beggar present whose "relish spread like a cloud of contentment over the square" and is its "eating monument." He, however, is not a Jew. Here as well is where Canetti inexplicably projects himself into the square's metaphysics, identifying with its warmth and density; he confesses that wherever else he wanders in the Mellah, he keeps returning to this square. As before, with the connection between "his murderous goal and the fate of the Armenian," one is not sure exactly what to make of this except to take it at face value. Perhaps it is the absence of beggars or the sort of cruelty he witnessed in the large open square by the city wall.

This square is secluded, within the district of Marrakesh that is enclosed by walls on all four sides. Its denizens, tradespeople for the most part, are distinctive for their "heterogeneity." Since Canetti specifically ascribes to it a quality that makes him feel that he "had reached the goal of his journey" (45), in tandem with its patina of "transmigration," one has to suppose that it affords him some imaginative *frisson*. Does its density and warmth somehow recall Ruschuk? Does it ground Canetti's own "eastern" Jewish origins, bestowing some wistful belonging? He says only that he "had been here hundreds of years ago but I had forgotten and it was all coming back to me" (45).

The visit to the Mellah moves on, however, and becomes less and less "enchanting," the term Canetti uses to describe the square earlier. He is distracted by a din and tracks it to a *heder* (a classroom), where "the Hebraic syllables fell like raindrops in the raging sea of the school" (47), and whose teacher "spoke no French, and I expected nothing of him" (46). Patting one student on the head, Canetti "praise[s] him—in French, but *that* he underst[ands]" (47). This detour leads him out onto a street in which, for the first time, he glimpses Jewish beggars, and, directed by a young man to *le cimitière israélite* ("these were the only words of French he spoke,"48), Canetti enters the Mellah's, and the chapter's and the whole book's innermost space, the Jewish cemetery.

It is as counter-Sebaldian an experience as one could imagine.[57] The decrepit cemetery is "a lunar landscape of death" from whose confines beggars begin to pursue Canetti to his horror and disdain. Not surprisingly, perhaps, it does afford the author an opportunity to expatiate upon his favored theme. In *The Secret Heart of the Clock: Notes, Aphorisms, Fragments 1973–1985*, Canetti says, "A person who has opened himself too early to the experience of death can never turn away from it again; a wound that becomes like a lung through which one breathes" (40). But in the immediate context, considering Canetti's own ambivalence about his identity here, the passage still reads startlingly. I quote it in full:

Nothing in it stood up to any height. The stones you could see and bones you could imagine were all *lying*. It was not a pleasant thing to walk erect; you could take no pride in doing so, you only felt ridiculous. Cemeteries in other parts of the world are designed in such a way as to give joy to the living. They are full of things that are alive, plants and birds, and the visitor, the only person among so many dead, feels buoyed up and strengthened. His own condition strikes him as enviable. Without admitting it to himself, he has something of the feeling of having defeated each one of them in single combat. He is sad too, of course, that so many are no more, but at the same time this makes him invincible. Where else can he feel that? On what battlefield of the world is he the sole survivor? Amid the supine he stands erect. But so do the trees and gravestones. They are planted and set up there and surround him like a kind of bequest that is there to please him. But in that desolate cemetery of the Jews there is nothing. It is truth itself, a lunar landscape of death. Looking at it, you could not care less who lies there. You do not stoop down, you make not attempt to puzzle it out. There they all lie like rubble and you feel like scurrying over them, quick as a jackal. It is a wilderness of dead in which nothing grows anymore, the last wilderness, the very last wilderness of all. (48–49)

The ultimate *midbar* for Canetti seems to be a Maghrebi Jewish burial ground (the cemetery, however, has been restored in recent years.). Yet again, he leaves the portrayal so abstract that one can only speculate on any correlation between the response this particular cemetery elicits in him and the shared identity of its Jewish dead. By itself, the spatial opposition between horizontal and vertical seems gratuitous anyway, not necessarily the sort common to all visitors of cemeteries everywhere, recognizably Canettian in its worldview (one recalls the passage in *Crowds and Power* about standing amid a heap of corpses as the surest form of self-assertion). It is by no means clear whether any passerby would share Canetti's indifference to who lies there and who they were in life. Moreover, it jars dramatically with what Canetti writes several years later about such graveyard tributes:

> Visiting the dead, establishing the locality of their life, is necessary, otherwise they disappear with uncanny rapidity. As soon as one touches their legitimate place, the place where they could exist if they existed, they come back to life with overwhelming speed. All of a sudden, you know again all the things you thought you had forgotten about them, you hear their talk, touch their hair, bloom in the glow of their eyes. Perhaps at the time you were never sure of the color of those eyes; now you see it without even posing the question. It is possible that everything about them is more intense now than it was; it is possible that only in this sudden flash of light do they become completely themselves. It is possible that every dead person waits for his perfection in the resurrection offered him by someone he has left behind. (*The Secret Heart of the Clock*, 81)

In the Jewish cemetery of Marrakesh, however, "*Abi, viator,*" rather than "*Sta," hasten away, traveler* rather than *pause,* describes Canetti's anomalous reaction, as the site engenders an interruption or bar across his visit, just as the Mellah's market square seemed to promise its goal.

The chapter concludes on an even more grotesque note. Canetti is assailed by Jewish beggars—so different from their blind Muslim counterparts—one of whom, one-legged, "hurled himself along with mighty thrusts of his crutches.... The low gravestones were no obstacle to him" (50). "Like some threatening animal he came hurtling at me. In his face there was nothing to arouse sympathy. Like his whole figure, it expressed a single violent demand: 'I'm alive! Give!' I had an inexplicable feeling that he wanted to slay me with his bulk; it was uncanny.... After the episode with the old man, however, the wilderness was no longer quite so desolate. He was its rightful occupant, keeper of the bare stones, the rubble, and the invisible bones" (50). Clearly, the cemetery is depopulated and repopulated at Canetti's imaginative and figural will. And just as plainly, such a tableau catches Canetti on the cusp of both keeping people alive with words and in the same manner (de)creating them.

We need not, nor should we, begrudge this particular visitor his particular responses, of course. After all, they belong to him. And as such, they individuate Canetti himself against the background "chaos of voices and faces" apart from which he, no less than others, needs to be "experienced individually." One of Canetti's more skeptical critics sees his entire oeuvre as progressive self-entombment, writing that "seals it[self] hermetically from the outside": "With each new text, it hardens and thickens into a monument that confronts death. A tombstone of enormous size, erected during life, in which single pieces fit together seamlessly like the square blocks of a pyramid." (Ursula Ruppel, quoted in *Critical Essays on Elias Canetti*, 263).[58] The analogy feels especially apropos here, alongside what I say above about the penchant for monumentalization. The memoirist's impulse, in his very *avoidance* of wishing to make the dead speak (which for de Man, through the trope of prosopopoeia, epitomizes the genre's untrustworthiness), has the eerie effect of defacing not Canetti himself but the Moroccan-Jewish dead along with the defiantly, albeit grossly and threateningly, alive beggar. He sets before us a conventional literary topos of the cemetery as tranquilizing, oddly liberating (Gray's *Elegy* being the most famous example), but then swiftly replaces it with something altogether more baroque—no less literary, however—that infinitely widens its distance from him. It is an avoidance that he himself enacts by rushing away from the importuning clutches of Jewish beggars.

As if the uncanny must nevertheless have its due,[59] he runs directly into "an entire population domiciled here . . . a jumble of men and women afflicted with every infirmity under the sun, an entire tribe almost" (50–51), which escorts him to a prayer chamber lit by hundreds of candles. "They did not take me for a Jew and I said no prayer. The guide pointed to the coins and I understood what was expected of me. I did not stay for more than a moment. I was awed by this little room in the wilderness that was filled with candles, that consisted of nothing but candles. They radiated a quiet serenity, as if nothing was quite over as long as they still burned. Perhaps these frail flames were all that was left of the dead" (51). Here, Canetti has found his space for aesthetic *Verwandlung*. The traveler can now briefly pause. But the respite does not last long, as the press of entreating and infirm Jews draws around, physically confining him.

> They seemed to be blessing every bit of my body. It was as if a throng of people had brought their mouths and eyes and noses, their arms and legs, their rags and crutches, everything they had, everything they consisted of, to bear upon praying to you. I was frightened, but I cannot deny that I was also deeply moved and that my fright was soon lost in the emotion. Never before had people come physically so close to me. I forgot about their dirt, I did not care, I forgot about lice. I could feel the seduction of having oneself dismembered alive for others. That terrible weight of worship seems to justify the sacrifice, and how could it not work miracles?

The allusion recalls Orpheus among the Maenads or a pagan frenzy, perhaps not the most native of cultural or religious signifiers for someone of Sephardic lineage, but hardly far-afield in the context of Canetti's catholic tastes. But again, the epiphany remains entirely aesthetic. Like Lily Briscoe at the end of Virginia Woolf's *To the Lighthouse*, Canetti has had his vision—even, to borrow Harriet Murphy's trenchant formulation, if it is still only one more "transient pose or performance *for the eyes and for the ears* of the spectator subject" (*A Companion to the Works of Elias Canetti*, 157). As with the marabout, the woman behind the grille, camels and donkey, the crying blind, and the Jewish poor, Canetti has once again found objective correlatives for his own metaphysic, his own "poetic anthropology,"[60] and, not least, his own flâneur's proprietary adventures.

The episode ends with its preoccupation with commerce intact. "But my guide took care that I did not remain in the beggars' hands. His claims were older, and nothing had yet been done to satisfy them" (52). He, too, is left monumentalized as Canetti departs: "I passed through the gate of the cemetery and my guide disappeared as swiftly as he had come, and at the same spot. It is possible that he lived in a crack in the cemetery wall and emerged only rarely. He did not go without first having accepted his due, and by way of farewell he said 'oui'" (53). "Oui" has served as his sole linguistic token, like the beggars' "Allah," or the brown bundle's "e-e-e-e-e-e-e," where language has been reduced to its purest dimension of near-silent exchange.

This is not the case, however, in the chapter that follows. In "The Dahan Family," Canetti's namesake repeatedly duns him with imperative requests to write him a letter so he can find employment ("write me" / "read it to me" / "translate it" / "put your address") that merely provokes Canetti's irritation and perhaps a certain degree of Jewish self-hatred. In the person of Élie Dahan, the Mellah's tradesmen and beggars have, as it were, been upscaled and made garrulous—as befits the Dahan home, which is "furnished in European style," and whose general effect "could have been that of any modest, petit-bourgeois home in France" (55). These are Moroccan Jews living as if *from elsewhere*—the new daughter-in-law wears a dress "that might have come from a French department store," her brother-in-law looks "as if he just stepped out of the window of a Paris outfitter's," with the only "foreign element" in the room being "their dark-brown skin" (56).

But this episode also marks the point in the work where Canetti stares into a distorting mirror. His interlocutor shares his name; he is asked pointedly whether he himself is Jewish; Élie's Jewish-centeredness, his Jewish "circumspection," strikes him as more "medieval" (66) than the Mellah itself. And the gist of the episode seems to be Canetti's resentment at being importuned altogether more vulgarly than before: "I should not have accepted these people's hospitality" (64). But the incident takes an unexpected turn that mollifies Canetti so completely that he "zealously fulfill[s] every one of [Dahan's] burdensome little wishes" (76). Canetti is introduced to the *pater familias*, whom we have already met as the hospitable profferer of an invitation for Purim, and whom Canetti is content simply "to have seen once" (76).

Why? Because he has laughing eyes and because, although he cannot speak a word of French, he transforms Canetti's name into something otherworldly . . . or other-linguistic:

> "E-li-as Ca-ne-ti?" the father repeated on a note of interrogation. He spoke the name aloud several times, pronouncing each syllable distinctly and separately. In his mouth the name became more substantial, more beautiful. He looked not at me but straight ahead of him, as if the name were more real than I and as if it were worth exploring. I listened in amazement, deeply affected. In his singsong voice my name sounded to me as if it belonged to a special language that I did not know. He weighed it magnanimously four or five times; I thought I heard the clink of weights. I felt no alarm, for he was not a judge. I knew he would find my name's meaning and true mass; and when he finished he looked up and his eyes laughed again into mine. He was standing there as if he wanted to say: the name is good. But there was no language in which he could have told me. I read it in his face and experienced an overpowering surge of love for him. . . . Awed, I remained perfectly silent. Perhaps I was also afraid of breaking the wonderful spell of the name-chanting. If he only understands why I cannot speak, I thought; if my eyes could only laugh the way his do. (74–75)

The insistent and multiform economy in the text discovers its apotheosis (the economy *of* the text, by contrast, will wait indefinitely). The measure of a name is found—rather than that of loaf or a woman's allure—prophetically, numinously, assayed.[61] The dream of post-Babel man finds its most pleasing approximation. Neither the cry of "Alláh" in the open square, nor the author's own "Alláh! Alláh! Alláh!" repeated to himself after his return from Marrakesh. Not "la-lo-ma-nu-she-ti-ba-bu," the Hebraic syllables that fell like raindrops in the schoolroom within the Mellah. Not the unseen's "e-e-e-e-e-e-e." Rather, "E-li-as Ca-ne-ti."

Yet, it is the second-to-last series of vocables—the melisma on "e"—that Canetti tells us comprised "the sound that outlived all the others" (103). Anne Fuchs speculates that we hear in it a pure utopian vision (or rather, sound), "not the tongue set free but the voice liberated from the dominance of the tongue."[62] Alternatively, it can be heard as the proper name reduced to its own purifying elemental particle, the "E" that begins "Elias," and thus one more furtive instance of self-inscription. We can never be entirely sure, since the meaning of the brown bundle's call remains "as obscure as its whole existence" (though as we have seen, Canetti supposes it may distil the name of God). Whatever the "e-e-e-e-e-e-e" does pronounce, in its relation to "E-li-as Ca-ne-ti" can be found the text's permanently mysterious innermost echo chamber—if not its secret heart then the lung or wound through which it breathes.

For do we know what "E-li-as Ca-ne-ti" portends, after all? In the mouth of the stately, etherealized Moroccan Jew, it becomes not only "more substantial, more beautiful," but according to the book's inveterate propensity, more monumental—more real than the writer whom it names, and therefore worth exploring. Whatever Élie Dahan's father may or may not have found, the work will not definitively satisfy our own investigative explorations of it. Canetti has made sure to keep his secrets. The name's true mass remains indistinct, and it is wise to recall that it is pronounced by one of the voices of Marrakesh, not one of which becomes fully audible—even Canetti's own.

One chapter in Canetti's book has been left to the end of this reading, yet it is not *its* last. For there is no reason why we trust Canetti's senses in the open square where he sees "the unseen"—"I sensed that I would never do anything to discover the bundle's secret" (102)—more reliably than elsewhere in the text to gain some final interpretive foothold. Rather, "Storytellers and Scribes" leaves us with a more satisfying parting view, if only because it represents a notably *scribal* meditation on borders that can more obviously be set alongside "the author function" itself. If I have devoted more attention to *The Voices of Marrakesh* as a whole than with either *The Tongue Set Free* or von Rezzori's *The Snows of Yesteryear*, it is, finally, because this oddly bounded text about a bounded city so willfully situates itself on the oblique, "border from border."

Canetti has left the confines of the Mellah for the one of larger precincts of Marrakesh, the large open square of Djema el Fna when the action of the chapter opens.

The largest crowds are drawn by the storytellers.... Their words come from farther off and hang longer in the air than those of ordinary people.... I sensed the solemnity of certain words and the devious intent of others. Flattering compliments affected me as if they had been directed at myself; in perilous situations I was afraid.... [The storytellers] spared few glances for the people by whom they were surrounded. Their gaze was on their heroes, their characters. If their eye did fall on someone who just happened to be there it surely gave him an obscure feeling of being someone else. Foreigners were simply not there as far as they were concerned, did not belong in the world of their words. At first I refused to believe I was of so little interest to them; this was too unfamiliar to be true.... The storyteller had seen me, of course, but to him I was and remained an intruder in his magic circle: I did not understand him. (77)

Nothing really new greets us here; versions of that same "as if" have been operative throughout the text, as Canetti personalizes one incident and encounter after another. Like a not-so-ancient mariner, he habitually bends others to his will. The storytellers, though, he cannot, for they already discharge that role more capably than he—which is why, given the locale, we may wish to recall Sartre's introduction to Frantz Fanon's *The Wretched of the Earth,* in which the colonized talk among themselves with their backs turned to us, rather than the more hospitable and culturally proximate narrators of Walter Benjamin's "The Storyteller."

What is new, however, is explicit reference to Canetti's vocation as writer. He tells us that as such the tale-telling voices of Marrakesh belong to "elder and better brothers to myself" (78). The difference is that he remains tethered to his non-geographically-specific room—his own private Mellah—while they "roam from place to place" (78). Alternatively, of course, it is they who are rooted—to Morocco, to Marrakesh—while he floats free of attachment to any place in particular. They live "among a hundred strange faces that are different each day, unburdened by cold, superfluous knowledge, without book, ambition, or empty respectability" (79).

But yet again, something awaits him farther on in the Djema el Fna, which prompts him to revise his distinctions and admit, "how seriously I had blasphemed against paper" (79). He approaches the stalls where the scribes set up shop. Unlike the theatrical, mesmeric storytellers, they do nothing in particular to recommend their skill. They are needed, nonetheless: "They themselves were barely present; all that counted was the silent dignity of paper" (79). That, and the transactions they conduct; for theirs too is a milieu of commerce.

This chapter comments on the two preceding. It does so structurally by dividing neatly in half; the "storytellers" tell ghost stories and fairy-tales of their own that rival or improve upon "A Visit to the Mellah," and the "scribes" recapitulate Canetti's own delegated service in writing a letter for the Dahans. In both cases, Canetti *the narrator-writer* is placed between them and us. The chapter concludes with the scene of a family (a revision, so to say, of the Dahans), "who had arranged themselves on two benches at right angles with the scribe between them" (80). "The father was an elderly, powerful-looking, magnificently handsome Berber, experience and wisdom plainly legible in his face. I tried to imagine a situation in which he would be inadequate and could think of none." In fact, his appearance before the scribe attests to that very situation which Canetti notes with dignified empathy, appropriate to the solemnity of the ensemble.

The scribe, who was very much smaller, accepted their respect. . . . He had probably asked for an account of the matter and was now considering how this could best be encompassed in terms of the written word. The group gave such an impression of unity that its members might have known one another forever and occupied the same positions since the beginning of time. So intimately did they belong together that I did not even ask myself what they had all come for, and it was not until much later, when I had left the square, that I began to think about it. What on earth could it have been that had required the whole family's attendance before the scribe. (80)

The explanation can only be imagined, and more immediately, readers are not bidden to hazard it. But if this text has trained them in its multileveled topographics, then they must turn the question back at themselves and at the storyteller-scribe who stands invisibly before them: what on earth can it have been that has required our attendance to *The Voices of Marrakesh*?

Ultimately, I do not believe the answer is the book before us, in its varied and colorful "goings-on." For, these appear as *stained* glass. And we are too often placed in relation to them as is Canetti vis-à-vis Marrakesh itself when he ascends to its rooftops and is rebuked for peering into the densities of chamber and courtyard. The book is at once too thin at its surface and too deep and webbed in its interstices. Like Calvino's Despina, what we see is a kind of border city between two deserts, constantly oscillating with respect to one or the other of two perspectives on it that do not know each other. Perhaps that is why it can only be "notes after a visit"—less a record of the visit than a story about the notes.

At the beginning of this section, a passage from Canetti's essay "Dialogue with the Cruel Partner" was suggested as a gloss on our reading of *The Voices of Marrakesh*, but only if we think about it precisely in terms of *our reading* and not the workings of the text: "It is the spectacle of two minds interpenetrating: they touch at certain points; at others, empty spaces form between them not to be filled in any way. The similar and the dissimilar are so close together as to force one to think." This, finally, seems to be the role played by this odd and consistently unsettling text. It does not really look backward to Marrakesh, just as the memoirs make a point of *not* revisiting Ruschuk. It is *lieu,* not *milieu,* a space configured in place of a place.

Is Marrakesh really like Despina, then—though real, an *invisible city*? Four aphorisms from *The Human Province*—the first a decade before Canetti's visit to Marrakesh; the second, contemporary with it; the third and fourth, from the year of the book's composition—provide a marker.

To live in a city until it becomes alien to you. (109)
What is it one loves so much in closed cities, in the cities wholly contained
    within walls, not running out into streets gradually and unevenly. (147)
Don't say: I was there. Always say: I was never there. (221)
The man from Asia, having settled in Africa, been driven to England, not
    arrived here. (268)

But what they signpost is not geography. Rather, it is the work, *The Voices of Marrakesh:* alien after one has resided in it for a time, closed and wholly contained within walls, an elsewhere that one cannot say one has really visited, having oneself not yet arrived.

Maghrebi voices, the voices of Marrakesh, are so very much unlike the inimitable voice of Dr. Sonne, whom Canetti regards with exceptional veneration in the third volume of his memoirs, *The Play of the Eyes,* and who under his given name, Avraham ben-Yitzhak, makes a reappearance in this book's concluding chapter in connection with the Israeli poet Dan Pagis. "I have never listened to anyone else so intently," Canetti writes of Sonne. "I forgot that the speaker was a human being, disregarded his peculiarities of speech, never regarded him as a character. If anyone had asked me to imitate him, I would have refused, and not only out of respect, I would have been quite incapable of playing him, the very thought strikes me even today not only as sacrilege but as an utter impossibility" (687). Only Élie Dahan's father approximates such reverence, but that is because he is able to connect with Canetti outside of language, or rather solely through the incantation of the name. Sonne, on the other hand, "*spoke* as [Robert] Musil *wrote* . . . founding whole countries in the mind of his listener" (688)[63]—just as Musil's work will be described as phenomenological "war of *conquest*" that earns it "the fascination comparable to that of a *map,* a map composed of human beings" (694).

The voices of Marrakesh, finally, are like the city itself, a bordered space between two deserts. Canetti eventually settles in England, just as Dr. Sonne emigrates to Palestine. But Marrakesh and its voices remain oblique, willfully imagined as Elsewhere, necessarily alien, of which one says, I never was there, hadn't arrived.

4

Border from Beyond
André Aciman's *Out of Egypt* and Edward Said's *Out of Place*

In Raissa, life is not happy. People wring their hands as they walk in the streets, curse the crying children, lean on the railings over the river and press their fists to their temples. In the morning you wake from one bad dream and another begins. At the workbenches where, every moment, you hit your finger with a hammer or prick it with a needle, or over the columns of figures all awry in the ledgers of merchants and bankers, or at the rows of empty glasses on the zinc counters of the wine shops, the bent heads at least conceal the general grim gaze. Inside the houses it is worse, and you do not have to enter to learn this: in the summer the windows resound with quarrels and broken dishes. And yet, in Raissa, at every moment there is a child in a window who laughs seeing a dog that has jumped on a shed to bite into a piece of polenta dropped by a stonemason who has shouted from the top of the scaffolding, "Darling, let me dip into it," to a young serving-maid who holds up a dish of ragout under the pergola, happy to serve it to the umbrella-maker who is celebrating a successful transaction, a white lace parasol bought to display at the races by a great lady in love with an officer who has smiled at her taking the last jump, happy man, and still happier his horse, flying over the obstacles, seeing a francolin flying in the sky, happy bird freed from its cage by a painter happy at having painted it feather by feather, speckled with red and yellow in the illumination of that page in the volume where the philosopher says: "Also in Raissa, city of sadness, there runs an invisible thread that binds one living being to another for moment, then unravels, then is stretched again between moving points as it draws new and rapid patterns so that at every second the unhappy city contains a happy city unaware of its existence."
        Italo Calvino, *Invisible Cities*

A Standing Jump

This would be the condition of nostalgia, an ache, a pang, a desire by turns melancholy and strangely sweet, the longing at the ambivalent heart of belonging at a near distance. Calvino's conceit enlarges to the contours of the city the kind of reverberant nostalgia made famous by Heinrich Heine's famous poem about the yearning of northern for southern tree:

Ein Fichtenbaum steht einsam	A pine is standing lonely
Im Norden auf kahler Höh;	In the North on a bare plateau.
Ihn schläfert; mit weićer Decke	He sleeps; a bright white blanket
Umhüllen ihn Eis und Schnee.	Enshrouds him in ice and snow.
Er träumt von einer Palme,	He's dreaming of a palm tree
Die, fern im Morgenland,	Far away in the Eastern land
Einsam und schweigend trauert	Lonely and silently mourning
Auf brennender Felsenwand.	On a sunburnt rocky strand.[1]

Or somewhat closer in space (as adopted home for Said and Aciman both) to this chapter's two *midbar*-texts, if only slightly closer in time (and much less so in language), from *In Nyu York* (1919), by the American-Yiddish poet Moyshe-Leyb Halpern:

Fartreybt men a mensh in di yoren fun heymland,	A man adrift from homeland,
Vert ibergerisen zeyn leben oyf zvey.	Irrecoverable, his life splits in two.
Eyn helft geyt arum in der fremd, un di zveyte benkt shtendig a heym.	One half goes around in a strange land, the second Pines constantly for home,
Un gor tif iz ir veh.	immersed in pain.[2]

In turn, every lost homeland might be thought of as Raissa writ large, a locus of sadness, which, pitched and pivoted by memory, can transform into rapture. The place itself is ultimately utopian, a set of borders that licenses the imperceptible shift into a realm beyond. One writes about home, in other words, from elsewhere. The filaments by which this omni-reterritorializable Raissa secures hold on the imagination alternately unravel and are stretched taut again by its once and future citizens who remain harnessed to and yet float free of it at one and the same time.

Border from Beyond

In 1914 on the eve of the Great War, one such citizen was Joseph Conrad, setting sail from England for Germany by the North Sea on a return trip to Poland. This marked the first time Conrad would set foot in Cracow since he had abandoned his native land for a berth before the mast in the French merchant marine in 1874. The journey back forty years later becomes the subject of a 1915 essay entitled "Poland Revisited." It is a curious document, typically Conradian in its temporal looping, in its movable or continuously absent center, and thus particularly intriguing for the amount of space it devotes to reverie about not Poland but England.

"Writing for Conrad," argues Edward Said in an essay on his first scholarly subject, "was an activity that constituted negation—of itself, of what it dealt with—and was also oral and repetitive. That is, as an activity Conrad's writing negated and reconstituted itself, negated itself again, and so forth indefinitely" (*The World, the Text, and the Critic*, 108). Many of these elements are on display in "Poland Revisited," for which the central question becomes: why not an essay that keeps faith with its title, that *revisits* Poland instead of holding Poland at bay as if it were a kind of Nostromo at the level of nation that will only take center stage late in the narrative naming it? Why does Conrad dwell instead and for so long on the journey by sea and his love of England, and devote comparatively few pages to the actual experience of homecoming? (The "wonderful, poignant two months" Conrad and family spent detained in Poland by the outbreak of war are dispatched in as many paragraphs.)

The essay is almost misnamed; it could rightly be called "The North Sea Revisited," for all the revisitation of Poland it actually narrates. It seems mostly to commemorate Conrad's first endeavor in English seafaring, and thus dovetails closely with *The Mirror of the Sea*, a book Conrad wrote, as "the best tribute my piety can offer to the ultimate shapers of my character, convictions, and in a sense destiny—to the imperishable sea, to the ships that are no more, and to the simple men who have had their day" (135). That book begins with the grand dialectic of a seaman's life and of a ship's career—landfall and departure—from which "Poland Revisited" seems to take its cue: "The Departure is not the ship's going away from her port any more than the Landfall can be looked upon as the synonym of arrival" (137). Neither is a sentimental regard; each marks a *professional*'s falling in with or away from the land.

Early in the essay, Conrad and his family leave their home in Kent as rain begins to descend on its parched fields.

A pearly blur settled over them, and a light sifted of all glare, of everything unkindly and searching that dwells in the splendor of unveiled skies. All unconscious of going towards the very scenes of war, I carried off in my eye, this tiny fragment of Great Britain; a few fields, a wooded rise; a clump of trees or two, with a short stretch of road, and here and there a gleam of red wall and tiled roof above the peace. And I felt that all this had a very strong hold on me as the embodiment of a beneficent and gentle spirit; that it was dear to me not as an inheritance, but as an acquisition, as a conquest in the sense in which a woman is conquered—by love, which is a sort of surrender. (*Life and Letters*, 199)

This is what *The Mirror of the Sea* will account a "sentimental 'goodbye'" (138). Later, on board the steamer, Conrad looks out upon the North Sea, which, though farther out than he was wont to travel when he himself sailed off the English east coast, makes him "deeply conscious of the familiarity of [his] surroundings."

It was a cloudy, nasty day.... For myself, a very late-comer into that sea and its former pupil, I accorded amused recognition to the characteristic aspect so well remembered from my days of training. The same old thing. A greygreen expanse of smudgy waters grinning angrily at one with white foamridges, and over all a cheerless, unglowing canopy, apparently made of wet blotting paper. From time to time a flurry of fine rain blew along like a puff of smoke across the dots of distant fishing boats, very few, very scattered, and tossing restlessly on an ever dissolving, ever reforming sky-line.... It might have been a day five and thirty years ago, when there were on this and every other sea more sails and less smoke-stacks to be seen. Yet, thanks to the unchangeable sea I could have given myself up to the illusion of a revised past, had it not been for the periodical transit across my gaze of a German passenger. (209–10)

In the very first part of this four-part essay, Conrad acknowledges that because of a desire to travel, his thoughts do not gather themselves toward the onset of war but rather incline regressively toward an Old Europe: "my eyes were turned to the past, not to future; the past that one cannot suspect and mistrust, the shadowy and unquestionable moral possession, the darkest struggles of which wear a halo of glory and peace" (194). After landfall, the subsequent passage through Germany is represented as vacuous, "as if it were pure space, without sights, without sounds. No whispers of the war reached my voluntary abstraction" (219). The arrival in Cracow itself takes up only eight of the essay's forty-odd pages; after a reminiscence of his father's public funeral (which he also relates in somewhat different form in the author's note to *A Personal Record,* written four years later), the essay concludes as the ship's head wings into the estuary of the Thames with premonitions of war dimly discerned in the form of guns "at work on the coast of Flanders, shaping the future" (231).[3]

It is a characteristic piece of late prose by Conrad, and no less odd for that. It purports to revisit Poland, and yet the nostalgia it records does not seem to be homesickness for Poland. In an essay about borders—for what is Poland since the late eighteenth century but a nation subject to partition and boundaries redrawn?—the keynote is memory always in traffic with a near distance, a "beyond." In her book *The Future of Nostalgia,* Svetlana Boym observes that outbreaks of nostalgia often follow revolutions. So it is with Conrad's perhaps. "Nostalgia is not always about the past; it can be retrospective but also prospective," writes Boym (xvi). So it is again with Conrad's; his reverie is not "confined to the planes of individual consciousness," but rather concerns "the relationship between individual biography and the biography of groups or nations, between personal and collective memory" (xvi) Conrad's essay is in perfect sync with a critical tradition of refashioned nostalgia Boym calls the "off-modern," which, as the essay demonstrates, "makes us explore sideshadows and back alleys rather than the straight road of progress," allowing us "to take a detour from the deterministic narrative of twentieth-century history" (xvii).

Of the two varieties into which nostalgia tends to sort itself, according to Boym, the *restorative,* which "stresses *nostos* and attempts a transhistorical reconstruction of the lost home," and the *reflective,* which "thrives in *algia,* the longing itself, and delays the homecoming—wistfully, ironically, desperately" (xvi), Conrad's expostulations conform mostly to the latter. (Yet, if we are to be most faithful to the essay, we should probably agree with André Aciman that nostalgia's true home is textual, for nostalgia is desire for the *record,* the transposition of place rather than the place itself.) The odd quality of the essay, apart from its telltale sensibility (it is contemporary with *Victory,* Conrad's novel about the isolated consciousness, or what Said calls "pure virtuality"), may be credited, I think, to the swerve *away* from Poland, or the postponement of arrival, that it seems to register. Fore-echoing his fellow Pole Gombrowicz—who "gets close" to Europe by indulging passionate intoxication with America (Argentina)—Conrad journeys to Poland, yet finds himself nostalgically diverted by the erotic pull of the Maritime and Britain. Poland, that is to say, arrives late: late in the essay, belated in the author's record of fidelities.

What Poland means in Conrad's writing is never a simple matter, anyway. If we heed the voice of Gombrowicz: "I do not think that our country ought to be confused with details, nor should Conrad and his native land be dragged by the hair towards one another."[4] One way to extend Said's insights might be to propose that the site of continuous negation, of the absent center in Conrad's oeuvre, is often where the Polish *nostos,* already subtracted from the map of Europe through successive partitions and reappropriations, will be (invisibly) sighted as well.[5] Jim's leap off the Patna and onto Patusan (both, as Czeslaw Milosz suggests, somewhat "blotted" versions of *"patria"*), Leggat's leap into the sea, the order to "shove off—push hard" at the end of *A Personal Record:* all can be read as analogues to Conrad's own push off landlocked Poland to commence a twenty-year career at sea, which comes to an end as he begins his second apprenticeship as a novelist. "I verily believe mine was the only case of a boy of my nationality and antecedents taking a, so to speak, standing jump out of his racial surroundings and associations" (*A Personal Record,* 113). But filling in the gap doesn't necessarily resolve or rectify it. As Said puts it in a collection of essays in which he shares space with André Aciman, "No matter how perfectly [Conrad] is able to express something, the result always seems to be an approximation of what he had wanted to say, and to have said too late, past the point where the saying of it might have been helpful" ("No Reconciliation Allowed," *Letters of Transit,* 92).

The counter-gesture, thus, to the standing jump, that is, the return homeward, will be conducted with cancelled momentum, less of a leap than a reluctant landfall. One thinks of the body of James Wait, true to its name, resistant at first, then giving in slowly to a downward plunge off the *Narcissus's* lifted planks into burial at sea. And so, the actual return to Poland culminates in the recollected ceremonies of mourning, as, similarly, the writings by Edward Said (1995–2003) and André Aciman (b. 1951) juxtaposed in this chapter both perform the service of memorialization for worlds that have ceased to be.

This fourth chapter of *The Elsewhere* commences with Conrad instead of Edward Said's *Out of Place* in part because Said's own career as a literary critic begins with a consideration of Conrad's autobiographical project (as it just about concludes with his own). And although neither in Aciman's memoir *Out of Egypt* nor in his essays on reflective nostalgia grouped under the title *False Papers: Essays on Exile and Memory* does Conrad or Cracow make an appearance—that author prefers the likes of Proust, Cavafy, and Lawrence Durrell, and such places as Illiers-Combray, New York City, and Alexandria—the narratives of expatriation, of loss and longing, told there could be said to have been christened by Conrad's modernist example: say, in Said's choice for exemplary exilic text, "Amy Foster." Said's and Aciman's memoirs measure what Conrad would call the "rhythmical swing" between Raissa's two poles of threnody and recollected delight; and from one to the other, they rehearse the bifold between restorative and reflective nostalgia.

This chapter also begins with Conrad instead of Said or Aciman because it recognizes something deeply and continually urgent in the way Conrad sublimated (or complicated) his sense of estrangement by means of his fiction and even in his autobiographical writings, as opposed to the risk of flogging or fetishizing it to which both Aciman and Said come dangerously close. Conrad's, one can argue, is thus the more compelling estrangement because it under- rather than overwrites literary production. It *predicates,* in the sense of making known, of risking its authoritativeness to speak in public, and in a language (one recalls), that Conrad had to learn as an adult. It also engenders a world over and above endorsing worldliness—a position both Said and Aciman insistently take up. While the autobiographical always lurks inside the critical as a live potentiality for "foreign interference"[6] (and surely Conrad's work is emblematic in this regard), there is something deeply *predicative* in Conrad's enterprise—transmuting the worldly, the real, the secular into fictive shape (even the memoirs like *A Personal Record, Mirror of the Sea,* and "Poland Revisited" qualify as such). Which is to say simply that Said and Aciman will interest us primarily here as *memoirists* writing in the same mode as, if not the style of Conrad, and less so as theorists or, in Said's case, ideologues. For it is in their memoirs, pulling abreast certain moments in their essays, that the effect of landfall and departure approaches something like Conradian meanings.

Additionally, this chapter pushes off Conrad as a way of re-signing a recommitment to the book's dual loyalties to the hinterland of east-central Europe and the eastern Mediterranean of the Levant—the "collision" of geographies, on display for instance, in Said's example of the European scholar Eric Auerbach composing *Mimesis* while exiled in Istanbul. In this chapter, as well as the concluding one, the Levant on a direct line through the Bosporus straits from a previous disembarkation in Canetti's Bulgaria will now occupy the foreground of our attention, as we briefly survey Aciman's Alexandria and Said's Cairo, Mandatory Jerusalem, and Dhour el Shweir in Lebanon. *The Elsewhere* proceeds, in other words, according to its own variant of the device Aciman invokes to justify the peculiar errancy, the diversionary tactics, of memory, which he calls "mnemonic arbitrage."

For Aciman, arbitrage defines a certain relation to the past the way his "palintropism" explained the machinery of deflected desire. Like "the purchase of securities in one market for resale in another" (*False Papers*, 151–52), Aciman's principle works by substitution—not unlike England exchanged for Poland, or the North Sea for the Polish Ukraine. "Arbitrageurs have seats on not one but two exchanges, the way the very wealthy have homes not in one but two time zones, or exiles two homes in the wrong places. One always longs for the other home, but home, as one learns soon enough, is where one imagines or remembers *other* homes" (152). It will perhaps not surprise readers of Aciman's reminiscences, so unself-consciously bourgeois are they, that the metaphor here is a monetary one. But more importantly, it will not surprise readers of this book, in light of previous chapters, that the essay by Aciman named after the metaphor (as well as its companion piece, "Alexandria: Capital of Memory") should culminate at the scene of a cemetery. So does Conrad's essay—at least a funeral procession on the way to the cemetery—and to that degree, they both share affinities with Said's *Out of Place*. While no cemetery scene appears in Said's memoir, still the entire work is so suffused with valediction in the wake of its author's diagnosis of leukemia and presided over by the sense of mortality (it concludes with the death of Said's mother), that it can plausibly be considered its own extended vigil. So once again, as a final explanation, Conrad's essay functions as an isthmus between Said's and Aciman's texts of *midbar*, which are each in their own way gravestone-elegies for the convergence of time and place.

The cemetery visit in Aciman's essay represents more of an anecdote or accident than an object lesson, although it does illustrate a point about the nostalgic spirit of place: cemeteries are the original *lieux de memoire*, and as such permanent founts of longing. The piquancy of Aciman's pilgrimage has to do with specificities of his family's origins in Egypt and the fact that subsequent to the expulsion of Egypt's remaining Jews in 1964, a Jewish cemetery there denotes a peculiarly orphaned site: the dead lie unvisited, and like its counterparts in the Bukovina or Lithuania that we have seen in previous chapters, the place itself epitomizes the extinction, not just the passing out of remembrance, of a collective presence. The void left behind, that sense of an all but irretrievable past, is the bridge connecting Aciman's and Said's memoirs, which are twinned, as palm tree to palm tree or spruce to spruce, on more levels than just their titles.⁷

Irremediably Secular

The memoirs are eerily akin. Each author spent all or part of his childhood in Egypt. Both come from wealthy families. Both went to the Cairene equivalent of Eton, Victoria College, and both were connected with Princeton University as graduate student or professor in comparative literature. Both esteem Beethoven. Both are dis- or nonbelievers, but also self-admitted secular *clercs*. Though nonfiction, both of their books by design or inadvertence flirt outside their precincts with the borders of fictionality.⁸ Those are merely fortuitous coincidences, however. Each of the memoirs places its author's familial idiosyncrasies against the background of much larger myths of exile and barred return. Each of them is thus "irremediably secular," to cite Said's phrase for the very nature of exile.⁹ And yet they will be discussed here "religiously," a term that requires some explanation.

Said frames his various essays collected in *The World, the Text, and the Critic* with a prologue and epilogue respectively entitled "secular criticism" and "religious criticism." The first introduces "circumstance and distinction where there had only been conformity and belonging," that is, "distance," as Said observes pointedly, "or what we might also call criticism" (15). To be secular is to be situated. It is also to be worldly, not just in the world, but tilted to the world, displaced within it.¹⁰ Both of the memoirists treated in this chapter are secular critics in exactly this sense. Moreover, to be secular is to be *exiled* (though Gombrowicz would say it is to be *émigré*): "It seems to me that theoretically speaking and bypassing material hardship, the immersing of oneself in the world, that is emigration, should constitute an incredible stimulus for literature. For lo and behold, the country's elite is kicked out over the border. It can think, feel, and write from the outside. It gains distance. It gains spiritual freedom. All bonds burst. One can be more of oneself. In the general din all the forms that have existed until now loosen up and one can move toward the future in a more ruthless way ("Reflections on Exile," *Altogether Elsewhere*, 154). And there is indeed nothing quite like Gombrowicz's peculiar brand of incorrigibility to deflate the hypertrophic bubble of the relentlessly exilic (and thus almost *religious*) consciousness. No doubt, Said would agree with the sentiment that "only he who knows how to reach deeper, beyond the homeland, only he for whom the homeland is but one of the revelations in an eternal and universal life, will not be incited to anarchy by the loss of his homeland" (155).

What is a permanent scandal for Said is salutary loss for Gombrowicz—a productive injury and different kind of "scrupulous (not indulgent or sulky) subjectivity" than Said endorses,[11] but that is because Gombrowicz writes as a displaced artist and Said writes as a critic on behalf of a displaced people (though even that distinction is vexing, considering Poland's long history of partition and appropriation at the hand of other nations). Indeed, for Said, exile is a wound or scandal transformed into criticism's posture, and a set of critical premises that takes its inspiration from a wound, even if daily experienced by others than himself (as he documents in *After the Last Sky: Palestinian Lives*).

"Religious criticism," by contrast, is an interpretive approach underwritten by "the extrahuman, the vague abstraction, the divine, the esoteric, the secret" (291). Said has the delphic quality of poststructuralism in mind, but he makes his critique anti-religious *tout court*, as when he laments "the current vogue for Walter Benjamin not as a Marxist but as a crypto-mystic" (292), a position that seriously undervalues the meaning of Benjamin's own transgredient sense of religiosity.[12] Religious criticism is any posture that stresses "the private and hermetic over the public and social." Yet such a line, at least between private and public, is notoriously difficult, and in some cases—like the genre of literary memoir—almost foolhardy to draw. Mikhail Bakhtin, by any reckoning a major secular critic (though "prosaics," Caryl Emerson and Gary Saul Morson's term, more accurately describes his critical predilections than "secularism"[13]), sustained a rapprochement throughout his long, multilinear career between ethical religiosity and situated, worldly criticism reflectively open to its own failings.

One might argue that, by Said's account, the allegorical use of biblical allusions in this book's introduction, or more pointedly the very trope of *midbar* itself, risks smuggling into a secular enterprise a "hermetic religiosity." And yet, one hopes that the critical posture endorsed and practiced throughout the chapters of this book—the choice, for example, of *midbar* over "diasporic" or "exilic"—is understood to be reconciling an antinomy between secular and religious or else transcending it entirely. Call it, then, secular criticism practiced religiously—criticizing situatedly, from a position in the world, but also exilically, which is to say not skeptically but ethically.[14] Emmanuel Levinas, no more cryptomystic than Walter Benjamin, expresses the idea this way, in an essay about exegesis and habits of reading: "More than just a listener, is not the human being the unique "terrain" in which exteriority can appear? . . . It is as if the multiplicity of persons—is this not the very meaning of the personal?—were the condition for the plenitude of 'absolute truth': as if every person, through his uniqueness, were the guarantee of the revelation of a unique aspect of truth, and some of its points would never have been revealed if some people had been absent from mankind" (*Beyond the Verse*, 133).[15]

Truth, then, reveals itself not relativistically, but, one could say—as indeed, has Said himself—*contrapuntally,* a term not drawn from his music criticism, however, as one might perhaps expect.[16] In the original version of "Reflections on Exile," entitled "The Mind of Winter: Reflections on Life in Exile," Said writes, "Most people are principally aware of one culture, but exiles are aware of at least two, and this plurality of vision gives rise to an awareness of simultaneous dimensions, and an awareness that—to borrow a phrase from music—is *contrapuntal*" (55). In an interview anthologized in *The Edward Said Reader,* he admits, "I'm interested in the possibilities for the interpreter to bring out voices that, to the author, or composer, may not have been apparent" (425). Finally, in *Freud and the Non-European,* he says, "I see [figures from the past whom I admire] contrapuntally, that is, as figures whose writing travels across temporal, cultural, and ideological boundaries in unforeseen ways to emerge as part of a new ensemble *along with* later history and subsequent art" (24). In books such as *Reflections on Exile* or the meditation on Freud, Said's interpretive paradigm is also contrapuntal to the degree that the critic polyphonically weaves themes on his own in-betweenness and obliquity, a standing that is also a studied and willed displacement.

While it does have Levinasian implications, "counterpoint" in this book, however, is closer to Said's sense of it in *Culture and Imperialism* where first- and third-world texts are made to overlap; it thus exchanges the dichotomy of religious versus secular criticism for the strategy of dialogic or contrapuntal criticism, a colloquy accomplished through the reciprocal voicing of texts, where the critic's function is, properly and etymologically speaking, *conspiratorial*—to make them breathe together. When Said's "place" is confined in this chapter to that of a memoirist, it means exploring his book and Aciman's (though already glossed in some way by their respective acts of criticism), as also mutually interpreted through the act of juxtaposition. Their memoirs share a contiguous border, in other words, and if these two works gesture toward a "beyond" in the space of interpretation, then it will epitomize the surplus meaning of texts that exceed their own borders in facing one another.

And just as "contiguity" itself denotes a core tenet of Said's methodology,[17] so the space of adjacency shared by this chapter's two palintropically Levantine authors will thus be *contrapuntal* in a different version of Said's characteristic deployment of the term. The interpretive surplus or margin thus produced should be seen as no less religious (hermeneutically speaking), than secular inasmuch as it follows from a reading posture that, in words of Said to be quoted again below minus the ellipsis, "*stands close* . . . to a concrete reality about which political, moral, and social judgments have to be made, and, if not only made, then exposed and demystified" (*The World, the Text, and the Critic*, 26). Yet, translated into by now familiar terms, such *standing close* goes by the name, "at a near distance." For judgment—in a strictly critical sense—can demystify only so much, in accord with individual texts' resistance to being wholly possessed by their demystifiers, something even more at issue in the concluding chapter on Pagis and Shammas.

As before in these analyses, what counterpoint expressly does *not* mean is equilibration. Said's prominence as a synthetic critic and public intellectual exceeds Aciman's by several orders of magnitude, which is why this chapter has spent more time with some of his distinctive critical concepts than with Aciman's. The warrant for juxtaposing the two *contrapuntally* as writers of literary memoir derives from what Said would call the various affiliative connections their books share. The practicability in doing so is demonstrated by the way each in facing its other brings some value out into the open that lay covered up by its own self-sedimentation, its own self-affiliation. This would be the specifically *intertextual* operation of the bringing out of voices unapparent to author or composer that Said adduces above. Counterpoint, then, is the critical terrain that permits exteriority, in Levinas's sense, to take shape.

But "contrapuntal" also coincides with the particular ethical posture proposed at this book's outset. The introduction asks how we might speak of readers as well as writers "dispossessed in acts of imaginative possession," as owners made tenants and even vagrants relative to the books they seem to inhabit. Neither fully religious nor fully secular, *contrapuntal criticism*, then, not only sets texts at a near distance from each other, but also insists on one's own purchase on them remaining slanted, approximate. That asks for a different sort of exilic sensibility than the one endorsed in common (though differently accentuated) by Said and Aciman; yet it will yield the interplay by which their respective experiences of place and elsewhere become voiced in counterpoint—even when the two memoirists' ironic or critical sensibilities, as in this case, sometimes exchange the self-aware for the self-serving, and thus partially strain against recuperative readings.

Place and Elsewhere

The title "out of place" in Said's memoir bespeaks more than a record of irrecoverable childhood and adolescence in Palestine and colonial Egypt, which is the ostensible motivation behind the memoir's composition. Rather, "out of place" is offered as a kind of professional calling card, or as one critic has put it, "something of a hometown."[18] Whether Said is subject of others' critical analyses and appreciations or of his own self-reflection, the phrase indicates a credential. For example, in Abdul R. JanMohamed's essay in *Edward Said: A Critical Reader,* Said's placelessness becomes the vehicle for a theoretical construct, "towards a definition of the specular border intellectual." On the other hand, in the next-to-last book published before Said's death, *Freud and the Non-European,* the figure of Freud, another precursor for him in the lineage of exiled intellectuals, discloses lineaments of Said's own biography: "The strength of this thought is, I believe, that it can be articulated in and speak to other besieged identities as well—not through dispensing palliatives such as tolerance and compassion but, rather, by attending to it as a troubling, disabling, destabilizing secular wound—the essence of the cosmopolitan, from which there can be no recovery, no state of resolved or Stoic calm, and no utopian reconciliation even within itself" (54).

However and wherever he is positioned, Said is necessarily atopian—*out of place*. "My background is a series of displacements and expatriations which cannot ever be recuperated," he remarks in an interview. "I am always in and out of things, and never really of anything for very long."[19] In his contribution to the essay collection *Letters of Transit: Reflections on Exile, Identity, Language, and Loss* edited by Aciman, he refers to "my sense of doubt and of being out of place, of always feeling myself standing on the wrong corner in a place that seemed to be slipping away from me just as I tried to define or describe it" (97). For Said, Levinas's "very meaning of the personal" from his essay on ethics and exegesis would seem to presage something almost exquisitely solitary. In one of the most beautifully written passages of

Out of Place, Said concludes a list of traits held in common with his mother that "imprinted and guided" him, with "a virtually unquenchable, incredibly various cultivation of loneliness as a form both of freedom and affliction" (12). It is to a program and existential formula that the title of Said's memoir attests, not solely a description of the author's formative years from 1935 to 1963 and his sense of impending mortality during the late 1990s. "[T]he more I think about it," he writes at the end of the book, "the more I believe [my father] thought the only hope for me as a man was in fact to be cut off from my family." "My search for freedom, for the self beneath or obscured by "Edward," could only have begun because of that rupture, so I have come to think of it as fortunate, despite the loneliness and unhappiness I experienced for so long. Nor does it seem important or even desirable to be 'right' and in place (right at home, for instance). Better to wander out of place, not to own a house, and not ever to feel too much at home anywhere, especially in a city like New York, where I shall be until I die" (294). Let one of Aciman's essays sound the *punctum contra punctum* here, as its author contemplates a park on the upper west side of New York (that happens to lie only a few blocks from Edward Said's former residence on Riverside Drive): "Any change reminds me of the thing I fear most: that my feet are never quite solidly on the ground, but also that the soil under me is equally weak, that the graft didn't take. In the disappearance of small things, I read the tokens of my own dislocation, my own transiency. An exile reads change the way he reads time, memory, self, love, fear, beauty: in the key of loss" (39). Aciman's essay is included in *False Papers* and reprinted in *Letters of Transit,* where it neighbors the essay by Said originally published as "Between Worlds: Edward Said Makes Sense of His Life" (a preparation for the narrative reminiscences of *Out of Place*). One notes the superadded tone of elegy or melancholy here that is absent from Said's less "essayistic" rhetoric. But then, Said construes the *form* of an essay very differently than does Aciman (for whom it answers to the contours of more belletristic literary magazines), as when he writes that what he means by criticism and consciousness "is directly reflected not only in the subjects of these essays but in the essay form itself," and that "the essay—a comparatively short, investigative, radically skeptical form—is the principal way to write criticism" (*The World, the Text, and the Critic,* 26).

So what is Said's sense of place, exactly, and how might it be correlated with his view of personal identity as either "perpetual reinvention or a constant restlessness" (*Letters of Transit,* 111)? In the essay "Secular Criticism," he writes,

The readiest account of place might define it as the nation, and certainly in the exaggerated boundary drawn between Europe and the Orient—a boundary with a long and often-unfortunate tradition in European thought—the idea of the nation, of a national-cultural community as a sovereign entity and place set against other places, has its fullest realization. But this idea of place does not cover the nuances, principally of reassurance, fitness, belonging, association, and community, entailed in the phrase *at home* or *in place*. . . . It is in culture that we can seek out the range of meanings and ideas conveyed by the phrases *belonging to* or *in a* place, being *at home in a place*. (*The World, the Text, and the Critic,* 8)

Place is projected rather than fixed, proposed instead of summed, a complex matter of qualified affiliative connections over and above bonds of filiation. (Aciman, in an essay about Freud called "Reflections of an Uncertain Jew" calls these connections "assimilationist," meaning not strictly "swallowed up, absorbed, and incorporated," but rather, "to become similar to, to simulate" (22). It is possible, indeed admirable, as Said demonstrates, to be saturated by and with culture—to be at home in it—and yet still one has to position oneself so as to critique it contrapuntally, by being at the very same time strategically out of place. Later in the same essay, stressing the vocation of criticism as situated, skeptical, and secular practice, and flagging what was to have been the original title of *The World, the Text, and the Critic*,[20] Said says, "To stand between culture and system is therefore to stand close to— closeness itself having a particular value for me—a concrete reality about which political, moral, and social judgments have to be made, and if not only made, exposed and demystified" (26). The qualification is important, as it doubly registers by itself a sort of appoggiatura.

One suspects one already understands the mutually informing relationship between *closeness* and being *at home in a place*. But what of closeness and being *out of* place, each of which can be said to have a "particular value" for Said? Self-evidently, "place" means more than a particular region or country; but the prepositional phrase cannot just mean "out of Palestine," like Aciman's "out of Egypt" (although Said is similarly "out of Egypt" by dint of his own sequential exodus from Cairo to Dhour in Lebanon and ultimately to the United States). Nor can it mean a shortage or insufficiency of place, as if one could be out of place the same way one could be out of time. It seems to connote something altogether more ambitious than de Certeau's *place* and Nora's localized and delimited *lieu*, something either excessively immanent or excessively transcendental, but in any event, something excessive. It is the oversound of the passage from Hugo St. Victor that Said likes to cite from one book of his to another: "The man who finds his homeland sweet is still a tender beginner; he to whom every soil is as his native one is already strong; but he is perfect to whom the entire world is as a foreign land. The tender soul has fixed his love on one spot in the world; the strong man has extended his love to all places; the perfect man has extinguished his" (*The World, the Text, and the Critic*, 7). Said sounds this note over and over again in critical writings, interviews, and autobiographical pieces. Is such extinguished love for the far as well as near so very different from the aphorisms of Canetti with which the previous chapter concludes? "To live in a city until it becomes alien to you." "Don't say: I was there. Always say: I was never there." "The man from Asia, having settled in Africa, been driven to England, not arrived here." And is it so very different from Aciman's plaintive note?

> New York is my home precisely because it is a place from which I can begin to be elsewhere—an analogue city, a surrogate city, a shadow city that allows me to naturalize and neutralize this terrifying, devastating, unlivable megalopolis by letting me think it is something else, that is indeed far smaller, quainter than I feared, the way certain cities on the Mediterranean are forever small and quaint, with just about the right number of places where people can go, sit, and like Narcissus leaning over a pool of water, find themselves at every bend, every store window, every sculptured forefront. (*False Papers*, 46–47)

Said would insist that it is, and while both Canetti and Aciman, on the one hand, and Said, on the other, could perhaps compare notes as exilic intellectuals, as cosmopolitans, secular critics, traveling theorists, and even types of Narcissus, to be out of place in Said's sense depends in part upon a uniquely affiliative background and upbringing and in part upon the positing of exile as always and already political.

"I, Hamlet, Horatio, and Claudius"

The first sentence of Said's memoir asserts that "*Out of Place* is a record of an essentially lost or forgotten world" (xi). The chosen term of record is Conrad's for his own autobiography as well, suggesting documentation, testimony, and memorial all at once. "Along with language," Conrad writes, "it is geography—especially in the displaced form of departures, arrivals, farewells, exile, nostalgia, homesickness, belonging and travel itself—that is at the core of my memories of those early years" (xiv).[21] This core is the vocabulary of *midbar*—or in Arabic, as Said explains in *After the Last Sky, fil-kharij* ["in the exterior"], in a state of *manfa* ["exile"] and *ghurba* ["estrangement"].[22] In a subsequent interview, when asked about the memoir, Said says that the book is shaped around "the places that irrevocably changed in my life: Egypt, Palestine, and Lebanon" (*The Edward Said Reader*, 420); indeed in writing it, Said consulted the archive of the feet by journeying to Jerusalem for the first time since leaving it with his family in 1947.

But principally, Said tells us, the memoir is meant to act as a span between past and present, unifying a life that its author fears—rightly, as it happened—is nearing its end. Thus, late in the text, he confesses that the record of a life and ongoing course of a disease "are one and the same, it could be said, the same but deliberately different" (216). Allusions to the latter, have mostly been "effaced in this story of my early life," but plainly the memoir tells a dual story about maturation, and mortality. (It is thus altogether a weightier and more portentous affair than *Out of Egypt*, whose mode is almost low-mimetic, in Northrop Frye's sense, by comparison.[23]) Like Canetti's *Memoirs*, Said's leave off just as the self gains a certain professional maturity: in Canetti's case, the acclaim garnered by the publication of his 1935 novel *Auto-da-Fé*; in Said's, the completion of five years as a graduate student at Harvard in 1963, yielding the publication of *his* first book, on Joseph Conrad. Most of the events recounted in *Out of Place* predate what Said has said was his moment of politicization—the Arab defeat by Israeli forces in 1967. And indeed the *naqba* ("catastrophe") of 1948, the Nasserite years in Cairo, the *naqsa* ("setback") of 1967, the war in Lebanon, are only peripherally present, if at all, in the course of the narrative. (They are, however, documented as they intersect with certain moments in Said's personal story in *After the Last Sky: Palestinian Lives*, which expressly concerns itself with recording the Palestinian experience *min al-dakhil*, "from the inside."[24])

Akin to Canetti's memoirs as well, Said's end with the death of his mother. To that end, it is really the first chapter rather than the preface that anticipates the memoir's driving force—the place Said assumes within a family: "All families invent their parents and children, give each of them a story, character, fate, and even a language. There was always something wrong with how I was invented and meant to fit in with the world of my parents and four sisters (3). To retrieve Said's own terms from his essay "Secular Criticism," we could say that *Out of Place* plots a story of filiation in tension with affiliative counter-force; the drama of the book alternates between Said's complex relationship with his parents, formative in one sense, and his schooling, formative in another.

Bestriding these two worlds is his own name, half Arabic, half English, the "Edward" suspended in quotation marks by the author throughout the memoir as Said makes sense of it.[25] Echoing Conrad's characterization of himself in one of his letters, Said is *homo duplex*—already hybridized by name, by competing languages, by improbable heritage (Christian, Arab, American, Palestinian). In the essay, however, the internal dynamics of filiation/affiliation are triple, not double, plotting a three-part narrative. Filial ties are replaced by those of affiliation, which, in turn, "reinstate vestiges of the kind of authority associated in the past with filiative order" (19). "If a filial relationship was held together by natural bonds and natural forms of authority—involving obedience, fear, love, respect, and instinctual conflict—the new affiliative relationship changes these bonds into what seem to be transpersonal forms—such as guild consciousness, consensus, collegiality, professional respect, class, and the hegemony of a dominant culture" (20). In this third step, mimicking the regnant claims of filiation, culture is transformed into what Said terms "possessing possession: the power to authorize, to dominate, to legitimate, demote, interdict, and validate" (9).

In the memoir, filiation in the obvious sense (and thus, not so different from Levinas's sense "filiality" or "fraternity," less matters of biological succession than of investiture by one generation of another), bequeaths a permanent self-consciousness about being ill-fit. It is "reproduced" at the affiliative level when Said makes common cause with displaced and disenchanted intellectuals like Erich Auerbach and Teodor Adorno (who, needless to say, lack a similarly complex family pedigree). Said, the secular critic, inserts himself "between culture and system," only partly affiliated with the former, the more successfully to scrutinize the latter by means of a willed displacement that echoes if not reproduces the gap between "Edward" and "Said." The missing piece here between Said's intellectual and familial trajectories is, of course, *ba'midbar,* in Hebrew, or more fittingly in Arabic, *fil-kharij*—the Saids' removal to Cairo after 1947 and the loss of their home in what is now referred to by Israelis as West Jerusalem.

> From the moment I became conscious of myself as a child, I found it impossible to think of myself as not having a discrediting past and an immoral future in store; my entire sense of self during my formative years was always experienced in the present tense, as I worked frantically to keep myself from falling back into an already established pattern, or from falling into certain perdition Being myself meant not only never being quite right, but also never feeling at ease, always expecting to be interrupted or corrected,

to have my privacy invaded and my unsure person set upon. . . . And thus I became "Edward," a creation of my parents whose daily travails a quite different but quite dormant inner self was able to observe, though most of the time was powerless to help. . . . Could "Edward's" position be anything but out of place? (19)

The terminal question braids together Said's createdness with each of his parents' compote of filiations and affiliations: Christian, Palestinian, American—all mingling as a blended entity "in" but also "out of" colonial Egypt. (It is of course a "terminal" question in an alternate sense in so far as Said's diagnosis of leukemia haunts the entire text even when not specifically mentioned; for he now experiences a *bodily* dislocation of a truly perilous kind.) The question also almost unavoidably summons what could be called the memory of genre, since Said's painful self-consciousness at this moment recapitulates the burden of being over-fathered to which so many memoirists before him—John Stuart Mill, for example, or even Joseph Conrad—so dutifully and conflictedly testify. In Said's case, however, the educative and inculcating part played by Mill senior and Apollo Korzeniowski[26] is enacted by Said's mother, Hilda, as the following quotation shows:

> The two of us sat in the front reception room, she in a big armchair, I on a stool next to her, with a smoky, smoldering fire in the fireplace on the left, and we read Hamlet together. She was Gertrude and Ophelia, I, Hamlet, Horatio, and Claudius. She also played Polonius as if in implicit solidarity with my father, who often admonishingly quoted "neither a borrower nor lender be" to me as a reminder of how risky it was for me to be given money to spend on my own. We skipped the whole play-within-a-play sequence as too bewilderingly ornate and complicated for the two of us. There must have been at least four, and perhaps even five or six, sessions when, sharing the book, we read and tried to make sense of the play, the two of us completely alone and together, for four afternoons after school, with Cairo, my sisters, father totally shut out. (52–53)

This offers itself as the comparatively uninflected and benign counterpart to those moments in Mill's *Autobiography* when his father is both unnervingly present and also uncannily absent and perhaps wished dead. As Wordsworth's poetry allowed Mill a certain margin of independence from his father's omnipresence (while replacing one father with another), and as reading about the death of the father in Marmontel's *Memoirs* permitted him the satisfaction of displacement, so the conjugation of parent and text in Said's anecdote cements a relationship and compensates for a breach.

There are other moments in Said's memoir like this one, when he is quite obviously and comfortably *in place,* as well as others where his sense of dislocation is acute. Writing of the separation from his mother while he was at school in the United States, he says, "I still find myself reliving aspects of the experience today, the sense that I'd rather be somewhere else—defined as closer to her, authorized by her, enveloped in her special maternal love, infinitely forgiving, sacrificing, giving— because being *here* was not being where I/we had wanted to be, *here* being defined as a place of exile, removal, unwilling dislocation" (218). But Said's rhetorical question about "Edward's" fate needs to be reintroduced, and by having done so, syncopated with Aciman's by means of some differentiating particulars. Doubtless, Said would blanch at the comparison. "I've never been convinced by Alexandria [Aciman's birthplace].... I have believed that one is either a Cairo person—Arab, Islamic, serious, international, intellectual—or an Alexandria amateur— Levantine, cosmopolitan, devious, and capricious," he writes, worrisomely for this chapter's purposes, in an essay in *Reflections on Exile* (337). But the counterpoint will be orchestrated nonetheless.

Marranism

Of the two, Aciman's memoir is the more frankly novelistic. There is something almost *too* secular, too meditated and detached about Said's discursive style. Conversely, as the blurbs on front and cover ("magical," "evocative," "beguiling") and its own self-description attests, Aciman's book reads almost like a theatricalization of the genre, a record of an exotic bygone past supplied, so to speak, by central casting.[27] One isn't surprised, to discover a certain fictional hand at play in the text. That is, Aciman will *render* the transgenerational story of a Jewish family against the background of cosmopolitan Alexandria, and not just decant the significance of such a world, as he does in one of his essays:

> And yet if the world of Alexandria had one wish—and that wish lasted for seventy-five years—it was precisely to be like Berlin, Vienna, Paris, Rome, Milan, and London, to be Berlin, Vienna, Paris, Rome, Milan, and London all in one. I won't repeat the clichés; everyone knows them: Alexandria was a city where all the religions and nationalities of the world were represented, and where each religion lived side by side with the others in perfect harmony. Perfect harmony may be an exaggeration, of course, but I mean it no less facetiously than when it is said of married couples living side by side in perfect harmony.... They thrived in this ideal panopolis, though, as

with immigrants elsewhere in the world, no one really expected to stay there permanently. No one identified with Alexandria, and everyone was too busy identifying with the entire culture of Europe to understand what having a single culture really meant. ("Reflections of an Uncertain Jew," 23)

If it lacks the seriousness and pathos of Said's memoir, it also stops short of the both the decentering technique favored by von Rezzori's *The Snows of Yesteryear* and the mystifying self-alienation practiced by Canetti in *The Voices of Marrakesh*. The story is told at an affectionate distance and concerns mostly the elder generations of Aciman's family, not himself. One suspects the title takes its cue as much from Isak Dinesen, who wrote inescapably as a colonialist, as from the story of exodus recited at the annual *seder*. And even if it is the Jewish family that is imperiled finally, the unreflective slide into the kind of stereotype—worldly, bourgeois, complicit in class domination and colonialism—that is the target of Said's aspersion above, makes it a less self-aware account than it otherwise might be. Aciman reserves self-reflection for his essays, where, however, it approaches excess. Clearly, the memoir is designed not so much as the re-creation of a consciousness (the author's) but of a world (the Aciman family's), a *tombeau* for the moment of exile.

Out of Egypt is divided into six chapters, "Soldier, Salesman, Swindler, Spy," "Rue Memphis," "A Centennial Ball," "Taffi Al-Nur!" "The Lotus-Eaters," "The Last Seder." The titles already transmit an unmistakably stylized patina. Unlike Said's book, which is strictly chronological (with occasional flash-forwards to its author's present state of health), Aciman's organizes its early chapters around specific family members—great-uncle, two grandmothers, mother—or else around the imminent expulsion by the Egyptian government in the early 1960s. Unlike Said's, which narrates after the *naqba* as well as before it, Aciman's is always leading up to the final moments before disappearance, a last Passover *seder* commemorating the exodus from Egypt on the eve of an exodus from Egypt. His family, as he puts it in an essay, *temporized* across the generations, first in Spain as Marranos and later, after emigrating from Turkey, as Alexandrian Jews waiting out the Holocaust, and subsequently keeping expulsion at bay in Nasserite Egypt.[28] The memoir inserts itself, so to speak, inside one of those caesurae, dilating time and holding it in abeyance because the text already knows that its world is on the verge of vanishing. It is thus a kind of fermata.

So to ask the same question differently: what is Aciman's sense of place? His essays convey a rather mannered and bourgeois cultivation of placelessness that always pivots according to the metropole: New

York, Paris, Rome. As with Said, ironically enough, a very definite elitism and class privilege remains, often unreferenced yet stubbornly present. There is the moment or event of exile or banishment, and there is also exile's cultivation thereafter as a constantly fecund breeder of metaphorical conceit.[29] Moreover, neither writer comes to English as Conrad did, late in life, and displacement in a foreign language is perhaps exile's most palpably felt anguish. (One sometimes wants, along with Ian Buruma, for the word itself to be reserved for the connotation of banishment and not merely loneliness:[30])

I am tempted to call Marranism temporizing because what I want to lay bare here is not so much the unavoidable connection between the two but what one could tentatively call a form of "Marranism of time." A Marrano, after all, is someone who practices two faiths simultaneously: one in secret, another in the open. Similarly, an exile is a person who is always in one place but elsewhere as well. An ironist is someone who says one thing but means another. A hypocrite is someone who upholds one thing but practices another. An arbitrageur is someone who buys in one market and sells in another. A temporizer is someone who exists in two time zones but who, for this very reason, does not exist in either. He has stepped out of time. The temporizer lives like others, with others, perhaps better than others—except that, like the Marranos in Spanish churches or like me in Egypt saluting the Egyptian flag every morning at school, knowing it represented anti-Semitism in its foulest manifestation, the temporizer lets time happen without being part of it. He is not touched—or hurt—by time. He lives in abeyance. ("Temporizing," 34)

Marranism, arbitrage, temporizing, living in abeyance: very possibly whether these comprise the "false papers" that give Aciman's essay collection its title, that is, a racket, a conscious deceit. At times in Said's writings as well as throughout Aciman's essays, one is struck by the clerisy-effect that attaches to being an always credentialed member of a very select group of persons: bourgeois citizens who regularly and secularly sound the voice of exile. Exile, paradoxically enough, becomes an almost religious vocation—which is especially vexing for two such zealous secularists as these two writers. Thus, the attachment to Egypt that Aciman describes in his essays is less a true homesickness than a conceit entertained, an essayist's (as opposed to fiction writer's) *figura*. One recalls, in contrast, the very different kind of metaphoricity we witnessed in Bruno Schulz, the trope of temporal "branch tracks" from *Sanatorium under the Hourglass:* "What it is to be done with events that have no place of their own in time; events that have occurred too late, after the whole of time has been distributed, divided, and allotted; events that have been left in the cold, unregistered, hanging in the air; homeless, and errant? Could it be that time is too narrow for all events? Could it be that all the seats within time might have been sold?" (*The Complete Fiction*, 131). In Aciman's case, such seats have been double-booked, or else brokered on the sly and at a profit by canny arbitrageurs.

Appropriately enough, *Out of Egypt* begins with the story of Great-uncle Vili, the soldier, salesman, swindler, spy—and surrogate Gentile— of the chapter title, a prodigy at substitution if there ever was one. Actually, Aciman's text begins with Uncle Vili's catch phrase, "so, are we or aren't we, *siamo o non siamo*?" on which it rings changes for the duration of the chapter. Aside from the obvious "local color," deeper reasons probably explain why the memoir begins this way, with this figure and with this particular cliché. It would be ascribing much more portent than it deserves to say that this book interrogates an ontological dilemma. Indeed, it is Said's memoir that rather programmatically depicts a certain state of being or problem of identity—"out of place"— whereas Aciman's concerns are by comparison phenomenological or ethnographic. Still, Great-uncle Vili's phrase does capture something peculiarly essential about this particular family, which had previously been severed by force from its Jewish roots through conversion under the Spanish monarchy.

It is at once a boast and a challenge; on the memoir's first page, a distinction is drawn between Aciman the nostalgic and his Great-uncle the *bricoleur:* "I tried to speak to him of Alexandria, of time lost and lost worlds, of the end when the end came, of . . . lives so far away now. He cut me short and made a disparaging motion with his hand, as if to dismiss a bad odor. 'That was rubbish. I live in the present,' he said almost vexed by my nostalgia. *Siamo o no siamo?* He asked, standing up to stretch his muscles, then pointing to he first owl of the evening" (3-4). We are prompted to compare Vili's presentist bravado with the fate of the Aciman family and with what Aciman affirms in his essays, "Arbitrage" and "Temporizing" about an always available fungibility of the present moment: "The temporizer . . . *forfeits the present* and . . . *moves elsewhere in time.* He moves from the present to the future, from the past to the present, from the present to the past, or, as I've already suggested in my essay 'Arbitrage,' he 'firms up the present by experiencing it from the future as a moment in the past'" (32). So what does "so are we, or aren't we" really signify? In a short history that works as a gloss for the memoir (though not included by it), Aciman writes,

The more westernized the Jews of Alexandria grew, the more they developed the sensibility of their German, French, and Italian Jewish counterparts: they too allowed their Jewish identity to be displaced, not by a national identity—which was almost entirely imaginary—but by a pan-European, equally imaginary one. We imagined every other city in the world in order not to see the one city we were very much a part of, the way we imagined every other culture in order to avoid seeing we were basically and just Jewish. Some of us could afford to go through all these antic moves because we knew—and feared—that, all things considered, the one thing that would never be taken away from us was precisely our Jewishness. And yet, was Jewishness something at the core, securely lodged, or was it something that had been dislodged and was now spinning forever out of orbit? ("Reflections of an Uncertain Jew," 23)

Vili intends his maxim to encapsulate gumption and indomitability—are we man enough, are we worth our salt, are we going ahead with it—which is exactly how he has feigned his way through two wars, on the side of the Italians against Germany in World War I, and as a supporter of Mussolini until the fate of European Jews became obvious in World War II, to end up finally under an assumed name, Dr. H. M. Spingarn, on a Georgian estate in Surrey. A "Turco-Italian-Anglophile-gentrified-Fascist Jew" (given name, Aaron) who ends up being overheard listening to the French-language shortwave broadcast from Israel and muttering a Jewish prayer behind his door after retiring for the night (though "he'll deny it if you ask him," 39), Vili is the very epitome of fictional identity. Its declension is pronounced later in the memoir: "'But what a survivor.' 'Not a survivor, a chameleon.' 'An opportunist.' 'A madman,' they agreed" (210). One may ask what difference separates Said's sometimes melancholy refrain about his own heterogeneity and Great-uncle Vili's exultation in his; to be sure, Aciman's pedigree offers one protypically Jewish history of polyglot, mongrelized genotype: ethnocultural identity as a function of persistent othering. For one thing, Said's public self-disclosures take place in the marketplace of earnest intellectualism and literary celebrity. By comparison, Vili is a tradesman, an arbitrageur in a much more flagrantly mercantile sense.

"So are we or aren't we?" works as an equivocal question about the permanent fact of familial equivocation. One reason that in his essays Aciman himself cultivates a destabilized idea of his own Jewish identity is that it functions that way across the generations of his family, an are-we-or-aren't-we attitude toward who one actually (though as an "uncertain Jew," he would dispute the term) is in relation to various cousins, in-laws, and even siblings. Having recounted a similar history of part-Jews, converted Jews, and mongrelized Jews in his own background, Primo Levi, in the *Periodic Table* frames Jewish identity itself as reagent and alloy: "I am the impurity that makes the zinc react, I am the grain of salt or mustard.... In order for the wheel to turn, for life to be lived, impurities are needed, and the impurities of impurities in the soil, too, as is known, if it is to be fertile. Dissension, diversity, the grain of salt are needed: Fascism does not want them, forbids them, and that's why you're not a Fascist; it wants everybody to be the same, and you are not" (34). And of course, Aciman's family, at least in the person of Great-uncle Vili, is capable of even temporarily becoming Fascist while *still* de-essentializing the zinc and salting the mix. But then the question becomes, *are* we worth our salt, after all? Have we learned the lessons of heterogeneity? For both Vili and Aciman, the blandishments of family wealth are difficult to resist; the memoir is as inhospitable to class-based or racial others as are some of the essays in *False Papers*, where a bourgeois Eurocentrism holds sway.

"Out of Egypt," therefore, does not betoken a particularly fraternal regard for non-Jewish or non-European Egyptians, who tend to be socially or economically inferior. Not unlike Said's portable resistance to being "of" a place for very long, Aciman is already "out of" Egypt even while residing in it. The story he narrates situates his Jewish family as provisionally part of Alexandria (only metaphorically, "of Egypt") as it had been provisionally part of Constantinople, where it had resided when Great-uncle Vili was a boy. The bygone Alexandria, "that part-Victorian half-decayed vestigial nerve-center of the British Empire," (*False Papers*, 4), Alexandria the "capital of memory " (Durrell, *The Alexandria Quartet*)—but also "a shabby little seaport built upon a sand reef" (also Durrell)—Aciman revisits, lending to it the same air of romance that he lent to America when he lived in Alexandria as a boy: that place has always been a vehicle instead of tenor for Aciman, Borgesian, one might say. Except that it has not been recreated imaginatively as von Rezzori re-imagined Czernowitz in the form of a made-up Czernopol. It had the function of an elsewhere from the start. "*He forfeits the present* and *he moves elsewhere in time*," writes Aciman. And what does von Rezzori admonish in the last sentence of *his* book? "You must never undertake the search for lost time in the spirit of nostalgic tourism."

Metaphor and Memory

One could conceivably make a similar argument for Said's Jerusalem, which strikes the reader as a more tenuous place of residence in *Out of Place* than Cairo, where the Said family had its primary place of business. But its loss has been dramatized and politicized by Said in a way that Alexandria simply is not by Aciman. The latter mentions the current Islamicization of Egyptian society in passing as a potentially more dangerous threat for, say, the Copts than Nasserite pan-Arab nationalism was for Jews: "In 1981, the assassination of President Anwar el-Sadat, in recent years the killings of tourists and Egyptian intellectuals, and in October 1995 the stabbing of the writer and Nobel laureate Naguib Mahfouz—are these the new plagues? Must I worry and remember for Egypt as well now?" (*False Papers*, 110). The force of the question has to do with the oxymoronic condition of a not-even nominally religious Jewish family that annually celebrates the exodus from Egypt, making the lived-in, present-day Egypt (or its ostensible metonym but really its metaphor, Alexandria) already the stuff of commemoration. Even the Ladino spoken by Aciman's older relatives "spoke of their homesickness for Constantinople" (55). And if Great-uncle Vili continues to "live in the present," he does so finally from the vantage of an English estate the symbolism of which "he had always secretly envied" (21), along with its acquired privileges: "A small incident occurred over dinner. A couple of Gypsies were observed through the dining room window roaming the grounds. Vili went into the drawing room, got his shotgun, and fired two shots in the air, rousing the dogs and horses.... 'Do you think I'm afraid of them? I'd go after every one of them—'... 'Me afraid of them? Me frightened? What do you think? Am I or aren't I?'" (37).

Passages like the following from a subsequent chapter alert us that this is not merely Vili's classist (and ironic) xenophobia but Aciman's on occasion as well: "Thus the summer hours would linger, and the Sudanese boy servant who had taken forever to bring out the rainbow assortment of sherbets, seemed to take yet another eternity to come back to clear the sticky dishes from the balcony" (51), or "Life at Smouha after the 1956 war had become too unsafe, and so unsavory, they said—too many vagrants, too much dust, so few Europeans" (217). A culpably Orientalist strain weaves in and out of Aciman's discourse, which, one supposes, is written as much with a localized *Commentary* (where three of the chapters were first published) or *New Yorker* readership in mind as the author's own predispositions. Indeed, the book's blurbs attest to a frankly naive reception that is bedazzled by the prospect of another lost—yet Eastern—Eden.

At one point in the memoir, one of Aciman's aunts, now old and dishabille gives voice to the other side of Great-uncle Vili's coin, a discomfiture about one's fixity or belongingness in the world that recalls Said's allegiance to the askew:

> "I cross the street on a slant, I always sit in the side rows at concert halls. I am a citizen of two countries but I live in neither, and I never look people in the eye," she said, as I, conscious of her effort to do so now, averted my own. "I'm honest with no one, though I've never lied. I've given far less than I've taken, though I'm always left with nothing. I don't even think I know who I am, I know myself the way I might know my neighbor: from across the street. When I'm here, I long to be there; when I was there, I longed to be here," she said, referring to her years in Alexandria. (85–86)

One wonders how much of this is Aciman's own ventriloquism, since Aunt Flora's pronouncements are of a piece with the meditations on his conceits of palintropism, arbitrage, and Marranism that link the thought-excursions in *False Papers*. In one essay, "Square Lamartine," Aciman goes as far as to say that it is France that represented the homeland to which he knew he would eventually return as an adult. "Here I was, a Jewish boy landlocked in Nasser's anti-Semitic Egypt, yearning to be back in a France I had never seen and did not even belong to" (51). This belies the note of *mal du pays* that Aciman sounds elsewhere for Alexandria itself as the site of nostalgia, and in both Aciman's and Said's cases (each of them, an expellee) one often detects the conflation of forced expatriation—one kind of estrangement—with the sense of rue with which one looks back on a lost childhood—another, and far more common, kind of alienation. *Midbar*, in other words, is wherever we happened to be when we hadn't yet crossed the bar to adulthood. The subtitle of *False Papers* is "essays on exile and memory," yet the one often appears to function as pretext for the other. Or in other words, border is always summoned wistfully from beyond.

> Egypt itself had become a metaphor, the way losing Egypt was a metaphor, the way reclaiming Egypt, or even trying to forget Egypt, was no less of a metaphor than writing about it. I had invented another Egypt, a mirror Egypt, an Egypt meant to be speculated about, an Egypt that stood beyond time, because although it gave every indication of having been lost, there was scant evidence that it had ever existed, an Egypt I kept frozen, tucked, secret, cosseted, and Egypt "on margin," an Egypt "on spec," an Egypt I

"castled" with every other place I might have called home, and Egypt from the past that kept intruding on the present to remind among so many other things that if I loved summoning the past more than the past I summoned up, and if it was not really Egypt I loved but remembering Egypt, this was also because my trouble was no longer with Egypt than with life itself. (160)

This is pretty but it is also indulgent. And as has already been suggested, the trouble is not with Egypt as metaphor but rather with Alexandria as metonymy, since what Aciman really means here is the way Alexandria's cosmopolitanism has already paved the way, socioculturally, for a metaphorical relation to place and elsewhere. Alexandria, in other words, is Europe in Egypt. While neither the Saids' Mandatory Jerusalem nor colonial Cairo fits the same bill, and despite Said's own resistance to exile-as-metaphor and his insistence that exile be regarded as the necessary reciprocal of nationalism, there is still something overdetermined about the way the biographical past in his case is marshaled toward an argument about its impersonal, politicized, and secular future. In an interview, Said calls *Out of Place* a "Proustian meditation"[31] (though as a species of genre it may bear more resemblance to Mill's autobiography with both its opacities and lacunae in plain sight, than to Proust's work). But interestingly, one of the most plaintive memories of Said's youth is not recorded there but in *After the Last Sky*, instead. The family has rented a house in Ramallah in 1942, and Said's mother takes him to a variety show at the local school.

During the second half, I had left the hall to go to the toilet, but for reasons I could not (and still do not) grasp, the boy-scout usher would not let me back in. I recall with ever-renewed sense of poignancy the sudden sense of distance I experienced from what was familiar and present—my mother, friends, the show; all at once the rift introduced into the cozy life I had led taught me the meaning of separation, of solitude, and of anguished boredom. There was nothing to do but wait, although my mother did appear a little later to find out what had happened to me. We left immediately, but not before I furtively took a quick look back through the door window at the lighted stage. The telescoped vision of small figures assembled in a detached space has remained with me for over forty years. (48)

In the book, Said's memory accompanies a Jean Mohr photograph of a terraced village near Ramallah at mid-distance, which Said says is a "private, crystallized, almost Proustian evocation of Palestine" (42). Yet it is still a tourist's memory, then and now; the tableau is at more than a near distance, a kind of memory of memory, one suspects, for a privileged Cairene family like Said's. Reviewing at many years' distance some home movies that his father shot when he was a boy, Said comments on "the artificial quality of what we were, a family determined to make itself into a mock little European group despite the Egyptian and Arab surroundings that are only hinted at as an occasional camel, gardener, servant, palm tree, pyramid, or tarbrushed chauffeur is briefly caught by the camera's otherwise single-minded focus on children and assorted relatives" (75).[32] When Said says that the "telescoped vision" he experienced in Ramallah as a boy "reappears in the adjusted and transformed center of the 1983 photograph" (43), it is memory that has worked the transformation and made the adjustment. This is not to gainsay his point à la Foucault about an innocent gaze made panoptic and punishing when widened to include the security forces of an occupying army. It is, however, meant to underscore the *uses* of metaphor as engineered by both these memoirists, and the slippage between a merely contiguous category (Alexandria for Egypt; telescoped vision for youthfully experienced separation anxiety) and a more all-encompassing substitution (Egypt as a name for exilic consciousness; or that same telescoped vision as *metaphor*).

To refer again to the construct from Bruce Robbins cited in chapter 1, Said's and Aciman's memoirs, juxtaposed this way, demonstrate first comparative, then discrepant cosmopolitanisms, even if, as Robbins puts it, "to catch an author in the act of belonging to a metropolis, even one who claims to belong nowhere, is a two-finger exercise, given that we believe in advance that everyone belongs somewhere, that there is no alternative to belonging" (249). Robbins wants to hedge bets on the vocation of worldliness as something less than a preconceived totality, where a given world, or worlds, may be "contested." "*Cosmos* (world) in *cosmopolitan* originally meant simply 'order' or 'adornment'—as in cosmetics—and was only later extended metaphorically to refer to 'the world.' Cosmetics preceded totality. Worlding, then, might be seen as 'making up the face of the planet'—something that can be done in diverse ways" (252). We see an analogous if not wholly identical extension at work for Said and Aciman, each of whom retrospectively *makes up* Palestine and Egypt (or rather, Jerusalem and Alexandria) metaphorically—a place invented, mirroring, on spec, standing beyond time.[33] And if too, these cities are sites of sadness, they are also cites of never-to-be repeated enchantment. And too, resembling Calvino's city of Raissa, there runs an invisible thread that binds, unravels, then is stretched again between moving points as it draws new and rapid patterns so that at every second the unhappy city contains a happy city unaware of its existence.

Palestine—that is, the place—enlarges or telescopes its horizons to become Palestine the metaphor even if Said's experience of exile bears, as he says, an anti-metaphoric burden. Alexandria possesses a similar function for Aciman, although exile for him has become so saturated with figuration that it is almost hyper-metaphoric. Arguably, the most redolent moment in *Out of Place* is a trope that is neither political nor particularly politicizable. It is, however, like the photograph of a village in Ramallah wedded to autobiographical anecdote in *After the Last Sky*, fundamentally visual, a specular, framed, and altogether coded moment. Said is sifting through his batch of super-8 movies and comes across a film of himself at a swimming pool in the midst of the crowd and his father's jerky camera-work:

> Watching this maelstrom I suddenly detected myself, a little boy in a pair of dark swimming trunks with a white belt, slipping between a phalanx of much larger bodies, and diving into the pool with scarcely a splash. It was as if I had caught my father unaware; the camera followed quickly, having abruptly located me, but I seem to have swum out of shot. The camera returns to the general confusion, and then, from an unexpected angle, running toward him with my head down, arms outstretched, I appear, and almost immediately disappear into the pool. He had missed me entirely the second time, although of course I appeared in the camera for a split second. (78)

For Said, the lesson of the unregistered cameo appearance is that he is allowed to escape briefly from his father's "fearsome strength," a liberating margin of private selfhood beneath the familial inventions and superimpositions of "Edward." Here, being out of place is a virtue. The condition is not all alienation and perturbation of identity's central core, we realize, but sometimes salutary escape and even dispossession of a sort.

Metaphor and Metaphysics

Where displacement is virtue made of necessity for Said, it is blessed accident for Aciman, who continues to draw from its well to slake an essayistic thirst. To that extent, if *Out of Egypt* did not share so many obvious points of tangency with Said's *Out of Place,* one might have preferred a more compelling narrative of being cut free from one's roots, to fit the only slot in *The Elsewhere* assigned to a Sephardi author—a memoir, say, by the previously mentioned Albert Memmi, or so-called Third-World Mizrahi writers, the Moroccan Albert Suissa, or Samir Naqqash and Shimon Ballas from Iraq.[34] From her article "Blowups in the Borderzones: Third World Israeli Authors' Gropings for Home," take the anthropologist Smadar Lavie's quotation from Na'im 'Araidi, a Druze writer who composes in Hebrew and who sounds uncannily like Edward Said:

> I don't feel grounded anywhere, I've come back to the village, but it feels like a hotel, not home. . . . This is where I live but it is not the home of my symbolic geography. . . . Here everyone lives on "village time," and I don't like it. When I lived in Haifa, I lived on Western time. I don't like that either. Now, back in the village, is a paradoxical conflict, I try to live in both times. But even so, my dubious freedom in Israel's mutation of a Western democracy is better for me than my own stagnant village. (*Displacement, Diaspora, and Geographies of Identity*, 55–56)

The opposite note, however, is struck in an essay from a volume of ethnographic essays entitled *Sephardi and Middle Eastern Jewries: History and Culture in the Modern Era* about a rural community in southern Morocco, whose Jews abscond. One silversmith in particular is described as "half-tempted and half-forced by a group of Arab acquaintances to get out of the bus that is about to take the remaining Jews to Marrakesh" and thence to resettlement in Israel.

> [The silversmith] relates how he sat down with his Arab friends, serving them tea and enjoying their company, until it occurred to him that he was the only Jew left in the village. In order not to invoke their suspicion, he left them in his house without even collecting his tea set and ran away from the village. As far as we know, his was the last Jewish presence in Oulad Mansour. This informant admits that he is afraid to visit Oulad Mansour again. More than thirty years after *aliyah* [emigration to Israel] he still expects retribution for his "desertion." (308)

Where the first example positions a partially westernized "Oriental" residing uncomfortably in an interspace between East and West, the second reverses the accepted view of Mizrahi immigration to Israel that imagines *aliyah* as a "return" (the legal and constitutional term); instead, the counter-fable configures departure as, improbably or not, a possible betrayal of one's village, one's Arab friends, and one's home. "Home," in other words, may still be an elsewhere.

Aciman acknowledges a diffuse relationship to both his Jewishness and his Sephardic heritage. The former he regards as a "form of diluted Judaism that longed for a Christian past" (*False Papers*, 141); the latter is rehearsed mainly as a vehicular circuit from Italy to Turkey to Egypt to Italy again, and the occasional reference to Ladino. Not particularly compunctious about possible betrayals, Aciman takes pleasure in a variety of palintropisms that enable him to be elsewhere while located somewhere in particular (New York, a revisited Alexandria, Illiers-Combray).[35] As such, he can avail himself of a particular rhetorical "place" located in advance for him by such Oriental Jewish writers as Jacques Derrida and Edmond Jabès. Ammiel Alcalay begins his remarkable book on remaking Levantine culture, *After Arabs and Jews*, with that very *topos*: "The modern myth of the Jew as pariah, outsider, and wanderer has, ironically enough, been translated into the postmodern myth of the Jew as 'other,' an other that collapses into the equation: writing=Jew=Book. By what sleight of hand? Metaphor? Metaphysics? Such an exclusive address (whether it is an open or closed book) ultimately obscures the necessity of mapping out a space in which the Jew was native, not a stranger but an absolute inhabitant of time and place" (1).[36]

When Aciman writes that nostalgia's telos is, at last, textual—"the act of recording the loss is the ultimate homecoming" (*False Papers*, 145) he has effectively captured his essays' *raison d'etre*. And the more the screw is turned, the more the homecoming is indefinitely postponed; or, looked at from another angle, incessantly restaged.

Aciman, however, takes this process one step further:

> The true site of nostalgia is not the original place (since there isn't one), nor is it just the text that will eventually record the absence of such an origin, or ponder the implied paradox of this. Nor is it the come-and-go traffic between one place and another, or between the text and its multiple versions. The true site of nostalgia is, of course, all of the above, coupled, however, with the realization that to be successful every literary return and every literary reminiscence, like every Proustian insight, must be incomplete and always eager to consider its own failure as such. (145)

At its close, this certainly sounds like something resembling Said's secular criticism—self-revising, open-ended. But in parallel to the way that Said sometimes risks a temporized politics (as evinced in the alteration of the title of his essay in *Letters of Transit* from "Between Worlds" to "No Reconciliation Allowed"), so Aciman, in taking this final, figural step, risks reifying the literary. That, finally, is how best to differentiate their exilic projects, one critical (a kind of autobiographical supplement to the ongoing work of criticism) and the other literary in a pictorial sense (a bending of the palintropic bow belletristically toward Alexandria and not enough toward itself).

Reading the two together, one notes how they complement each other but also expose each other's insufficiencies: how more tensile Aciman's memoir could be had it exerted a certain pressure on itself, politicizing a picturesque story; how more self-exploited Said's could be as an example of genre in tension with other genres (novel, autobiography, essay). In other words, of the five pairs of counterpointed texts that make up *The Elsewhere,* the two that specifically designate themselves as "memoir" are the ones that seem most homebound and, finally, most conservative. It is therefore to the plane of genre, troubled, refracted, bent back on itself, that this book turns now for its final chapter, from Raissa's unraveling and invisible thread to the raveled threads of our last invisible city, and to two final texts of *midbar,* two last cemetery vigils, two books that instruct their readers to pause, two way-stations in a redirected Talmudic itinerary that aim . . . beyond.

5

Beyond from Beyond
Dan Pagis's *Abba* and Anton Shammas's *Arabesques*

In Eudoxia, which spreads both upward and down, with winding alleys, steps, dead ends, hovels, a carpet is preserved in which you can observe the city's true form. At first sight nothing seems to resemble Eudoxia less than the design of that carpet, laid out in symmetrical motives whose patterns are repeated along straight and circular lines, interwoven with brilliantly colored spires, in a repetition that can be followed throughout the whole woof. But if you pause and examine it carefully, you become convinced that each place in the carpet corresponds to a place in the city and all the things contained in the city are included in the design, arranged according to their true relationship, which escapes your eye distracted by the bustle, the throngs, the shoving. All of Eudoxia's confusion, the mules' braying, the lampblack stains, the fish smell is what is evident in the incomplete perspective you grasp; but the carpet proves that there is a point from which the city shows its true proportions, the geometrical scheme implicit in its every, tiniest detail. It is easy to get lost in Eudoxia: but when you concentrate and stare at the carpet, you recognize the street you were seeking in a crimson or indigo or magenta thread which, in a wide loop, brings you to the purple enclosure that is your real destination. Every inhabitant of Eudoxia compares the carpet's immobile order with his own image of the city, an anguish of his own, and each can find, concealed among the arabesques, an answer, the story of his life, the twists of fate. An oracle was questioned about the mysterious bond between two objects so dissimilar as the carpet and the city. One of the two objects—the oracle replied—has the form the gods gave the starry sky and the orbits in which the worlds revolve; the other is an approximate reflection, like every human creation. For some time the augurs had been sure that the carpet's harmonious pattern was of divine origin. The oracle was interpreted in this sense, arousing no controversy.

Beyond from Beyond 241

> But you could, similarly, come to the opposite conclusion: that the true map of the universe is the city of Eudoxia, just as it is, a stain that spreads out shapelessly, with crooked streets, houses that crumble one upon the other amid clouds of dust, fires, screams in the darkness.
>
>   Italo Calvino, *Invisible Cities*

Threads

The city of Eudoxia, the city of "good opinion," may be an ultimately more reliable source of truth than the elegant, geometrical textile map transposing and correcting for its inscrutabilities. Or so ends Calvino's lesson. In the case of this last of our five prefatory invisible cities, we see in operation something like the reverse polarity for what de Certeau regards as the typical relation between text and reader. Here, it is the ostensibly original text that departs from the norms mapped by an authoritative reading of it. Here, it is the text that wanders, eluding the determinative quotients of fixity. Here, it is the city-space that is transitive, not keeping what it acquires, or doing so poorly (as de Certeau might say). Here, it is the city that "has no place" (*The Practice of Everyday Life*, 174), that exists in a kind of beyond, which is why its inhabitants are obliged to consult the carpet patterned to decipher it, not only to find out the truth about their own lives—Anton Shammas calls this operation "autocartography"—but also to make sense of their city's shapelessness. To the extent, then, that on the ground Eudoxia—the city of "beneficent truth"—holds definitive interpretation at bay, it could be said to resemble the movements of de Certeau's practitioners, poachers, and nomad readers: "As unrecognized producers, poets of their own acts, silent discoverers of their own paths in the jungle of rationalist functionality, consumers produce through their own signifying practices something that might be considered similar to the 'wandering lines' (*'lignes d'erre'*) drawn by autistic children . . . 'indirect' or 'errant' trajectories obeying their own logic . . . unforeseeable sentences, partly unreadable paths across a space" (*The Practice of Everyday Life*, xviii).

Presumably, the arabesques that comprise the totality of Eudoxia's design as reflected in the carpet are also present and somehow discernable in the city itself: "the geometrical scheme implicit in its every tiniest detail." Evidently, they cannot be perceived amidst its bustle and chaos, its errant trajectories and wandering lines. Arabesques read and revise the city abstractly, as the city itself (at least by one reckoning), reads and reflects the heavens above it (another beyond) in all their possible haphazardness. Whether in the arabesques is to be detected a truer picture of celestial form and motion, Calvino's exemplum cannot say for sure. What is undeniable is that the arabesques' "symmetrical motives whose patterns are repeated along straight and circular lines, interwoven with brilliantly colored spires, in a repetition that can be followed throughout the whole woof" define the very meaning of map and therefore of city. To live in Eudoxia is a kind of at-home diaspora; to read its truth in the carpet is to seek one's place.

In this final chapter, "Beyond from Beyond," *The Elsewhere* itself comes almost full circle. Each of its two *midbar* texts invokes obliquely a text from the first chapter in addition to conjuring each other. Dan Pagis, Israeli poet and author of *Abba*, comes from the same region of the Bukovina as Aharon Appelfeld, and it is in his late prose poems and prose pieces that Pagis mentions his hometown, Radautz, for the first time in print. The narrative scheme for Anton Shammas's novel *Arabesques* recalls W. G. Sebald's *The Emigrants* insofar as it too answers to a version of patterned yet meandering narrative lines—*midbar*-literature as arabesque.[1] To take a single example from Sebald's third memoir-novel, *The Rings of Saturn:* one rewoven thread belongs to the figure of Sir Thomas Browne, seventeenth-century writer of sonorous prose and labyrinthine sentences, singled out by the narrator because of his penchant for naturally recurring patterns, in particular, the *quincunx,* "which is composed by using the corners of a regular quadrilateral and the point at which its diagonals intersect" (20).

At the end of the book, Sebald retrieves this same thread in the course of a winding discussion about the silk industry. For, as the son of a silk merchant, Browne perhaps acquired an eye for what silk weavers see, which is yet again analogous to the narrator's own vision:

> That weavers in particular, together with scholars and writers with whom they had much in common, tended to suffer from melancholy . . . is understandable given the nature of their work, which forced them to sit bent over, day after day, straining to keep their eye on the complex patterns they created. It is difficult to imagine the depths of despair into which those can be driven, who, even after the end of the working day, are engrossed in their intricate designs and who are pursued, into their dreams, by the feeling that they have got hold of the wrong thread. (283)

In the tradition of English arabesque literature, Browne is rivaled perhaps only by Thomas De Quincey (1785–1859), the compulsive autobiographer not only obsessed with the Orient as phobic stimulus but also driven by arabesque-like narration as the structuring principle for all his prose. In his *Suspiria de Profundis* De Quincey makes that very case, in the course of which he manages to connect natural efflorescence to cityscape:

> The whole course of this narrative resembles, and was meant to resemble, a *caduceus* wreathed about with meandering ornaments, or the shaft of a tree's stem hung round and surmounted with some vagrant parasitical plant.... Just as in Cheapside, if you look right and left, the streets so narrow, that lead off at right angles, seem quarried and blasted out of some Babylonian brick-kiln. But if you enquire of the worthy men who live in the neighborhood, you will find it unanimously deposed—that not the streets were quarried out of the bricks, but on the contrary (most ridiculous as it seems), that the bricks have supervened upon the streets. The streets did not intrude amongst the bricks, but those cursed bricks came to imprison the streets. So, also, the ugly pole—hop-pole, vine-pole, espalier, no matter what—is there only for support. Not the flowers are for the pole but the pole is for the flowers. (455)[2]

In Browne, in De Quincey, in Sebald, arabesques exceed providing ornament. They insinuate themselves as the very logic of narrative elaboration. The same is true for Shammas's novel, which, whatever "arabesque" denotes, needs to be pursued in multiple contexts: literary modernism, twentieth-century Hebrew literature, *The Thousand and One Nights*. For it is a composite of autobiography, fiction, and history as commingled genres. Indirectly, *Arabesques* ('*Arabeskot,* in Hebrew)—which, when it was first published in translation, Irving Howe's review described, appositely enough, as "news from elsewhere"[3]—cites the Hebrew Bible and Israeli poets like Amir Gilboa and Natan Alterman in an exceptionally fluid Hebrew (some Israeli critics even faulted it for its highly wrought quality). But *Arabesques* just as often explicitly alludes to Willa Cather, Wallace Stevens, and Borges as well as Bialik, Nahman of Bratslav, and anonymous Palestinian refugee songs. The figure in its carpet is composed of multiple heterogeneous threads.

> But here I am traveling along the road to Silwad holding on to the thread he had interwoven with the warp and woof of my life. Like a weaver I yank at that thread and find myself wondering about the opportunity that has presented itself to me as a result of the new turn of events, and before I have sufficiently considered my next steps, I comb out the unraveled thread and card it again, then turn to impart to it a completely different color and to weave it once more into the frayed tapestry, mending what has unraveled.

What guarantee do I have that this act is not a proclamation of liberty on the part of that thread, once it has become unbound? All at once a story that had apparently come to its end is exposed to a capricious thread, which will stray it into unsuspected regions in an adventure whose outcome we cannot foresee. (*Arabesques*, 36)

The other compound text explored in this chapter is *Abba* ("Father," or "Dad"), a series of short prose fragments, which the Israeli poet Dan Pagis (1930–1986) left unpublished at the time of his death.[4] In its unfinished conclusion, *Abba* adverts to an ultimately unsuccessful metaphor (Pagis questions its utility in the margins[5]): the net.

The claim that this distress, the humiliation woven in dread that is woven in disgust, webs of knots, a fisherman's net that washes ankle-deep in water and catches nothing but the water, a fisherman's net that gathers water and releases water, and its knots are for naught, and it comes up from the water just as it had sunk into it, with dread and humiliation and disgust that is salty and foul—the claim that the web of distress is merely spoiled self-indulgence of someone who has everything (what do I lack? Not income, not a wife and children, not a house, not job security)—this claim usually extends to the argument that if I really had it bad I would have put things in proper perspective. . . . For the net of dread and distress and humiliation, only the holes in that net represent seemingly insignificant things, matters of work or books or relationships with people of the present, whereas the threads of the net and its web of knots represent the same death and suffering that the dim-witted present as a source of comfort. (*Kol ha'shirim*, 368)

The metaphor is overworked, but it offers a unifying image for *Abba* as a whole—a deliberately fragmentary work of recuperation, a web of knots and holes through and by means of which the author addresses his deceased father and his own past. As arabesques are to the formal and stylistic problems posed by Shammas's novel, so *Abba*'s prose fragments position themselves relative to their overall meaning and place in Pagis's oeuvre.

I am making bold to call these prose fragments *partzufim*[6] (or "faces") rather than knots or threads, very loosely adapting the term *partzuf* (singular) from the post-medieval symbol-system of Lurianic Kabbalah, where, as sefirotic visage, it connotes restoration and reconstitution after fragmentation. Although Pagis did not himself label the prose-pieces in this way, nor appeal to sixteenth-century mystical philosophy, I take the warrant from the fact that it is in these pieces—as is programmatically *not* the case in Pagis's famously elusive, self-concealing poetics—that the author dons a subjective, personal identity:

a face continuous with his biographical self.[7] Not only does each isolated fragment present itself, confessionally, as a feature for a face-in-the-making, but in the aggregate, as *partzufim*, they compose a self-portrait—name, patrimony, biography. Along with Sidra Ezrahi, I take these last writings of Pagis to be acts of recuperation—if not redress, exactly, for a singularly austere, self-distancing and fragmentary poetics, then a belated and oblique attempt at memoir or "speech in the wilderness." They are thus both *speaking faces* and perfect *metaphorai*.[8]

As final justification for my naming, not only is one of the six *partzufim* that collectively answer to the agency of *tikkun* (or reconstitution) called *abba* itself, a procreative and supernal force. But also, the last volume of poetry published while Pagis was still alive is the 1988 volume entitled *Shneim-asar panim* (Twelve faces). The arabesque and the recuperative fragment or *partzuf*, then, are the mechanisms by which Shammas and Pagis obliquely memorialize their pasts and their genealogies. To that degree, the two tropes function like the photographs and embedded stories in Sebald's fiction or the ritualized scenes of facing in Gombrowicz or stylized scenes of speech and hearing in Canetti's *Die Stimmen Von Marrakesh*—the latticework of the literature of *midbar*.

As in previous chapters, the analysis proceeds by reading Pagis and Shammas through a kind of double helix. Harold Bloom is famous for arguing that meaning does not inhere within texts but rather *between* them, that "there *is* something uneasily dialectical about literary meaning" (*Kabbalah and Criticism*, 106). Where his theory assumes a temporal relationship—a latter author's belated (and strong) "misreading" of a predecessor's text—the method in this book depends upon a *spatial* ligature, just as dialectical (though, admittedly, this is a strong misreading of Bloom, to match my idiosyncratic allusion to Lurianic symbology). "To interpret," writes Bloom, "is to revise is to defend against influence" (64) through a triadic movement of limitation, substitution, and representation that generates not only an idiosyncratic literary history but also an "antithetical criticism."[9] Here, on the other hand, to criticize is to contrapuntalize is to create influence—to fashion, *laterally,* a kind of echo-chamber. Revisionary ratios, as Bloom calls them, obtain between texts in contiguous space, and not just diachronically.

Parsimonious critics might insist that the only justification for ties binding Shammas and Pagis is their late acquisition and eventual mastery of Hebrew and the fact that both writers composed poetry; each also happens to mention Amir Gilboa as poetic influence; and each of their texts, *Arabesques* and *Abba*, was written within a few years of each other. But these parallels are merely coincidental. In other respects, differentially situated as citizens of the State of Israel, heirs of different cultural traditions, politicized by different forces, the two writers would seem to share little if anything in common.[10] Yet here too, this is only superficially the case. Moreover, the precedent for an intertwining of texts in this chapter is to be found in more than just the sequence of pairings from previous chapters. *Arabesques* itself is contrived as a juxtaposition of two languages, Hebrew and a simulated Arabic, and two narratives, "The Teller" and "The Tale" *(ha'misaper* and *ha'sipur)*, that interlace their strands like a caduceus (the former depicts Shammas as a writer of Hebrew; the latter places him as a young boy in the margin of a generational account of his extended family).[11] The colloquy to be fashioned in this final chapter, then, follows the precedent of text itself and thereby finds its own internal warrant. As before, the point is not an exhaustive account of each work but the intaglio-effect produced by interlamination between them.

The Impossibility of One's Own Place

As a native of Bukovina, passed through the refiner's fire of the *Shoah* to become an immigrant of Palestine-Israel, Pagis used biographical displacement as the basis for a poetics unique in the canon of twentieth-century Jewish literature. Like Aharon Appelfeld, Pagis's purchase on a new, Israeli, identity fundamentally involved *choosing* a language alongside other accoutrements of adoptive identity; nationality follows from the staking of a necessarily *linguistic* claim (and in fact, both Pagis and Appelfeld favor a spare, laconic Hebrew voice). Within four years, Pagis became proficient in a brand-new tongue. Adopting Hebrew meant "a radical displacement of his native language," writes Robert Alter in the introduction to the English translation of Pagis's selected poetry (xi). And the energy of choice was such that, within ten years, Pagis became the preeminent Israeli scholar most closely identified with medieval and post-medieval Hebrew verse.[12]

Anton Shammas also comes to Hebrew as a second language learned as an adolescent, upon moving to Haifa with his family from the Arab village of Fassuta in the Galilee. The epigraph to part 1 of *Arabesques* quotes Shaw's *Pygmalion:* "You told me, you know, that when a child is brought to a foreign country, it picks up the language in a few weeks, and forgets its own. Well, I am a child in your country." But Shammas also comes to the Israeli state as Bloom might put it, belatedly, being the kind of Israeli—a Christian Arab—as well as poet for whom the sentiments expressed in the *Hatikvah,* the National Anthem of Israel, sound alien in the mouth, as exclusivist as they are ill-fitting:

> While yet within the heart, inwardly,
> The soul of the Jew yearns,
> And towards the vistas of the East, eastward,
> An eye looks toward Zion,
> Our hope is not yet lost,
> The hope born of two thousand years,
> To be a free people in our land,
> In the land of Zion and Jerusalem,

Instead Shammas might ask, with Yehuda Amichai (but from the perspective of an insider who has been made an outsider, whom the first person plural fails to include), "What are we doing / In this dark land casting / Yellow shadows that slice our eyes?"[13] For Shammas, too, *choosing* to write in Hebrew expresses a governing displacement, or as Brian McHale characterizes it in his review of *Arabesques,* a calculated "seizing [of] the means of representation."[14]

It is through the arabesque and the *partzuf* that Shammas and Pagis respectively narrate their enduring sense of displacement as citizens perhaps only secondarily of Israel and foremost of the Elsewhere, a place that can only continually compensate, still hold out unfulfilled promise, for *midbar,* for place lost or ceded. Fittingly, Pagis appears twice in the Stanley Burnshaw-edited volume of modern Hebrew poetry, *The Modern Hebrew Poem Itself*—once as a poet in his own right and once again as a commentator on the very last poem published by Avraham Ben-Yitzhak (Canetti's Dr. Sonne), *"Ashrei ha'zor'im"* (Happy are the sowers) The poem of Pagis's reproduced in the volume is *"Yoman ha'shayit,"* (The log book), one of several poems on what Dalia Ravikovitch, the translator (and poet in her own right) calls "unsentimental leave-takings" (178). The poem narrates a journey that did not ultimately take place: to be somewhere—at the "island of death's treasures"—is to have cancelled the getting there. "For we, who did not set sail at all, have arrived. One must cast anchor and forget."

We can read in this lyric perhaps Pagis's own unsentimental attitude toward what the *partzufim* in *Abba* recurrently name "immigration"—a demythologizing that the prose fragments, unlike the poetry, grapple with autobiographically. As for the poem by Ben-Yitzhak (perhaps his most famous), one of its middle verses reads, "Happy are they who know their hearts cry out from the wilderness [*mi-midbar*] / And on their lips silence blossoms," and that concludes (as alternately translated by Pagis), "And their lot shall be a constant sacrifice accompanied by speechlessness." (Recall the verse from Exodus quoted in the introduction, "the wilderness [or, *speech*] has closed them in.")[15] Where Ben-Yitzhak's sower-poets "adhere" (Pagis's word) to silence, both Pagis and Shammas concentrate their voices like a laser through a refracted or fragmented idiom.

Ben Yitzhak's poem licenses a self-silencing, and indeed 1928, the year in which this poem appeared, was the last in which Abraham Sonne published poetry. Shammas and Pagis, on the other hand, must each attempt to *speak after* language's investiture, as it were: Pagis writes short, autobiographical prose passages after many years of publishing an idiosyncratic body of self-displacing poetry; Shammas takes on an entire literature whose prior voices meld Israeli nationality and Jewish identity without the dramatic fissure that underpins his anomalous case of Israeli-but-not-Jew. Shammas takes up residence in language as one would in a foreign country, accenting it and also estranging it more knowingly than would a native speaker (Conrad writing in English is the great exemplar here, with whom Shammas has more in common in this respect than does, say, Said or Aciman). Pagis abandons a lyric albeit dispersed persona for a prosaics that makes the intensely private accessibly public.[16]

Through a conversation between dead father and (in a double sense) surviving son, Pagis's *partzufim* perform a willed posthumousness, as is evident in the very first of them:

"So what, Daneleh, are you planning to write all of this and print it? Write, write, don't be shy. If somebody happens to read it, surely he won't believe it. The main thing is that you yourself truly believe it."

"You didn't understand your father," said the heavy-set man, Dad's card-playing partner, "you misunderstood him completely. You are like him, but only on the outside, if you forgive my bluntness." I get angry: "And so what? He needs to come back to life in order for me to understand him?" "No, no," says the card-playing partner, "you are the one who needs to come back to life. But if you forgive my bluntness, you don't have much of a chance of doing that." (341)

The first words belong to Pagis's father, and the second to an associate. Pagis himself speaks third, only to be tripped up and made to change places with the deceased father. Even in the prose passages, that is to say, when Pagis's writing finally speaks through a mask that resembles the self ("Dan P."), subjectivity is diminished.[17] The *partzufim* seem to ask, what happens to a self when it leaves and when it arrives elsewhere, when it immigrates? Can it claim itself as the same? Is there a figure in the carpet, like Eudoxia's map that can be used to locate and decipher it?

Unhomed in a deep and lasting sense, Dan Pagis concretizes de Certeau's assertion that "writing is born of the impossibility of one's own place [and] articulates the constantly initial fact that the subject is never authorized by a place . . . that he is always foreign to himself." The place that fails to authorize him, or rather the place that is never appealed to as authorizing four decades of poetry but comes to haunt the posthumously published prose, is Radautz (Radauti in present day Romania, Radevitz or Radowitz to Yiddish-speakers), thirty-five miles southwest of Czernowitz.[18] Writes Pagis in one of his last prose poems, "The Souvenir."

The town where I was born, Radautz, in the country of Bukovina, threw me out when I was ten. On that day she forgot me, as if I had died, and I forgot her too. We were both satisfied with that.

Forty years later, all at once, she sent me a souvenir. It was a new photograph, her latest winter portrait. A canopied wagon is waiting in the courtyard. The horse, turning its head, gazes affectionately at an elderly man who is busy closing some kind of gate. Ah, it's a funeral. There are just two members left in the Burial Society: the gravedigger and the horse.

But it's a splendid funeral; all around, in a strong wind, thousands of snowflakes are crowding, each one a crystal star with its own particular design. So there is still the same impulse to be special, still the same illusions. Since all snow-stars have just one pattern: six points, a Star of David in fact. In a minute they will all start melting and turn into a mass of plain snow. In their midst my elderly town has prepared a grave for me also. (*The Selected Poetry of Dan Pagis*, 9)

Place has become accessible through the trace of an unexpected found object. The long-lost, diaspora-producing home of Radautz is belatedly captured by the power of documentary evidence; a photograph of the present has made the past once again briefly visible.[19] Similarly—though Shammas is now an émigré, not an internal refugee—the place that keeps destabilizing itself by changing under its residents' and claimants' feet in *Arabesques* is the palimpsest village of Fassuta: "Our village is built on the ruins of the Crusader castle of Fassove, which was built on the ruins of Mishafta, the Jewish village that had been settled after the destruction of the Second Temple by the Harim, a group of deviant priests (11)." In its recurrent sedimentation, most recently a Palestinian village in the new Jewish State, Fassuta historically keeps revising itself—not unlike the earth in the Pagis poem entitled "Brothers': "Abel remains in the filed. Cain remains Cain. And since it was decreed that he is to be a wanderer, he wanders diligently. Each morning he changes horizons. One day he discovers; the earth tricked him all those years. *It* had moved, while he, Cain, had walked on one spot. Had walked, jogged, run, on a single piece of ground exactly as big as his sandals" (*The Selected Poetry of Dan Pagis*, 7).

In turn, the entire text of *Abba* (such as it stands, since Pagis probably intended to refine or add to it at the time of his death[20]) can be said to work in the fashion of a palimpsest. Not only does it coordinate several discrete temporalities, but it also layers itself by incorporating letters written by Pagis's mother, aunt, and grandmother to his father in 1934, which graft the Bukovinan past onto the pre-posthumous Israeli present. As Shammas's novel memorializes the bygone and superceded but also jars internally against a disjointed contemporary story that alternates with the chronicle of the Shammas family in Fassuta, so Pagis's *partzufim* progress sequentially but loosely and episodically, formally framed by three cemetery visits to his father's grave Pagis makes on the occasion of his *yortsayt* (death-anniversary). What weakens both works is probably also what gives them their strength—the extra-literary, psychological component that authenticates them as documents attempting to assimilate the unassimilable—Pagis's conflicted relationship with his father, Shammas's political and linguistic project. Both Shammas and Pagis treat the impossibility of one's own place as a kind of first principle; memoir has nowhere to go but backward, as if compelled to establish footholds that risk giving way or evanescing.

In the case of *Arabesques*, Shammas deliberately undermines his own authorial privilege at the end of his novel by suggesting that his entire discourse has been ventriloquized by an alter ego named Michael Abyad aka Anton Shammas. Abyad offers an Ariadne's thread for a labyrinthine text by way of explanation:

I decided to write my autobiography in your name and to be present in it as the little boy who died. A piece of the Palestinian fate that would confuse even King Solomon. . . . I didn't tell anyone about it. I locked it all up in the closet again after I'd come out of myself, you might say. And then a few days ago Larry told me that the members of the International Writing Program were going to be visiting him. I glanced absently at the list of members, and I saw my fictitious name there. Which is also your name. Take this file and see what you can do with it. Translate it, adapt it, add or subtract. But leave me in. (259)[21]

In other words, part and parcel of Christian Arab Israeli identity is to be fragmented at the core, to fail to resolve into a whole, substantive self. Strictly speaking, Shammas seems to say, my "place" is an impossibility, neither here nor there but elsewhere, such that my novel will not provide the Eudoxia's carpet to rectify the necessary and permanent confusion; it will merely reimagine it.

In an essay written after Shammas emigrated to America entitled "Autocartography," the author spins a twist on Calvino's conceit: the granddaughter of Palestinian refugees, living in America, counterfactually returns to Palestine by "drawing her own internal map of return and going *home* to Palestine but this time in Michigan, the Palestine that is on 45° latitude by 87° longitude, in the southwestern most tip of the Upper Peninsula, in a county called Menominee" (*The Geography of Identity*, 473). Quoting Walter Benjamin's "The Work of Art in the Age of Mechanical Reproduction," Shammas speculates that such a "replica" of Palestine can imaginatively be made to line up with the original, and thus "blow the whole concept of displacement from within." And yet, even the replica is vulnerable to becoming undone—an always unstable Eudoxia—for those whose lives are born under the sign of *midbar*. A Palestine, Michigan (though not identical with the identically named town in the Upper Peninsula), it turns out, was settled by American Zionists in the 1880s. Place lies still at a near distance.

In Pagis's "The Souvenir" above, the evacuation that happened once echoes in successive disappearances: a funeral reduced to a remnant, snowflakes shedding their distinctiveness when commingled. In one of the final *partzufim*, in reference to Pagis's choice of first-name upon immigration, his father tells him, "I never said anything. I understood that you wanted to disappear in the country, simply to be absorbed into it, like water into sand" (366). "The Souvenir" works as a bridge between Pagis's poetry and the prose pieces (though many of the latter seem positively anti-poetic such is their prosaism). It joins his specifically poetic concern with de-individualization (how to conceive of personal identity after the Shoah) with the *realia* of Pagis's past and pre-posthumous future: names, dates, family memorabilia, a father's jocosely querulous voice, the ritual of saying *kaddish*.

The *thrownness* to which Pagis refers in that poem is a sensibility Shammas shares as well. In an insistently decentered narrative, perhaps the most emblematic protagonist is not Shammas himself but rather the marginal figure of Laylah Khoury, brought by Shammas's father to Beirut from Fassuta as an orphan, expelled by Israeli soldiers to Jenin in 1948 and again across the border to Ramallah on Jordan's West Bank. The search for her and the meaning of her identity dovetails with ramifications of Shammas's own identity as narrator and Christian Arab Israeli writing in Hebrew, as the losing of one's place that follows from expulsion drives the narrative's need to claim and hold onto a voice.

> In my heart I was certain that this Laylah Khoury, should our paths be destined to cross eventually, would take her image as sketched by the family and blur it beyond recognition. Indeed, something of this anguished soul—who as a girl of ten was condemned to wander from her home to the land of the cedars and when she wished to return to the scene of her childhood was flung, instead, by fate's capricious hand to scenes which would in due time be exposed (since history loves repetitions), to that outstretched arm which yet again would deflect the course of her life, in 1948, to eternal exile within her own homeland—something of this anguished soul had seeped into my consciousness all these years and had formed relics of doubt, forbidden to the touch. (34)

The marginal figure of Laylah Khoury thus lies at the text's center, as the city of Radautz serves in some way as *Abba*'s hieroglyphic key.

Cherry Herring and Olive Oil

After the short *partzuf* in which Pagis and the card partner trade jibes, an anecdote relates Pagis's discovery of his father's death as he and his son, Yoni, arrive at Lod airport on a return-trip to Israel. A suitcase that contains a duty-free bottle of Danish cherry brandy purchased on the plane accidentally falls off the luggage cart, smashing the bottle. "An elderly man passes by us and says, 'What's happening with you? Is something broken?' And indeed, we are in the middle of a dark red puddle. The small suitcase is oozing sticky cherry brandy, bittersweet, disgusting, which covers the tile floor. I remove the pieces of broken glass, run to the faucet in an attempt to save the soaked papers and shirts, and to wipe the suitcase—of course, in vain. The super, sticky liquor resists. To this day there is still a remnant of it in the suitcase" (344). The liquid's permeating flow, the shards of glass, the offhand, unrelated but apropos remark, the remnant: these signal that something irretrievable has taken place. *Abba* is studded with uncanny moments such as this, when materiality changes state, when something comes into or goes out of the world. In another *partzuf*, Pagis's father arrives "slightly late—a green felt hat, an elegant jacket—high-spirited, almost sprightly" (34),[22] only to transform into a body donning *tachrimim* (burial shrouds) and laid out on the burial society's bier, which, like a latter-day Uzza putting forth his hand to the Ark of God,[23] "the son" (Pagis) "is forbidden to touch." In still another *partzuf*, entitled "Dream," Pagis's father sits with him on the bed one moment—"That's father, isn't it? Heavy snows cover him on this wide bed. I (it's me, isn't it?) sit next to him, looking at him. This is it, then. But no, he extends his hand to me, he's alive, full of life, the snow has vanished, and his body (so beautiful in photographs from his youth), and with its large moles, is swelling up" (36). And the very next moment, "[he] shrivels up, tears away from the bed, yellow and straight and dried-up like a stalk of straw, and floats in the air."

But the spilt and sticky brandy is surely the most arresting of these transfigurative instances, standing over the whole work (in his marginal note written in German, Pagis wonders aloud, "Remove this? If it stays, can be less symbolic even though everything is factual"). There is something eerily fateful about such accidents in life, where what is contained bleeds and leaks out into public space; certainly, the connection with mortality in Pagis's piece is unmistakable. It is as though one has wet oneself, as though one's insides were suddenly visible and exterior. The unsettling quality of the incident remains unrelieved by the story's coda, in which Pagis observes laconically, "On another trip—which one it doesn't really matter—I was careful to purchase a bottle of Cherry Herring and carry it in this small suitcase. It made it in one piece" (344). Because it stands for what won't stay put, for what seeps out, "Cherry Herring" is *Abba* writ even smaller: after death, life leaks. But what spills throughout all the *partzufim*, uniting them, is talk—Pagis to his father, his father to him. As Sidra Ezrahi puts it, "The poetics of self-transcendence yields to the prosaics of memory: the father's dematerialization through death suspends, for once, the imperative of surrealist *poetic* dematerialization and creates its own counter-imperative" (*Booking Passage*, 173). Thus, Pagis is accosted during mourning (the ritually torn clothes) in one of those encounters in which we find ourselves accidentally recognized without being at all recognized:

Dan P., how are you, are you going down from the holy city to have some fun in Tel Aviv?" I hide the tear in my shirt. "And how are you doing?" He finds an empty seat behind me and talks right into my ear. "Listen, I have been meaning for some time to ask you for a favor. I was told you have connections with publishers. I wrote an extraordinary story; I'm not saying it's a fine piece, let others decide that. But it's very strange, very distinctive, about family. Are you willing to read it and recommend it? Preferably in writing. Do you know that your shirt is torn? ("The Request," 350)

Even stray dogs are given voice: "The streets are empty. Only a puny dog that somehow looks familiar totters at my side. At the street corner he turns to me and says; 'Again you've succumbed. Your father, don't you know, arrived unannounced, you did not have to act the host. And besides, why this fumbling when all is already lost. . . . If you held your own, we'd have no qualm, as we say here on the street among the dogs'" ("Dan Pagis: Last Poems," Keller translation, 33–34).

Unlike the distended or atomistic lyric persona of Pagis's poetry (the speaker in "Written in Pencil in the Sealed Railway-Car,"[24] for example, invokes a posthumous hearer rather than speaking directly with him or her), the prose fragments in *Abba* entail conversation, a give-and-take between speakers beyond—or alongside—the grave. Eavesdropping on the most private of colloquies, we are indeed, as Pagis puts it, in the middle of a dark, red puddle.

In Shammas's *Arabesques,* the puddle is also dark, but olive-colored and composed of oil. "'I see three white horses standing near the oak tree by the monastery, guarding the treasure, and that is the place to dig. But now I see only oil.' She was looking with downcast eyes at her brother, who presided over the *mandal*. He begged her to look once more into the slick of olive oil floating on the water in the saucer before her" (17). These are Shammas's mother and uncle as children. The *mandal* is a vehicle for visions, and at this moment, Elias (the uncle), disappointed that his sister Elaine can see no further because the *mandal* has become inexplicably "sealed," tosses the saucer over the stairway railing in a fit of pique. "The water trickled through the pores in the stone, but the oil stain on one of the paving stones did not fade and will appear nine years later in one of the pictures in the family album that I so loved to look at when I was a child" (19). This is not the only time that olive oil is spilt in Shammas's novel. Fifty-one years later, in 1980, soldiers of the Israeli Defense Forces harass a woman named Surayyah Sa'id, formerly Layla Khoury, the mother of twin deaf-mute sons. "When she began to explain that the sons were deaf and couldn't hear the orders, they yelled at her to raise her hands and face the wall and shut up. Then the soldiers spilled the contents of two jars of olive oil upon the floor. . . . And the twins stood on one side and, like a pair of mute turtledoves, watched the olive oil seep into the earth" (33).

And later in the next installment of "The Tale," one of Fassuta's priests, who composes a work in careful calligraphy in a notebook, "which would glorify the Catholic Church among all the Arabic-speaking peoples" (67), is distressed to find that his cat has accidentally knocked the notebook into a large crock of oil, for he discovers that "the calligraphy that had adorned the pages of the notebook had returned to its liquid state" (68). Shammas's aunt interrupts the priest to tell him that her mother is dying, whereupon he gives her (with oil still on his hands, one presumes) an amulet in the form of a piece of paper to be immersed in a glass of water. When brought to her mother's lips, the water tastes to her not only of ink but, mysteriously, of oil.

Or again, situated at the entrance to the olive press at a later point in the story, Shammas watches

> the shadow of the horse cast by the weak lantern on the walls and on the heaps of olive husks, and my soul goes out to my father, whose hands now grasp the handle of the press and carefully lower the iron plate that squeezes the oil through the groaning sieves, set around the gleaming upright axle of the press. The oil than flows into the sump from which I can take a bit of oil to dip my bread into. . . . The rustle of the crispy bread I am eating fresh from the tin-domed oven distracts Abu Shacker to another realm of pleasure, and he breaks off a handful of the loaf and brings the crustiness to his mouth. I throw a last glance at the shadow of the horse plodding around the walls, at my father standing outside the circle, and escape into the night, cheeks burning. I throw the rest of the loaf into the heaps of olive husks and wipe my tears with a shrug of my sleeve. (114)

Olive oil, like tobacco, is an agrarian staple of Shammas's Galilean village life, so it is perhaps not surprising that it functions as one of the more lubricious textual objects in a novel that constantly recycles and re-embeds its metonyms—a pillow, a feather, various enclosures and apertures. In the instances above, it seems particularly associated with varying degrees of forfeiture or abridgement. The trail of dispossession, for example, forfeiture of the power to see visions, failure to author and authorize, to claim and protect what is inalienably one's own: Shammas's book narrates a veined saga of such losses—of property, of land, of object, of story.

Coupled this way, Shammas's and Pagis's texts are each *stained*, with liquor, with oil, which is how each palpably records its loss.

Cemeteries

The dominant mise-en-scène of *Abba*—a cemetery vigil—appears as a leitmotiv in *Arabesques* in the first chapter of part 2, "The Teller," situated at Père Lachaise cemetery in Paris. In this strand of the novel, Shammas has been invited to participate in an International Writer Program in Iowa City, where he will fraternize with fellow writers including an Israeli, Yehoshua Bar-On, a thinly disguised portrait of the novelist A. B. Yehoshua; a Palestinian; and a French woman, Jewish, named Amira and born in Alexandria. Before the conference begins, Shammas finds himself in Paris on a stopover; Bar-On and Amira are there as well, before they all fly to Cedar Rapids. A dream initiates the story line here, in which Amira, who draws close to Shammas later in the thread but at this point is involved with a married photographer, imagines herself to be in the Jewish cemetery of Alexandria, as her deceased father takes photographs of her in front of the tombstone. What the dream condenses and displaces is a series of visits to Père Lachaise, where she is posed among the tombs by her lover.

Shammas finds himself at the cemetery as well, searching for Proust's tomb and finding on the way the grave of one Mahmoud Al-Hamshari, a PLO representative born in the village of Em Khaled.

> Beyond the hedge, ten graves to the west, Marcel Proust lay buried. It must have been the French sense of humor that granted both of them, the man of the lost country and the man of the *temps perdu* nearly identical graves.... Fifty years separate the two lost times, the two darknesses. But both are equally lost under the flowers of remembrance.... And under the black marble lay the two lost men, each in the darkness of his own tomb, a Jew of Time and an Arab of Place. And apart from the almost matched graves and the avenue of trees reflected in the smoothness of the black marble, they appeared to share nothing at all. (136)[25]

Speculating on W. G. Sebald's "quarrel with Proust," my introduction proposed that it is the emplacement of a particular gravestone, its rootedness *here* as opposed to elsewhere, that authorizes and insists on the dogma of place. Conversely, in *Abba* and *Arabesques,* cemeteries possess a peculiarly de-authorizing power. Revenants converse after death; tombs ironically hail each other's occupants through proximity; ghosts and graves, all are each other's elsewhere.

In Pagis's case, what cemeteries do is to localize, individuate, and shelter a potentially displaceable, unmemorialized mass. The threads of his net (the sum of its holes, we recall), "accompany me daily," he writes in the last *partzuf*. "In every rectangular flowerbed I see a mass grave that was decorated later on, even in the rug in the room, even in—what else should I say?" (368). In the Pagis lexicon, perhaps a cemetery is merely one more "point of departure":

> —Hidden in the study at dusk,
> I wait, not yet lonely.
> A heavy walnut bureau opens up the night.
> The clock is a tired sentry,
> Its steps growing faint.
> —From where? In Grandfather's typewriter,
> An Underwood from ancient times,
> Thousands of alphabets are ready,
> What tidings?
> —I think not everything is in doubt.
> I follow the moment, not to let it slip away.
> My arms are rather thin.
> I am nine years old.
> —Beyond the door begins
> The interstellar space which I'm ready for.
> Gravity drains from me like colors at dusk.
> I fly so fast that I'm motionless
> And leave behind me
> The transparent wake of the past.
> (The Selected Poetry of Dan Pagis, 112)

Shammas's novel begins with a double death: of his grandmother Alia in 1954 and of his father in 1978. As in Pagis and in what Hanan Hever calls the "Arabian iconography of the arabesque," the different temporalities are pleated, tessellated. A portion of ground in Fassuta does get marked by a stone that covers a depth in this strand of the narrative ("The Tale"), yet it is not a graveyard, but rather a cave reputed to hide Crusader gold and that is stopped up by a boulder, a site of mythic origins that the text slyly deconstructs. It is thus really only in those scenes at Père Lachaise that Shammas's novel stages a pilgrimage to a cemetery, and it too, as in Pagis's poem above, signals a stopover or point of departure.

What other significations attach to cemeteries? One way to approach the question is to consider what informs each text at the broadest or most foundational level of rhetorical levels. *Abba* and *Arabesques* predicate or imply something about death and place in relation to their own prosaics by each staking a claim for the location of identity after personal and communal loss.[26] For Shammas, the personal is inextricably tied to the political and the linguistic, and to that degree, his novel could be said to inculcate (with qualification) the three-fold "revolutionary" premise of a minor literature as outlined by Gilles Deleuze and Félix Guattari in their oft-cited book about Kafka in which they formulate the trope of deterritorialization.[27] For Shammas isn't merely offering up another indigenous fiction that borrows from the magical-realist and postmodern and postcolonial palette of works like Marquez's *A Hundred Years of Solitude* or Rushdie's *Shame*. He is also writing in Hebrew, which, given his minority status in Israeli society, is roughly analogous to Kafka's use of German as a Czech Jew. In any event, *Arabesques* is a veritable prototype of how to become a nomad, a gypsy, an immigrant in one's own, or the master, language.[28]

The section of Shammas's novel that takes place at Père Lachaise (Hever calls it an intermezzo) is the novel's most out-of-place since it is located neither in Israel nor the United States. The action in "The Tale" takes place largely in the former, with the latter merely being mentioned as Michael Abayd's adopted home; most of "The Teller" takes place in Iowa, though Shammas, of course, comes from Israel (Haifa). Paris doesn't quite have the disaporic thrust of Argentina, where earlier generations of the Shammas family as narrated in "The Tale" find themselves expatriated or exiled, after first having left the environs of rural Syria in the nineteenth century. But Père Lachaise is effectively neither here nor there, one site in an ambient surround where artists and émigrés typically seek inspiration, acceptance, and solidarity and where Proust wrote and lies buried, but that Shammas passes through on the way to or from some place else.

As Shammas the author complicates a facile dichotomy between Jew and Arab through the supplementary compound of Arab Christianity (the author in the text does not unequivocally label himself, as does Said, a "Palestinian"[29]), so he makes ambiguous a simple polarity between the places of Israel and America (the respective locales for "The Tale" and "The Teller"), by adding the stopover point of Père Lachaise. Hever has suggested that *Arabesques* could be "the most truly Israeli novel yet written," because it is one that "imagines an Israeli essence through an intricate essence of negations" (50). In line with that appraisal, the narrative sequence at Père Lachaise would seem to negate (or at least qualify) both the American antithesis and Israeli thesis of Shammas's text in each locale for which the character-narrator of Shammas himself is already decentered. In discussing the text's two strands, Hever observes: "In fact, any differences between the two versions can be taken equally well as a contradiction or a simple matter of mutual indifference. Each story line has its own claim to reality, and the reader has no way of determining which reality is 'genuine'" (53). The liminal quality of the cemetery episode ensures that it works to similar effect: Père Lachaise becomes a point of intersection between three distinct yet connected narrations, that of Shammas himself in third-person; his Lebanese cousin Nadia who lives in Paris; and Amira, who, like Shammas, is about to leave for the International Writing Program—each of the three voices bleeds into the others, blurring the borders among them.

Interwoven, the voices form an arabesque, as does the near-contiguity of the Jew of Time and the Arab of Place in the Parisian cemetery (Proust, as Yael Feldman points out in "Postcolonial Memory, Postmodern Intertextuality: Anton Shammas's *Arabesques* Revisited," being the European high modernist "progenitor of this technique"—arabesque-like *mémoire involontaire*). If Fassuta and its narration orient themselves non-teleologically in time, in cyclical fashion, the cemetery of Père Lachaise marks the place where linear time meets its dead end—or, for religious believers, where a somber pause is interpolated before the onset of linear eternity. Cemeteries, especially those like the Parisian one in which notables are buried, serve the needs of the living as much as if not more than they do the dead—the need to arrive, to encamp, to hold vigil. In one of her sections from part 2, "The Teller," Amira says of the United States, "They could use a historical sense of death over there. Their tombstones are so much newer than ours. They'll just eat up an exhibition of death with some tradition behind it" (84). In a later section, speaking of her father in Alexandria, buried in the same cemetery, presumably, that André Aciman commemorates in *False Papers*, she says, "Do you know that the Hebrew letters that were fastened to his tombstone were stolen? An Arab stonecutter came and carved them into the stone. I was surprised to see Hebrew letters on it, because he lived his life in Arabic. So why should his death be in Hebrew? Come to think of it, maybe that is why Hebrew is the language of death for me" (93–94).

What Amira says here has already been partly anticipated by Shammas's choice of epigraph from a poem by Amichai for this section: "Dresses of beautiful women in blue and white. / And everything in three languages: / Hebrew, Arabic, and Death."[30] These are indeed the three linguistic centers of the novel, a rich and mesmeric spoken Arabic, an adaptive, multi-layered literary Hebrew that functions in part to render it, and a universalizing mortality that fixes (or transcends) the terms of the oppositions driving the novel: Arab/Jew, Hebrew/Arabic, Israeli/American. One reason for the narrative's pause at Père Lachaise, which it then abandons for further wandering or internal expatriation, is that settled spaces like cemeteries with the sharp boundaries they mark between the dead and the living (or for that matter, between row of grave and row of grave) clash with the infinite permutability of structures like the arabesque. One may make a vigil to Proust's tomb, in other words, but text proper is where one makes contact with the spirit of arabesque.

Late in the novel, Shammas explicates the meaning of *arabesque* as a motive for narrative design:

> [Uncle Yusef's] stories were plaited into one another, embracing and parting, twisting and twining in the infinite arabesque of memory. Many of his stories he told again and again, with seemingly minor changes, while other stories were granted only two or three tellings during the whole of his lifetime. All of them, however, flowed around him in a swirling current of illusion that linked beginnings to endings, the inner to the external, the reality to the tale. . . . That's how Yusef was. On the one hand, he was a devout Catholic, who like Saint Augustine, was utterly certain, as if the Virgin Mary herself had assured him, that the years of his life were but links in a chain leading to salvation. On the other hand, as if to keep an escape route open for himself, in case the only reality was dust returning to dust and the jaws of the beast of nothingness gaped wide, he could still believe that the circular, the winding, and the elusive, had the power to resist nothingness. . . . And here I am, his nephew, who served as an altar boy until I was twelve and since have trod among the alien corn, here I am trying to separate myself from Uncle Yusef's circular pagan-like time and follow the linear path of Christian time, which supposedly leads to salvation, to the breaking of the vicious circles. (227–28)[31]

To dramatize the opposition between linear and cyclical, oriental-pagan and occidental-Christian, Shammas ends the intermezzo at Père Lachaise with one of several instances in the novel of a floating signifier—the folkloric, "pagan" motif of a red cock's crimson feather (its referent is the mythic rooster Ar-Rasad, who stands guard over the entrance to the cave where the crusader treasure is reputed to lie buried). If Hebrew is associated with death in Amira's mind, it is the imaginative regenerative vehicle ("the language of grace," Yehoshua Bar-On calls it) for Shammas by which the tapestry of folk culture—as well as the postmodern crazy quilt of identity—gets woven.

Proust, Hebrew language, the arabesque: all these bearers of meaning are stilled at Père Lachaise and open out in the sections of the novel that enframe it—as in the concluding lines from a poem by Shammas published in 1979, "One language ahead, another one behind. / And I imagine things in my no-man's land."[32] The cemetery scene is the text's topographical dead center, not because it balances oppositions, holding them in equipoise, but because it freezes them and substitutes the publicly consecrated for the privately (Shammas) or communally (Fassuta) enlivened. At one point in the first section of "The Teller," Amira tells her lover, "It was a way to stay in touch with my father. Now it's become something else. . . . I only know that you're protected there behind your wife and behind your camera. And I'm exposed. And my being exposed is what you want to show in your pictures. A grave that's closed and sealed, against a woman who's exposed and defenseless" (88). In *Arabesques,* a cemetery is where both Hebrew and Arabic are outstripped by the third language, death.

Hunting for his father's grave the location of which he fears he has mistaken, Pagis writes, "What am I complaining for? It's not here that I lost you and this is not where I will find you. In our long polemic, you have the last word; it is inscribed on the tombstone in black letters, here in front of my eyes" ("1984," 357). Throughout the *partzufim* that take place at the cemetery, Pagis records a state of mind that is distinctly out of place, misplaced. Pagis's father dies on the ninth of Av, the enshrined date of mourning in the Hebrew calendar, which means that private mourning has already been subsumed, outdistanced, dislocated by the collective remembrance of national tragedies. On each of the three anniversaries narrated by the text, the cemetery is therefore bustling with mourners, cantors for hire, peddlers selling memorial candles. Freighted by obsequies, the cemetery is not where his father will be found, though it is where centripetal energies exercise their pull, as Sidra Ezrahi suggests.

But perhaps it is in talk, banter, colloquy. In an early *partzuf,* Pagis off-handedly and seamlessly segues from memorials of the vanished past, on the one hand, to the living language of Hebrew (as acquired by his father), on the other: "Remember, Daneleh, how we looked for the photographs mother sent me when you were four, a month before she died? I found them in the closet. Here you are maybe five, adorable in the Russian shirt. And Daneleh, I also have with me a report I must submit to the Bureau tomorrow. Do you mind going over the Hebrew?" (Keller, 33). Another *partzuf,* entitled "1983," begins, "Since his death a year ago, Dad speaks better Hebrew" (352). The *partzufim* constantly remind us that even though Pagis's father preceded him by twelve years as an immigrant to Palestine, he remains in part—as Shammas would have it—"a child in your country," that is, unlike Pagis himself, linguistically belated; his speech is rendered full of periphrases such as "I simply don't know how to phrase it" and "if this is the right form of the word" and "if you understand me."

Belatedness, linguistic or otherwise, is one of *Abba*'s overarching themes. Father and son have reconciled too late; each arrives too late relative to the other: reciprocal understanding has arrived late as well. In "The First Anniversary," at the gravesite, Pagis speaks:

> They all turned to leave and I linger a bit longer with you. It's good you didn't laugh this time. I was only four years old when you traveled away and left me, and seventeen when I traveled to you after the war. A simple reckoning, how many years? After that we lived in Israel close to each other, on both sides of those years. And at the very end, for no fault of mine, just by chance, I was not with you. You arrived late during your life, I arrived late for your death. The score leads towards a draw and may even not get to that. And it is really no longer needed; I absolve you of all your vows and all your promises and all your excuses. (351)

The cemetery merely picks up where quotidian life between father and son has left off: the two elude each other. Thus, in life,

> And of course always the same question that you keep coming back to, why didn't I wait for you in Haifa [when you arrived in Palestine]. I want to repeat my response to this because you tend to forget. No one knew when the boat would arrive. There were mines scattered in the open seas; there was no schedule. They told us they would let us know, but even Haifa's townspeople didn't know, let alone those of Tel Aviv. (351)

So in death,

> I happen to come here, Dad, to your big cemetery: the father of some friend died—you didn't know him—and I came to the funeral. The announcement said, as always: gather by the entrance gate. I came an hour early so I could visit you. I have on me a note with your address—block, plot, row, and the grave number. How do I get there? At the entrance, they told me: right and again another right, go straight and then left, and it's in that area. I march energetically to my destination.
>
> But what is this, there is no logic here, after block ten comes block twenty-six and after it block nine. In the distance I see a living person and ask him: excuse me, where is block twenty-five? He stretches his hands in a gesture of polite despair: he also is new to this place.

Time is running short, I am not sure how much will be left for both of us. True, I didn't come just for you, I caught a ride on somebody else's funeral, but so what? Immediately you have to take revenge, to hide, to let me get lost (now I am really running) amidst all these names?

I call you with a loud voice: "See you, Dad!" You will surely hear me from where you are. I have to get back to the entrance, to the dead stranger who is easy to find. ("Strange Burial," 355)

Nevertheless, at the same time, father and son can also uncannily keep pace. Pagis: "This year I decided: no cantor. We stand in front of the tombstone (they cheated us, we paid for second-rate and they provide third-rate)" (351). His father: "At the Jewish Agency, though they cheated me, I paid for first class and they stuck you in third class, but never mind" (352).

The cemetery in Shammas is an interlude. In Pagis, it is a place where things, persons, events, fail to align. Both *Arabesques* and *Abba* initiate one into private mental spaces overseen by gravesites, only to wave off and send away. One asks rightfully, therefore: what are we doing here in these texts, in the first place? Where, indeed, is *our* place, and does it indeed come "first"?

Reading as Poaching?

"The Art of Contraction"

At first he thinks the entire meadow in its abundance belongs to him, with all its thousands of green surprises. Then he realizes that he can't bear such chaos. True, the grass blades aren't very high, they reach no farther than his knees, maybe just his ankles, and yet they are a labyrinth, twisted, deceptive. There is not a single path, and thus an infinity of paths: free to choose any direction he wishes, he is irretrievably lost.

Well then, he chooses contraction. Not a meadow, but a patch of lawn. Not even that, but three blades of grass. Not three, not even one (and this, he feels, is the crux of the matter), not even a single blade of grass, but the picture of one. This is the essence.

Finally, after he hangs it on the wall, he understands: this painted blade of grass, which implies the entire meadow, also negates the entire meadow. (*The Selected Poetry of Dan Pagis*, 87)

This is an instructive lesson for the poet and for all students of mimesis. But the bystander, the traveler whom gravestones ask to pause, may meditate on it as well. The appropriate response to the art of contraction; its role for an ethics of reading; letting x "stand for" y; the proper thing to do with it when we suppose we have discovered the key to a textual riddle: these are all elements in the practical difficulty of reading tombstones—especially those in Hebrew, with their many acronyms and abbreviations. But these are also all questions presupposed by each of this chapter's texts, made unavoidable through their juxtaposition.

Both *Abba* and *Arabesques* circle back on themselves, to different degrees, as willfully ciphered works. Shammas produces the kind of fiction for which readers have to do almost too much work. Each by itself, parts 1 and 2 of the narrative make enormous demands on simple textual processing. Together, twined like De Quincey's caduceus, they require a prodigious reserve of hermeneutic generosity. Pagis's prose passages, on one hand, offer prosaic relief from an ingeniously puzzled poetics where part of the poems' unpacking involves guessing the identity of the speaker; they are consciously meditated riddles. On the other hand, even lying open as they do, they suggest an opaque mystery, and not only because we know they are written by the poet Dan Pagis. Almost banal in its descriptions, episodic, and unfinished, *Abba* reads as something we have inadvertently found, just as one of the *partzufim* relates Pagis's own discovery of letters written by his mother in 1934 and forgotten, it seems, by his father for more than four decades.

Another way to put all this is to propose that each of these works is an *occulted* or *secretive* text. Each is constructed to ensconce and, only with the proper hermeneutic regard, disclose a set of secrets. In the next to last and most knotted *partzuf* (the margins express the author's dissatisfaction), Pagis writes,

> (I was able to hide the fears at least ten-twelve years even from myself, it all broke out after Eichmann) and over time I could see that you were aware of it, not doing anything, not saying anything (and that went beyond the guilty feelings that you probably harbored, or that at least I choose to ascribe to you, over the fact that I suffered all the horrors because you did not take me to Israel in time). But at least you never resorted to the parable of "removing the goat from the house." Thank you for remaining silent. Even though you did not know that I too was about to die, not long after you. (367)

The parable of "removing the goat from the house," like "the story about under the bed: a man comes home and finds his wife" (352) and "the story about the woman and the playing cards" (354) are specimens of the father's propensity for the jocose. By comparison, Pagis's sense of humor, according to the same *partzuf*, from his father's perspective is "unique" (one has to remind oneself of course that the illusion of two voices here is authorial, for language play dots the landscape of the *partzufim*).[33]

But even if we smile at such moments, the puns don't really include us, as they suggest a voice-print whose proper resonating field is intimate, between father and son—a feature painfully evident, as above, in the *partzufim* that are wrenching rather than wry.

If *Arabesques* sounds shallower depths, it is only because discretely sorrowful events (Layla Khoury's successive expulsions, Shammas's aunt Almaza's inconsolable grief over the death of her child—the Anton for whom the author is named) are rendered through the distancing effect of arabesque structure and Scheherazade-style narration. The novel's secrets are on its surface, in any event, not hidden in its depths. The epigraph that stands over the entire text, from Clive James's *Unreliable Memoirs*, reads "Most first novels are disguised autobiographies. This autobiography is a disguised novel." Many Israeli readers—for whom the novel is expressly meant, as the author is subordinating an address to fellow Christian Arabs—initially expressed dismay over the novel's bewildering formal convolutions. Hillel Halkin, Dan Miron, and other literary power-brokers, predictably, favored the first part ("The Tale") over the second ("The Teller"), as the latter expressly concerned itself with Shammas's standing as an Israeli author who writes deliberately against certain patronizing stereotypes about Israel's minority populations.

Under Israeli eyes, many of the novel's wittiest reversals or sublations of dead-end oppositions read merely as postmodern excess. About "The Teller" sections, Halkin wrote, for example, "I felt cheated. No longer was I reading a magical novel about an ordinary yet wondrous Palestinian village, but rather a flat exercise in literary modernism, with its airplane flights and cocktail parties, its self-conscious artifice and look-at-me-ness, its multiple narrators, split identities, and writers writing about writers writing about writing. No doubt Shammas had his reasons for it all, and I supposed that I could guess what some might be, but were any of them worth the price of spoiling a little masterpiece?" (29). The economic figure is apropos. The novel's exchange value, from this perspective, is analogous to the indemnity benignly purchased by those contemporary American films that feature "magical" (ghostly, supernatural, otherworldly, beneficent) African-Americans who palliate white culture's wish to be guided and absolved without being aggressively confronted. In American Jewish literature, the prototype here is the black angel in Bernard Malamud's short story "Angel Levine" who reproves the Jew Manishevitz but from within the anodyne precincts of the "magical and wondrous." That story's punch line, "A wonderful thing, there are Jews everywhere," transposed to the wished-for remunerative economics of Shammas's novel, would read, "A wonderful thing, there are Israeli writers everywhere."

Clearly Shammas's political purposes lie not with the everywhere but with the *elsewhere*. If, indeed, he can claim to having become a "child in your country" then he will seize the foreign language subversively, as children do, to level the discursive playing field, dominated as it is by adults. One of the novel's secrets, then, is logic of the arabesque, which offers an alternative to not only the non-dialectical master narrative of Zionist history, as Hever argues, but also to the top-heavy scene of Israeli cultural politics. As mentioned before in relation to Schulz/Gombrowicz, the gauntlet thrown down by Robert Musil—"But life always makes you choose between two possibilities, and you always feel: one is missing! Always one—the uninvented third possibility"—is the one Shammas takes up in a distinctly Levantine register. To be sure, certain twists of plot—made visible through the caduceus-like structure of narrative, become visible by novel's end: Michael Abayd's identity, the question of who, finally, narrates. Similarly, successive readings tie up certain strands in "The Tale" that at first sight seem unconnected. But the novel's preeminent secret is what Deleuze and Guattari's manifesto calls for: "steal the baby from its crib, walk the tightrope" (19), that is, to speak both within and against Hebrew and deterritorializing it in ways "appropriate for strange and minor usage" (16). Or, in other words, *poach*.

This section shifts now to consider some of the ways in which such poaching presents itself as a power exercisable at text level by readers, and how Pagis and Shammas both do and do not make room for them. To begin with Pagis, the innermost sanctum of *Abba*, its holy of holies is the *partzuf* that narrates his discovery of his mother's, aunt's, and grandmother's letters, together with a reproduction of those texts translated into Hebrew. For years, Pagis and his father lived in polite estrangement, the result of a mutual misunderstanding only belatedly clarified. The question for Pagis was why his father never saw fit to correct what were his own unfounded suppositions. When challenged in another *partzuf*—"Now tell me everything in order, from the earliest to the latest, everything just as it happened"—the father is imagined saying: "How come, Daneleh, just as it happened? In life things don't happen in order, everything is interconnected, mixed, confused, always. And don't tell me that it is light philosophy. It's not philosophy at all, just the way things are. Everything that you would try to hear in some order, to feel according to some order, is phony. After all, you wanted the truth, though I can't understand why" (364).

In the same *partzuf*, Pagis goes as far to entertain aloud whether he is actually his father's biological child, since his mother's letter, delighting in the resemblance between them, at one point exclaims, "This is your child, definitely yours," which he reads suspiciously, apprehensively, rather than expansively. "I am confused, because she is writing again about the cute boy, adding, "The boy is yours, really yours." But wait a minute, I read again, "The boy is yours, really yours"—why, "really?" What does it mean, 'really?'" (364). Rehearsing his mistaken beliefs in the *partzuf* entitled "Letters," Pagis poignantly admits,

> I was told all that, I thought, in order to conceal from me that you had abandoned us perhaps for a woman, or perhaps for another adventure, and only after the war you regretted it, located me, and sent a certificate. I kept silent all those years, but I dreamed about it. And here, everything they told had been true, everything was in the letters, as if mom felt sorry for me and resent them in order to relieve me of all those suspicions. All the letters testified that you really had waited for us, you really had prepared everything for our arrival in '34. For thirty years the letters sat in the suitcase. I asked you if you agreed to give them to me and you responded immediately, "Take them, take them, why not," as if you didn't grasp their significance. And perhaps you really didn't. Now I will read them in your presence. As an apology that is too late and perhaps redundant for those suspicions. . . . And frankly, I am not apologizing in total sincerity: you have been guilty of such a prolonged forgetfulness. It didn't occur to you to show me the letters all these years simply because you forgot them. I am going to remind you. I will read them to you. This is my revenge. (358)

We learn the name of Pagis's mother (she signs the letter reproduced, "I am burning with longing for you. Yuli"); we learn the names of his aunts; we learn of his grandmother's anguish and guilt over a medical operation that results in the mother's death, we even read the death-announcement by telegram: "Yuli has passed away Stop we must all deal with this blow of fate Stop you too have to be strong Stop the boy is staying with us there is no point in you coming now letter on the way Stop" (360). By this point in the text we wonder whether we have overstayed our welcome. We also learn of the parents' polyglot heritage back in the Bukovina in a passage that, as it were, prepares a space for both his mother's looming effacement from eastern European Jewish terrain and Pagis's deliverance as Israeli poet-to-be on nonnative grounds: "And what are you doing about languages? Are you learning Hebrew and English? I haven't yet, because the teachers are not yet back from their summer vacation, and by the end of the fall I won't be here anymore. Imagine, your Russian and my German and on top of that we'll add two more languages! But most importantly, Hebrew" (359).

A few *partzufim* later, Pagis relates the story of discovering another envelope after his father's death, which turns out to contain only phone bills—"but I didn't dare ask: the letters were already more than I could bear" (this line is written by hand, and in the margin, Pagis writes, "Does he give me the will at this point? No, much later. Or do I find it after his death when I found the telephone bills?"). We never do learn Pagis's given name; there remain certain things to which we will not gain access, as *Abba* keeps some of its secrets:

> "Your name? Which one of them, if you don't mind? The name I gave you (well, actually it wasn't me, aunt Tzili suggested it), you erased that sonorous Latin name when you came to Israel. You chose the most ordinary one: Dan. I didn't protest. I figured that in Israel you wanted to blend in, to simply become absorbed into it like water in sand. As the saying goes, change your name and change your luck, right? But I thank you for not changing our family name too. Do you understand me?"
> "No, Dad." ("Your Name," 366)

But then the entire work is entitled "father" and can only be autobiographical on the oblique. *Abba* is still a literary artifact, not a confessional. And as Ezrahi observes, "'Dan' the persona, like Dan the writer, is only a marker or signifier of an 'original,' unrevealed identity" (*Booking Passage*, 172).

Clarifying where we stand as readers in relation to such a work, like the speaker in Pagis's poem "The Log Book," we are partly akin to those "who did not set sail at all, [but] have arrived." If not exactly thrown, we are *inducted* here, placed athwart a border dividing public and private space. Only we cannot easily cast anchor and forget; for manifestly, by planning to publish such intimacies as these, Pagis summons us to witness his reading the letter in his father's hearing. And of course, it is really we, silent auditors, who lend our ears. Pagis's father is merely conjured; we are situated.

Yuli's letter is an even more materially binding document than the photograph of Radautz (the grandmother's letter adds a postscript after signing "mom"—"woe is me, do I still have the right to sign this way"—and we might ask ourselves accordingly whether we can so liberally afford to call Pagis's mother by her first name); and it seems only to lead to further encounter with the jettisoned Romanian past, as will be suggested below. The "revenge" Pagis exacts by reading it to his father is really double-edged, because it forces readers into a kind of unwilled presence as well. Do we look away, distract ourselves, we wonder, at such a voyeuristic moment? The beginning of this *partzuf* speaks of "a bridge that would help us cross over all the long silences between us," but that seems to denote merely the quotidian affair of helping his father organize the cupboard in the kitchen balcony where the box of letters is discovered. After the letters are "read" to him, Pagis's father says, "It's good that you called me, Daneleh. It was good to listen to you read the letters. How could you have thought I forgot them" (361)? In any event, readers are made unsettlingly privy.

If the chronological sequence of *partzufim* is to be trusted as their organizing strategy, reading the letters only prompts further unearthing on Pagis's part: he looks up a volume of a periodical from 1936 in which a photograph of himself as a six-year old appears: "And below me appears my old name, which I had worked so hard to forget that I had actually succeeded. But now it rose and surfaced just like the corpse of a drowned person does after a while. Here he is. The paper's editor added a note: 'Our little Romanian is young but already a loyal reader of our paper'" (365). "Letters" ends with what can be taken as a rebuke to both Pagis's curiosity and ours; and it is why I ascribed a "sequestered" character to *Abba* along with Shammas's text. After his father's death, Pagis goes to the cabinet in which he knows a blue envelope lies concealed, but is intercepted by his father's widow. Some time later, while she is in the hospital, he uses a spare key to open the apartment, retrieves the keys to the cabinet, which were kept in a drawer, tremblingly opens the blue envelope, and finds a "bundle of documents" in which he supposes he will find additional footprints from the past.

I spread them in my hand in the shape of a fan, just like people hold poker cards and expose their edges slowly to be able to peek at them. Gambling. The first card turned out to be an old telephone bill that had been paid. Not important. And then, what, another such bill? With one movement of my arm, I flung them all, they fluttered confusedly and landed around me on the bed. They were, all of them, telephone bills from years ago, so many calls, so much for usage fee, and all of them bearing the rectangular mark of a rubber stamp: paid, paid, paid. (363)

We could call this the symbolic bookend to "Cherry Herring," a second, similarly quotidian spillage confirming the irretrievable. Pagis is blocked from any further foothold on the intimate past, any further belated message from it, and so are we. *Abba* is drawing to a formal close.

Two *partzufim* on, we read what may well stand as the most uncanny fragment of the lot:

Your steps had a special rhythm. Every step—a light click of the heel and then a springy step, optimistic, perhaps a bit contemptuous. Light and springy, light and springy. I walk differently, with heaviness, with decisiveness—just like now, when every step removes me farther from your grave. We were complete opposites. You were sweet, and superficial and cheerful, I am bland and bent over. And so, goodbye, this visit to the cemetery reaches its end, once again I am walking along, marching intently on the inner pathway leading to the gate.

Suddenly I hear, what, first a light click of the heel and then a springy step. Optimistic, perhaps a bit contemptuous. Light and springy, light and springy. I start running. Your steps are behind me, with me, running within me, your feet are my feet, your death is my death.

Stop! I order myself. Stop. Me, me only, not you, not you. I admit that we weren't complete opposites. I admit that we were very close, more than I wanted to admit, more than I wanted. But the difference between us is clear and will remain forever: my shoe size is large, 43, and yours—I remember that very well—was only 37. ("Steps," 367)[34]

This is the same mordant (or "unique") sense of humor that in the *partzuf* that questions paternity has the father exclaim, "our blood is identical" to which Pagis replies laconically, "so is the earth, also ours; I'm so happy, Abba," taking the measure of an irreducible distance in the midst of proximity.

For at bottom, like von Rezzori and Canetti's texts, like Schulz and Gombrowicz's, Said and Aciman's, Appelfeld and Sebald's, *Abba* plays out an elaborate arabesque between the nearer distances and the clearer mysteries. But it does so intra-familially in particularly stark fashion, almost comically so: inadvertently abandoned son survives the Shoah and reunites with father against the backdrop of a new homeland and new language, nigh yet enduringly at a remove. In the recuperative fragments written after death (the father's) but also before it (Pagis's own), father and son are repeatedly pitched forward at each other and away, with Pagis tracing their mutual reckoning as though it were a rapprochement between place abandoned and adopted-though-still-foreign home, with all the tenuousness that such relationship necessarily entails.

The valedicatory *partzuf* is entitled "The End as the Future."

In seven years, the tenth anniversary of your death, father, in a rare, sparkling hour of a Tel Avivian month of August, we will sit, you and I, on a small veranda. And as though it were much higher than just the third floor, it will unfold before us the big city, which will have long been foreign to us, weaving distant beads, amber lights.

And I will recite for you a foreign poem about a foreign cemetery dear to me. I will not be bashful and will recite for you, for the first time, a phrase of poetry: "The wind rises, we must try to live." And you will listen, attentively, for you respect my good memory, yet also somewhat mockingly, for what is the point? Still, the silence between us will be like thanksgiving.

Wind and counter-wind will twirl before our eyes, raising a tiny whirlpool of play. The curtains behind us will swell, turn into wide sails, but only for play. We won't sail anywhere, for we have already arrived, haven't we? And you will nod your head, agreeing with me." (Keller, 38)

The foreign poem referred to is *"La Cimetiere Marin"* (The cemetery by the sea) by Paul Valéry, and the verse, quoted from its last stanza, is *"Le vent se lève! Il faut tenter de vivre!"* But Pagis also quotes himself; the harmonics of the next-to-last verse of "The Log Book" sound above the prose: "For we, who did not set sail at all, have arrived" (so much of *Abba* concerns arrivals). Once again we are situated alongside the text's intimacies in such a way as to solicit not interpretive potency but a kind of *acknowledgment,* Stanley Cavell's word for a certain hopeless yet communal, even ritual, recognition before the fate of others.[35]

The tone in this last *partzuf* is more poetic than prosaic and we note the shift. We may be familiar with a conversational and familiar tone struck from time to time in Pagis's poetry, for instance in the poem, *"Likrat"* (The readiness):

> —I too, like all the apes in the neighborhood,
> grumble from branch to branch:
> the past age, which was filled with sun, has passed.
> Now it's too cold. The nuts are too hard.
> The carnivores are getting more and more supple.
> —This is it, I'm emigrating. Good-bye.
> Hey, what's happening,
> my tongue's tied in knots,
> my shoulders, where are my shoulders,
> suddenly I've got stature,
> erectness,
> suddenly I'm threatened with
> what, a high brow!
> Bulbs flickering bulbs.
>
> (*The Selected Poetry of Dan Pagis,* 21)

In the prose fragments of *Abba*, however, the same sort casualness disconcerts; perhaps it is because they are addressed to, and not simply titled, *Abba*. Or perhaps it is because they were never published in Pagis's lifetime but, rather, found among his working manuscripts, along with his last poems. And yet Pagis's final poems speak in an accomplished and recognizable Pagisian voice. The *partzufim* exercise a different rhetorical hold, and as such arrest or give pause—but only briefly. To be sure, we do not have before us anything like the stately cemetery scene in Sebald's *The Emigrants*, or the essayistic cemetery visit in Aciman, or even the other-worldly encounter on the fringes of the mellah in Canetti's *The Voices of Marrakesh*. In their stead, a certain levity of tone, a certain abstractness of place, a purposeful sketchiness preside. As the last word, *Abba* treads nimbly and unprepossessingly[36]—on the whole, like the father's tread: perhaps a bit contemptuous but also light and springy.

To call the envelope that contains only bills in "Letters," a rebuke means that the text may wish to keep some of its secrets, to discourage a thorough-going exegesis that as it were substitutes Pagis's gait for his father's. Once the illusion of two voices fades, we realize that Pagis is communing with himself, revisiting the past and cleaning house, or in Ezrahi's words, reclaiming a plot in Radautz. *Abba* sequesters but it also holds out against privative reading (this is also the father's characteristic maneuver with his understandably importunate son—a fending off, a keeping at bay). The *partzuf*, by its very nature, seeks a brief engagement with reading's overdetermination, especially with the sort of reading that has been instructed by the previous chapters' sometimes solemn reconnoiters and obsequies. One of the reasons that the *partzuf* and arabesque are paired in this final chapter is to highlight them as strategies deployed as counterweight to more conventional rhetorical practices, or, even more pointedly, to offer them as a kind of anti-ballast or buoyancy that recalls the midrash on the verse, "And Jacob lifted up his legs" from the introduction, and also Calvino's favored image of lightness: "resting his hand on one of the great tombs and being very nimble, Guido leaped over it and, landing on the other side, made off." Perhaps, this is also why Pagis, already dying of cancer, chooses to quote Valéry's poem at its most unbound and levitated moment: "The wind rises: we must try to live."

When we turn to Shammas's novel, the arabesque that serves as its opening gesture traces a winding line of nested or contiguous objects among which we find the following story of concealment:

The church was the walking distance of a single Ave Maria from our house. . . . At the end of the fifties an eccentric priest came to the village, who was apparently the first man to carry an open umbrella on the hot, dry days of summer. The white parasol protected the delicate priest from the ruthless sun but exposed him to many discreet smiles of ridicule and won him a prominent place on the list of eccentrics inscribed in village memory. Along with the parasol the priest brought a collection of old books and journals, which my brother Jubran coveted. Bit by bit this collection made its way to our bookcase, which was embedded in the thick wall. Its olive-colored door was locked with the yellow key that was kept in the cookie dish in the "armoire" that was brought disassembled from Beirut in 1940 in a truck and was loaded on the back of two camels in the village of Rmeish near the Lebanese border. Its doors, shelves, and drawers were covered by a fragile brown veneer, which had survived the journey, and there was a thick mirror on its middle door. Behind this looking glass was the full cookie dish, kept under lock and key. There was a custom in the family that the key to the bookcase could not be taken until the cookie dish was emptied by guests. However, everyone knew that my eldest brother, the book lover, who was systematically raiding the priest's library, had found a way to loosen the lock by lifting the lower-left hand corner of the mirrored door. . . . In time many books from the priest's library joined [a sword that my brother kept] in the bookcase in the wall. Later these books changed hands in order to blur their tracks, but I still have a copy of the *Al-Jinan* from 1874, the year my grandmother was born, in which I found the complete text of the law on growing tobacco. (8)

The priest's book corroborates an oral tradition that Grandmother Alia was indeed born in the same year the Ottoman tobacco law was published, a date calculated intuitively by Shammas's father with reference to other important events in the life of the Shammas paterfamilias, grandfather Jubran. Reading these opening pages of the novel, one is unsure which seemingly extraneous details will impinge on later events. "I comb out the unraveled thread and card it again, then turn to impart to it a completely different color and to weave it once more into the frayed tapestry, mending what has unraveled. What guarantee do I have that this act is not a proclamation of liberty on the part of that thread, once it has been unbound? (36). But the cumulative effect of the weaving serves as a training in what the novel later calls the "plaited" structure of arabesque, "embracing and parting, twisting and twining . . . in a swirling current of illusion that linked beginnings to endings, the inner to the external, the reality to the tale" (226–27).

The text want us to know that the marriage of Shammas's parents (the armoire from Beirut), the ambient surrounds of nineteenth-century

Ottoman rule (the tobacco law) and Arab Christianity (the church and priest), the counterpoint of oral tradition and literacy (village memory and the collection of filched books), familial custom (the "secret" of the locked bookcase), village habit (the discreet smiles of ridicule), and modernity (the 1950s, that is, after the State of Israel has been established) are all complexly folded in on one another, which is one meaning of arabesque: the axis of selection intertwined with the axis of combination, the bending of metaphor toward metonymy, a fugue of concatenating figures.

The scissors that belonged to my father, who had once been a barber, now lay alongside his other instruments in a damascene wooden box inlaid with mother-of-pearl, which had been bought in Beirut in the late 1930s as a betrothal gift to my mother. My father's pocketknife, with the black horn handle was not in that box, as I had expected it to be. Several days later I found it in his briefcase. This penknife, which I had never imagined I would one day play with to my heart's content, had in the past served my uncle Yusef "to bind the mouths of the wild beasts." . . . In time I found out that the incantation was nothing but the Christian Creed, which my uncle would mumble backwards over the drawn blade. . . . The penknife was not lying in the damascene box inlaid with mother-of-pearl, but there was a lock of graying hair from the head of Grandmother Alia wrapped in a page of an old religious journal that carried the end of an article in praise of the Inquisition and the beginning of one about the Canaanite woman who believed in Jesus after he exorcised the spirits from her daughter's body. The folded page had been tucked into the inner pocket of the faded leather cover of my father's notebook. Next to the notebook were two small blue velvet boxes, all that remained of the bridal jewelry that had been stolen out of this same damascene box, where it had been kept by my mother. She had come at the end of the 1930s to Fassuta to teach French and had fallen in love with the man now lying before her. For his sake she had given up her family in Beirut and the memories of her girlhood in the fishermen's alleys of Tyre, and now he was abandoning her to the diaspora[37] of her longings. (15–16)

This notebook, originally intended as a ledger and inscribed with the date of his grandmother's death, "Wednesday, the thirty-first of March, 1954, at ten to six in the evening," is re-inscribed two decades later with the date of Shammas's father's death, "Monday the nineteenth of June, 1978, at twenty to ten in the evening." Particulars shown to be contained or embedded—as the very the logic of the arabesque—thus demonstrate an interpretive method, the Eudoxia's carpet of correspondence and clarification. We are meant to sort through and sift out those same particulars, to notice how they are enfolded and with which other objects, dates, names they are made to mesh. As Brian McHale and Yael Feldman have each noted, the obtrusive motif of exact dating in the novel suggests an alternative history meant to "compete with the 'official' historical narrative on its own terms" ("Seizing the Means of Representation," 20), "to reconstruct mythic time while engaging historical memory ("Postcolonial Memory, Postmodern Intertextuality," 382).[38] Details are encoded, or secreted, because they aim at careful elucidation, the teasing out of specificities.

There are, however, certain features that do not yield to recoverability. At the level of decoding, the most crucial of these is the identity of the narrator, which, strictly speaking, remains undecidable. At the level of plot, an inscription used as an amulet in "The Tale," divided in half, remains stubbornly incomplete: the sequestered or eclipsed part is never found and never revealed. These two features are coefficient, teaching their own lesson about the vagaries of ferreting away.

> Forty golden coins were in the box, and a folded paper, yellowed and crumbling.... When the paper was spread out by the pale light of the lantern they saw that mysterious red letters were inscribed upon it. "It's the amulet that was found on the body of Karrarah, your teacher," said Mahmood El-Ibraheem to Zaki." And those are the magic words that if uttered at the right place in your village are supposed to open the door leading to the cave where the Crusaders' treasure is hidden. But the dervish who saw this paper said it's only half of the whole paper, and the door will never open unless the other half is found and the Word is completed. Therefore this paper is worthless by itself, but if Fortune smiles upon you and you find the other half of the paper, you will never lack for anything. (221)

The other half of the amulet is placed around the neck of the original Anton Shammas and is transferred to Michael Abayd, the narrator's *doppelganger*, bequeathed by him in turn to Laylah Khoury whom, as Surayyah Sa'id, the narrator finally visits, toward the end of the novel. Whether, indeed, the amulet she possesses contains the other half of the inscription, whether it is even the same amulet worn by the original Anton, whether there is any amulet at all remains unresolved by the narrative. If "sometimes they burn the tongue, the red candies of memory" (3), they also can be swallowed whole, their taste still a mystery. Thus, the dominant folkloric motif of the text—the Crusader gold hidden in a cave guarded by a red cock—along with its standing hermeneutic riddle—the question of authorship—mirror each other as dual figures for a booty that will not be yielded up.

By the same token, when the text wants to expose its secreted meanings, hold them to the light, it does so in a manner that satisfies both the needs of the decoder and the needs of the plot. Yael Feldman has painstakingly tracked one of these in her groundbreaking essay on the novel. She uncovers a surface ungrammaticality—the word *se'udah*, "meal"—that appears in the context of the amulet story line subtly, disturbing the mythic stone rolled over the cave motif, opening its entrance, so to speak, by connecting it not to legendary medieval treasure, but to "dry and hard political history" (382)—that is, the persecution of Lebanese Christians by Muslims and Druse in the 1860s, and subsequently the persecution of Fassutan Christians by nationalist Muslims in the Arab Revolt of 1936. That this minority historiography takes place in the register of Hebrew is all the more noteworthy, since Hebrew is not merely deconstructed or deterritorialized by Shammas but is also made to function, "paradoxically enough, as a haven, a neutral medium (as ironic as this may sound) outside the system of Arab nationalism" (385).

The intertext prompting Feldman's pursuit is a short clause omitted in the English translation (done with Shammas's help, curiously enough)—"those who were slaughtered and were not privileged to attend the meal were the Christians of Lebanon"[39]—which smuggles in an allusion to "Isaac," by Amir Gilboa, the most famous short poem about the *Shoah* before Pagis's "Written in Pencil": "*Abba, Abba,* quickly save Isaac so that no one will be missing at the midday meal. / It is I who am being slaughtered, my son, and already my blood is on the leaves."

(Could Pagis, another admirer of Gilboa's poetry, have had this poem in mind for the text of *Abba,* as well, one wonders?) As Feldman shows, "The purpose of the intertext . . . is to produce a final reversal no less startling (and by analogy no less crucial for the constructed identity of the speaker) than the one produced by the poem 'Isaac'" (380–81)— that is, the analogy between Jews persecuted in the *Shoah* and the minority of Arab Christians persecuted by their Muslim neighbors in nineteenth and twentieth century Galilee.[40] Self-evidently, Shammas wants his readers to sing for their supper, to be as determined and devious (the text wishes to be rubbed more than caressed, like Pagis's [41]) as Shammas and his brother are when they "loosen the lock by lifting the lower-left hand corner of the mirrored door" in order to liberate the priest's absconded books from the family bookcase set into the wall.

The Wilderness Rose Up to It

I want to conclude this chapter and this book with one of those very texts, dramatically invoked by Shammas in a middle chapter of the "The Teller." If less deeply interred than the Gilboa allusion, and with fewer political and sub-textual ramifications, it constitutes one of the more fascinating intertexts in the novel, the one that directly impinges upon a reading of both *Arabesques* and *Abba* as *midbar*-literature. "I was thinking about Proust and Al-Hamshari," writes Shammas, "and about how livid the man sitting next to me would be if he knew what odd twinnings and pairings were running through my mind." "As for me, I doubt I would have gotten to Iowa City were it not for Willa Cather's *My Ántonia*, the first novel I ever read, which I found in our olive-green bookcase, embedded in the thick wall. . . . It was in an Arabic translation, whose opening I used to know by heart" (138). The novel then quotes those famous paragraphs (it is the longest such passage in the novel). The braiding here is even odder than the pairing above: the Jew of Time, the Arab of Place, and the American modernist of the Nebraska heartland, the novelist who wrote, "There was nothing but land: not a country at all but the material out of which countries are made." In *My Ántonia*, of course, she is also the novelist of immigration, and of nostalgia for origins. "During that burning day when we were crossing Iowa, our talk kept returning to a central figure, a Bohemian girl whom we had both known long ago. More than any other person we remembered, this girl seemed to mean to us the country, the conditions, the whole adventure of our childhood" (*My Ántonia*, 2). Why, in addition to these self-evident points of correspondence, one wonders, are we reminded of this text as the *Ur*text of Shammas's literary education?

I think the answer lies in recognizing it as one of a number of mythic fictions that show how one can be invested, anchored by Elsewhere, that evince the *possibility*—albeit limited—of one's own place. Through this chapter's own odd twinning and pairing, Pagis's *Abba* and Shammas's *Arabesques* coincide, by contrast, in the distance each measures between place and a substantive, authorial self. If a past and a country can be owned by laying claim through an act of inscription—"He frowned at this a moment, then prefixed another word, making it 'My Ántonia.' That seemed to satisfy him"—then perhaps the dispossessed past, the de-authorized place can, paradoxically, be conjured and evanescently possessed through the fictions of arabesque and *partzufim*. If a plot is to be reclaimed in Radautz, if Fassuta, situated above a hole in the ground and its own sedimentations and interments is to be concretely anchored, then they each must draw the *midbar* up around them, conjure its voice, yet somehow not take dominion.

Shortly after the long quotation from Cather, as they wait in the airport for a flight to Cedar Rapids, Shammas and the Israeli writer Bar-On share between them a joke punctuated by another reference to American literary modernism. They quote Wallace Stevens's famous "Anecdote": "I placed a jar in Tennessee / And round it was, upon a hill. / It made the slovenly wilderness / Surround that hill / The wilderness rose up to it" (in the poem the line continues, "And sprawled around, no longer wild."). The poem is brokered in the text as a sexual prank, but its import for Shammas's and Pagis's texts alike is profound: a certain kind of formal abstraction compels and constrains the surrounding *midbar*. Yet, in the last two lines of Stevens's poem, we discover that the figure for calculating design "did not give of bird or bush / Like nothing else in Tennessee." In a virtuosic reading of the poem, contextualizing it with reference to the Stevens corpus, Frank Lentricchia writes,

> The eccentric is the base of *design:* eccentric signs would be signs unplotted, surprising. Eccentric design would resolve the greatest of antinomies because it would be both necessary and spontaneous; a form of determination, yet free. Jars—they're not that kind of design, and what's more they seem to have designs upon power. They take dominion, they can even make something as unmanageable as a wilderness shape up, imitate their structural roundedness. A jar can make a wilderness surround itself; a jar can make the very ground into a mirror. (*Close Reading the Reader*, 145)

As practices for writing and reading, the *partzuf* and the arabesque, alike knowing the eccentric to be the base of design, could be the things most diametrically opposed to jars. They seek a different commerce with the wilderness. If therefore, to recall once again the verse from Exodus, the wilderness has *closed in on* them, encompassed them (that is the counter-gesture to the dominion seized in Stevens's poem), then, at the same time, they have allowed themselves to be surrounded—addressed, founded, placed—by the redemptive possibilities of *midbar*-speech as well. And reciprocally, like speech, one's own place (to cite Stevens in an altogether different frame of mind) is also possible, possible, possible.

Envoi

And finally, there is something right about the vagrancy of the replacements. Nowhere can keep us too long. Let us look at it this way: for want of the fruit the garden was lost, for want of the garden the places were gained, for want of the places new places arrived, for want of new places we dreamed and we dreamed. We composed in the tiniest inner room all the chambers of the endless palace, opening on to each other, directly as well as indirectly, off unlit corridors, once entered and left, then lost, even if returned to at a later time and by a route that we could never have known to be circuitous, so much so that while we are in it, there is no way of getting it right. Once left, there is only what we say of it, which is never mistaken.
> "In Place of Place," John Hollander

Or mistaken even then and there, which is to say: speech is *also* a vagrancy and a wilderness. Set free, the tongue can sometimes but wander, its speakers and the invisible presences whom they address—emigrants all—transported elsewhere.

Notes

Preface and Acknowledgments

1. The presentation took place on October 15 at the 92nd Street Y, along with contributions by Susan Sontag and André Aciman. A description of the evening can be found in Alan Lookwood, "In Memoriam W. G. Sebald, Part 2: 10/01; W. G. Sebald at the 92nd St. Y," www.nonserviamnyc.com/al/alan_lockwood.html; and also in Ed Park, "The Precognitions: On the Posthumous Trail of W. G. Sebald and William Gaddis," *Village Voice Literary Supplement* (Fall 2002): www.villagevoice.com/vls/178/park.shtml.

Introduction

1. As glossed by R. Asher Meir, "Meaning in Mitzvot #58: chapter 95," *Yeshivat Har Etzion Israel Koschitzky Virtual Beit Midrash,* also online at www.ou.org/torah/tt/5762/ beshalach62/specialfeatures_mitzvot.htm. The mishna discussed in *Eruvin* 51a specifies how, while on a journey, one declares "his place" (four cubits around) once the Sabbath commences in order to derive the prescribed 2000 cubit limit *(tehum Shabbat)* for travel. Even though the *tehum* is a Rabbinical pronouncement, the Talmud seeks scriptural justification (called an *asmkakhta*) for the operative verse (Ex. 16:29) this way: "It was taught in a *baraita* [a Tannaitic ruling not included in the Mishna]: 'Let every man remain in his place' refers to the four cubits; 'No man shall go beyond his place' refers to the 2000 cubits." R. Hisda explains by means of an exegetical device known as *gezerah shava,* allowing different Biblical verses to be enchained around a common word. Thus, *place* in Ex. 16:29 is clarified by the identical word in the verse, 'And I have established a *place* whither he may flee' (Ex. 21:13), referring to the cities of refuge—*place* thus linked to *fleeing. Fleeing* [or *flight*] is clarified by the identical word in the verse, 'from the border of his city of refuge, whither he may flee' (Num. 35:26)—*fleeing* now linked to *border,* signifying a protective limit. *Border* is then clarified by the identical word in the next verse, 'And the blood avenger will find him beyond the *border*—that word now linked to *beyond*

(or "outside"), which is elucidated by the same word in the verse 'And you shall measure *beyond* the city' two thousand *amot* in each direction (Num. 35:5), referring to the environs of the special Levite cities. Thus *place* (four cubits) connects to *beyond* (2000 cubits), as residence is correlated with journey. The Schottenstein edition of *Eruvin*, vol. 1 (New York: Mesorah Publications Ltd., 1990) provides an import clarifying resource, as does the *Steinsaltz Talmud Reference Guide* by Adin Steinsaltz (New York: Random House, 1989). On the innovation of *"asmakhta"* and rabbinic interpretive procedures generally, see also David Weiss Halivni, *Peshat and Derash: Plain and Applied Meaning in Rabbinic Exegesis* (New York: Oxford University Press, 1991).

2. "Realm of memory" is the organizing concept for Pierre Nora's seven-volume *Les Lieux de Mémoire,* explained in the general introduction, "Between Memory and History," to *Realms of Memory: Rethinking of the French Past,* Vol. 1: *Conflicts and Divisions,* trans. Arthur Goldhammer (New York: Columbia University Press, 1996), 1–20. In *Landscape and Memory* (New York: Alfred A. Knopf, 1995), Simon Schama explains that the word "landscape" (from the Dutch *landschap*) originally signified a unit of occupation and jurisdiction (10). For a geographer's phenomenology of space, see J. Nicholas Entrikin's *The Betweenness of Place: Towards a Geography of Modernity* (Baltimore: Johns Hopkins University Press, 1991). For an ambitious materialist analysis of social space, see Henri Lefebvre's *The Production of Space,* trans. Donald Nicholson-Smith (Oxford: Blackwell, 1991). Finally, for general introductions to the construct of "place" itself, see Edward S. Casey, *Getting Back into Place: Toward a Renewed Understanding of the Place World* (Bloomington: Indiana University Press, 1993) and Roberto M. Dainotto, *Place in Literature: Regions, Cultures, Communities* (Ithaca: Cornell University Press, 2000).

3. *Shir Hashirim Rabbah,* 7. Compare the midrash on 2:1, 2: "'I am a Rose of Sharon.' R. Berekiah said: This verse is spoken by the wilderness [itself]." Also, *Bamidbar Rabbah* 1:1, 7 and 21:18, 26, where the *midbar* is compared to one's capacity to learn Torah or be open to others, a generative emptiness. Last, from the same tractate as above, *Eruvin* 54a: "A person who makes himself like a desert traversed by all [but also implicitly, a "speaker"]—Torah is given to him as a gift." Marc-Alain Ouaknin and José Faur draw attention to similar tropings in *The Burnt Book: Reading the Talmud,* trans. Llewellyn Brown (Princeton: Princeton University Press, 1996), 209, and *Golden Doves with Silver Dots: Semiotics and Textuality in Rabbinic Tradition* (Bloomington: Indiana University Press, 1986), 4–5. While not quite exploiting the lexical play on speech/wilderness, Hayim Nachman Bialik's famous 1905 poem "Metei Midbar" (The dead of the desert) nevertheless conjoins the two through lavish prosopopoeia of the following sort: "The desert moans in its dream of the cruelty of eternal waste in dumb ululation wails.... The desert shudders to silence, awed by precipitous heights, fumes again, inwardly mutters, utters a surly growl" (110). *Selected Poems, Bilingual Edition,* trans. Ruth Nevo (Jerusalem: Dvir and *Jerusalem Post,* 1981). For the parallel dualism of exile and homecoming (or as Bialik called it, "leaving and re-entering"), see also the essay "Jewish Dualism" along with the afterword by Zali Gurevitch in Hayim N. Bialik, *Revealment and Concealment: Five Essays* (Jerusalem: Ibis Editions, 2000).

4. As to writing vs. mapping, two late sixth century C.E. Byzantine floor mosaics depict the land of Israel in illuminating contrast. The first, a five hundred and sixty square foot mosaic map from a church in Madaba, Jordan, portrays the Holy Land according to its promised boundaries in Num 34:1-2. More or less a polychrome illustration of Eusebius's fourth-century *Onomastikon*, the Madaba Map images Biblical Israel as the site for pilgrimage with an out-of-scale Jerusalem at its center, an enormous Baedaker for local and itinerant believers. The second mosaic, measuring fourteen feet by nine feet, was discovered in the ruins of an ancient synagogue near Tel Rehov in Israel's Beth-Shean valley. It consists of twenty-nine lines of Hebrew, compiled from early rabbinic (Tannaitic) writings and the Palestinian Talmud, detailing various agricultural commandments incumbent upon Jews living in eretz Israel as well as a precise delineation of the land's halakhic borders (Jerusalem appears only implicitly through the mosaic's orientation in the synagogue's entrance, as the *mitzvot* regarding sacrificial service were no longer in effect after the destruction of the Second Temple and Jews were not permitted to live in Jerusalem until the end of the Byzantine period in the seventh century). In certain respects, the mosaics form an uncanny pair. Speculating on their *Sitz in Leben* as pedagogical devices, Aaron Demsky writes, "Both are mosaics. Both were located on the floors of houses of worship. Both date to the end of the Byzantine period in Palestine. Geographically, they were located only fifty-five miles apart, although on opposite sides of the Jordan river. [E]ach was intended to deliver a message—visually imparting to their respective worshippers the meaning of the Holy Land" (33). And yet, just as self-evidently, they differ radically. One is a map as iconograph, as picture; the other is a map as text. One visualizes the land (indeed, stepping over it as they entered the church, congregants could vicariously envisage themselves traversing the Holy land itself); the other textualizes it (although the Rehov mosaic, too, was large enough for worshippers to stand upon). Where the one takes imaginative possession by illustrating the land, the other takes up residence in the land inscriptively, representing it, for the sake of settlement and proper observance, in the spirit of *dibur* (from the same root as *medaber*)—as speech-commandment. "Is not reading a way of inhabiting?" Levinas will ask pointedly in an essay on revelation in the Jewish tradition. For Israel's "nostalgia for the land," he adds, "is fed on texts" (*Beyond the Verse*, 130). Demsky's comparison of the two mosaics can be found in "Christian and Jewish Views of the Holy Land: Visiting Sacred Sites vs. Working the Land," *Bible Review* 28.5 (October, 2002): 32-41, and "Holy City and Holy Land: A Conceptual Approach to Sacred Space," in *Sanctity of Time and Space in Tradition and Modernity*, ed. Anton Houtman, Marcel Poorthuis, and Joshua Schwartz (Boston: Brill, 1998), 285-96. A similar, aboriginal version of land-as-speech (or song) can be found in Bruce Chatwin's *The Songlines* (New York: Viking Penguin, 1987).

5. Compare Stanley Cavell's formulation from *The Senses of Walden* (Berkeley: University of California Press, 1989): "Words come to us from a distance: they were there before we were; we are born into them. Meaning them is accepting the fact of their condition. To discover what is being said to us, as to discover what we are saying, is to discover the precise location from which it is

said; to understand why is said from just there, and at that time. The art of fiction is to teach us distance—that the sources of what is said, the character of whomever says it, is for us to discover" (56).

6. See the chapter "Reading as Poaching" in *The Practice of Everyday Life,* trans. Stephen Rendell (Berkeley: University of California Press, 2002). As "poaching," for de Certeau reading is emblematic of the operations by which quotidian users intervene and innovate in the means and forms of production that constitute their cultural inheritance.

7. The critic Michael Seidel sums up the reciprocal relationship between literary fiction and exile this way: "exilic space is the metaphoric terrain of projected adventure, and exilic time a resource for narrative repatriation" (*Exile and the Narrative Imagination* [New Haven: Yale University Press, 1986], 198).

8. The example of Maurice Blanchot comes immediately to mind. "The poem is exile," Blanchot writes, "and the poet who belongs to it belongs to the dissatisfaction of exile. He is always lost to himself, outside, far from home" ("The Original Experience," *The Space of Literature,* trans. Ann Smock [Lincoln: University of Nebraska Press, 1989], 237). Other examples in this vein are "desert" and "arrière-pays" in the work of Blanchot's contemporaries, Edmond Jabès and Yves Bonnefoy.

9. The theoretical literature, too, finds such terms irresistible. Like emigrants and immigrants themselves, rhetorical terms like *exile, diaspora, displacement, margin, border, location* or constructs like the "poetics of pilgrimage," "going home as critical gesture," "exilic emplacement," "diasporic self-fashioning," insistently book passage—as demonstrated by the title of Sidra Ezrahhi's superb study, *Booking Passage: Exile and Homecoming in the Modern Jewish Imagination* (Berkeley: University of California Press, 2001). See also, for example, Avtar Brah, *Cartographies of Diaspora: Contesting Identities* (London: Routledge, 1996); Jana Evans Braziel and Anita Mannur, eds., *Theorizing Diaspora: A Reader* (Malden, MA: Blackwell Publishers, 2003; Rey Chow, *Writing Diaspora: Tactics of Intervention in Contemporary Cultural Studies* (Bloomington: Indiana University Press, 1993); James Clifford, *Routes: Travel and Translation in the Late Twentieth Century* (Cambridge: Harvard University Press, 1997); Angeletta K. M. Gourdine, *The Difference Place Makes: Gender, Sexuality, and Diaspora Identity* (Columbus: Ohio State University Press, 2002); Karim H. Karim, ed., *The Media of Diaspora* (London: Routledge Press, 2003); Nico Israel: *Outlandish: Writing Between Exile and Diaspora* (Stanford, CA: Stanford University Press, 2000); Smadar Lavie and Ted Swedenburg, eds., *Displacement, Diaspora, and Geographies of Identity* (Durham: Duke University Press, 1996); and Patricia Yaeger, ed., *The Geography of Identity* (Ann Arbor: University of Michigan Press, 1996).

10. As Bhabha's readers often discover, for example; see *The Location of Culture* (New York: Routledge, 1994). In the richness of its own analytical and discursive complexities, however, his essay—indeed the very theoretical approach it exemplifies—has been faulted for a demonstrable superficiality when it comes to addressing literary texts. See for instance, Marjorie Perloff, "Cultural Liminality/Aesthetic Closure? The 'Interstitial Perspective' of Homi Bhabha" wings.buffalo.edu/epc/authors/perloff/bhabha.html, and also Bruce Robbins's instructive essay, "Comparative Cosmopolitanisms" in *Cosmopolitics:*

Thinking and Feeling beyond the Nation, ed. Pheng Cheah and Bruce Robbins (Minneapolis: University of Minnesota Press, 1998), 246–64.

11. Lefebvre, *The Production of Space,* 140. De Certeau distinguishes between place *(lieu)*—the delimitation of a field—and space *(espace)*—the "practice" of place, the various operations that orient, situate, temporalize, and make it function. Place is the realm of the proper and the univocal, of *langue;* space is analogous to utterance, a *parole* that belongs to the improvisatory practices of speakers. But according to Lefebvre, this potentially misconstrues the differences between language as figuration and space as social practice: "The analogy between the theory of space and (and of its production) and the theory of language can be carried only so far. The theory of space describes and analyzes textures.... The production of space lays hold of such structures [the straight line, the curve, etc.] and integrates them into a great variety of wholes (textures). A texture implies a meaning—but a meaning for whom? For some reader? No: rather, for someone who lives and acts in the space under consideration, a 'subject' with a body—or, sometimes, a 'collective subject'" (*The Production of Space,* 132). Gilles Deleuze and Félix Guattari, de Certeau's contemporaries and fellow *soixante-huitards,* stand under a similar critique in their *Kafka: Toward a Minor Literature,* trans. Dana Polan (Minneapolis: University of Minnesota Press, 1980), and also *A Thousand Plateaus: Capitalism and Schizophrenia,* trans. Brian Massumi (Minneapolis: University of Minnesota Press, 1987). The critique can be followed in David Lloyd and Abdul JanMohamed, *The Nature and Context of Minority Discourse,* and Chana Kronfeld, *On the Margins of Modernism: Decentering Literary Dynamics* (Berkeley: University of California Press, 1994).

12. Compare the same spatial sense of the word as evoked by Emmanuel Levinas in the first sentence of *Totality and Infinity* (with its silent allusion to Rimbaud), "'The true life is absent.' But we are in the world. Metaphysics arises and is maintained in this alibi" (trans. Alphonso Lingis [Pittsburgh: Duquesne University Press, 1969], 33), and also by Roland Barthes in *Mythologies,* as cited by Jill Robbins: "the turnstile revolving" of myth is its "perpetual alibi: it is enough that a signifier has two sides for it always to have an 'elsewhere' at its disposal" (*Altered Reading: Levinas and Literature* [Chicago: University of Chicago Press, 1999], 18).

13. One might juxtapose the claim here with J. Hillis Miller's argument about the reciprocal relation between host and parasite in his much-anthologized essay on deconstructive criticism, "The Critic as Host," in *Modernism, Criticism, and Theory,* David Lodge, ed. (London: Longman, 1988), 278–85, along with the earlier essay by Miller's onetime influence, Georges Poulet, "The Phenomenology of Reading" *New Literary History* 1 (1969): 53–68.

14. "History: Science and Fiction," in *Heterologies: Discourse on the Other,* trans. Brian Massumi (Minneapolis: University of Minnesota Press, 1989), 221. "Ethics is articulated through effective operations, and it defines a distance between what is and what ought to be. This distance designates a space where we have something to do. On the other hand, dogmatism is authorized by a reality that it claims to represent and in the name of this reality, it imposes laws" (199).

15. In a symposium on Sebald after his death, Arthur Lubow muses upon

the Sebald/Proust connection as a contrast of temporal sensibilities. "When people call something 'Proust-ian,' they are usually referring to Proust's fascination with involuntary memory, the way in which sensory associations conjure up the past. Yet the French writer elaborated just as extravagantly on the joys and tortures of anticipation. (The present moment is what disappointed him.) Sebald, temperamentally, preferred to keep his eyes averted from the future, which for him impended heavily with disaster. And he accumulated his recollections not in windfalls, but through diligent dredging and mining." "A Symposium on W. G. Sebald," *Threepenny Review* 89 (Spring 2002): threepennyreview.com/samples/sebaldsympos_sp02.html. A comprehensive treatment of Sebald's writings can be found in *Understanding W. G. Sebald* by Mark McCulloh (New York: Columbia University Press, 2003).

16. For photographic correctives to the "romance of exile" and exile-as-metaphor, see *Migrations: Humanity in Transition* by Sebastião Salgado (New York: Aperture, 2000) and *Exiles*, photographs by Josef Koudelka, essays by Czeslaw Milosz (New York: Aperture, 1988).

17. As Sebald himself writes in *Vertigo*, "One inch of yew wood will often have upward of a hundred annual growth rings, and there are said to be trees that have outlasted a millennium and seem to have quite forgotten about dying" (trans. Michael Hulse [New York: New Directions, 2000], 70).

18. "Yew Trees," by Wordsworth, "Elegy in a Country Churchyard," by Gray," "Ash-Wednesday" and "Four Quartets," by Eliot, and "The Moon and the Yew Tree," by Plath. In a review of Robert Mack's *Thomas Gray: A Life,* Lawrence Lipking's observations on the "Elegy" bear on Sebald's methods as well: "A brilliant shift of pronouns (first noticed by Bertrand Bronson) helps to draw us in. The first stanza concludes with 'me.' But the poet or speaker never refers to himself in the first person again. Instead, by line ninety-three he has turned into "thee": "thee, who mindful of th' unhonour'd Dead / Dost in these lines their artless tale relate." Through a sort of osmosis, the sympathetic reader has now identified with the speaker of the poem, while the poet retreats to the second person. Then, in a final stroke, a "hoary-headed swain" invites us to read the epitaph, in which the poet mourns himself as "he," "A Youth to Fortune and to Fame unknown." Critics who try to unravel these shifts have come up with ingenious theories. But in practice few readers are bewildered. Captured by Gray's point of view, we find it easy to see ourselves in the churchyard, whether as tenants or as guests. The art of the poet erases distinctions of "me" and "thee" and "he," enfolding all singulars into eternal collectives" ("Location, Location," *New Republic*, Feb. 12, 2001, 38). See also Jonathan Rosenberg's study devoted to the form as practiced by later nineteenth-century writers, *Elegy for an Age: The Presence of the Past in Victorian Literature* (London: Anthem Press, 2005), and the biographies by Richard Holmes, *Footsteps: Adventures of a Romantic Biographer* (New York, Viking, 1985) and *Sidetracks : Explorations of a Romantic Biographer* (New York: Vintage, 2001), which, much like Sebald's texts, diligently track their subjects at ground level.

19. In her essay "The Return of the Dead: Memory and Photography in W.G. Sebald's *Die Ausgewanderten*," *German Quarterly* 74.4 (Fall 2001): 379-92, Stephanie Harris reads it as a defining image of unintelligibility: "As a lacuna in

the work, the image presents "'die Lagune der Erinnerungslosigkeit'" (A 259) or "'die von blinde Flecken durchsetzte Vergangenheit'" (A 80) that afflict not only the narrator's subjects but also the narrator's and our own relationship to the past. The first photograph thus brings together the fundamental issues of the novel—the imperative of memory and forgetfulness, the relationship to death and the past—that the linguistic text alone is unable to reconstitute." See also Arthur Williams, "W. G. Sebald: A Holistic Approach to Borders, Texts, and Perspectives," *German-Language Literature Today: International and Popular?* ed. Arthur Williams, Stuart Parkes, and Julian Preece (Bern: Peter Lang, 2000): 99–118.

20. The term used by Gray Kochnar-Lingren to describe Sebald's signature hybrid genre, in the essay "Charcoal: The Phantom Traces of W. G. Sebald's Novel-Memoirs," *Monatshefte* 94.3 (Fall 2002): 368–81.

21. One of the most incisive pieces on Sebald proposes that "Romanticism haunts these books in a way that argues a more than casual involvement, that it deeply 'informs' them. It is not an alternative site of origin for memory and history but rather a dialectic principle of mapping them." The essay identifies a set of concepts—impression, image, trace, layer, association, digression, and design—in addition to a lexicon of "afterlife"—eerie, sublime, spectral, ghostly, haunting—that attests to the underlying epistemology of British Romanticism and its characteristic stylization (in Wordsworth and Scott, for instance) of loss and consolation. See James Chandler, "About Loss: W. G. Sebald's Romantic Art of Memory," *South Atlantic Quarterly* 102.1 (2003): 235–62.

22. Attested to by "a tombstone, though not a tomb" (132), as Anthony Lane astutely observes in his review of *Vertigo,* "Higher Ground," *New Yorker* (May 29, 2000), 123–28.

23. Harris remarks, "In a sense, Sebald's entire work is a self-conscious examination of this problem of the narrator's 'wrongful trespass'" (381).

24. The scene has become a critical touchstone. Thus, Peter Brooks interprets Pip's childish construal of a lineage for himself from the letters on his parents' tombstones as the attempt to remotivate the graphic sign to yield a mimetic sense it nevertheless cannot authorize (*Reading for the Plot: Design and Intention in Narrative* [Cambridge: Harvard University Press, 1992], 116). *Person* is a set of letters from whose shape one "unreasonably derives" a fancy about origin and the identity of things. In *Practicing New Historicism* (Chicago: University of Chicago Press, 2000), Catherine Gallagher and Stephen Greenblatt write, "The letters in the churchyard promise no stories," as Pip locates himself within "a landscape like a blank sheet, ruled but not lettered" (171). *Place*—a churchyard bounded by marshes, river, and a lowering sky—is a set of horizontal lines, long and dense, that figure an "as yet unwritten social world."

25. A long section in *Austerlitz,* from which this book's epigraph is excerpted, treats this same kind of communicative paralysis. The narrators in Sebald's texts almost always become ill or break down at some point during their texts.

26. An entire study remains to be written on the simple motif of transported documents and mementos in Sebald's work as its own movement from place to beyond—the way, for instance, *The Emigrants* records the fate of certain photographs of the Litzmannstadt ghetto in Łodz, "which had been discovered in 1987 in a small suitcase, carefully sorted and inscribed, in an antique dealer's

shop in Vienna," (236), and which subsequently re-enter public space as relics in a photograph-exhibition in Frankfurt. (I thank Kendle Wade for this insight.) Chapter 1 discusses the same motif as a conspicuous element in Appelfeld's *The Iron Tracks*. An important three-part novel of life in the ghetto has recently appeared in English, Chava Rosenfarb's *The Tree of Life: A Trilogy of Life in the Lodz Ghetto*, Book 1: *On the Brink of the Precipice, 1939*, trans. Chava Rosenfarb and Goldie Morgentaler (Madison: University of Wisconsin Press, 2004).

27. "[T]his old photograph touches me: it is simply *there* that I should like to live. This desire affects me at a depth and according to roots I do not know. . . . Whatever the case (with regard to myself, my motives, my fantasy), I want to live there, *en finesse*." (*Camera Lucida*, trans. Richard Howard [New York: Hill and Wang, 1981], 38). Harris also discusses Barthes's notion of the *punctum* in her essay. See also Marianne Hirsch's important *Family Frames: Photographs, Narrative, and Postmemory* (Cambridge: Harvard University Press, 1997), and compare in this connection, Katherina Hall, "Jewish Memory in Exile: The Relation of W. G. Sebald's *Die Ausgewanderten* to the Tradition of the 'Yizkor' books," in *Jews in German Literature since 1945: German-Jewish Literature?*, ed. Pól O'Dochartaigh (Atlanta, GA: Rodopi, 2000):153–64.

28. *The Biography of Ancient Israel National Narratives in the Bible* (Berkeley: University of California Press, 2000), 102. Pardes's reading of the episode astutely borrows from Freud's essay on the Uncanny to account for the story's projected friction between male and female, adult and child. She also has some intriguing correlations between the Talmudic understanding of the "desert generation" and the Bialik poem "The Dead of the Desert," cited above. In the narrative we have already seen that places its own spin on homecoming and return—and the only instance within the Pentateuch of the term *meraglim* itself (Gen. 42:9)—while he is viceroy in Egypt, Joseph accuses his brothers of being spies come to see the nakedness of the land *(ervat ha'aretz)*.

29. The verb is also translated as "impressed." R. Samson Raphael Hirsch comments that *vayifga* "never means just a meeting, but always such a meeting where one makes an important impression on the other. Hence it is also used for the intentional going to meet with weapons, or to make a request, to attack, or to urge. So that here, too, it must have been a place to which he had been meaningfully attracted and held" (*Hirsch Commentary on the Torah*, trans. Isaac Levy [New York: Judaica Press, 1966], 458. Because "he came upon" has the root letters *peh, gimmel* and *ayin* which also appear in the word for "prayer," the verse is alternately read by the Talmud in *Berakhot* 26b as indicating Jacob's ordaining the Evening Service, or *Ma'ariv*. The companion verse to 28:10, "Jacob went on his way and angels of God *encountered* him" (Genesis 32:2) has been incorporated into the "traveler's prayer" *(tefila derekh)* in Jewish liturgy, recited before commencing any lengthy journey.

30. Notwithstanding the complexity of defining boundary and designating territory for this non-Western part of Europe and this not simply Middle East, I favor the term "Levant" and "Eastern Mediterranean" for the latter and "east-central Europe" (rather than *Mitteleuropa* or eastern europe or eastern/central Europe) for the former. Here, I follow the precedent of Ammiel Alcalay in *After Arabs and Jews Remaking Levantine Culture* (Minneapolis: University of

Minnesota Press, 1993), Marcel Cornis-Pope and John Nebauer in *Towards a History of the Literary Cultures in East-Central Europe: Theoretical Reflections* (ACLS Occasional Paper, No. 52, 2002), and Harvey Goldberg, *Sephardi and Middle Eastern Jewries: History and Culture in the Modern Era* (Bloomington: Indiana University Press, 1996).

31. Cioran's essay is entitled "The Advantages of Exile," from *The Temptation to Exist*, trans. Richard Howard (Chicago: University of Chicago Press, 1988), 74–78, and was reprinted in *Altogether Elsewhere: Writers on Exile*, ed. Marc Robinson (New York: Harcourt, 1996), 153–56. See also the essay "Defamation and Exile: Witold Gombrowicz and E. M. Cioran," by Katarzyna Jerzak, in *Gombrowicz's Grimaces: Modernism, Gender, Nationality*, ed. Ewa Płonowaska Ziarek (Albany: State University of New York Press, 1998), 177–209.

32. Thus, Salman Rushdie on the *apatride*-as-seer: "It may be argued that the past is a foreign country from which we have all emigrated, that its loss is part of our common humanity. Which seems to me self-evidently true; but I suggest that the writer who is out-of-country and even out-of-language may experience this loss in an intensified form. It is made more concrete for him by the physical fact of discontinuity, of his being present in a different place from his past, of his being 'elsewhere.' This may enable him to speak properly and concretely on a subject of universal significance and appeal" (*Imaginary Homelands: Essays and Criticism, 1981–1991* [New York: Penguin Books, 1992], 12). In contrast, Joseph Brodksy introduces a much-needed hedge against semantic aggrandizement when he affirms, "'Exile' covers, at best, the very moment of departure, of expulsion: what follows is both too comfortable and too autonomous to be called by this name, which so strongly suggests a comprehensible grief" ("The Condition We Call Exile," in *Altogether Elsewhere*, ed. Robinson, 9). Exiled or homeless writers, as Rob Nixon has noted in *London Calling: V. S. Naipaul, Postcolonial Mandarin* (New York: Oxford University Press, 1992), are often "metropolitans" by another name.

33. Edward Said captures the particular case of Conrad the memoirist as "the fixing of something as a point of reference from which the active mind immediately departs," in *Joseph Conrad and the Fiction of Autobiography* (Cambridge: Harvard University Press, 1966), 23. In a related essay, "Conrad: The Presentation of Narrative," from *The World, the Text, and the Critic* (Cambridge: Harvard University Press, 1983), Said points to a scene in *The Secret Agent* as a "strongly self-commenting" figure for the interminability of Conrad's own compulsive authorial project, each text being "the never-ending product of a continuing process." See also Aaron Fogel's brief but suggestive insights about *A Personal Record* as one more instance of Conradian "forced conversation" in *Coercion to Speak: Conrad's Poetics of Dialogue* (Cambridge: Harvard University Press, 1985), 37–42.

34. See also Carol Jacobs, "Walter Benjamin: Topographically Speaking," *Studies in Romanticism* 31.4 (Winter 1992): 501–25. Stephanie Polsky, "Anterior Devices: Walter Benjamin's Tactics of Procrastination," *Parallax* 5.1 (February 1999): 21–35. Bryan S. Turner discusses *A Berlin Chronicle* in relation to Edward Said's more recent memoir in "Edward Said and the Exilic Ethic: On Being Out of Place," *Theory, Culture & Society* 17.6 (December 2000): 125–29.

35. "Reading," from *The Space of Literature*, 191–97. Blanchot does also allow for reading's "light, innocent yes," but this he equates with readers' weightlessness and irresponsibility before the most ponderous of texts. Much of Blanchot's oeuvre entwines death, writing, and reading, in particular the novels and *récits, Aminadab* (1942), *L'Arrêt de mort* (1948), and more recently, *The Instant of My Death* (1974) and *L'Écriture du désastre* (1980).

36. Luc Sante writes of how photographs, like those in *The Emigrants,* exercise an impalpable claim on us: "Through the act of looking, we own these pictures, or, rather, they thrust themselves upon us. . . . The responsibility of witness that is thrust at us is too grave: when such a thing comes from a stranger, it is as if we had been entrusted with his or her existence" (*Evidence* [New York: Noonday Press, 1992], 63). Sante, a fellow Belgian and fellow expatriate but otherwise very remote from Paul de Man, continues, "Each photograph is a regret; it is an end: there is no sequel to what it depicts, no means of expanding it. . . . The terrible gift that the dead make to the living is that of sight, which is to say foreknowledge; in return they demand memory, which is to say acknowledgment" (98). Sebald himself says something very similar about "the mysterious quality peculiar to photographs when they surface from oblivion" in his most recent work, *Austerlitz:* "One has the impression of something stirring in them, as if one caught small sighs of despair . . . as if pictures had a memory of their own and remembered us, remembered the roles that we, the survivors, and those no longer among us had played in our former lives" (trans. Anthea Bell [New York: Random House, 2001]. 182).

37. More useful, I think, are the brief arguments about autobiography as merely a mode of the biographical, "an aesthetic of lived life" in the early essay "Author and Hero in Aesthetic Activity," in *Art and Answerability: Early Philosophical Essays,* trans. Vadim Liapunov (Austin: University of Texas Press, 1990), 4–256. Presupposing an entirely different philosophy of language than de Man's, Bakhtin accords a high value to autobiography as the most "realistic" of forms because it is "least transgredient to self consciousness" (151ff). Literary subjectivity poses no epistemological trap since autobiography is written by and for "others."

38. Said makes an interesting distinction between "potentate" and "traveler" as figures for academic identity that bears on Calvino's frame story as well as echoing de Certeau: whereas "the potentate sit[s], surveying all before [him] with detachment and mastery . . . , the image of the traveler "depends not on power but on motion . . . the traveler *crosses over,* traverses territory, and abandons fixed positions, all the time" (*Reflections on Exile and Other Essays* [Cambridge: Harvard University Press, 2000], 404).

39. "It is forbidden to see oneself, and I have reached the end of discovering myself. God turned Lot's wife into a pillar of salt—is it possible for me to survive my contemplation of myself." *The Pillar of Salt,* trans. Edouard Roditi (Boston: Beacon Press, 1992), 335.

40. Guillory actually cites de Certeau as something of a counter-figure to Foucault, whom he both admired as a thinker and critiqued as a historian. Guillory's bifurcated model of reading is sharply criticized by Joanna Zylinska in her review of *The Turn to Ethics,* "On the Impossibility of Finding One's Way to

Ethics," in *Culture Machine*, http://culturemachine.tees.ac.uk/Reviews/rev8.htm.

41. See also Altieri's contribution to *Renegotiating Ethics in Literature, Philosophy, and Theory*, ed. Jane Adamson, Richard Freadman, David Parker (London: Cambridge University Press, 1999), "What Differences Can Contemporary Poetry Make in Our Moral Thinking?" 113-33. Two programmatic alternatives to Nussbaum's ethic of reading, both geared toward Levinas and the postmodern, are offered by Steve McCaffrey, *Prior to Meaning: The Protosemantic and Poetics* (Evanston, IL: Northwestern University Press, 2001), and Andrew Gibson, *Postmodernity, Ethics, and the Novel: From Leavis to Levinas* (New York: Routledge, 1999).

42. I explore this idea in an article entitled "The *SARL* of Criticism: Sonority, Arrogation, and Letting-Be," *American Literary History* 13.3 (Fall 2001): 603-37.

43. The first pair of terms belongs to Edward Said from the same essay; the second, to Michael Seidel, from *Exile and the Narrative Imagination*.

44. Consider for example, how Jacqueline Kahanoff, a Jewish Cairene, explicates the meaning of "Levant" (as quoted by Ammiel Alacalay): "It is called 'Near' or 'Middle' East in relationship to Europe, not to itself. Seen from Asia, it could just as well be called the 'Middle West.' Here, indeed, Europe and Asia have encroached on one another, time and time again. . . . It is not exclusively western or eastern, Christian, Jewish or Moslem. Because of its diversity, the Levant has been compared to a mosaic—bits of stone of different colors assembled into a flat picture. To me, it is more like a prism whose various facets are joined by the sharp edge of difference, but each of which, according to its position in a time-space continuum, reflects or refracts light. Indeed, the concept of light is contained in the word Levant as in the word *Mizrah*, and perhaps the time has come for the Levant to reevaluate itself by its own lights, rather than see itself through Europe's sights." *After Arabs and Jews*, 72. Compare Edward Said's debatable but telling distinction between Cairo and Alexandra: "I've never been convinced by Alexandria. . . . I have believed that one is either a Cairo person—Arab, Islamic, serious, international, intellectual—or an Alexandria amateur—Levantine, cosmopolitan, devious, and capricious" (*Reflections on Exile*, 337).

45. Feigl Bisberg-Youkelson, ed., *The Life and Death of a Polish Shtetl*, trans. Gene Bluestein (Lincoln: University of Nebraska Press, 2000). A website devoted to assembling and translating memorial books can be found at www.jewishgen.org/yizkor/index.html.

46. Joseph Rosenberg, "Strzegowo Lives in My Imagination," in Bisberg-Youkelson, 117-18.

47. *The Ambassadors* (Cambridge: Riverside Press, 1960), 92.

48. As in the *mishna*, "R. Levitas of Yavneh used to say, 'Be exceedingly humble since the end of man is worms'" (*Avot:* 4:4).

49. "*Klangn-soydos*" ("Sound-Secrets"), in *The Fiddle Rose: Poems 1970-1972*, trans. Ruth Whitman (Detroit: Wayne State University Press, 1990), 41.

50. Dan Jacobson, *Heshel's Kingdom* (London: Hamish Hamilton, 1998), xi. At the end of the book, a more striking metaphor for the unredeemability of time: "Imagine swimming in a fluid which is all movement and light as you

stroke your way through it, but which petrifies instantly behind you into granite cliffs and peaks, never to be shifted or altered by human effort" (233).

51. There are extant Jewish temples within the confines of the Czernowitz cemetery, and a small, active synagogue (along with new *mikva*), but this cannot be what Appelfeld has in mind. See Bruce I. Reisch, "Back to Bukovina: A Trip to My Roots in Radauti and Sadagura—Photographs of Czernowitz," 1998, www.shtetlinks.jewishgen.org/radauti/czernowitz.html. My own enchaining of writers here in the context of a familial past that hovers just out of reach finds an unexpected but affirming echo in the final pages of Sebald's *Austerlitz*. The last of the book's myriad textual and historical allusions, *Heshel's Kingdom* by the South African writer Dan Jacobson, recounts the author's unsuccessful attempts to recover something of his family's occluded history in Lithuania. At one point in the narrative, Jacobson describes the precipice at the edge of the disused Kimberley and De Beers diamond mines, and Sebald writes, "The chasm into which no ray of light could penetrate was Jacobson's image of the vanished past of his family and his people, which, as he knows, can never be brought up from those depths again" (297).

52. See in this vein the dialogue with Czeslaw Milosz on Vilnius/Wilno/Vilna, "Dialogue about a City," and the essay "Jews and Lithuanians" in Tomas Venclova's *Forms of Hope* (Riverdale, NY: Sheep's Meadow Press, 1999), 5–52.

53. Something like that insufficiency explains the motivation of a very different chronicle of the search for Jewish roots in Lithuania, Jacobson's *Heshel's Kingdom*. Jacobson visits not only Kovno (Kaunas) and Vilna (Vilnius) but also the various sites there (in particular the infamous Fort IX) and in outlying townships where Jews were massacred in 1941–44. The cemetery vigil in this book is at once more piercing and more instructive than Schama's. Pausing before an inscribed granite memorial near the gate, Jacobson writes, "Here, the inscription is telling us, where so many of the dead have lain for so many generations, my grandfather among them, *had* been a cemetery once. Though they lie here still, it is not to be described as 'the Jewish cemetery of Varniai' now. It had ceased to be that in 1941, when the community which it 'used to' serve was destroyed" (189).

54. See *The Hooligan's Return: A Memoir*, trans. Angela Jianu (New York: Farrar, Straus Giroux, 2003).

55. Levinas speaks of the need to "'rub' the text to arrive at the life it conceals . . . to tear from [it] the secret that time and conventions have covered over with their sedimentations, a process begun as soon as these words appear in the open air of history." *Nine Talmudic Readings*, trans. Annette Aronowicz (Bloomington: Indiana University Press, 1990), 47. Levinas uses another beautiful figure borrowed from R. Haim of Volozhin about the interpreter's sustained exhalation that keeps alive the smoldering coal of text in *Beyond the Verse: Talmudic Readings and Lectures*, trans. Gary D. Mole (Bloomington: Indiana University Press, 1994), 210.

56. From Robert Frost's "Education by Poetry": "What I am pointing out is that unless you are at home in the metaphor, unless you have had your proper poetical education in the metaphor, you are not safe anywhere. Because you are not at ease with figurative values: you don't know the metaphor in its strength

and its weakness. You don't know how far you may expect to ride it and when it may break down with you" (Cox Hyde and Edward Connery Lathem, eds. *Selected Prose of Robert Frost* [New York: Collier Books, 1974], 35). See also Richard Poirier's discussion of Frostean "extra-vagance" in *Robert Frost: The Work of Knowing* (Stanford, CA: Stanford University Press, 1990).

57. Joseph Cohen, *Voices of Israel: Essays on and Interviews with Yehuda Amichai, A. B. Yehoshua, T. Carmi, Aharon Appelfeld, Amos Oz* (Albany: State University of New York Press, 1990), 133. André Aciman, "Conversations with Gregor von Rezzori," *Salmagundi* nos. 90–91 (Spring–Summer 1991): 17. Similarly, Aciman lays claim to a fellowship with Sebald in his review of *The Emigrants*: "That he and I are both emigrants—a cross of immigrant, exile, and extraterritorial—and that we have both written on the impact of personal as well as acquired memories, and that the question of Jewish suffering lies at the root of our work (though Sebald is not himself Jewish) are coincidences that should have drawn me to his book" ("Review of *The Emigrants*," *Commentary* 103.6 [June 1997]: 61). As a final, albeit unrealized example (since I ultimately chose not to include it among my paired texts), Albert Memmi's *La Statue de Sel*, a semi-autobiographical tale of guilty expatriation from Tunisia on the eve of decolonization, concludes with the protagonist's plan to sail to Argentina, where the fictional Alexandre Mordekhai Bennilouche could just possibly have crossed paths with a somewhat more chastened *depayseé*, Witold Gombrowicz. In the latter's case, however, it is Argentina, a displaced Poland, that beckons retrogressively just as he is "tearing away" from it; for Memmi's Benillouche, precisely to escape the self-destructive gazing back on the past that is signaled by the book's title, it is, rather, "the violent sea" ahead of him that "attracted . . . like a sorceress while it heaved and settled" (*The Pillar of Salt*, trans. Edouard Roditi [Boston: Beacon Press, 1992], 342). While Memmi's hero also shares with Gombrowicz a similarly ambivalent declaration of personal destiny—"it was always my fate to be always breaking with something" (329)—he makes an altogether more lachrymose and pallid figure of pained self-consciousness. Gombrowicz's idiosyncratic brand of *reversement* finds a more biting echo in Memmi's class-critique, in his later writing, of "Europeanized North African Jewish intellectuals" who belatedly come to oppose French colonialism; in far less self-critical (albeit no less ironic) parallel to Gombrowicz's pining for Argentina only as he leaves it behind, it is only "through an excess of loyalty to France—to a certain image of France, the finest image—[that such intellectuals] returned to their former loyalty to North Africa" ("Am I a Traitor?" *Commentary* 34.4 [April 1955]: 291). Only by having cast their eyes elsewhere do they, quite inadvertently, look back at their discarded origins, though the price of such reclamation, Memmi suggests, seems to be just another (collective) version of "the pillar of salt."

58. Like Borges's "Map of the Empire whose size was that of the Empire" from his story "Of Exactitude in Science" (*Collected Fictions*, trans. Andrew Hurley [New York: Penguin, 1999], 141), the critical literature on memoir is almost as vast as the terrain itself. Some general guides are: Elizabeth W. Bruss, *Autobiographical Acts: The Changing Situation of a Literary Genre* (Baltimore: Johns Hopkins University Press, 1976); Adriana Cavarero, *Relating Narratives: Storytelling*

and Selfhood, trans. Paul Kottman (London: Routledge, 2000); Paul John Eakin, *Fictions in Autobiography: Studies in the Art of Self Invention* (Princeton: Princeton University Press, 1985) and *The Ethics of Life Writing* (Ithaca: Cornell University Press, 2004); Richard Freadman. *Threads of Life: Autobiography and the Will* (Chicago: University of Chicago Press, 2001); Wojciech H. Kalaga and Tadeusz Rachwal, eds., *Memory—Remembering—Forgetting* (New York: Peter Lang, 1999); Philippe Lejeune, *On Autobiography* trans. Katherine Leary (Minneapolis: University of Minnesota Press, 1989); James Olney, *Memory and Narrative: The Weave of Life-Writing* (Chicago: University of Chicago Press, 1998).

1. Place from Place, and Place from Flight

1. *Six Memos for the New Millenium,* trans. Patrick Creagh (Cambridge: Harvard University Press, 1988), 71.

2. *Beyond Despair: Three Lectures and a Conversation with Philip Roth,* trans. Jeffrey M. Green (New York: Fromm International, 1994), 69. "To write things as they happened means to enslave oneself to memory, which is only a minor element in the creative process. To my mind, to create means to order, sort out, and choose the words and the pace that fit the work. The materials are indeed materials from one's life, but ultimately, the creation is an independent creature" (68). Appelfeld's preface goes into greater detail about the peculiarly intensified role assumed by memory in living past the Holocaust as well as testifying to it but distinguishes generically between memoir and his chosen medium, prose fiction. He returns to this distinction framed according to the opposing categories of memory and imagination in the preface to his own memoir, *Sipur hayim,* published in 1999, and translated as The Story of a Life, trans. Aloma Halter (New York: Schocken Books, 2004).

3. Gila Ramras-Rauch, *Aharon Appelfeld: The Holocaust and Beyond* (Bloomington: Indiana University Press, 1994), 192. See also her essay "Aharon Appelfeld: A Hundred Years of Jewish Solitude," *World Literature Today* 72:3 (Summer 1998): 493–502, and the definitive analysis by Yigal Schwartz in *Aharon Appelfeld: From Individual Lament to Tribal Eternity* (Hanover, NH: University Press of New England for Brandeis University Press, 2001).

4. "A Perpetual Story of Departure," interview with Michael March in *New Presence* (September 1997), originally published in *Na Kulturu* (March 1997), www.new-presence.cz/97/09/interview.htm.

5. "In Israel he is not yet too much appreciated. The critics and the professors like his work more than the people, probably because his work is so esoteric. [I]t is not the Israeli experience he writes about; it's the standard European Jewish experience" (*Voices of Israel,* 37). The following are the most important treatments of Appelfeld in Hebrew and English: Yitshak Ben Mordecai and Iris Parush, eds. *Bein kefor le'ashan: Mehkarim bitsirato shel Aharon Appelfeld* (Beersheba: Ben Gurion University of the Negev Press, 1997); Lily Rattok, *Bayit 'al belimah, omanut hasippur shel A. Appelfeld* (Tel Aviv: Heker, 1989); Gershon Shaked, "Requiem la'am hayehudi sheneherag" in *Between Frost and Smoke: Studies in the Writing of Aharon Appelfeld,* ed. Yitzhak Ben-Mordechai and Iris Parush (Be'ersheva: Ben-Gurion University Press, 1997), 15–57; and *Modern Hebrew Fiction*

(Bloomington: Indiana University Press, 2000), and most pertinently for the present analysis in its extended discussion of literature and place (and its extensive bibliography), Yigal Schwartz, *Kinat hayahid venetsah hashevet: Aharon Appelfeld—temunat 'olam* (Israel: Magnes Press, 1996)—English translation: Aharon Appelfeld: From individual lament to tribal eternity. See also Michael André Bernstein, *Foregone Conclusions: Against Apocalyptic History* (Berkeley: University of California Press, 1994) in concert with Emily Budick, *Aharon Appelfeld's Fiction: Acknowledging the Holocaust* (Bloomington: Indiana University Press, 2005); Alan Mintz, "The Appelfeld World" in *Hurban: Responses to Catastrophe in Hebrew Literature* (New York: Columbia University Press, 1984); Stanley L. Nash, "A Creative Sense of Impasse: Aharon Appelfeld's *Masot Beguf Rishon*," *Modern Hebrew Literature* 7.1/2 (1981/1982): 56-59; Naomi Sokoloff, *Imagining the Child in Modern Jewish Fiction* (Baltimore: Johns Hopkins University Press, 1992); Michael Taub, "Fables of Loss and Delusion," *Modern Judaism* 17.1 (1997): 91-96; Aryeh Wineman, "On Aharon Appelfeld's *Essays in the First Person*," *Conservative Judaism* 33.4 (1980): 93-94; Ruth Wisse, "Aharon Appelfeld, Survivor," *Commentary* 76 (August 1983): 73-76; Maurice Wohlgelernter, "Aharon Appelfeld: Between Oblivion and Awakening," *Tradition* 35.3 (2001): 6-19; and Leon Yudkin, "Appelfeld's Vision of the Past," in *Escape into Siege: A Survey of Israeli Literature Today* (London: Routledge and Kegan Paul, 1974). Some of these are discussed in Stanley L. Nash, "Critical Reappraisals of Aharon Appelfeld," *Prooftexts* 22.3 (Fall 2002): 334-402. Finally, *Encounter with Aharon Appelfeld*, ed. Michael Brown and Sara R. Zhorowitz (Oakville, Ontario: Mosaic Press, 2003) is a compact but important collection of interviews, essays, and bibliography.

6. "The Right Thread," *New Republic* (July 6, 1998): 39. Reprinted as "W. G. Sebald's Uncertainty" in *The Broken Estate: Essays on Literature and Belief*, 248-57. New York: Modern Library, 2000.

7. In her chapter on Appelfeld in *Booking Passage*, Ezrahi makes the following salient point about his narratorial strategy: "The survivors who populate Appelfeld's fiction are a new breed. Even the volume of autobiographical essays, which appears to have a confessional tone and in its original Hebrew version was entitled *Masot be-guf rishon* [Essays in the first person], is in fact cast almost entirely in the first-person *plural*—as is the novel *Mikhvat ha-or* [Searing light]. When a story is narrated in the singular—whether first or third person—the character rarely appears significantly differentiated from his or her comrades" (188). See also by Ezrahi, "Aharon Appelfeld: The Search for a Language, *Studies in Contemporary Jewry* 1 (1984): 366-80, and "Memory: Coming and Going." *Jewish Social Studies* 1.3 (1995) 161-73.

8. In a more recent magazine piece on a 1998 visit to Prague, "The Kafka Connection," *New Yorker* (July 23, 2001): 36-41, Appelfeld speaks of quarter- and half-Jews who "emerged, as if from hiding" (40), echoing descriptions of the same phenomenon in *The Iron Tracks*. Gila Ramras-Rauch has noted a resemblance between the "essays in the first person" (Appelfeld's designation is intentionally misleading) and the fiction: "In both, a direct description of the Holocaust is absent; in both, the main concern is with the life of the assimilated Jew before the war. In his factual account, Appelfeld uses a very literary, metaphoric

language, and by doing so, he avoids the merely memoiristic mode of expression. He talks about himself and his contemporaries, but he does not use 'I,' even for personal experiences" (*Aharon Appelfeld*, 36). Still, the *New Yorker* memoir marks a departure in both content and form, and as such is often in parallel with the distinctive idiom of *The Iron Tracks*. Yigal Schwartz's cautionary distinction between literary and imaginary autobiographical modes is salient here, however; see *Aharon Appelfeld*, 20-25.

9. The two books were also published within a year of each other. Appelfeld's memoir, published one year after his 1998 essay in the *New Yorker*, continues its thrust by disinterring the buried homeland of his past. While strategically occluding or telescoping important biographical details (his mother's death, for instance), it does share certain key features with *The Iron Tracks*: a tension between conscious memory and "bodily" memory, the loss of mother tongue and acquisition of a new language, a highly selective focus on marginal persons (children, the blind, the mad). Additionally, it retrieves Appelfeld's gradual acculturation as citizen of Israel, a particularly poignant element of which is the concluding vignette about the "New Life Club," which comprises fellow survivors from Galicia and Bukovina; and in this respect, the often reticent memoir bears indirectly upon *Abba*, the *midbar*-text treated in chapter 5, by Appelfeld's fellow Buokovinian, Dan Pagis. More recently, Appelfeld has composed an album reminiscence of his adolescence in Jerusalem with illustrations by his son, Meir, entitled *A Table for One: Under the Light of Jerusalem*, trans. Aloma Halter (New York: Toby Press, forthcoming).

10. "How should a stranger read your work?" "As a saga of Jewish sadness—long Jewish sadness that had different variations. And I am trying to pick up the last chapters" ("A Perpetual Story of Departure"). However, in an interview with Joseph Cohen from 1990, Appelfeld also says that in having written three novels on the lives of Jews in the Middle Ages, his intention is "to write about Jewish life in all its manifestations" (*Voices of Israel*, 133).

11. *For Every Sin*, trans. Jeffrey M. Green (New York: Weidenfeld & Nicolson, 1989), 3.

12. A few sentences after making the salient observation about Sebald's origins—"What fascinated me was the incontrovertible fact yielded up by his birth date: Sebald wasn't Jewish. How many Jews born in Germany in 1944 survived Hitler's ovens?" (283)—James Atlas corroborates my own intuitions: "Like Aharon Appelfeld, whose novels tend either to prefigure the Holocaust or to dwell on its lingering aftermath, Sebald chronicles the ripple effect of recent German history" ("W. G. Sebald: A Profile," *Paris Review* 41.151 [Summer 1999]: 278-95). In her review of *The Emigrants*, Cynthia Ozick also pauses to ruminate about the connection between the author's biography and his book: "For a German citizen to live with 1944 as a birth date is reminder enough.... It is just this extraterritorialism—this ineradicable, ever-recurring, hideously retrievable 1944—that Sebald investigates, though veiled and at a slant, in *The Emigrants* ("The Posthumous Sublime," *New Republic* [December 16, 1996]: 34).

13. Sebald's *The Emigrants* and Peter Schneider's *Paarungen* [Couplings] present exceptions. Of another example, Bernard Schlink's 1992 novel *The Reader*, Ozick argues that it offers a negative case in point as "a softly rhetorical

work that deflects from the epitome," in her essay "The Rights of History and the Rights of Imagination," first published in *Commentary* magazine and subsequently included in *Quarrel and Quandary* (New York: Alfred Knopf, 1999). Schlink's recent collection of short fiction, *Flights of Love: Stories*, trans. John E. Woods (New York: Vintage, 2002), specifically the story "Girl with Lizard" would seem to counterbalance that judgment.

14. This is something Appelfeld acknowledges as well, despite his own ambivalence about the German language, which he spoke growing up. Of Paul Celan, a fellow native of Czernowitz, he writes, "His cryptic poetry is certainly his secret, but it is also the collective secret of the Jews of Czernovitz, whose love for the German language and German literature was unbounded" ("Buried Homeland," *New Yorker* [November 23, 1998], 57).

15. See "Buried Homeland," 48–61.

16. "It is likely that Sebald borrowed this idea from Stendhal's autobiography, *The Life of Henri Brulard*, throughout which Stendhal litters his own often unreliable drawings and diagrams.... We are encouraged to look at the photograph, which then turns us away from itself, converting the passage, very movingly, into a meditation on visibility. The book's deep theme, after all, is visibility: how we see the past, and how it sees us" (Wood, "The Right Thread," 39). "[H]e, like James with his 1909 frontispieces, is acknowledging the uncanny ache that cries out from the silence of solid things. These odd pictures attach to Sebald's voice like an echo that cannot be heard, no matter how hard one strains; they lie in the crevices of print with a terrible helplessness, deaf-mutes without the capacity to sign" (Ozick, "The Posthumous Sublime," 34).

17. Ozick's remarks on photographs in *The Emigrants* should be compared with her empiricist argument about the camera-as-witness in "The Rights of History and the Rights of Imagination," an essay that construes photography as testimony. Reviewing Sebald's fiction, she unwittingly echoes Barthes ("what founds the nature of photography is the pose," *Camera Lucida*, 78) when she proposes, for instance, that "in their fierce time-bound isolations the [photographs] suggest nothing so much as Diane Arbus" (34). Yet they do not sustain the comparison when judged on an internal aesthetic, since they demonstrably betray the hand and eye of the *amateur;* surely it is this aspect—that they inadvertently want us to "look" while being "operated" on by adjacent narrative rather than photographer—that gives them their significatory power. As Christopher Gregory-Guider has reminded me, Sebald was not wholly solitary in this enterprise, for he frequently collaborated with visual artists like Jan Peter Tripp, Tess Jaray, and Franz Meier, as well as acquiring photographic material from his friends. In fact, Sebald's last completed work, *Unerzählt* (2003), features thirty-three close-ups of pairs of eyes: people who were personal or professional intimates.

18. I thank Jarron Sanderson for these insights.

19. James Chandler remarks, "It is seldom an easy matter in a Sebald narrative to tell whether one is moving in the direction of remembering or of forgetting; one is often doing both, and neither, all at once" ("About Loss," 245). Chandler suggests that "impression" is one of several concepts in Sebald underpinned by an epistemology and vocabulary drawn from the eighteenth-century

"theory of ideas" developed by Hutcheson and Hume and present in various texts of British Romanticism. See also the equally fine essay about memory and forgetting by Arthur Williams, "'Das Korsakowsche Syndrom': Remembrance and Responsibility in W. G. Sebald," in *German Culture and the Uncomfortable Past: Representations of National Socialism in Contemporary Germanic Literature*, ed. Helmut Schmitz (Hampshire: Ashgate, 2001), 65–86.

20. *One-Way Street and Other Writings*, trans. Edmund Jephcott and Kingsley Shorter (New York: Verso, 1979), 249–50, 243. A very different correlation of nearness and farness in specific relation to language rather than visual phenomena can be found in Benjamin's masterly essay on Karl Kraus, whom he quotes: "The more closely you look at a word, the more distantly it looks back," (*Selected Writings*, Vol. 2: *1927–1934*, trans. Rodney Livingstone et al. [Cambridge: Harvard University Press, 1999], 753). See also the essays in *Benjamin's Blind Spot: Walter Benjamin and the Premature Death of Aura*, eds. Lise Patt, Gerhard Richter, Marquand Smith (New York: Institute of Cultural Inquiry, 2001).

21. Ozick says that it is the *photographs* (Barthes would call them "eidolons") that are voiceless, not memoirist or reader: "These odd pictures attach to Sebald's voice like an echo that cannot be heard, no matter how hard one strains; they lie in the crevices of print with a terrible helplessness, deaf-mutes without the capacity to sign" ("The Posthumous Sublime," 34).

22. Charles Sanders Peirce characterizes photographs as both iconic (figural representations) and indexical (necessary, intrinsic relation between sign and object). "Photographs," he writes, "especially instantaneous photographs, are very instructive, because we know that in certain respects they are exactly like the objects they represent. But this resemblance is due to the photographs having been produced under such circumstances that they were physically forced to correspond point by point to nature. In that aspect, then, they belong to the ... class of signs ... by physical connection [the indexical class]" (Peirce, *Collected Writings*, 8 vols., ed. Charles Hartshorne, Paul Weiss, and Arthur W. Burks [Cambridge: Harvard University Press, 1931–58], 2:281 and 5:554).

23. "His method is to build up a collage of apparently random details—stray bits of personal history, historical events, anecdotes, passages from other books—and fuse them into a story; Sebald, borrowing the term from Claude Lévi-Strauss, calls it *bricolage*" (Atlas, "W. G. Sebald," 283).

24. Compare, however, the novel *The One Facing Us* [Ze im hapanim eleinu] by Ronit Matalon, trans. Marsha Weinstein (New York: Henry Holt, 1998), a story of Sephardic emigrants in Cameroon, each chapter of which begins with photos from a family album that are analyzed by the text, including those designated as "missing," as, for instance, the title photograph: "A man stands facing us at the edge of a pool, casting his shadow, trying, it seems to emerge. It is as if he is being projected onto the pool, being forced into the scene. He is being screened onto it in fragments, as something other than his true self, vaporized into parts that will soon be transported to another place, another time, that will regroup and try to appear once more. ... Situated in this pool scene, he himself is the pool scene: not a person but a place" (229–30). Incidentally, like the main stories' nesting of metadiegetic narratives in *The Emigrants*, Matalon's novel encloses an excerpt from the memoirs of the Jewish Cairene Jacqueline Kahanoff

(mentioned in my introduction), along with a photograph of her in the company of the narrator's family.

25. Sharing the trait Anthony Lane calls "diplomatic immunity," both the narrator here and Sebald himself, who refers to his birthplace, Wertach im Allgäu, as "W.," choose to conceal the proper name, prompting Lane to speculate whether the point is to "keep it encoded, or perhaps nudge it to the edge of the fiction" ("Higher Ground," 132). On the complex interplay between fact and fiction in Sebald's work, see both James Wood's essay "The Right Thread," and Peter Craven, "W. G. Sebald: Anatomy of Faction," *Heat* 12 (1999): 211–24.

26. See also Emil Benveniste, "Subjectivity in Language," in *Problems in General Linguistics,* trans. Mary Elizabeth Meek (Coral Gables, FL: University of Miami Press, 1971).

27. Other examples are: "I had to discover the story I did not know" (28); "If I intended to go to Ithaca, I ought not to defer" (105); "and so I went to Manchester again" (178).

28. The German equivalent of *style indirect libre* or free indirect discourse. See Ann Banfield, *Unspeakable Sentences: Narration and Representation in the Language of Fiction* (Boston: Routledge & Kegan Paul, 1982); Dorit Cohn, *Transparent Minds: Narrative Modes for Presenting Consciousness in Fiction* (Princeton, NJ: Princeton University Press, 1978); and Franz Karl Stanzel, *A Theory of Narrative* (Cambridge: Cambridge University Press, 1984).

29. "What he liked most, then, was to stand in one of the window bays toward the head of the room, half facing the class and half turned to look out, his face at a slightly upturned angle with the sunlight glinting on his glasses; and from that position on the periphery he would talk to us" (34). (Incidentally, the published fragment of what was to be Sebald's next novel places the perambulating narrator on the island of Corsica, poised on Europe's own periphery. See "Campo Santo," *Akzente: Zeitschrift fr Literatur* 1 [February 2003]: B 5384, 3–14.)

30. The act of telling one's own or another's story is fraught with exigency in *The Emigrants:* Paul is "consumed by inner loneliness" (44); Uncle Adelwarth is "filled with appalling grief" (111); "Tragedy in my youth struck such deep roots within me that it later shot up again, put forth evil flowers, and spread the poisonous canopy over me which has kept me in the shade and dark in recent years" (191), professes Max Ferber; and last but not least the narrator: "Often I could not get on for hours or days at a time, and not infrequently I unraveled what I had done, continuously tormented by scruples that were taking tighter hold and steadily paralyzing me" (trans. Michael Hulse [New York: New Directions, 1996], 230). The last memoir-novel, *Austerlitz* (New York: Random House, 2001), turns on the gradual revelation of the protagonist's forgotten origins in Prague and passage to Britain on the *Kindertransport.*

31. Emphasis on *word* is Bakhtin's. On Sebald's debt to Romanticism, see again Chandler's essay "About Loss." Marjorie Perloff discusses Bakhtin's use of Goethe along with what she insists is Homi Bhabha's misuse of both in her essay "Cultural Liminality/Aesthetic Closure? The 'Interstitial Perspective' of Homi Bhabha," cited in my introduction. While an emphasis on the visual in this essay by Bakhtin (making him complicit, for Bhabha, in "the fullness of narrative time and visual synchrony") may seem at odds with his characteristic

emphasis on voice, what is consistent across all his work is an authorial bias that often means inattention to the kind of hermeneutic I have in mind here; readers' lines of sight (or hearing)—as *explicit* variables—tend to be factored out of the dialogic. (P. N. Medvedev and V. N. Vološinov, however, typically speak of texts as an ideological bridge between authors and readers; see *The Formal Method in Literary Scholarship: A Critical Introduction to Sociological Poetics,* trans. Albert J. Wehrle (Baltimore: Johns Hopkins University Press, 1978), 52; and *Marxism and the Philosophy of Language,* trans. Ladislav Matejka and I. R. Titunik [New York: Seminar Press, 1973], 84–87.)

32. Stendhal and Kafka, as well. *Vertigo* contains a reconstructive homage to both.

33. Perloff explains: "When, for example, in a mountain valley south of Palermo, the guide explains 'how, long ago, Hannibal had given battle here and what stupendous feats of valour had taken place on this very spot,' Goethe irritatedly rejects what he calls an 'odious evocation of defunct ghosts' (*Italian Journey,* trans Robert R. Heitner [New York: Suhrkamp Publishers, 1989], 222)), there being no trace, in the landscape before him, of past acts of violence and war." Compare the passage from Sebald's *The Rings of Saturn,* in the chapter on the young exile Joseph Conrad, where the narrator from within a camera obscura on the plain of Waterloo remarks, "We, the survivors, see everything from above, see everything at once, and still we do not know how it was . . . no clear picture emerged" (125)—a silent echo too, perhaps, of Benjamin's "Angelus Novus."

34. For example, this seeming emblem of "Germany": "Directly across from me, even though there were plenty of seats free, a fat, square-headed man of perhaps fifty had plumped himself down. His face was flushed and blotched with red, and his eyes were very close-set and sharply squint. . . . I could not say whether the physical and mental deformity of my fellow passenger was the result of long psychiatric confinement, some innate debility, or simply beer-drinking and eating between meals" (219). Or Selwyn's servant, "a female personage of indeterminate age": "Elaine, as she was called, wore her hair shorn high up the nape, as inmates of asylums do. Her facial expressions and movements gave a distraught impression, her lips were invariably wet. . . . What we found particularly unsettling was her intermittent habit, when she was in the kitchen, of breaking into strange, apparently unmotivated, whinnying laughter that would penetrate to the first floor" (10).

35. Stendhal wrote about it in "The Salzburg Bough," an epilogue to the treatise "On Love. See the essay by A. Lockwood, "Beylisms in W. G. Sebald's Vertigo," *The Brooklyn Rail* 38 (July 2000): www.thebrooklynrail.org/archives/index.html.

36. "Reality and Its Shadow," in *Collected Philosophical Papers,* trans. Alphonso Lingis (Dordrecht: Martinus Nijhoff, 1987), 6. "A being is that which is, that which reveals itself in its truth, and, at the same time, it resembles itself, is its own image. . . . The whole of reality bears on its face its own allegory, its own revelation and its truth. In utilizing images, art not only reflects but brings about this allegory. In art allegory is introduced into the world, as truth is accomplished in cognition" (7). This essay is treated by Robert Eaglestone, *Ethical Criticism: Reading after Levinas* (Edinburgh: Edinburgh University Press, 1997)

and Jill Robbins, *Altered Reading*; I explore it as well in my *Narrative Ethics* (Cambridge: Harvard University Press, 1992) and *Facing Black and Jew: Literature as Public Space* (Cambridge: Cambridge University Press, 1998).

37. From the unsigned review of *Vertigo* in *The Guardian*, October 14, 2000, books.guardian.co.uk/reviews/travel/0,,382145,00.html. See, also in the *Guardian*, Stephen Moss, "Falling for Vertigo" (January 20, 2000), books.guardian.co.uk/critics/reviews/0,,124963,00.html.

38. The narrative breaks into two diegetic halves: the narrator's, which relates his limited knowledge of Bereyter as a student, and Mme. Landau's, which both fills in the missing background and carries the personal history forward to Paul's suicide. It thus anticipates the enchainment of discourse that characterizes "Ambros Adelwarth" and "Max Ferber." But as is also the case throughout the text, internal correspondences in this second section complicate what seem merely to be arbitrary transitions: for instance the twinning of the narrator's search for more information about Paul as "my investigations" and Mme. Landau's description of Paul's notes on suicidal writers as "his investigations."

39. "In Ardwick, Brunswick, All Saints, Hulme, and Angel Fields too, districts adjoining the centre to the south, whole kilometers of working class homes had been pulled down by the authorities, so that, once the demolition rubble had been removed, all that was left to recall the lives of thousands of people was the grid-like layout of the streets" (157). "And there were pictures of the ghetto—street cobbles, tram tracks, housefronts, hoardings, demolition sites, fire protection walls, beneath a sky that was grey, watery green, or white and blue—strangely deserted pictures, scarcely one of which showed a living soul, despite the fact that were as many as a hundred and seventy thousand people in Litzmannstadt, in an area of no more than five square kilometers" (236). One should also compare Sebald's essays on the Allied bombing campaign in Germany, *On the Natural History of Destruction*, trans. Anthea Bell (New York: Random House, 2003).

40. From the surname and locutions like "he was... a veritable Melammed" (56), we infer that she is Jewish; from the story she tells, we suspect that she and Paul were perhaps intimates late in their lives.

41. They are *And the last remnants memory destroys* ("Dr. Henry Selwyn"); *There is a mist that no eye can dispel* ("Paul Bereyter"); *My field of corn is but a crop of tears* ("Ambros Adelwarth"); *They come when night falls to search for life* ("Max Ferber"). The third of these is drawn from the lyric "The Claimant," written by the Elizabethan Chidiock Tichborne (ca. 1558–1586), the night before his execution for treason, although the wording has been altered slightly from "My crop of corn is but a field of tares." Sources for the others are more obscure.

42. Born in Mikhailovka, Russia, Tchernichovsky (1875–1943) is generally acknowledged to be the most important poet after Bialik in the generation of Hebrew writers who first became active in the Odessa of the 1890s. As Robert Alter says in a commentary to another poem by Tchernichovsky, his work "generally conveys a sense of being at home in a natural world, despite the physical uprootings and difficulties experienced by the man himself" *The Modern Hebrew Poem Itself*, 36. The poem "*Tavnit nof moladto*" concludes,

everything a wondering child comes across
on the dew-softened paths....
But when the days become many, and in the war of being
the scroll of his Book of Life is being interpreted—
then comes, one by one, each letter with its interpretation
and each symbol revealing past and future that was inscribed
in it when it was first opened.
Man is nothing but the landscape of his homeland.

43. Writes Yigal Schwartz, "*The Iron Tracks* refers to an enormous surrounding space that includes the Unites States. Argentina and Uruguay; Siberia, Copenhagen, and Naples, Australia, New Zealand, and Israel. Yet not a single plot event takes place in that enormous area; all events occur within a limited space bounded with precision by the oval course of the railroad stations" (*Aharon Appelfeld*, 75).

44. An inflected form of the verb-root SLL (*salal*, "to tread, to make a path"). In his Torah-commentary, Samson Raphael Hirsch explains that the word involves the idea of elevation and raising up: "*mesilah* would accordingly be a road leading upwards," *Commentary on the Torah*, trans. Isaac Levy (New York: Judaica Press, 1966), 373—as explicitly so in Num. 20: 19, "We will go up by the high road" (*ba'mesilah na'aleh*). It should also be noted that *barzel* ("iron") in biblical Hebrew often has constrictive connotations, as for instance, the *bur habarzel* ("crucible of iron") in Deut. 4:20 or *nichbdehem barzel* ("iron fetters") in Psalm 150, and often connotes human hardness. The prohibitions in Ex. 20:22 and Deut. 27:5, for example, specify that no iron tools be used in the construction of the Temple with the implication that their material would violate its peaceful purposes. Even more pertinently, the set of curses in Deut. 28 include: "Your heavens over your head will be copper and the land beneath you will be iron" (23) and "And he will put an iron yoke on your neck, until he destroys you" (48).

45. *The Path of the Just*, trans. Yaakov Feldman (Northvale, NJ: Jason Aronson Inc., 1996). Also online at www.shechem.org/torah/mesyesh/. Adventitiously, in the context of the novel's core theme of travel, "*Mesilat Yesharim*" is also the name of a street in the center of West Jerusalem. The schema for *Mesilat Yesharim* derives from a source verse in Deut. 10:11–13, "And now, Israel, what does Hashem your God require of you, but to fear Hashem your God, to walk in all His ways, and to love Him, and to serve Hashem your God with all your heart and all your soul, to keep the commandments of the Lord and His statutes, which I command you this day for your good?" After the rabbinic court in Frankfurt forbade him (in the year 1735) to continue teaching kabbalah, R. Luzzatto wrote a letter that eerily bears on a landscape in which stranded objects outnumber the Jews who once owned and used them: "The German Jews are whole and numerous, thank God—in Frankfurt alone there are some three hundred Torah scholars studying in *yeshivot*.... But behold, they waste their days in pointless casuistry, and there is no spirit of piety in them" (*Otzrot Ha-Ramchal* [Jerusalem: Sifriaty, 1992], 304). For estimations of R. Luzzato's work and influence, see Isaiah Tishby, *Messianic Mysticism of Moses Chaim Luzzato* (Oxford: Littman Library of Jewish Civilization, forthcoming), and "Kithvei ha-Kabbalah

le-RaMHaL be Polin uve-Lita" (Spreading of RaMHaL's kabbalistic writings in Poland and Lithuania), *Kiryath Sefer* 45.1 (1969): 127–54, which discuss his two other major works, as well, *Derech Hashem* ("The Way of God") and *Kalach Pis'chey Chochmah* ("One Hundred and Thirty-Eight Gates of Wisdom"); and Joëlle Hansel, "Défense et illustration de la cabale: *Le philosophe et le cabaliste* de Moïse Hayyim Luzzatto," *Pardès* 12 (1990): 44–66. Finally, an entire issue of *Daat: A Journal of Jewish Philosophy and Kabbalah* 40 (Winter 1998) is devoted to the figure of Luzzato.

46. *The Iron Tracks*, however, covertly quotes the book of Judges, as we will see. On the tradition of scriptural quotation or *melitsah* in modern Hebrew literature (*shibbutz* is a related device for creating intertext), see Robert Alter, *The Invention of Hebrew Prose: Modern Fiction and the Language of Realism* (Seattle: University of Washington Press, 1988). Gershon Shaked's *Modern Hebrew Fiction* discusses the hybrid of modern prose style and classical Hebrew known as "formulation." For an example of the same biblical motif as variously deployed by different Israeli writers, see Yigal Schwartz's "The Person, the Path, and the Melody: A Brief History of Identity in Israeli Literature," *Prooftexts* 20.3 (Autumn 2000): 318–39.

47. *Ashan* (Jerusalem: Akhshav, 1962); *Ba-gai ha'poreh* (Jerusalem: Schocken Books, 1964); *Kfor 'al ha'aretz* (Ramat Gan: Massada, 1965), especially the novella "In the Isles of St. George," which envisions the survivor as eternally wandering Jew, and, like the concluding gesture of *The Iron Tracks*, twins the protagonist with his Gentile opposite; *Adnai ha'nahar* (Tel Aviv: Ha'kibbutz ha'me'uhad, 1971). See also Lily Rattok's discussion of these stories in *Bayit 'al belimah*, 119–36.

48. Agnon, Kafka, and Sholem Aleichem represent Appelfeld's own precursor influences in *The Iron Tracks*. To take the last as another example, I am not the first to notice that the novel also "rewrites" *Ayznban Geshickhtes: Kvosim fun a komivoyzahner* (The railroad stories: Tales of a commercial traveler"), written in 1909–11. Appelfeld discusses Agnon's influence on him in his memoir, 151–55 and 162–66, in light of which one might also compare Levinas's short but very beautiful essay on Agnon, "Poetry and Resurrection," in *Proper Names*, trans. Michael B. Smith (Stanford, CA: Stanford University Press, 1996), 7–16

49. See the treatment of Agnon's story, in Arnold J. Band, *Nostalgia and Nightmare: A Study in the Fiction of S. Y. Agnon* (Berkeley: University of California Press, 1968) and the introduction by Anne Golomb Hoffman and Alan Mintz to Agnon's *A Book That Was Lost and Other Stories* (New York: Schocken, 1992), 3–29. See also Hoffman's full-scale study, *Between Exile and Return: S. Y. Agnon and the Drama of Writing* (Albany: State University of New York Press, 1991) and her essay "Topographies of Reading: Agnon through Benjamin," in *Prooftexts* 21.1 [Winter 2001]: 71–90).

50. David Suchoff addresses this point in an unpublished lecture on the novel that focuses on Siegelbaum as a figure who articulates the shared border between native and foreign, Jewish and Gentile languages and cultural legacies, because tradition, as he puts it, "is bilingual at its heart": "The successful murder of Nachtigel culminating the novel is ultimately superfluous. Not because vengeance belongs elsewhere, but because the Nazi "other" who murdered

Erwin's parents shares that same native tongue with him. The barbaric 'otherness' visited upon a national culture, or which vents on others, can never be eradicated by murder, because our most intimate possession—the mother tongue that holds our hand, as Appelfeld puts it in a beautiful figure—always comes from elsewhere, leaving traces that can never be erased. Neither murder, nor loyalty, nor memory can purify a tradition of its others, or make it safe for them." "The Twisted Path of Tradition in Aharon Appelfeld's *The Iron Tracks* [*Mesilat Barzel*]," International Society for the Study of European Ideas [ISSEI], Biannual Conference, University of Bergen, Norway (August 2000). Compare also Appelfeld's comments about speaking "a mix of Ukrainian and Yiddish" in the conversation with Eleanor Wachtel in *Encounter with Aharon Appelfeld*, 53.

51. Although its subject is the national inability to mourn as reflected in modern German cinema, Eric Santner's *Stranded Objects: Mourning, Memory, and Film in Postwar Germany* (Ithaca: Cornell University Press, 1990) should be consulted for the different formulation it assigns to "stranded object" as a token of loss within cultural inheritance whose working-through is actively resisted or repressed.

52. See the discussions of time and space in the introduction to Ramras-Rauch's *Aharon Appelfeld: The Holocaust and Beyond* and the chapter on Appelfeld in *Booking Passage* by Ezrahi.

53. And as Ezrahi explains in relation to Sholem Aleichem, trains thus create the perfect venue for telling stories (*Booking Passage*, 110–11). Like certain encounters outside of trains in *The Iron Tracks*, a disjunction is complexly marked out within them in Abramovitch's fiction between native and foreign: "an interior space whose physical boundaries are the dimensions of the railway car, but whose cultural boundaries are defined by the Yiddish speech within and the goyish landscape without" (111). Yet, part of Appelfeld's revision of this deliberate division and cordoning off has Siegelbaum riding in first class rather than the conventional third-class compartments of a bygone *Ostjüdisch* past.

54. The formulation belongs to Ezrahi. "The suspended narrative belongs to that third place, neither the Holy Land nor the European home, but the 'concentrationary' universe with a black hole as its center and *absence* as its aesthetic foundation" (*Booking Passage*, 187).

55. I borrow the phrase from Shelley Hornstein, whose article, "Fugitive Places," on the artists Chantal Ackerman and Vera Frankl, appears in *Art Journal* 59.1 (Spring 2000): 45–54. Although the towns and villages that Appelfeld names are almost all fictitious, one might also compare Sebald's own repeated itineraries through his native Bavaria, which included the village of his birth, Wertach im Allgu, and thence, Sonthofen, Innsbruck, Bichl, Jungholz, Vordere and Hintere Reutte, Weienbach, Haller, Tannheim, Schattwald (the Pfronten forests), and Krummenbach. (I thank Christopher Gregory-Guider for this information.)

56. In what may be one of the text's subtler collocations of *mesilat barzel* and *Mesilat Yesharim*, Siegelbaum recalls the words of agent Murtschik who "used to talk about the Jews' duty to execute the murderers and purge the world of its sins. Once he even told me that a religious man was obligated to carry out the sentence—for had the Jews not bought the religion of truth into the world?" (170).

57. Suchoff points out that the biblical text uses *pelitei*, corresponding to the modern Ivrit *peletim* or "refugees" to describe those wishing to enter the promised land. Interestingly, the word also appears in Gen. 14:13 in close proximity to the appellation *"Ivri"* ("the crosser-over"). (See page 352 for addendum.)

58. The denunciation is very clearly aimed not at the Nazi war machine but at local Gentile populations. In "Buried Homeland," Appelfeld writes, "Who could imagine that in this village, on a Saturday, our Sabbath, sixty souls, most of them women and children, would fall prey to pitchforks and kitchen knives" (52). The drama of the memoir centers on Appelfeld's request to be shown the mass grave, which the townspeople stonewall until one of them raises his arm and points; the gesture is repeated by several children: "Right away, they raised their hands and pointed" (54). One thinks as well of Jan T. Gross's *Neighbors: The Destruction of the Jewish Community in Jedwabne, Poland* (Princeton, NJ: Princeton University Press, 2001), which, in fact, commences one chapter, "What Do People Remember," with Appelfeld's article as a proof-text.

59. See also the contours of this very personal "politics of language" as sketched by the opening pages of *The Story of a Life*, and on 107–17. He begins, for example, by asking at what point does his memory begin, and supplies a single word in German, *Erdbeeren*, or "strawberries." A page later, he writes, "But the images I see in my memory have become so hazy since then that they are more like a dream. All the same, one word remains, and that is *mestameh*—'presumably.' The word is strange and incomprehensible, yet Grandmother repeats it several times a day" (95). In fact, it is Yiddish, the grandparents' tongue. Compare this with von Rezzori's and Canetti's accounts of their respective linguistic heritage in the following chapter.

60. As Gilead Moragh has noted however, it was Amichai himself in the 1963 novel *Not of This Time, Not of This Place* who suggested new narrative possibilities for representing the Holocaust in an Israeli tradition of literary fiction that has heretofore relegated a writer like Appelfeld to the margins. See "Israel's New Literature of the Holocaust: The Case of David Grossman's *See Under: Love*," in *Fiction Studies* 45.2 (1999): 457–79. Writes Moragh,

> Israel's prevailing cultural code was, for many years, articulated through the discourse of ideological Zionism. Within this discourse, the Holocaust was regarded as the inevitable culmination of diasporic conditions and the ultimate manifestation of a pathological diasporic mentality.... Zionist discourse did not deny the agony and the horror of the events of the Holocaust, but it did deny the *relevance* of these events to the Israeli experience and to the formation of Israeli identity. And since Israeli literature was intensely preoccupied with matters of Israeli experience and Israeli identity, the Holocaust was largely excluded from its domain.

> Survivor-immigrants to the State of Israel like Appelfeld (as his essays attest) thus faced a double bind: "Upon their arrival in Israel, the survivors were engulfed by the imperatives of integrating into a society that they were encouraged to call their own, but that regarded the totality of their past experiences as irrelevant, if not shameful. Their shame of being disdained outsiders was often compounded by the guilt evoked by the actual experiences of survival" (457–60).

61. The story is briefly told: in July 1941, Northern Bukovina, which had been part of the Soviet Union, was occupied by the German and Rumanian armies. For three days, the rioting soldiers carried out a massacre among the local Jewish population. Some five thousand Jewish residents of the Czernowitz and Stroznitz regions lost their lives. Those who remained alive were subjected to house curfew for twenty-one hours out of the day. The Jews were forced to wear badges, their property was confiscated, prayer and work were prohibited, and they were taken to forced labor. On October 11, 1941, a ghetto was established in Czernowitz, and within a few days, 40,000 Jews from Czernowitz and 35,000 from Southern Bukovina were loaded onto freight trains and transported to Transnistria. The terrible conditions and the inhuman labor led to the death of approximately half of the deportees.

62. Ruthenian (Rusyn, Carpathian, Carpatho-Rusyn) is spoken in the Transcarpathian Oblast of Ukraine, Slovakia, and Romania. It is sometimes called a dialect of Ukrainian, but speakers consider themselves distinct from Ukrainians. See Stefan M. Pugh, *Testament to Ruthenian—A Guide to the Rusyn Language* (Cambridge: Harvard University Press, 1996).

63. This is clarified in Appelfeld's essays, where far from a rootlessness that could not foresee its own destruction within Austro-Hugarian Europe, wandering connotes a post-Shoah rejection of the life lived before: "After the war a group of Jews wandered along the open seacoasts of Italy. They refused to live indoors, in sheds, and they earned their bread as migrant laborers in the villages. After the Holocaust, life under a roof seemed not only like a pure absurdity to them but also like the mute acceptance of the illusions inherent in culture, which had brought the darkest demons up from their dark lairs. They chose wandering over the comforts of a petit-bourgeois life. Theirs was a form of protest, perhaps also a hint of the kind of life fit for us after the Holocaust" (19). Schwartz explains the peculiar significance of this "Italian region," as an intermediary space between the Land of the Cattails (Europe) and the Land of Israel in *Aharon Appelfeld*, 59–63.

64. The *mezuzah*, which means "doorpost," contains the three paragraphs of the *shema*, the first of which explains the commandment itself: "And you shall write them on the doorposts of your house and on your gates" (Deut. 6:9).

65. Chapter 7 ends with Siegelbaum's memory of being placed in his father's care, and chapter 8 begins, "The train advances, and now it's close to the little village of Gruenwald" (52). Likewise, chapter 8 ends with the parallel memory of returning to his mother's care, and chapter 9 begins, "After three hours of rapid travel the train stops at Pracht" (60). Chapter 10 ends with the recollection of Bertha; chapter 11 begins, "The trip north from Sternberg is like a plunge into cold water" (73). Chapter 22 ends with memories of Siegelbaum's parents' murder by Nachtigel; chapter 23 begins, "I headed south, away from the iron tracks" (145).

66. Earlier in the story, one is led to believe that it is only Siegelbaum's father who exemplifies Jewish communism, hence, perhaps, his mother's silence; but later on, when his father passionately defends the work he does, we read, "My mother didn't speak much. But her mute face said, Nothing will force us to abandon our commitment to reforming the world" (68).

67. Compare the superb chapter on *Heart of Darkness* in Michael Levenson, *Modernism and the Fate of Individuality: Character and Novelistic Form from Conrad to Woolf* (Cambridge: Cambridge University Press, 1991), and the penetrating remarks on absent centers in Conrad in George Toles, "The Metaphysics of Style in *Tender is the Night*," *American Literature* 63.2 (1990): 423–44.

68. The term is of Bakhtinian provenance, from his essay, "Forms of Time and of the Chronotope in the Novel" in the *Dialogic Imagination*, 85–258, and Yigal Schwartz also applies it with rigor and subtlety (with direct implications for centripetal and centrifugal forces at work in *The Iron Tracks*), in the section "The Chronotopic Dimension of the Realm," in *Aharon Appelfeld*, 68–82.

69. In the same essay, however, Appelfeld proves Siegelbaum's fantasies correct, for Israel is described as restorative, alongside a willed forgetfulness: "Our bodies grew stronger, and we flourished in the fresh air.... With the fragrance of the earth we also soaked up our first Hebrew words written in books. The ancient language, which was new to us, was absorbed with clarity within our oblivion. With no regrets we divested ourselves of the few words we had brought from home, the way one takes off an old and worn-out garment" (17). See also 20–21. Schwartz's study of Appelfeld has much to say about the topographical meaning of the Land of Israel in Appelfeld's fiction, but perhaps the most relevant claim for the present analysis involves an analogy between Europe and the *midbar:* "The almost unending, cyclical character of the movement of Appelfeld's characters through narrative space explains another phenomenon: the parallel that is drawn between the journeys of the characters and those of the Israelites in the desert on their way to the Land of Canaan, which is described as an infinite journey. This parallel is meant to emphasize what was latent in the chronotopical structure of the stories: Appelfeld's characters belong to the generation of the desert, those who have left one place but will never arrive at their destination or return to their place of origin.... It takes place in a region that, it appears, is suitable for such a journey: a twilight region between myth and history" (74).

70. The gun is also aligned with Mrs. Groton, who bequeaths the *mezuzah:* "Years ago a tenant attacked Mrs. Groton and threatened to kill Mutzi, her little dog.... I headed for my room so I could come back and threaten him with the pistol.... The pistol is one of my precious secrets ... here in these uninhabited spaces, I unwrap it in the evening, take it apart, clean it with a soft rag, oil the delicate barrel, and put it back into place" (88).

71. In another instance of deferred homecoming in the promised land, Rabbi Zimmel, the novel's link to Gershom Scholem and the haven of Jerusalem for rescued books, plans to "prostrate himself on his ancestors' tombs, and then to join the refugees [*pelelim*] on their way to Palestine" (127). Instead, finding his synagogue in Sandberg intact along with its books, he stays on. "Since his return, Rabbi Zimmel has not left the place. If a wandering Jew finds his way there, he feeds him, lodges him in one of his rooms, and shows him the many books in his library" (127). The familiar stranger who praises Siegelbaum's rescue mission after he has murdered Nachtigel tells him that he plans to move to Israel, but in the same breath admits that he has "never thought of moving" there. "The thought of all those Jews crowded into one place depresses me, afflicts me, but what can I do, where shall I go?" (183).

72. We are thus prepared for the characteristic silence of Siegelbaum's mother, for instance, when earlier in the text, he records the following dialogue with Bella, "'What language did you speak at home?' 'Yiddish.' 'Have you forgotten it?' 'No.' That was all I managed to get out of her. Her replies were one word, sometimes one syllable, as if her tongue has been cut out" (20).

73. "When I was a child, Grandfather wanted to attract me to prayer but didn't know how. Grandmother would read the prayers with me, and I was certain that only women knew how to pray. For many days I sat here with Rabbi Zimmel. His way of reading was marvelous, as if he were touching a fruit and smelling its perfume" (129).

74. More specifically, a certain psycho-Lamarckism underpins the machinery of Jewish tradition: "Collectively, the group too represses the memory of profound events experienced early in its history and transmits them phylogenetically through the unconscious, 'independent of direct communication,' until what was repressed occasionally breaks forth much later in distorted form with but utterly compelling force" (30). In his 1989 novel, *Mr. Mani*, Appelfeld's contemporary A. B. Yehoshua invents just as radical an interrogation of Judaic origins as Freud, focusing not on repressed race-memories of a slain Moses but rather on the culturally defining episode of the *akedah*, the binding of Isaac. More complexly than the "historical novel" of Moses and Monotheism, Yehoshua's genuinely novelistic *Mr. Mani* replays and secularizes mythic generational tension on what Yehoshua terms "a credible psychological and realistic foundation" by, scandalously, actualizing what is merely a threatened sacrifice. See his essay on the novel, "Mr. Mani and the Akedah," *Judaism* 49.5 (Winter 2001): 61–65. See also the essays by Arnold J. Band, "The Archaeology of Self-Deception: A. B. Yehoshua's *Mr. Mani*," *Studies in Modern Jewish Literature* (Philadelphia: Jewish Publication Society, 2003), 299–314; Adam Katz, "The Originary Scene, Sacrifice, and the Politics of Normalization in A. B. Yehoshua's *Mr. Mani*," *Anthropoetics* 7.2 (Fall 2001/ Winter 2002): www.anthropoetics.ucla.edu/apo702/sacrifice.htm; and Bernard Horn, "The Shoah, the Akeda, and the Conversations in A. B. Yehoshua's *Mr. Mani*," *Symposium* 53.3 (Fall 1999): 136–50; together with Horn's own conversation with the novelist in *Facing the Fires: Conversations with A. B. Yehoshua* (Syracuse: Syracuse University Press, 1997), and Yehoshua's essays on what he calls the "neurotic condition" of the Jewish diaspora, in *Between Right and Right*, trans. Arnold Schwartz (Garden City, NY: Doubleday, 1981). Yehoshua, too, contemplates the dilemma of Jews caught between Judaisms terminable and interminable, the incongruent yet entwined pulls of peoplehood and religious self-definition. But like Appelfeld, he grounds it materially in place, the various spatial crossroads of modern Jewish history (the plot of his formally complex novel intersects with the Shoah from oblique angles, and thus finds points of conjuncture with both *The Iron Tracks* and *The Emigrants*). The fourth of its fifth sections, for example, set in Galician Poland in 1899, culminates in a railway suicide; just before he lowers himself onto the tracks, the text's second-generation Mani remarks, "Well, well . . . so there is a railway line here too. Who knows, perhaps in a few years you will be able to take a train straight from Jerusalem to that świecim of yours without having to brave the sea!" (*Mr Mani*, trans. Hillel Halkin [New York: Doubleday,

1992], 283). I juxtapose Sebald and Yehoshua in the essay "Not Quite Holocaust Fiction: W. G. Sebald's *The Emigrants* and A. B. Yeshoshua's *Mr. Mani*," in *MLA Options for Teaching Series: Teaching the Representation of the Holocaust*, ed. Marianne Hirsh and Irence Kacandes (New York: MLA, 2004): 422–30.

75. From a letter dated August 28, 1913, in Aldo Carotenuto, *A Secret Symmetry: Sabina Spielrein between Freud and Jung*, trans. Arno Pomerans, John Sheply, and Krishna Winston (New York: Pantheon Books, 1982), 120.

76. See appendix 2 in Yosef Hayim Yerushalmi, *Freud's Moses: Judaism Terminable and Interminable* (New Haven: Yale University Press, 1993), 104–5, which gives the Hebrew sources for the inscriptions and discusses the accompanying photographs of items in Freud's collection of antiquities. Of particular relevance are two kiddush cups (one embossed with the *luchot*, the Tablets of the Law) and a menorah, along with a picture postcard depicting the Arch of Titus (showing the sack of Jerusalem in year 70 C.E..) and inscribed by Freud, "Der Jude übersteht's!" ("The Jew survives it!"). The concluding chapter of Michel de Certeau's *The Writing of History*, trans. Tom Conley (New York: Columbia University Press, 1988), describes the nature of language (or writing) in Freud's text as manifesting "the place of itinerant alteration" (317). He makes the following salient point about Freud's *Moses and Monotheism:* "Membership is expressed only through distance, through traveling farther and farther away from a ground of identity. A name obliges, but no longer provides the thing, this nurturing land. . . . The work has no hereditary soil. It is nomadic. Writing cannot forget the misfortune from which its necessity springs. . . . Writing begins with an exodus. It proceeds in foreign languages. Its only recourse is the very elucidation of its travels in the tongue of the other: it is analysis" (319). This, of course, could be extended to the case of Appelfeld's *The Iron Tracks*. See "The Fiction of History: The Writing of *Moses and Monotheism*," *The Writing of History*, 308–54. For a discussion of *Freud's Moses* in the place of Yerushalmi's thought, see David Myers's introduction to *Jewish History and Jewish Memory: Essays in Honor of Yosef Hayim Yerushalmi*, ed. Elisheva Carlebach, John Efron, and David Myers (Lebanon, NH: University Press of New England, 1998), 1–24. Arnold J. Band considers Yerushalmi's book in conjunction with Emmanuel Rice's *Freud and Moses: The Long Journey Home* in "Back to Moses: Reflections on Reflections on Freud's Reflections on Jewish History" in *Studies in Modern Jewish Literature*, 23–33. Finally, see Richard J. Bernstein, *Freud and the Legacy of Moses* (Cambridge: Cambridge University Press, 1998).

77. See Wladyslaw T. Bartoszewski, *The Convent at Auschwitz* (New York: George Braziller, 1991) for an account of the controversy until that point, and also the film *Silent Witness* (1994) by the Canadian filmmaker Harriet Wichin. In 1996, the nuns agreed to remove their religious symbols and give up ownership rights to the cloister, for which they received $460,000 from the Polish government. The cloister was subsequently turned into an ecumenical education center.

78. In *Freud and the Non-European* (London: Verso Books, 2003), Edward Said offers a valedictory analysis of the Israeli-Palestinaian conflict as refracted through the optic of Freud's *Moses and Monotheism*, although the question of homeland and belonging could have greatly benefited from an Appelfeldian or Sebaldian prism, as well. I refer to Said's book again in chapter 4.

2. Flight from Flight, and Flight from Border

1. Letter to Maria Kasprowiczowa, in *Bruno Schulz: New Documents and Interpretations*, ed. Czeslaw Z. Prokopczyk (New York: Peter Lang, 1999), 22.

2. Timothy Brennan, "The National Longing for Form," in *Nation and Narration*, ed. Homi K. Bhabha (London: Routledge, 1990), 44–69.

3. A particularly trenchant analysis of such unswerving commitment can be found in Suzanne Sztajnberg's "Witold Gombrowicz's *I Am Where I Am Not*," in *Crosscurrents: A Yearbook on Central European Culture* 4, ed. Ladislav Matejka (Ann Arbor: University of Michigan, 1985): 99–112. Compare the postcolonial perspective advanced by Abdul R. JanMohamed in "Worldiness-without-World, Homelessness-as-Home: Toward a Definition of the Specular Border Intellectual," in *Edward Said: A Critical Reader*, ed. Michael Sprinker (Oxford: Blackwell, 1982), 96–120. Closer to Gombrowicz's predilections and those of his own Romanian precursor, Mihail Sebastian, however, Norman Manea writes: "What does being a 'dissident' mean? Someone dissenting even from dissidents?" (*The Hooligan's Return*, 17)

4. "Peace and Proximity," in *Alterity and Transcendence*, trans. Michael B. Smith (New York: Columbia University Press, 1999), 132. See also the essay "Nonintentional Consciousness," elsewhere translated as "Bad Conscience and the Inexorable"), in *Entre Nous: On Thinking of the Other*, trans. Michael B. Smith and Barbara Harshav (New York, Columbia University Press, 1998), 123–32.

5. Two complementary studies since Brennan's essay have extended to non-western Europe itself the argument of a foreign national or cultural backdrop as required for the image of "the European": Maria Todorova, *Imagining the Balkans* (Oxford: Oxford University Press, 1997) and Larry Wolff, *Inventing Eastern Europe: The Map of Civilization on the Mind of the Enlightenment* (Stanford, CA: Stanford University Press, 1996). See also the following three essays, all from *Crosscurrents: A Yearbook on Central European Culture*, ed. Ladislav Matejka: Danilo Kiš, "Variations on the Theme of Central Europe," in *Crosscurrents* 6 (Ann Arbor: University of Michigan Press, 1987), 1–14; Endre Bojtar, "Eastern or Central Europe?" (on Hungary) in *Crosscurrents* 7 (Ann Arbor: University of Michigan Press, 1988), 253–69; Jan Triska, "East Europe? West Europe? Both? Neither?" (on Poland) in *Crosscurrents* 1 (Ann Arbor: University of Michigan Press, 1982), 39–44.

6. Novelist and theorist V. Y. Mudimbe writes that the predication, "I know . . ." can connote dominance, or alternatively, a common, leveling humanity—as in the French *connaître* or Spanish *conocer* or Italian *conoscere*, all from the Latin *nasci*, "to be born (with)." See "Jewish Diaspora: A Dialogue," in the special *Diaspora and Immigration* issue, edited by V. Y. Mudimbe and Sabine Engel, of *South Atlantic Quarterly* 98.1–2 (Winter/Spring 1999): 95–116.

7. As noted in the previous chapter, Marjorie Perloff believes that Bhabha has neither followed Bakhtin's own more complex relationship to genre nor adequately adjudged Goethe's *Italian Journey* according to its own formal particulars as travel book. "Whereas Bhabha's cultural model is characterized by its hybridities and liminalities—the nation, we are told again and again, is an arena of contestation and rival performativities—the artwork has, evidently, no

more than instrumental value, illustrating and exemplifying the political and ideological thesis of the critic who happens to find it of use" ("Cultural Liminality / Aesthetic Closure?").

8. Issued monthly, and often referred to as *"Paryska Kultura,"* Kultura was published by Jerzy Giedroyc from 1947 until his death in 2000. Giedroyc's Literary Institute more commonly known by the name of its suburban site, Maisons-Lafitte, produced the magazine as a forum for writers in exile, like Gombrowicz, Czeslaw Milosz, and Gustaw Herling-Grudzinski, as well as writers in Poland, like Adam Michnik.

9. See the introduction by Stanislaw Baranczak in the Carolyn French and Nina Karsov translation of *Trans-Atlantyk* (New Haven: Yale University Press, 1994). The novel is also discussed by Vitaly Chernetsky in "Displacement, Desire, Identity, and the 'Diasporic Momentum': Two Slavic Writers in Latin America," *Intertexts* 7.1 (Spring 2003): 49–71, and Bogdan Czaykowski, "Witold Gombrowicz's Trans-Atlatyk: A Novel for the New Europe?" in *Crosscurrents: A Yearbook on Central European Culture* 12, ed. Ladislav Matejka (New Haven: Yale University Press, 1993): 69–77.

10. *Diary*, Vol. 2: *1957–62*, trans Lillian Vallee (Evanston, IL: Northwestern University Press, 1989), 19–20. "[T]he whole point is that the work is nothing but itself. It is not satire. It is not a 'settling of accounts with the national conscience.' It is not philosophy. It is not a philosophy of history. What is it then? A story I told. In which, among other things, Poland appears.... These are my adventures, not Poland's. Except that I just happen to be a Pole."

11. A photograph and description can be found at www.math.ualberta.ca/~amk/shoah /towns.html. See also www.shtetlinks.jewishgen.org/ Drohobycz/maps_con.htm and the selection from the Drohobycz *Yizkor* book at www.jewishgen.org/yizkor/Drohobycz/Drogobych.html, as well as the interview with Jerzy Ficowski *in Bruno Schulz: New Documents and Interpretations* that describes the Drohobycz Jewish community, 67–68.

12. The circumstances are recapitulated at the end of David Grossman's *See Under: Love,* trans. Betsy Rosenberg (New York Washington Square Press, 1990), whose second section mythologizes Schulz's "afterlife." Grossman alludes to it as well in his forward to *The Collected Works of Bruno Schulz,* ed. Jerzy Ficowski (London: Picador, 1998), vii.

13. The full account of Schulz's last days is recorded in Ficowski's *Regions of the Great Heresy: Bruno Schulz, a Biographical Portrait* (New York: W.W. Norton & Co., 2003). A comprehensive website on Schulz in Polish containing biography, multilingual bibliography, texts in Polish and English translation, artwork and illustrations, can be found at www.brunoschulz.org.

14. Celestine Bohlen, "Artwork by Holocaust Victim Is Focus of Dispute," *New York Times,* June 20, 2001, A1, and "From a Mural, New Life in a Debate over Memory," *New York Times,* June 24, 2001, WK4; Eli Zborowski, et al., "The Battle over the Murals of Pain" (letter to the editor) *New York Times,* June 22, 2001, A26. See also "Whose Art Is It Anyway?" *Time International* 158.2 (July 16, 2001): 24; Ian Traynor, "Murals Illuminate Holocaust Legacy Row," *Guardian* (July 2, 2001) www.guardian.co.uk/israel/Story/0,2763,515412,00.html; and Noah Adams and Linda Wertheimer, "Analysis: Controversy over Paintings by

Writer/Artist Bruno Schulz Removed from Ukraine and Brought to Israel," (NPR's *All Things Considered* [July 9, 2001]). The affair is covered meticulously by D. V. Powers in "Fresco Fiasco: Narratives of National Identity and the Bruno Schulz Murals of Drogobych," *East European Politics and Societies* 17.4 (November 2003): 622–53. See also "Bruno Schulz's Frescoes," an exchange of letters in the *New York Review of Books* between university professors and mostly Jewish respondents (including Aharon Appelfeld): 157.19 (November 29, 2001): 65, and 158.9 (May 23, 2002). In the wake of the controversy, Jewish leaders, museum professionals, U.S. State Department officials, and artists discussed issues of provenance in a forum on "The Legacy of the Artist: Claiming Jewish Cultural Property from the Holocaust," held in New York on July 16, 2001. Bernard Geissler's *Bilden Finden*, a documentary by the filmmaker who rediscovered the murals was first shown at Center for Jewish History in New York in 2002 and at Harvard University in 2003. "Harvard Death Fugue: On the Exploitation of Bruno Schulz," by James R. Russell in *Zeek Magazine* (http://www.zeek.net/art_04015.shtml) critiques both that film and the Harvard audience's troubling reaction. Sidra DeKoven Ezrahi's "Sacred Space: Individual and Social Reaction to the 9/11/01 Disaster," *Tikkun* (January–February, 2002): 24 (www.tikkun.org/magazine/index.cfm/action/tikkun/issue/tiko201/article/020111f.html), puts the whole affair in fascinating perspective (as, reversing the polarity and point of view, do two articles by Patricia Eszter Margit on the threatened destruction of Budapest's Jewish ghetto by urban developers who are partially financed by several Israeli investors and construction companies—see "Builders of Budapest" in *Jerusalem Report* 15.2 (October 4, 2004): 34–36, and "Fighting for the Ghetto," *Jerusalem Report* 15.17 (December 13, 2004): 30–31).

15. The letter, to the writer and editor Tadeusz Breza, begins, "I need a friend. I need the closeness of a kindred spirit." The plaintiveness of Schulz's letters is often just that bald (22).

16. "Bruno Schulz, a Jewish artist, was forced to illustrate the walls of the villa under duress, and was killed by an SS officer for the sole reason that he was a Jew. As a victim of the Holocaust, we believe that housing the sketches at Yad Vashem, the Holocaust Martyrs' and Heroes' Remembrance Authority, is fitting and proper. Here the works will be preserved for generations and may be viewed by the millions of tourists from all over the world that visit Yad Vashem each year" (www1.yadvashem.org/about_yad/press_room/press_releases/schulz.html). On purely pragmatic grounds, however, it appears that neither Polish nor Ukrainian governments nor Drohobycz municipal authorities can claim sufficient funds and/or expertise to preserve the mural fragments or convert the former Villa Landau into the kind of climate-controlled environment a museum would require.

17. For discussions of the generation of Shoah survivors in Israel in the specific context of the aforementioned David Grossman novel see Efraim Sicher, "The Return of the Past: The Intergenerational Transmission of Holocaust Memory in Israeli Fiction," *Shofar* 19.2 (Winter 2001): 26–40; Johanna Baum, "A Literary Analysis of Traumatic Neurosis in Israeli Society: David Grossman's *See Under: Love*," in *Other Voices* 2.1 (February 2000): www.othervoices.org/2.1/baum/seeunderlove.html; Moragh, "Israel's New Literature of the Holocaust";

and Sidra Dekoven Ezrahi, "The Future of the Holocaust: Storytelling, Oppression, and Identity—See Under: 'Apocalypse,'" in *Judaism* 201.51.1 (Winter 2002): 42–51.

18. After the fall of the Iron Curtain in 1989, as claims for Holocaust reparations were being pressed against the former East Germany and Soviet-Bloc countries, international attention was also focused on assets (monies, art, and real property—houses, land, wedding rings, dental crowns extracted from corpses) stolen by the Reich and deposited in Swiss, Swedish, French, and British bank and insurance accounts. See, among others, Gabriel Schoenfeld, "Holocaust Reparations: A Growing Scandal," *Commentary* 110.9 (September 2000): 25–34, www.commentary.org/ 0009/schoenfeld.html, along with reactions to the article and Schoenfeld's response in *Commentary* 111.1 (September 2001): 10–22, www.commentary.org/0101/schoenfeld.htm. See also the many official papers in "Documents Related to the Holocaust, War Crimes, and Genocide," www.ess.uwe.ac.uk/genocide/docments.htm.

19. Actually, several of the murals left behind—*Para Dzieci* ("A pair of children"), *Kot* ("The cat"), *Staruszka* ("Old woman"), *Krajobraz z Drzewem i Ptakiem* ("Landscape with tree and bird"), and *Jezdziec na Koniu* ("Rider on horse")—have themselves been freed of their Drohobycz moorings for a traveling exhibition of Schulz's artwork entitled *Bruno Schulz: Republic of Dreams*. One wonders how soon they will journey outside the confines of Poland or even Europe, making the forced migration of the Schulz frescoes all but complete. Ruth Franklin captures a similar irony in "The Lost: Searching for Bruno Schulz," *New Yorker* (December 16, 2002): 97–100.

20. The rabbis held that the ninth of Av was predestined to be a day of calamity because it coincides with the night the Israelites wept after hearing the report of the spies in Num. 13–14, and was therefore decreed to be a day of weeping in the Jewish calendar. The *mishna* in *Ta'anit* 4:6 specifies that not only were the First and Second Temples destroyed on that date, but also Betar was captured and Jerusalem ploughed up. On the same date in 1290 and 1492, Jewish expulsions were decreed by the English King Edward I and King Ferdinand of Spain. Finally, World War I began on the ninth of Av, precipitating three decades of catastrophe for European Jewry.

21. As conflicting answers to the question, consider the choices either to select Schulz, as in Daniel Schwartz's *Imagining the Holocaust* (New York: St. Martin's Press, 1999) or to deselect him, as in Ruth Wisse's *The Modern Jewish Canon: A Journey through Language and Culture* (New York: Free Press, 2000), as a representative twentieth-century Jewish writer.

22. In a letter to Roma Halpern, for instance, Schulz confesses, "My fiancée is Catholic. . . . I don't care to accept baptism, though. The only concession I made for her was to give up membership in the Jewish community" (134). It is not at all self-evident, then, as one letter to the editor in the *New York Times* insists, that "Schulz would have been amused; now suddenly, he is the best of Poles, an international figure, well beyond his provincial Jewish origins" (Wolitz, in Eli Zborowski, et al., "The Battle over the Murals of Pain"), as such fate could just as plausibly have been a consummation devoutly wished by him in his lifetime. Schulz drew a small number of scenes depicting *hasidim;* one disturbing print,

"Encounter: A Young Jew and Two Women in an Alley," reproduced as the frontispiece to *The Collected Works* shows a thin, feminized *hasid* obsequiously bowing to two modishly dressed women, epitomizing Schulz's penchant for depicting men abasing themselves in front of women. In fact, it is nearly identical to a pencil and india-ink wash reproduced in *Letters and Drawings with Selected Prose* (trans. Walter Arndt with Victoria Nelson [New York: Harper & Row, 1988], 104), which replaces the *hasid* with Schulz himself. In general, the specifically Jewish import of Schulz's work must be teased from linguistic cues; several Polish critics interpret Schulz's work from the perspective of *kabbalah* and Hebrew poetics, for instance, Bozena Shallcross, "'Fragments of a Broken Mirror': Bruno Schulz's Retextualization of the Kabbalah," *East European Politics and Societies* 11.2 (1997): 270–81; Jan Błoński "On the Jewish Source of Bruno Schulz," in *Crosscurrents: A Yearbook on Central European Culture* 12, ed Ladislav Matejka (New Haven: Yale University Press, 1993): 53–67. While Schulz's circle of friends was largely Jewish, they were, in Ficowski's apt phrase, "polonized" or "europeanized" Jews who spoke Polish rather than Yiddish and did not participate in the religious life of the community (*New Documents and Interpretations*, 67–68). (Compare the Wolitz letter above: "The Eastern European countries always claim important artists of Jewish origin as their own. . . . But historical truths must not be wiped out. Jews in Eastern Europe were always a distinct nationality.")

23. Catherine Chalier, *Levinas: L'utopie de l'humain* (Paris: Albin Michel, 1993) and Marie-Anne Lescourret, *Emmanuel Levinas* (Paris: Flamarrion, 1999).

24. The phrase comes from Schulz's essay on himself for S. I. Witkacy: "The migration of forms is the essence of life" (*Letters and Drawings*, 113).

25. By the same token, however, it is certain that Schulz would have wanted his work to be preserved anywhere that it could, even if that meant smuggling part of Drohobycz into Jerusalem. See, for instance, the Ficowski interview in Prokopczyk, *New Documents and Interpretations*, 56–61.

26. He did make "the ritual pilgrimage" there, however. See Adam Zagajewski's preface and Jerzy Ficowski's introduction to *Letters and Drawings with Selected Prose*, 13–29.

27. See Ficowski's discussion of Schulz's "Excursions Abroad" in *Regions of the Great Heresy*, 103–14.

28. [Schulz was] "a wanderer in foreign lands which open up in the heart of his hometown" writes Dorota Głowacka in "Sublime Trash and the Simulacrum: Bruno Schulz in the Postmodern Neighborhood," *New Documents and Interpretations*, 100. In "The Prisoner of Myth" *New Republic* (November 25, 2002): 33–41, a review of Ficowski's *Regions of the Great Heresy Bruno Schulz: A Biographical Portrait*, Jaroslaw Anders mounts a salutary and bitter critique of Schulz's self-serving hermeticism.

29. Compare Eric Santner's *On The Psychotheology of Everyday Life: Reflections on Freud and Rosenzweig* (Chicago: University of Chicago Press, 2001): "What makes the Other *other* is not his or her spatial exteriority with respect to my being but the fact that he or she is *strange*, is a *stranger*; and not only to me but to him- or herself, is the bearer of an internal alterity" (9). See also Edmond Jabès, *A Foreigner Carrying in the Crook of His Arm a Tiny Book*, trans. Rosemarie Waldrop

(Hanover: Wesleyan University Press, 1993): "The foreigner allows you to be yourself by making a foreigner of you" (1); and Michel de Certeau: "Within the frontiers, the alien is already there, an exoticism or Sabbath of the memory, a disquieting familiarity" (*The Practice of Everyday Life*, 129).

30. "Face" joins "Part," "Immaturity," and especially "Form" in Gombrowicz's specialized vocabulary for expressing the primacy of the interhuman. The following crucial explanation of the role played by Form in all of Gombrowicz's work comes from volume 1 of the *Diary*: "The most important, most extreme, and most incurable dispute is that waged in us by two of our most basic strivings: the one that desires form, shape, definition, and the other which protests against shape, and does not want form. . . . That entire philosophical and ethical dialectic of ours takes place against an immensity, which is called shapelessness, which is neither darkness nor light, but exactly a mixture of everything: ferment, disorder, purity, and accident" (93). Compare the extended remarks on Form in volume 2 of the *Diary* (3–5, 184–85); chapter 5 of *A Kind of Testament*, ed. Dominique de Roux, trans. Alastair Hamilton [London: New Calder and Boyars, 1973], 69–82); and of course the fictive exploration of this construct in the novels *Ferdydurke, Cosmos,* and *Pornografia*. See also Jakób Liszka's "The Face: I and Other in Gombrowicz's *Ferdydurke*," *Philosophy and Literature* 5 (1981): 62–72; and Tomasilaw Z. Longinović's *Borderline Culture: The Politics of Identity in Four Twentieth-Century Slavic Novels* (Fayetteville: University of Arkansas Press, 1993).

31. Compare the other set pieces of face-to-face in volume 2, 108–13, 231–39. The latter commences as follows: "Face to face. Alone. Hand to Hand. Foot to foot. Knee to knee. Face to face. Until this stupid identity begins to irritate me in the room, and I think, how is it that he repeats me, that I repeat him, face to face" (231). Later on in volume 3 of his *Diary*, Gombrowicz will indulge in a "close scrutiny of bodies": "I drew physical defects out of the crowds, oh look, flat chest, anemia of the neck, hunchback, twisted trunk, the tragedy of those limbs. . . . I was persistent about seeking out a certain defect, a kind of very French inelegance dancing about their very lips, noses, not of all Frenchman but quite a few" (*Diary*. Vol. 3: *1961–66*, trans. Lillian Vallee [Evanston, IL: Northwestern University Press, 1992], 87).

32. "Peace and Proximity," *Alterity and Transcendence*, 142. In an essay in the same volume, "The Prohibition against Representation and 'The Rights of Man,'" *dévisagé* is translated as "the perception that [merely] stares at the other" (126) rather than being awakened or called into question.

33. These terms are drawn from Levinas's essay, "Intentionalité et sensation," in *En découvrant l'existence avec Husserl et Heidegger* (Paris: Vrin, 1975), 137–44, where he construes sensation as the diachronic relation of "temporal distance" (155).

34. "What does it mean to traditional interpretations to have a body? It means tolerating it as an object of the external world. It weighs on Socrates like the chains that weigh him down in the prisons of Athens; it encases him like the very tomb that awaits him. The body is an obstacle. It breaks the free flight of the spirit and it drags it back down to earthly conditions, and yet, like an obstacle, it is to be overcome" ("Reflections on Hitlerism," 67). As this work predates

the trope of the face in Levinas's writings first announced in *Time and the Other* (1947) and crystallized in "Is Ontology Fundamental?" (1951), so it also anticipates what in *Existence and Existents* (also from 1947), Levinas will designate as the *il y a* or *there is*—"the irremissibility of pure existing" (*Time and the Other*, 47), "this impersonal, anonymous, yet indistinguishable 'consummation' of being, which murmurs in the depths of nothingness" (*Existence and Existents*, 57). In *Altered Reading* (91–101), Jill Robbins underscores Levinas's recourse to literary examples and allusions in describing the *il y a* (to that degree hardly atypical of Levinas's philosophical writing, but still pronounced), a counterpoint in keeping with the reverberation-effect among Levinas, Gombrowicz, and Schulz I wish to create here. For Levinas's programmatic encounter with various literary authors (most of them his contemporaries), see his essay collection, *Proper Names* and also *Outside the Subject,* trans. Michael B. Smith (Stanford: CA: Stanford University Press, 1993).

35. Philipe Lacoue-Labarthe, *La Fiction du politique: Heidegger, l'art, et la politique* (Paris: Christian Bourgois, 1987); Victor Farias, *Heidegger et le Nazism* (Paris: Lagrasse, 1987); Rüdiger Safranski, *Martin Heidegger: Between Good and Evil,* trans. Ewald Osers (Cambridge: Harvard University Press, 1998).

36. *De l'évasion* has been translated by Bettina Bergo as *On Escape* (Stanford, CA: Stanford University Press, 2003), and discussed at length by Jacques Rolland in a long introduction to the reissued essay (Paris: Fata Morgana, 1982); in the sharp and trustworthy treatment, *Interpreting Otherwise Than Heidegger: Emmanuel Levinas's Ethics as First Philosophy,* by Robert John Sheffler Manning (Pittsburgh: Duquesne University Press, 1993); in the first chapters of Howard Caygill, *Levinas and the Political* (New York: Routledge, 2002), Gibson, *Postmodernity, Ethics, and the Novel* , John Llewelyn, *Emmanuel Levinas: The Genealogy of Ethics* (New York: Routledge, 1995); and (along with a discussion of "Quelques reflexions"), Elisabeth Louise Thomas, *Emmanuel Levinas: Ethics, Justice, and the Human beyond Being,* New York: Routledge, 2004. One should also compare Julia Kristeva's ruminations about the upswell of paganism within Nazi ideology in *Powers of Horror: An Essay in Abjection,* trans. Leon S. Roudiez (New York: Columbia University Press, 1982).

37. Gombrowicz's dissection of Hitler in the *Diary* proceeds along different but equally characteristic terms, and here perhaps is an important place to mark cleavage with Levinas. Hitler, according to Gombrowicz, is a monster of the threshold exceeded, "that one unbelievable, impossible, completely unacceptable step . . . —he desired the cruelest life as the ultimate gauge of the capacity to live" (*Diary* 2:77). Moreover, there is that peculiarly Gombrowiczian math that turns on proliferating excess: "Imperceptibly, however, there came into play the action of a practically unnoticeable actor, namely, the number, the growing number of people. As the number grew, the group entered another dimension, almost inaccessible to one man. Too heavy, too massive, it began to live its own life" (77). Where Levinas privileges an almost abstract metaphor of expansion, Gombrowicz sees a crazed metonymy, Hitler's own ordinary and feeble humanity algorithmically magnified into a mass. "No one can back out," he writes, "because they are no longer in a 'human' but rather in an 'interhuman' or 'superhuman' realm" (78). The passage is key, since Gombrowicz

almost ineluctably modulates from "twos" to "multiples." The interhuman, which for Levinas begins in the face-to-face relation of ethics and is subsequently socialized by the intervention of the "third party" (the demands of distributive justice), for Gombrowicz, even if it does begin with self and other, almost immediately *spills* into multiplicative chaos.

38. "Idealism is not only exposed to the attacks of those who reproach it for sacrificing sensible reality, of mistaking and scorning the concrete and poignant exigencies of man in the clutches of his daily problems, and of consequently being incapable of directing and guiding him; it doesn't even have the excuse of escaping from being because, on the level where it leads us, it finds (under a more subtle form which invites false serenity) being still identical and renouncing none of its characteristics" (97).

39. It is also an occasion for perhaps the most spectacular, certainly most grotesque, instance of the "formal (i.e., mimetic) imperative" in the entire Gombrowiczian weft. No summary can do the tableau justice, from a *Diary* entry that recounts the sailing journey from Argentina back to Europe (3:79-80). But its brute uncanniness, its antic series of enchainments together with clever orchestrations of time, distance, and perspective all folded within the most extravagant staging of mimesis, makes for a witting and scrambled Gombrowiczian parody of almost every trope in Levinas's essay on evasion—from impossible escape to embodiedness to embarrassed self-presence to shame to suffering, and finally, to nausea.

40. Did Gombrowicz read Levinas? It is certainly possible. In an interview for a French journal, he recites a litany of *au courant* writers he has read—Greimas, Bourdieu, Jacobson, Macherey, Ehrmann, Barbut, Althusser, Bopp, Lévi-Strauss . . . Foucault, Genette, Godelier . . . Marx . . . Lacan and Poulet, and also Goldmann, Starobinski, Barthes—and this, simply by way of demonstrating familiarity with structuralist (and implicitly, poststructuralist) literary theory. His reading in philosophy was equally thorough and up to date, so one suspects a more than subliminal proximity. For Gombrowicz's miscellaneous writings, see the two-volume *Gombrowicz en Argentine 1939-1963* and *Gombrowicz en Europe 1963-1969*, ed. Rita Gombrowicz (Paris: DeNoël, 1984, 1988).

41. Quoted in Pierre Hayat's introduction to *Alterity and Transcendence*, xii. I wish to call attention to my own repeated and embedded use of the concept "figure" in this sentence because on a manifest level it speaks in a register Levinas himself forswears. "Visage," in short, is not a figure for Levinas, nor is it a metaphor, but rather it indicates the very mode of the other's non-phenomenal appearance and withdrawal in ethical encounter. As Jill Robbins puts this point in a perspicuous discussion of Levinas's 1950 essay, "Persons or Figures?" "To take on a character (une figure) is to risk becoming a figure, and thereby to lose what is human, to be turned into a statue, to be turned into stone. . . .To figure a face is to de-face it." (50, 57). Not only does this critique bear upon Levinas's own complex relation to the aesthetic, it also (altogether accidentally), finds Gombrowicz and Bruno Schulz in its sights as well, since each writer will rehearse his own version of such petrifaction or deformation—Gombrowicz, as we have seen, and Schulz in his essay on Josef Piłsudski, "The Formation of Legends," in *Letters and* Drawings, 59-64. See, therefore, Robbins's treatment of

the Levinas piece along with "Reality and Its Shadow" in *Altered Reading,* 39–54 and 82–90. For very different perspectives on the trope of prosopopoeia, also relevant to certain animating and de-animating impulses in Gombrowicz's and Schulz's figuration, see J. Hillis Miller, *Versions of Pygmalion* (Cambridge: Harvard University Press, 1990), and an essay by Genevieve Warwick, "Speaking Statues: Bernini's Apollo and Daphne at the Villa Borghese," *Art History* 27.3 (2004): 353–81, which invokes Marc Fumaroli's elegant account of the seventeenth-century culture of conversation to argue that "art objects demand viewer presence, even participation" (353).

42. See *Alterity and Transcendence;* and especially *Humanisme de l'autre homme* (Paris: Fata Morgan, 1972). See also Finkielkraut's consideration of these matters in the context of multiculturalism in *The Wisdom of Love,* trans. Kevin O'Neill and David Suchoff (Lincoln: University of Nebraska Press, 1997).

43. The predicate adjectives belong to Valérie Deshouliéres, from her essay, "Witold Gombrowicz: Toward a Romantic Theory of Incompleteness," in *Gombrowicz's Grimaces,* ed. Ziarek, 55. In briefly sorting through Gombrowicz's tropological anatomy, she writes, "the 'rump' and the 'mug' are the rhythms of the tragic history of a man in search of his face." According to Danuta Borchardt in the introduction to her translation of *Ferdydurke,* "while the 'mug' is Gombrowicz's metaphor for the destructive elements in human relationships, the pupa is his metaphor for the gentle, insidious, but definite infantilizing and humiliation that we inflict on one another" (*Ferdydurke,* trans. Danuta Borchardt [New Haven, CT: Yale University Press, 2000], xix).

44. See the astute essay by Jerzy Jedlicki, "Poland's Perpetual Return to Europe, " in *Crosscurrents: A Yearbook on Central European Culture* 12, ed. Ladislav Matejka (New Haven: Yale University Press, 1993), 78–88.

45. But what Gombrowicz says of Sartre could also be legitimately applied to Levinas's writing: "When you read *Being and Nothingness* you have the feeling which only truly creative works give you. It is a book which aims at *you,* you personally, and keeps its eye on you . . . and I, I suddenly recognized myself in it, when I laid hands on it, down there, in the Argentine" (148–49). As well, we should recall Derrida's famous remark on Levinas's thought in his essay on *Totality and Infinity* from *Writing and Difference,* trans. Allan Bass (Chicago: University of Chicago Press, 1980), that it is designed "to make us tremble" (82)—though Gombrowicz's sobering caveat hails us from a near distance: "Nothing compromises an artist more than another artist" (*Diary* 3:54).

46. Ewa Ziarek, from her introduction to *Gombrowicz's Grimaces,* "By writing from the periphery, frequently perceived as 'lagging behind' the development of the Western history, Gombrowicz brackets the revolutionary and proleptic claims of the avant-garde and juxtaposes them with the experience of cultural obsolescence and belatedness. This strategy is most strikingly deployed in *Trans-Atlantyk,* where the degraded and obsolete Baroque style is used to describe the modern experience of exile" (17).

47. In his introduction to *De l'évasion,* Jacque Rolland offers the following bridge between it and the later Levinasian text: "Subjectivity, in this sense, is *structured like escape,* which is to say an inversion into *something other than being* of the Me who identifies himself while persevering in his being, existing in the

rhythm of the essence" (50). At the end of the introduction, unifying the two works by Levinas from very early and very late moments in his intellectual development, Rolland says, "That it nonetheless required nearly forty years and several books (which were more than mere intermediaries) to go from one to the other and in order for the last book to keep the promise of the first suggests in its way a second dimension of philosophy's work and designates it as an exercise of the greatest possible patience" (53).

48. In an excursus on existentialism in *A Kind of Testament*, Gombrowicz writes, "Subjectivity, nothingness and liberty, the free creation of value: doesn't this all imply distance from Form? Consequently it is outside ourselves that we should search for man. On the other hand, isn't 'being for others' just as radical an assertion that we subject ourselves to other people's Form, that we are deformed by Form" (149).

49. See pages 129–30 in volume 2 of his *Diary*, and also 198: "When a single man says 'we,' he is misusing the word, since no one has authorized him to use it, he is allowed to speak only in his own voice. Whoever wants to get at his 'own reality' and support himself on it should avoid the plural form at all costs."

50. No less significantly for the parallel with Levinas's "Quelques reflexions," Gombrowicz immediately relates this to the historical context of prewar Europe: History came to my assistance. . . . I saw with amazement how, with the war, Europe, particularly central and eastern Europe, entered a demoniacal period of formal mobilization. The Nazis and Communists fashioned menacing, fanatical masks for themselves. . . . People were artificially putting themselves into artificial states, and everything—even, and above all, reality—had to be sacrificed in order to obtain strength. . . . Man, bereft of God, liberated and solitary, began to forge himself through other men. . . . It was Form and nothing else which was at the basis of these convulsions." (58).

51. Tomasilaw Longinović, "I, Witold Gombrowicz: Formal Abjection and the Power of Writing in *A Kind of Testament*," in *Gombrowicz's Grimaces*, ed. Ziarek, 35.

52. In addition to the Jill Robbins title cited above, the following all discuss the vexed question of Levinas's relation to the aesthetic: Gerald Bruns, "The Concepts of Art and Poetry in Emmanuel Levinas's Writings," in Robert Bernasconi and Simon Critchley, eds. *The Cambridge Companion to Levinas* (Cambridge: Cambridge University Press, 2002), 207–32. Seán Hand, "Shadowing Ethics: Levinas's View of Art and Aesthetics," in *Facing the Other: The Ethics of Emmanuel Levinas* (Richmond: Curzon, 1996), 63–87; Steve McCaffery, "The Scandal of Sincerity: Toward a Levinasian Poetics," in *Prior to Meaning*, 204–30; and Edith Wyschogrod, "The Art in Ethics: Aesthetics, Objectivity, and Alterity in the Philosophy of Emmanuel Levinas," in *Ethics as First Philosophy*, ed. Adriaan Peperzak (New York: Routledge, 1995), 137–47. Finally, for essays on Levinas as reader of the Bible, see the collection, *Levinas and Biblical Studies*, ed. Tamara Eskenazi and Gary A. Phillips (Boston: Brill, 2003).

53. One of the most arresting and revealing passages in the *Diary* shows us that unease even while in the prehensile grasp of theatrical and ironizing consciousness:

I know, I feel, that the "how" and "whence" and "why" of this other's "approaching" or "emerging" and what our "disposition" is toward one another should not be a matter of indifference; I know that it should be more fundamental than one can express in words; and that it should be "introductory," or "preceding" my other sensation constituting something like a background. I try to adjust myself to the theory as if I were declaiming a role. And this lends my actions a half-hearted quality. . . . The oppressive complexity on the horizon, heavy and dirty vomit of the sky hanging over the speeding and boiling confusion of this million-strong incomprehensible nightmare. (*Diary* 3:23)

54. In *Interpreting Otherwise Than Heidegger,* Manning explains, "Clearly, Levinas is on the way to discussing the emergence of human being from being in general as the solution to the origin of being, but in '*De l'évasion*' the issue remains a paradox because he has not yet developed his notion of impersonal being in general the *there is,* which, as we shall see, makes the issue so much more clear in *Existence and Existents*" (36–37).

55. This is an unacknowledged echo perhaps, in Levinas's scrupulously non-particularist text, of the Israelites' acceptance of doing before hearing in Exodus 27:7, a phenomenon to which in later essays he will refer often. See, for instance, "From Ethics to Exegesis," in *In the Time of Nations,* trans. Michael B. Smith (Bloomington: Indiana University Press, 1994), 111, and also the discussion of Esther 9:27 in "For a Place in the Bible," 27–29.

56. In a steely entry on Bruno Schulz, he writes, "I hail, as I have said, from the landed gentry, and this is a burden almost equally strong and only a bit less tragic than to have behind one those thousand years of Jewish banishment. . . . A landowner will always harbor distrust of culture, for his remoteness from the great centers of human activity makes him resistant to human confrontations and products. And he will have the nature of master. He will demand that culture be for him, not he for culture; all that is humble service, devotion, sacrifice, will appear suspect in him" (*Diary* 3:8).

57. See *Diary* 3:67, and also the article by Suzanne Sztajnberg, "Witold Gombrowicz's *I Am Where I Am Not.*"

58. Yet, Gombrowicz very tellingly upbraids Proust in the *Diary*. As with Sebald, the French modernist represents a counter-influence to be strategically resisted: "Heavy! This cousin of mine crushes me. Because I do belong to the same family after all—I, the refined . . . I am from the same milieu. Except without Paris. I do not have Paris" (*Diary* 2:64). Proust is censured for an "exaggerated, naïve faith in the power of art" (his criticism of Schulz, as well), cumbrous and protracted psychological analysis, monotony of plot and mannerist effect, a narrow social world, "an intentional lack of loyalty to life," and finally, overrefinement. Moreover, Gombrowicz suspects his own retrospection, which supplies a kind of corrective lens to his reminiscences in *A Kind of Testament* and *Diary:* "The present is always too aggressive, even when life is waning, and the more this present life is molded, polished, defined, the further it plunges into the troubled waters of the past in order to fish out what alone can be of use to it in the present and can improve its present form" (*A Kind of Testament,* 33). This bears comparison with Schulz's explanation of his retrograde propensities as

"spiritual genealogy" in the short essay "The Mythologizing of Reality" and his description of *Cinnamon Shops* in a letter to Stanislaw Witkiewicz (*Letters and Drawings*, 110–17).

59. See, for instance, *A Kind of Testament*, 64–66. Immaturity just happens to represent one of the notable lacunae in Levinas's phenomenology, and few topics divide it from Gombrowicz's representational landscape as widely. His is a strenuously grown-up world of adult responsibilities and adult sensation; youth or children are reserved for what is called "filiality," a supercession of the erotic bond that is superior both temporally and ethically.

60. Eros is so overt, so unsublimated and flaunted in the memoirs that one chafes at taking it entirely at face value. Levinas writes that one doesn't respect a text unless it solicits one to do so. Gombrowicz's texts are so boldfacedly solicitous (in both the Levinasian sense of frictional challenge and just plain cheekiness) that without gainsaying his acknowledged departures from "heteronormativity," an equally powerful narrative about home and elsewhere gets played out if one takes the text up on its multilayered *sollicitation* (Levinas's term: see Annette Aronowicz's explanation in her excellent introduction to *Nine Talmudic Readings*). Thus, entwined with a recounting of his forays into *demi-monde*, Gombrowicz consciously threads a parallel (and ongoing) story about place and location that concludes with a bicycle trip to the beach with some young workmen: "When we arrived I was so intoxicated I was unable to stop my bicycle, and raced around the square in circles. . . . Is that why I subsequently decided to spend my life in the Argentine? Was the Argentine already contained within it? I become a little mystical when I gaze at my past" (*A Kind of Testament*, 39–40). A trenchant essay that explores the links between national, cultural, and gendered forms in Gombrowicz is Agnieszka M. Sołtysik's "Witold Gombrowicz's Struggle with Heterosexual Form: From a National to a Performative Self," in *Gombrowicz's Grimaces*, ed. Ziarek, 245–66.

61. *Diary* 2:20.

62. Compare with pages 74–75: "No, it's not that I loved her, but I wanted to have myself in love with her and apparently I needed desperately to get close to Europe in no other way except in a state of passionate intoxication with Argentina, with America."

63. The only comparable moment, in my view, consists of the final stretch of twelve mostly short and cryptic (incoherent?) entries that were supplied by Gombrowicz's widow, Rita, after his death. Repeated invocations of the names "Henry" and "Rosa," Nabokov-like play with sound and sense, an opaque narrative revolving around a "half-mulatto [who] shows up on my doorstep with a tender 'daddy'": Gombrowicz's literary departure is perhaps the most dramatic of all, if only because so unexpected and chthonic, while surreal to the last: "29.iii.68 I sold it for two hundred and fourteen thousand dollars, including the grounds, panorama, the son, and the mulatto. Nothing is left!" (*Diary* 3:207).

64. The phrase is drawn from the end of Schulz's essay, "The Republic of Dreams" (*Letters and Drawings*, 222). As a shadowy excrescence, the mug is thus akin to a *symptom* in the Lacanian sense: summoned in the act of being warded off. See Slavoj Žižek's explanation of the dual meaning of this concept,

alternately personalist and semiotic, in *The Sublime Object of Ideology* (London: Verso, 1989); see also Hanjo Berressem's *The "Evil Eye" of Painting: Jacques Lacan and Witold Gombrowicz of the Gaze* (Albany: State University of New York Press, 1995), and *Lines of Desire: Reading Gombrowicz's Fiction with Lacan* (Evanston, IL: Northwestern University Press, 1999).

65. Excerpted from "The Old Age Pensioner" in *Sanatorium under the Sign of the Hourglass*, trans. Celia Wieniewska, intro. by John Updike (New York: Penguin, 1979), Schulz's most Gombrowiczian story in its depiction of adult juvenility. It also features a momentary glimpse of what Levinas would call possible rather than impossible escape: "You are unburdened, feel light, empty, irresponsible, without respect for class, for personal ties, for conventions. Nothing holds me and nothing fetters me. I am boundlessly free." And yet: "The strange indifference with which I move lightly through all the dimensions of being should be pleasurable in itself. But . . . that lack of anchorage, the would-be careless animation and lightheartedness—but I must not complain" (*The Complete Fiction*, trans Celina Wieniewska [New York: Walker and Co., 1989], 294).

66. In the introduction to the Spanish edition of *Ferdydurke*, Gombrowicz addresses his readers in closing, "I therefore beg you to keep silent. . . . For the time being, if you wish to let me know that the book pleased you, when you see me touch your right ear. If you touch your left ear, I shall know that you didn't like it, and if you touch your nose, it will mean you are not sure. . . . Thus we shall avoid uncomfortable and even ridiculous situations and understand each other in silence. My greetings to all" (trans. Eric Mosbacher [London: Macgibbon & Kee, 1961], 9). In her lecture "Translating Witold Gombrowicz's *Ferdydurke*," *Exquisite Corpse: A Journal of Letters and Life* 5: www.corpse.org/issue_5/critical_urgencies/borchar.htm, Danuta Borchardt quotes the novel's closing words, omitted from the previous translation: "It's the end, what a gas / And who's read it is an ass."

67. "How many names, as Shakespeare says, 'should I write in the book that I read each day'! . . . The note in *Kultura* that I finally snagged my first award (Good God!) mentions Wittlin and Sandauer as those who said to my corpse: rise! But if Jélenski wrote this note, then he forgot to add to all the editions of my works in other languages should be stamped 'thanks to Jélenski.' Sometimes I see nothing but a forest of enemies around me. And sometimes, when I look, I spot a benefactor" (*Diary*, 3:7).

68. *The Pianist*, by Wadylsaw Szpilman (New York: Picador, 1999), and Avraham Sutzkever, *Selected Poetry and Prose*, trans. Barbara Harshav and Benjamin Harshav (Berkeley: University of California Press, 1991).

69. Rolland adds an important parenthesis:

(But being-riveted-to-Judaism nevertheless does not identify itself to that which it would be the model, being-riveted-to-being. Why? Because it is positively election, which is to say service, but is thus already an ethical deliverance with respect to being as a trajectory. This brings to mind a text hardly later than the period we are occupied with here, "The Spiritual Essence of Anti-Semitism According to Jacques Maritain," published in the fifth number of the 1938 *Peace and Justice* [pp. 3–5]: A stranger to the world, the Jew would be its ferment he would arouse it from its torpor, he would convey to it his impatience and his uneasiness for the good. Fixedness, like tension, has for its object not being but the Good, which is to say, as the later work will teach us, that which, beyond being, is *better* than it.) (105)

"Levinas's early years in Lithuania and the Ukraine, and his response to the interwar "crisis of historicism" are both pertinent here. See Samuel Moyn, "Emmanuel Levinas's Talmudic Readings: Between Tradition and Invention," *Prooftexts* 23 (2003): 338-64; and several of the interviews in *Is It Righteous to Be? Interviews with Emmanuel Levinas,* trans. Jill Robbins (Stanford, CA: Stanford University Press, 2001).

70. Schulz himself offers the following corroborative apologia in "A Description of the Book *Cinnamon Shops*" for an Italian publisher: "Here the author feels closet to the sensibility of classical antiquity; he regards his creative imagination and its phantasmagoric inclination as being derived from a 'pagan' concept of life—having to do with the fact that for the ancients, too, the genealogy of the clan became steeped at two or three generations' remove, and the backward look exposed a family history which found its solution and dissolution in mythology" (*Letters and Drawings,* 154).

71. See Zagazewski's preface and Ficowski's introduction to *Letters and Drawings* as well as the latter's interview with Głowacka in *New Documents and Interpretations* for an assessment of Schulz's fame and professional fortunes during his lifetime. He was far from obscure, as Zagajewiski says, "supported and protected in the literary world by those in the political and literary mainstream" (14). Yet his correspondence, most especially the newly retrieved letters and applications to regional and national school authorities, evinces an embittered attitude toward a teaching burden as a secondary-school drawing and crafts teacher that continues to cramp and vitiate his artistic energies.

72. One of Schulz's lost manuscripts, mentioned several times in his letters, was a novella entitled *Die Heimkehr* ("Homecoming"), written in German for Thomas Mann.

73. To this extent, it bears comparison with the figure of the "proud and sad demiurge," the Franz Joseph I in *Sanatorium under the Sign of the Hourglass,* the guarantor of unpassable frontiers and circumscribed boundaries, who "squared the world like paper, regulated its course with the help of patents, held it within procedural bounds, and insured it against derailment into things unforeseen, adventurous, or simply unpredictable" (*The Complete Fiction,* 177).

74. Zagajewski connects this, importantly, with the discourse of letter-writing as a kind of literary backwater (or channel). Just as "Schulz needed to be bound to the provinces the way he needed air to breathe," so he maintained unflagging contact with his correspondents, whose "dilemmas and conflicts were emblematic of the peripheral, of everything that was borderline" (*Letters and Drawings,* 14).

75. One of his letters begins, "Dear Classmate, of course I remember you, and your face springs vividly before my eyes" (*Letters and Drawings,* 89).

76. See in this connection the analysis of the "Schulzian sublime" in Andreas Schönle, "Of Sublimity, Shrinkage, and Selfhood in the Works of Bruno

Schulz," *Slavic and East European Journal* 42.3 (Autumn 1998): 467-82, and David A. Goldfarb, "The Vortex and the Labyrinth: Bruno Schulz and the Objective Correlative," *East European Politics and Societies* 11.2 (Summer 1997): 257-69.

77. From John Updike's introduction to *Sanatorium under the Sign of the Hourglass,* xiii–xiv.

78. Compare also the story "Sanatorium under the Sign of the Hourglass," for the description of a man-dog: "How great is the power of prejudice! How powerful the hold of fear! How blind I had been! It was not a dog, it was a man. A chained man, whom by a simplifying metaphoric error, I had taken for a dog"(*The Complete Fiction,* 269).

79. The "Schulzian chronotope" is the subject of several recent essays. See, for example, "'Stumps Folded into a Fist': Extra Time, Chance, and Virtual Reality in Bruno Schulz," by Sven Spieker, *East European Politics and Societies* 11.3 (Fall 1997): 282-98; Diana Kuprel, "Errant Events on the Branch Tracks of Time: Bruno Schulz and Mythical Consciousness," *Slavic and East European Journal* 40.1 (1996): 100-117; and the following articles in the special issue of *Chicago Review* 40.1 (1994) on Schulz: "Bruno Schulz and the Map of Poland," by David Jarrett, 73-84, and "A Ticket to Elsewhere," by Tadeusz Rachwal, 85-97.

80. In his "Open Letter to Bruno Schulz" from two years earlier, Gombrowicz accuses his compatriot of a mandarin façade that remains opaque to the common reader ("the doctor's wife"), exhorting him at the end to "show us this expression on your face, give us one look at it, how gentle Bruno shakes off the opinion of the doctor's wife from Line 18" (*Letters and Drawings,* 119). Schulz's riposte was witty and unafraid and certainly places Gombrowicz's assessment of him there and in his *Diary* in a different light. Two years after this exchange, Schulz published a review of *Ferdydurke* in the journal *Skamander* in 1938, which, to use Gombrowicz's terms, reflects almost undistilled "symbiosis." This exchange provides Dorota Głowacka's point of departure for her essay, "The Heresiarchs of Form: Gombrowicz and Schulz" in *Gombrowicz's Grimaces,* ed. Ziarek, 65-88. Głowacka's piece mounts an argument roughly parallel to this book's own in respect to both writers' desire for an "escape beyond Form," as well as their contrasting anti-mimetic strategies toward that end. "Each writer has to disentangle himself from mimesis and remain unblemished by resemblance to a previous model." (83) Where I would like to appeal to a (quasi-Levinasian) rupture on the plane of reading and writing alike whose fissures are ethical, political, and ultimately historical, Głowacka confines her argument to a philosophical stance that for both authors answers to a wholly aesthetic imperative: "For Gombrowicz as well as Schulz, writing happens as a gesture of transcendence ... a moment of exteriority that incessantly traverses Form and bounces back on itself" (83).

81. One can thus say of the prose's sexual energies that, unlike Gombrowicz's, there is no *friction.* It is worth pursuing the question of eros as a differentiating category for these two writers, say, along lines suggested by Barthes's distinction between texts of *plaisir* and those of *jouissance* in *The Pleasure of the Text,* trans. Richard Miller (New York: Noonday Press, 1975). If texts of pleasure can be linked to a "comfortable practice of reading," and texts of bliss to "a state of loss" or discomfort (14), Gombrowicz and Schulz might be

thought of, likewise, in terms of the text that chafes or abrades, on the one hand, and the text that slides and slips away, on the other.

82. "He was a fanatic of art, its slave. He entered this cloister and submitted to its rigors, carrying out its strictest injunctions with great humility in order to attain perfection. . . . Falling to his knees before the Spirit, he experienced sensual pleasure. He wanted to be a servant, nothing more. He craved nonexistence" (*Diary* 3:7). See also Głowacka's essay, 73–75.

83. Schulz's references to the organic and material represent the most troubling aspects of these pieces in light of Levinas contemporaneous essay. For example, in a passage that sets up an analogy between Wierzyński the young poet and the myth of Piłsudski, he writes, "The entrance of the collective body from phantom regions of an historically marginal existence into the living flesh and blood of historical life assumes the general form of euphoria, a sort of overflow from its outer edges and borders. The biological is a symbol, a transposition of historical reality. In the microcosm of this representative and splendid youth, an enormous historical fact finds its shape: the revival of a nation's existence, a provisional shape, still illusive and flickering. This is one side of the coin; the winged genius of freedom, intoxicated with the recovery of its flesh" (*New Documents and Interpretations,* 45). While the other side of the coin, represented by Wierzyński's book of Piłsudski poems, *Tragic Freedom,* may again "hew out the face of freedom—but how differently," Schulz does not forswear this paean to the flesh in the wake of what Levinas far more acutely registers as the triumph of the biological and the concomitant degradation of the ideal in and through Hitlerism.

84. This is the title in French of *The Other Heading: Reflections on Today's Europe,* trans. Michael B. Naas and Pascale-Anne Brault (Bloomington: Indiana University Press, 1992), which asks how a "European cultural identity can be responsible for itself, for the other, before the other" (16). It deserves particular mention in this context because of Derrida's several allusions to writings by Paul Valéry which compare the continent of Europe (or its capitals), with human countenance. "Valéry observes, looks at, and envisages Europe; he sees in it a face, a persona and he thinks of it as a leader, that is, as a head" (20). In reference to the essay *Présence de Paris* (written shortly before Gombrowicz left Poland for Argentina), Derrida says, "Just before this, the 'figure' of the face has guided the analysis of this capital of capitals. One actually looks the capital in the face. One distinguishes the face, the head, and the forehead" (119) (the translator notes that Valéry writes "*Europe*" not "*L'Europe,*" as though the continent were a person.) Derrida's argument is reviewed in an essay by Jonathan Boyarin, "From Derrida to Fichte? The New Europe, the Same Europe, and the Place of the Jews," in *Thinking in Jewish* (Chicago: University of Chicago Press, 1996), 109–39. See also his brief allusion to the political essays of the 1930s in *Adieu to Emmanuel Levinas,* trans. Pascale-Anne Brault and Michael Nass (Stanford, CA: Stanford University Press, 1999). (Appropriately enough, a film made in 2000 by Safaa Fathy about the "transitory nature of place" in Derrida's own work is entitled *Derrida's Elsewhere.*) In the introduction to *Nation and Narration* (London: Routledge, 1990), Homi Bhabha speaks of the "Janus-faced discourse of the nation" as an index of the doubling and ambivalence at the core of the nation-space (4).

Most presciently, however—that is, closest to the nationality and literary fortunes of Gombrowicz and Schulz—Geoffrey Galt Harpham points to the figural place assigned to Poland in the fiction of the Polish writer born Jósef Teodor Konrad Nałęcz Korzeniowski: "Thus, we can mark the appearance of Poland in such unlikely sites as the crushed face in the mud by the river in Conrad's first book, *Almayer's Folly*" (*One of Us: The Mastery of Joseph Conrad* [Chicago: University of Chicago Press, 1996], 12). Finally, Gerard Richter discusses rhetorical figures of physiognomy in Walter Benjamin's writings and their link to "the face of facism" in "Face-Off," *Monatshefte* 90.4 (Winter 1998): 414-44.

85. See Ezra Mendelsohn, *The Jews of East Central Europe between the Two World Wars* (Bloomington: Indiana University Press, 1993) and the exchange between Iztván Deák and Abraham Blumberg in the *New York Review of Books* 48.14 (September 20, 2001), 91-93, www.nybooks.com/articles/article-preview ?article_id=14531, and 48.18 (November 15, 2001): 64-65, www.nybooks.com/ articles/14800). See also the discussion of Piłsudski in Carl Tighe's "Cultural Pathology: Roots of Polish Literary Opposition to Communism," *Journal of European Studies* 23.3 (September 1998): 267-309, and *Politics of Literature: Poland 1945-1985* (Cardiff: University of Wales Press, 1999).

86. A connection between the Schulz murals controversy and Gross's revelations about the Jedwabne massacre is ventured by Harold Ticktin in "Jedwabne and Bruno Schulz: Jews and Poles Apart," *Midstream* 48.3 (April 2002): 9-10. See also the Ezrazhi essay cited earlier, "Sacred Space."

87. *The Wandering Jews*, trans. Michael Hoffmann (New York: W. W. Norton & Co., 2001), 20. See also the essay by the same name in *Report from a Parisian Paradise: Essays from France 1925-1939*, trans. Michael Hoffmann (New York: W. W. Norton & Co., 2003), 145-51.

88. The original version in French of *A Kind of Testament* (Talks with Dominique de Roux) (Paris: Pierre Belfond, 1990) commences with an epigraph from Martin Buber's *Tales of the Hasidim:* "Sayings of Rabbi Moshe Loeb: 'Passage through this world is like a knife's edge: on this side, torment, and on the other, the abyss; and between the two, the way of life'" (4).

3. Border from Border

1. *An Anthropologist on Mars: Seven Paradoxical Tales* (New York: Vintage, 1996), 169. Sacks's example is Franco Magnani, a Funes the Memorious of the plastic arts, who retains a near-photographic recall of the Tuscan town of Pontito, which he left thirty years earlier and reproduced in paintings with total fidelity ever since. "He is not at liberty to misremember, nor is he at liberty to stop remembering," writes Sacks (169). The eidetic capacity interests me less here in connection with Canetti and von Rezzori than the immediate reason for Magnani's compulsion to remember and represent: Pontito was occupied by the Nazis in 1942, all its townspeople evicted, and its countenance effectively despoiled, its agrarian economy ruined. Except for a small number of elderly people, all former occupants, including Magnani (who currently lives in San Francisco), moved elsewhere. Like von Rezzori at the end of *The Snows*

of Yesteryear, Sacks ends his essay with an account of Magnani's return to Pontito, which even though essentially unchanged, assails him in its presentness and leaves him both emotionally and sensorily torn between an old, recreated Pontito of his imagination and a new Pontito, seen again, revisited, and far more haunting.

2. Von Rezzori is quoted in Nancy Yanes Hoffman, "The Temptations of Betrayal: Von Rezzori on Anti-Semitism," *Southwest Review* (Summer 1983): 234–50. In the epilogue to *The Snows of Yesteryear,* von Rezzori writes, "But if one seeks to achieve [fictionalizing the real] by drawing—as I do—on the autobiographical, paraphrasing and transforming it and inserting it into fictional and hypothetical happenings, then one runs the danger of falling into one's own trap, with the result that one no longer knows what is real and what is not" (*The Snows of Yesteryear: Portraits for an Autobiography,* trans. H. F. Broch de Rothermann [New York: Knopf, 1989], 278). For generally dependable reviews of the memoir, see John-Paul Himka, "The Snows of Yesteryear," in *Crosscurrents: A Yearbook on Central European Culture* 11, ed. Ladislav Matejka (New Haven: Yale University Press, 1991): 67–72, Michael Ignatieff, "The Old Country," *New York Review of Books* 37.2 (February 15, 1990): 3–5, and Gabriele Annan, "*The Snows of Yesteryear* by Gregor von Rezzori," *London Review of Books* 12:23 (Dec. 6, 1990): 23–24. Von Rezzori's novel, *Memoirs of an Anti-Semite,* trans. Joachim Neugroschel (New York: Penguin Books, 1982), much of which also takes place in Czernowitz, has received comparatively greater critical attention than the memoir, but since it is the latter that is coupled with Canetti's autobiographical writings as opposed to the Applefeld/Sebald pairing of fictive memoir in the previous chapter, the novel is not discussed here.

3. Martin Bollacher's "'I Bow to Memory': Elias Canetti's Autobiographical Writings," in *Essays in Honor of Elias Canetti,* trans. Michael Hulse (New York: Farrar, Straus and Giroux, 1987), 255–70, explores the Goethe connection. One observation of Canetti's about Goethe may be applied with equal relevance to himself in this context, although it cuts both ways: "The thing that often seems so boring about Goethe: the fact that he is always there *complete*" (*The Human Province,* trans. Joachim Neugroschel [New York: Seabury Press, 1978], 235). See Canetti's lavish encomium for Goethe on pp. 34–35.

4. Claudio Magris makes an excellent point in this regard:

The whole of Austrian literature in the twentieth century consists of an unmasking of this crisis: from Hofmannsthal to Musil, from Andrian to Rilke, from Alternberg to Broch, and Canetti, Austrian writers diagnose the insufficiency of the word, which can no longer express experience and give order to the uncertain flux of life—and they announce the foundering of the subjective self, which is no longer capable of placing the net of language between itself and the chaos of life but instead is lost in a whirlwind of sensations and images. . . . Reality becomes an endless chain of individual centers. (275)

See "The Writer in Hiding," in *Critical Essays on Elias Canetti,* ed. David Darby (New York: G. K. Hall, 2000), 279–91.

5. Stefan H. Kaszyński, "Dialogue and Poetics: On the Dialogical Character of Canetti's Notebooks," in *Essays in Honor of Elias Canetti*, 211-23. Kaszyński borrows the concept from Mikhail Bakhtin as one "which would be quite acceptable to Canetti" (216). In addition to studies of Canetti paired with Nietzsche and with Rousseau, Canetti himself has most recently been placed in dialogue with the anthropologist Baermann Steiner in Michael Mack's *Anthropology as Memory: Elias Canetti's and Franz Baermann Steiner's Responses to the Shoah* (Tübingen: Niemeyer, 2001), the most important new work on Canetti as social thinker. See also "Language of Dark Times: Canetti, Klemperer, and Benjamin" in *Diogenes* 48.189 (Spring 2000): 11-22, by Olivier Remaud, which examines the relationship between language and violence in Canetti's *Crowds and Power*; Jeffrey J. Folks, "'Memory Believes before Knowing Remembers': Faulkner, Canetti, and Survival," *Papers on Language & Literature* 39.3 (Summer 2003): 316-32; and Marilya Veteto-Conrad, "German Minority Literature: Tongues Set Free & Pointed Tongues," *International Fiction Review* (January 2001): 78-87, a treatment of Canetti and the German Indian poet Anant Kumar.

6. Bernd Witte makes a similar observation in his essay "The Individual and His Literature: On Elias Canetti's Conception of the Writer," in *Critical Essays on Elias Canetti*, ed. Darby, 227-38: "With a storyteller's equanimity, he sees that justice is done to them all. In this process the individuality of each character is emphasized to the point of caricature. At the same time, however, they seem so tailor-made to the fit the life of the individual who has written the text that one could mistake them for freakish products of the author's imagination" (230). See also in the same volume, Gerhard Melzer's "The Only Sentence and Its Sole Possessor: The Symbolic Power of Elias Canetti," 215-26.

7. Yet compare the claim from *The Human Province*: "I am interested in living people and I am interested in living characters. I despise any cross between them" (189). As I say later on, however, it is both potentially facile and risky to pick through Canetti's notations for something resembling a "summary judgment."

8. "Nostography" is a coinage belonging to André Aciman, from his interview with von Rezzori, "Conversations with Gregor von Rezzori." See also Aciman's essay on *The Snows of Yesteryear*, "Family Fictions," in *Salmagundi* 90-91 (Spring-Summer 1991): 33-45.

9. In his *Jewish Self-Hatred: Anti-Semitism and the Secret Language of the Jews* (Baltimore: Johns Hopkins University Press, 1986), Sander Gilman discusses a passage in the second volume of the memoirs, *The Torch in My Ear*, as illustrative of the Westernized Jew's repudiation of his *Ostjüdisch* counterpart. As is often the case, however, Canetti's notations supplement his major works with an important gloss of their own, as in this 1944 entry from *The Human Province*:

The greatest intellectual temptation of my life, the only one I have to fight hard against is: to be a total Jew.... I scorned my friends for tearing loose from the enticements of many nations and blindly becoming Jews again, simply Jews. How hard it is for me now not to emulate them. The new dead, those dead before their time, plead with one, and who has the heart to say no to them? But aren't the new dead everywhere, on all sides, in every nation? Should I harden myself against the Russians because there are Jews, against the Chinese because they are far away, against the Germans because they are possessed by the devil? Can't I still belong to all of them, as before, and nevertheless be a Jew? (51)

Ritchie Robertson rehearses the question in "'Jewish Self-hatred'? The Cases of Schnitzler and Canetti," in *Austrians and Jews in the Twentieth Century: From Franz Kafka to Waldheim*, ed. Robert S. Wistrich (New York: St. Martin's Press, 1992), 82–96. See also Stuart Ferguson, "Elias Canetti and Multiculturalism," *Poetica* 29.3–4 (1997): 532–95; Sara R. Horowitz, "The Wounded Tongue: Engendering Jewish Memory," in *Shaping Losses: Cultural Memory and the Holocaust*, ed. Julia Epstein and Lori Hope Lefkovitz (Urbana: University of Illinois Press, 2001) 107–27; and especially, Michael Mack's "Elias Canetti Response to the Shoah: Masse und Macht," in *A Companion to the Works of Elias Canetti*, ed. Dagmar C. G. Lorenz (Rochester, NY: Camden House, 2004): 289–312.

10. Aciman describes von Rezzori in turn as a Romanian expatriate who is a German writer who also writes in English ("Conversations," 37). Compare also the Romanian expatriate Norman Manea: "We come out of Egypt every year as they did, without ever leaving it behind altogether, we relive other Egypts again and again, their fate is ours, just as our fate is theirs, forever and ever" (*The Hooligan's Return*, 215).

11. In addition to Appelfeld, one should compare the various descriptions of the Bukovina and Czernowitz in Norman Manea's *The Hooligan's Return*, in particular pp. 79–84.

12. And indeed, this is how Canetti defines that entity, by which he means the fictional "I" (*sujet d'enonciation*) of a diary or memoir: "It is always at hand, it never turns away. It never feigns interest, it is not polite. It does not interrupt, it lets one finish speaking. It is not only curious, it is also patient. I can speak only of my own experience: yet I am always amazed that there is someone listening to me as patiently as I listen to others. Still, one should not imagine that this listener makes things easy for one. . . . He is not only patient, he is also malicious. He won't let anything pass, he sees through everything. . . . Never in my entire life have I met such a dangerous interlocutor" (*The Conscience of Words*, trans. Joachim Neugroschel [New York: Seabury Press, 1979], 46). When Canetti does finally admit the subsidiary importance of another kind of partner, it is not, as one might suspect, the reader, but rather those speech interlocutors in real time whose ripostes and interjections the diarist *records* in his text. Indeed, Canetti speaks specifically of encoding such dialogue in the diary—keeping it secret—so it cannot be easily deciphered. "Thus I can write down whatever I like, never hurting or damaging another person, and when I am finally old and wise, I can decide whether to make it disappear entirely or confine it to some secret place, where it would be found only by chance, in some harmless future" (48).

13. See, for instance, David Denby, "Learning to Love Canetti: The Autobiography of a Difficult Man, " *New Yorker* (May 31, 1999): 106–13; Edward Rothstein, "The Secret Life of Elias Canetti: Dreams of Disappearance," *New Republic* (January 8, 1990): 33–38; and Peter Conradi's biography of Iris Murdoch

(with whom Canetti had a three-year affair), *Iris Murdoch: A Life* (New York: W. W. Norton & Sons, 2001).

14. Later in the book, he confesses that looking at his mirrored reflection caused him to feel like "a mechanical toy, the driving motor of which whirred relentlessly while I remained timeless in another dimension of my being and beyond the image in the mirror's depth. There my emotions were no longer my own, nor did I miss the heart I lacked" (267).

15. A more pertinent contrast than Nabokov, therefore, might be made with Sebald himself (whose literary criticism happened to focus primarily on Austrian literature). A salutary article by Jeanne Marshall about Sebald's reputation in contemporary German literary circles, "History, Through a Glass Darkly," *National Post* (February 4, 2002): B4, can be found at www.nationalpost.com/search/story.html?f=/stories/20020204/1331429.html. Mark McCulloh compares *The Emigrants* with von Rezzori's novel *Memoirs of an Anti-Semite* in his *Understanding W. G. Sebald*, 56.

16. When André Aciman reminds him that his reviewers often characterize his writing as "Baroque," von Rezzori replies, "The German language, as a language, is a magnificent instrument, and I use it, always claiming that I am not a German writer. And the Germans know it. They don't consider me a German writer" (26).

17. Entitled "Word Attacks," the address describes his compulsion in the past to scribble down isolated words, an "ambush" or "onslaught" of language that serves as a totem of the "private sphere" that speaking and writing in German not infrequently signify for him.

18. In an earlier section, Canetti says, "People often talked about languages: seven or eight different tongues were spoken in our city alone, everyone understood something of each language. Only the little girls, who came from villages, spoke just Bulgarian and were therefore considered stupid. Each person counted up the languages he knew; it was important to master several" (27). See the essay by Anne Fuchs, "'The Deeper Nature of My German': Mother Tongue, Subjectivity, and the Voice of the Other in Canetti's Autobiography" (*A Companion to the Works of Elias Canetti*, ed. Lorenz, 45–60).

19. The phrase belongs to William Collins Donahue, from his essay, "Goodbye to All That: Elias Canetti's Obituaries, " *A Companion to the Works of Elias Canetti*, ed. Lorenz, 37). Irene Stocksieker Di Maio points to the identical episode as in her essay, "Space in Canetti's Autobiographical Trilogy," in *A Companion to the Works of Elias Canetti*, ed. Lorenz, 176–97, as a multivalent expression of how Canetti will locate himself, figure and ground, center and margin, within both the world and his own life history. The essay sketches a brilliant discussion of Canettian topographics in all its guises: countries and cities, nature and the outdoors, streets, interiors, and even furniture, pictures, and human bodies. It is worth noting that while the German subtitle for *The Tongue Set Free*. Volume 1 of *The Memoirs of Elias Canetti*, trans. Joachim Neugroschel (New York: Farrar, Straus and Giroux, 1999) leaves "childhood" unqualified, the English translation by Neugroschel renders it "European childhood."

20. One is reminded of Julia Kristeva's distinction between "semiotic" (pre-Oedipal) and "symbolic" drives or fields of signification, categories to which

Anne Fuchs appeals in order to account for a differential relationship to language as sound or meaning in "The Dignity of Difference: Self and Other in Canetti's *Voices of Marrakesh*," in *Critical Essays on Elias Canetti*, ed. Darby, 201–12. It is worth recalling that Kristeva and Canetti share both a homeland and a history of emigration; see the chapter "Bulgaria, My Suffering" in Kristeva's *Crisis of the European Subject*, trans. Susan Fairfield (New York: Other Press, 2001).

21. In an illuminating moment in his essay on Kraus, Walter Benjamin says, "Language has never been more perfectly distinguished from mind, never more intimately bound to eros, than by Kraus in the observation, 'The more closely you look at a word, the more distantly it looks back'" (*Walter Benjamin: Selected Writings* 2:753).

22. Other intriguing congruences: 1) Like von Rezzori, Canetti has a Romanian wet-nurse—"The Danube is very wide in its Bulgarian lower reaches. Giurgiu, the city on the other bank, was Rumanian. From there, I was told, my wet-nurse came, my wet-nurse who fed me her milk. She had supposedly been a strong healthy peasant woman and also nursed her own baby, whom she brought along. I always heard her praises, and even though I can't remember her, the word 'Rumanian" has always had a warm sound for me because of her" (*The Tongue Set Free*, 9). And like Canetti, von Rezzori had a milk-brother whom he "longed to meet and be reunited with . . . forever after in brotherly love" (*The Snows of Yesteryear*, 32). 2) Like Canetti in his mother's hands, von Rezzori in his "was both tool and weapon with which to overcome her emptiness" (59). 3) Like Canetti, Von Rezzori is made complicit in a tryst he is too young to comprehend, bribed not with the threat of a knife applied to his tongue, but with a cavalryman's saber itself, with which "I could relish to the full the agonizing thrill of drawing the naked blade from its heavy, dull-metal scabbard, letting it glitter in the sun and then using it for nothing more martial than the beheading of nettles" (38). 4) Finally, like Canetti, von Rezzori also registers the constant portentousness of death; "the death fear would henceforth be with me, inextinguishably and forever, and it would hollow out my whole being: even if fleetingly I might forget it, it would rise in me at some moment and gnaw at my happiness or joy, or be ready to sink down to the bottom of my soul like a heavy stone" (42).

23. See Alice Yaeger Kaplan, "On Language Memoir," in *Displacements: Cultural Identities in Question*, ed. Angelika Bammer (Bloomington: Indiana University Press, 1994): 59–70.

24. Svoboda Alexandra Dimitrova and Penka Angelova's "Canetti, Roustchouk, and Bulgaria: The Impact of Origin in Canetti's Work, " in *A Companion to the Works of Elias Canetti*, ed. Lorenz, 26287, makes essential reading. The authors trace the Canetti family history back to the Spanish expulsion in 1492 and carefully sift through all references in *The Tongue Set Free* to Canetti's six years spent in Bulgaria, comparing them with the city's actual environs and sociocultural history.

25. Martin Bollacher refers to the following passage in *The Torch in My Ear*

Contrary to most people, particularly those who have surrendered to a loquacious psychology, I am not convinced that one should plague, pester, and pressure memory or expose it to the effects of well-calculated lures; I bow to memory, every person's memory. I want to leave memory intact, for it belongs to Man, who exists for his freedom. And I will not conceal my abhorrence of those who perform surgery on a memory until it resembles anyone else's memory. Let them operate on noses, lips, ears, skin, hair as much as they like; let them—if they must—implant eyes of different colors, even transplant hearts that manage to beat along for another year; let them touch, trim, smooth, level everything—but let them leave memory alone. ("'I Bow to Memory,'" 261)

Yet Bollacher also omits the sentences that precede these, in which Canetti sounds a different note when he defends the machinery not of memory but of memoir:

I had seen many things in Berlin that stunned and confused me. These experiences have been transformed, transported to other locales, and, recognizable only by me, have passed into my later writings. It goes against my grain to reduce something that now exists in its own right [i.e., as *Dichtung*] and to trace it back to its origins [*Wahrheit*]. That is why I prefer to cull out only a few things, from those three months in Berlin—especially things that have kept their recognizable shape and have not vanished altogether into the secret labyrinth from which I would have to extricate them and clothe them anew. (*The Torch in My Ear*, vol. 2 of *The Memoirs of Elias Canetti*, 534)

    26. Friederike Engler discusses Canetti in relation to de Man in "'Fissures in the Monument': Reassessing Canetti's Autobiographical Works," *Critical Essays on Elias Canetti*, ed. Darby, 266-67.

    27. "From that moment, Canetti's life and writing are determined by the 'original taboo against killing.' The most enduring obsessions of his thinking, the struggle against the outrage of death and the scorn for power and those who possess it can be derived from this taboo" (Gerhard Melzer, "The Only Sentence," 216). Canetti himself calls the event "my Sinai" and "my shalt not"; "my true religion," he says, "thus originated in a very definite, personable, unatoneable event, which, despite its failure, adhered to me" (*The Tongue Set Free*, 214).

    28. It should be noted that this first of Canetti's "refugees" is left mostly in outline, abstract, iconic, but perhaps that is also how Canetti preserves his essential *mysteriousness*. In "At the Edge of Silence: 'Mystery' in the Work of Elias Canetti," in *Critical Essays on Elias Canetti*, ed. Darby, 189-200, and in the context of the ax episode in "The Murder Attempt," Gerhard Melzer argues that Canetti's wish to kill Laurica goes underground to continue in all of subsequent writing. "In *his* way, Canetti has never stopped attacking Laurica; and just as he wanted to strike at her, he strikes at all those who play in a similar way on his powerlessness.... It can be summed up thus: Canetti kills by writing. Or better: there are sentences in his texts that carry out symbolically what was forbidden to the boy Canetti" (216). (However, Melzer proves Canetti right by *not* making the connection between ax and Armenian.)

29. In "Discourse in the Novel," Mikhail Bakhtin writes, "Consciousness finds itself inevitably facing the necessity of *having to choose a language*. With each literary-verbal performance, consciousness must actively orient itself amidst heteroglossia, it must move in and occupy a position for itself within it; it chooses, in other words, a 'language'" ("Discourse in the Novel," in *The Dialogic Imagination*, 295).

30. This is a notion drawn from the work of Roland Barthes, which bears comparison with Mikhail Bakhtin's idea about the internal otherness and thus alienness of language, that the "words of others carry with them their own expression, their own evaluative tone, which we assimilate, rework, and reaccentuate" ("The Problem of Speech Genres," in *Speech Genres and Other Essays*, trans. Vern W. McGee [Austin: University of Texas Press, 1989], 89.) Closer to home, compare the following notation from Canetti's *The Human Province*: "All the places that words have been to! In what mouths! On what tongues! Who can, who may know them all, after these wanderings" (97).

31. In part four of *The Tongue Set Free*, recounting his Zurich teachers, Canetti writes, "They are non-interchangeable, one of the supreme qualities in the hierarchy; their having become figures as well takes nothing away from their personalities. The fluid boundary between individuals and types is a true concern of the real writer" (150). See, additionally, Mark H. Gelber's discussion of the figure of Sonne (Avraham ben Yitzakh) in Canetti's memoirs in "Abraham Sonne und *Das Augenspiel*: Jüdisches Bewusstsein in Elias Canettis Autobiographischen Schriften," in *Canettis Aufstand gegen Macht und Tod*, ed. John Pattillo-Hess and Mario R. Smole (Vienna: Verlag, 1996), 69–79.

32. "The silence made me aware of the lack of some dearly familiar sounds from the past: what was missing were the rough shouts of 'Hoh!' with which the Jewish hackney drivers had shooed inattentive pedestrians out of the way of their horses, and the whirring twitter of swarms of sparrows that everywhere greedily awaited the plentiful fall of damply steaming horse apples" (279).

33. In the interview with Aciman, von Rezzori explains straightforwardly, "The city was no longer inhabited by the same population. And therefore it had completely changed" (21).

34. In her essay "A Passion for People: Elias Canetti's Autobiography and Its Implications for Exile Studies" from *Essays in Honor of Elias Canetti*, 249–60, Harriet Murphy remarks, "There is thus little in Canetti's autobiography on what it "means" to have to leave, or choose to leave, a linguistic, cultural, religious, or national home, not least because Canetti rejects definitions of home which equate home with geographical *space*" (251). A contemporary visit to Canetti's birthplace is recounted by Richard Bernstein in "A City and Its Noted Son, Hurt by 'Eruption of Crowds': Down the Danube/ Remembered Glory," *International Herald Tribune*, September 2, 2003. www.iht.com/articles/108461.html.

35. See Fuchs's "The Dignity of Difference," 201, and Melzer's "At the Edge of Silence," 194.

36. For a general study of the ideological slant in European travel-writing like Cunningham-Graham's, see Mary Louise Pratt, *Imperial Eyes: Travel Writing and Transculturation* (New York: Routledge, 1992), and also compare the

reverse-angle perspective of Nabil I. Matar's *In the Lands of the Christians: Arab Travel Writing in the Seventeenth Century* (New York: Routledge, 2002).

37. Engler's "Fissures in the Monument," 271. "Rhetorically, the aphorisms and notes are governed by repetition and metonymic substitution, features that underscore their fragmentary and open-ended character. The autobiography, by contrast, relies heavily on metaphors and a symbolic organization of events implying a meaningful telos and closure." *The Voices of Marrakesh* might therefore be best described as a hybrid, lying at an architectonic midpoint between the notations and the memoirs.

38. Cecile Zorach, "The Outsider Abroad: Canetti in Marrakesh," *Modern Austrian Literature* 16.3-4 (1983): 47-64. A very different critique of the book's privileged detachment and aestheticism can be found in Harriet Murphy's "'Gute Reisende sind herzlos': Canetti in Marrakesh" in *A Companion to the Works of Elias Canetti*, ed. Lorenz, 157-73. Murphy argues that the key to understanding its enigmas lies in Gnostic doctrines of imprisoned matter and unredeemed flesh. Canetti's Gnoticism is "a vote of confidence in the primitive and atavistic, or the non-intellectual and ant-intellectual," she says, but at the same time "is fully endorsed to the extent that it resists being synthesized into a rhetorical argument about the wider context of exploitation, misery, injustice, or cruelty, upon which . . . Canetti is himself parasitically dependent for his own momentary experiences" (160). Other essays that discuss the text are Anne Fuchs's mentioned above, and Ofelia Marti Peña's "Die Stimmen von Marrakesh," in *Homenje a Elias Canetti/Festschrift Elias Canetti*, ed. Roberto Corcoll and Marisa Siguán (Kassel: Reichenberger; Barcelona: Promociones y Publicaciones Universitarias, 1987), 165-80.

39. Comparing Canetti's philosophical attitude toward death with Levinas's, Engler notes that, rather than assigning it a metaphysical meaning, Canetti views it as a violent rupture, for "ultimately any death carries with it an element of murder" ("Fissures in the Monument," 270).

40. It should be noted also that the essay dates from 1965, just two years before the publication of *The Voices of Marrakesh*.

41. The question is also asked directly in a helpful introduction to Canetti's life and work by Ingo Seidler, "Who Is Elias Canetti?" in *Crosscurrents: A Yearbook on Central European Culture* 1, ed. Ladislav Matejka (Ann Arbor: University of Michigan, 1982): 107-24. Equally instructive is Dagmar C. G. Lorenz's introduction to the valuable collection of essays, *A Companion to the Works of Elias Canetti*, 1-11.

42. In fact, in the Mellah portion of the narrative, Canetti refers to the "little square I called its 'heart'" (53).

43. Nora, *Realms of Memory*. Nora's analytic crucible is *memoire* in a collective and artifactual sense, commemorative but also "vestigial" (as object or place that exceeds the limits of history). It contrasts, thus, with Canetti's and von Rezzori's individualized orientations to both "vestige" and nostalgia. See also the discussion of historical vs. autobiographical memory in Maurice Halbawchs, *The Collective Memory*, trans. Francis J. Ditter Jr. and Vita Yazdi (New York: Harper, 1950), and Edward Said's essay about the dialectic of geography

and human imagination, "Invention, Memory, and Place," *Critical Inquiry* 26.2 (Winter 2000): 175-92.

44. The list of adjectives is Murphy's from her essay (162).

45. Compare the following notation from *The Human Province* for the year 1954: "Languages fail, the constantly employed words do not count. When I had to speak to Englishmen in Morocco, I was ashamed for them merely because I spoke to them; they were very alien to me there. Even more alien were the French, who are the masters there, and indeed masters in the moment before being thrown out. The others, however, the people who have always lived there and whom I didn't understand—they were like myself to me" (148). An earlier notation begins, "The fact that there are *different* languages is the most sinister fact in the world. It means that there are different names for the same things; and one would have to doubt that they are the same things" (7).

46. In an entry for the year 1954 in *The Human Province,* Canetti provides an alternate version of this scene: "To think that every day since you left, they have kept calling, to think that the blind are calling now, while you sit here: 'Alláh! Alláh! Alláh!'" (147). And six years later, "It is good to think of certain words and keep saying them to oneself. It is not good that only words like 'God' have achieved this highest intensity of repetition. The Allah-sayers in Marrakesh reminded me of this, and I would now like to serve many splendors of language in the very same way" (190).

47. "Ideally, all are equal there," Canetti continues; "no distinctions count, not even that of sex. The man pressed against him is the same as himself. He feels him as he feels himself. Suddenly it is as though everything were happening in one and the same body. This is perhaps one of the reasons why a crowd seeks to close in on itself: it wants to rid each individual as completely as possible of the fear of being touched," *Crowds and Power,* trans. Carol Stewart (New York: Farrar, Straus and Giroux, 1984), 15-16. Written after his Morrocan journey although published seven years before *The Voices of Marrakesh* appeared in print, *Crowds and Power* suggests its own gloss of *Die Stimmen* as a text intimately concerned with the scrutinizing *power* of an outsider's anthropologic gaze as he attaches himself to yet continually circles around a preconstituted *crowd*. Significantly, then, Richard Lawson says that in coming to terms with the later book, "it is probably relevant to know that when he wrote *The Voices of Marrakesh,* Canetti had come to an impasse with *Crowds and Power,* which he had been working on for the better part of two decades" (*Understanding Elias Canetti* [Columbia: University of South Carolina Press, 1991], 94).

48. In the chapter entitled "The Dahan Family," Canetti records the following encounter:

I liked the aunt. She was a well-developed young woman and she was looking at me in a wondering and far from servile way. She put me in mind at first glance of the kind of oriental women Delacroix painted. She had the same elongated and yet full face, the same eyes, the same straight, slightly overlong nose. I was standing very close to her in the tiny courtyard and our glances met in response to a natural pull. I was so affected that I dropped my eyes, but then I saw her strong ankles, which were as attractive as her face. I would have liked to sit beside her. . . . I tried to imagine her husband, envying him. I bowed, shook hands with her mother and her, and turned to go. (68)

Earlier in the same chapter, a similar incident is recounted, whose reversal reads like repression:

I was thinking that the beautiful, silent person sitting opposite me had shortly before risen from her bridal bed. I was the first stranger she had seen since this crucial change in her life had occurred. My curiosity about her was as great as hers about me. . . . I remember that during that session a quite absurd hope filled me. I hoped that she was mentally comparing me with her groom. . . . I made a wish that she would prefer him to me. . . . I wished him my defeat, and his marriage had my blessing. (56–57)

49. Harriet Murphy sees the fascination with trade in human flesh as an essential component in Canetti's "revived Gnosticism." See pp. 162–68 in her essay in *A Companion to the Works of Elias Canetti*, ed. Lorenz.

50. As famously anti-Freudian as Nabokov, Canetti once wrote, "Redeem psychiatry from itself: five hundred or a thousand precise accounts, and not a word of division of explanation" (*The Human Province*, 123).

51. "The Only Sentence," 217.

52. Its *political* unconsciousness lies not far removed. Other than a brief metalepsis in the chapter, "The Dahan Family," about the Glaoui (the Moroccan Pasha) and the Freedom Party's assassination attempt on the new Sultan, Morocco's colonial past and present remain a blank. Interestingly enough, in "Sheherazade," the homosexual husband of the young woman proffered to Canetti is revealed to be a favorite of the Glaoui's son; the woman herself is being courted by one of his cohorts, who forms a ménage à trois with both husband and wife. At such a crisscrossing, one must say, the ante on what Canetti's text doesn't explicitly register gets raised considerably.

53. According to André Chouraqui, the word "mellah" was first seen in a Judeo-Arabic letter, dated 1541 and meant: "place where the Jews lived." As it also means "salt" in both Aramaic and Hebrew, it may well have been associated with the unpleasant task assigned to Jews to salt the severed heads of their enemies brought back as trophies by returning Muslim soldiers, so as to preserve them when they were displayed in public squares. See Chouraqui, *Between East and West: A History of the Jews of North Africa*, trans. Michael M. Bernet (Philadelphia: Jewish Publication Society of America, 1968), and also the article by Harvey E. Goldberg, "The Mellahs of Southern Morocco: Report of a Survey," *Maghreb Review* 8.3–4 (1983): 61–69.

54. If the last three but one are read as I have grouped them, then only two chapters, "Storytellers and Scribes" (chapter 9) and "The Unseen" (chapter 14) seem to stand alone; yet each, as I will suggest, functions reflexively, commenting at a strategic juncture upon what has preceded it—the former, indirectly on chapters 7 and 8, the latter, in relation to the entire text.

55. Among European Diaspora communities, Sephardic Bulgarian Jewry

was singular for its assimilated character combined with relative freedom from anti-Semitic persecution. Bulgarian Jews had been on good terms with both Ottoman Christians and Muslims. Independence following the Turco-Russian war of 1878 offered a new model for collective identity, and many Bulgarian Jews became staunch Zionists (as Canetti attests in the chapter "The Orator" from *The Torch in My Ear*). Separatist it no doubt was, as we learn from the very first pages of *The Tongue Set Free*. But it was also urbanized and bourgeois, and, by the time of Canetti's youth, only nominally religious. Especially pertinent where Canetti is concerned was the close affiliation between Bulgarian Zionists and their counterparts in Berlin and Vienna (the first translation of Herzl's *Der Judenstadt* was into Bulgarian), as well as the active role played by the French *Alliance Israélité Universelle* in educating middle-class Bulgarian youth. By both cultural background and disposition, therefore, Elias Canetti was already well-distanced from Jewish religious expression before he visited Marrakesh and predictably found its Jews so "strange." Di Maio makes an important point when she observes, "Canetti draws a distinction between his Sephardic heritage, which he calls Spanish or 'spaniolisch' (the German equivalent for Ladino), implicitly making it Western, and his roots in the Balkans and Turkey, which he calls Oriental . . . and contrasted his 'commercial' Jewish ancestors, who had led an Oriental life in the Balkans, with their 'intellectual, creative' Jewish ancestors in medieval Spain" (*A Companion to the Works of Elias Canetti*, ed. Lorenz, 179). On his Sephardic roots, see Gloria J. Ascher, "Elias Canetti and His Sephardic Heritage," *Shofar* 8.3 (1990): 16–29; Yaier Cohen, "Elias Canetti: Exile and the German Language," *German Life and Letters* 42.1 (1988): 32–45; and María Esformes, "The Sephardic Voice of Elias Canetti," *European Judaism* 33.1 (2000): 109–17. On Bulgaria's Jewish community, see Guy Haskell, *From Sophia to Jaffa* (Detroit: Wayne State University Press, 1994). On the Sephardic/Mizrahi communities of the Ottoman Empire, Maghreb, and Levant, see Harvey Goldberg, *Sephardi and Middle-Eastern Jewries*.

56. It is worth noting that of the many allusions to religion in Canetti's notations, Judaism occupies a very minor place. Islam, Confucianism, Hinduism, and Taoism receive far more attention, an index perhaps of certain Orientalist leanings. See, for instance, *The Human Province*, 63, 109, 117, 162–65, 256. The spread of years in which Canetti seems to have penned most of his few notations about Jews, not surprisingly, was 1942–45; see *The Human Province*, 15, 51, 53, 69, 71.

57. In *Austerlitz*, for example, the protagonist tells the Sebaldian narrator, "walking among the gravestones erected in a vaguely segregated part in memory of the members of the Woefflin, Wormser, Mayerbeer, Ginsburg, Franck, and many other Jewish families, I felt as if, despite knowing nothing of my origins for so long, I had lingered among them before, or as if they were still accompanying me. I read all the euphonious German names and retained them in my mind" (258). To be sure, the Jewish cemetery in Marrakesh was not laid out by seventeenth-century Hospitalers like the Cimitiére de Montparnasse, nor do its gravestones (if even legible to Canetti) contain euphonious German names. But the *reverence*, and its absence (or repression) in Canetti, is what immediately strikes home.

58. By contrast, Melzer sees Canetti's work more fluidly as "a scene of fusions. Autobiographical, fictional, and reflective-essayistic elements merge into each other, even if Canetti himself apparently makes strict generic distinctions" ("At the Edge of Silence," 192).

59. The escape and its aftermath is prefigured earlier in the chapter when Canetti describes his encounter with "an ancient, withered crone . . . looking like the oldest thing on earth": "When at last she had gone by me I turned to look after her. She felt my eyes on her, because she slowly swiveled round, as slowly as she walked, and turned her gaze full on me. I hurried on; and so instinctive had been my reaction to her look that it was not for some time that I noticed how much faster I was walking" (42). One should also note that the reciprocity of gaze Canetti has wished from veiled, underage, or attractive women otherwise inaccessible to him in other places of the text has here been turned upon him with a vengeance. Commerce, interchange, the trade of ocular buying and selling: these alternately charm and repel him.

60. The term belongs to Melzer, from "At the Edge of Silence," 190.

61. One of the *Aufzeignungen* reads, "He feel calibrated, but he doesn't know the measure" (*The Human Province*, 212). A decade earlier, Canetti wrote, "People's fates are simplified by their names " (90), and "The letters of one's name have a dreadful magic as though the world were composed of them" (77).

62. From her essay, "'The Deeper Nature of My German': Mother Tongue, Subjectivity, and the Voice of the Other in Canetti's Autobiography," in *A Companion to the Works of Elias Canetti*, ed. Lorenz, 58. Fuchs ties this incident to the figure of Sonne (whom we will meet again in chapter 5), whose transcendence for Canetti derives from the fact that he has not only renounced all worldly attachments but also represents a voice without bodily needs, an apotheosis of a voice that does not need to be housed in a body (55–56).

63. Chana Kronfeld calls him thus "a sort of oral vehicle (one is tempted to say almost an embodiment of) modernist poetics." See the introduction to her study of the literary politics of Hebrew and Yiddish, *On The Margins of Modernism*.

4. Border from Beyond

1. Translated by Hal Draper, from *The Complete Poems of Heinrich Heine: A Modern English Version* (Cambridge, MA: Suhrkamp/Insel Publishers Boston, Inc., 1982), 62. The poem is quoted in Svetlana Boym's *The Future of Nostalgia* (New York: Basic Books, 2001), about which she writes, "This is not a comforting national love affair. The two rather anthropomorphic trees share solitude and dreams, not roots. Longing for a fellow nostalgic, rather than for the landscape of the homeland, this poem is a long-distance romance between two 'internal immigrants,' displaced in their own native soil" (14).

2. Moyshe-Leyb Halpern, *In Nyu York* (New York: Farlag Winkel, 1919), 53. I thank Marcela Sulak for this reference.

3. Sebald's *The Rings of Saturn* narrates Conrad's shore leave in Lowestoft, Suffolk, on the North Sea, and his travels thence to the Belgian Congo and later to Belgium itself.

4. "The Statue of Man upon the Statue of the World," reprinted in *Conrad under Familial Eyes*, ed. Zdzisław Najder, trans. Halina Carroll Najder (Cambridge: Cambridge University Press, 1983), 174–76. See also Czeslaw Milosz's discussion of Conrad's complex allegiances in the essay "Joseph Conrad's Father" in *Emperor of the Earth: Modes of Eccentric Vision* (Berkeley: University of California Press, 1981), 157–85.

5. This is the argument advanced by Geoffrey Galt Harpham in *One of Us*. Harpham cites Michael Fried's argument that scenes of erasure in Conrad's texts emblematize a certain stance toward writing and the blank page, extending it to a claim about the place of Poland in Conrad's work: "Fried leaves this symptomatic blankness, this obsessive smudging of a prior act of writing . . . historically orphaned when its proper home is Poland, the black origin of blank origins in Conrad" (61). If so, the argument is perfectly apposite for "Poland Revisited" where, on the way homeward over the North Sea, a "smudgy" sea is overseen by a cloudy "canopy apparently made of wet blotting paper."

6. Harpham uses this term borrowed from Levinas to articulate an insistent energy in Conrad's writing: "Often praised for its 'polish' or 'purity,' Conrad's style—especially his early style—is, in fact, marked by foreign interferences and for this reason constitutes a foreign interference in English literature. At its most polished, Conrad's style is most Polish" (*One of Us*, 64).

7. The only other treatment of them as juxtaposed texts is a short essay by Roger Porter, "Autobiography, Exile, Home: The Egyptian Memoirs of Gini Alhadeff, André Aciman, and Edward Said," in *Biography: An Interdisciplinary Quarterly* 24.1 (Winter 2001): 302–14.

8. In Said's case, not only is the memoir constructed in such a way that its length belies a narrative strategy that sometimes retells the same time period (if not events) from multiple perspectives. It also tells a modified version of his upbringing in Cairo as opposed to the Jerusalem-centered account he had given in interviews over the years. Questions about Said's veracity were first raised by Justus Reid Weiner in "'My Beautiful Old House' and Other Fabrications by Edward Said," in *Commentary* 108.2 (September 1999): 23–28 and rebutted in "Defamation, Zionist Style" in *Al-Ahram Weekly* no. 444 (26 August–1 September 1999): www.zmag.org/saidreply.htm. "Exile Runes" by Mustapha Marrouchi in *College Literature* 28.3 (Fall 2001): 88–128, discusses the controversy but is unfortunately partisan itself. A more satisfying treatment can be found in Amahl Bishara, "House and Homeland: Examining Sentiments about and Claims to Jerusalem and Its Houses" *Social Text* 75 (2003): 141–62. The character of Uncle Vili in *Out of Egypt*, Samir Raffat has suggested, bears more than slight resemblance to the figure of Maurice-George Levi in Raffat's *Maadi 1904–1962: History and Society in a Cairo Suburb* (Cairo: Palm Press, 1994). See "André Aciman's *Out of Egypt*," *Egyptian Gazette* (December 21 1996): www.egy.com/judaica/96-12-21.shtml; and "Aciman Encore: *Out of Egypt*—Great Uncle Vili Mystery Resolved at Last," *Egyptian Mail* (February 1 1997): www.egy.com/judaica/97-02-01.shtml, both by Raffat.

9. "Is it not true that the views of exile in literature, and, moreover, in religion obscure what is truly horrendous: that exile is irremediably secular and unbearably historical; that it is produced by human beings for other human

beings; and that, like death but without death's ultimate mercy, it has torn millions of people from the nourishment of tradition, family, and geography" ("Reflections on Exile," in *Altogether Elsewhere,* ed. Robinson, 138).

10. See again Abdul JanMohamed's discussion of the ambiguity at work in Said's successive definitions of "secular criticism" in his essay "Worldliness-without-World, Homelessness-as-Home." Compare also the related discussions by Jonathan Boyarin, "Reading Exodus into History," *New Literary History* 23.3 (1992): 523–54; Henry A. Giroux, "Edward Said and the Politics of Worldliness: Toward a 'Rendezvous of Victory,'" *Cultural Studies/Critical Methodologies* 4.3 (2004): 339–49; Joseph Massad, "The Intellectual Life of Edward Said," *Journal of Palestine Studies* 33.3 (2004): 7–22; Bryan S. Turner, "Edward Said and the Exilic Ethic: On Being Out of Place." *Theory, Culture & Society* 17.6 (December 2000): 125–29; Alain Epp Weaver, "On Exile: Yoder, Said, and a Theology of Land and Return," *Cross Currents* 52.4 (2003): 439–61; and Ella Shohat, "Antinomies of Exile: Said at the Frontiers of National Narrations," *The Edward Said Reader,* 121–43, along with her fascinating essay "The 'Postcolonial' in Translation: Reading Said in Hebrew," *Journal of Palestine Studies* 33.3 (2004): 55–75.

11. "Reflections on Exile," 147.

12. Said's *Freud and the Non-European,* in arguing for cosmopolitan consciousness, goes even farther in delegitimating peoplehood when defined sectarianly and religiously—that is, "Jewish" but not "Judaic." When he writes, for example, "Most distressing of all is the growing resemblance between professed political neoconservatives and the religiously inclined critics, for both of whom the privatized condition of social life and cultural discourse are made possible by a belief in the benign quasi-divine marketplace" (292), he seems to have reintroduced something like the critique of "huckerism" as an expression of Jewish identity that one finds in Marx's "On the Jewish Question": "Selling [*verausserung*] is the practical aspect of alienation [*Entausserung*]," writes Marx (in)famously. "Just as man, as long as he is in the grip of religion, is able to objectify his essential nature only by turning it into something *alien,* something fantastic, so under the domination of egoistic need he can be active practically, and produce objects in practice, only by putting his products, and his activity, under the domination of an alien being, and bestowing the significance of an alien entity—money—on them." (Karl Marx, *Selected Writings,* ed. David McClellan [Oxford: Oxford University Press, 2000], 63.)

13. See Caryl Emerson and Gary Saul Morson, *Mikhail Bakhtin: The Creation of a Prosaics* (Stanford, CA: Stanford University Press, 1990).

14. The distinction is borrowed from William Hart, *Edward Said and the Religious Effects of Culture* (Cambridge: Cambridge University Press, 2000), 12. See especially Hart's "Preliminary Remarks" and "Concluding Remarks." Hart's book is instructive for its founding a discussion of Said's contributions to criticism upon "a conflict now latent now manifest between religion and secularism" and culture "as a battleground on which the responsible intellectual struggles" (14). His study is based on three interlocking themes: the religious effects of culture, the religious seduction of the secular thinker, and the return of repressed religiosity.

15. In an essay from *In the Time of Nations* entitled "From Ethics to Exegesis," Levinas says, "But my work, which is situated in the fullness of the documents, beliefs and moral practices that characterize the positive fact of Judaism—in its empirical and historical content, which is constantly enriched and renewed by the ongoing contributions of the religious experience, lived yet unpredictable; bearing exegetic traits, but new—attempts to return to the structures or modalities of the spiritual that lends itself, or consents to, or even tends toward, such treatment" (108). This is an aspect effectively obscured by Said's delimited notions of the function of criticism in the essay "The World, the Text, and the Critic," the title essay to the volume, which results, for example, in the rabbinic tradition's being uncritically assimilated into "Biblical interpretation," and therefore to what a favored critic of Said's, Giambattista Vico, calls "Gentile history." But plainly, "religious criticism," in this alternate sense, is nothing more or less than liberating interpretivity, a strenuous ethics of listening which is therefore also political, or "contrapuntal." That project is illustrated quite nicely by the following "midrashic" exegesis applied to the word *midbar* itself by Marc-Alain Ouaknin, one of Levinas's students. The fourth book of the Pentateuch, Numbers, is called *Bamidbar* ("in the wilderness") in Hebrew, because of its opening word. That phrase can also, however, be parsed ("misread"), as *bam dabar*, "in them—speech," which not only recalls this book's point of departure but for Ouaknin suggests the multiplicity of meaning in any single book—a Book becomes "books"—because it necessarily "contains more than it contains. . . . The structure of the Book, the fact that it can contain, makes the relationship to the book possible—reading and interpretation" (*The Burnt Book*, 157, 170).

16. A pianist, musicologist, and music critic for *The Nation*, Said was the author of *Musical Elaborations* (New York: Columbia University Press, 1991), and, with Daniel Barenboim, *Parallels and Paradoxes: Explorations of Music and Society* (New York: Pantheon Books, 2002).

17. See Hayden White's essay, "Criticism as Cultural Politics," *Diacritics* 6.3 (1976): 8–13. Says White, "In Said's world view, things exist side-by-side with one another, not in hierarchies of relative reality or ordered series of dynastically created groups. But the principle of contiguity here embraced is not a mechanistic one" (12).

18. From the review of *Out of Place* by Chris Colin in *Salon* (October 4, 1999): www.salon.com/books/it/1999/10/04/said/. Extended readings of Said's memoir can be found in Paul B. Armstrong, "Being 'Out of Place': Edward W. Said and the Contradictions of Cultural Differences," *Modern Language Quarterly* 64:1 (2003): 97–121, and Edmund White, "*Out of Place*, by Edward Said," *Raritan* 19.3 (Winter 2000): 135–43.

19. *Edward Said: Criticism in Society* (New York: Routledge Press, 1997), 122–48. In *The Burnt Book*, on a Talmudic extract that deals with the "Journey of the Ark," departure, and settling, in Numbers 10:35–36, Marc-Alain Ouaknin writes, "Atopia is the refusal of the place without hope of a place. The place of atopia is, radically, the non-place (*non-lieu*). On the other hand, utopia is a temporary nonplace, linked to the place by hope, or by demand, for example" (151).

20. In "The Problem of Textuality: Two Exemplary Positions," *Critical Inquiry* 4.4 [Summer 1978]: 673–714), Said announced the title of his forthcoming work as *Between Culture and System*, which appears as the title of the longest essay, "Criticism between Culture and System," in *The World, the Text, and the Critic*.

21. At one point, for example, shades of Conrad, the memoir subverts the paradigmatic immigrant's arrival narrative: "We were entering the West, something I had dreamed about, but it was neither Hollywood nor the mythic canyons of New York City: a small, utterly silent and unpopulated little town whose character it was impossible that morning to make out from the *Saturnia*'s deck" (134). See, in this connection, the two essay-length treatments of Said's book, Mustapha Marrouchi's "Exile Runes" and Alon Confino, "Remembering Talbiyah: On Edward Said's *Out of Place*," *Israel Studies* 5.2 (Fall 2000): 182–98.

22. See the chapter "Interiors," 51–86.

23. I refer to Frye's typology of discourse in the first chapter of *Anatomy of Criticism: Four Essays* (Princeton: Princeton University Press, 2000), myth, romance, high mimetic, low mimetic, irony.

24. See especially pages 18–19, 47–48, 88–91, 116–20, and 154–55.

25. In *After the Last Sky: Palestinian Lives*, Said emphasizes not his first name but rather the middle initial W. for Wadie (later William), which is his father's name, and the surname adopted by his father after several years in the United States, "Said," which replaced "Ibrahim," the name of his grandfather. In this case, identity is subject to deformations at the end of the instead of the beginning: "I, like many Palestinians, am the product of a society of names constructed and trafficked in according to European norms" ([New York: Pantheon Books, 1986]. 88). He does not, however, mention there that he was named "Edward" after Edward, Prince of Wales.

26. See respectively, Mill's *Autobiography* (New York: Oxford University Press, 1971) and the Milosz essay, "Joseph Conrad's Father," cited earlier.

27. To take one non-arbitrary choice, Gregor von Rezzori's pro forma blurb: "This is not only the marvelous saga of a genuinely Levantine family but also the tale of a vanished and multicultural world from the Istanbul of the sultans to the Alexandria of Egypt up to Nasser and of the life of a young man doomed to say goodbye to its charms. A touching and highly amusing, masterfully written book."

28. "Temporizing," in "How True to Life is Biography?" with Edith Kurzweil, Jeffery Meyers, and Michael Govrin, *Partisan Review* 68.1 (February 15, 2001): 31–56. Compare also "Gardens and Ghettos," *Commentary* 89.1 (1990): 55–59 and "Le Juif Antérieur," *Pardès* 29 (2000): 39–56.

29. As Joseph Brodsky writes, "'Exile' covers, at best, the very moment of departure, of expulsion: what follows is both too comfortable and too autonomous to be called by this name, which so strongly suggests a comprehensible grief" ("The Condition We Call Exile," 9).

30. "The Romance of Exile," *New Republic* (February 12, 2001): 33–37. www.tnr.com/021201/buruma021201.html.

31. "An Interview with Edward W. Said," *The Edward Said Reader*, 420. See also "On Writing a Memoir" in the same volume, 399–418.

32. Perhaps even on the order of the following snapshot of Jewish Jerusalem: "Jerusalem, moreover, seemed to have a more homogeneous population, made up mainly of Palestinians, although I do recall the briefest of glimpses of Orthodox Jews and one visit to or very near Mea Sharim, where I felt a combination of curiosity and distance, without assimilating or understanding the startlingly different presence of the black-suited, -hatted, and -coated Orthodox Jews" (111). In fact, at the time when the Said family resided intermittently in Jerusalem, Talbieh was itself a heterogeneous neighborhood with an even mixture of Palestinian Jews and Arabs.

33. The function of metaphor in these cases, as a kind of personalized cosmopolitanism, goes in the direction opposite that charted by Homi Bhabha in the essay, "DissemiNation," originally published in *Nation and Narration* and reissued in *The Location of Culture* (New York: Routledge, 1994). Taking his cue from some of Said's parameters for secular criticism, Bhabha argues that we should be "alive to the metaphoricity of the peoples of imagined communities— migrant or metropolitan—then we shall find that the space of the modern nation-people is never simply horizontal. Their metaphoric movement requires a kind of 'doubleness; in writing: a temporality of representation that moves between cultural formations and social processes without a 'centered' causal logic" (*The Location of Culture*, 140). See also Said's own essay "Invention, Memory, and Place."

34. See interviews with and discussions of these and other Mizrahi writers in Ammiel Alcalay, ed. and trans., *Keys to the Garden: New Israeli Writing* (San Francisco: City Lights, 1996).

35. Said's thesis in *Freud and the Non-European* is that limits on a monolithic Jewish identity are symbolized by Freud's suggestion that the founder of Jewish identity, Moses, "was himself a non-European Egyptian" (54). This, in turn, provides a model for hospitality to the non-Israeli, non-European in its midst that the state of Israel should be duty-bound to practice. By Aciman's definition, it is a perfect palintropism and one that might very well appeal to an exiled Alexandrian-Jewish cosmopolite.

36. On Jewish otherhood inside and outside Europe and postcolonial studies, see Jonathan Boyarin, "The Other Within and the Other Without," in *The Other in Jewish Thought and History: Constructions of Jewish Culture and Identity*, ed. Laurence J. Silberstein (New York: New York University Press, 1994), 424–51.

5. Beyond from Beyond

1. Neither Sebald's writing nor Shammas's imitates the arabesque structure of narrative exemplified by a text like *Alf Layla wa-Layla (The Thousand and One Nights)*, but each in its own way connects with the fundamental logic of that sort of figuration. Sandra Naddaff explains it succinctly in her book *Arabesque, Narrative Structure, and the Aesthetics of Repetition in the 1001 Nights* (Evanston, IL: Northwestern University Press, 1991): "Nonfigural and thus necessarily antimimetic, the arabesque takes at its point of departure the denatured, indeed unnatural, threads of a leaf pattern and spins a self-perpetuating, potentially infinite design. Unable to point to any external phenomenon as its

representational source, the arabesque, with its ever-repeating extension of an initial pattern, can ultimately establish only itself as the element it signifies. It alone engenders itself, instigates its own unfolding, and thereby supplies the information by which the figure it makes achieves meaning. It is at once the means of signification and the thing signified" (115). See also Ernst Kuhnel, *Arabesque: Meaning and Transformation of an Ornament* (Graz: Verlag fur Sammler, 1977).

2. *Confessions of an English Opium-Eater,* ed. Malcom Elwin (London: Macdonald & Co., 1956). J. Hillis Miller discusses this and other pertinent passages in an analysis of De Quincey's peculiarly vagrant and digressive writing style in *The Disappearance of God: Five Nineteenth-Century Writers.* Champaign: University of Illinois Press, 2000. He also quotes Baudelaire in this particular context: "De Quincey's thought is not merely sinuous; the word is not strong enough: it is naturally spiral" (39). Naddaff, as well, cites a related passage that begins "Qu'est-ce qu'un thyrse?" For other implications of De Quincey's orientalism, however, see John Barrell's fascinating, *The Infection of Thomas De Quincey: A Psychopathology of Imperialism* (New Haven: Yale University Press, 1991) and E. S. Burt, "Hospitality in Autobiography: Levinas Chez De Quincey," *English Literary History* 71 (2004): 867-97.

3. "News from Elsewhere," *New York Review of Books* (April 14, 1988): 5, www.nybooks.com/articles/article-preview?article_id=4462.

4. In addition to Ezrahi's treatment in *Booking Passage,* Robert K. Baruch traces the composition and publication history of the work in "Rereading Dan Pagis's 'Abba,'" in *History and Literature: New Readings of Jewish Texts in Honor of Arnold J. Band,* ed. William Cutter and David C. Jacobson. (Providence, RI: Brown University Judaic Studies, 2002), 369–77. Baruch compares *Abba* with Kafka's "Letter to His Father": "Both of these Jewish writers spoke similar forms of German characteristic of the eastern extremity of the old Hapsburg realm and shared a Germanic literary and cultural frame of reference. Moreover, the writings of both authors reflect the destruction of that peculiar German-Jewish *Kulturkreis* from the opposite vantage point of before and after. [Finally,] Kafka's 'Letter to his Father' and Pagis's 'Abba' share the impulse to reenact a complex and destructive Oedipal struggle, a battle that results, ultimately, in the vitiation of the son's strength" (371). Hanan Hever also discusses the father-son polarity in "She-harei kvar higanu, nachon?" (For we have already arrived, right?). *Davar* (February 1992), 26.

5. Pagis's marginal note reads, "I regret that I got stuck using this image of the net. It is confusing and distracting."

6. Oona Ajzenstat juxtaposes the metaphor of knots found in the work of the thirteenth-century Kabbalist Abraham Abulafia with the trope of *partzufim* central to Isaac Luria's (1534–1572) cosmogony, both with reference to the recurrent image of "face" in Emmanuel Levinas's philosophy, in *Driven Back to the Text: The Premodern Sources of Levinas's Postmodernism* (Pittsburgh, PA: Duquesne University Press, 2001). Compare Jill Robbins's use of a similar figure derived from a short story by Agnon in *Altered Reading* and Susan Handelman's separate analyses in *fragments of Redemption: Jewish Thought and Literary Theory in Benjamin, Scholem, and Levinas* (Bloomington: Indiana University Press, 1991), especially for its the parallels between Levinasian trace, Benjaminian fragment,

and Scholemian symbology. Eric Zakim's "Between Fragment and Authority in David Fogel's (Re)Presentation of Subjectivity," *Prooftexts* 13.1 (January 1993): 22–35, discusses Benjamin's aesthetic of the fragment in relation to modern Hebrew poetry. See also the chapter "The Aesthetics of Transience" in Beatrice Hanssen, *Walter Benjamin's Other History: Of Stones, Animals, Human Beings, and Animals* (Berkeley: University of California Press, 2000); Charles Rosen's "The Ruins of Walter Benjamin," in *On Walter Benjamin: Critical Essays and Recollections*, ed. Gary Smith (Cambridge: MIT Press, 1988), 129–75; and Benjamin's own essay "The Task of the Translator" along with Hannah Arendt's introduction in *Illuminations*, trans. Harry Zohn (New York: Schocken Books, 1969) and *The Origin of German Tragic Drama*, trans. John Osborne (London: NLB, 1977. In the AriZal's (R. Luria's) system, the symbolism of the Partzufim is a further development of the Kabbalistic notion of Adam Kadmon, Primordial Man, and illustrates the notion that the world, as a whole, mirrors and is mirrored in the erotic, psychic and personal life of humankind. In *Kabbalah and Criticism*, Harold Bloom sees the *partzufim* as both "psychic and linguistic, defense mechanisms and rhetorical tropes" (42), amounting to a representational agency; through *tikkun*, they become "acts of mediation, acts that lift up and so liberate the fallen sparks of God" ([New York: Continuum, 1983], 43), after their descent earthward in what R Luria called *shevirah ha'kelim*, the breaking of the vessels. Sidra Dekoven Ezrahi's discussion of Pagis's transition from poetry to prose fragment is apposite here: "The poetry of four decades attests to a process whereby the private domain, the "point of departure," had been all but erased. Rather than any coherent *picture* of reality, there remained the "thingness" or discrete "factuality" of reality, punctuating the poems like fallout from an extinguished star" (*Booking Passage*, 164). The classic studies of the kabbalah to consult are Scholem's *Major Trends in Jewish Mysticism*, trans. Ralph Manheim (New York: Schocken Books, 1961) and *Origins of the Kabbalah*, trans. Allan Arkush (Philadelphia: Jewish Publication Society, 1987), and Moshe Idel's *Absorbing Perfections: Kabbalah and Interpretation* (New Haven: Yale University Press, 2002) and *Kabbalah: New Perspectives* (New Haven: Yale University Press, 1988).

7. In an interview with Haim Chertok, Pagis remarks that his scholarship in medieval Hebrew poetry as well as Renaissance and Baroque historical backgrounds "has nothing to do with my own poetry or theory of poetry. You know, I published my first poems before I became a student and long before I decided to become a scholar" (67). See *We Are All Close: Conversations with Israeli Writers* (New York: Fordham University Press, 1989), a volume that also contains interviews with Appelfeld, Amichai, and Yehoshua. In the same interview, he also takes issue with some of Harold Bloom's estimations of the Hebrew poetic traditions, and insists that while he has journeyed outside of Israel to France, England, and the United States, he would never revisit eastern Europe.

8. That has specifically linguistic implications, too, especially considering Pagis's later acquisition of Hebrew. Quoting Shmuel Trigano, Marc-Alain Ouaknin says that not only is Hebrew "metaphorical," but also, philosophically considered, it can be seen as "a trace," in Levinas's sense of the concept. "It is a function of this language which has the ability to burst open, to pulverize itself

into a thousand pieces to work a derealization of reality 'by which the proud self-assurance of all the realities of this world, the clear conscience of idolatry, fall in ruins into the emptiness of their vanity'" (*The Burnt Book*, 73-74).

9. See the discussion of criticism's *clinamen* (the Lucretian concept of change in equilibrium due to infinitesimal deviation) in relation to a strong poet's performance of the same trope in Bloom's *The Anxiety of Influence: A Theory of Poetry* (New York: Oxford University Press, 1997).

10. In "Finding Palestine," an article published in *Harper's Magazine* 292.1753 (June 1996): 24-28, Shammas writes that with the establishment of the Jewish state, which meant, of course, the creation of a new homeland for Pagis, the "Big Bang of 1948 — the scattering of the Palestinians upon the face of all the earth, as a biblical writer would have it — he [Shammas writes in the third-person] became a refugee." What authorizes Pagis to speak in Hebrew as newly reterritorialized muffles Shammas as a refugee, who, paradoxically enough, also finds his voice in the Hebrew language: "The Palestinian noise of identity has been muffled for nearly a century.... But above all, since World War II, the Palestinian voice was muffled because it had to pass through the man-made black hole of the Holocaust, and so it was almost never heard." The piece is excerpted from "Autocartography: The Case of Palestine, Michigan," in *The Geography of Identity*, ed. Patricia Yaeger (Ann Arbor: University of Michigan Press, 1996), 466-75.

11. In his review of the novel, Hillel Halkin explains that Shammas first conceived it in two discrete parts, and only subsequently decided to alternate them in a fashion like De Quincey's metaphor. See "One Hundred Years of Multitude," *New Republic* 198.18 (May 2, 1988): 28-33.

12. It is extremely telling that, as Ezrahi points out, among the marginalia in the manuscript of *Abba* that suggest a final shape these pieces might assume (along with copies of his father's will and photographs), some are written in German. As Radautz itself had reentered Pagis's imaginative life in the form of a photograph, so his native language reasserts itself at the moment, late in a literary career, when autobiography begins to be consolidated. Compare Appelfeld's recounting of his conflicted acquisition of Hebrew and its replacement of German in his memoir, *The Story of a Life*, 107-17.

13. Amichai is cited in the novel several times. The verse comes from "Jews in the Land of Israel," which reads, in part,

> What are we doing, coming back here with this pain?
> Our longings were drained together with the swamps,
> the desert blooms for us, and our children are beautiful.
> Even the wrecks of ships that sunk on the way
> reached this shore,
> even winds did. Not all the sails.
>
> What are we doing
> in this dark land with its
> yellow shadows that pierce the eyes?

> (Every now and then someone says, even after forty
> or fifty years: "The sun is killing me.")
>
> What are we doing with these souls of mist, with these names,
> with our eyes of forests, with our beautiful children,
> with our quick blood?
>
> Spilled blood is not the roots of trees
> but it's the closest thing to roots
> human beings have.

Selected Poetry of Yehudah Amichai, trans. Chana Bloch and Stephen Mitchell (New York: Harper and Row, 1986), 87. Compare the counter-poem, "We Journey Towards a Home," by the Palestinian poet Mahmoud Darwish:

> We journey towards a land not of our flesh
> Not of our bones its chestnut trees,
> Its stones unlike the curly goats
> Of the Song of Songs.
> And the pebbles' eyes are not lilies.
> We journey towards a home
> That does not halo our heads with a special sun.
> Mythic women clap:
> A sea around us, a sea against us.
> If wheat and water do not reach you,
> Eat our love and drink our tears.
> Black veils of mourning for the poets. . . .
> You have your victories and we have ours,
> We have a country where we see only the invisible.

From *Unfortunately It Was Paradise: Selected Poems,* trans. Munir Akash and Carolyn Forché (Berkeley: University of California Press, 2003), 10. Compare also by the same poet, "We Travel Like Other People," 11.

14. "With this gesture Shammas (like Rushdie in *The Satanic Verses*) preempts the classic imperialist strategy whereby a "western" discourse claims to represent the "Orient" [to the world—to the "West," it goes without saying, but also to the "Orient"] itself. . . . In *Arabesques* Anton Shammas has staged a kind of uprising of his own, seizing from both the Israeli Jews (and the Hebrew language) and from us "Westerners" the means of representation and self-representation that are his by birthright" (20). "Seizing the Means of Representation," *American Book Review* 11.6 (January–February 1990): 4+.

15. The opening lines of Ben-Yitzhak's poem, "Happy the sowers that will not reap / For they will wander a long way off," according to Chana Kronfeld, "can be read as an ambiguous midrash on the success/failure of his—and Hebrew's—minor modernism. In abdicating a high modernist canonicity, in resisting reterritorialization, identity, and income, Ben-Yitzhak both asserted and denied the possibility of his project ever leaving a mark" (*On the Margins of*

Modernism, 17). The dovetail with Pagis's own poem in *The Modern Hebrew Poem Itself* makes for further fascinating if accidental midrash. Ben Yitzhak's miniscule oeuvre has recently been translated into English: *Collected Poems*, trans. Peter Cole (New York: Small Press Distribution, 2003). Contemporary poet Edward Hirsch has written a short appreciation of Ben-Yitzhak in "Poet's Choice: Avraham Ben-Yitzhak," *Washington Post*, June 27, 2004, BW12.

16. Yet there is little place for readers in these texts as invisible addressees or cowitnesses. Rarely has reading felt more like poaching. Ezrahi notes, "As full of *presence* as these prose texts are, what is missing is precisely the absences—all the circumlocutions and open-ended mysteries—that had characterized a Pagis text. A poetry of unfathomable depths poised at the borders of language, of enigmatic signals sent directly to the reader, yields to a sane set of surfaces that beckon the reader merely to eavesdrop" (176).

17. Baruch notes that not only do the "ostensibly paternal words 'don't be ashamed' actually induce shame," but the card-partner's 'you don't have many prospects for that' "apparently comprise a judgment the poet imposes upon himself." (372-73).

18. See Bruce Reisch's essay on Radautz, "Back to Bukovina: A Trip to My Roots in Radauti and Sadagura" cited in chapter 2.

19. As Ezrahi explains, Pagis probably saw the photograph at an exhibition, "The Last Jews of Radautz" at the Diaspora Museum in Tel Aviv. Penetratingly, she says of the poem that memento has become memento mori: "the place of origin, the town that 'threw him out' when he was ten, becomes the matrix for the poet's final return, the only possible grave for a life that has been haunted by— as the poetry has been enabled by—weightlessness" (*Booking Passage*, 166).

20. See Ezrahi's note 42 in her chapter on Pagis in *Booking Passage*, 299-300.

21. Shammas is canny enough to make the two versions of Abayd's origins in "The Teller" and "The Tale" disagree in certain particulars, for instance, the date of Abayd's emigration to America (1949, not 1948), and the identity of the servant in his childhood Beirut home (Alamaza, Shammas's aunt, not Layla Khouri, a Palestinian orphan). Abayd's authority over his fictionalized autobiography is in turn undermined by the controlling authorial hand of Anton Shammas, who mimics the discourse of Cather's *My Antonia* and appeals to Borges: "If Michael were the teller, he would have ended it like this: 'He opened a drawer and took out a pencil and wrote on the file: My Tale. He frowned at this a moment, then he used an eraser, leaving only the single word Tale. That seemed to satisfy him.' But maybe, out of polite arrogance, he might have finished with a paraphrase of Borges: "Which of the two of us has written this book I do not know'" (259).

22. From "Dan Pagis: Last Poems," trans. Tsipi Keller, *Quarterly Review of Literature* 31 (1993): 3-61. All other translations are mine in consultation with Abraham Marcus, unless noted. On Pagis's final output, see Shimon Sandbank, "The Last Poems of Dan Pagis," *Modern Hebrew Literature* 11 (1993): 33-36, the general introduction in Robert Alter, "Dan Pagis and the Poetry of Displacement," *Judaism* 45.4 (1996): 399-402, and Wendy Zierler, "Footprints, Traces, Remnants: The Operations of Memory in Dan Pagis's *Aqebot*," *Judaism* 41.4 (1992): 316-33.

23. Book of Samuel 6:6-8.

24. "Written in Pencil," perhaps Pagis's most famous poem, reads as follows:

> here in this carload
> i am eve
> with abel my son
> if you see my other son
> cain son of man
> tell him that I

Pagis also treats the Cain/Abel motif in the previously cited "Brothers" and "Autobiography."

25. Shammas exploits such "twinnings and pairings" throughout the novel. Surayyah Sai'd (Layla Khoury) has two twin sons; Shammas has two mirroring Jewish lovers (Shlomith and Amira); Shammas and Bar-On are said to "constitute schizophrenia, two faces of the same person" (145); and Jews and Arabs (or Hebrew and Arabic) trace parallel patterns, for example: "There are two great black stones in the world, the late Abu Mas'ood used to say, the black stone in the Ka'bah in Mecca, which was quarried by almighty Allah himself, and the black stone on Herzl's tomb, which was quarried by the mortal Abu Mas'ood himself, and both of them are sites of pilgrimage (39).

26. Shammas's explicit thoughts on this matter are to be found in a series of articles, in particular "Ashmat ha'babushka" (The fault of the babushka), *Politika* (February-March, 1986): 44-45, "Al galut v'sifrut" (On exile and literature), *Igra* 2 (1987): 67-70, and an interview with Dalya Amit in *Proza* (May-June 1988): 73-79. See also Avraham Balaban, "An Arab-Israeli's Novel," *Michigan Quarterly Review* 29.1 (1990): 145-51; "Anton Shammas: Torn between Two Languages," *World Literature Today* 63.3 (1989): 418-21; and Alex Zehavi, "Solitude Is a Bitter Thing: On Anton Shammas's *No-Man's Land*," *Modern Hebrew Literature* 6.1/2 (1980): 43-46. Pagis, predictably, is less informative in this respect outside of the signals to be gleaned from the shift in his literary output marked by *Abba*. In the biographical *Lev pit'omi* (Sudden heart) (Tel Aviv: Am Oved, 1995), however, his wife clarifies some of the ambivalences and conflicts here, and Pagis did as well in a 1983 interview with Yaira Genoosar, "Dan Pagis: Likro bishem, linkot 'emda" ("Calling it by name, taking a stand") in *Iton 77*.38 (February 1983): 33.

27. See Hanan Hever's discussion of the interface in "Hebrew in an Israeli Arab Hand: Six Miniatures on Anton Shammas's *Arabesques* in *The Nature and Context of Minority Discourse*, ed. Abdul JanMohamed and David Lloyd (New York: Oxford University Press, 1990), 264-93.

28. Deleuze and Guattari's description from *Kafka: Toward a Minor Literature*, 17. See Hever, and also the discussions by Rachel Feldhay Brenner, "In Search of Identity: The Israeli Arab Artists in Anton Shammas's *Arabesques*," *PMLA* 108.3 (May 1993): 431-45 and "The Search for Identity in Israeli Arab Fiction: Atallah Mansour, Emile Habiby, and Anton Shammas," *Israel Studies* 6.3 (Fall 2001): 91-112; and by Yael S. Feldman, "Postcolonial Memory, Postmodern Intertextuality: Anton Shammas's *Arabesques* Revisited," *PMLA* 114.3 (May

1999): 373–89; and "Memory in a Minor Key: Postmodernist Arabesques and the Critic," in *Bein historya lesifrut: Festschrift for Isaac Barzilay,* ed. Stanley Nash (Tel Aviv: Hakibbutz Hameuchad, 1997), 51–63.

29. This is Feldman's argument, and it respresents the most sophisticated analysis of the complexities of Shammas's novel to date in English.

30. The poem is "Memorial Day for the War Dead" from *Amen,* trans. Ted Hughes (New York: Harper and Row, 1977), 34.

31. Compare Naddaff:

The foundation of the arabesque, then, is the repeat unit, the horizontal and vertical mirroring of the design which ensures its spatial perpetuation.... In much the same way that narrative repletion impedes the temporally determined progress of a tale from beginning to end, the repetition of pattern in arabesque stalls, for all intents and purposes, the spatial movement of its design by turning it back on itself, by making it repeat its earlier self. What seems to be the progress of a design in space is, in fact, only the repetition, the replaying of an initially determined pattern. What seems to be the end of a design is, in fact, only another manifestation of its beginning, of a point that, given the movement of repetition, could potentially antecede its beginning. (*Arabesques,* 112)

32. *Shetah Hefker* (Tel Aviv: Hakibbutz Hameuchad, 1979), 46.

33. For example, Pagis writes, "And why won't you tell me how you decided to immigrate, how you immigrated on your own, how you found a job, and became a widower, and got remarried, and reflected (meaning, you suddenly acquired a grown-up son; just kidding). The word *"hitbonen"* (reflected) is turned into a pun that depends on the word *"ben"* for "son."

34. In one of the many convergences linking individual fragments, this one is echoed by the *partzuf* entitled "Shoes," in which Pagis's father exasperatedly recounts his son's arrival in the land of Israel and their subsequent interpersonal belonging-at-a-near-distance that picks up where separation on the plane of geography leaves off:

And you, for example, what, Danaleh, you were so right? Hell, you made me miserable, you know, during all these years since you immigrated to Israel. Suddenly I had a son, almost seventeen years old, a new immigrant, confused, if you see what I mean. All my love, if you forgive the expression, wanted to go out to you. Yet it didn't reach you. In the beginning you didn't stop talking about the Jew you met as a child in Marduz. On the way to the boat he stole your backpack. You couldn't stop talking about him and you said that you would no longer trust anyone. But Tel Aviv charmed you and you wanted to learn Hebrew quickly. Toward me you showed a kind of politeness or should I say impenetrability.... I am not claiming that you were condescending, if this is the right form of the word, but you remained distant. A stranger. (347)

It ends with father and son, awkwardly positioned at ground level:

"Yes, Dad, I give you credit for much more. You tried with various gestures. Do you remember, one winter, when I came late in the evening for visit from the kibbutz. The shoes were very muddy, and I left them outside the door. And then in the morning, surprise, they were next to the bed, shining black: You polished them! You polished my shoes!"

"Don't make a big drama out of that, Danaleh, I always enjoyed shining things." (347)

35. The essays in which Cavell develops the formulation are "Knowing and Acknowledging" and "The Avoidance of Love: A Reading of *King Lear*" in *Must We Mean What We Say? A Book of Essays* (New York: Charles Scribner's Sons, 1969). In the latter essay, Cavell explains,

A character is not, and cannot become aware of us. . . . I will say: We are not in their presence. They are in our presence. This means, again, not simply that we are seeing and hearing them, but that we are acknowledging them (or specifically failing to). . . . Tragedy shows that we are responsible for the death of others even when we have not murdered them, and even when we have not manslaughtered them innocently. . . . But doesn't the fact that we do not or cannot go up to them mean that we do not or cannot acknowledge them. One may feel like saying here: The acknowledgement cannot be *completed*. But this does not mean that acknowledging is impossible in a theater. Rather, it shows what acknowledging, in a theater, is. And acknowledging in a theater shows what acknowledgment in actuality is. (332–34)

36. The second-to-last *partzuf*, which even Pagis laments in the margins as disjointed and confusing, reminds us, however, that the text still straddles the border between psychological immediacy and literary artifact. Any assessment of its unified meaning has to remain tentative in light of its unfinished state.

37. The word in Hebrew actually denotes "exile," which is closer to the novel's general sense of forced displacement.

38. Feldman asks, "And what is all this chronology doing in a work modeled on Proust's involuntary memory? Was not the point of Bergson's subjective time, the philosophical matrix of Proust's technique, to deny the reign of the clock and the controlling power of the calendar. . . . What are the historian's tools doing in this unruly Borgesian text, one that in the last chapter overturns any imaginable narrative component: place time, characters—even the assumed identity of the author?" (382)

39. "The problem is that it's the Lebanese Christians who have been slaughtered far more often" is the corresponding sentence as rendered in English. In a prefatory note on the translation, Shammas freely admits that "frequently both the words and the music of the English version diverge from the original Hebrew."

40. Feldman, "Postcolonial Memory, Postmodern Intertextuality," 379–85.

41. Compare Marc-Alain Ouaknin: "But the Text withdraws only if we let it; the interruption of the demonstration of transcendence, the movement of necessary withdrawal depends, above all, on the interpreter, on his way of

being as he reads the text, on his approach. We call this way of being the 'caress.' . . . The interpreter experiences things by caressing: never seizing anything, he allows himself to be carried, negatively and infinitely, from one meaning to another, so that if one had to locate (in the Text) a center, an origin of meaning, a god that gives the meaning, one would find it only in the void, empty of writing, the 'blanks of writing'" (*The Burnt Book*, 64).

Addendum to chapter 1, note 57, p. 305: *Shibboleth* connotes surging waters (among other things), and is discussed by Derrida as a trope for *partage* (parting, border, scission, but also participation) in the essay on Jewish identity, "Shibboleth: For Paul Celan," translated by Joshua Wilner in *Acts of Literature* (New York: Routledge, 1991), 370–413. On *Ivri* ("the crosser-over"), Ouaknin elaborates: "The Hebrew, in his etymological meaning, is a passer-through *(la'avor)*, a breaker-off *('avera)*, a transgressor *('avera)*, a passer-on, a producer and a creator *(ubar, me'uberet, ibur hahodesh)*; he is also someone who takes into account that which is outside of himself *(ba'avur she)* These are all words from the root 'I, V, R. The Hebrew tears himself away, protests, passes through The Hebrew-passer-through 'not only invites us to go from one riverbank to the other [*passeur*, lit."ferryman"], but to head every-where where there is a passage to be achieved, while maintaining this between-two-banks that is the truth of the passing' [Blanchot]" (*The Burnt Book*, 73).

Works Consulted

Aciman, André. "Conversations with Gregor von Rezzori, *Salmagundi* 90-91 (Spring-Summer 1991): 12-32.
———. *False Papers*. New York: Farrar, Straus and Giroux, 2000.
———. "Family Fictions." *Salmagundi* 90-91 (Spring-Summer 1991): 33-45.
———. "Gardens and Ghettos." *Commentary* 89.1 (1990): 55-59.
———. "Le Juif antrieur." Pardès 29 (2000): 39-56.
———, ed. *Letters of Transit: Reflections on Exile, Identity, Language, and Loss*. New York: W. W. Norton, 1999.
———. *Out of Egypt: A Memoir*. New York: Farrar, Straus & Giroux, 1994.
———. "Out of Novemberland." *New York Review of Books* 45.19 (December 3, 1998): 44-47.
———. "Review of *The Emigrants*." *Commentary* 103.6 (June 1997): 61-63.
———. "Reflections of an Uncertain Jew." *Threepenny Review* 81 (Spring 2000): 22-24. www.threepennyreview.com/samples/aciman_sp00.html.
———. "Temporizing," *Partisan Review* 118.1 (February 15, 2001): 31-56.
Agnon, Y. S. *A Book That Was Lost and Other Stories*. Anne Golomb Hoffman and Alan Mintz, eds. New York: Schocken Books, 1992.
Ajzenstadt, Oona. *Driven Back to the Text: The Premodern Sources of Levinas's Postmodernism*. Pittsburgh: Duquesne University Press, 2001.
Alcalay, Ammiel. *After Arabs and Jews: Remaking Levantine Culture*. Minneapolis: University of Minnesota Press, 1993.
———. "Cultural Exchange." *Jerusalem Post Magazine* (December 12, 1986): 18.
———, ed. and trans. *Keys to the Garden: New Israeli Writing*. San Francisco: City Lights, 1996.
Annan, Gabriele. "*The Snows of Yesteryear* by Gregor von Rezzori." *London Review of Books* 12.23 (December 6, 1990): 23-24.
Alter, Robert, "Dan Pagis and the Poetry of Displacement." *Judaism* 45.4 (1996): 399-402.
———. *The Invention of Hebrew Prose: Modern Fiction and the Language of Realism*. Seattle: University of Washington Press, 1988.

Altieri, Charles. "Lyrical Ethics and Literary Experience." *Mapping the Ethical Turn: A Reader in Ethics, Culture, and Literary Theory*, ed. Todd F. Davis, Kenneth Womack, 30–58. Charlottesville: University of Virginia Press, 2001.

———. "What Differences Can Contemporary Poetry Make in Our Moral Thinking?" *Renegotiating Ethics in Literature, Philosophy, and Theory*, ed. Jane Adamson, Richard Freadman, David Parker, 113–33. London: Cambridge University Press, 1999.

Amichai, Yehudah. *Amen*. Trans. Ted Hughes. New York: Harper and Row, 1977.

———. *Not of This Time, Not of This Place*. Translated by Shlomo Katz. London: Vallentine Mitchell, 1973.

———. *Selected Poetry of Yehudah Amichai*. Trans. Chana Bloch and Stephen Mitchell. New York: Harper and Row, 1986.

Anders, Jaroslaw. "The Prisoner of Myth." *New Republic* (November 25, 2002): 33–41.

Anijdar, Gil. *Our Place in Al-Andalus: Kabbalah, Philosophy, Literature in Arab Jewish Letters* Stanford, CA: Stanford University Press, 2002.

Annan, Gabriele. "*The Snows of Yesteryear* by Gregor von Rezzori." *London Review of Books* 12.23 (December 6, 1990): 23–24.

Appelfeld, Aharon. *Adnai ha'nahar*. Tel Aviv: Ha'kibbutz ha'me'uhad, 1971.

———. *Ashan*. Jerusalem: Akhshav, 1962.

———. *Ba-gai ha'poreh*. Jerusalem: Schocken, 1964.

———. *Beyond Despair: Three Lectures and a Conversation with Philip Roth*. Trans. Jeffrey M. Green. New York: Fromm International, 1994.

———. "Buried Homeland." *New Yorker* (November 23, 1998): 48–61.

———. *For Every Sin*. Trans. Jeffrey M. Green. New York: Weidenfeld & Nicolson, 1989.

———. *The Iron Tracks*. Trans. Jeffrey M. Green. New York: Schocken Books, 1998.

———. "The Kafka Connection." *New Yorker* (July 23, 2001): 36–41.

———. *Kfor 'al ha'aretz*. Ramat Gan: Massada, 1965.

———. *Mesilat barzel*. Jerusalem: Keter 1991.

———. *Od ha-yom gadol: Yerushalayim: ha-zikaron veha-or* (It is yet high day: Jerusalem: the memory and the light). Yerushalayim: Keter, 2001.

———. "A Perpetual Story of Departure," interview with Michael March. *The New Presence* (September 1997). www.pritomnost.cz/index.php?clanek =1015. Originally published in *Na Kulturu* (March 1997).

———. *Sipur hayim*. Jerusalem: Keter, 1999.

———. *The Story of a Life*. Trans. Aloma Halter. New York: Schocken Books, 2004.

———. *A Table for One: Under the Light of Jerusalem*. Trans. Aloma Halter. New York: Toby Press, forthcoming.

Appelfeld, Aharon, et al. "Bruno Schulz's Wall Paintings." *New York Review of Books* 49.9 (May 23, 2002). www.nybooks.com/articles/15424.

Armstrong, Paul B. "Being 'Out of Place': Edward W. Said and the Contradictions of Cultural Differences." *Modern Language Quarterly* 64.1 (March 1, 2003): 97–121.

Arnold, Heinz Ludwig. *Text + Kritik: W. G. Sebald*. München: Richard Boorberg Verlag, 2003.

Ascher, Gloria J. "Elias Canetti and His Sephardic Heritage." *Shofar* 8.3 (1990): 16-29.

Ashcroft, Bill and Ahluwalia, Pal. *Edward Said: The Paradox of Identity.* New York: Routledge, 2001.

Atlan, Henri. "Niveaux de signification et athéis, de l'écriture." In *La Bible au present.* Paris: Gallimard, 1982.

Atlas, James. "W. G. Sebald: A Profile." *Paris Review* 41.151 (Summer 1999): 278-95.

Bakhtin, Mikhail M. "Author and Hero in Aesthetic Activity." In *Art and Answerability: Early Philosophical Essays,* trans. Vadim Liapunov, 4-256. Austin: University of Texas Press, 1990.

———. *The Dialogic Imagination: Four Essays.* Trans. Caryl Emerson and Michael Holquist, Austin: University of Texas Press, 1981.

———. "The Problem of Speech Genres." In *Speech Genres, and Other Essays,* trans. Vern W. McGee, 60-103. Austin: University of Texas Press, 1989.

Balaban, Avraham. "An Arab-Israeli's Novel ." *Michigan Quarterly Review* 29.1 (1990): 145-51.

———. "Anton Shammas: Torn between Two Languages." *World Literature Today* 63.3 (1989): 418-21.

Balibar, Etienne. "The Borders of Europe." In *Cosmopolitics: Thinking and Feeling beyond the Nation,* ed. Cheah and Robbins, 217-29.

Band, Arnold J. *Nostalgia and Nightmare: A Study in the Fiction of S. Y. Agnon.* Berkeley: University of California Press, 1968.

———. *Studies in Modern Jewish Literature.* Philadelphia: Jewish Publication Society, 2003.

Banfield, Ann *Unspeakable Sentences: Narration and Representation in the Language of Fiction.* Boston: Routledge & Kegan Paul, 1982.

Barrell, John. *The Infection of Thomas de Quincey: A Psychopathology of Imperialism.* Yale University Press, 1991.

Barthes, Roland. *Camera Lucida.* Trans. Richard Howard. New York: Hill and Wang, 1981.

———. *The Pleasure of the Text.* Trans. Richard Miller. New York: Noonday Press, 1975.

Bartoszewski, Wladyslaw T. *The Convent at Auschwitz.* New York: George Braziller, 1991.

Baruch, Robert K. "Rereading Dan Pagis's 'Abba.'" *History and Literature: New Readings of Jewish Texts in Honor of Arnold J. Band.* Ed. William Cutter and David C. Jacobson. 369-77. Providence, RI.: Brown University, 2002.

Baum, Johanna. "A Literary Analysis of Traumatic Neurosis in Israeli Society: David Grossman's *See under Love.*" *Other Voices* 2.1 (February 2000): www.othervoices.org/2.1/baum/seeunderlove.html.

Beinen, Joel. *The Dispersion of Egyptian Jewry: Culture, Politics, and the Formation of a Modern Diaspora.* Berkeley: University of California Press, 1998.

Ben Mordecai, Yitshak, and Iris Parush, eds. *Bein kefor le'ashan: Mehkarim bitsirato shel Aharon Appelfeld.* Beersheba: Ben Gurion University of the Negev Press, 1997.

Ben Yitzhak, Avraham. *Collected Poems*. Trans. Peter Cole. New York: Small Press Distribution, 2003.
Benjamin, Walter. *Selected Writings*, Vol. 2: *1927–1934*. Trans. Rodney Livingstone et al. Cambridge: Harvard University Press, 1999.
———. *Illuminations*. Trans. Harry Zohn. New York: Schocken Books, 1969.
———. *One-Way Street and Other Writings*. Trans. Edmund Jephcott and Kingsley Shorter. New York: Verso, 1979.
———. *The Origin of German Tragic Drama*. Trans. John Osborne. London: NLB, 1977.
———. *Reflections: Essays, Aphorisms, Autobiographical Writings*. Ed. Hannah Arendt. New York: Random House, 1986.
Benveniste, Emil. "Subjectivity in Language." In *Problems in General Linguistics*, trans. Mary Elizabeth Meek, 223–30. Coral Gables, FL: University of Miami Press, 1971.
Bernstein, Michael André. *Foregone Conclusions: Against Apocalyptic History*. Berkeley: University of California Press, 1994.
Bernstein, Richard. "A City and Its Noted Son, Hurt by 'Eruption of Crowds': Down the Danube/Remembered Glory." *International Herald Tribune*, September 2, 2003. www.iht.com/articles/108461.html.
Bernstein, Richard J. *Freud and the Legacy of Moses*. Cambridge: Cambridge University Press, 1998.
Berressem, Hanjo. *The "Evil Eye" of Painting: Jacques Lacan and Witold Gombrowicz of the Gaze*. Albany: State University of New York Press, 1995.
———. *Lines of Desire: Reading Gombrowicz's Fiction with Lacan*. Evanston, IL: Northwestern University Press, 1999.
Bhabha, Homi K. *The Location of Culture*. New York: Routledge, 1994.
———. *Nation and Narration*. London: Routledge, 1990.
Bialik, Hayim Nahman. *Revealment and Concealment: Five Essays*. Jerusalem: Ibis Editions, 2000.
———. *Selected Poems, Bilingual Edition*. Trans. Ruth Nevo. Jerusalem: Dvir and Jerusalem Post, 1981.
Bisberg-Youkelson, Feigl, ed. *The Life and Death of a Polish Shtetl*. Trans. Gene Bluestein. Lincoln: University of Nebraska Press, 2000.
Bishara, Amahl. "House and Homeland: Examining Sentiments about and Claims to Jerusalem and Its Houses." *Social Text* 75 (2003): 141–62
Blanchot, Maurice. *Aminadab*. Trans. Jeff Fort. Lincoln: University of Nebraska Press, 2002.
———. *Death Sentence*. Trans. Lydia Davis. Barrytown, NY: Station Hill Press, 1998.
———. *The Space of Literature*. Trans. Ann Smock. Lincoln: University of Nebraska Press, 1989.
———. *The Writing of the Disaster*. Trans. Ann Smock. Lincoln: University of Nebraska Press, 1995.
Blanchot, Maurice, and Jacques Derrida. *The Instant of My Death: Demeure: Fiction and Testimony*. Trans. Elizabeth Rottenberg. Stanford, CA: Stanford University Press, 2000.

Błoński, Jan. "On the Jewish Source of Bruno Schulz." In *Crosscurrents: A Yearbook on Central European Culture* 12. ed. Ladislav Matejka, 53–67. New Haven, CT: Yale University Press, 1993.
Bloom, Harold. *The Anxiety of Influence: A Theory of Poetry.* New York: Oxford University Press, 1997.
——. *Kabbalah and Criticism.* New York: Continuum, 1983.
Bohlen, Celestine. "Artwork by Holocaust Victim Is Focus of Dispute." *New York Times,* June 20, 2001 p. A1.
——. "From a Mural, New Life in a Debate over Memory." *New York Times,* June 24, 2001, p. WK4.
Bojtar, Endre. "Eastern or Central Europe?" In *Crosscurrents: A Yearbook on Central European Culture* 7, ed. Ladislav Matejka, 253–69. Ann Arbor: University of Michigan Press, 1988.
Borchardt, Danuta. "Translating Witold Gombrowicz's *Ferdydurke.*" *Exquisite Corpse: A Journal of Letters and Life* 5. www.corpse.org/issue_5/critical_urgencies/borchar.htm.
Borges, Jorge Luis. *Collected Fictions.* Trans. Andrew Hurley. New York: Penguin, 1999.
Boyarin, Jonathan. "From Derrida to Fichte? The New Europe, The Same Europe, and the Place of the Jews." In *Thinking in Jewish,*109–39. Chicago: University of Chicago Press, 1996.
——. "The Other Within and the Other Without." In *The Other in Jewish Thought and History: Constructions of Jewish Culture and Identity,* ed. Laurence J. Silberstein, 424–51. New York: New York University Press, 1994.
——. "Reading Exodus into History." *New Literary History* 23.3 (1992): 523–54.
Boym, Svetlana. *The Future of Nostalgia.* New York: Basic Books, 2001.
Brah, Avtar. *Cartographies of Diaspora: Contesting Identities.* London: Routledge, 1996.
Braziel, Jana Evans, and Anita Mannur, eds. *Theorizing Diaspora: A Reader.* Malden, MA: Blackwell Publishers, 2003.
Brennan, Timothy. "The National Longing for Form." In *Nation and Narration,* ed. Homi K. Bhabha, 44–69. London: Routledge, 1990.
Brenner, Rachel Feldhay. "In Search of Identity: The Israeli Arab Artists in Anton Shammas's *Arabesques.*" *PMLA* 108.3 (May 1993): 431–45.
——. "The Search for Identity in Israeli Arab Fiction: Atallah Mansour, Emile Habiby, and Anton Shammas." *Israel Studies* 6.3 (Fall 2001): 91–112.
Brooks, Peter. *Reading for the Plot: Design and Intention in Narrative.* Cambridge: Harvard University Press, 1992.
Brown, Michael, and Sara R Zhorowitz, eds. *Encounter with Aharon Appelfeld.* Oakville, Ontario: Mosaic Press, 2003.
Brown, Russell E. "Bruno Schulz and World Literature." *Slavic and East European Journal* 34.2 (1990): 224–46.
——. *Myths and Relatives: Seven Essays on Bruno Schulz.* München: Verlag Otto Sagner, 1991.
Brumberg, Abraham. "Neighbors: An Exchange." *New York Review of Books.* 158.18 (November 15, 2001): 64–65. www.nybooks.com/articles/14800.

Bruns, Gerald. "The Concepts of Art and Poetry in Emannuel Levinas's Writings." In *The Cambridge Companion to Levinas,* ed. Robert Bernasconi and Simon Critchley, 207-32. Cambridge: Cambridge University Press, 2002.
Bruss, Elizabeth W. *Autobiographical Acts: The Changing Situation of a Literary Genre.* Baltimore: Johns Hopkins University Press, 1976.
Budick, Emily. *Aharon Appelfeld's Fiction: Acknowledging the Holocaust.* Bloomington: Indiana University Press, 2005.
———. "Literature, Ideology, and the Measure of Moral Freedom: The Case of Aharon Appelfeld's *Badenheim 'ir nofesh.*" *Modern Language Quarterly* 60.2 (1999): 223-49.
Burnshaw, Stanley, T. Carmi, and Ezra Spicehandler, eds. *The Modern Hebrew Poem Itself.* New York: Holt, Rinehart and Winston, 1965.
Buruma, Ian. "The Romance of Exile." *New Republic* (February 12, 2001): 33-37.
Burt, E. S. "Hospitality in Autobiography: Levinas Chez De Quincey." *English Literary History* 71 (2004): 867-97
Calvino, Italo. *Invisible Cities.* Trans. William Weaver. New York: Harcourt, 1978.
———. *Le citt a'invisibili.* Torino, Einaudi, 1972.
———. *Six Memos for the Next Millennium.* Trans. Patrick Creagh. Cambridge: Harvard University Press, 1988.
Canetti, Elias. *The Conscience of Words.* Trans. Joachim Neugroschel. New York: Seabury Press, 1979.
———. *Crowds and Power.* Trans. Carol Stewart. New York,: Farrar, Straus and Giroux, 1984.
———. *Das Augenspiel: Lebensgeschichte, 1931-1937.* Munchen: C. Hanser, 1985.
———. *Die Fackel im Ohr: Lebensgeschichte 1921-1931.* Munchen: C. Hanser, 1980.
———. *Die gerettete Zunge: Geschichte einer Jugend.* Munchen: C. Hanser, 1980.
———. *Die Stimmen von Marrakesch; Aufzeichnungen nach einer Reise.* Munchen: C. Hanser, 1967.
———. *The Human Province.* Trans. Joachim Neugroschel. New York: Seabury Press, 1978.
———. *The Memoirs of Elias Canetti.* Trans. Joachim Neugroschel. New York: Farrar, Straus and Giroux, 1999.
———. *Notes from Hampstead: The Writer's Notes, 1954-1971.* Trans. John Hargraves. New York: Farrar, Straus and Giroux, 1998.
———. *The Secret Heart of the Clock: Notes, Aphorisms, Fragments, 1973-1985.* Trans Joel Agee. New York: Farrar, Straus and Giroux, 1989.
———. *The Voices of Marrakesh: A Record of a Visit.* Trans. J. A. Underwood. New York: Seabury Press, 1978.
Carlebach, Elisheva, John Efron, and David Myers, eds. *Jewish History and Jewish Memory: Essays in Honor of Yosef Hayim Yerushalmi.* Lebanon, N.H.: University Press of New England, 1998.
Carotenuto, Aldo. *A Secret Symmetry: Sabina Spielrein between Freud and Jung.* Trans. Arno Pomerans, John Sheply, Krishna Winston. New York: Pantheon Books, 1982.
Casey, Edward S. *Getting Back into Place: Toward a Renewed Understanding of the Place World.* Bloomington: Indiana University Press, 1993.

Cavarero, Adriana. *Relating Narratives: Storytelling and Selfhood.* Trans. Paul Kottman. London: Routledge, 2000.
Cavell, Stanley. *Must We Mean What We Say? A Book of Essays.* New York: Charles Scribner's Sons, 1969.
———. *The Senses of Walden.* Berkeley: University of California Press, 1989.
Caygill, Howard. *Levinas and the Political.* New York: Routledge, 2002.
Chalier, Catherine. *Levinas: L'utopie de l'humain.* Paris: Albin Michel, 1993.
Chandler, James. "About Loss: W. G. Sebald's Romantic Art of Memory." *South Atlantic Quarterly* 102.1 (2003): 235-62.
Chatwin, Bruce. *The Songlines.* New York: Viking Penguin, 1987.
Chernetsky, Vitaly. "Displacement, Desire, Identity, and the 'Diasporic Momentum': Two Slavic Writers in Latin America." *Intertexts* 7.1 (Spring 2003): 49-71.
Chertok, Haim. *We Are All Close: Conversations with Israeli Writers.* New York: Fordham University Press, 1989.
Chouraqui, André. *Between East and West: A History of the Jews of North Africa.* Trans. Michael M. Bernet. Philadelphia: Jewish Publication Society of America, 1968.
Chow, Rey. *Writing Diaspora: Tactics of Intervention in Contemporary Cultural Studies.* Bloomington: Indiana University Press, 1993.
Clifford, James. "Diasporas." *Cultural Anthropology* 9.3 (1994): 302-28.
———. *Routes: Travel and Translation in the Late Twentieth Century.* Cambridge: Harvard University Press, 1997.
Cohen, Joseph. *Voices of Israel: Essays on and Interviews with Yehuda Amichai, A. B. Yehoshua, T. Carmi, Aharon Appelfeld, Amos Oz.* Albany: State University of New York Press, 1990.
Cohen, Yaier. "Elias Canetti: Exile and the German Language." *German Life and Letters* 42.1 (1988): 32-45.
Cohn, Dorit. *Transparent Minds: Narrative Modes for Presenting Consciousness in Fiction.* Princeton, N.J.: Princeton University Press, 1978.
Colin, Chris. Review of *Out of Place. Salon Magazine* (October 4, 1999): www.salon.com/books/it/1999/10/04/said/.
Confino, Alon. "Remembering Talbiyah: On Edward Said's *Out Of Place.*" *Israel Studies* 5.2 (Fall 2000): 182-98.
Conrad, Joseph. *A Personal Record* and *Mirror of the Sea.* New York: Penguin Books, 1998.
Conradi, Peter. *Iris Murdoch: A Life.* New York: W. W. Norton & Sons, 2001.
Cornis-Pope, Marcel, and John Neubauer. *Towards a History of the Literary Cultures in East-Central Europe: Theoretical Reflections.* ACLS Occasional Paper, No. 52, 2002.
Craven, Peter. "W. G. Sebald: Anatomy of Faction." *Heat* 12 (1999): 212-24.
Czaykowski, Bogdan. "Witold Gombrowicz's Trans-Atlantyk: A Novel for the New Europe?" In *Crosscurrents: A Yearbook on Central European Culture* 12, ed. Ladislav Matejka, 69-77. New Haven, CT: Yale University Press, 1993.
Dainotto, Roberto M. *Place in Literature: Regions, Cultures, Communities.* Ithaca, NY: Cornell University Press, 2000.
Darby, David, ed. *Critical Essays on Elias Canetti.* New York: G. K. Hall, 2000.

———. "A Literary Life: The Textuality of Canetti's *Autobiography.*" *Modern Austrian Literature* 25.2 (1992): 37–49.
Darwish, Mahmoud. *Unfortunately It Was Paradise: Selected Poems.* Trans. Munir Akash and Carolyn Forché. Berkeley: University of California Press, 2003.
De Certeau, Michel. "History: Science and Fiction." In *Heterologies: Discourse on the Other,* trans. Brian Massumi, 1992-21. Minneapolis: University of Minnesota Press, 1989.
———. *The Practice of Everyday Life.* Trans. Stephen Rendell. Berkeley: University of California Press, 2002.
———. *The Writing of History.* Trans. Tom Conley. New York: Columbia University Press, 1992.
De Man, Paul. *The Rhetoric of Romanticism.* New York: Columbia University Press, 1984.
De Quincey, Thomas. *Confessions of an English Opium-Eater.* Ed. Malcom Elwin. London: Macdonald & Co., 1956.
De Roux, Dominique. *Entretiens avec Gombrowicz.* Paris: P. Belfond, 1968.
Deák, Iztván. "Neighbors: An Exchange." *New York Review of Books* 48.14 (September 20, 2001): 91–93. www.nybooks.com/articles/article-preview?article_id=14531.
Deleuze, Gilles and Guattari, Félix. *Kafka: Toward a Minor Literature.* Trans. Dana Polan. Minneapolis: University of Minnesota Press, 1980.
———. *A Thousand Plateaus: Capitalism and Schizophrenia.* Trans. Brian Massumi. Minneapolis: University of Minneapolis Press, 1987.
Demsky, Aaron. Christian and Jewish Views of the Holy Land: Visiting Sacred Sites vs. Working the Land. *Bible Review* 28.5 (October 2002): 32–41
———. "Holy City and Holy Land as Viewed by Jews and Christians in the Byzantine Period: A Conceptual Approach to Sacred Space." In *Sanctity of Time and Space in Tradition and Modernity,* ed. Anton Houtman, Marcel Poorthuis, and Joshua Schwartz, 285–96. Boston: Brill, 1998.
Denby, David. "Learning to Love Canetti: The Autobiography of a Difficult Man." *New Yorker* (May 31, 1999): 106–13.
Derrida, Jacques. *Adieu to Emmanuel Levinas.* Trans. Pascale-Anne Brault and Michael Nass. Stanford, CA: Stanford University Press, 1999.
———. "Circumfession: Fifty-nine Periods and Periphrases." In *Jacques Derrida,* Geoffrey Bennington and Jacques Derrida. Chicago: University of Chicago Press, 1993.
———. *Contre-allé.* With Cathereine Malabou. Paris: La Quinzaine Litteraire et Louis Vuitton, 1999.
———. *Monolingualism of the Other; or, The Prosthesis of Origin.* Trans. Patrick Mensah. Stanford, CA: Stanford University Press, 1998.
———. *The Other Heading: Reflections on Today's Europe.* Trans. Michael B. Naas and Pascale-Anne Brault. Bloomington: Indiana University Press, 1992.
———. *Points . . . : Interviews, 1974–1994.* Trans. Peggy Kamuf. Stanford, CA: Stanford University Press, 1995.
———. "Shibboleth." In *Acts of Literature,* 370–413. New York: Routledge, 1991.
———. *Writing and Difference.* Trans. Allan Bass. Chicago: University of Chicago Press, 1980.

Eakin, John. *Fictions in Autobiography: Studies in the Art of Self Invention.* Princeton, NJ: Princeton University Press, 1985.
——. *The Ethics of Life Writing.* Ithaca, NY: Cornell University Press, 2004.
Eaglestone, Robert. *Ethical Criticism: Reading after Levinas.* Edinburgh: Edinburgh University Press, 1997.
Efraim Sicher. "The Return of the Past: The Intergenerational Transmission of Holocaust Memory in Israeli Fiction." *Shofar* 19.2 (Winter 2001): 26–40.
Emerson, Caryl, and Gary Saul Morson. *Mikhail Bakhtin: The Creation of a Prosaics.* Stanford, CA: Stanford University Press, 1990.
Entrikin, J. Nicholas. *The Betweenness of Place: Towards a Geography of Modernity.* Baltimore: Johns Hopkins University Press, 1991.
Esformes, Mara. "The Sephardic Voice of Elias Canetti." *European Judaism* 33.1 (2000): 109–17.
Eskenazi, Tamara Cohn, and Gary A. Phillips, eds. *Levinas and Biblical Studies.* Boston: Brill, 2003.
Ezrahi, Sidra DeKoven. "Aharon Appelfeld: The Search for a Language." *Studies in Contemporary Jewry* 1 (1984): 366–80.
——. *Booking Passage: Exile and Homecoming in the Jewish Imagination.* Berkeley: University of California Press, 2001.
——. "Conversation in the Cemetery: Dan Pagis and the Prosaics of Memory." *Holocaust Remembrance* (1994): 121–33.
——. "The Future of the Holocaust: Storytelling, Oppression, and Identity—See under: 'Apocalypse.'" *Judaism* 201,51.1 (Winter 2002): 42–51.
——. "Memory: Coming and Going." *Jewish Social Studies* 1.3 (1995): 161–73.
——. "Sacred Space: Individual and Social Reaction to the 9/11/01 Disaster." *Tikkun* (January–February 2002): 24. www.tikkun.org/magazine/index.cfm/action/tikkun/issue/tiko201/article/020111f.html.
Farias, Victor. *Heidegger et le Nazism.* Paris: Lagrasse, 1987.
Faur, José. *Golden Doves with Silver Dots: Semiotics and Textuality in Rabbinic Tradition.* Bloomington: Indiana University Press, 1986.
Feldman, Yael S. "Memory in a Minor Key: Postmodernist Arabesques and the Critic." *Bein historya lesifrut: Festschrift for Isaac Barzilay,* ed. Stanley Nash. Tel Aviv: Hakibbutz Hameuchad, 1997, 51–63.
——. "Postcolonial Memory, Postmodern Intertextuality: Anton Shammas's *Arabesques* Revisited." *PMLA* 114.3 (May 1999): 373–89.
Ferguson, Stuart. "Elias Canetti and Multiculturalism." *Poetica* 29.3–4 (1997): 532–95.
Ficowski, Jerzy. *Regions of the Great Heresy: Bruno Schulz, a Biographical Portrait.* New York. W. W. Norton & Co., 2003.
——. "W poszukiwaniu partnera kongenialnego" (In search of a kindred spirit). In *Czytanie Schulza,* ed. Jerzego Jarzębskiego, 176–81. Kraków: Instytutu Filologii Polskiej UJ, 1994.
Finkielkraut, Alain. *The Wisdom of Love.* Trans. Kevin O'Neill and David Suchoff. Lincoln: University of Nebraska Press, 1996.
Fogel, Aaron. *Coercion to Speak: Conrad's Poetics of Dialogue.* Cambridge: Harvard University Press, 1985.

Folks, Jeffrey J. "'Memory Believes before Knowing Remembers': Faulkner, Canetti, and Survival." *Papers on Language & Literature* 39.3 (Summer 2003): 316-32.
Franklin, Ruth. "The Lost: Searching for Bruno Schulz." *New Yorker* (December 16, 2002): 97-100.
Freadman, Richard. *Threads of Life: Autobiography and the Will.* Chicago: University of Chicago Press, 2001.
Frost, Robert. *Selected Prose.* New York: Collier Books, 1974.
Gallagher, Catherine, and Stephen Greenblatt. *Practicing New Historicism.* Chicago: University of Chicago Press, 2000.
Gelber, Mark H. "Abraham Sonne und 'Das Augenspiel' Jüdisches Bewusstsein in Elias Canettis autobiographischen Schriften." *Canettis Aufstand gegen Macht und Tod,* ed. John Pattillo-Hess and Mario R. Smole, 69-79. Vienna: Verlag, 1996.
Gibson, Andrew. *Postmodernity, Ethics, and the Novel: From Leavis to Levinas.* New York: Routledge, 1999.
Gilman, Sander. *Jewish Self-Hatred: Anti-Semitism and the Secret Language of the Jews.* Baltimore: Johns Hopkins University Press, 1986.
Gilman, Sander L. and Milton Shain, eds. *Jewries at the Frontier: Accommodation, Identity, Conflict.* Urbana: University of Illinois Press, 1999.
Giroux, Henry A. "Edward Said and the Politics of Worldliness: Toward a "Rendezvous of Victory." *Cultural Studies—Critical Methodologies* 4.3 (August 2004): 339-49.
Goethe, Johan Wolfgang von. *Italian Journey.* Trans Robert R. Heitner. New York: Suhrkamp Publishers, 1989.
Goldberg, Harvey, ed. *Sephardi and Middle Eastern Jewries: History and Culture in the Modern Era.* Bloomington: Indiana University Press, 1996.
———. "The Mellahs of Southern Morocco: Report of a Survey." *Maghreb Review* 8.3-4 (1983): 61-69.
Goldfarb, David A. "The Vortex and the Labyrinth: Bruno Schulz and the Objective Correlative" *East European Politics and Societies* 11.2 (1997): 257-69.
Gombrowicz, Rita. *Gombrowicz en Argentine 1939-1963.* Paris: DeNoël, 1984.
———. *Gombrowicz en Europe 1963-1969.* Paris: DeNoël, 1988.
Gombrowicz, Witold. *Diary.* Vol. 1: *1953-56.* Trans. Lillian Vallee. Evanston, IL: Northwestern University Press, 1988.
———. *Diary.* Vol. 2: *1957-62.* Trans. Lillian Vallee. Evanston, IL: Northwestern University Press, 1989.
———. *Diary.* Vol. 3: *1961-66.* Trans. Lillian Vallee. Evanston, IL: Northwestern University Press, 1992.
———. *Dziela vols 2. Ferdydurke—3. Trans-Antlantyk—7. Dziennik 1953-1956—8. Dziennik 1957-1961—9. Dziennik 1961-1966.* Krakow: Wydawn. Literackie, 1986.
———. *Ferdydurke.* Trans. Danuta Borchardt. New Haven, CT: Yale University Press, 2000.
———. *Ferdydurke.* Trans. Eric Mosbacher. London: Macgibbon & Kee, 1961.
———. *Gombrowicz en Argentine: Temoignages et Documents, 1939-1966.* Ed. Rita Gombrowicz. Paris: Denoel, 1984.

———. *A Kind of Testament*. Ed. Dominique de Roux. Trans. Alastair Hamilton. London: New Calder and Boyars, 1973.

———. "The Statue of Man upon the Statue of the World." Reprinted in *Conrad under Familial Eyes*, ed. Zdzisław Najder, trans. Halina Carroll Najder, 174–76. Cambridge: Cambridge University Press, 1983.

———. *Trans-Atlantyk*. Trans. Carolyn French and Nina Karsov. New Haven, CT: Yale University Press, 1994.

Gorner, Rudiger, ed. *The Anatomist of Melancholy: Essays in Memory of W. G. Sebald*. Munich: Iudicium, 2003.

Gourdine, Angeletta K. M. *The Difference Place Makes: Gender, Sexuality, and Diaspora Identity*. Columbus: Ohio State University Press, 2002.

Graham, Cunninghame R. B. *Mogreb-El-Acksa: A Journey in Morocco*. Evanston: Northwestern University Press, 1997.

Gross, Jan T. *Neighbors: The Destruction of the Jewish Community in Jedwabne, Poland*. Princeton, NJ: Princeton University Press, 2001.

Grossman, David. *See Under: Love*. Trans. Betsy Rosenberg. New York: Washington Square Press, 1990.

Grumberg, Karen. "The Poetics of Place: Unravelling Home and Exile in Jewish Literature from Israel and the United States." PhD diss., University of California, Los Angeles, 2004.

Guillory, Jon. "The Ethical Practice of Modernity: The Example of Reading." In *The Turn to Ethics*, ed. Marjorie Garber, Beatrice Hanssen, and Rebecca L. Walkowitz, 29–46. New York: Routledge, 2000.

Halbawchs, Maurice. *The Collective Memory*. Trans. Francis J. Ditter Jr. and Vita Yazdi. New York: Harper, 1950.

Halkin, Hillel. "One Hundred Years of Multitude." *New Republic* 198.18 (May 2, 1988): 28–33.

Hall, Katharina. "Jewish Memory in Exile: The Relation of W. G. Sebald's 'Die Ausgewanderten' to the Tradition of the "Yizkor" Books." In *Jews in German Literature since 1945: German-Jewish Literature?* ed. Pól O'Dochartaigh, 153–64. Atlanta, GA: Rodopi, 2000.

Halpern, Moyshe-Leyb. *In Nyu York*. New York: Farlag Winkel, 1919.

Hand, Seán. "Shadowing Ethics: Levinas's View of Art and Aesthetics." In *Facing the Other: The Ethics of Emmanuel Levinas*, , 63–87. Richmond: Curzon, 1996.

Handelman, Susan. *fragments of Redemption: Jewish Thought and Literary Theory in Benjamin, Scholem, and Levinas*. Bloomington: Indiana University Press, 1991.

Hanssen, Beatrice. *Walter Benjamin's Other History: Of Stones, Animals, Human Beings, and Animals*. Berkeley: University of California Press, 2000.

Hansel, Joëlle. "Défense et illustration de la cabale: *Le philosophe et le cabaliste* de Mose Hayyim Luzzatto." *Pardès* 12 (1990): 44–66.

Harpham, Geoffrey Galt. *One of Us: The Mastery of Joseph Conrad*. Chicago: University of Chicago Press, 1996.

Harris, Stephanie. "The Return of the Dead: Memory and Photography in W. G. Sebald's *Die Ausgewanderten*." *German Quarterly* 74.4 (Fall 2001): 379–92.

Hart, William. *Edward Said and the Religious Effects of Culture*. Cambridge: Cambridge University Press, 2000.

Haskell, Guy. *From Sophia to Jaffa: The Jews of Bulgaria and Israel.* Detroit: Wayne University Press, 1994.

Hever, Hanan. "She-harei kvar higanu, nachon?" (For we have already arrived, right?). *Davar* (February 1992), 26.

Himka, John-Paul. "The Snows of Yesteryear." *Crosscurrents: A Yearbook on Central European Culture* 11, ed. Ladislav Matejka, 67–72. New Haven, CT: Yale University Press, 1991.

Hirsch, Edward. "Poets Choice: Avraham Ben-Yitzhak." *Washington Post,* June 27, 2004, BW12.

Hirsch, Marianne. *Family Frames: Photographs, Narrative, and Postmemory.* Cambridge: Harvard University Press, 1997.

Hirsch, Samson Raphael. *Commentary on the Torah.* Trans. Isaac Levy. New York: Judaica Press, 1966.

Hoffman, Anne Golomb. *Between Exile and Return: S. Y. Agnon and the Drama of Writing.* Albany: State University of New York Press, 1991.

———. "Topographies of Reading: Agnon through Benjamin." *Prooftexts* 21.1 (Winter 2001): 71–90.

Hoffman, Eva. *Lost in Translation: A Life in a New Language.* New York: Penguin Books, 1990.

Hoffman, Nancy Yanes. "The Temptations of Betrayal: Von Rezzori on Anti-Semitism." *Southwest Review* (Summer 1983): 234–50.

Hollander, John. *In Time and Place.* Baltimore: Johns Hopkins University Press, 1986.

———. "It All Depends." In *Home: A Place in the World,* ed. Arien Mack, 27–45. New York: New York University Press, 1993.

Holmes, Richard. *Footsteps: Adventures of a Romantic Biographer.* New York: Viking, 1985.

———. *Sidetracks : Explorations of a Romantic Biographer.* New York: Vintage, 2001,

Horn, Bernard. *Facing the Fires: Conversations with A. B. Yehoshua.* Syracuse: Syracuse University Press, 1997.

———. "The *Shoah,* the *Akeda,* and the Conversations in A. B. Yehoshua's *Mr. Mani."* *Symposium* 53.3 (Fall 1999): 136–50.

Hornstein, Shelley. "Fugitive Places." *Art Journal* 59.1 (Spring 2000): 45–54.

Horowitz, Sara R. "The Wounded Tongue: Engendering Jewish Memory." In *Shaping Losses: Cultural Memory and the Holocaust,* ed. Julia Epstein and Lori Hope Lefkovitz, 107–27. Urbana: University of Illinois Press, 2001.

Howe, Irving. "News from Elsewhere." *New York Review of Books* (April 14, 1988): 5. www.nybooks.com/articles/article-preview?article id=4462.

Howe, Irving, Khone Shmeruk and Ruth R. Wisse, eds. *The Penguin Book of Modern Yiddish Verse.* New York: Penguin Books, 1987.

Hulse, Michael, trans. *Essays in Honor of Elias Canetti.* New York: Farrar, Straus and Giroux, 1987.

Hussein, Abdirahman A. *Edward Said: Criticism in Society.* New York: Routledge Press, 1997.

Idel, Moshe. *Absorbing Perfections: Kabbalah and Interpretation.* New Haven, CT: Yale University Press, 2002.

———. *Kabbalah: New Perspectives.* New Haven, CT: Yale University Press, 1988.

Ignatieff, Michael. "The Old Country." *New York Review of Books* 37.2 (February 15, 1990): 3-5.
Israel, Nico. *Outlandish: Writing Between Exile and Diaspora*. Stanford, CA: Stanford University Press, 2000.
Jabès, Edmond. *A Foreigner Carrying in the Crook of His Arm a Tiny Book*. Trans. Rosemarie Waldrop. Hanover, NH: Wesleyan University Press, 1993.
———. *From the Desert to the Book: Dialogues with Marcel Cohen*. Trans. Pierre Joris. Barrytown, NY: Station Hill Press, 1990.
Jacobs, Carol. "Walter Benjamin: Topographically Speaking." *Studies in Romanticism* 31.4 (Winter 1992): 501-25.
Jacobson, Dan. *Heshel's Kingdom*. London: Hamish Hamilton, 1998.
Jaggi, Maya. "The Last Word." *Guardian*, December 21, 2001. books.guardian.co.uk/departments/generalfiction/story/0,6000,624750,00.html.
James, Henry. *The Ambassadors*. Cambridge: Riverside Press, 1960.
———. *Art of the Novel*. New York: Charles Scribner's Sons, 1934.
JanMohamed, Abdul."Worldliness-without-World, Homelessness-as-Home: Toward a Definition of the Specular Border Intellectual." In *Edward Said: A Critical Reader*. ed. Michael Sprinker, 96-120. Oxford, Basil Blackwell, 1992.
JanMohamed, Abdul, with David Lloyd. *The Nature and Context of Minority Discourse*. New York: Oxford University Press, 1990.
Jarrett, David. "Bruno Schulz and the Map of Poland." *Chicago Review* 40.1 (1994): 73-84.
Jedlicki, Jerzy. "Poland's Perpetual Return to Europe." *Crosscurrents: A Yearbook on Central European Culture* 12, ed. Ladislav Matejka, 78-88. New Haven, CT: Yale University Press, 1993.
Kalaga, Wojciech H. and Tadeusz Rachwal, eds. *Memory—Remembering—Forgetting*. New York: Peter Lang, 1999.
Kaplan, Alice Yaeger. "On Language Memoir." In *Displacements: Cultural Identities in Question,* ed. Angelika Bammer, 59-70. Bloomington: Indiana University Press, 1994.
Karim, Karim H., ed. *The Media of Diaspora*. London: Routledge Press, 2003.
Katz, Adam. "The Originary Scene, Sacrifice, and the Politics of Normalization in A. B. Yehoshua's *Mr. Mani*." *Anthropoetics* 7.2 (Fall 2001/Winter 2002): www.anthropoetics.ucla.edu/ap0702/sacrifice.htm.
Kenney, Padraic, István Deák, et al. "Bruno Schulz's Frescoes." *New York Review of Books* 157.19 (November 29, 2001): 65. www.nybooks.com/articles/14876.
Kiš, Danilo "Variations on the Theme of Central Europe." In *Crosscurrents: A Yearbook on Central European Culture* 6, ed. Ladislav Matejka, 1-14. Ann Arbor: University of Michigan Press, 1987.
Klemperer, Viktor. *I Shall Bear Witness: The Diaries of Victor Klemperer, 1933-41*. Trans. Martin Chalmers. New York: Phoenix, 1999,
———. *The Lesser Evil: The Diaries of Victor Klemperer, 1945-59*. New York: Phoenix, 2004.
———. *To the Bitter End: The Diaries of Victor Klemperer, 1942-45*. Trans. Martin Chalmers. New York: Phoenix, 2004.

Kochnar-Lingren, Gray. "Charcoal: The Phantom Traces of W. G. Sebald's Novel-Memoirs." *Monatshefte* 94.3 (Fall 2002): 368–81.
Koudelka, Josef. *Exiles*. Essays by Czeslaw Milosz. New York: Aperture, 1988.
Kristeva, Julia. *Crisis of the European Subject*. Trans. Susan Fairfield. New York: Other Press, 2001.
———. *Nations without Nationalism*. Trans. Leon S. Roudiez. New York: Columbia University Press, 1993.
———. *Powers of Horror: An Essay in Abjection*. Trans. Leon S. Roudiez. New York: Columbia University Press, 1982.
———. *Strangers to Ourselves*. Trans. Leon S. Roudiez. New York: Columbia University Press, 1994.
Kronfeld, Chana. *On the Margins of Modernism: Decentering Literary Dynamics*. Berkeley: University of California Press, 1994.
Kuhnel, Ernst. *Arabesque: Meaning and Transformation of an Ornament*. Graz: Verlag fur Sammler, 1977.
Kuprel, Diana. "Errant Events on the Branch Tracks of Time: Bruno Schulz and Mythical Consciousness." *Slavic and East European Journal* 40.1 (1996): 100–117.
Lacoue-Labarthe, Philippe. *La Fiction du politique: Heidegger, l'art, et la politique*. Paris: Christian Bourgois, 1987.
Lane, Anthony. "Higher Ground." *New Yorker* (May 29, 2000): 123–28.
Lavie, Smadar, and Ted Swedenburg, eds. *Displacement, Diaspora, and Geographies of Identity*. Durham: Duke University Press, 1996.
Lawson, Richard. *Understanding Elias Canetti*, Columbia: University of South Carolina Press, 1991.
Lefebvre, Henri. *The Production of Space*. Trans. Donald Nicholson-Smith. Oxford: Blackwell, 1991.
Lejeune, Philippe. *On Autobiography*. Trans. Katherine Leary. Minneapolis: University of Minnesota Press, 1989.
Lentricchia, Frank, and Andrew DuBois. *Close Reading: The Reader*. Durham: Duke University Press, 2003
Lescourret, Marie-Anne. *Emmanuel Levinas*. Paris: Flamarrion, 1999.
Levenson, Michael. *Modernism and the Fate of Individuality: Character and Novelistic Form from Conrad to Woolf*. Cambridge: Cambridge University Press, 1991.
Levi, Primo. *The Periodic Table*. Trans. Raymond Rosenthal. New York: Schocken Books, 1984.
Levinas, Emmanuel. *Alterity and Transcendence*. Trans. Michael B. Smith. New York: Columbia University Press, 1999.
———. *Beyond the Verse: Talmudic Readings and Lectures*. Trans. Gary D. Mole. Bloomington: Indiana University Press, 1994.
———. *De l'évasion*. Ed. Jacques Rolland. Paris: Fata Morgana, 1982.
———. *Entre Nous: On Thinking of the Other*. Trans. Michael B. Smith and Barbara Harshav. New York: Columbia University Press, 1998.
———. *Existence and Existents*. Trans. Alphonso Lingis. Pittsburgh: Duquesne University Press, 2001.

———. *In The Time of Nations*. Trans. Michael B. Smith. Bloomington: Indiana University Press, 1994.
———. *Humanisme de l'autre homme*. Paris: Fata Morgan, 1972.
———. "Intentionalité et sensation." In *En découvrant l'existence avec Husserl et Heidegger*, 137–44. Paris: Vrin, 1975.
———. *Is It Righteous to Be? Interviews with Emmanuel Levinas*. Trans. Jill Robbins. Stanford, CA: Stanford University Press, 2001.
———. *Nine Talmudic Readings*. Trans. Annette Aronowicz. Bloomington: Indiana University Press, 1990.
———. *On Escape*. Trans. Bettina Bergo. Stanford, CA: Stanford University Press, 2003.
———. *Outside the Subject*. Trans. Michael B. Smith. Stanford: CA: Stanford University Press, 1993.
———. *Quelques reflexions sur la philosophie de l'hitlerisme*. With an essay by Miguel Abensour, "Le mal élémental." Paris: Payot & Rivages, 1997.
———. "Reality and Its Shadow." In *Collected Philosophical Papers*, Trans. Alphonso Lingis, 1–15. Dordrecht: Martinus Nijhoff, 1987.
———. "Reflections on the Philosophy of Hitlerism." Trans. Seán Hand. *Critical Inquiry* 17 (1990): 63–71.
———. *Time and the Other*. Trans. Richard Cohen. Pittsburgh: Duquesne University Press, 1987.
———. *Totality and Infinity: An Essay on Exteriority*. Trans. Alphonso Lingis. Pittsburgh: Duquesne University Press, 1969.
Lipking, Lawrence "Location, Location: Review of *Thomas Gray: A Life* by Robert L. Mack." *New Republic* (February 12, 2001): 38–42.
Liszka, Jakób. "The Face: I and Other in Gombrowicz's *Ferdydurke*." *Philosophy and Literature* 5 (1981): 62–72.
Llewelyn, John. *Emmanuel Levinas: The Genealogy of Ethics*. New York: Routledge, 1995.
Long, J. J., and Anne Whitehead. *W. G. Sebald: A Critical Companion*. Edinburgh: Edinburgh University Press, 2004.
Longinović, Tomislav Z. *Borderline Culture: The Politics of Identity in Four Twentieth-Century Slavic Novels*. Fayetteville: University of Arkansas Press, 1993.
Lookwood, Alan. "Beylisms in W. G. Sebald's Vertigo." *Brooklyn Rail* 38 (July 2000): www.thebrooklynrail.org/archives/index.html.
———. "In Memoriam W. G. Sebald, Part 2: 10/01; W. G. Sebald at the 92nd St. Y." www.nonserviamnyc.com/al/alan_lockwood.html.
Loqaui, Franz, ed. *W. G. Sebald: Porträt 7*. Eggingen: Edition Klaus Isele, 1997.
Lorenz, Dagmar C. G., ed. *A Companion to the Works of Elias Canetti*. Rochester, N.Y.: Camden House, 2004
Lubow, Arthur. "A Symposium on W. G. Sebald." *Threepenny Review* 89 (Fall 2003): www.threepennyreview.com/samples/sebaldsympos_sp02.html.
Luzzato, R. Moshe Hayyim. *Mesilat yesharim*. Tel Aviv: Mahbarot le-sifrut, 1964.
———. *Otzrot ha-Ramchal*. Jerusalem: Sifriaty, 1992.

———. *The Path of the Just*. Trans. Yaakov Feldman. Northvale, N.J.: Jason Aronson Inc., 1996.

Mack, Michael. *Anthropology as Memory: Elias Canetti's and Franz Baermann Steiner's Responses to the Shoah*. Tübingen: Niemeyer, 2001.

Manea, Norman. *The Hooligan's Return: A Memoir*. Trans. Angela Jianu. New York: Farrar, Straus Giroux, 2003.

Manea, Norman, with Geoffrey Hartman, Leonard Michaels, and Stanley Crouch, "Ways of Writing about Oneself." *Partisan Review* 118.1 (February 15, 2001): 57–90.

Manger, Itzik. *The World According to Itzik: Selected Poetry and Prose*. Trans. Leonard Woolf. New Haven, CT: Yale University Press, 2002.

Manning, Robert John Sheffler. *Interpreting Otherwise Than Heidegger: Emmanuel Levinas's Ethics as First Philosophy*. Pittsburgh: Duquesne University Press, 1993.

Margit, Patricia Eszter. "Builders of Budapest." *Jerusalem Report* 15.2 (October 4, 2004): 34–36.

———."Fighting for the Ghetto." *Jerusalem Report* 15.17 (December 13, 2004): 30–31.

Marrouchi, Mustapha. "Exile Runes." *College Literature* 28.3 (Fall 2001): 88–128.

Marshall, Jeanne "History, Through a Glass Darkly." *National Post* (February 4, 2002): B4. www.nationalpost.com/search/story.html?f=/stories/20020204/1331429.html.

Marx, Karl. *Selected Writings*. Ed. David McClellan. Oxford: Oxford University Press, 2000.

Massad, Joseph. "The Intellectual Life of Edward Said." *Journal of Palestine Studies* 33.3 (2004): 7–22.

Matalon, Ronit. *The One Facing Us*. Trans. Marsha Weinstein. New York: Henry Holt, 1998.

———. *Ze im hapanim eleinu*. Tel Aviv: Am Oved, 1986.

Matar, Nabil I. *In the Lands of the Christians: Arab Travel Writing in the Seventeenth Century*. New York: Routledge, 2002.

McCaffrey, Steve. *Prior to Meaning: The Protosemantic and Poetics*. Evanston, IL: Northwestern University Press, 2001.

McCulloh, Mark. *Understanding W. G. Sebald*. New York: Columbia University Press, 2003.

McHale, Brian. "Seizing the Means of Representation." *American Book Review* (January–February 1990): 4+.

Medvedev, P. N. *The Formal Method in Literary Scholarship: A Critical Introduction to Sociological Poetics*. Trans. Albert J. Wehrle. Baltimore: Johns Hopkins University Press, 1978.

Meir, R. Asher. "YHE-Kitzur: Meaning in Mitzvot # 58: Chapter 95." *Yeshivat Har Etzion Israel Koschitzky Virtual Beit Midrash*. www.ou.org/torah/tt/5762/beshalach62/specialfeatures_mitzvot.htm.

Memmi, Albert. "Am I a Traitor?" *Commentary* 34.4 (April 1955): 287–92.

———. "An Impossible Existence: The Way Out." *Sources of Contemporary Jewish Thought* 6 (1975): 19–78.

———. "Does the Jew Exit?" *Commentary* 42.5 (November 1966): 73–76.

---. "Jews, Tunisians, and Frenchmen." *Literary Review* 41.2 (Winter 1998): 223–28.
---. *Le Nomade Immobile*. Paris: Arléa, 2000.
---. *The Pillar of Salt*. Trans. Edouard Roditi. Boston: Beacon Press, 1992.
Mendelsohn, Ezra. *The Jews of East Central Europe between the Two World Wars*. Bloomington: Indiana University Press, 1993.
Midrash Rabbah on Esther and Song of Songs. Trans. Maurice Simon. London: Soncino Press, 1983.
Midrash Rabbah: mefurash peirush mada'i hadash be-tseiruf "ein ha-derash"/ mar'eh mekomot le-kol ma'amarei ha-midrash me-et Mosheh Aryeh Mirkin. Tel Aviv: Hotsa'at "Yavneh," 1956–82.
Miller, J. Hillis. "The Critic as Host." In *Modern Criticism and Theory: A Reader*, ed. David Lodge, 278–85. London: Longman, 1988.
---. *The Disappearance of God: Five Nineteenth-Century Writers*. Champaign: University of Illinois Press, 2000.
---. *Versions of Pygmalion*. Cambridge: Harvard University Press, 1990.
Miloscz, Czeslaw. "Joseph Conrad's Father." In *Emperor of the Earth: Modes of Eccentric Vision*, 157–85. Berkeley: University of California Press, 1981.
---. *Native Realm: A Search for Self-Definition*. Trans. Catherine S. Leach. Berkeley: University of California Press, 1981.
Minczeles, Henri. *Vilna, Wilno, Vilnius: la Jérusalem de Lituanie*. Paris: Ed. La Découverte, 2000.
Mintz, Alan. *Hurban: Responses to Catastrophe in Hebrew Literature*. New York: Columbia University Press, 1984.
Moragh, Gilead. "Israel's New Literature of the Holocaust: The Case of David Grossman's *See Under: Love Modern*." *Fiction Studies* 45.2 (1999): 457–79.
Moss, Stephen. "Falling for Vertigo." *Guardian* (January 20, 2000): books.guardian.co.uk/critics/reviews/0,,124963,00.html.
Moyn, Samuel. "Emmanuel Levinas's Talmudic Readings: Between Tradition and Invention." *Prooftexts* 23 (2003): 338–64.
Mudimbe, V. Y. "Jewish Diaspora: A Dialogue." In *Diaspora and Immigration* issue, edited by V. Y. Mudimbe and Sabine Engel. *South Atlantic Quarterly* 98.1–2 (Winter/Spring 1999): 95–116.
Musil, Robert. *The Enthusiasts*. Trans. Andrea Simon. New York: Performing Arts Journal Pubs., 1983.
Nabokov, Vladimir. *Speak Memory: An Autobiography Revisited*. New York: Vintage, 1989.
Naddaff, Sandra. *Arabesque, Narrative Structure, and the Aesthetics of Repetition in the 1001 Nights*. Evanston, IL: Northwestern University Press, 1991.
Nash, Stanley L. "A Creative Sense of Impasse: Aharon Appelfeld's *Musul Beguf Rishon*." *Modern Hebrew Literature* 7.1/2 (1981/1982): 56–59.
---. "Critical Reappraisals of Aharon Appelfeld." *Prooftexts* 22 (2002): 334–402.
Nelson, Victoria. "The New Science of Witold Gombrowicz." *Salmagundi* 85–86 (Winter–Spring, 1991): 314–25.
Newton, Adam Zachary. *Facing Black and Jew: Literature as Public Space in Twentieth Century America*. Cambridge: Cambridge University Press, 1998.

———. *The Fence and the Neighbor: Yeshayahu Leibowitz, Emmanuel Levinas, and Israel among the Nations*. Albany: SUNY Press, 2001.

———. *Narrative Ethics*. Cambridge; Harvard University Press, 1992.

———. "Not Quite Holocaust Fiction: W. G. Sebald's The Emigrants and A. B. Yeshoshua's Mr. Mani." In *MLA Options for Teaching Series: Teaching the Representation of the Holocaust*, ed. Marianne Hirsh and Irence Kacandes, 422–30. New York: MLA, 2004.

———. "The SARL of Criticism: Sonority, Arrogation, and Letting-Be." *American Literary History* 13.3 (Fall 2001): 603–37.

Nixon, Rob. *London Calling: V. S. Naipaul, Postcolonial Mandarin*. New York: Oxford University Press, 1992.

Nora, Pierre. *Realms of Memory: Rethinking of the French Past*, Vol. 1: *Conflicts and Divisions*. Trans. Arthur Goldhammer. New York: Columbia University Press, 1996.

Olney, James. *Memory and Narrative: The Weave of Life-Writing*. Chicago: University of Chicago Press, 1998.

Ouaknin, Marc-Alain. *The Burnt Book: Reading the Talmud*. Trans. Llewellyn Brown. Princeton, NJ: Princeton University Press, 1996.

Ozick, Cynthia. "The Posthumous Sublime." *New Republic* (December 16, 1996): 33–36.

———. "The Rights of History and the Rights of Imagination." *Commentary* 107.3 (March 1999): 22–27.

———. *Quarrel and Quandary*. New York: Alfred Knopf, 1999.

Pagis, Ada, *Lev pit'omi* (Sudden heart). Am Oved: Tel-Aviv, 1995.

Pagis, Dan. "Dan Pagis: Last Poems." Trans Tsipi Keller. *Quarterly Review of Literature* 31 (1993): 3–61.

———. "Interview with Yaira Genoosar: *Dan Pagis: Likro bishem, linkot 'emda*." *Iton 77*.38 (February 1983): 33–36.

———. *Kol ha-shirim; Abba: (pirke prozah)*. Tel Aviv: ha-Kibuts ha-me'uhad; 1991.

———. *The Selected Poetry of Dan Pagis*. Trans Stephen Mitchell. San Francisco: North Point, 1989. Originally published as *Variable Directions*.

———. *Shneim-asar panim* (Twelve faces). Tel Aviv: HaKibbutz Hameuchad, 1988.

Pardes, Ilana. *The Biography of Ancient Israel: National Narratives in the Bible*. Berkeley: University of California Press, 2000.

Park, Ed. "The Precognitions: On the Posthumous Trail of W. G. Sebald and William Gaddis." *Village Voice Literary Supplement* (Fall 2002). www.villagevoice.com/vls/178/park.shtml.

Patt, Lise, ed., *Searching for Sebald*. Los Angeles: Institute of Cultural Inquiry Press. Forthcoming.

Patt, Lise, with Gehard Richter, Marquand Smith, eds. *Benjamin's Blind Spot: Walter Benjamin and the Premature Death of Aura*. New York: Institute of Cultural Inquiry, 2001.

Peña, Ofelia Marti. "Die Stimmen von Marrakesh." In *Homenje a Elias Canetti/Festschrift Elias Canetti*, ed. Roberto Corcoll and Marisa Sigun, 165–80. Kassel: Reichenberger; Barcelona: Promociones y Publicaciones Universitarias, 1987.

Peirce, Charles Sanders. *Collected Writings*. 8 vols. Ed. Charles Hartshorne, Paul Weiss, and Arthur W Burks. Cambridge: Harvard University Press, 1931-58.

Perloff, Marjorie. "Cultural Liminality/Aesthetic Closure? The 'Interstitial Perspective' of Homi Bhabha." wings.buffalo.edu/epc/authors/perloff/bhabha.html.

Poirier, Richard. *Robert Frost: The Work of Knowing*. Stanford, CA: Stanford University Press, 1990.

———. *A World Elsewhere*. New York: Oxford University Press, 1966.

Polsky, Stephanie. "Anterior Devices: Walter Benjamin's Tactics of Procrastination." *Parallax* 5.1 (February 1999): 21-35.

Porter, Roger. "Autobiography, Exile, Home: The Egyptian Memoirs of Gini Alhadeff, André Aciman, and Edward Said." *Biography: An Interdisciplinary Quarterly* 24.1 (Winter 2001): 302-14.

Poulet, Georges. "The Phenomenology of Reading." *New Literary History* 1 (1969): 53-68.

Powers, D. V. "Fresco Fiasco: Narratives of National Identity and the Bruno Schulz Murals of Drogobych." *East European Politics and Societies* 17.4 (November 2003): 622-53.

Pratt, Mary Louise. *Imperial Eyes: Travel Writing and Transculturation*. New York: Routledge, 1992. Prokopczyk, Czeslaw Z., ed. *Bruno Schulz: New Documents and Interpretations*. New York: Peter Lang, 1999.

Proust, Marcel. *In Search of Lost Time*. 7 vols. Trans. C. K. Scott-Moncrieff, Terence Kilmartin, D. J. Enright. New York: Modern Library, 1998.

Pugh, Stefan M. *Testament to Ruthenian: A Guide to the Rusyn Language*. Cambridge: Harvard University Press, 1996.

Rachwal, Tadeusz. "A Ticket to Elsewhere." *Chicago Review* 40.1 (1994): 85-97.

Raffat, Samir. *Maadi 1904-1962: History and Society in a Cairo Suburb*. Cairo: Palm Press, 1994.

———. "André Aciman's *Out of Egypt*." *Egyptian Gazette*, December 21, 1996. www.egy.com/judaica/96-12-21.shtml.

———. "Aciman Encore: *Out of Egypt*—Great Uncle Vili Mystery Resolved at Last." *Egyptian Mail*, February 1, 1997. www.egy.com/judaica/97-02-01.shtml.

Ramras-Rauch, Gila. "Aharon Appelfeld: A Hundred Years of Jewish Solitude." *World Literature Today* 72.3 (Summer 1998): 493-502.

———. *Aharon Appelfeld: The Holocaust and Beyond*. Bloomington: Indiana University Press, 1994.

Rattok, Lily. *Bayit 'al belimah, omanut hasippur shel A. Appelfeld*. Tel Aviv: Heker, 1989.

Reisch, Bruce I. "Back to Bukovina. A Trip to My Roots in Radauti and Sadagura—Photographs of Czernowitz," 1998. www.shtetlinks.jewishgen.org/radauti/czernowitz.html.

Remaud, Olivier. "Language of Dark Times: Canetti, Klemperer, and Benjamin." *Diogenes* 48.189 (Spring 2000): 11-22

Rezzori, Gregor von. *Anecdotage: A Summation*. Trans Susan Bernofsky. New York: Farrar, Straus Giroux, 1996.

———. *Blumen im Schnee: Portraitstudien zu einer Autobiographie, die ich nie schreiben werde; auch: Versuch der Erzahlweise eines gleicherweise nie geschriebenen Bildungsromans. Munchen: C. Bertelsmann, 1989.

———. *Memoirs of an Anti-Semite.* Trans. Joachim Neugroschel. New York: Penguin Books, 1982.

———. *The Snows of Yesteryear: Portraits for an Autobiography.* Trans. H. F. Broch de Rothermann. New York: Knopf, 1989.

Richter, Gerard. "Face-Off," *Monatshefte* 90.4 (Winter 1998): 414–44.

Robbins, Bruce. "Comparative Cosmopolitanisms." In *Cosmopolitics: Thinking and Feeling beyond the Nation,* ed. Pheng Cheah and Bruce Robbins, 246–64. Minneapolis: University of Minnesota Press, 1998.

Robbins, Jill. *Altered Reading: Levinas and Literature.* Chicago: University of Chicago Press, 1999.

Robertson, Ritchie. "'Jewish Self-hatred'? The Cases of Schnitzler and Canetti." In *Austrians and Jews in the Twentieth Century: From Franz Kafka to Waldheim,* ed. Robert S. Wistrich, 82–96. New York: St. Martin's Press, 1992.

Robinson, Marc, ed. *Altogether Elsewhere: Writers on Exile.* New York: Harcourt, 1996.

Rosen, Charles. "The Ruins of Walter Benjamin." In *On Walter Benjamin: Critical Essays and Recollections,* ed. Gary Smith, 129–75. Cambridge: MIT Press, 1988.

Rosenberg, Jonathan. *Elegy for an Age: The Presence of the Past in Victorian Literature.* London: Anthem Press, 2005.

Rosenfarb, Chava. *On the Brink of the Precipice, 1939.* Book 1 of *The Tree of Life: A Trilogy of Life in the Lodz Ghetto.* Madison: University of Wisconsin Press, 2004.

Roth, Joseph. *Report from a Parisian Paradise: Essays from France 1925–1939.* Trans. Michael Hoffmann. W. W. Norton & Co., 2003.

———. *The Wandering Jews.* Trans. Michael Hoffmann. New York: W. W. Norton & Co., 2001.

Rothstein, Edward. "The Secret Life of Elias Canetti: Dreams of Disappearance." *New Republic* (January 8, 1990): 33–38.

Roumani, Judith. "Albert Memmi and the North African Jewish Identity: Two Phases of the Return to Roots." *Jewish Frontier* 49.10 (1982): 12–15.

Rushdie, Salman. *Imaginary Homelands: Essays and Criticism, 1981–1991.* New York: Penguin Books, 1992.

Russell, James R. "Harvard Death Fugue: On the Exploitation of Bruno Schulz." *Zeek Magazine.* www.zeek.net/art_04015.shtml.

Sacks, Oliver. *An Anthropologist on Mars: Seven Paradoxical Tales.* New York: Vintage, 1996.

Safranski, Rüdiger. *Martin Heidegger: Between Good and Evil.* Trans. Ewald Osers. Cambridge: Harvard University Press, 1998.

Said, Edward W. *After the Last Sky: Palestinian Lives.* Photographs by Jean Mohr. New York: Pantheon Books, 1986.

———. "Defamation, Zionist Style." *Al-Ahram Weekly* no. 444 (26 August–1 September 1999): www.zmag.org/saidreply.htm.

———. *The Edward Said Reader.* Ed. Moustafa Bayoumi and Andrew Rubin. New York: Vintage Books, 2000.

———. *Freud and the Non-European*. New York: Verso, 2003.
———. "Invention, Memory, and Place." *Critical Inquiry* 26.2 (Winter 2000): 175–92.
———. *Joseph Conrad and the Fiction of Autobiography*. Cambridge, Harvard University Press, 1966.
———. *Musical Elaborations*. New York: Columbia University Press, 1991.
———. *Out of Place: A Memoir*. New York: Knopf, 1999.
———. "The Problem of Textuality: Two Exemplary Positions." *Critical Inquiry* 4.4 (Summer 1978): 673–714.
———. *Reflections on Exile and Other Essays*. Cambridge: Harvard University Press, 2000.
———. *The World, the Text, and the Critic*. Cambridge: Harvard University Press, 1983.
Said, Edward, with Daniel Barenboim. *Parallels and Paradoxes: Explorations of Music and Society* New York: Pantheon Books, 2002.
Salgado, Sebastião. *Migrations: Humanity in Transition*. New York: Aperture, 2000.
Sandbank, Shimon. "*The Last Poems* of Dan Pagis." *Modern Hebrew Literature* 11 (1993): 33–36.
Sante, Luc. *Evidence*. New York: Noonday Press, 1992.
Santner, Eric. *On the Psychotheology of Everyday Life: Reflections on Freud and Rosenzweig*. Chicago: University of Chicago Press, 2001.
———. *Stranded Objects: Mourning, Memory, and Film in Postwar Germany*. Ithaca, NY: Cornell University Press, 1990.
Sartre, Jean-Paul. Preface to *The Wretched of the Earth*, by Frantz Fanon. Trans. Constance Farrington. New York: Grove Press, 1986.
———. *"What Is Literature?" and Other Essays*. Trans. Steven Ungar. Cambridge: Harvard University Press, 1988.
Schama, Simon. *Landscape and Memory*. New York: Alfred A. Knopf, 1995.
Schlant, Ernestine. *The Language of Silence: West German Literature and the Holocaust*. New York: Routledge, 1999.
Schlink, Bernard. *Flights of Love: Stories*. Trans. John E. Woods. New York: Vintage Books, 2002.
Schneider, Judith Morganroth. "Albert Memmi and Alain Finkielkraut: Two Discourses on French Jewish Identity." *Romanic Review* 81.1 (1990): 130–36.
Schneider, Peter. *Paarungen*. Reinbeck: Rowohlt. 1994.
Schoenfeld, Gabriel. "Gabriel Schoenfeld and His Critics." *Commentary* 111.1 (September 2001):10–22. www.commentary.org/0101/schoenfeld.htm.
———. "Holocaust Reparations: A Growing Scandal." *Commentary* 110.9 (September 2000): 25–34. www.commentary.org/ 0009/schoenfeld.html.
Scholem, Gershom. *Major Trends in Jewish Mysticism*. Trans. Ralph Manheim. New York: Schocken Books, 1961.
———. *On the Kabbalah and Its Symbolism*. Trans. Ralph Manheim. New York: Schocken Books, 1996.
———. *Origins of the Kabbalah*. Trans. Allan Arkush. Philadelphia: Jewish Publication Society, 1987.
Schönle, Andreas. "Of Sublimity, Shrinkage, and Selfhood in the Works of Bruno Schulz." *Slavic and East European Journal* 42.3 (Autumn 1998): 467–82.

Schulz, Bruno. *The Collected Works of Bruno Schulz*. Ed. Jerzy Ficowski. London: Picador, 1998.
——. *The Complete Fiction*. Trans. Celina Wieniewska. New York: Walker and Co., 1989.
——. *Letters and Drawings with Selected Prose*. Trans. Walter Arndt with Victoria Nelson. New York: Harper & Row, 1988.
——. *Sanatorium under the Sign of the Hourglass*. Trans. Celia Wieniewska. Introduction by John Updike. New York: Penguin, 1979.
Schwartz, Daniel. *Imagining the Holocaust*. New York: St. Martin's Press, 1999.
Schwartz, Yigal. *Aharon Appelfeld: From Individual Lament to Tribal Eternity*. Hanover, NH: University Press of New England for Brandeis University Press, 2001.
——. *Kinat hayahid venetsah hashevet: Aharon Appelfeld—temunat 'olam* Jerusalem: Magnes Press, 1996.
——. "The Person, the Path, and the Melody: A Brief History of Identity in Israeli Literature." *Prooftexts* 20.3 (Autumn 2000): 318-39.
Sebald, W. G. *After Nature*. Trans. Michael Hamburger. New York: Random House, 2002.
——. *Austerlitz*. Trans. Anthea Bell. New York: Random House, 2001.
——. "Campo Santo." *Akzente: Zeitschrift für Literatur* 1 (Februar 2003): B 5384, 3-14.
——. *Campo Santo*. Trans. Anthea Bell. New York: Random House, 2005.
——. *Die Ausgewanderten: Vier lange Erzählungen*. Franfurt am Main: Vito von Eichborn GmbH & Co Verlag KG, 1992.
——. *Die Ringe des Saturn, Eine englishe Wallfart*. Franfurt am Main: Vito von Eichborn GmbH & Co Verlag KG, 1995.
——. *The Emigrants*. Trans. Michael Hulse. New York: New Directions, 1996.
——. *On the Natural History of Destruction*. Trans. Anthea Bell. New York: Random House, 2003.
——. *The Rings of Saturn*. Trans Michael Hulse. New York: New Directions, 1998.
——. *Schwindel. Gefühle*. Frankfurt Am Main: Eichborn Verlag, 1998.
——. *Unerzählt*. München: Carl Hanser Verlag, 2003.
——. *Vertigo*. Trans. Michael Hulse. New York: New Directions, 2000.
Seidel, Michael. *Exile and the Narrative Imagination*. New Haven, CT: Yale University Press, 1986.
Seidler, Ingo. "Who Is Elias Canetti?" *Crosscurrents: A Yearbook on Central European Culture* 1, ed. Ladislav Matejka, 107-24. Ann Arbor: University of Michigan, 1982.
Shaked, Gershon. *Modern Hebrew Fiction*. Bloomington: Indiana University Press, 2000.
——. "Requiem la'am hayehudi sheneherag." In *Between Frost and Smoke: Studies in the Writing of Aharon Appelfeld*, ed. Yitzhak Ben-Mordechai and Iris Parush, 15-57. Be'ersheva: Ben-Gurion University Press, 1997.
Shallcross, Bozena. "'Fragments of a Broken Mirror': Bruno Schulz's Retextualization of the Kabbalah." *East European Politics and Societies* 11.2 (1997): 270-81.

———. "Pencil, Pen and Ink: Bruno Schulz's Art of Interference." In *The Heart of Nation. Proceedings of PIASA International Congress*, ed. James Pula, ed. 57-68. New York: PIASA & Columbia University Press, 1994.
Shammas, Anton. "Al Galut v'Sifrut." *Igra* 2 (1987): 67-70.
———. *'Arabeskot*. Tel Aviv: 'Am 'oved ve-Sifre Maikelmark, 1986.
———. *Arabesques*. Trans. Vivian Eden. New York : Harper & Row, 1988.
———. "Ashmat ha-Babushka." *Politika* (February-March 1986): 44-45.
———. "Autocartography: The Case of Palestine, Michigan." *Palestine-Israel Journal of Politics, Economics and Culture* 9.2 (2002): 111-19. Originally printed in *The Geography of Identity*, ed. Patricia Yaeger, 466-75. Ann Arbor: University of Michigan Press, 1996.
———. "Finding Palestine" *Harper's Magazine* 292.1753 (June 1996): 24-28.
———. "Ha-kesamim she-me'ever le-gader : re'ayon im Anton Shamas / me-et Sh. Shifrah" (The enchantments on the other side of the fence). Interview with Sh. Shifra." *Davar* 21 (June 1974): 1.
———. "Interview with Dalya Amit." *Proza* (May-June 1988): 73-79.
———. *Shetah Hefker*. Tel Aviv: Hakibbutz Hameuchad, 1979.
Shohat, Ella. "The 'Postcolonial' in Translation: Reading Said in Hebrew." *Journal of Palestine Studies* 33.3 (2004): 55-75.
Silberstein, Laurence J., ed. *The Other in Jewish Thought and History: Constructions of Jewish Culture and Identity*. New York: New York University Press, 1994.
Sokoloff, Naomi. *Imagining the Child in Modern Jewish Fiction*. Johns Hopkins University Press, 1992.
Spieker, Sven. "'Stumps Folded into a Fist': Extra Time, Chance, and Virtual Reality in Bruno Schulz." *East European Politics and Societies* 11.3 (Fall 1997): 282-98.
Stanzel, Franz Karl. *A Theory of Narrative*. Cambridge: Cambridge University Press, 1984.
Stendhal [Henri Beyle]. *On Love*. Trans. H. B. V. and C. K. Scott-Moncrieff. New York: Grossett & Dunlap, 1967.
———. *The Life of Henri Brulard*. Trans. Jean Stewart and B. C. J. G. Knight. Chicago: University of Chicago Press, 1986.
Steinsaltz, Adin. *Steinsaltz Talmud Reference Guide*. New York: Random House, 1989.
Sztajnberg, Suzanne. "Witold Gombrowicz's *I Am Where I Am Not*." In *Crosscurrents: A Yearbook on Central European Culture* 4, ed. Ladislav Matejka, 99-12. Ann Arbor: University of Michigan, 1985.
Suchoff, David. "The Twisted Path of Tradition in Aharon Appelfeld's *The Iron Tracks* [*Mesilat Barzel*]." International Society for the Study of European Ideas Biannual Conference. University of Bergen, Norway, August 2000.
Sutzkever, Avraham. *The Fiddle Rose: Poems 1970-1972*. Trans. Ruth Whitman. Detroit: Wayne State University Press, 1990.
———. *Selected Poetry and Prose*. Trans. Barbara Harshav and Benjamin Harshav. Berkeley: University of California Press, 1991.
Szpilman, Wadylsaw. *The Pianist*. New York: Picador, 1999.
Talmud Bavli. Jerusalem: Hatham Sofar, 1966-67.

Talmud Bavli. Shottenstein Edition. Tractate *Eruvin*. Vol. 1. New York: Mesorah Publications Ltd., 1990.

Taub, Michael "Fables of Loss and Delusion" *Modern Judaism* 17.1 (1997): 91–96.

Tchernikowsky, Saul. *Shirim*. Tel Aviv: Devir, 1966.

Thomas, Elisabeth Louise. *Emmanuel Levinas: Ethics, Justice, and the Human beyond Being*. New York: Routledge, 2004.

Ticktin, Harold. "Jedwabne and Bruno Schulz: Jews and Poles Apart." *Midstream* 48.3 (April 2002): 9–10.

Tighe, Carl. "Cultural Pathology: Roots of Polish Literary Opposition to Communism." *Journal of European Studies* 23.3 (September 1998): 267–309.

———. *Politics of Literature: Poland 1945–1985*. Cardiff: University of Wales Press, 1999.

Tishby, Isaiah. "Kithvei ha-Kabbalah le-RaMHaL be Polin uve-Lita" (Spreading of RaMHaL's kabbalistic writings in Poland and Lithuania). *Kiryath Sefer* 45.1 (1969): 127–54.

———. *Messianic Mysticism of Moses Chaim Luzzato* Oxford: Littman Library of Jewish Civilization, forthcoming.

Todorova, Maria *Imagining the Balkans*. Oxford: Oxford University Press, 1997.

Toles, George. "The Metaphysics of Style in *Tender Is the Night*." *American Literature* 63.2 (1990): 423–44.

Traynor, Ian. "Murals Illuminate Holocaust Legacy Row." *Guardian* (July 2, 2001). www.guardian.co.uk/israel/Story/0,2763,515412,00.html.

Triska, Jan. "East Europe? West Europe? Both? Neither?" In *Crosscurrents: A Yearbook on Central European Culture* 1, ed. Ladislav Matejka, 39–44. Ann Arbor: University of Michigan Press, 1982.

Turner, Bryan S. "Edward Said and the Exilic Ethic: On Being Out of Place." *Theory, Culture & Society* 17.6 (December 2000): 125–29.

Yad Vashem. " Statement regarding the sketches by Bruno Schulz. " www1.yadvashem.org/about_yad/press_room/press_releases/schulz.html.

Venclova, Tomas. *Forms of Hope*. Riverdale, NY: Sheep's Meadow Press, 1999.

Veteto-Conrad, Marilya."German Minority Literature: Tongues Set Free and Pointed Tongues." *International Fiction Review* 28 (January 2001): 78–87.

Vološinov, V. N. *Marxism and the Philosophy of Language*. Trans. Ladislav Matejka and I. R. Titunik. New York, Seminar Press, 1973.

Warwick, Genevieve. "Speaking Statues: Bernini's Apollo and Daphne at the Villa Borghese." *Art History* 27.3 (2004): 353–81.

Weaver, Alain Epp. "On Exile: Yoder, Said, and a Theology of Land and Return." *Cross Currents* 52.4 (2003): 439–61.

Weiner, Justus Reid. "Exchange with Amos Elon." *New York Review of Books* 47.3 (February 24, 2000): www.nybooks.com/articles/218.

———. "'My Beautiful Old House' and Other Fabrications by Edward Said." *Commentary* 108.2 (September 1999): 23–28.

Weiss-Halivni, David. *Peshat and Derash: Plain and Applied Meaning in Rabbinic Exegesis*. New York: Oxford University Press, 1991.

White, Edmund. "*Out of Place*, by Edward Said." *Raritan* 19.3 (Winter 2000): 135–43.

White, Hayden. "Criticism as Cultural Politics." *Diacritics* 6.3 (1976): 8–13.
Williams, Arthur. "'Das Korsakowsche Syndrom': Remembrance and Responsibility in W. G. Sebald." In *German Culture and the Uncomfortable Past: Representations of National Socialism in Contemporary Germanic Literature*, ed., Helmut Schmitz, 65–86. Hampshire: Ashgate, 2001.
———. "W. G. Sebald: A Holistic Approach to Borders, Texts, and Perspectives." In *German-Language Literature Today: International and Popular?* Ed. Arthur Williams, Stuart Parkes, and Julian Preece, 99–118. Bern: Peter Lang, 2000.
Wineman, Aryeh. "On Aharon Appelfeld's *Essays in the First Person*." *Conservative Judaism* 33.4 (1980): 93–94.
Wisse, Ruth. "Aharon Appelfeld, Survivor." *Commentary* 76.2 (August 1983): 73–76.
———. *The Modern Jewish Canon: A Journey through Language and Culture*. New York: Free Press, 2000.
Wolff, Larry. *Inventing Eastern Europe: The Map of Civilization on the Mind of the Enlightenment*. Stanford, CA: Stanford University Press, 1996.
Wohlgelernter, Maurice. "Aharon Appelfeld: Between Oblivion and Awakening." *Tradition* 35.3 (2001): 6–19.
Wood, James. "An Interview with W. G. Sebald." *Brick* 59 (1998): 23–29.
———."The Right Thread." *New Republic* (July 6, 1998): 38–41. Reprinted as "W. G. Sebald's Uncertainty" in *The Broken Estate: Essays on Literature and Belief*, 248–57. New York: Modern Library, 2000.
Wyschogrod, Edith. "The Art in Ethics: Aesthetics, Objectivity, and Alterity in the Philosophy of Emmanuel Levinas." In *Ethics as First Philosophy: The Significance of Emmanuel Levinas for Philosophy and Religion*, ed. Adriaan Peperzak, 137–47. New York: Routledge, 1995.
Yaegar, Patricia, ed. *The Geography of Identity*. Ann Arbor: University of Michigan Press, 1996.
Yehoshua, A. B. *Between Right and Right*. Trans. Arnold Schwartz. Garden City, N.Y.: Doubleday, 1981.
———. *Mr Mani*. Trans. Hillel Halkin. New York: Doubleday, 1992.
———. "*Mr. Mani* and the *Akedah*." *Judaism* 49.5 (Winter 2001): 61–65.
Yerushalmi, Yosef Hayim. *Freud's Moses: Judaism Terminable and Interminable*. New Haven, CT: Yale University Press, 1993.
Yudkin, Leon. *Escape into Siege: A Survey of Israeli Literature Today*. London: Routledge and Kegan Paul, 1974.
Zagajewski, Adam. *Two Cities: On Exile, History, and the Imagination*. Trans. Lillian Vallee. Athens: University of Georgia Press, 1992.
Zborowski, Eli, et al. "The Battle over the Murals of Pain" (Letter to the Editor). *New York Times*, June 22, 2001, p. A26.
Zehavi, Alex "Solitude Is a Bitter Thing: On Anton Shammas's *No-Man's Land*," *Modern Hebrew Literature* 6.1/2 (1980): 43–46.
Ziarek, Ewa Ponowska, ed. *Gombrowicz's Grimaces: Modernism, Gender, Nationality* Albany: State University of New York Press, 1998.
Zierler, Wendy, "Footprints, Traces, Remnants: The Operations of Memory in Dan Pagis's *Aqebot*." *Judaism* 41.4 (1992): 316–33.

Žižek, Slavoj. *The Sublime Object of Ideology*. London: Verso, 1989.
Zorach, Cecile. "The Outsider Abroad: Canetti in Marrakesh." *Modern Austrian Literature* 16.3–4 (1983): 47–64.
Zornberg, Avivah Gottlieb. *The Beginning of Desire: Reflections on Genesis*. New York: Doubleday, 1995.
Zylinska, Joanna. "On the Impossibility of Finding One's Way to Ethics." *Culture Machine*. http://culturemachine.tees.ac.uk/Reviews/rev8.htm.

Index

Abba (Pagis), 244, 250, 253-54, 266-72
abstraction, in Canetti's and von Rezzori's works, 162
Aciman, André, 26-27, 48; arbitrage, 214, 228, 229, 233; on assimilation, 221; belonging or fixity in works, 233; biographical information, 215; borders, 233-34; on Canetti, 38; Canetti compared with, 222; cemeteries in works, 14, 214-15; classicism or xenophobia in works, 232-33; on dislocation, 220; Egypt in works, 233-34; exile in works, 227-28; *False Papers*, 9, 37, 212-14, 220, 222, 228, 231-34; fictional identity in works, 230; France in works, 233; on Freud, 221; identity and, 229-30, 237; on Jewishness, 226-27, 229-30, 237; *Letters of Transit*, 212, 219, 220, 238; marranism, 227-28, 233; on memory, 213-14; metaphor in works, 235; nostalgia and, 229, 238-39; *Out of Egypt*, 212, 223, 227-28, 229, 236; palintropism and, 37; place in works, 227-28; "Reflections of an Uncertain Jew," 221, 226-27, 230; reification of the literary by, 238; Said compared with, 215, 220, 222, 226-27, 238-39; on Sebald, 7, 50, 293n57; secularism and, 215; as Sephardic, 236-37; "Temporizing," 227-28, 229; and von Rezzori, 38, 328n8; 333n33

Adorno, Theodor, 224
advenience, 24, 25, 38, 48
Aeneid (Virgil), 73
After the Last Sky (Said), 216, 222-23, 234-35, 236, 342n25
Agnon, S. Y. ("A Book That Was Lost"), 75-76, 105, 303nn48-49
Alcalay, Ammiel, 238, 343n34
Aleichem, Sholem, 303n48
Alexandria, 226, 229, 231, 233, 234, 236, 256, 259; as cosmopolitan, 234; Said on, 291n44
The Alexandria Quartet (Durrell), 213, 231
alibi, 7, 23, 27, 285n12
allusion: Appelfeld's works and precursor texts, 74-76, 303n46; in *Arabesques* (Shammas), 243-44, 278; in Pagis's works, 271; in Sebald's works, 301n41
alphabet letters: as relics, 74; as stolen, 259
Alter, Robert, 246, 301n42
Alterman, Natan, 243
Altieri, Charles, 26
Amichai, Yehuda, 80, 247, 294n5, 346-47n13
Anders, Jaroslaw, 152
"Anecdote of the Jar" (Stevens), in *Arabesques*, 278
Angelus Novus (Klee), 112
apatride: palintropism and, 27, 60; as seer, 289n32

Appelfeld, Aharon: assimilation and, 47; "Buried Homeland," 33, 35, 45, 73, 159, 296nn8-10, 297n14, 305n58; on Canetti, 38; critics on, 77, 294-95n5; death in works of, 73, 76-77, 92; Hebrew as language of works, 44, 80; on Holocaust and memory, 294n2; Holocaust as subject of works, 44; identity issues, 44, 80, 93; Israel and, 296n9; Jewish identity, 93, 295-96n8; "The Kafka Connection," 295n8; language in works, 303-4n50, 305n59; movement in works, 46; narrative stance of, 295-96n8, 295n7; Pagis and, 296n9; "A Perpetual Story of Departure," 296n10; precursor texts for, 74-76, 303n48; Proust and, 44; Sebald compared with, 46-47; *Sipur Hayim (Story of a Life)*, 45, 294n2, 296n9, 305n59; stasis in works, 46; wandering in works, 75. *See also The Iron Tracks* (Appelfeld)
arabesque, 241-42; critics on, 265-66; as literary structure, 242-43, 343n1, 350n31; *midbar* and literary structure, 245; as rhetorical strategy, 272-74
Arabesques (Shammas), 242, 245-47, 249-50, 254, 256-59, 261-65, 277; allusion in, 243-44, 278; doubles or doubling in, 258, 266, 275, 348n21, 349n25; language in, 246; as occulted text, 272-73, 275-76; weaving images, 273
'Araidi, Na'im, 237
arbitrage, 214, 228, 229, 233
Archimboldo, Guiseppe, 152
archive of the feet, *xiii*, 34, 223
Arditti, Bernhard, 176
Argentina: Gombrowicz and, 97, 99, 100-101, 127, 129-30; as reduplication or displaced Poland, 99, 153, 293n57
art: as alienating, 111-12; *Angelus Novus* (Klee), 112; *The Blinding of Samson* (Rembrandt), 177; creative destruction, 67-68; as cultural possession, 102-4; Levinas on, 112, 125; paintings as nets in Canetti's works, 177; Schulz's murals, 102-7, 135, 152, 312n16; in Sebald's *The Emigrants*, 66-68

"The Art of Contraction" (Pagis), 263
The Aspern Papers (James), 168
assimilation: Aciman on, 221; Appelfeld and, 47, 92; as impossible, 250
Atlantic City (Malle), 130
Auerbach, Erich, 213, 224
Auerbach, Frank, 66-67
aura, 55-56, 58, 72, 111-12, 158
Auschwitz, 91, 309n77
Austerlitz (Sebald), *vii, xii*, 287n25, 290n36, 299n30, 337n57
Austria and Austrian identity, 160, 327n4
autobiographical writing: *Arabesques* (Shammas) as, 265; Canetti on autobiographical "I," 329n12; Canetti on forgery in, 161; de Man on, 16-17; as enchantment, 68; instability of autobiographic discourse, 18-22, 42-43, 61; mastery of language or "language memoir," 166-67; Pagis's *Abba* as, 268; as privative, 56-57; Shammas's on, 265; subject "decentered" in, 20, 162, 250, 251-52; subjective authority and, 20, 290n37. *See also* memoirs
autocartography, 241
"Autocartography" (Shammas), 251

Babel, Isaac, 158
Babylonian Talmud. *See Talmud Bavli*
Bakhtin, Mikhail, 5-6, 29, 43, 65-66, 99, 100, 216, 290n37, 307n67, 333nn29-30
Barthes, Roland, 24, 49, 285n12, 288n27, 297n17, 324n81, 333n30; on photographs, 56, 288n27
belonging. *See* longing/belonging
Benjamin, Walter, 100, 172, 251, 289n34, 298n20, 345n6; on aura, 55, 158; on Kraus, 331n21; on language, 331n21; on memoir, 19; on memory, 21-22; Said on, 216; Sebald's works and, 47
Ben-Yitzhak, Avraham (Sonne), 205, 206, 247-48, 347-48n15
Bhabha, Homi K., 7, 100, 284n10, 299-300n31, 310n7, 325n84, 343n33
Bialik, Hayim Nachman, 243, 282n3
Bishop, Elizabeth, 68

Index

Blanchot, Maurice, 21, 284n8, 290n35
The Blinding of Samson (Rembrandt), 177
Bloom, Harold, 245-46, 345nn6-7
books: in Appelfeld's works, 74, 75-76, 77, 79, 82, 89-90; in Canetti's works, 191, 203; in Shammas's works, 272-73, 276-77; as tomb or gravestone, *xiii*, 21, 28; in von Rezzori's works, 175-76; *yizker bicher* (memorial books), 14, 31, 33, 36
A Book That Was Lost and Other Stories (Agnon), 74-75
borders, 30; in Aciman's works, 233-34; cultural borders and permeability of tradition, 80; enclosures in *The Voices of Marrakesh* (Canetti), 202; of *eretz Israel*, 283n4; language as wandering across, 164-65; on photographs, 67; Said on boundaries, 221
Borges, Jorge Luis, 243, 293n58, 348n21
Botticelli, Sandro, 144
Boym, Svetlana, 211, 338n1
Brennan, Timothy, 98, 99-100
bricolage, 229, 298n23
Brodsky, Joseph, 4, 16, 37, 298n32, 342n29
Brooks, Peter, 287n24
"Brothers" (Pagis), 250
Browne, Sir Thomas, 242
Bukovina, 16, 160-61, 165, 169, 246, 249n51, 306n61
"Buried Homeland" (Appelfeld), 33, 35, 45, 73, 159, 296nn8-10, 297n14, 305n58
Buruma, Ian, 228

caduceus, 243
Cain as wanderer, 250
Cairo, 213, 223, 225, 226, 232
Calvino, Italo, 22; *Invisible Cities*, 42, 66, 71, 72, 96, 155-57; Despina, 155-157; Ersilia 41-43; Eudoxia, 240-242; Moriana, 96-97; on lightness, 36-37; Raissa, 207-8; *Six Memos for the Next Millennium*, 36; Zora, 22
camels, 184
Canetti, Elias, *vii*, 33; Aciman and Appelfeld on, 38; Aciman and Said compared with, 222; Allah in, 186-87, 201; on Canetti family, 164-65; on characters and writing, 158, 171, 333n31; *Crowds and Power*, 190, 197, 335n47; death in works, 197-200; "Dialogue with the Cruel Partner," 156, 161, 180, 205; on diaries, 180; exchange or commerce in works of, 336n49; on forgery in autobiographical writing, 161; Fuchs on, 202; Gnosticism and, 334n38, 336n49; *The Human Province*, 158, 160, 162, 163, 335nn45-46; identity issues, 179, 182; Jewish identity and, 160, 194-200, 328-29n9, 336-37n55; on Jewishness, 195-96; on language, 94, 176, 180, 330n18, 335nn45-46; language as subject of works, 163-65; on memoirs, 332n25; on memory, 331-32n25; metamorphosis *(verwandlung)* in works, 158, 182, 189, 199-200; *midbar* and, 161; "midpoint" and the interhuman, 158, 180-81; narrative stance of, 162, 179; as nostographer, 159; *Notes from Hampstead*, *vii*; Other and Otherness, 158; on paintings as nets, 177; precursor texts for, 157-58, 168-69, 180; Proust and, 157, 161; on Ruschuk, 169, 171, 177; *The Secret Heart of the Clock*, 197-98; sexuality, 336n49, 336n52; *The Tongue Set Free*, 163-65, 169-70, 333n31; *The Torch in My Ear*, 158, 176-79, 328-29n9; on travel narratives, 180; violence in works of, 332nn27-28; von Rezzori compared with, 331n21; women in works of, 335-36n48, 338n59; writing as self-entombment, 198-99. *See also The Voices of Marrakesh* (Canetti)
Carlyle, Thomas, 124
carpets, 240-42
Cather, Willa, 243, 277, 348n21
Cavafy, Constantine, 59, 212
Cavalcanti, Guido, 36
Cavell, Stanley, 271, 283-84n5, 351n35
cemeteries: in Aciman's works, 14, 214-15; in Appelfeld's works, 14; in Bocaccio's *Decameron*, 36; in Canetti's works, 14, 196-200; as de-authorizing, 256-57;

cemeteries *(continued)*
    in de Man's works, 20; familial heritage and, 292n53; in *Great Expectations* (Dickens), 287n24; identity located in, 257-58; Jacobson and, 292n53; in Pagis's works, 14, 162-63, 249, 250, 256-58, 271; Père Lachaise, 258-61; photo in *The Emigrants*, 9, 53-54; as points of departure, 257; reading of, 13-14; in Said's works, 14, 214; Schamma's visit to Jewish cemetery in Punsk, 34-35; in Schulz's works, 14; in Sebald's works, 12, 337n57; in Shammas's works, 256, 258-61; in von Rezzori's works, 14. *See also* gravestones
Chandler, James, 297-98n19
characters, Canetti on, 158, 171, 328n7, 333n31
cherry herring in Pagis's works, 252-53
Chotkowski, Charles, 104, 106
chronotope, 307nn68-69, 324n79
churchyards. *See* cemeteries
Cinnamon Shops (The Street of the Crocodiles, Schulz), 124-25, 142-44, 323n70
Cioran, E. M., 16, 289n31
cities: in Applefeld's works, 24; as central to narrative, 30; as human countenance, 97; marginocentric cities, 29-30, 160; in Sebald's works, 24; webs of relationship as metaphor for city space, 41-42. *See also Invisible Cities* (Calvino); *specific cities*
Citizen Kane (Welles), 177
City Lights (Chaplin), 116
Claudel, Paul, 151
collision with place, 15-16, 28, 37
comparatavism, 49
Conrad, Joseph, 18-19, 179, 209, 224, 228, 248, 289n33, 307n67, 339n5; autobiographical writing, 213; on geography, 222; *The Mirror of the Sea*, 209-10, 213; *A Personal Record*, 18, 211, 212, 213; "Poland Revisited," 40, 209, 213; premonitions of war in works, 210-11; Said on Conrad, 289n33
conversation, in *Abba* (Pagis), 253-54

Corsica, 299n29
cosmopolitanism, 235
counterpoint, 217-19
Courbet, in Sebald's works, 11
creative destruction, 66-67
critical methodology, 22-24, 37, 213, 216-17, 242; pairings of texts, 38, 46-47, 217, 245, 272; "route" of book, *vii*, 38-40
criticism: contrapuntal criticism, 216-19; as "interpretive contest," 48; as poaching, 25; secular *vs.* religious criticism, 215-16
Crowds and Power (Canetti), 190, 197, 335n47
Czernopol (fictionalized Czernowitz), 173
Czernowitz, 33, 159, 160, 162, 173-75, 306n61; Appelfeld on, 197n14; cemetery in, 292n51; descriptions of, 33; as Other, 174; Radautz and, 249; as "spacialized" by reading, 175; in von Rezzori's works (Czernopol), 173-74

darkness and magic, 130
Darwish, Mahmoud, 347n13
death: in Appelfeld's works, 73, 76-77, 92; Canetti's attitude toward, 334n39; in Canetti's works, 197-200; Heidegger and Levinas on, 115; in Pagis's works, 267; reading as summoning the dead, 20-21; in Said's works, 214, 223; Schulz and, 102, 144, 311n13; in Sebald's works, 53-54, 61, 70-71; in Shammas's works, 257, 259, 261, 274. *See also* cemeteries
Decameron (Bocaccio), 36
de Certeau, Michel, 5, 14, 28, 77, 241, 315n29; on metaphor, *vii*; on place and space, 285n11; on poaching, 6, 106; on reading, 6, 24-25, 284n6; on writing and place, 249
déjà entendu, 22
Deleuze, Gilles, 258
De l'évasion (Levinas), 39, 99, 106, 113-14, 115, 117, 123, 125, 135-36, 320n55
de Man, Paul, 16, 17, 20-21, 22, 56-57, 61, 199, 290n37

Index

departures: cemeteries as points of departure, 257; exiles as, 342n29; in Gombrowicz's works, 126, 130; Pagis and "unsentimental leave-takings," 247; Poland as point of departure, 126, 209; as "sentimental" good-byes, 209-10

deportation, 72

De Quincey, Thomas, 242-43, 264, 344n2

Derrida, Jacques, 150, 238, 318n45, 325n84, 352

desert (wilderness), 4-5; in *Invisible Cities*, 155-57. *See also midbar*

desire: longing and belonging, 28-29; memoirs and, 156

despoliation, 14-15

deterritorialization, 258

detours, 20, 34-35; in *The Emigrants*, 37; in *The Iron Tracks* (Appelfeld), 75, 78, 84, 86

"Dialogue with the Cruel Partner" (Canetti), 180, 205

Diary (Gombrowicz), 99-102, 106, 108, 109-12, 117-18, 120-21, 124, 127-34, 144-45, 315nn30-31, 319-20n53

diaspora, 40, 95

Dickens, Charles, 13

Dickinson, Emily, 68

"Discourse on the Novel" (Bakhtin), 5-6

dislocation or displacement: Aciman on, 220; in autobiography, 20; illness as bodily dislocation, 225; language and exile, 228; memoirs and, 4-5; narrative as, 5-6; in Pagis's works, 247; in Shammas works, 247

distancing, 23; aura and, 72; Benjamin on, 298n20; closeness and being at home in a place, 221; detached observation in *The Voices of Marrakesh* (Canetti), 192-93; distance in Canetti's works, 179-80; in *The Emigrants* (Sebald), 65; Kraus on, 298n20; mimesis and, 68; proximity and facing texts, 218; "telescoping vision" in Said's works, 234-35

Don Quixote, 124, 140

doorways or portals, in *The Iron Tracks* (Appelfeld), 82-83

doubles or doubling: in *Arabesques* (Shammas), 258, 266, 275, 348n21, 349n25; in arabesque style, 350n31; Argentina as reduplication of Poland, 99, 153, 293n57; in *The Emigrants* (Sebald), 61; face as double agent, 111; in Gombrowicz's works, 99, 101-2, 153; in *The Iron Tracks* (Appelfeld), 80-81, 91-92; in *The Voices of Marrakesh* (Canetti), 200

Drohobycz, 102-7, 139-41

Dumas, Alexandre, 116

Durrell, Lawrence, *The Alexandria Quartet*, 212, 231

Egypt, 6, 14-15, 231-32, 233-34. *See also* Alexandria; Cairo

elegy, 28

Eliot, T. S., 10

Ellison, Ralph, 22

elsewhere, 27-30, 48; as alibi, 7; itinerary and topography of, vii; Jewish Europe as, 69; and place, 219-22; as pre-occupied, 17

embodiment: embodied subjectivity, 115; face and, 111, 315-16n34; in Gombrowicz's works, 117-18; human body as landscape, 73; race or racism and, 114-15; *The Voices of Marrakesh* (Canetti), 199

The Emigrants (Sebald), 42, 44, 49-73; aura in, 58; critical responses to particular photographs in, 50-52; detours in, 37; distance in, 65; doubling in, 61; Holocaust as oblique subject of, 67-71; as memoir or autobiography, 42-43; memory in, 64-65; Nabokov in, 62; names in, 47-48; narrator in, 43-44, 45; place names in, 59; as post-Romantic, 66; railway tracks in, 69-71; as reading lesson, 62; reviews of, 8-9; sensation and ideation in, 54; transported documents and mementos in, 287-88n26. *See also* photographs in *The Emigrants*

enchainment (bondage), 114, 116. *See also* escape *(évasion)*

England: in Conrad's works, 209; in Sebald's works, 9-11, 56, 60-61
epitaphs, 20
Eros, in Gombrowicz's works, 129-30
eroticism, in *The Voices of Marrakesh* (Canetti), 191-93
errancy. *See* wandering
Essay Upon Epitaphs (Wordsworth), 20
escape *(évasion)*: Canetti and, 157; geographic dispossession and, 128, 131; Gombrowicz's works and, 113, 116-19, 121-23, 126, 128; inbetweeness and, 128; Levinas on, 99, 106, 113-14, 115, 117, 123, 125, 135-36; need for *(besoin d'évasion)*, 116, 119-20, 123-24; Schulz's works and, 322n65; selfhood and, 116; subjectivity and, 318-19n47; von Rezzori and, 157
ethics, 22-27; contrapuntal awareness and, 218; distance and, 285n14; of *midbar*, 8; pairing of texts and, 37-38; practice and, 25-26; of reading, 24-26, 263-64; reading as restorative of, 8
Europe: Alexandria as metonymy for, 234; in Canetti's works, 165; east-central Europe, use of term, 288-89n30; eastern Europe as "Second World," 98; in *The Emigrants* (Sebald), 69; Levinas on, 120; as lost world, 159; as uninhabitable, 77; Valéry on "face" of, 234, 325n84
évasion. *See* escape
Evidence (Sante), 55, 290n36
exchange or commerce, in *The Voices of Marrakesh* (Canetti), 185-86, 188, 193, 200, 203-4, 336n49
exile: in Aciman's works, 227-28; Brodsky on, 298n32, 342n29; in Conrad's works, 212-13; as contrapuntal awareness, 217; as credential of writers, 219, 228; in *The Emigrants* (Sebald), 72; expulsion from Paradise, 178; of Jacob, 15-16; as literary trope, 284nn89; Said and, 234; in Said's works, 215-16; secularism as, 215; von Rezzori as exilic writer, 160; writing as exilic and fugitive, 6-7, 16-19, 160, 284n7

Exodus, Book of: despoiling of Egypt, 14-15; flight from Egypt, 4, 329n10; forty-years' wandering, 14-15; travel prohibitions in, 3; wilderness in, 4, 248
exodus, deportations as, 72
expulsion, 11, 178
Ezrahi, Sidra, 86, 245, 253, 268, 295n7, 304n53

faces (human countenance): art as face, 111; in Canetti's works, 184; Canetti's writing as a face, 158; being defaced, 112-13; as elsewhere, 154; embodiment and, 111, 315-16n34; face-offs, 97, 110-11, 175; *vs.* figure, 317-18n41; in Gombrowicz's works, 117-20, 145, 152; as homeless or migratory, 141-42; as imposed or impressed, 124-25, 143-44; Kristeva on the foreign face, 109, 142; Levinas and trope of, 99; as maps, 154, 206; as masks, 144, 151; as other, 109, 110-11, 118-19; Pagis's prose fragments as *partzufim*, 244-45; Schulz on encountering new persons, 102; Schulz's self-portraits, 144-45; in Schulz's works, 141-45, 152; self-consciousness and, 111
facing texts, 24, 217
False Papers (Aciman), 9, 37, 212-14, 220, 222, 228, 231-34, 259
family names, 31-33
Farias, Victor, 114
Fascism, 231
"Fatherland" (Schulz), 138-39
fathers: in Pagis's works, 248-49, 250, 253-54, 261-63, 264, 266-67, 270-71; in Said's works, 220, 223-26; in Schulz's works, 139-40; in Shammas's works, 257
Feldman, Yael, 259, 275, 351n38
Ferdydurke (Gombrowicz), 100, 111, 113, 117-18, 127
figure *vs.* face, 317-18n41
fil-kharij, 222-23, 224
"Finding Palestine" (Shammas), 346n10
Finkielkraut, Alain, 119

first-person: Appelfeld and use of first-person plural, 295n7; in Appelfeld's works, 45; Canetti on autobiographical "I," 329n12; Gombrowicz use of first-person, 123, 124; as inherently unstable, 61; in Sebald's works, 43
Fitzgerald, F. Scott, *xi*
flight: Levinas and subjective being as, 114; Talmud on, 281-82n1; trains as gravity defying, 73
folklore in Shammas's works, 257, 260, 275
Form: Gombrowicz and, 119-20, 319n50; national Form, 98, 99-100; Schulz on impression of, 124-25
Foucault, Michel, 25
France: in Aciman's works, 233; Gombrowicz on Frenchmen, 101; Kristeva on, 108-9
freedom, 148-49
Freud, Sigmund, 92-93, 95, 309; Aciman on, 221; Said on, 217, 219; Yerushalmi on, 88-89
Freud and the Non-European (Said), 217, 219, 309n78, 340n12, 343n35
friendship: in *The Iron Tracks* (Appelfeld), 87; Schulz on, 103, 312n16
From the Desert to the Book (Jabès), 4-5
Frost, Robert, 38, 292n56
Frye, Northrup, 342n23
Fuchs, Anne, 202
fugitivity, 19; in Gombrowicz's work, 122, 130; of place, 78, 304n55; writing as fugitive, 130

Galicia, 138
Genesis, Book of, 14-15, 28, 37, 288n29
genre, 16-22
German language, 163, 164, 171, 297n14, 305n59, 330n16
Germany: flight from as diaspora, 95; Sebald and, 47; in Sebald's works, 11-12, 59-60
Gilboa, Amir, 243, 245, 276
Gilman, Sander, 328n9
Głowtska, Dorota, 152, 153
Gnessin, Uri Nissan, 44

Gnosticism, 334n38, 336n49
Goethe, Johann Wolfgang von, 65-66, 100, 124, 157-58, 310n7, 327n3
Gombrowicz, Witold, 4, 16-17; Argentina and, 97, 99, 127, 153, 293n57; Argentina in works, 129-30; on art, 111; on being defaced, 112-13; biographical information, 152-53; bondage or enchainment in works, 122; on Cioran, 16-17; on Conrad and Poland, 212; *Diary*, 99-102, 106, 108, 109-12, 117-18, 120-21, 124; faces (human countenances) in works, 97, 101-2, 109-11, 145, 315nn30-31; *Ferdydurke*, 100, 111, 113, 117-18, 122, 127; Form and, 119-20, 122, 123, 126, 315nn30-31, 319n50; fugitivity and, 122, 130; on Hitler, 316-17n37; identity issues, 108, 125, 293n57; immaturity in works, 126-28, 131, 321n59, 322n65; inbetweeness and, 128, 131, 145; on institutionalization of art, 106; *A Kind of Testament*, 97-99, 101, 107, 108, 119-20, 122-23, 126-28, 130, 131, 319n48, 320-21n58; Levinas and, 113, 119-24, 317n40; nausea in works, 117; on near distance, 29; Other and Otherness in works, 122-23, 126, 131; on paintings, 111-12; parody in works, 107, 123, 124, 127; Poland and, 98-99, 108, 126, 129-30, 151-52; Polish identity, 101-2, 122; *Pornografia*, 111, 127; Proust and, 98, 127, 320n58; readership or audience and, 322n66; Said compared with, 215-16; Sartre and, 121, 130, 145, 203; on Schulz, 132-35, 320n56, 324n80; Schulz compared with, 128-29, 141-42, 144-45; on the self, 125; self-amputation, 122, 123; sexuality, 128, 321n60; on subjectivity, 119-20, 319n48; *Trans-Atlantyk*, 101, 122; use of first person, 123, 124
Graham, R. B. Cunninghame, 179, 182
gravestones: Canetti's works as monolithic gravestone, 199; inscriptions on, 12-13, 20-21, 259, 261, 264, 287n24; in Pagis's works, 256; Schulz's murals

gravestones *(continued)*
　　as monument, 104, 107, 140; in Shammas's works, 256; text as, *xiii*
gravity: weight, 114; in works considered, 36–37
Gray, Thomas, 10, 199, 286n18
Great Expectations (Dickens), 13
Green, Jeffrey M., 294n2
Gross, Jan, 84, 151, 326n86
Grossman, David, 135, 305n60, 311n12, 312n17
Grünewald, Matthias, 67, 177
Guattari, Félix, 258
Guillory, John, 25–26, 290n40
guns, 86–87, 92

Halkin, Hillel, 265
Halpern, Moyshe-Leyb, 208
Harpham, Geoffrey Galt, 326n34, 339nn5–6
Harris, Stephanie, 286–87n19
Hatikvah, 247
Hauser, Kasper, 51, 54
Hebrew: Appelfeld and, 80; as chosen language, 237, 246; "formulation," 303n46; as haven, 276; as language of authorship, 44, 243, 246–47, 258; as language of death, 259–60; letters in *The Iron Tracks* (Appelfeld), 74; in Pagis's works, 161–62, 267–68; in Shammas's works, 260, 276; as trace, 345–46n8
Heidegger, Martin, 114, 115, 121, 137
Heine, Heinrich, 208
heterological, de Certeau on, 8
Hever, Hanan, 257, 258
Hirsch, R. Samson Raphael, 288n29, 302n44
Hitler, Adolf, 147, 316n37
Hitlerism, 120, 136
Hoffman, Eva, 4
Hollander, John, 279
Holocaust: Appelfeld on memory and, 294n2; in Appelfeld's works, 296n12; as context for Schulz's works, 150; Czernowitz and, 306n61; impending war as context, 210–11; literary silence in response to, 46; in literary tradition, 305n60; reparations and, 313n18; in Sebald's works, 11, 68–71, 296n12; as subject matter, 44, 46, 69
home: Canetti on "straying" home, 182; in Canetti's works, 159–60; as elsewhere, 237; Europe as uninhabitable, 77; Gombrowicz, 153; language as, 163; railways as mobile homeland, 73; Said on, 221–22; as unfixed to land, 72; in von Rezzori's works, 159–60
homelessness: in Gombrowicz's works, 131; in *The Iron Tracks* (Appelfeld), 79–80, 86; nostalgia and, 208; Said and, 224–25; Schulz and, 132–33, 153; in Schulz's works, 139; being "un-homed," 115
Hornstein, Shelley, 304n55
Howe, Irving, 243
The Human Province (Canetti), 158, 160, 162, 163, 335nn45–46
Husserl, Edmund, 121

identity: Aciman and, 229–30, 237; of Alexandrian Jews, 227, 229–30; belonging and, 48, 98; cemeteries as centers of identity after loss, 257–58; choice of language and, 246; de-individualization and, 251; as enchained, 125; face and, 111; language and, 91; national identity, 100, 112, 150–51; in Pagis's works, 267–68; proper names and, 34; the subjective self, 114, 115. *See also* Jewish identity; specific authors
illness or disease: as context for Pagis's works, 272; Said and, 223; in Said's works, 225; in Sebald's works, 287n25
immaturity: in Gombrowicz's works, 126–28, 131, 321n59, 322n65; *midbar* and, 233
immigration in Pagis's works, 247–48
impression, 288n29; of place, 55
inbetweeness: escape *(évasion)* and, 128; in Gombrowicz's works, 131; of Poland, 98; in Gombrowicz's works, 128

"inner emigration" *(Daheimgebliebenen)*, 72
In Nyu York (Halpern), 208
inscriptions, 12–13, 20–21; as amulets, 275; in photographs, 51; Wordsworth on, 20
the interhuman: Canetti's "midpoint" and, 158, 180–81; Gombrowicz and, 112–13, 131; Levinas and, 126–27; proximity to the Other, 174–75
intersections, in *The Iron Tracks* (Appelfeld), 91–92
intertextuality: ethical pairing of texts and, 37–38. *See also* allusion
invisibility, 22–23; Bakhtin on Realist and Romantic optics, 65–66
Invisible Cities (Calvino), 22–23, 41, 66, 155–57, 207, 240–41
The Iron Tracks (Appelfeld), 42–47, 73–95; belonging in, 92; books and libraries in, 90; detours in, 84; doorways or portals in, 82–83; doubles or doubling in, 80–81, 91–92; intersections in, 92; Israel in, 85–86; Jewish identity in, 87–88; landscapes in, 73, 92; language in, 81–84, 91; maternal/paternal dichotomies in, 81–84; as memoir or autobiography, 42–43; *mesilat barzel*, 74–75, 90, 95; *Mesilat Yesharim* (The Path of the Just) and, 74; Nachtigel plot, 78–79, 85, 87, 93; the Other in, 91; place names in, 75, 77–78; postwar Europe as setting of, 45; railway tracks in, 73; relics in, 74, 76, 77, 78, 79, 82–83, 84, 86, 89, 90; silence in, 81, 88, 94; sleep in, 83–84, 85–86; title of, 90; tradition in, 84, 90, 94; vagrancy in, 46; webs of relationship, 84–85
"Isaac" (Gilboa), 276
Israel: Appelfeld on, 307n69; as deferred destination, 307n71; in *The Iron Tracks* (Appelfeld), 85–86; maps of, 283n4
itinerary and topography of book, *vii*

Jabès, Edmond, 4–5, 28, 238, 314–15n29
Jacobs, Carol, 289n34
Jacobson, Dan, 292n51
James, Henry, xi, 32, 168, 174, 182–83, 195

JanMohamed, Abdul R., 219
Jedwabne, Poland, 150
Jerusalem, 213, 223, 224, 232, 234, 235; 283n4
Jewish Europe: cultural inheritance of, 102–4; as political illusion, 80; ritual objects as vestiges of, 76
Jewish identity, 309n76, 343n35; Appelfeld and, 295–96n8; Canetti and, 160, 194–200, 328–29n9, 336–37n55; in *The Iron Tracks* (Appelfeld), 93; Levi on, 231; literature as definitive ("People of the Book"), 89; Pagis and, 249; Schulz and, 108, 134–35, 136; in *The Voices of Marrakesh* (Canetti), 201
Jewish Lamarckism, 88–89

Kabbalah, 244, 314n22, 344n6
Kafka, Franz, 44, 76, 108, 158, 167, 258, 300n32, 303n48
"The Kafka Connection" (Appelfeld), 295n8
Kahanoff, Jacqueline, 291n44
A Kind of Testament (Gombrowicz), 97–99, 101, 107, 108, 119–20, 122–23, 126–28, 130, 131, 319n48, 320–21n58
knots, 244, 344n6
Kochnar-Lingren, Gray, 287n20
Kraus, Karl, 158, 298n20, 331n21
Kristeva, Julia, 37, 137, 330–31n20; on being foreign, 108–9; on the foreign face, 142; on national identity, 112
Kronfeld, Chana, 338n63, 347n15
Kundera, Milan, 37

labyrinth, memoir as, 19–20
Lacan, Jacques, 322n64
"La Cimetiere Marin" (Valéry), 271
Lacoue-Labarthe, Philippe, 114
Landau, Felix, 102
Landscape and Memory (Schama), 34–35
landscapes: as embodied, 73; in *The Emigrants* (Sebald), 10; etymology of term, 282n2; in *The Iron Tracks* (Appelfeld), 92; man as, 302n42; mimetic transfer in, 63–64; national identity and, 100

Lane, Anthony, 287n22, 299n25
language: in *Arabesques* (Shammas), 246; as Babel, 164–66; Bakhtin and, 6; Benjamin on, 331n21; bilingualism and adversary languages, 91; Canetti on, 94, 180, 330n18, 335nn45–46; in Canetti's works, 163–65, 176, 186; as chosen, 165, 237, 246, 333n29; as culture, 79–80; displacement and exile, 228; German language, 163, 164, 171, 297n14, 305n59, 330n16; as home, 163; identity and, 91, 104, 163, 165, 195, 260, 346n10; in *The Iron Tracks* (Appelfeld), 91; as magic or enchantment, 170, 172; Marrakesh as antedating, 186; as medium for exchange, 200; mother tongues and language associated with the maternal, 80, 81, 163–64, 171, 172; in Pagis's works, 248, 264–65, 267–68; place transported by, 171; polyglossia, 164–65, 172, 267–68; Ruthenian language, 306n62; in Shammas's works, 248, 260, 276; stealth and thievery associated with, 187; in *The Voices of Marrakesh* (Canetti), 188–89, 202; von Rezzori on, 330n16; as wandering across borders, 79, 164–65; wordplay in Pagis's works, 264–65, 350n33; Yiddish, 31, 80, 91–92, 304n53, 305n59, 308n72. *See also* Hebrew
The Language of Silence (Schlant), 46
La Statue de Sel (Memmi), 23, 293n57
Lavie, Smadar, 237
Lefebvre, Henri, 7; on space, 285n11
Leibowitz, Yeshayahu, 31
Lentricchia, Frank, 278
Leonardo De Vinci, 111, 144
letters: in *Abba* (Pagis), 250, 266, 267–69; alphabet letters as relics, 74; alphabet letters as stolen, 259; in Pagis's works, 264; Schulz's correspondence, 97, 103, 107, 135, 144–45
Letters and Drawings (Schulz), 103, 127, 138–39, 144, 146–47, 323n70

Letters of Transit (Aciman), 212, 219, 220, 238
Levant: as focus of works, 213–14; use of term, 288–89n30, 291n44
Levi, Primo, 231
Levinas, Emmanuel, 15, 31, 35, 68; "The Actuality of Maimonides," 136; on art, 112, 125; *Beyond the Verse*, 216–17; *De l'évasion*, 39, 99, 106, 113–14, 115, 117, 123, 125, 135–36; on destiny and being, 134; *Difficult Freedom*, 35; on escape *(évasion)*, 99, 106, 113–14, 115, 117, 123, 125, 135–36; "Ethics and Exegesis," 341n15; filiality or fraternity, 224; on freedom and bondage, 114, 116, 148–49; Gombrowicz and, 113, 119–24, 317n40; on humans and trees, 35; National Socialism and Hitlerism, 114–16; "Peace and Proximity," 120; the personal, 219–20; "Persons and Figures," 151, 318n41; "Promised Land or Permitted Land," 15; "Quelques reflexions sur la philosophie de l'hitlerisme," 39, 99, 119, 124; on reading and inhabiting, 283n4; on reading and truth, 216–17; "Reality and Its Shadow," 125, 151, 300n36; "rubbing" of text, 292n55; subjective being, 114; subjectivity and, 125; *Totality and Infinity*, 118–19, 134, 285n12, 318n45
Lévi-Strauss, Claude, 121
lieu (Nora): *vs. espace*, 205, 285n11; *vs. milieu*, 205
lightness: Calvino on, 36; *vs.* gravity in works, 36–37
"*Likrat*" (Pagis), 271
Lingis, Alphonso, 300n36
literacy: alphabet letters as relics, 74; in Canetti's works, 170, 176; repudiation of written language, 165–66; in Said's works, 225; in von Rezzori's works, 175. *See also* books; reading; writing
Łodz, 59
"The Log Book" (Pagis), 247, 268

longing/belonging, *xiii;* in Aciman's works, 233; belonging as being bound to Form, 98; cemeteries as site of, 214–15; defined, 29; desire, 28–29, 156; in Gombrowicz's works, 128–29; identity and, 48, 98; in *Invisible Cities* (Calvino), 156; in *The Iron Tracks* (Appelfeld), 92; national Form and longing, 99–100; national identity and *natio,* 112; nostalgia and, 211
Lubow, Arthur, 285–86n15
Lukács, Georgy, 99
Luria, R. Isaac, 244, 344n6
Luzzatto, Moshe Hayim (RaMCHaL), 74, 302–3n42

Magris, Claudio, 182, 327n4
Malamud, Bernard, 265
Manchester, 59–60
Manea, Norman, 4, 37, 329n10
Manger, Itzik, 16
Mann, Klaus, 72
Mann, Thomas, 108, 178, 323n72
maps: faces as maps, 154, 206; frontispiece, *vii;* mosaic maps of the Holy Land, 283n4
Märchen: memoirs as, 7, 68; Schulz's murals, 102–4
Marrakesh: as elsewhere, 205–6; as *lieu vs. milieu,* 183–84, 205. See also *The Voices of Marrakesh* (Canetti)
marranism, 227–28, 233
Marx, Karl, 340n12
masks, 144, 151, 158
Massumi, Brian, on ethics, 285n14
Matalon, Ronit, 298–99n24, 298n24
maturation in memoirs, 223
McHale, Brian, 247, 275
Meir, R. Asher, 281n1
Melzer, Gerhard, 183, 194
Memmi, Albert, 23, 290n39, 293n57
memoirs: Aciman's work as, 40, 48; in Appelfeld's work, 7, 12; Appelfeld's work as, 42, 44, 75 (*See also* "Buried Homeland" [Appelfeld]); *vs.* autobiography, 40; Benjamin on, 19, 21–22;

Canetti on, 332n25; Clive James and, 265; desire and, 156; estrangement or dislocation and, 4–5; as exterior narratives, 157; as labyrinths, 19–20; as *Märchen* or enchantment, 7, 68; maturation in, 223; as *midbar* literature, 4, 21, 40; Said's work as, 40, 48; Sebald's works as, 13–14, 21, 42, 66; as subject in Sebald's works, 13–14, 58, 61, 62, 66; texts under consideration as, 213
memory: Aciman on, 213–14; anamnesis, *xiii;* archive of the feet, *xiii,* 34, 223; Canetti on, 331–32n25; in Canetti's works, 169, 178; eidetic memory and preservation of place, 326–27n1; forgetting and, 297–98n19; Jewish tradition and, 90; language and, 305n59; of memory, 234–35; mnemonic arbitrage, 214; Sacks on, 156; in Said's works, 234–35; in Schulz's works, 139; in Shammas's works, 275; in von Rezzori's works, 169
meraglim, 15
Mesilat Yesharim (The Path of the Just), 74, 302n45
metamorphosis: Canetti and, 167; in Canetti's works, 158, 167, 169; Schulz and transmigration of forms, 125, 144; transfiguration in Pagis's works, 252–54
metaphor: as elsewhere, 7; in Aciman's works, 235; Alcalay on Jew as Other, 238; Bhabha on, 7; de Certeau on, 6; as elsewhere or difference, 7; ethics of, 24–25; Frost on the strength of, 292–93n56; intertextuality and, 38; in Said's works, 235; Schulz on, 142; *tourniquets* (revolving door or *schwindel*), 19–20, 38, 57, 94; travel and, 6
metaphorai, vii, 8
"*Metei Midbar*" (Bialik), 282n3, 288n28
mezuzah, 82–83, 86, 87–88, 306n64
Mickiewicz, Adam, 34
midbar, 3–16, 42, 153, 161, 197, 214, 216–17, 222–23, 242, 341n15; arabesque as literary pattern, 242, 245; cemetery as

midbar (continued)
  wilderness, 197; childhood or immaturity and, 233; criticism as expression of, 24; described and defined, 27; as elegiac, 36; *fil-kharij* and, 222–23, 224; as generative emptiness, 282n3; as genre, 4; language as transportative, 279; memoir as literature of, 4, 21, 40; in midrash, 4, 282n3; photographs and, 50; reading of, 8, 24; as speech/wilderness (desert), 4–5, 27–28, 167, 247–48, 278, 282n3

Middlemarch (Eliot), 58

migration: deportations as, 72; "inner migration" and opposition to National Socialism, 72

Mill, John Stuart, 225–26, 234

Miller, J. Hillis, 285n13, 318n42

Milosz, Czeslaw, 4, 212, 286n16

Midrash Rabbah, 282n3

The Mirror of the Sea (Conrad), 209–10, 213

The Modern Hebrew Poem Itself (Burnshaw), 247, 348n15

Mogreb el Acksa (Cunninghame Graham), 179, 182

Morocco in Canetti's works. *See The Voices of Marrakesh* (Canetti)

Moses and Monotheism (Freud), 88–89, 93

mothers or maternal figures: language or mother tongues, 80, 81, 163–64, 171, 172; in Pagis's works, 266–69; in Said's works, 223, 225–26, 234; in Schulz's works, 139–40; in von Rezzori's works, 165–66

Mudimbe, V. Y., 310n6

murals (Schulz), 102–7, 135, 152, 312n16, 313n19

Murphy, Harriet, 200, 333n34, 336n49

Musil, Robert, 206, 266

My Ántonia (Cather), 243, 277

Nabokov, Vladimir, 4, 52, 54, 62, 163; in *The Emigrants* (Sebald), 52, 53

Nahman of Bratslav, 243

Naipaul, V. S., 4

names: Allah in *The Voices of Marrakesh* (Canetti), 186–87, 201–2; in Appelfeld's works, 47–48, 304n55; concealment of, 299n25; cultural identity and, 80; as hybridization of language and heritage, 224; identity and proper names, 34; as link to land and language, 12; in Pagis's works, 267–68; place names, 30–36; proper names, 33–36; in Said's works, 224, 225, 342n25; in Sebald's works, 299n25; surnames, 31–34; in *The Voices of Marrakesh* (Canetti), 201–2

naqba and *naqsa*, 223

Naqqash, Samir, 237

narration: as device in *Invisible Cities* (Calvino), 22; narrative as dislocation or displacement, 5–6; place-flight-border-beyond as kernel of narrative, 3–4; trains as narrative space, 304n53

narrators: Appelfeld's narrative stance, 295–96n8, 295n7; Canetti's narrative stance, 162, 179; instability of the first person voice, 61

national identity: Kristeva on, 112; landscapes and, 100; of Poland, 150–51

National Socialism, 114–16; Levinas on, 148; opposition to, 72

nation and national Form, 98; Bhabha on, 100; Goethe on nationhood, 100; Gombrowicz and Poland, 108

nausea, 116–17, 123. *See also* escape (*évasion*)

"near distance," 29, 131, 172; standing close as, 218

Neighbors (Gross), 151, 305n59

nets, 177, 244; weaving, images of, 240–42, 244

Nietzche, Friedrich, 93

nomadism. *See* wandering

Nora, Pierre, 183, 282n2, 334n43

nostalgia: Aciman on, 238; in Aciman's works, 229; Boym on, 211; Canetti on, 161; Cather and, 277; in Conrad's works, 209–11; for death, 115; in Gombrowicz's works, 130–31; in Heine's works, 208; for land, 283; in memoir, 40; Nabokov and, 163; nostography, 159, 328n8; restorative *vs.* reflective, 211; Sebald and, 163; von Rezzori on, 161

nostography, 159, 328n8
Notes from Hampstead (Canetti), *vii*
Novogrodsky family, 31–32
Numbers, Book of, 14–15, 341n19
Nussbaum, Martha, 26

olive oil in Shammas's works, 254–55
The One Facing Us (Matalon), 298n14
One Hundred Years of Solitude (Marquez), 258
On Escape (Levinas). See *De l'évasion*
"On the Jewish Question" (Marx), 340n12
Orientalism, 179
Other and Otherness, 8; barriers between self and, 91; Canetti and, 158; Czernowitz as Other, 174; the Elsewhere and, *xii*; Elsewhere as, 37; faces as the Other, 118–19, 141–42; in Gombrowicz's works, 122–23, 131; internal otherness and language, 333n30; Jew as Other, 238; Kristeva on being foreign in France, 108–9; language and, 303–4n50; as strangers, 112–13, 314n29; tradition and, 80, 85; walls or barriers as delineation of the Other, 174
Ouaknin, Marc-Alain, 19, 282n3, 341n15, 345n8, 351–52n41
Out of Egypt (Aciman), 212, 223, 227–28, 229, 236
Out of Place (Said), 212, 214, 219–23, 232, 234, 236
Ovid, 167
Ozick, Cynthia: on documentary photography, 49; on *The Emigrants* (Sebald), 51–52, 296n12, 298n21; on Sebald's works, 47, 57, 296

paganism, 136–37, 316n36
Pagis, Dan, 205; *Abba*, 244, 250, 253–54, 266–72; allusion in works, 271; Appelfeld and, 296n9; "The Art of Contraction," 263; "Brothers," 250; cemeteries in works, 250, 256–58; death in works, 253–54, 261–63, 267; familial dynamics as scene of works, 279; father as figure in works, 248–49, 250, 253–54, 261–63, 264, 266–67, 270–71; Hebrew as chosen language, 246; identity issues, 244–45; immigration in works, 247–48; Jewish identity, 249; language in works, 161–62; "*Likrat*," 271; "The Log Book," 247, 268; loss in works, 252–53, 255; mother figure in *Abba*, 266–69; poetics of, 244, 246, 253, 345nn6–7; Shammas compared with, 245–46, 263; *Shneim-Asar Panim*, 245; subjectivity in works, 249; "The Souvenir," 249, 251; transfiguration in works, 252–54; *Twelve Faces*, 245; wordplay in works, 264–65, 350n33; "Written in Pencil," 276, 349n24
Palestine, 236; as reduplicated in Michigan, 251; in Said's works, 234–35
palimpsest, 29, 67–68, 74, 249, 250
palintropism, 26–27, 37, 238; in Aciman's works, 233; in Gombrowicz's works, 128
Paradise, expulsion from, 178
Pardes, Ilana, 15
Paris, 107–8
the particular, 48
partzufim, use of term, 244–45, 344–45n6
Pascal, Blaise, 122
The Path of the Just (Mesilat Yesharim), 74, 302n45
patride/apatride, 60; palintropism and the *apatride*, 27
pedestrianism: cemeteries and, 14; *meraglim*, 15
Peirce, Charles Sanders, 298n22
Père Lachaise, 258–60
The Periodic Table (Levi), 231
Perloff, Marjorie, 299–300n31, 300n33, 310n7
"A Perpetual Story of Departure" (Appelfeld), 296n10
A Personal Record (Conrad), 18, 211, 212, 213
photographs: in *After the Last Sky* (Said), 234–35; aura of, 55–56, 58; Barthes on, 49; Benjamin on, 55; camera-as-witness, 297n17; of the dead, 290n36; film in Said's works, 236; of Freud's

photographs *(continued)*
 antiquities, 309n76; gaze and ownership of, 55; as haunting, 52; in Matalon's works, 298-99n24; *midbar* and, 50; Ozick on, 49, 297n17; of photographs, 52-53; Pierce on iconic and indexical photos, 298n22; reading of, 52; Sante on, 290n36; as signifiers, 52; and silence, 56-57; subjectivity and, 55. *See also* photographs in *The Emigrants*
photographs in *The Emigrants*, 9-10, 12, 14, 57, 297n16; of blackthorn twig, 56-57, 67-68; as evidence of memory, 64-65; of newspaper story/glacier, 52-53; Ozick on, 297n16, 298n21; railway tracks, 11, 69-71; Sebald on, 49; of teas-made, 56; voicelessness and, 298n21; web of relationship between, 58; of yew tree, 53-54, 286n17-18
Piłsudski, Jozef, 97, 99, 134, 146-49, 153-54, 325n83
Pirke Avot, 90, 291n48
place: as atemporal, 76; atopia *vs.* utopia, 341n19; as choice of language, 165; collision with place, 15-16, 28, 37; and/as elsewhere, 59-60, 219-22; in *The Emigrants* (Sebald), 59-60; as flight or buoyancy, 37; as landscape, 10; linked to identity in Canetti's works, 165; as palimpsest, 249-50; possession of one's own place through fiction, 277-78; privatizing and mystification of place, 27-28; relocation of, 105; Sacks on memory and, 156; Said and, 219, 220-21; *vs.* space (*lieu vs. espace*), 205, 285n11; as substitute for person, 63; Talmud on, 281-82n1; transported by language, 171
place-flight-border-beyond: Calvino's *Invisible Cities* and, 23-24; as narrative kernel, 3-4
place name, 30-33; in Canetti's works, 182; in *The Emigrants* (Sebald), 59; in *The Iron Tracks* (Appelfeld), 75, 77-78, 84, 93; of obliterated towns, 33; in travel writing, 182

poaching: in cemeteries, 13; literary criticism as, 25; mimesis as, 32; reading as, 5, 7-8, 241, 263-65, 284n6; removal of Schulz murals characterized as, 104, 105; touring or exploring as, 15
Poirier, Richard, 16
Poland: Argentina as reduplication of, 99, 153, 293n57; and Argentina in Gombrowicz's works, 129-30; Conrad and, 209, 212; Drohobycz, 102-7, 139-41; Gombrowicz and, 98-99, 100-101, 108, 126, 129-30, 151-52, 153; inbetweeness and, 98; native anti-Semitism in, 150-51; Piłsudski as "face" of, 150-51; Schulz on the face of, 97; as site of departure, 209
"Poland Revisited" (Conrad), 40, 209, 213
polyglossia, 164-65, 172, 267-68, 330n18
Pornografia (Gombrowicz), 111, 127
practice, use of term, 25-26
The Practice of Everyday Life (de Certeau), vii, 5-6, 7-8, 241
Prokopczyk, Czeslaw Z., 146
"Promised Land or Permitted Land" (Levinas), 15
proper names, 33-36
property/land ownership, 34, 320n56
prosopopoeia, 199, 318n41
Proust, Marcel: Aciman on, 26-27; Appelfeld and, 44; Canetti and, 161; Gombrowicz and, 98, 127, 320n58; Said and, 234; Sebald and, 9, 13; Shammas and, 256, 277; von Rezzori and, 161
Punsk, cemetery at, 35
Pygmalion (Shaw), 243

"Quelques reflexions sur la philosophie de l'hitlerisme" (Levinas), 39, 99, 119, 124

Radautz, Bukovina, 249, 346n12, 348nn18-19
railway tracks: in Appelfeld's works, 77; de Certeau on train travel as dispossession, 77; in *The Emigrants*, 11, 69-71; in *The Iron Tracks*, 73; trains as narrative space, 304n53; as writing or script, 74; in Yehoshua's works, 308-9n74

Ramras-Rauch, Gila, 44
Rashi, 5, 15
Rasselas (Johnson), 22
"The Readiness" (Pagis), 271
reading: as acknowledgment, 271; of cemeteries, 13–14; *The Emigrants* (Sebald) as reading lesson, 62; as enchantment, 68; ethics and, 8, 24–26, 263–64; as inhabiting, 283n4; as intimate encounter, 180; lay *vs.* professional readers, 25; lyrical power of (as transport), 26; of photographs, 52; as poaching, 5, 7–8, 241, 263–65, 284n6; as repetition of writing, 14; repudiation of written language, 165–66; as summoning the dead, 20–21; as travel, 6, 15; in *The Voices of Marrakesh* (Canetti), 191–92; as voyeurism, 268–69; as web of relationships, 274–75; webs of relationship constructed during, 54–55
Realism, 43, 65–66
reciprocal texts (facing texts), 24, 217
reconstitution, 245
recursion or repetition: in arabesque style, 343–44n1, 350n31; in Conrad's works, 51; *The Emigrants* (Sebald), 51, 242; as enchantment, 76; *The Iron Tracks* (Appelfeld), 75–76, 84, 93–94; in Pagis's works, 264; in Shammas's works, 264; writing and, 51. *See also* doubles or doubling
"Reflections of an Uncertain Jew" (Aciman), 221, 226–27, 230
"Reflections on Exile" (Said), 27, 215, 217, 226
refraction in texts, 52–53
relics (stranded objects): in *The Emigrants* (Sebald), 287–88n26; faces as, 145; in *The Iron Tracks* (Appelfeld), 74, 76, 77, 78, 79, 82–83, 84, 86, 89, 90, letters as, 264, 266; Luzzatto on, 302n42; Pagis's *Abba* as unpublished fragments, 272; photographs as *objets trouvés* and catalysts, 49; Schulz's murals, 102–7, 135, 152; in Shammas's works, 274
religion: in Canetti's works, 337n56; Gnosticism, 334n38, 336n49; marranism,

228; secular *vs.* religious criticism, 215–16
Rilke, Rainer Maria, 108
The Rings of Saturn (Sebald), 242, 300n33, 338n3
Robbins, Jill, 285n12, 316n34, 317n41
Robbins, Bruce, 48, 235
Rolland, Jacques, 115, 116–17, 135–36, 318–19n47, 322–23n69
Romanticism: cemetery scenes and, 20; *vs.* Realism, 65–66; Sebald and, 287n21, 299–300n31; in Sebald's works, 10
roots and legs, 34–36
Rosenfarb, Chava, 288n26
Roth, Joseph, 153
Roth, Philip, interview with Appelfeld, 44, 92
Rousseau, Jean-Jacques, 18, 28, 124
"rubbing" text, 292n55
Ruppel, Ursula, 199
Ruschuk, 159, 162, 169, 171, 176–79, 182, 196, 205; Marrakesh as substitute for, 182
Rushdie, Salman, 258, 289n32
Ruthenian language, 306n62

Sabbath, travel prohibitions, 3, 281n1
Sacks, Oliver, 156
Safranski, Rüdiger, 114
Said, Edward, 48; Aciman compared with, 215, 220, 222, 226–27, 238–39; *After the Last Sky*, 216, 222–23, 234–35, 236, 342n25; as atopian or "out of place," 219–22, 229, 236; biographical information, 215; on boundaries, 221; Canetti compared with, 222; on Conrad, 18, 209, 212, 289n33; contrapuntal criticism, 216–19; on exile and detachment, 27; exile in works, 215–16, 234; father figures in works, 220, 223–26; *fil-kharij* or *midbar* and, 224; *Freud and the Non-European*, 217, 219, 309n78, 340n12, 343n35; Gombrowicz compared to, 215–16; on home, 221; identity and, 220–21, 229; illness and, 223, 225; as "in place," 225–26; on intent of memoir, 223; JanMohamed on, 219; literacy in works, 225; Mill and,

Said, Edward *(continued)*
234; mother figures in works, 223, 225–26, 234; *Out of Place,* 212, 214, 219–23, 232, 234, 236; on place, 220–21; political content in works, 223, 238; Proust and, 234; "Reflections on Exile," 27, 215, 217, 226; secular criticism, 215–16, 220–21
Salgado, Sebastião, 286n16
Sanatorium under the Sign of the Hourglass (Schulz), 142, 143, 144, 151, 323n73
Sante, Luc, 55, 290n36
Santner, Eric, 154, 304n51, 314n29
Sartre, Jean-Paul, 121, 130, 145, 203, 318n45
Schama, Simon, 34–35, 282n2
Schlant, Ernestine, 46
Schlink, Bernard, 296n13
Schneider, Peter, 296n13
Schulz, Bruno: biographical information, 153; *Cinnamon Shops,* 124–25, 142–44, 323n70; correspondence of, 97, 103, 107, 135, 144–45 *(See also Letters and Drawings under this heading);* death and, 102, 144, 311n13; Drohobycz as perfected in the imagination of, 139–41; escape *(évasion)* and works of, 322n65; essays and short fiction of, 99, 146; faces (human countenances) in works, 97; "Fatherland," 138–39; on *Ferdydurke* (Gombrowicz), 127; as fictional character in Grossman's works, 135; as fixed in identity, 152; on friendship, 103; Gombrowicz and, 153; Gombrowicz on, 132–34, 320n56, 324n80; on greatness, 147–49; on history of collective myth, 147–49; Holocaust as context of works, 150; identity issues, 105–7; on imagination and mythical reality, 149–50; as Imagi-Native, 138; on impression of form, 124–25; Jewish identity of, 108, 134–35, 136, 313–14n22; *Letters and Drawings,* 103, 127, 138–39, 144, 146–47, 323n70; metamorphosis or transmigration of forms, 125, 144; mural controversy, 102–7, 135, 152, 312n16, 313n19; paganism and mythos of, 136–37; Piłsudski essays, 134, 146–49, 153–54, 325n83; place and, 107–8; as Polish or bound to Poland, 108, 135, 137–39; *Sanatorium under the Sign of the Hourglass,* 142, 143, 144, 151, 323n73; self-portraits of, 144–45; *The Street of the Crocodiles* (See *Cinnamon Shops* under this heading); as "the Jew in the world," 137; time in works, 144, 228–29; "Tragic Freedom," 134
Schwartz, Yigal, 302
Sebald, W. G.: Aciman on, 7; Appelfeld compared with, 46–47; *Austerlitz, vii, xii,* 287n25, 290n36, 299n30, 337n57; autobiographic discourse and works, 43; as *bricoleur,* 298n23; *Campo Santo,* 299n30; collaboration and works, 297n17; critics on, 44; death in works of, 53–54, 61, 70–71; death of, xi–xii; on destruction of cities, 71; Holocaust as context for works, 296n12; on language, *vii; On the Natural History of Destruction,* 301n39; Proust and, 9, 13, 285–86n15; *The Rings of Saturn,* 242, 300n33, 338n3; Romanticism and, 66, 287n21; Shammas compared with, 242; *Unerzählt,* 297n17; *Vertigo,* 286n17, 300n32. See also *The Emigrants* (Sebald)
seclusion, 190
The Secret Heart of the Clock (Canetti), 197–98
secrets: *Arabesques* (Shammas) as secretive text, 272–73, 275–76; Canetti and, 202; diaries as secretive, 181; in *Abba* (Pagis), 272; suppressive or secretive texts, 264–65
"secular criticism" (Said), 220–21
secularism: in Aciman's works, 215; in Said's works, 215–16, 220–21
See Under: Love (Grossman), 90, 135, 305n60, 311n12
Seidel, Michael, 284n7
selfhood, escape *(évasion)* and, 116
Sephardim, 236–37, 336–37n55

Index 395

September 11, 2001, *xi*
sexuality: in Canetti's works, 336n49, 336n52; Gombrowicz and, 128, 321n60; in *The Voices of Marrakesh* (Canetti), 193-94
Shaked, Gershon, 303n46
Shakespeare, William, 38, 124, 140, 322n67
Shame (Rushdie), 258
Shammas, Anton: "autocartography," 241; Cather and, 243, 277; displacement in works, 247; father family, 257; "Finding Palestine," 346n10; Hebrew as chosen language, 246-47; Hebrew as language of authorship and, 258; identity in works, 250-52, 258, 259; as "Israeli" author, 258; language in works, 248; loss in works, 254-55; Pagis compared with, 245-46, 263; polyvocality in works, 243, 258-61; Sebald compared with, 242. *See also Arabesques* (Shammas)
Shibboleth, 79, 305n57
sight: Bakhtin on Realist and Romantic optics, 65-66; dispossession of the land and, 77; spies or sightseers, 15
silence, 56-57; in Appelfeld's works, 306n66; in autobiography, 17; in Canetti's works, 163; in *The Emigrants* (Sebald), 298n21; in *The Iron Tracks* (Appelfeld), 81, 88, 94; as maternal, 306n66, 308n72; opposition to National Socialism and, 72; self-silencing in Ben-Yitzhak's works, 248; in *The Voices of Marrakesh* (Canetti), 189-90
Sipur Hayim (Appelfeld), 45, 294n2, 296n9, 305n59
Six Memos for the Next Millenium (Calvino), 36
sleep or rest, 83-84, 85-86
The Snows of Yesteryear (Von Rezzori), 33, 39, 159-63, 166-67, 169, 175, 326-27nn1-2, 328n8, 331n22
solitude: cemeteries and, 28; Gombrowicz on isolation, 101; the personal and, 219-20; seclusion, 181, 190
Song of Songs, 4
Sonne, Dr. *See* Ben-Yitzhak, Avraham

sound: acoustic masks, 158; memory and, 21-22
"Sound-Secrets" (Sutzkever), 32-33
"The Souvenir" (Pagis), 249, 251
Speak Memory (Nabokov), 163
speech/wilderness (desert) homograph, 4-5, 27-28, 167, 247-48, 278, 282n3
spying or voyeurism, 15, 190, 268-69
squares, 196, 202-3
The Statue of Salt (Memmi), 23, 293n57
sta viator, 7, 16, 198
Steiner, George, 35
Stendhal (Henri Beyle), 35, 297n16, 300n32
Stevens, Wallace, 243, 278
Stifter, Adalbert, 47
Story of a Life (Appelfeld), 45, 294n2, 296n9, 305n59
Strangers to Ourselves (Kristeva), 37, 108-9, 142
The Street of Crocodiles. See Cinnamon Shops (Schulz)
Strzegowo, 31, 33, 34, 291n45
subjective authority, 20, 32, 290n37
subjectivity: Gombrowicz on, 319n48; in Gombrowicz's works, 118; in Pagis's works, 249
substitution: place for person, 63; place for place, 99, 153, 182, 235-36, 251
Suchoff, David, 79-80, 82-83, 91, 303-4n50, 305n57
Suissa, Albert, 237
Sutzkever, Abraham, 32-33, 135
Szpilman, Wadyslaw, 135

Tales of the Hasidim (Buber), 326n88
Talmud Bavli: as history of dispersal, 5; Tractate *Eruvin*, 3-5; Tractate *Peah*, v; Tractate *Shabbat*, *xiii*; Tractate *Sota*, 15
Tchernichovsky, Saul, 73, 301 2n42
The Thousand and One Nights, 22, 343n1
Tichborne, Chidock, 301n41
tikkun, 245
time, 50-51; belatedness in Pagis's works, 161; as elsewhere, 9, 168-69; linked to writing in Canetti's works, 178; in Pagis's works, 250, 257, 351n38; the

time *(continued)*
    past as elsewhere, 168–69; place as atemporal, 76; Proust and, 9, 285–86n15; in Schulz's works, 144, 228–29; Sebald on, 9; in Shammas's works, 257; temporal sensibility in Sebald and Proust, 285–86n15; as unredeemable, 291–92n50. *See also* nostalgia
Titian, 111
The Tongue Set Free (Canetti), 161–67, 169–70, 176, 333n31
The Torch in My Ear (Canetti), 158, 176–79, 328–29n9
Totality and Infinity (Levinas), 118–19, 134
To the Lighthouse (Woolf), 195
tourniquets, 19–20, 38, 57, 94
tradition: in *The Iron Tracks* (Appelfeld), 76, 80, 90; memory and forgetting in Jewish tradition, 90; as permeable, 80; Yerushalmi on, 88–89
"Tragic Freedom" (Schulz), 134
Trakl, Georg, 72
Trans-Atlantyk (Gombrowicz), 101, 122
translation: as revisiting the past, 171–72; used by author, 40; in von Rezzori's works, 172
travel: Canetti's works as travel narratives, 179–81, 195; metaphor as travel, 6; as travail, xii
trees or forests: in Heine's works, 208; Israel as forest in *The Iron Tracks* (Appelfeld), 86; as subject in Sebald's works, 11; and Jews, 34–36; yew tree photo in *The Emigrants* (Sebald), 53–54, 286nn17–18
Twelve Faces (Pagis), 245
tzitzit, 15

Unerzählt (Sebald), 297n17
unhoming and *unheimlich*, xii
Unreliable Memoirs (James), 265

vagrancy. *See* wandering
Valéry, Paul, 271–72, 325n84
Venclova, Tomas, 292n52
Venice, 168

Vertigo (Sebald), 286n17, 300n32
verwandlung. *See* metamorphosis under Canetti, Elias
Villa Landau (Drohobycz), 102–3
Vilna, 32, 292n52
violence: in Canetti's works, 169, 177, 184, 332nn27–28; paintings as pugilistic, 111–12
visibility, 50, 297n16
The Voices of Marrakesh (Canetti), 158–59, 162–63, 167–68, 336n49; audibility in, 180, 186; blindness in, 186–88, 188, 190–91; camels in, 184; cemeteries in, 196–200; critics on, 179–80; detached observation and distancing in, 192–93; doubles or doubling in, 200; embodiment in, 199; enclosure or barriers in, 183, 202; eroticism in, 191–93; exchange or commerce in, 185–86, 188, 193, 200, 203–4; Jewish identity in, 201; language in, 188–89; as memoir, 334n37; names in, 201–2; narrative stance in, 162, 179; reading in, 191–92; seclusion in bounded spaces, 181; sexuality in, 193–94; silence in, 189–90; spying or voyeurism in, 190; storytelling as subject in, 202–3; symbolic patterning in, 184–85; time linked to writing in, 178; town squares, 183; violence in, 184; women in, 189–90, 191; writing as exchange, 203–4; writing in, 181–82, 202
von Rezzori, Gregor: Aciman and, 328n8; Aciman interview with, 328n8, 333n33; on Appelfeld and Canetti, 38; biographical information, 331n21; Canetti compared with, 331n21; as exilic writer, 160–61; identity and the self, 162; on language, 330n16; literacy in works, 165–66; on memoir, 157; *midbar* and, 161; mother tongues and language associated with the maternal, 165–66; as nostographer, 159; precursor texts for, 168–69; Proust and, 157, 161; *The Snows of Yesteryear*, 33, 39, 159–63, 166–67, 169, 175, 326–27nn1–2, 328n8, 331n22

walking: archive of the feet, *xiii*, 34, 223; in cemeteries, 14; *meraglim*, 15; rhetoric of walking, 5

wandering: after Exodus out of Egypt, 14–15; in Appelfeld's works, 75; Cain as wanderer, 250; de Certeau on, 241; the literary as errancy or vagrancy, 5–7; nomadism, *xiii*; in Pagis's works, 250; as rejection of pre-Holocaust life, 306; writing as, 203

The Wandering Jews (Roth), 153

weaving, images of, 44–45, 240–42, 244

webs of relationships: in Appelfeld's works, 44–45; in Canetti's works, 170–71; between facing texts, 217; in *Invisible Cities* (Calvino), 72, 207; in *The Iron Tracks* (Appelfeld), 84–85; as metaphor for city space, 41–42; between photographs in *The Emigrants* (Sebald), 58; reading as construction of, 54–55; in Sebald's works, 44–45

wilderness, 4–5; cemetery as wilderness, 197; in *Invisible Cities*, 155–57; as speech/wilderness (desert), 4–5, 27–28, 167, 247–48, 278, 282n3

Wirblbahn (The Iron Tracks), 24, 75–78, 84, 93–95

women: in Canetti's works, 189–90, 191, 335–36n48, 338n59; Schulz's depictions of, 314n24

Wood, James, 44–45, 49; on Sebald, 50, 57

Wordsworth, William, 11, 20, 225

writing: as enchantment, 68; as exilic or fugitive, 6–7, 309n76; inscriptions, 12–13, 20–21, 51, 259, 261, 264, 287n24; as negation, 209; reading as repetition of, 14; repudiation of written language, 165–66; as self-entombment, 198–99; as violence, 332n28; in *The Voices of Marrakesh* (Canetti), 202, 203–4; as wandering, 203; writers as readers, 32

"Written in Pencil" (Pagis), 276, 349n24

Yehoshua, A. B., 256, 308–9n74

Yerushalmi, Yosef Hayim, 88–89; on Freud, 93, 95

yews, 9–10, 53–54, 286nn17–18

Yiddish, 31, 80, 91–92, 304n53, 305n59, 308n72

yizker bicher (memorial books), 14, 31, 33, 36, 288n27, 291n45

Zagajewski, Adam, 138–39, 140, 323n71, 323n74

Ziarek, Ewa, 318n46

Zionism, 176

Zorach, Cecile, 179–80

Zornberg, Avivah, 16, 37